ENCYCLOPEDIA OF HISPANIC-AMERICAN LITERATURE

ENCYCLOPEDIA OF HISPANIC-AMERICAN LITERATURE

Luz Elena Ramirez

An imprint of Infobase Publishing

Encyclopedia of Hispanic-American Literature

Facts On File, Inc.
An imprint of Infobase Publishing
132 West 31st Street
New York NY 10001

Library of Congress Cataloging-in-Publication Data

Ramirez, Luz Elena.
  The Facts On File encyclopedia of Hispanic-American literature /
Luz Elena Ramirez. — 1st ed.
     p. cm. — (Encyclopedia of American ethnic literature)
  Includes bibliographical references and index.
  ISBN 978-0-8160-6084-9 (hc : alk. paper) 1. American literature—Hispanic-American
authors—Encyclopedias. I. Facts on File, Inc. II. Title. III. Title: Encyclopedia of Hispanic-
American literature.
  PS153.H56R36 2008
  810.9'868073003—dc22   2007034805

Facts On File books are available at special discounts when purchased in bulk quantities for businesses, associations, institutions, or sales promotions. Please call our Special Sales Department in New York at (212) 967-8800 or (800) 322-8755.

You can find Facts On File on the World Wide Web at http://www.factsonfile.com

Text design by Rachel L. Berlin
Cover design by Takeshi Takahashi

Printed in the United States of America

VB KT 10 9 8 7 6 5 4 3 2 1

This book is printed on acid-free paper and contains 30 percent postconsumer recycled content.

This book is for my son,
Ian Matthew Habich Ramirez,
and for his father,
Matthew Martin Habich.

TABLE OF CONTENTS

ACKNOWLEDGMENTS

I am indebted to the contributors to this volume, who submitted entries, provided feedback, and created a dynamic and productive climate for writing about Latino literature.

In editing this encyclopedia, I thank for his expertise and direction Executive Editor Jeff Soloway of Facts On File. In addition, I would like to thank the copy editor, Katy Barnhart, who was thorough and thoughtful in her work.

Entries were subject to peer review and, once in manuscript form, the encyclopedia was read afresh by the following contributors: Ritch Calvin, Kevin Cole, Ethriam Cash Brammer de Gonzales, Yolanda Martinez, Rolando Perez, and Betsy A. Sandlin.

I am also grateful for the support of colleagues and administrators at California State University, San Bernardino, especially for the sabbatical in 2007 that allowed me to complete the project. Finally, I would like to thank Matthew Habich for his support and his daughter Kate Habich for ensuring the completeness of the manuscript.

INTRODUCTION

∽⟨⟩∽

Hispanic-American literature represents the ethnic, linguistic, and religious mixture of cultures in the Latino communities of the United States. The *Encyclopedia of Hispanic-American Literature* is designed for students and general readers looking for an introduction to this rich canon of literature. This volume includes entries on the major Latino authors (such as Gary Soto and Nicholasa Mohr), important Latino texts (José Antonio Villarreal's *Pocho* and Piri Thomas's *Down These Mean Streets*), important events that have affected Latino literature (the Treaty of Guadalupe Hidalgo and the Cuban Revolution), and relevant topics and terms (*mestizaje* and Santería).

A few explanations are in order about the terms that appear throughout the volume. The descriptor *Hispanic-American* is used in government publications to categorize people of Spanish-speaking cultures who live in the United States. It is the adjective that is also used by the Library of Congress, and, therefore, we use it here, although we also use the term *Latino*, which many writers prefer.

According to the estimate of the 2002 U.S. Census, Mexican Americans represent the largest number of U.S. Hispanics (66 percent), followed by Central and South American immigrants (14.3 percent), Puerto Ricans (8.6 percent),

Cubans (3.7 percent), and "Other" Hispanic groups (including Dominicans, 6.5 percent). As a whole, Hispanics live mostly in the West (44 percent) and the South (34.8 percent), with notable populations in the Northeast (13.3 percent) and Midwest (7.7 percent) (Census 2002). Because Mexican Americans, Puerto Ricans, Cuban Americans, and Dominican Americans make up the primary populations of Hispanic-Americans in the United States, it is not surprising that this encyclopedia focuses on writers from these communities. The literary world has taken note, however, of an increasing number of Latin American authors, ranging from Mexican poet Alurista to Chilean novelist Isabel Allende, who have made the United States their home and who have published works about their experiences. The biographies of Latin American authors living primarily in the United States are therefore also included in this volume.

Settings for Hispanic-American literature include the border, the barrio, the *campo* (the fields or the country), and inner-city tenements, as well as the landscapes of the Northeast, Miami, Chicago, Los Angeles, and San Antonio. These settings give rise to very different kinds of stories, as life, for example, on the U.S.-Mexico desert frontier differs from tropical life in the Caribbean.

In terms of their approach to writing Latino authors often combine historical events and personalities with fictional ones. We can appreciate this technique in Rodolfo "Corky" Gonzales's epic poem *Yo soy Joaquín/I Am Joaquín* (1967), which surveys the major events of the last 500 years of Mexican and Mexican-American history. Likewise, Julia Alvarez's *In the Time of the Butterflies* centers on the lives of the real Mirabal sisters during Rafael Leónidas Trujillo's regime (1930–61) in the Dominican Republic. Hispanic-American literature uses the act of writing to create an awareness of history, whether that history is autobiographical or collective. Writing memoirs, poems, narratives, and essays is a way for Latino authors to situate themselves in the present and to preserve the memories or ways of being from the past. When Latino writers reflect on their colonial heritage, debates over land, class, language, and self-expression often occupy their attention. Specific themes include the role of the individual in the community—as with Esperanza, the young protagonist of Sandra Cisneros's *The House on Mango Street*—and the importance of memory and storytelling in forging connections between generations—as in Pat Mora's *House of Houses* or Cristina García's *Dreaming in Cuban.*

Because many of the families of the writers profiled have emigrated from Latin America, plot lines frequently center on an individual's adaptation to new surroundings, in the face of translocation and migration. Protagonists and narrators reflect on the cost of assimilating to white, English-speaking mainstream society in the United States. In *Hunger of Memory,* Richard Rodriguez writes about the loss that accompanies assimilation; for him the expression of identity is bound up in the language a writer chooses to use. In Rodriguez's case the choice is primarily English, but readers will find that Latino authors refuse to "stay" in one language, and they use English and Spanish in dynamic ways. Poets such as Tato Laviera incorporate Spanglish, a hybrid of English and Spanish, into their writing, while Latino characters can be heard "code switching," or shifting between languages, as in the work of Junot Díaz. This linguistic activity represents the experience of living in both English- and Spanish-speaking worlds.

The volume also surveys writers who depict gender roles in largely patriarchal, Catholic Latino communities. In recalling his own coming of age in Mexico, for example, Ilan Stavans observes: "In school, boys are required to constantly test their stamina and muscular strength, *ser muy macho* [be very macho]. Girls can cry, express their inner emotions, but men are encouraged to remain silent instead of sharing their psychological ups and downs. To open up, *abrirse,* is a sign of feminine weakness, whereas to penetrate, *meter,* means to demonstrate superiority" (*The Hispanic Condition: Reflections on Culture and Identity in America,* 135). Stavans's thoughts can be used as a framework for many of the tensions between husbands and wives, girlfriends and boyfriends in the Latino narrative, especially in the work of Denise Chávez and Ana Castillo.

The contributors to this volume take care to point out how Latino literature upsets many of the expectations of a mainstream audience. Latino authors seek, in many ways, to rewrite history from their own point of view, correcting stereotypes, such as that Latinos are overly sexual, lazy, or superstitious; that they work illegally or steal jobs from Americans; that they are all ignorant laborers and maids or drug dealers and thugs. Perhaps because stereotypes and irony are, for better or worse, closely aligned, we see them used comically in many works, such as John Leguizamo's *Freak,* Erika Lopez's *Flaming Iguanas,* and Guillermo Gómez-Peña's performance art.

Survey of Hispanic-American Literature

What follows is a survey of Latino literature, with a brief discussion of its colonial roots. Hispanic-American literature emerged from Spanish colonial writing of the Americas. In 1492 Christopher Columbus issued missives about his 33-day voyage from the Canary Islands to the Caribbean. For the admiral no words could express the beauty of what would be called the Caribbean; nevertheless, Columbus uses a rich, descriptive language to describe the islands and peoples of the Caribbean in a style that would become characteristic of New World travel writing.

In his accounts Columbus recognizes that the tendrils of nature extend to him and his men, inviting the sea-worn Spanish explorers into a sultry land of tribal cultures and mysterious legends about cities of gold. He comes to learn of Taino myths that foretell the coming of the white and fair-haired foreigners, myths that will eventually be found elsewhere among the indigenous peoples of the Americas (notably among the Aztec and Maya). Columbus leverages the prophecies about the coming of the white man to advance the "civilizing" mission of the Spanish monarchs Isabella and Ferdinand. By converting the natives of the Americas to Christianity, Columbus and Spanish conquistadores could make trade and exportation of goods from the New World to the Old a safer proposition. In the minds of the Spanish, Christian natives would be more obedient than pagan ones. And, at least, according to the Spanish historian Bartolomé de Las Casas, this indeed proved to be the case in the conquest of the Caribbean.

The activities of Columbus and his counterparts set the stage for indigenous conversion to Catholicism and for the use of slave and indentured labor throughout Latin America. As an early contributor—if not founder—of Hispanic-American literature, Columbus set up in his writing an important binary between the European self and the American "other" that is registered in Hispanic-American narratives, poems, plays, performances, and essays. After Columbus's first contact with the natives of the Caribbean, Spain expanded its empire through the efforts of conquistadores such as Hernán Cortés in Mexico, Francisco Pizarro in Peru, and Álvar Núñez Cabeza de Vaca in what is now Florida and the Southwest. By the 1500s the notion of the "other" became more complex, as the Spanish increasingly mixed with the indigenous inhabitants of the Americas. So, too, did the introduction of West African slaves in the Americas broaden the diversity of Latin America, especially on its coasts. Many Latino authors reconstruct in their work the fateful meeting between the Spanish and the indigenous and West African peoples, notably Rodolfo Acuña, Guillermo Gómez-Peña, and Aurora Levins Morales. Hispanic-American literature, as we shall see, reckons with the complexity of Spanish, West African, and indigenous cultures that have met, clashed, and merged with one another.

Taken together, audiences can read Mexican-American, Puerto Rican, Cuban-American, and Dominican-American literature as an ongoing conversation within one's family and community. It is a lively dialogue between Latino groups, and it is an engagement with mainstream society—a conversation that involves introspection and debate. As Columbus learned in his own attempts to capture the unique experience of life in Caribbean, language sometimes fails to express reality. Notwithstanding such difficulty, Hispanic-American authors have shared with their audiences a diverse cast of narrators, characters, and lyrical voices in a literature rich in pathos and vision.

The following surveys the various subgroups of Hispanic-American literature.

Cuban-American Literature

Cuban-American literature often reckons with its Spanish colonial roots. It started as a literature of protest. In 1891, nearly 400 years after Columbus advertised the wealth of the Caribbean and right after the last African slaves of the Americas had been freed in Brazil, Cuban revolutionary José Martí published his famous essay entitled "Our America." In it Martí argues that the countries of the Americas, including the Caribbean and Latin America, ought to celebrate their indigenous, African, and mestizo roots. Martí takes inventory of the indigenous cultures of the Caribbean as well as the impressive accomplishments of the Aztec of Mexico and the Inca of Peru. Unlike many statesmen of the 19th century, Martí regards ethnic diversity favorably. In addition he views the peasant, rather than the aristocrat, as an individual uncorrupted by modernity, imperial power, and European ways. For Martí the peasant works hard and lives close to nature; because of his simple ways, the peasant can resist tyranny and foreign ideas, especially those from the United States, Spain, and France. Thus Martí establishes a theme that will become important in Latino literature: the validation of the local and the struggle of ordinary people.

The most compelling argument in "Our America" is to create; Martí emphasizes the importance of making decisions, writing, and living life in ways that reflect the "American" character. He says America should not blindly imitate the United States or Europe, that it rather ought to establish a government that is unique and appropriate to the Americas.

Since the publication of Martí's essay, Cubans and Cuban Americans have migrated back and forth from the island to the United States, settling first in Miami and New York, but now as far as Los Angeles. One impetus for the migration of Cubans was Fidel Castro's assumption of power in 1959 and the establishment of his communist regime. Since 1959 Cuba has been enmeshed in a complex political and economic international situation, which involves U.S. sanctions against the island, U.S. occupation of the island's Guatánamo Bay, and Cuban-American resistance to Castro's regime. Only one thing is certain: Castro stirs up heated debate among Cuban-American writers. His brother, Raúl Castro, may be more acceptable to Cuban Americans now that he has taken Fidel's place as president.

Well-known Cuban-American writers include novelists Oscar Hijuelos and Cristina García, as well as cultural commentators such as Gustavo Pérez Firmat. A prolific author, Pérez Firmat contemplates the experience of living between two cultures in his poetry collection *Bilingual Blues.* Hijuelos represents the life of immigrant laborers in *Empress of the Splendid Season,* in which the character Lidia leaves her life of privilege in Cuba and becomes a maid in New York. And García uses the interplay between Cuba's history and the experience of family exile to track characters who move back and forth between the United States and the island in *The Agüero Sisters.*

Dominican-American Literature

In addition to Columbus, the Spanish priest Bartolomé de Las Casas is an important figure in early Dominican writing. Las Casas defended the rights of Hispaniola's indigenous in *The Devastation of the Indies: A Brief Account* (1552). In this critical history of the encounter between the Spanish and the islanders, Las Casas writes:

> And of all the infinite universe of humanity, these people are the most guileless, the most devoid of wickedness and duplicity, the most obedient and faithful to their native masters and to the Spanish Christians whom they serve. They are by nature the most humble, patient, and peaceable, holding no grudges, free from embroilments, neither excitable nor quarrelsome.... The sons of [Spanish] nobles among us, brought up in the enjoyments of life, are no more delicate than are these Indians, even those among them who are of the lowest rank of [Indian] laborers ... Yet into this sheepfold, into this land of meek outcasts there came some Spaniards who immediately behaved like ravening wild beasts, wolves, tigers, or lions that had been starved for many days. And Spaniards have behaved in no other way during the past forty years, down to the present time, for they are still acting like ravening beasts, killing, terrorizing, afflicting, torturing, and destroying the native peoples, doing all this with the strangest and most varied new methods of cruelty, never seen or heard of before, and to such a degree that this Island of Hispaniola, once so populous (having a population that I estimated to be more than three millions), has now a population of barely two hundred persons (27–28).

By the 19th century authors such as Manuel Galván seized upon Las Casas's argument about preserving the Taino nobility of Hispaniola. In *Enriquillo* Galván honors the Spanish priest Las Casas by making him a historical character in the novel's plot.

Nevertheless, the racial reality of the Dominican Republic is that it is more mulatto (a mixture of African and Spanish heritages) than Taino in its ethnic makeup. By the 20th century President Trujillo led a "whitening campaign" to lighten the appearance of islanders (through facial creams, hair straightening, and the invitation of European immigrants, who could lighten the race with their children). Afro-Caribbean authors such as Alan Cambeira, Loida Maritza Pérez, and Junot Díaz reflect on their West African and Spanish heritage in their fiction. The island's West African slave roots are both a source of inspiration and racial conflict in Dominican politics.

Having lived within the sphere of Trujillo's influences, Julia Alvarez and Rhina Espaillat recall the harrowing experience of life on the island. Alvarez writes about Trujillo in *How the García Girls Lost Their Accents* and other novels, while Espaillat contemplates in her autobiographical poetry the effect of Trujillo's regime on her family. Taken together, the work of Cambeira, Pérez, Alvarez, Espaillat, and Díaz bring to life a wide range of exile and immigrant experiences.

Mexican–American Literature

It should be pointed out that although the terms *Chicano* and *Mexican-American* are often used interchangeably in literary circles, they really are two distinct adjectives reflecting different generations and ideologies. The word *Chicano* reflects the Mexican-American resistance to U.S. and Mexican forms of authority and often marks differences between older Mexican Americans and a political generation of writers who came of age in the 20th century. Not all writers accept the term; for example, José Villarreal, the Mexican-American author of *Pocho,* insists on being recognized as an American writer and rejects the label Chicano.

As with Spanish-American colonial accounts of the Caribbean, Mexican-American literature has its roots in the writings of soldiers, explorers, and priests. Though it is difficult to choose one text as foundational, Fray Bernardino de Sahagún's Florentine Codex anticipates many of the conflicts and themes of Mexican-American literature. In this history of the Spanish Conquest, we have the first indigenous perspective of the European encounter and the events that followed. In the codex Aztec warriors recount their meeting with Hernán Cortés and his men. Conveying their

stories in their own language, Nahuatl, the Indian narrators describe European dress and forms of warfare. As with Columbus's writing and that of Las Casas, the Florentine Codex reinforces the theme of opposition between the European self and the indigenous other that has shaped Hispanic-American writing. As important, the codex depicts one of the most important female figures in Mexican history: La Malinche. Malinche (Malintzín) was Cortés's interpreter and mistress and bore him a son. This son represents a new race of people in the Americas: the mestizo born of Spanish and Indian blood. This mixture of cultures and bloodlines is a significant theme in Mexican-American literature; writers and characters often ask the questions: Am I Spanish, or am I Indian? Am I neither, or am I both?

After Cortés's arrival in 1519, Spanish colonization of Mexico took root and continued until the country's independence from Spain in 1821. In this period Mexico held the territory that is now the U.S. Southwest. With the signing of the Treaty of Guadalupe Hidalgo in 1848 after the U.S.-Mexican War, Mexicans in the Southwest became Mexican Americans overnight, as the treaty's provisions ceded the territory to the United States for $15 million. The United States, in turn, agreed to respect the cultural and property rights of Mexicans living in the Southwest. For Mexican Americans whose ancestors were "Americanized" after the 1848 signing, the treaty is a topic of legal debate. Descendants of Mexicans who owned ranches affected by the treaty have launched land tenure suits to secure their rightful property, especially in New Mexico, where such documentation is often more readily available than elsewhere. The issue of land is one that occupies many Mexican-American narratives.

Although there were signs of cultural validation of Mexican-American culture in the work of such authors as Josephina Niggli and Fabiola Cabeza de Vaca, the Chicano civil rights movement really set the scene for a widespread affirmation of individual and collective Mexican-American identity. Civil rights activists and writers such as Corky Gonzales and Cesar Chavez and their counterparts made visible to the U.S. public issues affecting Latino communities: working conditions, job opportunities, access to education, and the right to speak Spanish.

By recognizing their mestizo heritage, both Indian and Spanish, Mexican Americans exposed discrimination and racism at school, in the workplace, and in the military. Mexican Americans also created local and national organizations to secure their civic rights and began using the name *Chicano*. Mexican-American farm laborers joined the United Farm Workers Movement founded by Cesar Chavez; he and his colleagues exposed the harsh conditions of migrant farm labor, an issue that informs such works as Tomás Rivera's classic novel . . . *Y no se lo tragó la tierra* (. . . *And the Earth Did Not Devour Him*). One of the most important works of the period is Rodolfo Gonzales's *Yo soy Joaquín/I Am Joaquín*, which examines the civil rights movement as a postcolonial reaction to first Spanish and later U.S. forms of colonialism. Similarly, legal and social issues surface in border literature, dealing with the fate of illegal immigrants and female factory workers, as in Luis Alberto Urrea's *Across the Wire: Life and Hard Times on the Mexican Border* (1993), Ramón "Tianguis" Pérez's *Diary of an Undocumented Immigrant* (1991), and Alicia Gaspar de Alba's *Desert Blood: The Juárez Murders* (2005).

Puerto Rican Literature

Like their Dominican and Cuban counterparts, Puerto Rican writers have inherited a Spanish colonial literary tradition. Puerto Rican literature in the 19th century bears the mark of Spanish colonial rule in that most of the writers came from the upper class and imitated European ways of being and thinking. After the Spanish-American War in 1898, Puerto Rico celebrated independence from Spain, and islanders were excited about the possibility of severing ties from Europe so that they could establish their own Puerto Rican identity. But these hopes were frustrated when the United States invaded the island and claimed Puerto Rico as a U.S. commonwealth. This event, perhaps more than any other, has divided islanders ever since.

Puerto Rican literature expresses the historical changes that islanders have faced, especially given the transition from Spanish colony to U.S. commonwealth and the impending transition from U.S. commonwealth to either nationhood or U.S. state status. Cultural critic Juan Flores explains:

The first Puerto Ricans to write about life in the United States were political exiles from the independence struggle against Spain, who came to New York in the late decades of the nineteenth century to escape the clutches of the colonial authorities. Some of Puerto Rico's most prominent intellectual and revolutionary leaders, such as Eugenio María de Hostos, Ramón Emeterio Betances, Lola Rodríguez de Tío, and Sotero Figueroa, spent more or less extended periods in New York, where along with fellow exiles from Cuba they charted further steps to free their countries from Spanish rule. The lofty ideals of "Antillean unity" found concrete expression in the establishment of the Cuban and Puerto Rican Revolutionary Party, under the leadership of the eminent Cuban patriot Jose Martí. This early community was largely composed of the radical patriotic elite, but there was already a solid base of artisans and laborers who lent support to the many organizational activities. It should also be mentioned that one of these first settlers from Puerto Rico was Arturo Alfonso Schomburg, a founder of the Club Dos Antillas and, in later years, a scholar of the African experience. The writings that give testimonial accounts and impressions of those years in New York are scattered in diaries, correspondences, and the often short-lived revolutionary newspapers and still await compilation and perusal.

Some Puerto Rican writers, such as Esmeralda Santiago, focus on the benefits of the island's commonwealth relationship with the United States. Other novelists, such as Pedro Juan Soto, the author of *Spiks,* advocate Puerto Rican independence and fiercely criticize the United States, viewing it as an imperial power.

Analyzing Puerto Rican literature is challenging because many Puerto Ricans live both on the island and on the mainland. As both Magali García Ramis and Santiago demonstrate in their autobiographical works, Puerto Ricans travel to and from the mainland and the island with frequency. García Ramis's novel *Happy Days, Uncle Sergio* explores the vexed situation of being both Puerto Rican and American. In the novel Lidia considers her life on the island and relationship to the United States and realizes that she has many unresolved questions about her own identity, about the influence of European knowledge, art, and forms, as well as about the need to maintain one's autonomy. She expresses herself through a letter to Uncle Sergio, who, like hundreds and thousands of Puerto Ricans, has returned to New York after moving back and forth between the island and the mainland. Similarly, Santiago's *When I Was Puerto Rican* illustrates the challenges and dangers of relocating to New York from the island in a compelling coming-of-age story and narrative about assimilation.

Depending on their attitudes and their upbringing, Puerto Rican authors write in Spanish and/or English. Authors such as Piri Thomas write in English, while authors from the island, such as Manuel Zeno Gandía and Ana Roqué, choose Spanish as their means of communication. Puerto Rican literature explores a wide range of themes, from country living (Ana Roqué) to prison life (Miguel Piñero).

Bibliography

Census Bureau, U.S. "The Hispanic Population in the United States: March 2002." June 2003. Available online. URL: http://www.census.gov/prod/2003pubs/p20-545.pdf. Accessed September 17, 2007.

Flores, Juan. *ADE Bulletin* 91 (Winter 1998). Available online. URL: http://www.ade.org/ade/bulletin/N091/toc/091toc.htm. Accessed September 17, 2007.

Las Casas, Bartolomé de. *The Devastation of the Indies: A Brief Account.* Translated by Herma Briffault, Baltimore, Md.: Johns Hopkins University Press, 1992.

Stavans, Ilan. *The Hispanic Condition: Reflections on Culture and Identity in America.* New York: HarperCollins, 2001.

Luz Elena Ramirez

A TO Z
ENTRIES

Acuña, Rodolfo (1932–) (historian, teacher, activist)

Rodolfo Acuña was born in the Boyle Heights area of Los Angeles, California, in 1932 to Mexican parents. He earned his B.A. from Los Angeles State College (now California State University, Los Angeles) and an M.A. and Ph.D. in Latin American studies from the University of Southern California in 1968. During the 1960s he was involved in the civil rights movement and belonged to the Latin American Civic Association. He began his training in history as a Latin Americanist and came to focus on Mexican-American communities. He began his career in education teaching in high school, but by 1966 he offered a groundbreaking Mexican-American history course at Mount St. Mary's College in California. Since 1969 Acuña has been a professor at California State University, Northridge, where he helped found one of the nation's first, and now the largest, Chicano/a studies programs. Acuña has published more than 15 books, including ANYTHING BUT MEXICAN: CHICANOS IN CONTEMPORARY LOS ANGELES (1996) and the seminal history text OCCUPIED AMERICA: A HISTORY OF CHICANOS (1972).

In the 1990s he contributed a column for the *Los Angeles Times*; during this time he was also compelled to pursue a discrimination law suit against the University of California, Santa Barbara. This lawsuit, which took place from 1991 to 1996, is documented in his book *Sometimes There Is No Other Side: Chicanos and the Myth of Equality* (1998). Acuña was awarded a settlement, which he used to found a Chicana and Chicano studies foundation. His numerous honors include a National Association for Chicano Studies Scholar Award, the Emil Freed Award from the Southern California Social Science Library, the Gustavus Myers Award, and a Liberty Hill Founder's Award. Acuña's work creates a critical context for the study of CHICANO LITERATURE and BORDER LITERATURE.

Bibliography

Acuña, Rodolfo. *Anything but Mexican: Chicanos in Contemporary Los Angeles*. London: Verso, 1996.
———. *Occupied America: A History of Chicanos*. San Francisco, Calif.: Canfield Press, 1972.
———. *Sometimes There Is No Other Side: Chicanos and the Myth of Equality*. Notre Dame, Ind.: University of Notre Dame Press, 1998.
Calderón, José. "We Have a Tiger by the Tail: An Interview with Rudy Acuña." *Color Lines: Race, Action, Culture* 2, no. 2 (Summer 1999): 21–23.
Pitt, Stephen. "Rodolfo Acuña." *The Latino/a History Project*. Edited by Stephen Pitt. 2004. Available online. URL: http://www.latinohistory.com/people.php?id=106&keywords=mexican&print=1. Accessed September 17, 2007.

Alex Feerst

Adventures of Juan Chicaspatas, The
Rudolfo Anaya (1985)

The Adventures of Juan Chicaspatas is a mock epic poem that explores historical and mythological roots of Chicano culture. The main characters are

3

two "Chicano homeboys," Juan Chicaspatas and Al Penco. Juan Chicaspatas translates literally as "Johnny Little Feet" and is a slang term that means "Chicano." Al Penco's name is a variation of a street word for a womanizer. As both stereotypes and archetypes of Chicano culture, Juan and Al set out to find "the truth of AZTLÁN" (14), the mythic homeland of Chicanos. It is the place of the seven caves from which the Aztec migrated south into the Valley of Mexico centuries ago. Juan and Al are Chicano folk heroes whose duty is to remind the people in "Chicanoland" that the Southwest is Aztlán, the homeland to which they belong and with which they have an ancient covenant with the earth.

In Anaya's poem the secret of Aztlán offers a powerful corrective to the dark despair of the barrios, the "streets of neglect / and poverty and discrimination" (11) where the Chicano factory workers and farm laborers suffer because they are enslaved: "'Greed and the Gringo way have killed the spirit of our leaders'" (10). Anaya uses the picaresque qualities of Juan and Al to convey the probable cultural demise if Chicanos continue to go the "Gringo way" and forget the legacy of Aztlán. Juan and Al must therefore journey to the origin of Chicano culture, to Aztlán, to find a way to help the people remember the past.

The poem begins with Juan invoking a radical variant of classical epic introductions, saying, "Arms of the women, I sing" (5). The arms of which Juan sings are not weapons raised in warfare but rather the "arms of the women" that embraced and nurtured the Chicano people through the cataclysms of conquest. The women Juan praises are La MALINCHE, *Madre de los mestizos* (5), the Virgen de Guadalupe (Virgin of Guadalupe), La LLORONA (the Weeping Woman), and his *jefita* (mother). Juan asks the Virgen de Guadalupe, the synthesis of Indian and Catholic spirituality, to light his way "so the world may know / the beauty / and pride" of Chicanos (5). He sings to La Llorona in whom he "found [his] manhood," and he praises the strength, love, hard work, and sacrifices made on his behalf by his *jefita.* These women symbolize hybrid spirituality, sexuality, and family, which Anaya posits as the bases of

Chicano culture. Through Juan's celebration of these women Anaya asserts the importance of women in Chicano culture and exposes feminine qualities too often overshadowed by machismo. Central to the epic is La Malinche (Malintzin or Doña Marina), the Indian woman who served as Hernán Cortés's translator during the Spanish Conquest of Mexico and bore him a son. Anaya presents Malinche as the "mother of all Chicanos" (5), a "woman betrayed by Cortés," thereby removing the traitor stigma often associated with her. It is Madre Malinche who leads Juan and Al through time and space to teach them "the secret of Aztlán" (11) so that they can carry the stories back to the barrios and "Tell [the Chicano people] that their Eden and their Camelot / are in Aztlán. Their covenant is with / the earth of this world" (40), with the southwestern United States and its Indian cultures. Madre Malinche directs Juan and Al to Moctezuma, the Aztec ruler when Cortés invaded Mexico, and to Coatlicue, an Aztec goddess and the mother of the Aztec war god Huitzilopochtli. Coatlicue begs Juan and Al to return Huitzilopochtli to her, which means retrieving him from Tenochtitlán (Mexico City) on the eve of the Spanish Conquest. When Moctezuma obeys Coatlicue and orders Huitzilopochtli to return to Coatlicue in Aztlán, the people of Mexico are "robbed of their war spirit" (42). Mexico is therefore conquered in part because of Huitzilopochtli's absence. Malinche explains, "History has turned and twisted, / and now a new time is being born" (44) in which *la raza* (the people) must reestablish their "covenant with the earth of Aztlán" (48).

For Anaya, place and spirituality cannot be separated, nor can the Chicano present be divorced from the Indian past. His poem ends with Malinche promising the Chicano people that now is the time for the return of the ancient gods Huitzilopochtli and Quetzalcoatl who, along with "Christo and the kachinas" (44), will restore harmony with the earth and balance to the lives of Chicanos. This poem, and Anaya's work more broadly, can be read within the context of both CHICANO LITERATURE and BORDER LITERATURE.

Bibliography

Anaya, Rudolfo. *The Adventures of Juan Chicaspatas.* Houston, Tex: Arte Público Press, 1985.

———. "Aztlán." *The Anaya Reader.* New York: Warner Books, 1995, pp. 371–383.

Beekman Taylor, Paul. "Chicano Secrecy in the Fiction of Rudolfo A. Anaya." *Journal of the Southwest* 39, no. 2 (1997): 239–265.

Fernández Olmos, Margarite. *Rudolfo A. Anaya: A Critical Companion.* Westport, Conn.: Greenwood Press, 1999.

Lamadrid, Enrique R. "The Rogue's Progress: Journeys of the Picaro from Oral Tradition to Contemporary Chicano Literature of New Mexico." *MELUS* 20, no. 2 (1995): 15–34.

Sandra L. Dahlberg

Agosín, Marjorie (1955–) *(memoirist, poet)*

Marjorie Agosín was born in Bethesda, Maryland, in 1955 and raised in Santiago, Chile. She studied at the Instituto Hebreo in Santiago and later, when she returned to the United States, earned a B.A. in Spanish and philosophy from the University of Georgia, where her father was a visiting professor. By 1971, while her father was teaching in Georgia, political conditions in Chile under Salvador Allende's government compelled her family to remain in the United States. And it is in the United States, with memories of and visits to Chile, that Agosín has remained. She pursued a Ph.D. from Indiana University in Latin American literature, with a dissertation on Latin American author María Luisa Bombal. Since 1982 Agosín has taught Spanish and Latin American literature at Wellesley College.

In addition to her family narratives *A CROSS AND A STAR: MEMOIRS OF A JEWISH GIRL IN CHILE* (1994), *ALWAYS FROM SOMEWHERE ELSE: A MEMOIR OF MY CHILEAN JEWISH FATHER* (1998), and *The Alphabet in My Hands: A Writing Life* (2000), Agosín has published collections of poetry and short stories, critical essays on writers such as Gabriela Mistral and Pablo Neruda, and anthologies of writing by Latin American women. Her recognitions include a Latino Literature Prize in 1995 for *Toward the Splendid City* (1994), the 1995 Letras de Oro Prize for *Noche estrellada* (1996; published in English as *Starry Night*), a Peabody award for *Scraps of Life: Chilean Arpilleras* (1987), and human rights awards, including a United Nations Leadership Award, the Jeanette Rankin Award, and Hadassah's Henrietta Szold Award. For its political themes and interest in family life and Chilean history, Agosín's work can be read alongside that of ISABEL ALLENDE and ARIEL DORFMAN.

Bibliography

Agosín, Marjorie. *The Alphabet in My Hands: A Writing Life.* Translated by Nancy Abraham Hall. Piscataway, N.J.: Rutgers University Press, 2000.

———. *Always from Somewhere Else: A Memoir of My Chilean Jewish Father.* Translated by Celeste Kostopulos-Cooperman. New York: Feminist Press at CUNY, 1998.

———. *A Cross and a Star: Memoirs of a Jewish Girl in Chile.* Translated by Celeste Kostopulos-Cooperman. Albuquerque: University of New Mexico Press, 1995.

———. *Scraps of life: Chilean Arpilleras.* Translated by Cola Franzen. London: Zed, 1987.

———. *Toward the Splendid City.* Translated by Richard Schaaf. Tempe, Ariz.: Bilingual Press/Editorial Bilingüe, 1994.

Horan, Elizabeth. "Agosín, Marjorie." In *Jewish Writers of Latin America: A Dictionary,* edited by Darrell B. Lockhart, 7–13. New York: Garland, 1997.

Alex Feerst

Agüero Sisters, The Cristina García (1997)

Born in 1958, CRISTINA GARCÍA emigrated with her family from Cuba to the United States when she was two years old; she was raised in New York. García's *The Agüero Sisters* focuses on multiple generations of the Agüero family, who represent various aspects of Cuba's history from its 1898 independence to the 1990s. Characters include Blanca Mestre Agüero and her husband, Ignacio Agüero; both are naturalists from Pinar del Río (located in the westernmost region of the island). The novel focuses on Blanca's daughters—Reina and Constancia.

Throughout the novel García links the Agüero family and its tangled fortunes to the political life and future of Cuba. We can appreciate García's suggestive play on the word *agüero,* which in Spanish means "omen"; accordingly, there are many twists and turns in the plot that make this title satisfying. For example, the author uses the foreboding presence of an owl to announce the birth of Ignacio Agüero, who is born on the day that President Tomás Estrada Palma (1835–1908) visits the people of Pinar del Río. Because Estrada Palma was Cuba's first president, this is a moment that suggests the union of the islanders as a nation, a coming together of the Cuban government and the agricultural workers. This point is emphasized when we are introduced to Reinaldo Agüero, Ignacio's father. A first-generation Cuban from Spain, Reinaldo reads to the peasants at the tobacco factory, thereby spreading the fruits of his intellectual labor. But when Reinaldo Agüero dies, so too does the optimistic era he comes from; his son, Ignacio, abandons the occupation of lector to pursue a university education as a scientist. Ignacio meets Blanca while conducting fieldwork, and they marry, despite her ambivalence.

Blanca gives birth to Constancia and to Reina, but only Constancia is Ignacio's child. Though she carries Ignacio's last name, Reina Agüero's biological father is kept a mystery; her first name, in any case, means "queen" in Spanish, and indeed she is equally sensual and regal in her bearing. Readers know only that Reina's father is a towering, well-dressed mulatto "with a touch of oriental blood" and that he has a place in Blanca's heart (265). Not much is known about Constancia and Reina's teenage years. But by 1959 Constancia leaves Cuba during FIDEL CASTRO's revolution with her second husband, Heberto Cruz. Gonzalo Cruz was Constancia's first husband and father to her son, Silvestre. Although they flee Cuba with very little, Heberto and Constancia Cruz settle in New York and prosper; they have one daughter, Isabel. The owner of an upscale tobacco shop, Heberto is an advocate of dismantling Castro's regime; he dies during a Miami-based invasion of Cuba. Reina Agüero, meanwhile, names her daughter Dulce

Fuerte, in honor of her lover, the revolutionary José Luís Fuerte. Until the 1990s Reina supports Castro's government; however, her incredible survival of an electric shock, her estrangement with Constancia, and her perusal of family documents prompt her to reconsider her fidelity to "El Comandante" (Castro). Reina will ultimately move to Florida to be with Constancia and to start a new life as a middle-aged woman in her sexual prime.

The Agüero Sisters presents the stories of Constancia and Reina and their geographical and ideological dislocation as Cubans caught up in *la revolución* (Castro's overthrow of Batista Fulgencio's regime in 1959). The sisters' experiences are conveyed through their own perspectives and therefore give rise to competing versions of the same events, truths, and even lies. Though sharing a mother, the girls are raised separately; as adults, the women contend with loyalties that often set them in opposition to each other. The fragmented construction of the narrative highlights the compromises they make; at the same time, familial, cultural, and gender negotiations ensure their growth as individuals. The narrative traces how Constancia and Reina respond to situations of confusion about their identity (they think they share the same father) and how they confront the fact that Ignacio Cruz murdered their mother. Ultimately, *The Agüero Sisters* conveys a message of reconciliation between the two women and, by extension, between Cubans living in the United States and those on the island.

The novel depends on the classical technique of storytelling in which readers search for clues to unlock a hidden treasure. In this case the treasure comes in the form of family secrets, which are soon to be disclosed as Constancia finds her family's trunk on the grounds of the old Mestre farm in Camagüey, Cuba. The prologue, meanwhile, provides cryptic answers to questions that will soon arise concerning the brutal death of Blanca Mestre Agüero. It is 1948, and Blanca, once estranged from her husband (probably because of her love of Reina's father), has agreed to join Ignacio for a trip to the Zapata Swamp. The married couple has embarked on a hunting expedition for ruddy ducks for a new museum collection in Boston. Ignacio takes aim at a bee hummingbird but, for inexplicable reasons (although he could have been jealous), shoots his wife instead. While the reasons for her murder are unclear, we do know that Blanca has special powers of intuition and insight that her husband, Ignacio, a man trained in enlightened thought and scientific observation, cannot understand. She carries a bone in her belt, which is a token to nature, the spirit world, and perhaps an emblem of SANTERÍA. Her relationship to nature emphasizes the gap in sensitivities between men and women and highlights García's feminist insistence on the validation of female powers in the narrative.

After the shooting episode the author interweaves Ignacio's voice with the voices of Constancia, Reina, and their children to indicate the perplexing web of family relations. In its unfolding of events the novel explains Blanca's murder as a fatal occurrence that illustrates how the past is inextricably woven into the events of the present and the future. The author moves from voice to voice to signal the onset of a new generation of Cubans living in the 1990s and the departure of a way of life that existed before *la revolución* (a life that was traditional, comfortable, sometimes decadent, and amenable to foreign investors and residents of the 1940s and 1950s).

By the 1980s we find the feminine and fair-skinned Constancia living in New York City with her successful husband, Heberto; the Cruz family has acculturated to American mainstream culture. Once widowed, Constancia becomes a successful cosmetics saleswoman and maintains her own beauty and slim figure—a testament to the efficaciousness of her products. After she moves to Miami, she launches her own line of cosmetic products, vials and bottles that bear on the label the face of her beautiful mother. Though well adjusted to American life, Constancia has not abandoned her beliefs in *milagros* (good luck charms) or the foretelling of the future through Santería.

Meanwhile, Reina has remained in Cuba and supported Castro's government. She is a strong woman and a skilled electrician who works throughout the Cuban countryside. Respected by her coworkers, she is called the *"compañera amazona"* (*compañera* and *compañero* are the terms that revolutionaries use to express solidarity and friendship). Sensuous and statuesque (she is nearly six feet tall), Reina has many admirers and lovers; her character allows the author to subvert the Latin American double standard that men may have many affairs without much censure but women are criticized if they do the same.

By the time the narrative leads the reader into the 1990s, we see that Constancia and Reina differ in virtually every respect: in their allegiances to each of their parents, in their appearances, and in their love lives. The memories the two sisters have of Blanca and Ignacio are completely different, and in this way they represent the multiple memories and lineages of the islanders. The sisters' arguments are necessary and culminate in a tentative reconciliation with Constancia's return to Cuba. She seeks the remains of Heberto, who has died in a failed attempt to recover Cuba from Castro's communist government. She also finds the buried trunk her uncle has left for her; this trunk will give her the answers she is anxious to have about her mother, Blanca. The trunk contains her father's papers, as well as a declaration handwritten by Ignacio; Constancia reads with her own eyes that her father killed Blanca. Constancia also finds in the trunk the bone Blanca used to carry, and remembering that her sister asked her for it, she decides to take it for her to Miami. The bone becomes the symbol of reconciliation and hope, perhaps for a world much wider than the Cubans divided by time and geography.

Throughout her novel, García uses many narrative voices and shifts in chronology from the early 1900s to the 1990s. This nonlinear and complex structure recalls her other novels, *DREAMING IN CUBAN* (1992) and *MONKEY HUNTING* (2003), as well as Latin American works such as Gabriel García Márquez's *Chronicle of a Death Foretold* (1981) and Mario Vargas Llosa's *Who Killed Palomino Molero?* (1986). *The Agüero Sisters* has been well received among literary critics and was designated a notable book by the *New York Times*. Because of its dual setting between Cuba and Florida, García's novel can be read within the context of CUBAN-AMERICAN LITERATURE as well as SPANISH-AMERICAN CARIBBEAN LITERATURE.

Bibliography

García, Cristina. *The Agüero Sisters.* New York: Alfred A. Knopf, 1997.

García Márquez, Gabriel. *Chronicle of a Death Foretold.* Translated Gregory Rabassa. London: Jonathan Cape, 1982.

Luis, William. *Dance Between Two Cultures: Latino Caribbean Literature Written in the United States.* Nashville, Tenn.: Vanderbilt University Press, 1997.

Marmolejo-McWatt, Amparo. "Blanca Mestre as Ochún in *The Agüero Sisters.*" *Afro-Hispanic Review* 24, no. 2 (Fall 2005): 89–101.

Vargas Llosa, Mario. *Who Killed Palomino Molero?* Translated by Alfred MacAdam. New York: Farrar, Straus, Giroux, 1987.

Amparo McWatt

Alburquerque Rudolfo Anaya (1992)

In *Alburquerque*, RUDOLFO ANAYA takes on the large-scope novel of urban politics and class division. In the title and throughout the book, Anaya restores the *r* that was removed from the word *Alburquerque* when an Anglo stationmaster could not pronounce it (the name of the city today is *Albuquerque*). To Anaya the diminution of the very name of the city is emblematic of the injury to the Chicano culture and sense of self that the Anglo occupation of the Southwest has inflicted.

As in Anaya's novel *BLESS ME, ÚLTIMA* (1972), *Alburquerque* incorporates elements of Chicano history and mythology; in his settings, plots, and characterizations, Anaya combines indigenous beliefs with those of Catholicism while keeping in mind the intimate relationship between humankind and nature. He also focuses on the clash of cultures between the dominant English-speaking society and the Spanish-speaking mestizo peoples of the Southwest.

Alburquerque is a novel concerned with identity. The narrative seeks to learn the identity of the father of Abrán González, who learns in the first pages that he was adopted and is the son of a wealthy Anglo girl and her Chicano boyfriend. This search takes the former Golden Gloves champion from the barrio to the wealthiest suburbs and into a high-stakes prizefight in the midst of a bitter political struggle to determine the future of Alburquerque. The people touched by his search are also deeply concerned with identity, one Anglo trying to forge a political identity as a descendant of the original duke of Alburquerque, another trying to hide his wife's Marrano (Spanish Jewish convert to Christianity) heritage. Others are just struggling to determine how they fit into the jigsaw puzzle of cultures and communities that is the city and its environs.

Alburquerque is infused with Anaya's characteristic mysticism and mythmaking and is written in a controlled version of his expansive, sumptuous style. His concern with the sacredness of nature and the environment becomes a major subplot in which one of the mayoral candidates aims to build an ambitious casino-canal entertainment district that will destroy the communal lands of the surrounding pueblos and the Mexican-American land-grant communities. One of his major concerns is the tension Chicanos face in trying to negotiate the gulf between their own community and that of the Anglos, who hold most of the money and power in the area. This struggle is embodied in Abrán, the *coyote* (child of Anglo and Chicano or Indian parents), as he crosses and recrosses the divide between his parents' cultures, trying to learn who he is. His quest continues even after Doña Tules, an old *CURANDERA* (healer), tells him, *Tú eres tú* ("You are you", 23).

Abrán's best friend, Joe Calabasa, another *coyote*, has avoided his family's pueblo ever since he returned shell-shocked and alcoholic from Vietnam. In the course of the novel, however, Joe is forced to take up his responsibilities to family and pueblo in order to defeat the casino-canal plan and its attempt to take his people's traditional water rights. By the end of the book, with the intervention of Coyote, the Indian trickster god, Joe is instrumental in revealing Abrán's father to him.

As in so many of Anaya's novels, the *curandera* figure is central to the plot. Not only does the wise Doña Tules provide Abrán with insights necessary in his search for identity, but Lucinda Córdova, another *curandera* whom he meets at his dying mother's bedside, brings him support, love, and a new direction for his life. She also teaches him about the mysticism of the land that brings inner power. Abrán's darkest moment comes when the pregnant Lucinda learns he has betrayed her with the beautiful incumbent mayor, Marisa Martínez, and refuses to see him any longer. Suddenly Abrán realizes that Doña Tules was right: He had everything he needed as long as he had Lucinda's love. Lucinda's return and the discovery of his father restore Abrán to wholeness.

Anaya's work has received significant critical recognition, but it is only in the past decade that he has been published by a major New York trade publisher. In their reading of Anaya's work, Julio Cañero Serrano examines the representation of Mexican-American politics, while Carmen Flys Junquera examines Anaya's environmental concerns. Both approaches help us to read Anaya's contribution to CHICANO LITERATURE as well as BORDER LITERATURE.

Bibliography

Anaya, Rodolfo. *Alburquerque*. Albuquerque: University of New Mexico Press, 1992.

———. *Bless Me, Última*. New York: Warner Books, 1999.

Bruce-Novoa, Juan D. *Chicano Authors: Inquiry by Interview*. Austin: University of Texas Press, 1980, pp. 183–202.

Cañero Serrano, Julio. "Politics of 'Chingado': Chicano Political Misrepresentation in *Heart of Aztlán* and *Alburquerque*." In *(Mis)Representations: Intersections of Culture and Power,* edited by Fernando Galván, Julio Cañero Serrano, et al., 157–171. Bern, Switzerland: Peter Lang, 2003.

Dick, Bruce, and Silvia Sirias, eds. *Conversations with Rudolfo Anaya*. Jackson: University Press of Mississippi, 1998.

Fernandez Olmos, Margarite. *Rudolfo A. Anaya: A Critical Companion*. Westport, Conn.: Greenwood Press, 1999.

Flys Junquera, Carmen. "Nature's Voice: Ecological Consciousness in Rudolfo Anaya's Alburquerque Quartet." *Aztlán* 27, no. 2 (2002): 119–138.

Vasallo, Paul, ed. *The Magic of Words: Rudolfo A. Anaya and His Writings*. Albuquerque: University of New Mexico Press, 1982.

Linda Rodriguez

Algarín, Miguel (1941–) *(poet, editor, translator)*

Born in Santurce, Puerto Rico, a suburb of San Juan, Miguel Algarín moved to the U.S. mainland with his family in the 1950s. He settled first in New York City's Spanish Harlem and then eventually moved to Queens. He holds a B.A. from the University of Wisconsin and an M.A. in English from Pennsylvania State University. Algarín received his Ph.D. in English from Rutgers University, where he was a faculty member of the English and Caribbean Studies Departments; he is now professor emeritus of Rutgers, an honor accorded to him for his more than 30 years of service. He has also taught at Brooklyn College and New York University.

Algarín is best known as the founder of the NUYORICAN POETS CAFE and its literary legacy from the 1970s to the present. The Nuyorican Poets Cafe has featured the readings and performances of such poets as TATO LAVIERA, MIGUEL PIÑERO, and VICTOR HERNÁNDEZ CRUZ. Initially a gathering of artists at Algarín's house on the Lower East Side, the group later relocated to a storefront on East 3rd Street. The Nuyorican Poets Cafe is now an international forum for writers, actors, performance artists, and musicians.

Throughout his career Algarín has cultivated the "slam" poetry movement whereby artists compete against one another with their "spoken word" performances. The recipient of six American Book Awards, Algarín is the author of more than 10 books of poetry, editor of several anthologies, and the sole translator of Chilean Nobel Prize winner Pablo Neruda's *Songs of Protest* (1976). He has edited or coedited such works as *Nuyorican Poetry: An Anthology of Puerto Rican Words and Feelings* (1975), *Aloud!: Voices from the Nuyorican Poets Cafe* (with Bob Holman, 1994), and *Action: The Nuyorican Poets Cafe Theater Festival* (with Lois Griffith, 1997). In the late 1970s Algarín helped to launch a new series in Nuyorican literature through Arte Público Press. His awards include grants from the Samuel Rubin Foundation for the Nuyorican Theater Festival, the Judy Peabody Foundation, and the New York State Council of the Arts. Algarín has directed El Puerto Rican Playwrights'/Actors Workshop and the Nuyorican Theater Festival. He was a visiting poet at Naropa University in California and has given poetry readings across the United States, as well as in the Netherlands, France, and Algeria.

Algarín's writing concerns his Puerto Rican past and his place in the United States, especially his status as a Nuyorican (a Puerto Rican living in New York). Algarín experiments with poetry by writing in both Spanish and English, a form of CODE SWITCHING. Pushing the barriers of contemporary poetry, he has composed works that incorporate French, Spanish, and English. But more than that, Algarín weaves into his work jazz and salsa rhythms, as well as avant-garde elements. He writes on topics as eclectic as Rome, outer space, and the values and concerns that drive our age. His own books, *Mongo Affair: Poetry* (1978), *On Call* (1980), *Body Bee Calling from the Twenty First Century* (1982), *Time's Now/Ya es tiempo* (1985), and *Love Is Hard Work: Memorias de Loisaida/Poems* (1997) have all moved toward the same reconciliation of living in a strange land. *Memories of Loisaida,* the subtitle of *Love Is Hard Work,* refers to the Lower East Side; the work delves into Algarín's sexuality and brings to light his awareness that he is HIV-positive. His struggle with the disease creates a bridge from his earlier poetry to a more personalized vision of his reality, a vision that helps readers to understand LATINO GAY LITERATURE. *Love Is Hard Work* exhibits Algarín's ability to use images that draw the reader directly into the action of the poem. The speaker of the poem "HIV" asks, "Can it be that I am the bearer of plagues? / Am I poison to desire? / Do I have to deny yearning for firm full flesh / so that I'll not kill what I love?" (*Aloud* 297). Like the work showcased in the café, Algarín's own creations jump from the page and blur the lines between art and life.

Bibliography

Algarín, Miguel. *Body Bee Calling from the Twenty First Century.* Houston, Tex.: Arte Público Press, 1982.

———. *Love Is Hard Work: Memorias de Loisaida/ Poems.* New York: Scribner, 1997.

———. *Mongo Affair.* New York: Nuyorican, 1978.

———. *On Call.* Houston, Tex.: Arte Público Press, 1980.

———. *Time's Now/Ya es tiempo.* Houston, Tex.: Arte Público Press, 1985.

Algarín, Miguel, and Bob Holman, eds. *Aloud: Voices from the Nuyorican Poets Cafe.* New York: Henry Holt, 1994.

Algarín, Miguel, and Lois Griffith, eds. *Action: The Nuyorican Poets Cafe Theater.* New York: Simon & Schuster, 1997.

Algarín, Miguel, et al., eds. *Nuyorican Poetry: An Anthology of Puerto Rican Words and Feelings.* New York: Morrow, 1975.

Esterrich, Carmelo. "Home and the Ruins of Language: Victor Hernández Cruz and Miguel Algarín's Nuyorican Poetry." *MELUS* 23, nos. 3, 5 (Fall 1998). Available online. URL: http://www.findarticles.com/p/articles/mi_m2278/is_3_23/ai_54925293. Downloaded November 27, 2007.

Neruda, Pablo. *Songs of Protest.* Translated by Miguel Algarín. New York: Quill, 1976.

Turner, Faythe, ed. *Puerto Rican Writers at Home in the USA: An Anthology.* Seattle, Wash.: Open Hand Publishing, 1991.

Anne Marie Fowler

Allende, Isabel (1942–) *(novelist, memoirist)*

Isabel Allende was born in Peru in 1942 but considers Chile her homeland. Much of her writing centers on the political situation of Chile in the 1960s and 1970s. On September 11, 1973, a military coup in Chile toppled the administration of President Salvador Allende, the first democratically elected Socialist government in Latin America. Whether by his own hand or as a victim of the military junta, Allende died in Santiago's presidential palace. General Augusto Pinochet assumed dictatorial control of a regime that would last for roughly two decades. The early years of the dictatorship were especially brutal, and opponents of the new government were persecuted or disappeared. Given the violence surrounding the overthrow and death of the Chilean president, Isabel Allende went into exile in 1975 after receiving threats on her own life. Allende was the goddaughter of the deceased president; she called him uncle, though in reality he was her father's cousin.

As a young woman, she had secretly been aiding dissidents and those opposing the Pinochet dictatorship. Allende took up residence in Venezuela and struggled to adapt to life as an Andean exile. Allende tried for years to make sense of what had happened to her country and family. In 1981 Allende learned of her grandfather's declining health, and after working full days as both a school administrator and a journalist, she drafted a letter to him, assuring him that his memory would live on after his death. This farewell letter to her grandfather morphed and developed over time into the novel *La casa de los espíritus,* first published in Spain in 1982. By 1985, when the English translation (*The HOUSE OF THE SPIRITS*) appeared, Allende's first novel had already garnered her accolades and prizes in France, Germany, and her homeland of Chile. In 1988 she moved to the United States. In addition to *The House of the Spirits,* which was made into a film with Jeremy Irons and Winona Ryder, Allende is the author of *The INFINITE PLAN* (1993), *PAULA* (1994), *DAUGHTER OF FORTUNE* (1999) and *My Invented Country: A Nostalgic Journey through Chile* (2003), among many other works. As a Chilean American whose work is equally imaginative, political, and somewhat autobiographical, her work can be read alongside that of MARJORIE AGOSÍN and ARIEL DORFMAN.

Bibliography

Allende, Isabel. *Daughter of Fortune.* New York: HarperCollins, 1999.
———. *The House of the Spirits.* Translated by Magda Bogin. New York: Bantam Books, 1993.
———. *My Invented Country: A Nostalgic Journey through Chile.* Translated by Margaret Sayers Peden. New York: HarperCollins, 2003.
Feal, Rosemary G., and Yvette E. Miller, eds. *Isabel Allende Today: An Anthology of Essays.* Pittsburgh, Pa.: Latin American Literary Review, 2002.
Levine, Linda G. *Isabel Allende.* New York: Twayne, 2002.
Ramblado-Minero, María de la Cinta. *Isabel Allende's Writing of the Self: Trespassing the Boundaries of Fiction and Autobiography.* Lewiston, N.Y.: The Edwin Mellen Press, 2003.

Timothy K. Nixon

Almost a Woman   Esmeralda Santiago (1998)

ESMERALDA SANTIAGO's *Almost a Woman* records the narrator's move from Puerto Rico to New York. Whereas Santiago's first memoir, *WHEN I WAS PUERTO RICAN* (1993), is dominated by questions of cultural displacement, *Almost a Woman,* her second memoir, takes the formation of a female identity as its central concern.

The formation of identity and the feeling of dislocation are related in meaningful and troubling ways. The memoir is divided into 20 chapters and is narrated by Negi (a nickname for Esmeralda), who is coming of age in New York. Readers learn early on that she is *casi señorita* or "almost a woman." When the phrase is explained by her mother, *casi señorita* becomes a warning and a correction, serving as a reminder of the standards of behavior and sense of responsibility that she is expected to adhere to. Negi tries to seek a balance between what is acceptable and what is self-effacing:

> Having heard countless stories of deceitful men and wily women, I decided never to become one of those calculating *putas* [whores], but neither would I become a *pendeja* [a woman who has been taken advantage of], who believed everything a man told her, or looked the other way while he betrayed her. There was a midpoint between a *puta* and a *pendeja* that I was trying to figure out, a safe space in which

decent women lived and thrived and raised their families (14).

In the narrative Negi is becoming a woman and even more specifically a Puerto Rican woman who has been displaced. She is displaced because she has grown up on the island of Puerto Rico, which although being part of the United States, is located in the Caribbean and farther away from Florida than Cuba is. Her challenge is to adapt to life in Brooklyn, a borough of New York City made up of many ethnic communities and social boundaries.

The early chapters of the text cover Negi's acculturation as a student and her eventual acceptance into and graduation from the renowned New York Performing Arts School (the setting for the television series *Fame*). Though the similarities between *Almost a Woman* and *When I Was Puerto Rican* are striking, Santiago begins her second memoir with an expanded version of the events that concluded the first. The two books, when read in conjunction, provide a detailed account of the author's life from the age of four to 20. Chronologically speaking, the texts are continuous, one beginning literally at the point where the other leaves off. To a certain extent, then, both of the texts explore themes common to urban, autobiographical, migrant fiction. In particular, Santiago's writing centers on poverty, discreet and overt forms of racism, the experience of absent fathers, and the hybrid condition (being both Puerto Rican and American). *Almost a Woman,* like Santiago's first memoir, is a bildungsroman (coming-of-age narrative typified by the protagonist's psychological and intellectual growth). It is a narrative that explores the self as part of an island and later a northeastern urban community.

Negi faces tremendous obstacles, overcomes the squalor of her circumstances, and as a result thrives as a young woman; her successes are hard won. The motif of overcoming obstacles helps to explain the drastic shift that occurs halfway through the narration. Whereas the first chapters deal with Negi's high school experiences and the emergence of the self, the last half of the text concentrates on a variety of romantic entanglements and unlikely episodes. These range from Negi's

early work as a film extra, to starring in Children's Theater productions on Broadway and becoming romantically involved with such colorful figures as a Texas millionaire, a German expatriate, and an airplane thief. The most pivotal relationship in the text takes place with Ulvi, a Turkish film director. Negi's affair with Ulvi reveals an important shift in the narrative, the kind of shift that RICHARD RODRIGUEZ theorizes in *Hunger of Memory* (1981), DAYS OF OBLIGATION (1992) and BROWN: THE LAST DISCOVERY OF AMERICA (2002). Rodriguez writes about the division between the private life of the home, which is the site of cultural memory and practice, and the public life of the individual, who, once out in the world, sheds the language and cultural of the home. By the later chapters of Santiago's memoir, the family, which has hitherto occupied center stage, disappears into the background as Negi's experimental and emerging sexual identity takes center stage.

Once Negi is able to negotiate family and the cultural dynamics of moving to New York, she brings her story full circle. Through her romantic and sexual relationship with Ulvi, Negi is able to begin the process of reclaiming an identity she believes she has lost. She finally moves beyond the sense of paralyzing fragmentation that has thus far defined her. She recognizes that her much older lover is a classic father substitute, a man in whose arms she once again becomes simply a young *jíbara* (country girl). The fact that Negi allows Ulvi to determine even the most minute details of her life is both an enactment of this father substitute and an acknowledgment that Negi, more than anything, longs to be taken care of. With Ulvi the complications of her identity subside somewhat because she abdicates control and relies instead on his opinions. It is within this context that Negi recognizes that her greatest desire is to become the person she may have been—an uncomplicated, simple Puerto Rican country girl—though finally she also faces the impossibility of this desire. When Ulvi asks Negi to travel abroad with him, leaving behind her family, she surprisingly refuses him. In the end the woman she vows not to become, the longing for her absent father, and the desire to return to her homeland (Puerto Rico) remind her that she has a new identity. Negi maintains her loyalty to her mother and assumes a hybrid, bicultural life in New York.

In its themes and plot devices *Almost a Woman* can be read in the context of PUERTO RICAN LITERATURE. The novel *Almost a Woman* has much in common with other coming-of-age stories, namely JUDITH ORTIZ COFER's *SILENT DANCING: A PARTIAL REMEMBRANCE OF A PUERTO RICAN CHILDHOOD* (1990) and SANDRA CISNEROS's *The HOUSE ON MANGO STREET* (1984). Finally, Ulvi and Negi's relationship anticipates the story line of Santiago's following memoir, *The Turkish Lover* (2004).

Bibliography

Cisneros, Sandra. *The House on Mango Street.* Houston, Tex.: Arte Público Press, 1983.

Cofer, Judith Ortiz. *Silent Dancing: A Partial Remembrance of a Puerto Rican Childhood.* Houston, Tex.: Arte Público Press, 1990.

Flores, Juan. *Divided Borders: Essays on Puerto Rican Identity.* Houston, Tex.: Arte Público Press, 1993.

Grosfoguel, Frances, et al., eds. *Puerto Rican Jam: Rethinking Colonialism and Nationalism.* Minneapolis: University of Minnesota Press, 1997.

Rodriguez, Richard. *Brown: the Last Discovery of America.* New York: Penguin, 2002.

———. *Hunger of Memory: The Education of Richard Rodriguez.* New York: Bantam Books, 1982.

Santiago, Esmeralda. *Almost a Woman.* New York: Vintage Books, 1998.

———. *América's Dream.* New York: HarperCollins, 1996.

———. *The Turkish Lover.* Cambridge, Mass.: Da Capo Press, 2004.

———. *When I Was Puerto Rican.* New York: Vintage-Random House, 1993.

Lorna Pérez

Alurista (Alberto Baltazar Urista) (1947–) *(poet, activist)*

Alurista was born Alberto Baltazar Urista in the Mexican state of Morelos in 1947. He immigrated to the United States when he was 14.

He received his B.A. from San Diego State University (1970) and went on to receive an M.A. (1979) and a Ph.D. (1983) from the University of California, San Diego. In addition to being an important poetic voice in CHICANO LITERATURE, he has also been a devoted activist, fighting for the rights of Mexican Americans. He supported CESAR CHAVEZ and the United Farm Workers' effort to organize migrant workers in California; he also participated in the student protests of the late 1960s and early 1970s that advocated the Chicano movement. So, too, has he been an advocate of AZTLÁN, which was both a political plan and a cultural vision, reflecting a mixture of imagination and civic protest. Advocates of Aztlán emphasize that for many Mexicans the border crossed them and not vice versa. Alurista is the author of *RETURN: POEMS COLLECTED AND NEW* (1982), as well as of *As Our Barrio Turns: Who the Yoke b On?* (2000) *Spik in Glyph* (1981), *Timespace Huracán: Poems, 1972–1975* (1976), and *Floricanto en Aztlán* (1971).

Bibliography

Alurista. *As Our Barrio Turns: Who the Yoke b On?* San Diego, Calif.: Calaca Press, 2000.

———. *Floricanto en Aztlán.* Los Angeles: Chicano Cultural Center, University of California, 1971.

———. *Return: Poems Collected and New.* Yosilanti, Mich.: Bilingual Press, 1982.

———. *Spik in Glyph.* Houston, Tex.: Arte Público Press, 1981.

———. *Timespace Huracán: Poems, 1972–1975.* Albuquerque, N.Mex.: Pajarito Publications, 1976.

Jaime Rodríguez-Matos

Alvarez, Aldo (1965–) *(fiction writer, editor)*

Aldo Alvarez was born and raised in Mayagüez, Puerto Rico. Currently a professor of English at Wilbur Wright College in Chicago, he received a B.A. from Xavier University in 1987, an M.F.A. in creative writing from Columbia University in 1991, and a Ph.D. in English from Binghamton University in 2000. In 1997 he founded and edited *Blithe House Quarterly* (*BHQ*), a gay online literary journal that *Out* magazine has called "the central publishing arm of new queer fiction." *BHQ* was also nominated for the GLAAD (Gay and Lesbian Alliance Against Defamation) Media Award, which recognizes the "fairness, accuracy, quality, originality and impact of media representations of the LGBT [lesbian, gay, bisexual, and transgender] community." In 2003 Alvarez edited a special issue on Puerto Rican gay literature that included short stories by Moisés Agosto-Rosario, Edgardo A. Alvarado-Vázquez, Rane Arroyo, Larry La Fountain-Stokes, Angel Lozada, and Guillermo Román.

Alvarez's most important publication to date is his book of short stories, *Interesting Monsters* (2001), a collection of 16 interlinked texts that explore gay experiences and other forms of marginality. Nine of these stories focus on a small group of characters: Mark Piper, a 40-year-old, semi-closeted, gay white "has-been pop star" and record producer; his boyfriend, the New York–based, (white) Puerto Rican auction house appraiser and antiques collector Dean (formerly Dino) Rodríguez, who has AIDS; Mark's friend and work colleague Kip, a white heterosexual sound engineer; Dean's college friend Mary, a white heterosexual television writer; and Dean's former work colleague, a big-hearted but not very talented or intelligent gay white artist-photographer, Bob Koehr. These characters' lives and friendships are explored in a nonchronological way so that readers have the feeling of jumping back and forth through time as the book progresses. The other seven texts include metaliterary declarations by the author ("A Note on the Aesthetics and Ideology of Interesting Monsters" and "Up Close"), a detective story set in France ("Death by Bricolage"), a story about Anglican heaven ("A Small Indulgence"), a science-fiction story about a Latino professor of English named Serge Ruiz, whose gay white partner has AIDS ("Flatware"), and a fantasy story about a heterosexual Latino artist named Rog (Rogelio) who carries around in a briefcase a bloody placenta that is attached to his body by his umbilical cord ("Rog & Venus Become an Item").

In Alvarez's literary universe, Latinoness is portrayed as monstrous and/or exotic; most of the Latino characters are abject in one way or another, be it through physical deformity (Rog), illness (Dean), or prejudiced temperament, as in the case of Claudia Ferrier, the Puerto Rican real estate agent in the city of Mireya (Mayagüez) who does not want to help Mark and Dean purchase a home because of Dean's health status ("Property Values"). The relationships of Latino characters with each other—what it means for them to be Latino—is rarely discussed in detail. Latinos never date, befriend, or become sexually involved with other Latinos but, rather, interact only with Anglos. Only one word of Spanish appears in the entire book, *encantados* ("charmed," 93), although many characters frequently drop phrases in French and Italian. In this sense Alvarez's work can be seen as sharing similar aesthetics with the gay Chicano essayist RICHARD RODRIGUEZ, who uses British and European cultural referents. At times the book is also reminiscent of James Baldwin's *Giovanni's Room,* in which the African-American author focuses mostly on gay white American characters in Paris.

Specific references to Latino/a culture and locations are mostly limited to literary references (Serge Ruiz teaches texts by Jorge Luis Borges and Carlos Fuentes) and stylistic influences ("Death by Bricolage" seems indebted to Borges's metaliterary writing and interest in detective narratives). The one story from *Interesting Monsters* that takes place in Puerto Rico, "Property Values," presents the island as a location for dying, the place where Dean wishes to retire to spend his last days; people in Puerto Rico are portrayed as either supportive of or violently opposed to his desires. Interestingly enough, another young writer from Mayagüez, Angel Lozada, has also portrayed that city as hostile to gays in his novel *La patografía* (1998).

Alvarez's postmodern vision is for the most part, shaped by the feelings and experiences of white and assimilated Latino characters, particularly regarding issues of homosexuality, heterosexuality, and AIDS, rather than by the specificities of Latino/a experiences. Nevertheless, his work can be read within the context of PUERTO RICAN LITERATURE as well as LATINO GAY LITERATURE.

Bibliography

Alvarez, Aldo. *Interesting Monsters.* Saint Paul, Minn.: Greywolf Press, 2001.

Alvarez, Aldo, ed. Aa: Aldo Alvarez Cited. "About Interesting Monsters." Available online. URL: http://www.blithe.com/aa. Accessed November 27, 2007.

Lawrence La Fountain–Stokes

Alvarez, Julia (1950–) *(novelist, poet)*

Dominican-American Julia Alvarez is one of the most widely read Latina authors today. Her publications include novels, poetry, critical essays, short stories, and books for children. Alvarez was born on March 27, 1950, in New York City, to a physician and his wife but was raised in the Dominican Republic until the age of 10. Fleeing Rafael Trujillo's regime, her family returned to New York in 1960, and since then Alvarez has lived in the Northeast, primarily in New York and Vermont. She graduated from Middlebury College in 1971, earned an M.F.A. from Syracuse in 1975, and attended the Bread Loaf School of English in Vermont from 1979 to 1980. Alvarez is the recipient of the Hispanic Heritage Award in Literature (2002), the *Latina* Magazine Woman of the Year Award, (2000), a National Endowment of the Arts Grant (1987–88), the Robert Frost Poetry Fellowship (1986), and the Third Woman Press Award for Narrative (1986), among many other accolades. She is a member of the Academy of American Poets and a member of the Latin American Writers' Institute.

As an aspiring writer in the 1980s, Alvarez traveled across the United States with her "portable homeland of the imagination" (Heredia 32). She has read her poetry in elementary schools, nursing homes, community centers, and colleges. While writing and presenting her work, she has held writer-in-residence jobs at different universities across the country, including a tenured teaching position at Middlebury College. Most recently Alvarez has divided her time between Vermont and the Dominican Republic, where, with her husband, she manages the coffee farm Alta Gracia and helps to promote education within the mountain community.

Like her characters, Alvarez has experienced firsthand being uprooted and migration. Most of her work centers on life experiences—whether her own or those of others—in such novels as *In the Time of the Butterflies* (1994), *How the García Girls Lost Their Accents* (1991), *¡Yo!* (1997), *In the Name of Salomé* (2000), *Before We Were Free* (2002), and *Saving the World* (2006).

She has gone back and forth between the Dominican Republic and the United States, which has given her an opportunity to explore the consequences of migration and exile, especially for women.

How the García Girls Lost Their Accents, winner of the 1991 PEN Oakland/Josephine Miles Award, tells the story of four Dominican-American sisters (Carla, Sandra, Yolanda, and Sofía) who immigrate to the United States and struggle to adjust to life in the Northeast while maintaining their island heritage. The García girls' sheltered lives parallel the political history of the Dominican Republic, particularly the political unrest of the Trujillo regime (1930–61). The García family saga continues in the novel *¡Yo!* in which the voices of Yo(landa)'s family members take center stage in telling their own stories—as well as Yolanda's. We can view this as Alvarez's response to James Joyce's "portrait of the artist" insofar as family members craft the image of Yo, the writer-protagonist.

One pivotal area of concern that characterizes Alvarez's literature is the need to return to one's roots as a means of self-discovery. The recovery of the past through the search for identity also appears in Alvarez's second novel, *In the Time of the Butterflies,* and in *In the Name of Salomé.* In both novels the author revisits the past by going back to the island. Through the voice of the only surviving Mirabal sister, Dedé, *In the Time of the Butterflies* tells of the lives (and deaths) of Las Mariposas (The Butterflies)—María Teresa, Minerva, Patria, and Dedé Mirabal—whose involvement in the struggle to overthrow Trujillo's dictatorship culminated in their murder. Alvarez transforms Dedé's family's story into an intensely personal act, one that tries to explain the country's social, political, and economic history from the 1940s to the 1990s.

Alvarez similarly uses fiction to re-create the historical figure of Salomé Ureña and her daughter Camila Salomé in *In the Name of Salomé*. History and fiction cross boundaries again in her most recent novel, *Saving the World,* in which Alvarez intertwines the lives of two courageous women two centuries apart from each other and tries to find meaning in their lives through their commitment to humanitarian missions. In many of her works Alvarez points out the role of women in the preservation of a collective memory and the construction of a national identity. She elevates the role of women as active participants on a political stage that for many years had been occupied exclusively by men. She also strives to make this legacy available to a wider audience outside the borders of the Dominican Republic.

Major themes in Alvarez's writing are identity and culture, exile and home, hybridity and assimilation, the negotiation of the past and the present, and language and memory. In this regard she belongs to a much wider community of daughters of migration that includes JUDITH ORTIZ COFER, CRISTINA GARCÍA, and ESMERALDA SANTIAGO and, more broadly, to the diversity of Latino authors writing in the United States. For its themes and use of history Alvarez's work can be read in the context of DOMINICAN-AMERICAN LITERATURE as well as SPANISH-AMERICAN CARIBBEAN LITERATURE.

Bibliography

Alvarez, Julia. *Before We Were Free.* New York: Laurel Leaf Books, 2002.

———. *Homecoming: New and Collected Poems.* New York: Plume, 1996.

———. *How the García Girls Lost Their Accents.* New York: Algonquin Books, 1991.

———. *In the Name of Salomé.* New York: Plume, 2000.

———. *In the Time of the Butterflies.* Chapel Hill, N.C.: Algonquin Books, 1994.

———. *The Other Side/El otro lado.* New York: Plume, 1996.

———. *Saving the World.* Chapel Hill, N.C.: Algonquin Books, 2006.

———. *Something to Declare.* New York: Plume/Penguin Books, 1999.

———. *The Woman I Kept to Myself.* Chapel Hill, N.C.: Algonquin Books, 2004.

———. *¡Yo!* Chapel Hill, N.C.: Algonquin Books, 1997.

Heredia, Juanita. "Citizen of the World: An Interview with Julia Alvarez." In *Latina Self-Portraits: Interviews with Contemporary Women Writers,* edited by Juanita Heredia and Bridget Kevane, 19–32. Albuquerque: University of New Mexico Press, 2000.

Johnson, Kelli Lyon. *Julia Alvarez: Writing a New Place on the Map.* Albuquerque: University of New Mexico Press, 2005.

Sirias, Silvio. *Julia Alvarez: A Critical Companion.* London: Greenwood Press, 2001.

Yolanda P. Martínez

Always from Somewhere Else: A Memoir of My Chilean Jewish Father Marjorie Agosín (1998)

Always from Somewhere Else: A Memoir of My Chilean Jewish Father is about the life of Moíses Agosín, as written by his daughter, Marjorie, in memoir form. It is Agosín's second installation in a set of family memoirs she has called "the genealogies of memory and the cartographies of love" ("Journey" 425). *Always from Somewhere Else* is preceded by *A CROSS AND A STAR: MEMOIRS OF A JEWISH GIRL IN CHILE* (1994), about Marjorie Agosín's mother, and followed by the author's own story, *The Alphabet in My Hands: A Writing Life* (2000). Together the three volumes can be considered the Agosín family's testimony to the experiences of European Jews who migrated to Chile in the early 20th century.

As noted by Elizabeth Horan in the book's introduction (14), a major theme of *Always from Somewhere Else* is the predicament of Chilean Jews who fall outside the Chilean ruling class's cultural history, light skin, and Catholicism. Moíses Agosín, for example, faced considerable social and professional obstacles: While a medical student at the University of Chile in Santiago, he was "viewed with suspicion," and a university classmate complimented him for possessing musical sensitivity and careful manners, which distinguished him from typical "loud and vulgar" Jews, (as related in *Always from Somewhere Else* 133). Later, as a professor at the University of Chile, his candidacy for chair of medical chemistry brought death threats, and his appointment led to a mass resignation by his colleagues, many of whom, his daughter remembers, had "visited our house and stayed drinking wine until very late at night" (151). After moving to the United States in 1971, prejudice affected Agosín's life in new ways, as the professional barriers against Jews in Chile were replaced by the stigma of being regarded as a "third-world" scientist in America. For her part, Marjorie, a blond Jewish Chilean living in Georgia, upsets the expectations of her American classmates who had different suppositions about what Latin Americans and Jews looked like. In this regard Agosín's work can be read alongside that of ILAN STAVANS, who likewise has assumed a complex identity as a Spanish-speaking Mexican Jew living in the United States and writing in English.

Stylistically, Agosín notes that whereas *A Cross and a Star* experimented with the overlapping voices of mother and daughter, this text documents her father's lonely journey in a more linear fashion, yielding "a book that creates a dialogue between a daughter who narrates, and writes" and a father who is the son of immigrants ("Journey" 428). In its subject matter and interest in Chilean history, Agosín's work can be read alongside that of ISABEL ALLENDE and ARIEL DORFMAN.

Bibliography

Agosín, Marjorie. *The Alphabet in My Hands: A Writing Life.* Translated by Nancy Abraham Hall. Piscataway, N.J.: Rutgers University Press, 2000.

———. *Always from Somewhere Else: A Memoir of My Chilean Jewish Father.* Translated by Celeste Kostopulos-Cooperman. Introduction by Elizabeth Rosa Horan. New York: Feminist Press at CUNY, 1998.

———. *A Cross and a Star: Memoirs of a Jewish Girl in Chile.* Translated by Celeste Kostopulos-Cooperman. New York: Feminist Press at CUNY, 1995.

———. "A Journey through Imagination and Memory: My Parents and I, between the Cross and the Star." Translated by Roberta Gordenstein. *Judaism* 51, no. 4 (Fall 2002): 419–428.

Bing, Jonathan, et al. Review of *Always from Somewhere Else: A Memoir of My Jewish Father. Publishers Weekly* 245, no. 46 (November 16, 1998): 63.

Horan, Elizabeth. "Agosín, Marjorie." In *Jewish Writers of Latin America: A Dictionary,* edited by Darrell B. Lockhart, 7–13. New York: Garland, 1997.

Scott, Nina. "Marjorie Agosín as Latina Writer." In *Breaking Boundaries: Latina Writings and Critical Readings,* edited by Asunción Horno-Delgado, et al., 235–249. Amherst: University of Massachusetts Press, 1989.

Alex Feerst

América's Dream　**Esmeralda Santiago** (1996)

América's Dream is ESMERALDA SANTIAGO's first foray into fiction. The narrative explores the complicated emotional terrain of domestic abuse and the conditions that have given rise to it. *América's Dream* is set within the locales of the Puerto Rican diaspora; it begins in Vieques, Puerto Rico, and then moves to Westchester County, an affluent collection of suburbs north of New York City. The novel ends in the Bronx, an ethnically mixed borough of New York City. Santiago tells the story of América González, a single mother who breaks away from her abusive lover and flees to the U.S. mainland. The protagonist's name evokes a number of important references beginning with Amerigo Vespucci, the 15th-century mapmaker of the Americas. Second, the name recalls the racially mixed Latin American identity in the work of Cuban revolutionary JOSÉ MARTÍ, who published in 1891 his famous essay "Nuestra América" ("Our America"). Martí conceived "Our America" as a cultural and psychological space that would validate the African, Indian, and mestizo identities of Latin America. Finally, her name sets up the expectation that América González will seek the American Dream of making a better life for herself in the United States.

In Santiago's novel América's translocation to the mainland becomes an opportunity to slowly and painfully reclaim her identity; in the process she begins to recognize the rich and tattered patterns of a difficult life. Santiago opens the novel in Puerto Rico, introducing the reader to Rosalinda González. Rosalinda is América's 14-year-old daughter who has run off with her boyfriend; this episode allows readers entry into the González familial history. Here we learn that the González family is a family of single mothers and daughters, three generations of women who are each, in their own way, entirely self-destructive. Esther, América's mother, is an alcoholic, while América maintains a codependent abusive relationship with Correa, the father of Rosalinda. The reader finds it easy to imagine Rosalinda following in their unfortunate footsteps. Upon her return home Rosalinda refuses to speak to her mother and grandmother, eventually opting to live with her father's relatives in Fajardo. Interestingly, América calls her daughter's departure *el problema con Rosalinda* (the problem with Rosalinda), though the situation is clearly attributable to family dynamics as a whole. As Correa continues to beat América, readers come to understand that family dysfunction comes from her inability to conceptualize an identity independent of a man. In this sense *América's Dream* is perhaps the most deeply feminist of all of Santiago's texts, as América's ability to dream involves a disturbing self-inventory.

When América realizes she is spending her time fantasizing about ways to kill Correa, she makes the radical decision to flee his abuse by leaving her job as a hotel housekeeper and her home on an island off the Puerto Rican coast. She accepts a position as a domestic in the household of the rich Leverett family of Westchester County. Upon their invitation, she boards a plane headed to New York, telling only her mother and daughter that she is leaving. Though the cultural shock and uncertainty of América's first moments in New York leave her cold (it is February) and ready to flee back to Vieques, she soon falls into a routine with the Leveretts. Much of her time is occupied by her job, and she finds her freedom is circumscribed by professional obligations to the Leveretts; nevertheless, she finally has the safety and security to think about her own needs. As América gradually gains self-awareness, she also starts to gain a sense of her place within the world—a place that includes both privilege and dependence. Her friendship with Latina *empleadas* (employees) opens her eyes to both the poverty of her ambition and the fortuity of her citizenship.

While her status as a Puerto Rican makes her a U.S. citizen (Puerto Rico is a U.S. commonwealth), the doors that her American citizenship should open—the very avenues barred to the other foreign *empleadas* because their immigration status prevents them from doing anything else—seem closed to her. América is a domestic by choice, though it is arguable that she has few options available. She becomes a domestic by default because it is all she ever has bothered to dream of doing. Finally free of the man who made her life decisions for her, América begins the delicate and uncertain process of learning how to dream for herself.

A large part of this new ability to self-conceptualize is also about understanding herself as part of the Latino communities in New York. Her friendship with the *empleadas* from other Latin American countries exposes her to a Latino culture that is larger than just Puerto Rico. América finds refuge from drudgery in the English-speaking world by enjoying a state of being Latina—*Latinidad.* Similarly, her extended kinship network finally gives América the opportunity to participate in family life in an emotionally supportive and loving way. The effects of this community, however, also pose a dormant danger for América. She jarringly realizes that Puerto Rico, Vieques, the Bronx, and Westchester County are all intimately connected locations. For América, being part of this circuit of movement and community places her in a precarious position, as her fear of Correa finding her becomes much more feasible in this world of interconnection.

These fears are legitimated when Correa finds América and flies to New York to bring her back to Vieques. América's attempts to avoid their inevitable reunion result in a violent confrontation in the Leveretts' home. In the altercation that follows Correa stabs América. To defend herself she kicks him in the groin, and he falls back and hits his head on a table; he dies from the injury. However satisfying Correa's death may be to some readers, this conclusion creates a problematic and violent dream of feminism: the emasculation and death of the abusive patriarch. The América who emerges from this encounter becomes, much to her surprise, something of an underground feminist icon. Ultimately then, the American Dream for América is the final emergence of a woman with an inalienable right to her safety, self, and liberty.

América's Dream was published in the years between Santiago's two memoirs, WHEN I WAS PUERTO RICAN (1993) and ALMOST A WOMAN (1998). Santiago's work can be read within the context of PUERTO RICAN LITERATURE.

Bibliography

Duany, Jorge. *The Puerto Rican Nation on the Move: Identities on the Island and in the United States.* Chapel Hill: University of North Carolina Press, 2002.

Martí, José. *Nuestra América.* Barcelona: Ariel, 1970.

Philip S. Foner, ed. *Our America: Writings on Latin America and the Struggle for Cuban Independence.* Translated by Elinor Randall, et al. New York/London: Monthly Review Press, 1977.

Rivera, Carmen S. *Kissing the Mango Tree: Puerto Rican Women Rewriting American Literature.* Houston, Tex.: Arte Público Press, 2002.

Santiago, Esmeralda. *Almost a Woman.* New York: Vintage Books, 1998.

———. *América's Dream.* New York: HarperCollins, 1996.

———. *When I Was Puerto Rican.* New York: Vintage-Random House, 1993.

Lorna Pérez

Anaya, Rudolfo Alfonso (1937–   )
(novelist, poet)

Born on October 30, 1937, in Pastura, New Mexico, Rudolfo Alfonso Anaya is considered one of the founders of the Chicano literary movement. The son of Martín Anaya and Rafaelita Mares and the fifth in a family of 10 children, Anaya graduated from Albuquerque High School in 1956 and later pursued studies in Browing Business School. Anaya's first novel, BLESS ME, ÚLTIMA (1972), won the Premio Quinto Sol, a national Chicano literature award, and is considered a classic of CHICANO LITERATURE.

A prolific writer, Anaya has published short fiction, children's literature, essays, novellas, plays, and several novels. He has also edited a number of anthologies showcasing the work of younger Chicano authors and founded the Rio Grande Writers Association, an organization to support Mexican-American writers and those who publish and teach their work. He has received many awards, including two National Endowment of the Arts fellowships, the W. K. Kellogg Fellowship, the Mexican Medal of Friendship, the Award for Achievement in Chicano Literature, the National Medal of Arts, and five honorary doctorates.

Anaya earned his B.A. and M.A. in English from the University of New Mexico. He also holds a master's in guidance and counseling and has taught in the Albuquerque public schools. After he was awarded the Premio Quinto Sol for *Bless Me, Última*, Anaya accepted a fellowship at the University of New Mexico and eventually became a professor in the Department of English Language and Literature. In 1993 he retired from University of New Mexico with the title of Professor Emeritus.

Anaya has earned national acclaim for his involvement in literary events that promote the development of Chicano literature. His most important enterprise is the Premio Aztlán, an award he and his wife established for writers in 1993. This annual national literary award encourages Chicano writing, and past recipients of this award include ALICIA GASPAR DE ALBA and DENISE CHÁVEZ.

The international status of his writing can be measured by the numerous translations of Anaya's work. He is especially well known for his first novel, yet in order to continue his project of self-exploration, Anaya drew on childhood memories, places, experiences, and mythical beliefs to create a trilogy. In 1976 Anaya published the second of the trilogy, *Heart of Aztlán*, and in 1979 the last installment, *Tortuga*. In these narratives myth helps readers understand the role of the individual within the community. Reality therefore acquires a mythical dimension, and both exist in spiritual communion. *Heart of Aztlán* takes the protagonist, Clemente, to the heart of the Mexican-American mythical homeland, AZTLÁN. Clemente returns from the journey with power enough to lead a strike against the railroads that exploit the workers. Winner of the Before Columbus Foundation's American Book Award in 1980, *Tortuga* tells the coming-of-age story of Benji, nicknamed Tortuga (turtle). Like *Bless Me, Última, Tortuga* is somewhat autobiographical in that Anaya, like Tortuga, suffered a serious spinal injury as a boy.

In 1985 Anaya published *The ADVENTURES OF JUAN CHICASPATAS.* This mock epic surveys the history and folklore of Mexican-American culture and can be read as a response to Corky Gonzales's epic 1967 poem *I AM JOAQUÍN.*

In the 1990s Anaya published *ALBURQUERQUE* (1992), *ZIA SUMMER* (1995), *RIO GRANDE FALL* (1996), and *SHAMAN WINTER* (1999). *Alburquerque,* which preserves the original Spanish spelling of the city, received the PEN Center USA West Award for fiction in 1993. *Alburquerque* examines Mexican-American values through its protagonist, Abrán González.

While maintaining his interest in these values and in myth, Anaya's writing explores a new literary direction in his trilogy: *Zia Summer, Rio Grande Fall,* and *Shaman Winter.* These works constitute Anaya's Sonny Baca mystery novels. Sonny, a private investigator, is the great-grandson of the legendary New Mexican lawman Elfego Baca. *Zia Summer* touches on Chicano history and folklore. *Rio Grande Fall* deals with Sonny's case of psychic shock (*susto*). This novel also explores the Mesoamerican myth of the *nahual,* or animal side of the soul. Sonny Baca stands at the intersection of contemporary society and the traditions of his people.

Anaya's work also appears in an anthology of his writings, *The Anaya Reader* (1995). Anaya's most recent publications include *Jalamanta: A Message from the Desert* (1996), *Maya's Children: The Story of La Llorona* (1997), *Elegy on the Death of César Chávez* (2000), and a southwestern version of the *Arabian Nights* called *Serafina's Stories* (2004).

Bibliography

Anaya, Rudolfo A. *Adventures of Juan Chicaspatas.* Houston, Tex.: Arte Público Press, 1985.

———. *Alburquerque.* Albuquerque: University of New Mexico Press, 1992.

———. *The Anaya Reader.* New York: Warner Books, 1995.

———. *Bless Me, Última.* New York: Warner Books, 1999.

———. *Elegy on the Death of César Chávez.* El Paso, Tex.: Cinco Puntos Press, 2000.

———. *The Farolitos of Christmas.* New York : Hyperion Books for Children, 1995.

———. *Heart of Aztlán.* Albuquerque: University of New Mexico Press, 1992.

———. *Jalamanta: A Message from the Desert.* New York: Warner Books, 1996.

———. *Jemez Spring.* Alburquerque: University of New Mexico Press, 2005.

———. *The Legend of La Llorona: A Short Novel.* Berkeley, Calif.: Tonatiuh–Quinto Sol International, 1984.

———. *Lord of the Dawn: The Legend of Quetzalcoatl.* Albuquerque: University of New Mexico Press, 1987.

———. *Maya's Children: The Story of La Llorona.* New York: Hyperion Books, 1997.

———. *Rio Grande Fall.* New York: Warner Books, 1996.

———. *Serafina's Stories.* Albuquerque: University of New Mexico Press, 2004.

———. *Shaman Winter.* New York: Warner Books, 1999.

———. *The Silence of the Llano: Short Stories.* Berkeley, Calif.: Tonatiuh–Quinto Sol International, 1982.

———. *Tortuga.* Albuquerque: University of New Mexico Press, 1988.

———. *Zia Summer.* New York: Warner Books, 1995.

Bryan, Howard. *Incredible Elfego Baca: Good Man, Bad Man of the Old West.* Foreword by Rudolfo Anaya. Santa Fe, N.Mex.: Clear Light Publishers, 1993.

Fernández Olmos, Margarite. *Rudolfo A. Anaya: A Critical Companion.* Westport, Conn.: Greenwood Press, 1999.

González, César A., and Phyllis S. Morgan. *A Sense of Place: Rudolfo A. Anaya, an Annotated Bio-Bibliography.* Berkeley, Calif.: Ethnic Studies Library Publications Unit, 2000.

Marian Pozo Montaño

. . . And the Earth Did Not Devour Him
See THIS MIGRANT EARTH.

Anything but Mexican: Chicanos in Contemporary Los Angeles Rodolfo Acuña (1996)

Anything but Mexican by scholar and activist RO-DOLFO ACUÑA was published in 1996 and received the Gustavus Myers Award for Best Book on Human Rights in 1997. It advances a history of Chicanos in Los Angeles and describes "their political, economic, and cultural presence" (x). Compared to Acuña's sweeping historical text, OCCUPIED AMERICA (1972), *Anything but Mexican* focuses on the late 20th century, with the purpose of defining an "emerging Chicano/Latino political space . . . which challenges Eurocentric interests that want to preserve the national identity of the United States as a Western European nation" (xii).

The book's title refers to the situation of Mexicans in California: Acuña analyzes a two-sided problem—"the prevailing Euroangeleno evaluation of Mexicans" and the "Mexicans' view of themselves" (xv). "Los Angeles is a great place for Mexicans" Acuña explains, "so long as they make no claim to the city's history or to a place in its political life" (1). Acuña's text sets out to replace the region's debunked "fantasy heritage," in which words such as *Hispanic, Spanish,* and *discovery* obscure a violent colonial history. *Anything but Mexican* rewrites Eurocentric versions of California history that underplay white violence against Mexican Americans. He offers statistical research and blow-by-blow accounts of electoral races, as well as analyses of labor disputes, immigration laws, and education policies.

Though panoramic in its treatment of Mexican Americans in California, the core of *Anything but Mexican* is politics. Acuña writes: "Minorities in general, and Chicanos in particular, are obsessed with electoral politics; victories in this arena have become measures of empowerment" (xi). The text thus focuses in great detail on California electoral politics as it affects and has been affected by Chicano citizens. The ascendance of Chicano politicians such as Eddie Roybal in the 1950s and 1960s and Gloria Molina in the 1980s and 1990s are covered at length; the background and implications of several of the most notorious California ballot initiatives, Propositions 13, 184, and 187, are also given close attention.

The inhabitation of public space is also a significant element for Acuña. He chastises the preference of economic elites for "buildings over bodies," an architectural manifestation of "Anything but Mexican" psychology, in which picturesque images of "Spanish" America eclipse the contemporary presence of Chicanos. The chapter entitled "Taking Back Chicano History" details the struggle during the 1980s between the Latino community, other ethnic groups, and the state of California over the preservation of Olvera Street and the renaming of Brooklyn Avenue as Cesar E. Chavez Avenue (23). In presenting the details of such disputes, Acuña calls attention to how the naming of public space crystallizes issues of community memory and embodies the assertion of identity.

Acuña also documents particular struggles and accomplishments of Chicanas, whose existence has been obscured by a predilection among journalists and scholars to focus on Mexican-American men. Underwritten by Acuña's painstaking attention to detail and informed by his capacious historical consciousness, *Anything but Mexican* offers an account of Chicano/a community in Los Angeles that not only informs, but also, like all of Acuña's work, aims to bolster and enrich the activist work and everyday lives of Chicano/as who "instinctively . . . yearn for that sense of historically based community" (22). Given this work and his others, Acuña has created an important historical framework for CHICANO LITERATURE.

Bibliography
Acuña, Rodolfo F. *Anything but Mexican: Chicanos in Contemporary Los Angeles.* New York: Verso, 1996.
———. *A Community under Siege: A Chronicle of Chicanos East of the Los Angeles River, 1945–1975.* Los Angeles: University of California Chicano Studies Research Center, 1984.
———. *Occupied America: A History of Chicanos.* New York: Longman, 2003.

————. *Sometimes There Is No Other Side: Chicanos and the Myth of Equality.* Notre Dame, Ind.: University of Notre Dame Press, 1998.

————. *U.S. Latino Issues.* Westport, Conn.: Greenwood Press, 2003.

García, Juan R. Review of *Anything but Mexican: Chicanos in Contemporary Los Angeles. Labor History* 38, no. 4 (Fall 1997): 542–544.

Alex Feerst

Anzaldúa, Gloria (1942–2004) *(essayist, poet)*

Gloria Anzaldúa was an important contributor to CHICANO LITERATURE and to cultural studies in the United States. Born in Texas, in 1942, the eldest of four children, Anzaldúa described herself as a mestiza, a woman of Indian and Spanish heritage. Her family lived in poverty and, at age 11, Anzaldúa began working as a migrant worker to help support her siblings and parents. Her father died when she was a teenager, and Anzaldúa was forced to continue working while attending school. No doubt her years as a migrant worker were the motivating force behind her involvement with the United Farm Workers movement in the 1960s and 1970s.

Anzaldúa's parents did not encourage their daughter to pursue an education, reflecting a common belief among Latino families at the time that females should not be well educated. Anzaldúa nonetheless graduated from high school and went on to earn a bachelor's degree in English, art, and secondary education at Pan American University in Texas in 1969. Anzaldúa obtained an M.A. in English and education at the University of Texas, which she completed in 1973. She began working on a Ph.D. in Chicano and feminist studies at the University of Texas and then transferred to the University of California, Santa Cruz. At the time of her death she was preparing to submit her doctoral dissertation.

Anzaldúa coedited with CHERRÍE MORAGA the groundbreaking anthology *This Bridge Called My Back: Writing by Radical Women of Color* (1981), which won the Before Columbus Foundation American Book Award. This work was Anzaldúa's reaction to the frustration she felt when she attempted to participate in feminist groups that were dominated by privileged white women. It includes personal and theoretical essays, poems, and prose by African-American, Asian-American, Latina, and Native American feminists, including doris davenport, Nellie Wong, AURORA LEVINS MORALES, and Naomi Littlebear. The writers identify themselves both as feminists and radical women of color. The collection discusses several topics, among them how their race and culture relate to feminist theory, the impact of the largely white middle-class feminist movement, the differences among women of color; writing as a means of self-preservation and change, and the future of third world feminism. Contributors to *This Bridge Called My Back* seek to bridge the division between women of color and those white feminists who they felt have excluded them. This idea of bridging cultures is a prominent theme in Anzaldúa's work; she encourages white feminists to be more inclusive in the struggle for equal rights. As well, the work tries to unite women of color with an "uncompromised definition of feminism." *This Bridge We Call Home: Radical Visions for Transformation* (coedited with Ana Louise Keating, 2002) is a follow-up to *This Bridge Called My Back*. The collection contains more than 80 works by and women of different races and ethnicities.

Anzaldúa is perhaps best known for her work *BORDERLANDS/LA FRONTERA: THE NEW MESTIZA* (1987), which was selected by the Library Journal as one of the 38 best books of 1987. The autobiographical work combines genres and is written using SPANGLISH. The first section features essays that confront cultural concerns; the second half of the collection features Anzaldúa's poetry. Anzaldúa identifies herself as a woman of the border, a place of cultural complexity because of its Spanish- and English-speaking communities. She explains that the book illustrates the conflict that she experienced as she attempted to develop a sense of self in a place that was rife with white prejudice against and exploitation of Mexican and Mexican-American workers.

In 1990 Anzaldúa published *Making Face, Making Soul/Haciendo caras: Creative and Critical Perspectives by Women of Color* to address the need for more multiethnic materials for women's studies classes. The contributors are women of color, including SANDRA CISNEROS, JUDITH ORTIZ COFER, and Barbara Smith, and features poems, stories, and essays. While the writers continue to attempt to establish a bridge with white feminists, Anzaldúa explains that these writers' primary goal is to reaffirm their own identities.

Anzaldúa, who was considered to be a radical feminist, was one of the first openly gay Chicana authors. Anzaldúa began her teaching career in a bilingual preschool and then worked in a special education program. She taught creative writing, Chicano studies, and feminist studies at a number of colleges and universities throughout the country, including the University of Texas at Austin, San Francisco State University, and the University of California at Santa Cruz. She won numerous awards, including the Lambda Lesbian Small Book Press Award, a National Endowment for the Arts Award for fiction, and the Sappho Award of Distinction. Her work can be read within the context of BORDER LITERATURE and LATINA LESBIAN LITERATURE.

Bibliography

Anzaldúa, Gloria. *Borderlands/La frontera: The New Mestiza*. San Francisco, Calif.: Aunt Lute Books, 1987.

Azaldúa, Gloria, ed. *Making Face, Making Soul/Haciendo caras: Creative and Critical Perspectives by Women of Color*. San Francisco, Calif.: Aunt Lute Books, 1990.

Anzaldúa, Gloria E., and AnaLouise Keating, eds. *This Bridge We Call Home: Radical Visions for Transformation*. New York: Routledge, 2002.

Moraga, Cherríe, and Gloria Anzaldúa, eds. *This Bridge Called My Back: Writings by Radical Women of Color*. Watertown, Mass.: Persephone Press, 1981.

Reuman, Ann E. "Coming into Play: An Interview with Gloria Anzaldúa." *MELUS* 25, no. 2 (2000): 3–45.

Woo, Elaine. "Obituaries: Gloria Anzaldúa, 61; Feminist Academic Edited 'This Bridge Called My Back.'" *Los Angeles Times*, May 22, 2004, B17.

Diane Todd Bucci

Arenas, Reinaldo (Reinaldo Arenas Fuentes) (1943–1990) (novelist, poet)

Born in Cuba in 1943, Reinaldo Arenas was a prolific author who lived in the United States from 1980 until his death. Considered by critics to be one of the most important voices in both SPANISH-AMERICAN CARIBBEAN LITERATURE and CUBAN-AMERICAN LITERATURE, Arenas came of age when FIDEL CASTRO and his counterparts toppled Fulgencio Batista's regime in 1959. Growing up in the Cuban countryside, Arenas's experiences as a child helped to inspire much of his writing, including his views on nature, women, men, and sexuality. *BEFORE NIGHT FALLS* is a memoir in which Arenas reflects on his impoverished but carefree life in the Cuban countryside. He grows up without his father and with his mother and grandmother in Perronales County, and he speaks about his early years with nostalgia, but also with the recognition that, as an illegitimate son, he was outside the family structure.

Initially a supporter of Castro's Twenty-sixth of July movement to dismantle Batista's regime, Arenas withdrew his support once conditions in Cuba became detrimental to writers and individuals who did not promote the new regime. Arenas began to openly criticize the CUBAN REVOLUTION, especially as it shifted from a socialist to Marxist-Leninist government in 1961. During and after this shift, homosexuals and counterrevolutionaries were persecuted and excluded from most productive aspects of Cuban life. Gays were seen as a by-product of the Western capitalist influence Castro sought to remove from the island. Arenas's only solace was his writing, but in order to avoid censorship he smuggled or had others smuggle his manuscripts out of Cuba; this strategy allowed him to share his view of the conditions under which Cubans lived in the 1960s and 1970s. In a 1982 interview with Liliane Hasson, Arenas stated that what caused him to oppose the regime was its persecution of homosexuals. Ian Lumsden explains: "At the outset of the Cuban Revolution, machismo was deeply ingrained in the fabric of Cuban society. Gender roles were clearly identified and sharply differentiated. Men were expected to be strong, dominant, and sexually compulsive. Women were expected to be vulnerable and chaste" (55). Arenas deviated from this view of masculinity.

While he lived much of his adult life in Havana, Arenas seized the opportunity to enter into exile through the port of Mariel, 25 miles west of the capital. In 1980 Arenas made it to Key West, Florida, and once settled in his new circumstances as an exile, Arenas launched a literary crusade to denounce the conditions under which many Cubans lived on the island. These conditions were detailed, in part, by descriptions of the UMAP (Military Units to Aid Production) camps, labor camps set up to "reform" counterrevolutionaries and to which many homosexuals were sent.

Arenas wrote about living in rural and urban areas of Cuba, about his struggle as an artist under a Communist regime, and about his appreciation for intellectual and sensual pleasures. His major publications include *Antes que anochezca: Una autobiografía* (1992; *Before Night Falls: A Memoir,* 1993), *El central* (1981; *El Central: A Cuban Sugar Mill,* 1984), *La vieja Rosa* (1980; *Old Rosa,* 1989), *Arturo, la estrella más brillante* (*The Brightest Star,* both 1984), and *El mundo alucinante* (1969; *Hallucinations, or The Ill-Fated Peregrinations of Fray Servando,* 1971). These works are renowned for their detailed accounts of life in Cuba. Themes such as death, the sea, writing, and sex are present in these texts, as well as in the five novels that make up *Pentagonía* (*Pentagony,* both 1994): *Celestino antes del alba* (1968; *Singing from the Well,* 1987), *El palacio de las blanquísimas mofetas* (1980; *The Palace of the White Skunks,* 1990), *Otra vez el mar* (1982; *Farewell to the Sea,* 1985), *El color del verano* (1991; *The Color of Summer, or The New Garden of Earthly Delight,* 2000), and *El asalto* (1991; *The Assault,* 1994). In this five-part series every character dies and is in some way "reborn" in the next novel (with the exception of the main character in *El asalto*). Many of the plots of these novels can be read within the context of LATINO GAY LITERATURE.

As a result of his defiance against the Cuban government, one might say that Arenas lived his life in a series of prisons—physical, psychological, and intellectual. He became a marginalized individual in a patriarchal society that scrutinized his behavior, as gays and intellectuals were seen as "immoral" and outside the purview of the Cuban Revolution. His mentors, José Lezama Lima and Virgilio Piñera, suffered the same persecution; however, unlike them, Arenas was able to reappropriate what had been taken from him once he went into exile as part of the Mariel exodus. He decided to use his newfound freedom to condemn his enemies in a speech entitled "La represión (intelectual) en Cuba" ("[Intellectual] repression in Cuba"). At a gathering of dissidents at Columbia University in 1980, Arenas avowed:

For the first time I am a free man and, as such, for the first time I exist. My life until now has transpired between two dictatorships: first Batista's and later the communist dictatorship. Precisely because I am in a free country for the first time I can speak. And since I can speak, I can say things that many citizens of this free country will not like, least of all its leaders. Of course, if I were in a totalitarian country (as in today's Cuba) I would have to say what the dictator wanted me to say, or not say anything at all. This is where the advantages of being in a free country lie (translation by Morales-Díaz).

Here Arenas creates a counterdiscourse to Castro's official policy of creating equality on the island (a policy ideally, though not in practice, based on the platform of JOSÉ MARTÍ, a figure of Cuban independence). Arenas's writing adopts an antirevolutionary stance against the established order; this stance can then be described as Arena's own revolutionary agenda. In order to accomplish this task Arenas created characters associated with both the revolution and his personal life. This technique allowed him to criticize the revolution, its attitudes toward gays, and its repressive measures.

Though he managed to seek asylum in the United States, by the 1980s Arenas was dying of AIDS. His memoir, *Before Night Falls,* dictated into a tape recorder on his deathbed, is a literary act of defiance against the Castro government. Rather than allow his illness to control him, Arenas chose to end his life the same way he lived it, on his own terms. He committed suicide in December 1990.

Bibliography

Arenas, Reinaldo. *The Assault.* Translated by Andrew Hurley. New York; London: Viking, 1994.

———. *Before Night Falls.* Translated by Dolores M. Koch. New York: Viking, 1993.

———. *The Color of Summer, or The New Garden of Earthly Delights.* Translated by Andrew Hurley. New York: Viking, 2000.

———. *El Central: A Cuban Sugar Mill.* New York: Avon Books, 1984.

———. *Farewell to the Sea: A Novel of Cuba.* Translated by Andrew Hurley. New York: Viking, 1985.

———. *Hallucinations, or The Ill-Fated Peregrinations of Fray Servando.* Translated by Gordon Brotherston. London: Cape, 1971.

———. *Old Rosa/The Brightest Star: 1 novel in 2 stories.* Translated by Ann Tashi Slater and Andrew Hurley. New York: Grove Press, 1989.

———. *The Palace of the White Skunks.* Translated by Andrew Hurley. New York: Viking, 1990.

———. *Singing from the Well.* New York: Viking, 1987.

Lumsden, Ian. *Machos, Maricones and Gays: Cuba and Homosexuality.* Philadelphia: Temple University Press, 1996.

Ocasio, Rafael. *Cuba's Political and Sexual Outlaw: Reinaldo Arenas.* Miami: University Press of Florida, 2003.

Soto, Francisco. *Reinaldo Arenas.* New York: Twayne Publishers, 1998.

———. *Reinaldo Arenas: The Pentagonía.* Miami: University Press of Florida, 1994.

Enrique Morales-Díaz

Autobiography of a Brown Buffalo, The Oscar Zeta Acosta (1972)

Oscar Zeta Acosta writes in his 1972 memoir, *The Autobiography of a Brown Buffalo,* that he is "a hick from the sticks, a Mexican boy from the other side of the tracks" (71). Born in El Paso, Texas, but raised in rural California, Acosta's account narrates his transition from jaded urban lawyer to Chicano activist. In this work the character Brown Buffalo (who represents Acosta) invites the reader to consider the dual impulses of self-destruction and self-reflection as he travels from the San Francisco Bay Area, through the West, to Mexico and back to the United States, with a stop in East Los Angeles.

Acosta's trip begins on July 1, 1967, with the narrator looking in the mirror of his San Francisco apartment. The narrator initiates a dialogue with his former psychologist, Dr. Serbin, to whom he confessed sexual and peptic problems. While the problems may be, in Serbin's estimation, due to either his mother or his race, the narrator suspects his difficulties have other sources (19). Indeed, upon arriving at his job at Legal Aid in Oakland, California, Acosta comments that "my stomach aches and my heart burns every day," which suggests a lack of integration between what he does for work and who he is (20). He admits that "we're just overburdened, mealy-mouthed, chickenshit lawyers who wouldn't know what the hell to do with a real case if our licenses depended on it" (20). When he learns that his trustworthy secretary has died of cancer, the narrator takes Stelazine pills (taking drugs is another theme), decides that he can no longer face his job, and makes plans to leave the city.

As Acosta prepares to depart, he recalls episodes from his life in San Francisco, some salacious and some touching, and the individuals who have shaped his life while living there, particularly friends from his favorite bar, Trader JJ's. The ex-lawyer summons up memories of sexual encounters, drug experimentation, moments of trust and help, as well as old disputes and stories as he goes about his last night of debauchery in the city. The evening culminates with a Harley Davidson ripping into Trader JJ's as Acosta slips away with money lent by the proprietor.

In chapter 6 Acosta has begun his trip eastward, in the green Plymouth his father gave him for having graduated from law school, and the next several chapters consist of his recollections of growing up in Riverbank, California. Acosta describes the racial divisions of his hometown into three parts, "Mexicans, Okies, and Americans. Catholics, Holy

Rollers and Protestants" (78), and noting that "these California Mexicans were not much higher than the Okies with whom they lived" (77). His father, a Mexican immigrant, had been drafted into the navy during World War II and ran the lives of his two sons according to the guidelines laid out in the *Seabee's Manual*. In the narrative, Acosta describes life as a Mexican-American youth in the San Joaquin Valley.

Acosta also details his relationships with the prostitutes of the valley and includes his first sexual encounter with the madam of a local bordello. As a youth, he falls in love with two Anglo girls, Jane and Alice, neither of whom returns his affection. Jane is at first fascinated and then embarrassed by Acosta, humiliating him in front of his classroom and leaving the boy feeling that "I am nothing but an Indian with a sweating body" (94). In Alice's case the girl's Okie stepfather forbids her to date a Mexican-American boy, compelling Acosta's parents, and a police officer, to separate the couple.

An impulsive character, Acosta throws himself into the air force band and later into the Baptist church, both of which he eventually abandons. After this long journey he enrolls in junior college and takes up creative writing under the tutelage of his professor Doc Jennings. After a few encounters with the police in Los Angeles, Acosta moves to San Francisco and decides to study law, ". . . not to practice law. But just to get a job so I could write my life history without having to put up with scags who thought only they knew what literature was all about" (155).

The end of the narrative flashes back to Acosta's travels through Nevada, Idaho, and Colorado and the people he meets along the way. He tries peyote for the first time, is at the scene of several parties and civil disruptions (including one in which he rolls his car off a cliff in Alpine, Colorado), and ultimately flees southward after warrants for his arrest have been issued.

Acosta works briefly in Vail, Colorado, and decides to return to El Paso, his place of birth. From El Paso he crosses the border to Juárez, Mexico. After a decisive night on the border Acosta concludes, "I am neither a Mexican nor an American. I am neither a Catholic nor a Protestant. I am a Chicano by ancestry and a Brown Buffalo by choice" (199). The text closes with Acosta leaving the El Paso for East Los Angeles to join fellow Chicanos in their quest for equality.

In his only other book, *The Revolt of the Cockroach People* (1973), Acosta writes of his participation in the civil rights movement, an interest catalyzed by the Chicano identity he assumes at the end of *Autobiography of a Brown Buffalo*. Though he was only able to publish these two books before his untimely disappearance in Mexico in 1974, he remains an important contributor to CHICANO LITERATURE.

Bibliography

Acosta, Oscar Zeta. *The Autobiography of a Brown Buffalo*. San Francisco, Calif.: Straight Arrow Books, 1972.

———. *The Revolt of the Cockroach People*. San Francisco, Calif.: Straight Arrow Books, 1973.

Hames-Garcia, Michael Roy. "Dr. Gonzo's Carnival: The Testimonial Satires of Oscar Zeta Acosta." *American Literature* 72, no. 3 (September 2000): 463–493.

Smethurst, James. "The Figure of the Vato Loco and the Representation of Ethnicity in the Narratives of Oscar Z. Acosta" *MELUS* 20, no. 2 (Summer 1995): 119–132.

Anna M. Nogar

Aztlán

Aztlán is both the mythical Aztec homeland, and the Chicano name for the Southwest (Texas, New Mexico, Colorado, Arizona, and California). Even so, Aztlán is much more complex than merely being a mythical site or geographical area of the United States. To properly understand Aztlán one must recognize that there are two primary constructions separated by more than six centuries. Initially Aztlán was conceived of as the homeland that the Mexica, one of the tribal units collectively known as the Aztec, left on their way to establish their imperial home at Tenochtitlán (present-day Mexico City). According to many historians Aztlán helped to legitimize the Mexica imperial rule of central Mexico. Following the foundation of their "empire," Aztlán remained an important idea for indigenous elites but lost ground with the arrival of Spanish conquistadores. During the colonial period of the 16th century, Aztlán became associated with the European construct of Cibola, one of the legendary Seven Cities of Gold (although the name may possibly be a distortion of the Zuni word *shiwina*).

During the late 1960s young Chicanas/os revived this ancient indigenous notion as a way to legitimize their presence in the United States. For these activists the U.S. Southwest was, and continues to be, Aztlán, and by turning to indigenous history, they converted Aztlán into a rhetorical tool and a call to arms for working-class Mexican Americans. Aztlán indeed plays a unique role in the Chicana/o struggle for self-determination.

Aztlán must be analyzed as a hybrid site that combines both indigenous Mesoamerican and European (both Hispanic and Anglo) worldviews. As such, many contemporary Chicana/o critics have voiced their opinions that Aztlán is in fact a continuation of earlier indigenous manifestations, albeit one mediated by both Hispanic and Anglo-American perspectives. Although the manner in which Aztlán historically functions has transformed across time and space, preceding constructions of Aztlán are always visibly embedded in newer manifestations.

Unfortunately there only survive approximately 20 colonial texts, both native and European, that address the Mexica migration from Aztlán. Among these there are seven that substantially narrate the Aztlán tale. These codices, which vary in the amount of European or indigenous iconography they contain, were not meant to be read as one presently reads; rather, these codices were expected to serve as mnemonic devices to aid in the remembering of historic events.

From these documents historians have gleaned the generalities of the migration narrative. The Mexica (then known as the Aztec) left Aztlán in 1168 following the mandate of Huitzilopochtli. In many of the codices Huitzilopochtli is featured prominently and shown being carried in a sacred bundle. Following their departure from Aztlán, which is usually translated as the "land of whiteness" or the "place of herons," the Mexica spent time at Chicomoztoc and Colhuacán. In 1325 the Mexica established Tenochtitlán after nearly two centuries of travel. During the Aztec-Mexica reign of power, Aztlán served an important role signifying their past as a warring and migratory people and the sedentary and agricultural practices of Teotihuacán.

Shortly before the arrival of Europeans in Tenochtitlán, Mexica rulers remained interested in the function of Aztlán. In approximately 1450 the great *tlatoani*, or leader, Moctezuma Ilhuicamina sent an expedition north in an attempt to find the exact location of Aztlán. The mission turned up little, but during the mid-16th century Spanish forces combined knowledge of Aztlán with multiple Iberian medieval and Renaissance traditions. For instance, a 734 C.E. Portuguese legend envisioned the discovery of seven cities of gold isolated on a distant and abandoned island. This myth, combined with indigenous migration stories, influenced Viceroy Antonio de Mendoza to send Marcos de Niza in search of Cibola in 1539. In approximately 1600 Aztlán and Cibola disappeared from popular discourse. For nearly four centuries the concept of Aztlán remained semidormant until Chicana/o activists popularized it during the late-1960s.

The most important text during the Chicana/o struggle for self-determination during the 1960s and 1970s was El Plan Espiritual de Aztlán (The Spiritual plan of Aztlán), anonymously written at the Chicano Youth Liberation Conference in March 1969. This document served as the impetus to forge a national unified voice and movement within the Mexican-American–cum–Chicano community.

Although published and disseminated without the individual name of an author, the preamble to the collectively written Plan Espiritual de Aztlán has been credited to ALURISTA. According to the Plan:

Brotherhood unites us, and love for our brothers makes us a people whose time has come and who struggles against the foreigner "gabacho" who exploits our riches and destroys our culture. With our heart in our hands and our hands in the soil, we declare the independence of our mestizo nation. We are a bronze people with a bronze culture. Before the world, before all of North America, before all our brothers in the bronze continent, we are a nation, we are a union of free pueblos, we are *Aztlán*.

Bibliography

Anaya, Rudolfo, and Francisco Lomelí, eds. *Aztlán: Essays on the Chicano Homeland.* Albuquerque: University of New Mexico/Academia/El Norte, 1989.

Fields, Virgina M., and Victor Zamudio-Taylor. *Road to Aztlán: Art from a Mythical Homeland.* Los Angeles/Albuquerque: Los Angeles Museum of Art: University of New Mexico, 2001.

Forbes, Jack D. *Aztecas del norte: Chicanos of Aztlán.* Greenwich, Conn.: Fawcett, 1973.

Maiz, Apaxu. *Looking for Aztlán: Birthright or Right for Birth.* Lansing, Mich.: Sun Dog, 2004.

Navarette Linares, Federico. *La migración de los mexicas.* Mexico City: Tercer Milenio Consejo Nacional la Cultura y las Artes, 1998.

Dylan A. T. Miner

Azúcar! The Story of Sugar Alan Cambeira
(2001)

Dominican-American writer Alan Cambeira published his first novel, *Azúcar! The Story of Sugar,* in 2001. Cambeira was born on the Samaná Peninsula of the Dominican Republic in 1941 and immigrated first to Barbados and then to the United States (New York and Pennsylvania). He graduated from Pennsylvania State University with a B.A. in Spanish and holds an M.A. in Latin American and Caribbean literature from Brooklyn College, as well as a doctorate in Latin American and Caribbean cultures from Clark Atlanta University. At present he teaches Spanish at the Citadel. Cambeira's studies of Dominican and Caribbean sociopolitical history and culture appear in both English and in Spanish.

Azúcar! The Story of Sugar is the first in a trilogy of novels and tells the story of Azúcar Ferrand St. Jacques. The second novel in the series is *Azúcar's Sweet Hope . . . : Her Story Continues* (2004). The third novel in the trilogy, *Tattered Paradise: Azúcar's Trilogy Ends!* (2007), takes place 10 years after the end of the first novel and examines the issue of worker exploitation carried out by the hotel and tourism industries.

Azúcar! The Story of Sugar depicts the modern-day plight of sugarcane field workers in the Dominican Republic. The narrative reveals the perpetuation of slavelike conditions on the plantations and how globalization has reenforced the status quo. Most of the novel takes place on a sugar plantation named Esperanza Dulce (which translates as "sweet hope"). The name of the plantation offers a stark contrast to the actual situation of the cane-cutters (*braceros*) who work in the cane fields and dwell in the *batey* (the workers' settlement). Cambeira describes the *batey* as an abominable place with no electricity or plumbing; living quarters are overcrowded and squalid. It is an environment where children often cannot attend school; rather, they work under a scorching sun in the fields in order to support their families. Although the setting of the novel seems to take place in the late 20th century, the living and working conditions closely resemble those of colonial slavery. The novel lyrically portrays the sense of desperation, abuse, and economic bondage suffered in the *batey* through the story of the title character, Azúcar Ferrand. We learn at the beginning of the novel that this young and lovely 13-year-old suffers rape at the hands of Mario, the plantation foreman's son.

Through Ferrand's coming of age Cambeira's novel paints a vivid portrait of daily life for the workers in the *batey*. While their lives and living conditions seem tragic, the author also illustrates their everyday humanity in showing loving family relationships as well as strong community interactions. After a series of recent abuses on the plantation, Ferrand's grandmother arranges a vodou ceremony to call on ancestor spirits to protect Azúcar and the rest of the settlement. Cambeira shows the community joining together through a traditional ceremony with dance, drumming, song, and offerings honoring the ancestors.

While the immediate threats and aggressors to the community seem to be the plantation foreman and his family members, Cambeira makes clear that the people who actually own and control the plantation are mostly North Americans. He reveals that it is a global market for sugar that is part of the oppression of the locals. In the story, however, Azúcar has a life-changing chance encounter with a Canadian scientist that brings her a new life and new possibilities in Canada.

Cambeira's distinctive writing style is highly descriptive and detailed. The compelling story line is what drives the novel forward. Originally written and published in English, Cambeira often interjects phrases and sayings throughout his book in Spanish or in Haitian Creole giving greater texture to the linguistic landscape in which the *batey* exists.

With the Azúcar novels Cambeira joins a literary conversation with JULIA ALVAREZ (*IN THE TIME OF THE BUTTERFLIES*), Loida Maritza Pérez (*GEOGRAPHIES OF HOME*), and JUNOT DÍAZ (*DROWN*) about life in the Dominican Republic. With its themes and settings Cambeira's work can be read within the context of DOMINICAN-AMERICAN literature and, more broadly, SPANISH-AMERICAN CARIBBEAN LITERATURE.

Bibliography

Alan Cambeira Web site. Available online. URL: http://www.cambeira.com.

Alvarez, Julia. *In the Time of the Butterflies.* New York: Plume/Penguin, 1994.

Cambeira, Alan. *Azúcar's Sweet Hope . . . : Her Story Continues.* Frederick, Md.: PublishAmerica, 2004.

———. *Tattered Paradise: Azúcar's Trilogy Ends!* Frederick, Md.: PublishAmerica, 2007.

———. *Azúcar! The Story of Sugar.* Kearney, Neb.: Morris Publishing, 2001.

Díaz, Junot. *Drown.* London: Faber, 1997.

Pérez, Loida Maritza. *Geographies of Home.* London: Viking, 1999.

Jo-Anne Suriel

B

Before Night Falls **Reinaldo Arenas** (1992)
Cuban author REINALDO ARENAS recorded his lyrical and compelling autobiography shortly before he died of AIDS in 1990. It was later transcribed by friends word for word and published in Spanish in 1992 as *Antes que anochezca: Autobiografía.* It appeared in English translation the following year. *Before Night Falls: A Memoir* is an expression of Arenas's identity as a child in Perronales County and as a youth caught up in FIDEL CASTRO's CUBAN REVOLUTION. It is also a record of Arenas's life as a rebellious writer and lover in Havana and, ultimately, as a Cuban exile dying of AIDS in New York. As such, it is an interesting and politically important contribution to LATINO GAY LITERATURE. The memoir became the basis for the film *Before Night Falls* (2002), directed by Julian Schnabel. Schnabel's beautiful, playful, and heartbreaking portrait of Arenas also incorporates stories from Arenas's novels *Celestino antes del alba* (1967; *Singing from the Well,* 1987) and *El color del verano o, Nuevo "Jardín de las delicias": Novela escrita y publicada sin privilegio imperial* (1999; *The Color of Summer, or The New Garden of Earthly Delights,* 2000).

Perhaps one of the most poignant moments in Arenas's autobiography is the "suicide" letter published at the end of the book. In this letter he pleads with Cubans on and off the island to continue their struggle for a *Cuba libre,* and he maintains his invective against Castro and his regime. He pledges to his audience:

> You are the heirs of all my terrors, but also of my hope that Cuba will soon be free. I am satisfied to have contributed, though in a very small way, to the triumph of this freedom. I end my life voluntarily . . . The sufferings of exile, the pain of being banished from my country, the loneliness, and the diseases contracted in exile would probably never have happened if I had been able to enjoy freedom in my country. I want to encourage the Cuban people out of the country as well as on the Island to continue fighting for freedom. I do not want to convey to you a message of defeat but of continued struggle and of hope. Cuba will be free. I already am (317).

This letter conveys important aspects of Cuba as Arenas remembers it. First, Arenas holds Castro responsible for all the suffering he has endured, from incarceration in El Morro (a prison in Havana) and detention in the UMAP (Military Units to Aid Production) camp, a military labor camp. He rails against the regime's use of forced labor and its relentless censorship. For Arena, the censorship of his writing, as well as the control of his sexuality, concluded in the "disappearance" of another Cuban intellectual who opposed the revolution.

The freedom of expression that Arenas sought, according to his autobiography, was connected to his typewriter, his most prized possession. The typewriter became an emblem of Arenas's life and intimately connected to the ecstasies of his imagination. When he was diagnosed with AIDS, he was unable to continue his creative process; this symbolized an end to everything that mattered in his life. Sex and writing for Arenas complemented each other, often feeding into each other inspiration and ideas for his literary production.

In his autobiography Arenas affirms his desire to control his own life on his own terms, even if that means choosing death. He admits:

> I really cannot say that I want to die; yet I relieve that when the alternative is suffering and pain without hope, death is a thousand times better . . . If you cannot live the way you want, there is no point in living. In Cuba I endured a thousand adversities because the hope of escaping and the possibility of saving my manuscripts gave me strength. At this point, the only escape for me was death (ix).

Arenas's sentiments in this passage mirror those that he felt as a child, especially in his sense of loss, displacement, and the phenomenon of being both inside and outside his own family. His memoir comes full circle as he thinks about his birthplace and his beautiful island from his deathbed in New York. With his suicide impending, the memoir can be considered both an act of destruction and liberation; it can also be interpreted as a catalyst for the reappropriation not only of his writing but also of his life. Through his writing the Cuban author succeeds in reclaiming a marginalized voice by breaking away from the repressive measures of Castro's regime and exposing them. The writer's suicide is not an act of cowardice but an affirmation of his life, his experiences and struggles. The one obstacle that he cannot overcome, and yet was able to manipulate and cheat, is his illness. For its themes and settings Arenas's work can be read within the context of CUBAN-AMERICAN LITERATURE and SPANISH-AMERICAN CARIBBEAN LITERATURE.

Bibliography

Arenas, Reinaldo. *Antes que añochezca: Autobiografía.* Barcelona: Tusquets, 1992.

———. *Before Night Falls: A Memoir.* Translated by Dolores M. Koch. New York: Viking, 1993.

———. *The Color of Summer, or The New Garden of Earthly Delights.* Translated by Andrew Hurley. New York: Viking, 2000.

———. *Singing from the Well.* Translated by Andrew Hurley. New York: Viking, 1987.

Ocasio, Rafael. *Cuba's Political and Sexual Outlaw: Reinaldo Arenas.* Miami: University Press of Florida, 2003.

Schnabel, Julian, dir. *Before Night Falls.* Grandview Pictures. Los Angeles: Twentieth Century Fox, 2002.

Soto, Francisco. *Reinaldo Arenas.* New York: Twayne Publishers, 1998.

———. *Reinaldo Arenas: The Pentagonía.* Miami: University Press of Florida, 1994.

Enrique Morales-Díaz

Before We Were Free **Julia Alvarez** (2002)
Born in New York and raised in the Dominican Republic until the age of 10, JULIA ALVAREZ's *Before We Were Free* conveys, from a first-person point of view, the tumult of the Dominican Republic from 1960 to 1961, when the brutal dictatorship of Rafael Trujillo was brought to an end. In the course of this coming-of-age novel, much of personal and political significance takes place in the life of Anita de la Torre. The lively 12-year-old protagonist is called Cotorrita (little parrot) because she likes to talk. Anita's garrulousness becomes a problem given the island's volatile environment of clandestine meetings in which individuals must be silent or speak in code. Although its ending is hopeful, an ominous tone pervades almost the entire novel: Schools are closed because of the political crisis, embassies are vacated, family members flee for safety, goods are in short supply as a result of an embargo, and terror is just down the hall or around the corner.

Before We Were Free explains how Anita's family is involved in the movement to rid the country of General Trujillo's tyranny. The de la Torre house is regularly searched by the secret police, the SIM (Servicio Inteligencia Militar), and her father and uncle are under suspicion and surveillance. Her uncle Toni is in hiding to avoid persecution. While Anita's father runs the family concrete block business to provide materials for hurricane-proof housing, Construcciones de la Torre, he also organizes others to free his country of the dictatorship of El Jefe (Trujillo). The political context of the story allows Alvarez to explore themes of individual responsibility, courage, sacrifice, and the fight for freedom. Like her namesake, Anne Frank, Anita is forced to go into hiding to save her life, during which she keeps a diary, offering young readers of this novel an example of the value of using writing to reflect on one's experiences. Writing and reflection is a common thread in Alvarez's work, especially with Yolanda García's fanciful fictions in *¡Yo!* (1996) and with young Mate Mirabal's diary in *IN THE TIME OF THE BUTTERFLIES* (1994). In fact, Alvarez prepares readers for reading *In the Time of the Butterflies* in chapter 2 of *Before We Were Free*. In this episode Anita asks her father, who is saddened, about a car "accident" involving women who are called Las Mariposas (the butterflies). The butterflies is a code name for three Mirabal sisters who were murdered for their participation in the Fourteenth of June movement to overthrow Trujillo. Mr. de la Torre cannot answer this or other questions his daughter poses throughout the novel, revealing a politically charged climate.

Anita experiences a number of rites of passage: her first crush, first romantic kiss, and first menstrual period. Anita's classmate and love interest Oscar Mancini is a smart and attractive character for teenage audiences. We see him from the beginning to the end of the novel questioning authority and the status quo; he seeks explanations of what others may take for granted in the world around them. Mancini lives next door to the de la Torre family, and he attends the same American school as Anita; he represents the positive aspect of U.S. influences in the Dominican Republic. Likewise, the presence of the United States in these rough times is implied by the benevolent and watchful character of Mr. Washburn, the American consul

who arranges for visas for members of the de la Torre family. Historically, however, the U.S. role in the Dominican Republic is more complex than this book can readily convey through Mr. Washburn's character. The United States in fact supported Trujillo's procapitalist and anticommunist stance from the 1930s until very late in the dictator's administration, when it issued a crippling embargo that Alvarez mentions in the text.

Before We Were Free is framed by the observation of two Thanksgiving holidays, the first at the American school Anita attends in the Dominican Republic and the second at the García's house in Queens, New York. This novel may prompt young readers to interrogate what they too may be thankful for. By the novel's end Anita's mother (Mami), brother (Mundín), sister (Lucinda), and she have escaped the regime and relocated to snowy New York City. Anita is relieved to be free, but she cannot forget that her beloved father and uncle have been executed by Trujillo's henchmen. Still, the dictatorship is overthrown by 1961, and the Dominican Republic will hold its first free elections in 31 years. There is cause for optimism for a better life.

With its disturbing story of the Trujillo regime in the Dominican Republic, *Before We Were Free* exemplifies the genre of young adult historical fiction. Alvarez captures the lives of heroic individuals who worked together to free their country from a military dictatorship. The brutality of force and the jailing, torture, and murder of dissidents are serious topics for youth, but in the world in which we live, they are ones worthy of their consideration. Suspenseful and sensitive, this novel can raise young adult readers' political consciousnesses, as it explores the meaning of freedom and what it can take to win it for ourselves and others.

Alvarez explains her motivations for writing this novel in the author's note at the end of the text. Though her own family fled Trujillo's regime in 1960, she considered what it must have been like for her cousins to live during the darkest days of the Trujillo regime. She explains that she wanted to re-create the Dominican fight for freedom:

I chose to base the story on the Trujillo regime in the Dominican Republic because it was one under which I had myself had lived. But this story could have taken place in any of the dictatorships in Nicaragua, Cuba, Chile, Haiti [which shares the island of Hispaniola with the Dominican Republic], Argentina, Guatemala, El Salvador, or Honduras—a sad but not uncommon experience in the southern half of *our America* not too long ago (emphasis added, 166).

The author's note participates in the literary conversation that JOSÉ MARTÍ had begun with his essay "Nuestra América" (1891; "Our America," 1977); Alvarez recognizes that the calamity of one Latin American nation is often shared by others. On a related note, Anita's journal coincides with the Latin American tradition of the eyewitness account, the *testimonio* (testimony) of survivors who fought for freedom and equality. Within the context of Alvarez's work, *Before We Were Free* shares characters (members of the de la Torre family and the García family) with her first novel, How THE GARCÍA GIRLS LOST THEIR ACCENTS (1991) and her semiautobiographical novel *¡Yo!*. *Before We Were Free* also has much in common with SANDRA BENÍTEZ's El Salvadoran–based novels *Bitter Grounds* (1997) and *The Weight of All Things* (2000). *Before We Were Free* was awarded the American Library Association Best Book for Young Adults, as well as the Pura Belpré Award. It can be read within the context of both DOMINICAN-AMERICAN LITERATURE and SPANISH-AMERICAN CARIBBEAN LITERATURE.

Bibliography

Alvarez, Julia. *Before We Were Free*. New York: Alfred A. Knopf, 2002.

———. *How the García Girls Lost Their Accents*. New York: Plume, 1992.

———. *In the Time of the Butterflies*. New York: Plume/Penguin, 1994.

———. *¡Yo!* Chapel Hill, N.C.: Algonquin Books, 1997.

Benítez, Sandra. *Bitter Grounds*. London: Sceptre, 1997.

———. *The Weight of All Things*. New York: Hyperion, 2000.

Jacques, Ben. "Julia Alvarez: Real Flights of Imagination." *Américas* 53 (2001): 22–29.

Julia Alvarez: Official Author Web site. Available online. URL: http://www.alvarezjulia.com.

Martí, José. *Our America: Writings on Latin America and the Struggle for Cuban Independence*. Translated by Elinor Randall. London: Monthly Review Press, 1977.

G. Douglas Meyers

Belli, Gioconda (1948–) *(novelist, poet, activist)*

Born in Nicaragua in 1948, Gioconda Belli is one of the most noteworthy Nicaraguan-American writers of her time. In 1970 Belli began to participate in the Frente Sandinista de Liberación Nacional (Sandinista National Liberation Front, FSLN). The FSLN was a revolutionary movement that fought to remove Nicaraguan dictator Anastasio Somoza Debayle from power. During the 1970s Belli participated in clandestine military operations of the FSLN within Nicaragua and then once in exile continued to support the revolutionary cause. After the Sandinistas' victory over Somoza in 1979, she worked for the newly established government. Belli's work was featured in the national literary supplement *La Prensa Literaria*, and the author won a poetry prize, the Premio de Poesía Mariano Fiallos Gil, in 1972. Belli's award-winning poetry, which celebrates female sexuality and female power, has evoked shock in some of its readers.

Since the electoral defeat of the Sandinistas in 1990, Belli and her family have lived in the United States and Nicaragua. Combining political commitment and her artistic vision, Belli has established herself as an internationally acclaimed author through numerous collections of poetry, an autobiography, and novels. In 2001 she published *El país bajo mi piel: Memorias de amor y guerra* (2001; *The Country Under My Skin: A Memoir of Love and War*, 2003). Her novels include *La mujer habitada* (1988; *The Inhabited Woman*, 2004), *Sofía de los presagios* (1990; Sophia of the presages) and *Waslala* (1996).

Home to Rubén Darío, an important modernist writer, Nicaragua is often regarded throughout Latin America as the land of poets. When Belli began her literary career in the 1970s, very few Latin American women poets had achieved regional, national, or international recognition. And, while a number of female artists in Nicaragua attained a certain level of recognition for their works in the 1960s, it was not until Belli's generation that women consolidated their status as authors on the Nicaraguan and international scenes. Belli's works stand out for their mixture of mystical eroticism and affirmation of women's political, social, cultural, and physical liberation.

Sobre la grama (1975; On the grass), Belli's first collection of poetry, celebrates woman's physical and creative power. In "Y Dios me hizo mujer" ("And God made me a woman"), God lovingly and purposefully creates the body, mind, and spirit of the woman-poet, who is proud of her sex and power to create life. In addition to writing autobiographical poems on such historically taboo topics as menstruation and breast-feeding in "Uno no escoge" ("One does not choose"), Belli calls upon her fellow Nicaraguans to assume responsibility for their country's future. Perhaps more overt in its revolutionary content regarding the Sandinista cause, *Línea de fuego* (1978; Line of fire), Belli's second collection of poetry, won the CASA DE LAS AMÉRICAS Prize for poetry in 1978. The principal themes in this work are national liberation, women's freedom—erotic, social, and political—and a combination of both. Oftentimes intertwined with these topics is a utopian dream of a society in which all the people of Nicaragua participate in a democracy of love and equality. Some of the oft-referenced poems this volume includes are "Huelga" ("Strike"), "Hasta que seamos libres" ("Until we are free"), "¿Qué sos Nicaragua?" ("What are you, Nicaragua?"), and "Amo a los hombres y les canto" ("I love men and sing to them").

In celebration of the Sandinistas' victory over the Somoza dictatorship, Belli wrote one of her more renowned political poems, "Patria libre: 19 de julio de 1979" ("Free fatherland: July 19, 1979"), and published a third collection of poetry, *Truenos y arco iris* (1982; Thunder and rainbow). In her fourth collection of poetry, *De la costilla de Eva* (1987; *From Eve's Rib,* 1993), Belli returns to the question of women's liberation and civic freedom. Differing from her work of 1970s that focused on Nicaragua's liberation from Somoza, *From Eve's Rib* uses poetry to criticize the U.S. support of the Contras' attacks on the Sandinista government. The poet revisits the topic of eroticism and gender roles in "Pequeñas lecciones de erotismo" ("Brief lessons in eroticism") and "Reglas del juego para los hombres que quieren amar a mujeres" ("Rules of the game for men who want to love women"). As in many of Belli's works, this latter poem establishes a correlation between political revolutions and rebellion against traditional gender roles.

With a mixture of wit and nostalgia *Apogeo* (1998; Apogee) expands on Belli's often autobiographic discussion of women and society while meditating on women's physical changes, as well as their wisdom, spirituality, and social position in the apogee, or zenith, of their lives. Perhaps Belli's most thematically varied collection, *Mi íntima multitud* (2003; My intimate multitude), won the fifth Premio Internacional de Poesía "Generación del 27." Themes in Belli's works—women, the power to create, utopia, Nicaragua, and eroticism—are framed by Belli's personal reflections on her life in both Nicaragua and the United States and by historical events. Such events include the violence of civil war, the concern about life after the new millennium, and the despair associated with Hurricane Mitch (1998), which caused massive damage throughout Central America. With a note of nostalgia, Belli reflects on the loss of the dreams of the FSLN and mourns the poverty and hopelessness of Nicaragua in the present. She also ponders the role of the poet and the creative word in the future, addressing contemporary topics such as cyberspace, computers, and modernity in general. Belli has also published the following anthologies of her poetry: *Amor insurrecto* (1984; Insurgent love), *El ojo de la mujer* (1991; The woman's eye), and

Érase una vez una mujer (1998; Once upon a time there was a woman). For its themes and images, Belli's work can be read within the context of Central American literature.

Bibliography

Belli, Gioconda. *The Country Under My Skin: A Memoir of Love and War.* Translated by Kristina Cordero. New York: Knopf, 2003.

———. *From Eve's Rib.* Translated by Steven F. White. Willimantic, Conn.: Curbstone Press, 1993.

———. *The Inhabited Woman.* Translated by Kathleen March. Madison: University of Wisconsin Press, 2004.

———. *The Scroll of Seduction.* Translated by Lisa Dillman. New York: HarperCollins Publishers, 2006.

Hanzen, Sozy. Giocanda Belli. "Lies and Revolution" [Interview and compilation of articles on Belli]. Available online. URL: http://www.arlindo-correia. com/020303.html. Accessed November 27, 2007.

Analisa de Grave

Benítez, Sandra (1941–   ) *(novelist, educator)*
Born Sandra Jeanette Ables on March 26, 1941, in Washington, D.C., to Martha Ables Benítez and James Ables, Sandra Benítez is a writer and educator of Puerto Rican heritage. James Ables's work for the U.S. State Department took the family to Mexico and El Salvador, where he was appointed the commercial attaché to the U.S. embassy. While living in El Salvador, Benítez witnessed the conditions that would lead to the country's civil war in 1980, a war between the militia-backed government and the peasantry who took up arms. Benítez incorporated her understanding of history and her memories of Mexico and El Salvador into her fiction, most notably in *Bitter Grounds* (1997) and *The Weight of All Things* (2000).

Upon her family's return to the United States, Benítez attended college and graduate school in Missouri and has long enjoyed a long career as an educator. After teaching high school Spanish and English until 1968, Benítez worked as a Spanish-English translator and marketing representative.

In 1980 she married James F. Kondrick and taught creative writing at the University of Minnesota in Duluth with the Split Rock Arts Program. At this time Benítez started her writing career and took her mother's maiden name. She published her first novel, *A Place Where the Sea Remembers* (1993), at the age of 52. *A Place Where the Sea Remembers* is set in a Mexican coastal town called Santiago and tells the story of two sisters, Chayo and Marta. A family dispute arises over the impending birth of Marta's child, who is the product of rape. Chayo and her husband have agreed to raise Marta's child, but Chayo reneges on her promise when she discovers she, too, is pregnant. Two boys, Richard and Tonito, are born to Marta and Chayo, respectively; however, Richard is washed out to sea by a flood. Remedios, a CURANDERA (healer), waits for Marta's son to wash up on shore. Critics lauded *A Place Where the Sea Remembers* for its lively narrative style and character development. The text won the Barnes and Noble Discover Great New Writers Award in 1993 and the Minnesota Book Award for Fiction in 1994. *A Place Where the Sea Remembers* was also chosen as a finalist for the *Los Angeles Times* Book Award and earned Benítez membership in the National Writers' Voice Project.

In 1997 Benítez published her second novel, *Bitter Grounds*. The story centers on two families living in El Salvador from the 1930s to the 1970s, when military control of the peasantry had become intolerable. Readers are introduced to members of the wealthy Contreras family, as well as to Mercedes and Jacinta Prieto, a mother and daughter who have come to work as servants on the Contreras plantation. By surveying the generations of the Prieto and Contreras families, Benítez brings to light the region's political and economical instability; this instability arises in part from the terrible working and living conditions of the coffee harvesters, many of whom, like Mercedes Prieto, are Pipil Indians. The title of *Bitter Grounds* refers to a coffee industry expanded on contested lands to satisfy foreign consumption of the beans, to the role that harvesting plays in daily life, and to the burial or hiding of the dead who are part of this agrarian economy.

The novel earned critical praise for its rich prose style and historical elements. *Bitter Grounds* won an American Book Award (1998) and received a nomination for the United Kingdom's Orange Fiction Prize.

Following the success of *Bitter Grounds* Benítez published *The Weight of All Things* in 2000. In this, Benítez combines fiction and history to introduce readers to her nine-year-old protagonist, Nicolás de la Virgen Veras. Veras and his mother have come to pay their respects to the Archbishop Oscar Romero, who has been brutally assassinated (this assassination took place in 1980); however, chaos breaks out when the militia open fire on thousands of mourners, including Nicolás's mother, who dies protecting her child. In the remainder of the narrative Nicolás Veras will have to learn how face his loss by negotiating the lines between the guerrilla (armed peasants) and the U.S.-supported and state-sponsored El Salvadoran militia. As in *Bitter Grounds,* Benítez portrays the complexity of human brutality and generosity. She also shows the extreme suffering of Salvadorans during the civil war, which caused poverty, homelessness, and countless deaths (countless because not all the bodies have been found). *The Weight of All Things* won praise for its striking prose and compelling narrative technique and drew comparisons to JULIA ALVAREZ and her treatment of the Trujillo regime in IN THE TIME OF THE BUTTERFLIES (1994).

Benítez uses her midwestern background in her fourth novel, *Night of the Radishes* (2004). The story begins as Annie Rush recalls the death of her twin sister from a childhood accident. She leaves Minnesota to find her older brother, Hub, who left after the incident. Annie discovers him in Oaxaca, Mexico, where she learns how to cope with her loss and guilt. *Night of the Radishes* displays Benítez's ability to narrate human emotions and to depict vastly different settings (Minnesota and Oaxaca) in a vivid manner. The novel also expresses Benítez's feelings about the death of her own twin sister, Susana, who died soon after the twins were born.

Benítez's novels have been translated into a half-dozen languages. Her work frequently appears in anthologies, such as *A Place Called Home: Twenty Writing Women Remember* (1996) and *Sleeping with One Eye Open: Women Writers and the Art of Survival* (1999). Her first nonfiction text deals with chronic illness—ulcerative colitis—and is entitled *Bag Lady: A Memoir* (2005).

Benítez's academic career is impressive. In 1997 she was the Keller-Edelstein Distinguished Writer in Residence at the University of Minnesota. In 2001 she was selected as the Knapp Chair in Humanities as associate professor of creative writing at the University of San Diego. She lives in Edina, Minnesota, and since 2004 is the Judith Anderson Stoutland Writer-in-Residence at St. Olaf College in Northfield, Minnesota. In 2004 the author earned one of the greatest honors for Latinos, the National Hispanic Heritage Award for Literature, and in 2006 she was awarded a Gund Fellowship.

Bibliography

Alvarez, Julia. *In the Time of the Butterflies.* Chapel Hill, N.C.: Algonquin Books, 1994.

Baxter, Kevin. "Rediscovering Roots Through Her Writing." *Los Angeles Times,* October 28, 1997, p. E3.

Benítez, Sandra. *Bag Lady: A memoir.* Edina, Minn.: Benítez Books, 2005.

———. *Bitter Grounds.* New York: Hyperion, 1997.

———. *Night of the Radishes.* New York: Hyperion, 2004.

———. *A Place Where The Sea Remembers.* Minneapolis, Minn.: Coffee House Press, 1993.

———. *The Weight of All Things.* New York: Hyperion, 2000.

Habich, John. "Mother Country." *Star Tribune,* March 25, 2001, p. E1.

Kallet, Marilyn, and Judith Ortiz Cofer, eds. *Sleeping with One Eye Open: Women Writers and the Art of Survival.* London: University of Georgia Press, 1999.

Pearlman, Mickey, ed. *A Place Called Home: Twenty Writing Women Remember.* New York: St. Martin's Press, 1996.

Sandra Benítez Web site. Available online. URL: http://www.sandrabenitez.com.

Dorsía Smith Silva

Bilingual Blues Gustavo Pérez Firmat (1995)
Readers of *Bilingual Blues* and other works by GUS-TAVO PÉREZ FIRMAT come to realize that the Cuban-American author's preoccupation is not with Cuba, per se. Instead, as an exiled writer, Pérez Firmat fixates on the cultural hyphen that at once divides and unites his Cuban roots and his American ways of being. He considers himself Cuban and in exile; he teaches, writes, and lives in New York. In *Bilingual Blues* Pérez Firmat considers the language barrier between himself, his American wife, his children, and his Cuban relatives. The lack of a shared language is one of the "blues" conveyed in this book of poetry.

Bilingual Blues expresses the challenges of a bicultural life, one divided by being Cuban and living in the United States. Bringing together poems that were written between 1981 and 1994, one-third of the book is in Spanish and is entitled "Equivocaciones" ("Misunderstandings"). "Equivocaciones" is sandwiched in between the English sections, "Justified Margins" and "Unintelligible Ballads." Even these sections, however, switch back and forth between English and Spanish, and in this regard Pérez Firmat employs the technique of CODE SWITCHING.

As an intensely self-conscious writer, one who has grappled with the dynamics of moving between English and Spanish, Pérez Firmat opens *Bilingual Blues* with the admission that writing in English "already falsifies" what he wants to tell us. In this moment he brings to mind Shakespeare's island character, CALIBAN, who has learned his master's language only to be able to curse him in it. The new language weighs heavily on Caliban, and yet he can communicate in no other way with Prospero.

Pérez Firmat finds his English both a curse and a blessing. He explains the notion of falsification in his critical work *Tongue Ties* (2003), where he points out that "Even among people who have been raised bilingually, the relation of languages is not symmetrical . . . The notion of balanced bilingualism or *equilingüismo* is as much a fiction as that of bilingualism without pain . . . I am not talking about fluency but about affect" (8). The author's unease about being able to truly say what he wants

to say has less to do with finding the equivalent words in English than it does with being able to say in English what he might more authentically convey in Spanish.

In spite of their different linguistic and affective registers, Spanish and English are tied to the author's conclusion in *Bilingual Blues* that he belongs "no where else" but in English (3). His wife is American; his children, David and Miriam—both of whom he writes about in *Bilingual Blues*—are American by birth, not Cuban like he is. Several poems give rise to the tug of war Pérez Firmat contends with; for example, in "Seeing Snow" the poet sits in North Carolina, bewildered by the sight of the icy white flakes outside. This contemplative moment brings the autobiographical speaker to his past. If his father or grandfather had been asked whether Pérez Firmat would ever see snow, "they certainly—in another language— / would have answered / no . . ." (4). In Cuba, only 90 miles from Key West, Florida, snow is merely a word, *nieve,* having no connection to an actual reality. His Cuban relations would have little idea about the emotional experience that comes from seeing snow fall. Corresponding with the imagery of winter is the poet's observation of the summer party celebrated with Fourth of July fireworks, American food (Cokes, burgers, hot dogs), and country music. This summer holiday reminds the exiled author of his own U.S. nationality, as well as his estrangement from the sentiment of U.S. patriotism (he is reluctant to vote).

In the poem "Natives Like Us" the speaker seeks to reconcile the "half-life," the state of being in and out of *Cubanidad* (being Cuban), and the "whole life" (19). The title of *Bilingual Blues* is derived, in part, from the sundering that comes from living in between two cultures and trying to understand them. "Split Routines" centers on the speaker's divorce (from his first wife) and the double life his children begin to lead. They spend half their time with their mother and the other half with their father: "Such double lives they lead! / Even their hearts must be cleft in two" (114). This cleft heart is also his own and that of other Latino immigrants and exiles. Pérez Firmat shuttles back and forth every week between Chapel Hill, North Carolina, and his job at Columbia University in New York City, and he thinks back at what his children must have gone through during those early years of the divorce with "two blankets, two pillows, two turtles . . ." (114). But his children, he writes, already know what it took him 40 years to learn: "there's always another toothbrush / another blanket, another bed" (115).

Being divided between two families, two cultures, and two languages, while enriching, is nevertheless a painful experience. No wonder, then, he writes, *"vivir sin historia es vivir"*: to live without history is to live—by which the author means living free of the past (68). In the poem "Bilingual Blues" (also published as "The Last Mambo"), which gives the book its title, the author writes: *"Soy un ajiaco de contradicciones,"* which literally translates to "I am a stew of contradictions." Pérez Firmat follows this declaration with the confession, "I have mixed feelings about everything" (28). For the author these mixed feelings make the *ajiaco,* the stew, *tan sabroso,* so delicious.

Within a broader context the theme of negotiating two cultures can be found in CRISTINA GARCÍA's *DREAMING IN CUBAN* (1992), OSCAR HIJUELOS's *EMPRESS OF THE SPLENDID SEASON* (1999), and much of CUBAN-AMERICAN LITERATURE.

Bibliography

Dick, Bruce Allen. "A Conversation with Gustavo Pérez Firmat." *Michigan Quarterly Review* 40, no. 4 (Fall 2001): 682–693.

Hijuelos, Oscar. *Empress of the Splendid Season.* New York: HarperFlamingo, 1999.

García, Cristina. *Dreaming in Cuban.* New York: Knopf: 1992.

Gustavo Pérez Firmat Web site. Available online. URL: http://www.gustavoperezfirmat.com.

Pérez Firmat, Gustavo. *Bilingual Blues: Poems, 1981–1994.* Tempe, Ariz.: Bilingual Press/Editorial Bilingüe, 1995.

———. *Life on the Hyphen: The Cuban American Way.* Austin: University of Texas Press, 1994.

———. *Tongue Ties: Logo-Eroticism in Anglo-Hispanic Literature.* New York: Palgrave Macmillan, 2003.

Rolando Pérez

Black Cuban, Black American: A Memoir
Evelio Grillo (2002)

Evelio Grillo has devoted most of his life to the cause of civil rights. As an activist and community leader, Grillo has fought for fair access to education and military service. Born in 1919 to an Afro-Cuban family in Tampa, Florida, Grillo visited his Cuban relations as a very young boy. He went to the island with his father, who was suffering from tuberculosis; after his father died, Grillo returned to his mother and siblings in Tampa. As a boy and young man, he suffered the consequences of the Jim Crow laws and bore the prejudice of his white Cuban counterparts in Florida, despite the fact that he and they belonged to the same immigrant group. *Black Cuban, Black American: A Memoir* (2002) is the account of how all these experiences shaped his identity and activism.

Black Cuban, Black American represents episodes of Grillo's life in Ybor City, in Tampa, where he was raised; in Washington, D.C., where he went to high school; and in New Orleans, Louisiana, where he attended Xavier University (a historically black college). The memoir is divided into three sections: "Ybor City," "Going Up North," and "At War." In the first section Grillo allows readers a look at the racial politics during the 1920s and 1930s, when being black in the South was a liability with the enforcement of the Jim Crow laws. He explains the divisions between white Cubans and black Cubans, as well as between black Americans and black Cubans. The narrative then unveils the practices of segregation in the army during World War II; this was a time when military officials had little compunction in sending a disproportionate number of blacks (and Hispanics) to the front lines. As the title of his memoir suggests, Grillo poses important questions about ethnic and national identities. Grillo reflects on decades of struggling for equality and the use of strategic alliances to create social change, an approach that rejects an allegiance to one culture or racial category—black or Cuban or American.

Black Cuban, Black American compels the reader to look at Cuban immigration to the States as a long-standing phenomenon, dating back to the second half of the 19th century, especially as a result of the wars of independence (1868–78, 1895). The shifts in the cigar-making industry also became a factor in Cuban migration, as were the opportunities to emigrate more freely before 1959, when FIDEL CASTRO overthrew Fulgencio Batista's regime. Cubans who were part of the working-class migration in the early part of the 20th century were not fleeing revolution but instead making one. Grillo's parents left Cuba to work in the cigar factories of Ybor City, in Tampa. He writes:

> My father, Antonio, worked as a "finisher," a very prestigious job involving the final sculpture of the cigars into identical shapes. My mother, Amparo, worked as a *bonchera,* a "buncher." She gathered the inner leaves of the cigars into the long, rounded shapes to which the finishers applied the final, prime, wrapping leaf (6).

In this regard, his family's migration predates the economically successful, politically conservative, and predominantly white exodus of the 1950s and 1960s. His family's move from the island to Florida differs, too, from the Cuban migration of the 1980s, which, while including many Afro-Cubans, was nevertheless a controversial exodus because prison inmates and patients of mental institutions were among those who were able to leave the island.

When the Grillo family arrived in Florida, they saw a system of white supremacy that cut across class boundaries and nationalities. Legal statutes in the South aimed at keeping races separate in all public spaces: schools, parks, accommodations, buses, and trains. While blacks experienced discrimination in Cuba, the distance from their white compatriots was even greater in Florida. In Tampa, Grillo (who was more mullatto than black) found that speaking Spanish and being Cuban did not matter to people who looked at him; they regarded him in the same prejudicial light as they did African Americans.

Grillo's memoir incorporates these realities into a narrative that combines the structure of a bildungsroman (a coming-of-age story expressed through one's intellectual and psychological growth) with chapters that remind readers of a wartime diary. The sections entitled "Ybor City" and "Going Up North" recount Grillo's childhood experiences and his education in institutions exclusively devoted to the instruction of blacks. Having experienced the "separate but equal" classroom, Grillo found that his assimilation into the African-American community provided him a strong sense of identity, though not the one he was born with. Grillo decided to acculturate (to integrate into a different culture), not by "whitening" and thereby capitulating to the group that had excluded him, but rather by allying himself with African Americans.

The last section of the narrative, "At War," covers his four years of service in an all-black unit in the China-Burma-India theater of operations during World War II. If education gave him the possibility to transcend his humble origins, his wartime experience convinced him of his capacity to organize people to defend their civil rights. One key episode summarizes his rejection of the indignities of racial oppression. Black soldiers traveling by sea to India to support the war effort were subject to abuses that recall the infamous passage from Africa suffered by slaves (such as segregated quarters and inadequate access to food and water). Grillo organized black soldiers to present a formal complaint to their superiors in order to change the conditions under which they were living.

Grillo's memoir suggests a fluid identity bridging cultural and ethnic gaps between Afro-Cubans, Afro-Americans, and other minorities. This ultimately prepared him to work effectively in different social services. After the war he studied Latin American history at Columbia University. He later earned a master's degree in social welfare at the University of California at Berkeley. In the 1980s he was director of the Alexander Community Center in Oakland, California. During the administration of Jimmy Carter, Grillo worked in the Department of Health, Education, and Welfare. *Black Cuban, Black American* sketches salient moments in the life of a committed man who redefined his identity to seek racial equality. The memoir also constitutes a recollection of small battles to achieve the civil rights of African Americans and black Latinos. The memoir can be read within the context of CUBAN-AMERICAN LITERATURE.

Bibliography

Grenbaum, Susan D. *More Than Black: Afro-Cubans in Tampa*. Gainesville: University Press of Florida, 2002.

Grillo, Evelio. *Black Cuban, Black American: A Memoir*. Houston, Tex.: Arte Público Press, 2000.

———. *Report for the Oakland Interagency Task Force on Illicit Drug Traffic*. Oakland, Calif.: The Associates, 1984.

———. *Report to the City of Oakland, Covering the Period September 1, 1984 to December 31, 1984*. Oakland, Calif.: The Council, Oakland Interagency Council on Drugs, 1984.

Grillo, Evelio, and Harriet Nathan, eds. *Experiment and Change in Berkeley: Essays on City Politics*. Berkeley: Institute of Governmental Studies, University of California, 1978.

Luis Duno Gottberg

Bless Me, Última   Rudolfo Anaya   (1972)

Set in rural New Mexico, RUDOLFO ANAYA's first novel depicts a family of Mexican-American farmers whose quiet life is altered by the arrival of Última, a CURANDERA (healer). The family's three eldest sons are on the battlefront during World War II, while the youngest, Antonio Márez Luna, is entering adolescence and confronting for the first time the problems of living in a world of contradictions and opposing forces. How to reconcile these forces, such as the two elements of his family name, becomes a focal point of the narrative. As a Márez, he is expected to grow brave and wild as the sea; as a Luna, he is expected to become a priest, a calm and reflective man like his uncles from El Puerto. The story is narrated in the first person and from the perspective of an adult Antonio, a writer remembering his childhood.

Education and faith constitute important themes in the narrative. Upon entering school Antonio discovers a new reality, that of English supplanting his mother tongue, Spanish. In order to avoid alienation at school his sisters speak English—even at home, despite the fact that their parents do not understand the language. Catholicism provides a moral compass in Antonio's life. On Easter Sunday, Antonio is about to receive his First Communion but experiences an uneasiness. His friends mock the sacrament and, as a joke, they have him play the role of the priest taking their confessions, forcing him to distribute hard penances. As a consequence of this parody, Antonio's faith stumbles, and later on, upon taking the Holy Host, his expectations turn into disappointment as his questions about Catholicism remain unanswered.

Última becomes the child's refuge, providing the harmony lost in his encounter with the church. Through her teachings Antonio learns to look for balance in nature and appreciate the marvels hidden to inexperienced eyes that look without seeing. He learns to show respect for his elders and to love all creatures, as well as to keep Última's most intimate secrets; in fact, he helps the *curandera* heal his uncle Lucas and accompanies her in most of her tasks.

The realm of the supernatural is paramount in the narrative, especially for the rest of the inhabitants of the village of Guadalupe. Unlike Antonio, they fear the *curandera,* but they do not hesitate to call her when they need her to fight evil in their lives. The *curandera* heals inexplicable illnesses, breaks spells, confronts spirits locked in haunted houses, and works tirelessly to bring peace to her loved ones. As a witness to Última's actions, Antonio takes the reader into a world of mystery. Anaya creates a magical atmosphere that envelops Antonio and Última and at the same time separates them from the rest of the characters. The connection established between them grows so strong that both Última and her companion, the owl, appear repeatedly in Antonio's dreams. These dreams frequently serve as premonitions, but they also provide information about past events, such as Antonio's birth. Legendary figures such as La LLORONA also appear in the narrative and reflect Anaya's aim of preserving his people's culture and traditions through his writing.

Última's character occupies a position between a saint and a witch—this constitutes one of Anaya's main strategies in developing a mystical climate throughout the narrative. Última's final blessing upon Antonio and her death do not resolve doubts among the villagers and the reader; however, Antonio announces that her spirit will protect him for the rest of his life.

The novel was awarded the Premio Quinto Sol in 1972 and can be read within the context of BORDER LITERATURE and CHICANO LITERATURE.

Bibliography

Anaya, Rudolfo. *Bless Me, Última.* Berkeley, Calif.: Quinto Sol Publications, 1972.

Day, Frances Ann. *Latina and Latino Voices in Literature: Lives and Works.* Westport, Conn./London: Greenwood Press, 2003.

Fernández Olmos, Margarite. *Rudolfo A. Anaya: A Critical Companion.* Westport, Conn./London: Greenwood Press, 1999.

Imelda Martín-Junquera

Bodega Dreams Ernesto Quiñonez (2000)

Ernesto Quiñonez was born in Ecuador to a Puerto Rican mother and an Ecuadorean father in 1965. The youngest of five children, he grew up in East Harlem, in New York City. He earned a B.A. in English and Latino studies in 1995 from the City College of New York and has taught bilingual fourth grade in the south Bronx. He currently lives in Harlem and writes about life there.

Quiñonez's first novel, *Bodega Dreams,* was published in 2000 to critical acclaim. It was included among the Notable Books of the Year by the *Los Angeles Times* and *New York Times* and selected as a Barnes and Noble Discover Great New Writers title and a Borders Bookstore Original New Voice. The New York Library listed *Bodega Dreams* as one of its 25 Books to Remember. A Spanish translation by Edmundo Paz Soldan, *El vendedor de sueños,* was published in 2001. *Bodega Dreams* is narrated by Julio "Chino" Mercado, a married supermarket shelver and night school student. Through Mercado we learn the story of Willie "Bodega" Irizarry, a community-minded drug dealer of Spanish Harlem. Bodega, a former member of the Puerto Rican activist group the Young Lords, uses business profits to finance his vision of community renewal. He buys and renovates housing projects and offers college scholarships to individuals in the neighborhood who show promise and focus. He is also determined to win back his childhood sweetheart, Veronica Saldivia, who has married a wealthy Miami Cuban, anglicized her name to Vera, and shed her Puerto Rican identity for a mainstream upper-middle-class lifestyle. With a style that draws on both detective fiction and the protest novel, *Bodega Dreams* portrays Bodega's heroic rise and eventual fall after the betrayal by his ambitious partner and lawyer, Edwin Nazario.

Bodega Dreams represents the social, spatial, and linguistic texture of Spanish Harlem. Cultural references include Chino's business of spray painting R.I.P. memorials for fallen neighbors (drawn from Quiñonez's own teenage practice); local landmarks, such as the now closed J.H.S. 99 JULIA DE BURGOS school; and frequent use of SPANGLISH dialogue. Studded with references to local literary and activist traditions, *Bodega Dreams* situates itself in a tradition of Nuyorican (Puerto Ricans living in New York) culture. Quiñonez uses PIRI THOMAS's seminal autobiography, DOWN THESE MEAN STREETS, as a springboard from which to relate Chino's personal past (86). In his epigraphs Quiñonez quotes poetry by Pedro Pietri and MIGUEL PIÑERO, star performers at the NUYORICAN POETS CAFE. The closing scene includes cameo appearances from the "East Harlem Aristocracy," including MIGUEL ALGARÍN, MARTIN ESPADA, Lucky Cienfuegos, Edward Rivera, and Jack Agüeros (208).

Within the context of American literature *Bodega Dreams* self-consciously echoes F. Scott Fitzgerald's *The Great Gastby.* In both works a bootstrapping hero, enriched by illegal activity, is brought down by a futile love. (Chapter 4 of *Bodega Dreams,* for example, is entitled "A Diamond as Big as the Palladium," after Fitzgerald's short story "A Diamond as Big as the Ritz.") Critic June Dwyer notes the formal similarity of the two works: Both feature a semidetached narrator telling the story of the protagonist's worldly rise and dramatic fall. But whereas Gatsby's class aspirations lead him to an indulgent lifestyle, Bodega is a socially conscious (though criminal) entrepreneur, who hopes to leverage his drug fortune into affordable housing and scholarships for neighborhood youths. Gatsby sought to launder both his money and his humble background to leave his past behind, while Bodega plans to reinvest in his community and underwrite a promising future for Spanish Harlem and its residents. The novel concludes with a dream visitation from Bodega, who exhorts Chino to recognize the artistic potential of barrio life. Bodega explains that "Spanglish is the future. It's a new language being born out of the ashes of two cultures clashing with each other." Chino looks out from the fire escape onto the neighborhood below and thinks about the future of Spanish Harlem (212–213).

Quiñonez's second novel, *Chango's Fire,* simultaneously released in Spanish as *El fuego de Chango,* was published in 2004. Both works contribute to the rich tradition of PUERTO RICAN LITERATURE both on the island and in New York.

Bibliography

Casey, Maud. "Bad Influencia." *New York Times Book Review* (March 12, 2000), 11.

Dwyer, June. "When Willie Met Gatsby: The Critical Implications of Ernesto Quiñonez's *Bodega Dreams.*" *LIT: Literary Interpretation Theory* 14 (2003): 165–178.

Finn, Robin. "Spanish Harlem's Emerging Literary Voice." *New York Times,* March 15, 2000, p. B2.

Kevane, Bridget A. *Latino Literature in America.* Westport, Conn.: Greenwood Press, 2003.

Quiñonez, Ernesto. *Bodega Dreams.* New York: Vintage Press, 2000.

———. *Chango's Fire.* New York: HarperCollins, 2004.

Alex Feerst

Borderlands/La frontera: The New Mestiza
Gloria Anzaldúa (1987)

GLORIA ANZALDÚA was an important contributor to CHICANO LITERATURE and cultural studies of the border. Anzaldúa is perhaps best known for her work *Borderlands/La frontera: The New Mestiza,* which was selected by *Library Journal* as one of the 38 best books of 1987. The autobiographical work combines genres and is written using a combination of English, Spanish, SPANGLISH, and Nahuatl (the native language of the Aztec). She uses this combination to create a new language of the borderlands and to celebrate her rich ethnic heritage. The first section of the text features essays that confront a multitude of cultural concerns, and the second half of the collection contains poetry written by Anzaldúa.

Anzaldúa grew up in Texas and lived in bicultural, English- and Spanish-speaking communities; her work, therefore, contributes to BORDER LITERATURE. According to Anzaldúa, the borderland is not just the physical border that separates the United States and Mexico but also the "psychological," "sexual," and "spiritual" borders that divide the countries. She describes the border as a "place of contradictions," with those on each side of the border challenging the beliefs of the other. She writes to express a sense of self in a place that is full of discord and exploitation. By using the image of the borderlands, which has become a prominent one in many disciplines, Anzaldúa argues that it is necessary to form a new consciousness and heal the division experienced by conflicting cultures. She proposes a new mestiza reality in which one acquires a tolerance for ambiguity, a defining element of the borderland. As a mestiza, a woman of Indian and Spanish heritage, Anzaldúa declares that she has no race, homeland, or culture and is therefore a sister to all. In addition Anzaldúa proposes that Mexican Americans pursue a relationship with white, English-speaking society in order to both confront and accept cultural differences.

Anzaldúa also discusses her own Mexican-American border culture and her rebellion against a largely Catholic, patriarchal social order. She admits to feeling little approval within her Mexican culture, which she explains has very explicit rules regarding prescribed gender roles. She criticizes her male-dominated community for pushing women to be subservient and for offering them limited choices: to become a nun, a prostitute, or a wife and mother. Anzaldúa says that it is as a result of these attitudes that she chose to live her life as a lesbian, "the ultimate rebellion . . . against her native culture," a political as well as lifestyle choice. Anzaldúa, who was considered to be a radical feminist, was one of the first contributors to LATINA LESBIAN LITERATURE.

In part 1, "Crossing Borders," Anzaldúa discusses the history of Mexico. She explains that the original settlers of the southwest were Spanish, Indian, and mestizo ancestors and that Chicanos are the descendants of those people. As a result of the U.S.-Mexican War in the 1840s, the United States took possession of a great deal of land that was once Mexican with the TREATY OF GUADALUPE HIDALGO.

In more recent years the influx of U.S. factories along the border and the terrible living conditions in Mexico have compelled many Mexicans to enter the United States—legally and illegally—in order to survive. Many, like Anzaldúa's own family, have been forced to work as migrant workers under poor conditions for low wages. Her concern for Mexicans disenfranchised by economic and political conditions is apparent throughout the work, and within a larger context this concern is common in border literature.

In the poems included in part 2 of the collection, many of which are in Spanish, Anzaldúa continues to examine the same themes that she discusses in her essays, such as the role of women and the conflict between Mexican Americans and white, English-speaking authorities.

"We Call Them Greasers" exposes the discrimination and indignities that Mexicans experienced at the hands of Anglo authorities. In this poem Anzaldúa describes from the perspective of a white man his unscrupulous treatment of Mexican landowners and his rape and murder of a Mexican woman while her husband is forced to watch. In "El sonavabitch" she conveys images of illegal Mexican workers in a migrant camp who work from dusk to dawn, only to be turned over to immigrant officials by the boss so that he does not have to pay them. The collection also includes one of Anzaldúa's most important poems, "To live in the Borderlands means you." In it she explains that

we need to accept cultural differences rather than allow them to divide us, an important argument in Chicano literature.

Bibliography

Aigner-Varoz, Erika. "Metaphors of a Mestiza Consciousness: Anzaldúa's *Borderlands/La Frontera*." *MELUS* 25 (2000): 47–62.

Anzaldúa, Gloria. *Borderlands/La frontera: The New Mestiza*. San Francisco, Calif.: Aunt Lute Books, 1987.

Fowlkes, Diane L. "Moving from Feminist Identity Politics to Coalition Politics Through a Feminist Materialist Standpoint of Intersubjectivity in Gloria Anzaldúa's *Borderlands/La Frontera: The New Mestiza*." *Hypatia* 12 (1997): 105–124.

Reuman, Ann E. "Coming into Play: An Interview with Gloria Anzaldúa." *MELUS* 25 (2000): 3–45.

Diane Todd Bucci

border literature

The U.S.-Mexican border traverses several geographies—Southern California and the Southwest. Each border city is a region of its own, evidenced by its unique geography, history, languages, political and cultural sensibilities, cuisine, music, art, and, especially, literature. The body of literature inspired by the border is so unique and so large that one can now refer to a border canon.

Border literature defies simple definitions. Its origins existed before the modern-day border was established in 1848 with the the TREATY OF GUADALUPE HIDALGO. This treaty is one of the most important events in both U.S. and Mexican history because with it, the United States grew significantly while Mexico lost a great deal of territory north of the Río Bravo (Rio Grande). One finds a rich literary tradition—*corridos* (ballads), memoirs, histories, autobiographies, and dramas—in the region long before 1848. There is no official definition of border literature, and few writers label themselves exclusively as "border writers," but broadly speaking, border literature refers to works written between 1848 and the present that are unified by their attention to and influence of the border. Several genres—stories, poems, plays, memoirs, and novels—contribute to border literature, all unified by myriad aspects of a complex border experience that have inspired their authors. A work of border literature need not be situated on or near the border; for instance, a novel about migrant workers living and working in Minnesota or in the San Joaquin Valley of California would be considered a work of border literature because of its themes. These themes include but are not limited to the significance of northern Mexican music and folklore; political, cultural, religious, racial, and social conflict; the conflict between democracy and capitalism; cultural dislocation and assimilation; economic and social injustice; the centrality of family; sense of place; and the loss and search for identity.

Another unique aspect of Latino border writers is that they do not conceive of the border strictly as a geographic, political, and cultural dividing line between two nations. Notwithstanding their literary achievements, many Anglo-American border writers often stress these divisions and often rely on stereotypes associated with Mexicans and Mexican Americans (as with Helen Hunt Jackson's *Ramona*). Perhaps because so many were born and raised in the border region, Hispanic border writers—who certainly recognize the cultural divisions of the border—see the frontier less as a dividing line and more as a channel through which exists a rich exchange of traditions, literary forms, and themes. This vision results in a richer, more enlightened understanding of the sensibilities, ethos, and character of the border.

One of the most significant contributors to border literature is the novelist, musician, poet, folklorist, and scholar AMÉRICO PAREDES. He is arguably the first to recognize and write about the concept of a border literature. His first book, *WITH HIS PISTOL IN HIS HAND* (1958), is unique in American literature, consisting of commentary on the *corrido* of Gregorio Cortez and social and political commentary on border politics and poetics. Paredes also wrote three works of fiction largely situated on the border: two novels, *George Washington Gomez: A Mexico-Texan Novel* (1990) and

The Shadow (1998), and a collection of short stories, *The Hammon and the Beans and Other Stories* (1994). Along with a host of scholarly essays and presentations, Paredes edited three books central to a thorough understanding of border literature: *Folktales of Mexico* (1970), *A Texas-Mexican Cancionero: Folksongs of the Lower Border* (1976), and *Folklore and Culture on the Texas-Mexican Border* (1993).

Early on Paredes recognized the significance of the *corrido,* a narrative folk song unique to the border region. Typically it consists of four-line stanzas, each line of eight syllables. The *corrido* originated in Mexico during the 19th century but experienced considerable development along the border between 1848 and 1910. *Corridos* are still written and sung today. A *corrido* can be about anything but usually the subjects are of local and regional interest and praise a hero or underdog, such as the famous Gregorio Cortez. The *corrido* can tell the story of a bandit, describe a natural disaster, lament lost love or an unfaithful lover, satirize corrupt officials, or make a legend of faithful and fast horses.

In terms of lyrical poetry, a tradition inspired by the border begins to emerge in the 1960s. Alberto Baltazar Urista, better known as ALURISTA, is considered by some to be the foremost Chicano poet of the 20th century. His subject matter is wide ranging, but in poems such as "When raza?" and "i can't" one sees images and themes connected to the border. Other poets share Alurista's interest in the frontier. In *Al cielo se sube a pie* (1961; One gets to heaven on foot), SABINE ULIBARRÍ addresses themes of solitude and disjointedness in being uprooted from northern Mexico. In her first collection, *Bajo cubierta* (1976; Undercover), Miriam Bornstein-Sonoza addresses the political and social plight of women on the border as they seek to forge their own identities. Ricardo Aguilar Melantzón explores settings and themes in both real and imagined border cities. In two of his collections, *Caravana enlutada* (1975; Mourning caravan) and *En son de lluvia* (1980, In praise of the rain), the poems reflect on the history and culture of the speaker in the movement back and forth across the border. RICARDO SÁNCHEZ is one of the border's most prolific, vibrant, and unique voices. As a young man, Sánchez spent time in prison but eventually became a university professor and devoted much time to teaching prisoners and helping them publish their poetry. Among other works, *Obras* (1971; Works) and *Canto y grito mi liberación* (1971; I sing and shout my liberation) illustrate his powerful, energetic voice and border sensibilities. Finally, two poets have given sustained attention to the migrant experience in the San Joaquin Valley. GARY SOTO, an extraordinarily versatile and prolific writer, portrays migrant workers in Fresno in the 1950s in *The Elements of San Joaquin* (1977) and *Where the Sparrows Work Hard* (1981). And in Diana García's *When Living Was a Labor Camp* (2000), one hears strident voices that in many ways undermine comforting bucolic myths about agricultural America.

Border fiction in the latter half of the 20th century and early 21st century has seen the greatest expansion in terms of numbers of writers and published works. So many new writers have emerged in the last 20 years that one can think of a "classic" generation and a new generation of border fiction. The classic generation of writers gives significant attention to the migrant worker, in part because many border writers grew up in migrant families. This tradition addresses all aspects of migrant life: thirst, heat, illness, low wages, poor education, injustice, violence, and cultural dislocation, as well as endurance, hope, and the sacredness of family. Many still consider John Steinbeck's landmark 1939 novel, *The Grapes of Wrath*, as the authoritative literary work on migrant workers, but to acquire a complete understanding of the American migrant experience, one should be familiar with border literature that recounts the Mexican and Mexican-American migrant experience. TOMÁS RIVERA's *. . . Y no se lo tragó la tierra* (1987; *. . . And the Earth Did Not Devour Him*, also published as *THIS MIGRANT EARTH*), VICTOR EDMUNDO VILLASEÑOR's *Macho* (1973), and Genero Gonzalez's *Rainbow's End* (1988) represent the classic generation of migrant fiction. More recently, HELENA MARÍA VIRAMONTES's novel *UNDER THE FEET OF JESUS* (1995) and Elva Treviño Hart's memoir *Barefoot Heart: Stories of a Migrant Child* (1999) have made significant contributions to this genre.

Four classic fiction writers who have devoted much if not most of their art to the border are Miguel Méndez, ROLANDO HINOJOSA SMITH, JOSÉ ANTONIO VILLARREAL, and JOHN RECHY. Méndez, who writes mostly in Spanish, is one of the most unique and underrated writers in American literature. As seen in his 1974 novel *Peregrinos de Aztlán (Pilgrims in Aztlán)* and his 1979 short story collection, *Cuentos para niños traviesos* (Stories for mischievous children), Méndez is an ambitious writer. He provides a window into the oral traditions of the border, revisits Indian and Mexican folklore, forges a means of resurrecting lost identities for his characters, and delivers an elegant indictment of how colonization has compromised the lives of the Yaqui and Mexican. Méndez's themes extend beyond the border to universal themes of human suffering, as seen in his 1975 collection of poetry, *Los criaderos humanos épica de los desamparados y sahuaros* (The human hatcheries [epic of the forsaken] and saguaros). Meanwhile, one might think of Hinojosa Smith as the William Faulkner of border fiction because he creates a veritable universe in the fictional Belken County—in the valley of South Texas—the setting for his acclaimed *KLAIL CITY* (1987) and the Klail City Death Trip series of novels. Similar to Faulkner's novels set in Yoknapatawpha County, the themes of Hinojosa Smith's novels are both regional and universal in scope.

As many scholars have noted, another prominent concern of border literature is identity when characters or narrators face tensions and contradictions caused by class, race, religion, gender, and nationality. Villarreal's *POCHO* (1959) is an exemplary novel in this respect. The word *pocho* is rich in denotation and connotation: It can mean "faded" or "without color," "disillusioned," and someone who is ashamed of his identity. The son of a Mexican mother and Scottish father, Rechy explores similar problems of identity—including gay identity—in three novels: *City of Night* (1963), *Numbers* (1962), and *The Day's Death* (1969).

Perhaps the most striking difference between the classic and new generation of writers is the number of border works written by women. Alongside recent works by ARTURO ISLAS's *The RAIN GOD* (1991), Oscar Casares's *Brownsville Stories* (2003), and Richard Yañez's *El Paso del Norte: Stories on the Border* (2003), one also encounters MONTSERRAT FONTES's *First Confessions* (1991), SANDRA CISNEROS's *WOMAN HOLLERING CREEK AND OTHER STORIES* (1991), ALICIA GASPAR DE ALBA's *DESERT BLOOD: THE JÚAREZ MURDERS,* (2005), DENISE CHÁVEZ's *FACE OF AN ANGEL* (1994), Kathleen Alcalá's *Spirits of the Ordinary: A Tale of Casas Grandes* (1998), Lucrecia Guerrero's *Chasing Shadows* (2000), Estela Portillo Trambley's *Trini* (2003), and Ann Jaramillo's *La Línea* (2006).

One of the most critical studies of the border, consisting of poetry and social commentary, is GLORIA ANZALDÚA's *BORDERLANDS/LA FRONTERA: THE NEW MESTIZA.* Analyses of the U.S.-Mexican border by Mexican authors include Carlos Fuentes's *La frontera de cristal* (1997; *The Crystal Frontier*) and *El gringo viejo* (1985; *The Old Gringo*). Octavio Paz has also written about Mexican identity in *El laberinto de soledad* (1950; *The Labyrinth of Solitude*), the most famous essay of which is probably "MEXICAN MASKS." Interest in border literature continues to expand dramatically in high school, college, and graduate school curricula. More scholars are also devoting attention to border literature. These are all significant developments that shed light on the Mexican and American experience.

Bibliography

Calderón, Héctor. *Narratives of Greater Mexico: Essays on Chicano Literary History, Genres, and Borders.* Austin: University of Texas Press, 2004.

Castillo, Debra A. and Maria-Socorro Tabuenca Cordoba. *Border Women: Writing from la Frontera.* Minneapolis, Minn.: University of Minneapolis Press, 2002.

Paredes, Américo. *Folklore and Culture on the Texas-Mexican Border.* Austin, Tex.: Center for Mexican American Studies, 1993.

———. *A Texas-Mexican Cancionero: Folksongs of the Lower Border.* Urbana: University of Illinois Press, 1976.

Torrans, Thomas. *Magic Curtain: The Mexican American Border in Fiction, Film, and Song.* Fort Worth: Texas Christian University Press, 2002.

Kevin L. Cole

Brief Wondrous Life of Oscar Wao, The
Junot Díaz (2007)

The Brief Wondrous Life of Oscar Wao reflects a turbulent period in the history of the Dominican Republic. Díaz makes more human and immediate to readers the historical drama that unfolds in the novel and, while doing so, examines a family drama of recent times. Díaz explores the pain, sympathy, and outrage of his characters as well as their discoveries and revelations.

In *The Brief Wondrous Life of Oscar Wao,* the effect of the Dominican Republic's Trujillo dictatorship is felt in disturbing and direct ways that affect the lives of three generations of Dominicans and Dominican Americans. Although Trujillo himself is present in only three scenes in the novel, it is fair to say that the infamous general and dicator is a major presence—as he is in novels such as JULIA ALVAREZ's *IN THE TIME OF THE BUTTERFLIES.* Raphael Trujillo ruled the Dominican Republic from 1930 until his assassination in 1961. The opening pages of the novel describe a kind of family curse and present Trujillo as "a hypeman of sorts, a high priest," of the curse, or *fukú.* Diaz proceeds, in one of the novel's characteristic devices, to offer a long footnote on Trujillo's reign, within which is a fascinating physical description:

> A portly, sadistic, pig-eyed mulatto who bleached his skin, wore platform shoes, and had a fondness for Napolean-era haberdashery, Trujillo (also known as El Jefe, the Failed Cattle Thief, and Fuckface) came to control every aspect of the DR's political, cultural, social and economic life through a potent (and familiar) mixture of violence, intimidation, massacre, rape, co-optation, and terror; treated

the country like it was a plantation and he was the master. (2–3)

Although the protagonist, Oscar de León (nicknamed Wao) is born a dozen years after the assassination of Trujillo, the impact of Trujillo's rule is acute in the psychological makeup of Oscar's mother, and the wave of terror becomes a kind of curse on the family.

Díaz introduces the 300-pound Oscar Wao as "GhettoNerd at the End of the World," through the voice of Yunior, who is the main figure of Díaz's *DROWN*. Oscar is an unlikely protagonist compared to the hard-hitting, dope smoking, sexually frustrated characters of *Drown*. We learn that Oscar: "wasn't no home-run hitter or a fly *bachetero*, not a playboy with a million hots on his jock" (11). Instead, Oscar is an obese escapist, preoccupied with science fiction and fantasy, with role playing fantasy games with *Star Trek,* Japanese anime, and comic books. We follow Oscar through childhood and high school, into Rutgers University, to a short-lived career as a teacher at his alma mater, Don Bosco High School, and back to his *abuela's* (grandmother's) home in the Dominican Republic. Throughout, there is a pall of unhappiness over Oscar, as he is devoted first to girls and later to women, feeling a desire that is not reciprocated. His defeats grow into self-defeat and lethargy, and his unproductive response to his plight is to indulge in food.

Díaz offers an intersting portrait of several members of the de León family. Oscar Cabral is the beginning and end point of the family saga, which stretches back to Abelard Cabral, his maternal grandfather. Abelard, a surgeon and owner of shops and factories, lives a prosperous life in the Dominican Republic, until he runs afoul of Trujillo's tyranny. Abelard Cabral's daughter becomes an object of desire for Trujillo's rapacious appetite, and the family resists. We also learn of the story of Oscar's mother, Beli, orphaned by the terrible consequences of her father's resistance to Trujillo. Perhaps one of the most compelling narratives is that of Oscar's young sister Lola and her youthful rebellion against her mother's iron control. Lola runs away from home to the arms of a no-account boyfriend on the New Jersey shore. This rebellion takes place at the same time her mother's body is wracked with the initial but virulent stages of breast cancer, making the strength of Lola's resolve more dramatic, the consequences more tragic.

And there is the presence of Yunior, who functions as the antithesis to Oscar. Also Dominican American, Yunior is a runner and a weightlifter, while Oscar is mired in obesity and sloth. Against Oscar's virgin yearnings, Yunior has outgrown his awkward boyhood (depicted in *Drown*) and acts the part of suave playboy, a serial cheater even when he is happily paired with Oscar's beautiful, smart, lively sister. But there is in Yunior a reader and an inner nerd that connects with Oscar, who speaks the language of Tolkein's Middle Earth and *The Matrix* and shares with Oscar the desire to express his life in writing.

Ten years in the making, *The Brief Wondrous Life of Oscar Wao* has been hailed by critics as a fitting follow-up to the widely acclaimed *Drown* and won the Pulitzer Prize in fiction in 2008. *New York Times* reviewer Michiko Kakutani concluded her glowing evaluation of Díaz's prose by stating that this is "a book that decisively establishes him as one of contemporary fiction's most distinctive and irresistible new voices." Still, there may be elements of the new novel that may disappoint fans of *Drown* and won the Pulitzer Prize in fiction in 2008. The framing device of *fukú,* for instance, sometimes seems forced. Other elements are incongruous—as with the melding of the street voice and that of the Tolkien fan, or some of the asides that demonstrate the author's expectation of an academic readership (a vicious beating is described as being like "one of those nightmare eight-a.m. MLA [Modern Language Association] panels: endless" [299]).

Yet what remains for the reader will most likely be the authentic portrayals of desperate human experience, such as Oscar's devotion to "love," even when it presents itself inadequately and inappropriately (in the form of part-time prostitutes and gorgeous co-eds with no intention of romance with the love-addled fat boy); the dignity of Abelard Cabral, broken in Trujillo's prisons; and the fierce autonomy of Oscar's mother, Beli. For its flaws, this novel is a tour de force that shows the very human face in the grand scheme of history.

Bibliography
Díaz, Junot. *The Brief Wondrous Life of Oscar Wao.*
   New York: Riverhead Books, 2007.
———. *Drown.* Riverhead Books, 1996.
                               Brian F. Doherty

Brown: The Last Discovery of America
Richard Rodriguez (2002)

In *Brown: The Last Discovery of America* award-winning essayist and journalist RICHARD RODRIGUEZ celebrates the "browning" of America. The "Last Discovery of America" is a reference to Christoper Columbus's entry into the Caribbean in 1492; in this regard Rodriguez contributes his memoir to the diverse canon of Spanish-American, Mexican, and Mexican-American literature. *Browning* is a term Rodriguez uses to suggest a significant phenomenon in the American melting pot: the growth of the Latino population. Yet, rather than assimilate new immigrants into an American "whiteness," the "browning" of America melts away whiteness and reveals hitherto inconceivable cultural constructions of identity, such as "Blaxican" and "Baptist Buddhist."

Brown is the final installment of a trilogy in which Rodriguez explains the intersection between "American public life and my private life." The first in the trilogy, the memoir *Hunger of Memory: The Education of Richard Rodriguez* (1981), was quickly adopted as a required text for courses on Chicano and Latino studies. Since its publication, *Hunger of Memory* has proved highly controversial, especially within the Mexican-American community, because of Rodriguez's denunciation of bilingual education and affirmative action. The second book of the trilogy, DAYS OF OBLIGATION: AN ARGUMENT WITH MY MEXICAN FATHER (1992), earned Rodriguez praise for his literary skill and treatment of family relations and identity formation.

Brown celebrates MESTIZAJE (the mixed race) by investing in the word *brown* a new linguistic significance. He presents *brown* as one of America's primary ethnographic colors, along with white, black, yellow, and red (in other words, Hispanic, white, black, Asian/Pacific Islander, and Native American/Eskimo). But his redefining of the word as "impurity" allows it to signify the mix of contradictions that constitute Americans. When Rodriguez describes his own brownness, he refers not only to the color of his skin but also to the accidental mixture of economic and erotic forces that constitute his life in San Francisco. He explains in *Brown* his own unique identity: as a gay mestizo. Here Rodriguez uses shorthand to explain complex relations and conditions. He is a "meztizo" because of his Indian and Spanish ancestry. Given the conservative Catholic culture in which he was raised, his homosexuality may challenge suppositions about his manliness. But Rodriguez is not a minority in California; instead, he appears as one of many "brown" individuals in a coastal culture associated with beach tans, bleached blonds, and surfing.

Rodriguez conceived *Brown,* the final book in his trilogy, as a meditation on the question What do Hispanics mean to the life of America? In answering this question Rodriguez provides a peculiarly American notion of identity. This notion moves between a call for authenticity (owing much to a Puritan avoidance of playfulness) and a recognition of the libratory power of the theatrical (what Rodriguez describes as self-invention). Rodriguez suggests that Latinos can offer America a rich definition of race, and correspondingly, Americans can offer Latin America a more "playful" definition of culture. Latin America could share its myriad terms for identifying an individual's ethnic mixture, and the United States would no longer be saddled with racial essentialism that for half of the 20th century looked at the world as black and white.

Rodriguez's second impetus for writing *Brown* came when the mainstream media announced that Hispanics were surpassing African Americans as the United States's "largest minority." Disturbed by what he views as an attempt to compare Hispanics (who are defined by culture and not by blood) to African Americans (who present themselves as a race), Rodriguez argues that a new model is necessary to avoid the continual subgrouping of Americans. Rather than find an analogy with the civil rights struggles of the 1960s—an analogy that would only encourage competition among "minorities"—Rodriguez celebrates those individuals who transgress racial, ethnic, class, sexual, and religious borders.

Brown's first four chapters ("The Triad of Alexis de Tocqueville," "In the Brown Study," "The Prince and I," and "Poor Richard") provide a rereading of the American "Founding Sin." This sin is the European introduction of African slaves to the American continent and is the subject of the chapter "Indian Eye." The following two chapters ("Hispanic" and "The Third Man") explore the consequences of O.M.B. Statistical Directive 15. O.M.B. Statistical Directive 15 came out of the administration of Richard Nixon in the early 1970s and resulted in the decision to add the term *Hispanic* to the census form. By creating the United States's only official identity category based on culture rather than on blood, the government not only created a people from groups previously separated by nationalities but also initiated the inevitable "browning" of any attempt at ethnic or racial categorization. *Brown's* final three chapters ("Dreams of a Temperate People," "Gone West," and "Peter's Avocado") demonstrate how this continual browning of America has realigned the national axis from east-west to north-south and requires a similar realignment of personal identities.

As with the first two books of the trilogy, critics have noted Rodriguez's literary skill in *Brown*. Many acknowledge the book's basic thesis about browning, but at the same time some audiences begrudge Rodriguez his use of literary allusions, historical facts, and pop-cultural references. Meanwhile, fellow writer LUIS ALBERTO URREA acknowledges that Rodriguez's subtlety of argument—his flirtatious and teasing approach to the subject of identity—risks misinterpretation by ideologues from every political persuasion.

As an autobiographical form of cultural criticism, *Brown* may be read alongside the work of GLORIA ANZALDÚA, who writes about borders, identity, and gender. Indeed, *Brown* encourages a rereading of Rodriguez's collective work as much as it urges a new coloring of U.S. ethnic relations.

Bibliography

Anzaldúa, Gloria. *Borderlands/La frontera: The New Mestiza.* San Francisco, Calif.: Aunt Lute Books, 1999.

De Castro, Juan E. "Richard Rodriguez in 'Borderland': The Ambiguity of Hybridity." *Aztlán* 26, no. 1 (Spring 2001): 101–126.

Foster, David William. "Other and Difference in Richard Rodriguez's *Hunger of Memory.*" In *Postcolonial and Queer Theories: Intersections and Essays,* edited by John C. Hawley, 139–153. Westport, Conn.: Greenwood, 2001.

Rodriguez, Richard. *Brown: The Last Discovery of America.* New York: Penguin Books, 2002.

———. *Days of Obligation: An Argument with My Mexican Father.* New York: Penguin Books, 1992.

———. *Hunger of Memory: The Education of Richard Rodriguez.* New York: Bantam, 1981.

Urrea, Luis Alberto. "The 'Brown' Bomber; Richard Rodriguez takes no prisoners in wide-ranging, probing look at America." *San Diego Union-Tribune,* April 7, 2002, Books section, p. 1.

Jeffrey Charis-Carlson

Burgos, Julia de (1914–1953) *(poet)*

One of Puerto Rico's most beloved and well-known poets, Julia de Burgos was born in the rural neighborhood of Santa Cruz, in Carolina. She was one of 13 children, six of whom died of malnourishment. Despite the family's poverty, Burgos was able to attend school where she excelled and developed an appetite for reading. She earned a degree at the University of Puerto Rico's Normal School in 1933 and worked briefly as a teacher and later as a journalist. She held a variety of odd jobs during her lifetime. In addition to financial difficulties, she endured watching her mother die of cancer and her father suffer from alcoholism.

Because of her lifelong struggles with poverty, depression, and physical illness owing to her own alcoholism, Burgos is portrayed by biographers as a courageous but tragic figure. Considered a woman ahead of her time, she often went against social norms in her native Puerto Rico. She married twice, divorced, and was a longtime lover of a Dominican physician and politician, Juan Jimenes Grullón. Grullón lived with her but never married her, and some biographers say her love was unrequited, at least in part, because she was not only from the lower class but also a mulatto (of West African and Spanish blood).

Burgos was an admirer and supporter of Pedro Albizu Campos, the leader of the nationalist movement, and she became an active member of the Nationalist Party despite a political climate that was hostile to Campos and his followers. She was an *independentista,* or one who argues that Puerto Rico should be an independent nation, not a U.S. state or commonwealth. Burgos was also known as a social activist who spoke for the rights of women, workers, politically oppressed peoples, and children.

Because of her unconventional life and open challenge to the patriarchal ways of thinking, she has become an important foremother for Puerto Rican feminists. Puerto Rican writer Jack Agüeros has translated her poems in *Song of the Simple Truth: Obra poética completa/The Complete Poems of Julia de Burgos* (1997). One of her best-known poems is "A Julia de Burgos" ("To Julia de Burgos") from the 1938 collection *Poema en veinte surcos* (Poem in twenty furrows), which illustrates her preoccupation with identity formation. The poem critiques the social construction of "woman" and emphasizes the contrast between the authentic "I" and the inauthentic "you"; this poem tries to reconcile the expectations for women in private and in the public. Rejecting the "prejudices of men," the poetic I chastises her public self; she protests the fact that "everyone commands you."

Another popular poem from the same collection, "El Río Grande de Loíza" (Loíza's great river) focuses on female sensuality, an uncommon theme for women at the early 20th century. It shows Burgos's love for Puerto Rico and its island landscape, using images such as the sea that have come to characterize the poet's work.

In addition to *Poema en veinte surcos,* Burgos wrote *Canción de la verdad sencilla* (1939; Song of the simple truth) and *El mar y tú, otros poemas* (The sea and you, other poems), published posthumously in 1954. These later works primarily deal with romantic love as pleasure and pain, death, and solitude. Literary critic Carmen Esteves acknowledges artistic self-reflexivity as another constant in Burgos's poetry, as she struggled not only to define what it meant to be a woman but also a poet.

Burgos's move to New York City anticipated the arrival of many Puerto Ricans from the 1950s to the present day. She lived in the city in 1940 and then from 1942 until her death in 1953, though she resided briefly in Havana, Cuba, and Washington, D.C. (with her second husband). Although letters written to her sister, Consuelo, reveal that she felt like an outsider in New York, she was unable to return to her beloved island. While her poetic production in New York was scant, Burgos wrote two poems in English, "Farewell in Welfare Island" and "The Sun in Welfare Island," both composed from Goldwater Memorial Hospital in 1953.

The ambiguous circumstances of her death have captured the public's curiosity, catapulting her to the status of cultural icon in Puerto Rico. Unable to find steady employment, Burgos's health and financial situation worsened in New York, and during the 1950s she spent the last few years of her life in and out of hospitals. Having been diagnosed with cirrhosis of the liver, she collapsed on the corner of Fifth Avenue and 104th Street. Since she carried no form of identification, after her death she received a pauper's burial in Potter's Field, where she remained for a month until her body was recovered and returned to Puerto Rico for a proper memorial in 1953.

Although she has been called many things— icon, myth, legend, precursor, foremother—Burgos desired only one label: As she wrote in "Poema para mi muerte" (Poem for my death) from *El mar y tú,* *"me llamarán poeta"* (they will call me poet). Her poetry was lyrical, rich in metaphor, and socially aware; as such, Burgos is an important contributor to PUERTO RICAN LITERATURE and SPANISH-AMERICAN CARIBBEAN LITERATURE more broadly.

Bibliography

Burgos, Julia de. *Song of the Simple Truth: The Complete Poems of Julia de Burgos.* Translated by Jack Agüeros. Willimantic, Conn.: Curbstone Press, 1997.

Esteves, Carmen. "Julia de Burgos: Woman, Poet, Legend." In *A Dream of Light and Shadow: Portraits of Latin American Women Writers,* edited by Marjorie Agosín, 221–236. Albuquerque: University of New Mexico Press, 1995.

Zavala-Martínez, Iris. "A Critical Inquiry into the Life and Work of Julia de Burgos." In *The Psychosocial Development of Puerto Rican Women,* edited by Cynthia T. García Coll and María de Lourdes Mattei, 1–30. New York: Praeger, 1989.

Betsy Sandlin

Cabeza de Vaca, Álvar Núñez (c. 1488– c. 1559) *(soldier explorer, historian)*

In 1542 Spanish-born Álvar Núñez Cabeza de Vaca wrote *La relación (The Account,)* also known as *Los naufragios* (The ship-wrecked men), a report of his travels from Florida to Mexico City. In 1555 he revised the text and included his expedition to South America in a work called *Comentarios* (Commentary). The narratives include the tale of the metamorphosis of a fame-seeking soldier, from bloody conquest in Europe to peaceful coexistence in the "paradise" of the Americas. In *La relación*, Cabeza de Vaca offers a historical record of the Spanish Conquest. Though part of a colonial mission, Cabeza de Vaca's work reveals a more humanitarian view of the indigenous of the Southwest than might be expected from Spanish conquistadores.

Many of the critical writings about Cabeza de Vaca have built upon earlier histories, often without verifying facts, thus much about the life and lineage of Cabeza de Vaca has been reported inaccurately throughout history. Genealogical records reveal that he was the eldest son of seven children of Francisco de Vera and Teresa Cabeza de Vaca. Recent research has uncovered details about Cabeza de Vaca that attempt to set the record straight. Many previous works mistakenly refer to Cabeza de Vaca's using *Núñez* as his last name, assuming that *Núñez* was his father's surname based on the

Spanish tradition of adding the mother's surname after the father's. It has been conjectured by some researchers, however, that *Núñez* may have been a middle name given in honor of a relative by the name of *Nuño*. Spanish archival records indicate that Cabeza de Vaca was married to María Marmolejo, but little is known of his wife and less about any children they may have produced.

The Spanish philosophies of domination and globalization of the late 15th and early 16th centuries influenced his expeditions. At the time Cabeza de Vaca participated in military campaigns in Europe, Hernan Cortés was conquering natives in Mexico and sending reports back to Spain of the extensive wealth to be had in the New World. *La relación* demonstrates the particular demands placed on the explorer by Spanish colonialism to publish reports depicting untold riches. The tendency of explorers to exaggerate, along with several discrepancies in facts in his texts, has led many to question the credibility of Cabeza de Vaca's travel reports and the validity of his findings. Some of the discrepancies could be considered the result of a flawed memory due to illness and a time lapse, since Cabeza de Vaca wrote his first text more than 10 years after the events occurred, and also a result of faulty interpretations by early ethnographers and translators.

Strong influences of both family and fellow countrymen such as Columbus, who predated

Cabeza de Vaca by about 35 years, affected the young man's career. As his family belonged to the middle class, an education was afforded him. Taking his mother's surname but following in the footsteps of his paternal grandfather, Pedro de Vera Mendoza, who conquered the Grand Canaries, Cabeza de Vaca entered into the service of the king of Spain as an explorer and conquistador. His early military experiences brought him success and prepared him for appointment as the second-highest ranking officer on the ill-fated expedition initially commanded by Pánfilo de Narváez.

Cabeza de Vaca's adventures led him on forays into the wilderness of both North and South America. On the first expedition he departed Spain in 1527; shipwrecked several times, he survived hurricanes, tropical storms, and clashes with native tribes, and he escaped death numerous times. He spent more than six years wandering hungry in the North American wilderness as a captive of the natives. He escaped from the natives in the land then called La Florida that became Florida, Alabama, Mississippi, Louisiana, Texas, New Mexico, Arizona, and California. He returned to Spain in 1537. Of the 600 men who left Spain in that expedition, only four survived, and Cabeza de Vaca was the only one to return to Spain. The explorer's 1540 expedition took him to the Río de la Plata in South America as *adelantado* (governor) of the area now called Paraguay. He returned home in chains, much the same as his predecessor Columbus. He stood trial for false accusations made by several corrupt countrymen as a result of Cabeza de Vaca's orders that forbade mistreatment of the natives. Though Cabeza de Vaca's titles, estates, and pensions were eventually reinstated after he was cleared of wrongdoing (several years after the accusations), he never really regained the status of a noble.

Cabeza de Vaca's writing, like that of BARTOLOMÉ DE LAS CASAS, influenced policies regarding indigenous populations. His texts cross many intellectual boundaries, as demonstrated by the historians, ethnographers, anthropologists, geographers, naturalists, philosophers, and travel writers who have studied them. Though Cabeza de Vaca lived his last years without contemporary acclaim, his voice echoes today through scholars who have studied his work, particularly his construction of the "other." A visionary, a man ahead of his times in his interaction with American natives, Cabeza de Vaca established a philosophy of social relations that many of his day did not share; he both shaped and was shaped by the New World he explored as he lived among the native peoples, who named him "Child of the Sun." He wrote narratives that subtly changed the course of history by setting the tone for the peaceful "taming" of the American Southwest.

Cabeza de Vaca's writing created a new kind of interaction in the Americas by demonstrating that peoples of different cultures could mutually learn and benefit from one another instead of fighting. Without his accounts men such as Francisco Vásquez de Coronado and Fray Marcos de Niza would have lacked a guide to the American wilderness. Without his accounts much of the stories of the indigenous peoples and the flora and fauna of the New World would have been lost. Though Cabeza de Vaca did not conquer vast lands filled with untold wealth, as did Cortés and Columbus, nor discover new overland routes and major rivers, as did the explorers who followed in his footsteps, his narratives created a historical context for BORDER LITERATURE.

Bibliography

Cabeza de Vaca, Álvar Núñez. *The Narrative of Cabeza de Vaca*. Translated by Rolena Adorno and Patrick Charles Pautz. Lincoln and London: University of Nebraska Press, 2003.

Cindy Noble Marsh

Caliban

Caliban is a character in William Shakespeare's *The Tempest* (1611); since publication of that play, Caliban has become an important literary and cultural figure in Latin American criticism. In Shakespeare's play Caliban is the wild and illegitimate son of a witch; he lives alone on a deserted island. Prospero, an Italian lord who shipwrecks on this same island, makes a home there with his lovely daughter, Miranda, along with crew members who have survived the wreck. Prospero wastes no time in summoning his magical powers and seizing authority on the island. Through the use of his knowledge and his governance of the men who have survived the wreck, he enslaves Caliban. Caliban is taught how to speak English and is introduced to the "civilized" ways of Europeans. The tense relationship between the enlightened master, Prospero, and his uncultured slave, Caliban, raises the debate of what is a "natural man" within the cultural context of the 17th century. In his play Shakespeare demonstrates a European awareness that the natives peoples of the Americas are not animals but rather individuals with a sense of will. BARTOLOMÉ DE LAS CASAS had made this very argument the basis of his life's work in his defense of the Indians of the Caribbean, Mexico, Nicaragua, and Peru. The Shakespearean construction of Caliban as a primitive islander, however, dominated European thought until the 20th century.

Although the location of the island seems to be in the Mediterranean, scholars have read *The Tempest* as part of the furious output of writing about the Americas during the Encounter. This reading has credence as Shakespeare used shipwreck narratives from the Caribbean to write his own Encounter drama. Caliban has since been regarded as a Shakespearean version of the American native. As such, he is considered the "natural man" (uncorrupted, close to nature, barbaric but pure) because Caliban exhibits both negative and positive qualities resulting from the European Encounter with the New World. He is stuck somewhere in between civilization and barbarism.

Caliban acts on impulse and desire to commit wicked deeds throughout the play. He enlists Stephano to murder Prospero, and he attempts to rape Miranda so that they can people the island with their children. He is unsuccessful, but he poses the threat of a colonized figure mixing with a European woman. Caliban personifies the villainous nature of a natural man, a tamed and uncultivated person whose exploits are controlled by primitive instincts, not by societal rules. This negative characterization is further supported by the fact that his very name is an anagram of *Canibal,* or *cannibal* (man-eater). This view of Caliban as flesh eater (though not a man-eater) is presented in Robert Browning's Victorian poem "Caliban upon Setebos." In this fascinating poem Caliban tries to re-create the natural order of the world by capturing various kinds of animals and maiming their limbs so that they are dependent on him; at the same time Browning's Caliban is fearful of the cosmos, of the world beyond his beach that he does not understand.

From yet another perspective Caliban could be considered a tamed version of the natural man. Through his teacher, Prospero, Caliban learns how to communicate and how to be take responsibility for his own moral character. In *The Tempest,* Caliban's farewell soliloquy could be interpreted as a final note of hope and possibility for humanity's restoration to grace, which is made possible because of contact with Europeans. One less optimistic representation of Caliban can be found in the work of Martinique author Aimé Césaire. In *A Tempest* (*Une tempête,* 1969, an adaptation of Shakespeare's play), Césaire makes more obvious the master-slave relationship between colonizer and colonized by framing the play within an Afro-Caribbean context.

By 1971 Cuban poet and Marxist literary critic ROBERTO FERNÁNDEZ RETAMAR took up the figure of Caliban as the centerpiece for his book *Caliban and Other Essays.* Retamar exposes the colonial and neocolonial thinking about the figure of Caliban. At the heart of his argument is the insistence that *The Tempest* be read from the native's perspective. Retamar interprets Caliban, not the nobleman Prospero, as the true protagonist of the play. With Caliban staged as the protagonist, Retamar argues that the issue is not how Caliban as a natural man may have been socialized but rather how a Latin American identity (specifically one from the Spanish Caribbean) is constructed. Retamar first transforms the disobedient savage and the island primitive into the unjustly oppressed native. Retamar also brings to light the master-slave dichotomy, which is an essential feature of Shakespeare's play.

Retamar begins his essay by first recognizing that Latin America is uniquely the result of hybridity, a process of grafting and crossovers of ideas, peoples, and identities between divergent cultures, languages, and communities. It is a site of hybridity because Latin America is racially mixed and depends, with few exceptions, on the language of the colonizers to communicate. Accordingly, Retamar pays tribute to the Cuban author and revolutionary JOSÉ MARTÍ and his famous essay, "Our America" (1891). Martí celebrates the MESTIZOS (people of Spanish-Indian descent) and mulattos (people of Spanish-African descent) of Latin America. Entering into this conversation about reckoning with one's heritage, Retamar uses the mestizo identity for his anticolonial critique (5). Retamar quotes act 1, scene 2, from *The Tempest*, in which the enslaved Caliban uses the very language taught by Prospero to curse his master: "You taught me language, and my profit on't / Is, I know how to curse. The red plague rid you / For learning me your language!"(362–364). And with this association and through the Spanish language of the colonizers, Retamar—a Cuban who dutifully returned to his homeland after the ousting of Fulgencio Batista in 1959 to be part of the revolutionary change—puts forward Caliban as the central figure for his discourse about hybridity.

Retamar shapes his analysis by tracing the etymology of *cannibal* back to the word *carib* as it appears in Christopher Columbus's log books. The Carib lived in the Caribbean, the sea named after the indigenous group. Columbus and his men witnessed the cannibalism that took place on the islands of the Carib. *Caliban,* as an etymological relative of *carib*, therefore becomes, for Retamar, a colonized figure of the Caribbean and Latin America. Retamar suggests that Caliban's role as a natural man (one unchecked by the conventions of society) could be read instead as a figure of resistance to the civilizing and imperial presence of Prospero (who stands for Europe).

Retamar's work operates in a longer literary debate between civilization and barbarism that Domingo Faustino Sarmiento had raised in the 19th century with his 1845 book, *Facundo*. Retamar takes on the arguments in Sarmiento's *Facundo* and offers a direct response to José Enrique Rodó's *Ariel* (1900). In *Ariel* Rodó suggests that Caliban is a symbol of materialism and barbarism, while the character of Ariel is the intellectual symbol of Latin America. Although Retamar's essay "Caliban" was written as homage to Rodó on the centenary of his birth, he nevertheless challenges Rodó by rereading and rewriting Caliban as an important figure for Latin America. Retamar does so because he seeks to go beyond just merely presenting a Latin American sense of hybridity; Retamar considers the mestizo to be the embodiment of resistance to a colonial order.

In this rereading of *The Tempest* and literary reply to Rodó, Retamar endows the Shakespearean islander with a Latin American identity. Retamar offers Latin American readers a postcolonial symbol of the struggle for autonomy and dignity.

Bibliography

Césaire, Aimé. *A Tempest. [Une tempête].* Translated by Richard Miller. St. Paul, MN: TCG Books, 2002.

Fernández Retamar, Roberto. *Caliban and Other Essays.* Translated by Edward Baker. Minneapolis: University of Minnesota Press, 1989.

Rodó, José Enrique. *Ariel.* Mexico City: Editorial Novara, 1900.

Sarmiento, Domingo. *Facundo: Or, Civilization and Barbarism.* Translated by Mary Peabody Mann, introduction by Ilan Stevans. New York: Penguin, 1998.

Shakespeare, William. *The Tempest.* Edited by Peter Hulme and William H. Sherman. W.W. Norton, 2003.

Nhora Lucia Serrano

Campobello, Nellie (María Francisca Moya Luna) (1900–1986) (dancer, folklorist, memoirist)

Nellie Campobello offered one of the few female eyewitness accounts of the MEXICAN REVOLUTION. Her work *Cartucho* (1931; *Cartridge*), which was translated into English in 1988, helps readers to appreciate cultural references to such figures as Pancho Villa in CHICANO LITERATURE. Born María Francisca Moya Luna in Villa Ocampo, Durango, in Mexico, on April 7, 1900, she was known as "Xica." Despite racial and class differences Campobello, who was white, developed close ties to the north Mexican peasant community. Raised without a father, Campobello and her half sister, Gloria, were very close with their mother, Rafaela, as well as with each other. She spent her youth watching the events of the Mexican Revolution (1910–20) unfold in her town. She listened attentively to her mother's stories—stories that tried to explain the violent incidents and terrible losses of the war-torn community. These narratives and her young age gave her a unique perspective when she later chronicled the revolution.

In 1923 Campobello's mother died, causing the sisters to move to Mexico City. There, they changed their Spanish surnames to the English name *Campbell* (which Nellie later changed to *Campobello*) when they attended the Colegio Inglés. While in Mexico City, the sisters received dance instruction; by 1927 they were well known for their artistic abilities and for their insights about indigenous Mexican dance and folklore.

In 1929, under the name Francisca, Campobello published her first creative work, *¡Yo!,* but it went largely unnoticed by critics and the reading public. Undeterred, Campobello spent 1929 and 1930 writing and traveling in Cuba. Upon her return to Mexico she published her second work, *Cartucho.* This work is perhaps her most well known partly because it is one of the few female chronicles of the Mexican Revolution. Some critics have cast *Cartucho* as naïve, due to Campobello's unapologetic loyalty to Pancho Villa, who was from Durango; nevertheless, the text offers a unique view of war through the eyes of a young girl. The violence depicted is realistic and graphic. She openly criticizes war as a waste yet celebrates the tenet of the revolution to redistribute the land, which had been controlled by Spanish colonists, then Mexican governments, and finally foreign businesses. Her mother plays a central role in *Cartucho,* becoming

a symbol of emerging feminism. The book enjoyed limited success, and Campobello was never recognized with other canonical writers. Her view of the revolution was all but forgotten until her works were rediscovered by scholars such as Doris Meyer.

In 1937 Campobello published *Las manos de mamá* (Mother's hands), which recalls her mother's narratives that helped her daughters to understand postrevolutionary Mexico. In the 1960s Campobello taught, danced, and wrote about the Taurahumara indigenous population of Durango; at this time she published *Mis libros* (1960; My books). Even after her sister Gloria's death in 1968, the author continued to work on her study of traditional dance and folklore, as well as her writing. In 1984 the state of Durango awarded her the Francisco Zarco Medal for her work as a regional artist, writer, dancer, and folklorist.

Campobello lends a unique view into the world of revolutionary Mexico and the role women play in the emerging nation. In this regard she helps provide a context for Mexican-American accounts of the Mexican Revolution, and in so doing her work creates a critical context for plot details in JOSEPHINA NIGGLI's MEXICAN VILLAGE (1945), SANDRA CISNEROS's CARAMELO (2002), and ARTURO ISLAS's *The RAIN GOD* (1984).

Bibliography

Campobello, Nellie. *Cartucho and My Mother's Hands.* Translated by Doris Meyer and Irene Matthews. Austin: University of Texas Press, 1988.

Meyer, Doris, ed. *Rereading the Spanish American Essay: Translations of 19th and 20th Century Women's Essays.* Austin: University of Texas Press, 1995.

Peters, Kate. "The Arrested Message of War in *Cartucho* by Nellie Campobello." *Genre: Discourse and Culture* 32, no. 4 (1999): 329–338.

Dustin Crawford

Canícula: Snapshots of a Girlhood en la Frontera **Norma Elia Cantú** (1995)

The title of NORMA ELIA CANTÚ's *Canícula* refers to the dog days of summer. In her memoir Cantú depicts a Mexican-American family and the community of Laredo from the 1940s to the 1960s. In the author's own estimation the text, consisting of 85 episodes, may be considered a "fictional autobioethnography." She uses the term *auto* because she is writing about a self and *bio* because she is recording a life. The inclusion of the word *ethnography* brings Cantú's creative vision into alignment with the disciplines of anthropology and sociology. The author plays with literary and historical conventions by incorporating real photographs and aspects of her own life, as well as episodes and imagery that are not wholly factual. The narrator, Azucena, for example, shares the author's last name, though not her first, and there are clear parallels between Azucena's childhood and adolescence and the author's own background. In any case Azucena (also called Nena) is more of a lens to view the rites of passage—baptism, First Communion, *quinceaños* (the coming-out/15th birthday celebration for girls), marriage, parenting, and mourning—in Mexican-American culture rather than a fully developed character. It is through her eyes and those of her loved ones and neighbors that the reader glimpses "snapshots" of life in Laredo, Texas, and Nuevo Laredo, Mexico (Cantú's hometown). The story is roughly chronological, although Cantú jumps back and forth in time so that moments from Azucena's toddler years appear at the end of the book, while references to her adult life appear in the beginning.

The text opens with three quotations, one of which is from GLORIA ANZALDÚA's *BORDERLANDS/ LA FRONTERA: THE NEW MESTIZA* (1987). The line reads: "The U.S.-Mexican border *es una herida abierta* [is an open wound] where the Third World grates against the first and bleeds" (25). Cantú's quotation of Anzaldúa sets up the expectation that her narrative will rely on CODE SWITCHING between Spanish and English. Cantú views critically the border, often forced, between the United States and Mexico, and describes memories that are personal as well as generational. *Canícula* follows the logic set up by the Anzaldúa quotation, especially in Cantú's vignette, "Crossings." "Crossings" centers on the effect of the Bracero program

on the narrator's grandmother Bueli (a nickname for *abuela*). The Bracero program was a U.S. agricultural and political initiative of the 1930s and 1940s to employ Mexican labor during harvesting seasons. As part of an agreement between the U.S. and Mexican governments, Mexican workers toiled in the fields in the United States (usually in Texas and the Midwest) and then were sent back across the border after the crops had been picked. Oftentimes Mexican-American families were also deported, even though they were U.S. citizens who had every right to remain in the United States. Azucena's grandmother Bueli gets caught in the deportation, though she feels fortunate enough to have been driven to Laredo rather than "being packed in trains to the border . . ." (5). Life is not easy for the Cantú family, but they weather strife, and Bueli's daughter gives birth to Azucena by 1947.

In her first three years of life Azucena enjoys the generous attention of her parents, but as each new child (usually a girl) comes, Azucena yields her special place, and her responsibilities grow. In essence she becomes less of a child and more of a parental figure in looking after her 10 younger siblings (Dahlia, Esperanza, Margarita, Azalia, Teresita, Rosa, Xochitl, Rolando, David, and Tono). She picks up her sisters and brothers when they need to be carried, she feeds them, she tries to keep them out of trouble, and she plays with them. Despite this great burden, Azucena does not complain, but sometimes she makes a grave mistake. While arguing with Tono over what to watch on television, they start to struggle over the knob; Azalia, her six-month-old sister, starts to fall from her arms. Azalia's leg has been either pulled out of its socket or broken. Azucena tells her mother what happened: "It's Sunday and they take her to the emergency room. The baby Lala [Azalia] comes back with a fat white cast on her leg" (25–26). Azalia recovers, but the family will not know if there is permanent damage to her leg until she is a teenager. In the interim Azucena feels an overwhelming guilt, which only subsides once her younger sister becomes a cheerleader in high school, doing cartwheels across the football field. Azucena had felt especially bad because Bueli had visited her from the grave to warn her: "Cuida la niña" [take care of the little girl] (25).

As with the work of ROLANDO HINOJOSA SMITH and TOMÁS RIVERA, who also write about this time and this region, the operative word in *Canícula* is *forbearance,* especially in the midst of conflict or mishap, as in the story about an older couple who want children. Azucena's neighbor, Doña Carmen, lives alone with her husband, Don Vicente. Don Vicente has retired from his job downtown at Salinas Fine Fashions and tends to the fruit trees on the property. Doña Carmen, meanwhile, sells fabric remnants out of the family home and prays for a child of her own. Arrangements are made with a young Mexican woman from across the border, and Doña Carmen and Don Vicente are parents for six months, but one day the adopted baby dies of a fever. The reader learns only after the infant's death that Doña Carmen is deaf. She could not hear the infant's cries and noticed her child's suffering too late:

> She blamed herself for being deaf and not hearing the child's cries, for not knowing how to mother, for trusting God. She was broken, lost so much weight that her clothes and her skin hung from her bones like sackcloth.... Depressed and alienated she didn't want anything to do with anyone, fought with the neighbors, with Don Vicente, even with Mami, her comadre (65).

The loss of the child compels Cantú's audience on many levels to feel compassion for the infant, for Doña Carmen who has retreated irreversibly into her sorrow, for Don Vicente who has died essentially from grief, and for the biological mother who will never know what happened to her baby.

Even with these tragedies and worries Azucena is able to delight in the small pleasures of life: a red-checkered gingham dress, her mother's garden of herbs and flowers, and the academic challenge of *la declamación* (a classroom exercise that requires recitation). Cantú's skill as a writer is evident in her portrait of farmers and manual laborers and her picture of a new generation of Mexican Americans—of which Azucena is one—a generation who will have new educational and professional opportunities, though they will leave valuable aspects of the past behind.

Canícula draws on conventions from the autobiography and the novel, as well as the photodocumentary. In his correspondence with the author Timothy Adams analyzes where the lines between fact and fiction break down. Adams notes, for example, references to photos that do not reflect their descriptions by comparing "the actual photographs to the prose that describes them" (59). Cantú has obviously (and self-consciously) tampered with family pictures; for example, she has pasted the name *Azucena* over her own name in the passport image. In interpreting why Cantú plays with the snapshots and her narrative descriptions, Adams also calls attention to the constructions of identity that Mexican Americans sometimes depend on. People crossing the border are compelled to use two sets of descriptors about their race, depending on which way they are traveling. In one document Azucena's color is *blanco* (white), and in another document she is *moreno,* which means "brown." The author's depiction of Mexican-American ethnicity has, therefore, much in common with RICHARD RODRIGUEZ's memoir, *BROWN: THE LAST DISCOVERY OF AMERICA* (2002). Both authors demonstrate that race is a cultural as well as political "fact." For this kind of complexity and for the richness of its vision *Canícula* has been very well received and earned one of the highest honors of Chicano letters, the Premio Aztlán. The memoir can be read within the context of CHICANO LITERATURE and BORDER LITERATURE.

Bibliography

Adams, Timothy. "'Heightened by Life' vs. 'Paralyzed by Fact': Photography and Autobiography in Norma Cantú's *Canícula.*" *Biography* 24 (Winter 2001): 57.

Cantú, Norma Elia. *Canícula: Snapshots of a Girlhood en la Frontera.* Albuquerque: University of New Mexico Press, 1995.

Luz Elena Ramirez

Cantú, Norma Elia (1947–) *(scholar, memoirist)*

Norma Elia Cantú was born on January 3, 1947, in Nuevo Laredo, Mexico, to Virginia Ramón Becerra and Florentino Cantú Vargas. By 1948 she and her family crossed the Mexican border to settle in Laredo, Texas, though her relations had been moving back and forth across the border for decades. An essayist, storyteller, and cultural critic, Cantú made her debut as a memoirist with CANÍCULA: SNAPSHOTS OF A GIRLHOOD EN LA FRONTERA (1995). Her writing can be read alongside the work of ROLANDO HINOJOSA SMITH, TOMÁS RIVERA, and GLORIA ANZALDÚA.

As a young girl Cantú witnessed the effect that U.S. border policies had on people who crossed *la frontera* (the border) on a daily basis—sometimes willingly, sometimes by compulsion or by law. She saw the emergence of the civil rights movement in the 1950s, and she contributed to it in the 1960s through her participation in the Raza Unida (the United People or United Race, a party that fought for equal access to education, land, and job opportunities). By the 1970s Cantú had earned an undergraduate degree in English and political science from Texas A&M International University at Laredo (1973) and finished her master's in English at Texas A&M University at Kingsville (1975).

Awarded the Ford Foundation Chicano Dissertation grant, she earned her Ph.D. in English in 1982 from the University of Nebraska–Lincoln. From 1980 to 2000 Cantú returned to Laredo to teach at Laredo State University/Texas A&M International University, with only short stints away. Cantú is currently a professor of English and U.S. Latino/a literature at the University of Texas, San Antonio.

Cantú writes about the cultures and traditions of the U.S.-Mexico borderlands. She was awarded the 1995 Premio Aztlán National Literary Prize in Fiction for *Canícula,* a story about the experiences of a Mexican family settling in the United States during the 1940s. She recently finished another novel, *Cabañuelas: A Love Story,* and is working on two others, tentatively titled *Champú, or Hair Matters,* and *Papeles de mujer.* Her published short stories include "Se me enchina el cuerpo al oír tu cuento," "Bailando y cantando," "Police Blotter," "El Luto," and "Adios en Madrid." Her published poems include "Decolonizing the Mind," "Migraine," "Trojan Horse," "Reading the Body," "Las diosas," and "Fiestas de diciembre." Cantú is also at work on an ethnography, *Soldiers of the Cross: Los matachines de la Santa Cruz,* a religious dance drama from Laredo, Texas; and a collection of poetry, *Meditación fronteriza: Poems of Life, Love, and Work.*

An editor as well as narrator Cantú has published the anthology *Chicana Traditions: Continuity and Change* (2002) with Olga Nájera Ramírez, as well as *Flor y ciencia: Chicanas in Mathematics, Science and Engineering.* Cantú is also editor of a book series, *Río Grande/Río Bravo: Borderlands Culture and Traditions,* for Texas A&M University Press.

Cantú reads her creative work, gives community presentations, and conducts workshops in national and international venues. She serves on the board of trustees of the American Folklife Center at the Library of Congress and is chair-elect of the National Association of Chicana/o Studies.

Bibliography

Cantú, Norma. *Canícula: Snapshots of a Girlhood en la frontera.* Albuquerque, N.Mex.: University of Albuquerque Press, 2002.

Cantú, Norma, and Olga Nájera-Ramirez, eds. *Chicana Traditions: Continuity and Change.* Urbana: University of Illinois Press, 2002.

"Norma Elia Cantú." University of Texas, San Antonio Web site. Available online. URL: http://colfa.utsa.edu/cantu/vita2000.html. Accessed October 2, 2007.

Society for the Study of Gloria Anzaldúa Web site. Available online. URL: http://www.ssganzaldua.org.

Kati Pletsch de García and Patricia González

Caramelo Sandra Cisneros (2002)

In *Caramelo,* SANDRA CISNEROS demonstrates how a young Mexican-American girl travels back and forth across the borderlands of the United States and Mexico. Like the immensely popular *THE HOUSE ON MANGO STREET* (1984), Cisneros's second novel, *Caramelo,* is autobiographical and explores the process of becoming a Chicana and being "caught between here and there," or between the United States and Mexico (434). The title refers to the caramel-colored striped *rebozo* (traditional Mexican shawl) that becomes a Reyes family heirloom. But, as in RICHARD RODRIGUEZ's *BROWN: THE LAST DISCOVERY OF AMERICA* (2002), caramel is also the skin color of many Mexican Americans. As such, caramel symbolizes a MESTIZO heritage, a combination of Spanish and Indian ancestry.

The protagonist of *Caramelo* is a young girl, Celaya Reyes, otherwise known as "Lala." Celaya's mother, Zoila, defies her husband and names their daughter in honor of the site where Pancho Villa met his nemesis during the MEXICAN REVOLUTION. Not surprisingly, then, readers find Celaya to be rebellious, a characteristic she has inherited from her mother and perhaps her grandmother, too. In any case Celaya's journeys become the readers' journeys as well; Cisneros takes us along Route 66 from Chicago to Mexico City and back, a road trip filled with anecdotes and lively conversations. Like a *telenovela* (soap opera), the stories of the Reyes family are filled with lies, romances, and secrets.

Caramelo consists of three parts with 86 vignettes, including long footnotes and a chronology of historical events at the end of the text. In each episode Cisneros utilizes CODE SWITCHING between English and Spanish. This movement between two languages allows the author to bring to life the conversations and arguments of the Reyes family. At the same time *Caramelo* follows the contours of the history of Mexico and the United States, especially the MEXICAN REVOLUTION and World War II. In doing so the author offers commentary, whether in the story itself or in one of the many footnotes, about racism in the 1930s and 1940s, about expectations for Mexican women and men, and about cultural exchanges with other immigrant communities of Chicago. Cisneros's notion of the border can be aligned with GLORIA ANZALDÚA's observation that Mexican Americans did not cross the border, but rather *la frontera,* the border, crossed them.

Celaya, like Cisneros, is the only daughter of a Mexican father and a Mexican-American mother. She is the youngest child born after her six brothers (Rafael, Refugio, Gustavo, Alberto, Lorenzo, and Guillermo). Inocencio Reyes, her father, works in the upholstery business, as do his brothers. The novel begins with the Reyes' annual trip from Chicago to Mexico, but this time Inocencio's brothers (Uncle Fat-Face and Uncle Baby) are coming along, headed to see their mother, Soledad, in Mexico City. Celaya calls her Soledad "the Awful Grandmother," but it is clear that she has a special connection to her. The stories and histories are narrated by Celaya and inspired by her grandmother and, later, Soledad's ghost. Ultimately, by retelling the stories of her Mexican-American family—their moves from Mexico City to Chicago, to San Antonio, and back again to Chicago—Celaya recounts her own coming of age. Recognizing that Soledad's *rebozo* reflects a tradition of wool dyeing and weaving, Celaya seeks to reclaim her grandmother's *rebozo* as her own.

Cisneros divides *Caramelo* into three parts. The first part, "Recuerdo de Acapulco" (Memory of Acapulco), is set in Little Grandfather and Awful Grandmother's house on Destiny Street in Mexico City. It dramatizes the conflicts between Soledad and Celaya's mother. In a public market Inocencio is asked to choose one of them—mother or wife.

The second part, "When I Was Dirt," reveals the stories of Celaya's forefathers and foremothers. This section focuses on Soledad's miserable childhood, which explains why she became who she is: the Awful Grandmother. The third part, "The Eagle and the Serpent or My Mother and My Father," tells "Father's story and Mother's history" (310). Disputes within the Reyes family, along with financial hardship, compel Inocencio to move from Chicago to San Antonio. In the end the family is reconciled in Chicago. When Awful Grandmother, Soledad, dies, her passing is understood as the ending of a generation; Celaya then tells the grandmother's story as her own.

One of Cisneros's central themes is a room of one's own, a concept established by the English author Virginia Woolf. Like the narrator of *A*

Room of One's Own, Celaya longs for a place all for herself because, in a deeper sense, the room is a metaphor of female liberation. Like Soledad and her mother, Celaya desires a place where she can live her life. She wants to escape a place where a woman is cavalierly labeled a prostitute—*prostituta, puta, perra, perdida.* This is the same struggle ESMERALDA SANTIAGO expresses in her Puerto Rican memoir *ALMOST A WOMAN* (1998).

Caramelo illustrates how a male-centered society imposes on women their roles as daughters, wives, and, especially, mothers. Celaya's friend Viva observes, "If you can't control your own body, how can you control your own life?" (399). Cisneros criticizes patriarchal attitudes that take the Mexican-American woman (her industriousness, her endurance, and her fertility) for granted. Like *The House on Mango Street, Caramelo* moves the women of the narrative toward self-realization. In this regard Cisneros's writing has much in common with other stories about coming of age or coming into consciousness in CHICANO LITERATURE, especially NORMA ELIA CANTÚ's *CANÍCULA: SNAPSHOTS OF A GIRLHOOD EN LA FRONTERA* (1995), and TOMÁS RIVERA's . . . *Y no se lo tragó la tierra* (1971; *THIS MIGRANT EARTH.*

Bibliography
Cisneros, Sandra. *Caramelo.* New York: Alfred A. Knopf, 2002.
———. *The House on Mango Street.* New York: Vintage, 1991.
Morales, Ed. "Imaginary Homeland." *Criticas* 2 (2002): 29–31.
Stavans, Ilan. "Familia Face." *Nation* 276 (2003): 30–34.

Heejung Cha

Casa de las Américas
Casa de las Américas is a renowned publishing house, art gallery, cultural center, and classroom space in the Vedado district of Havana, Cuba. Under the leadership of famed author ROBERTO FERNÁNDEZ RETAMAR, Casa de las Américas welcomes the public to its national and international literary readings, musical performances, and art exhibitions. Established in 1959 by Haydee de Santamaría, the center is best known in the literary world for its prestigious Premio Literario Casa de las Américas (Casa de las Américas Literary Prize). This prize is frequently given to authors of SPANISH-AMERICAN CARIBBEAN LITERATURE and Latin American literature more broadly. However, there have been recipients of this prize in the United States, including ROLANDO HINOJOSA SMITH. Casa de las Américas also awards prizes to young artists, essayists, musicologists, and those involved in theater.

In recent years Casa de las Américas has opened its doors to U.S. faculty and students. Despite the U.S. embargo against Cuba and restrictions on U.S. travel to the island, Casa de las Américas has been instrumental in maintaining academic programs with U.S. campuses such as the University of California, California State University, Duke, Fordham, and Harvard. These unusual programs are made possible by academic visas issued by the Cuban government and academic licenses issued by the U.S. Treasury Department; however, under the administration of George W. Bush these academic licenses have been more difficult to obtain. Typically such programs involve various coordinators from Casa de las Américas, as well as guest faculty from the Universidad de Habana, who deliver lectures on such topics as U.S.-Cuban relations, economic conditions under Castro, and Cuban music, literature, history, and art.

Luz Elena Ramirez

Castillo, Ana (1953–) *(essayist, novelist, poet)*
Ana Castillo was born in Chicago on June 15, 1953. As a first-generation Mexican American living in Chicago, Castillo experienced many forms of prejudice, as did her entire family. Castillo's dark-skinned mother faced the racism of the 1950s when her landlord made her scrub the stairs of the front entrance of their building every Saturday morning for 10 years. Her light-skinned father, on the other hand, was able to "pass" for Italian; he eventually changed his last name to *Costello,*

thereby aligning himself with Chicago's European immigrant community. The rest of the family kept the name *Castillo* and consequently faced the stereotypes associated with being Mexican in the United States. Although both her mother and father endured prejudice as Mexicans, her mother was doubly disadvantaged as a Mexican woman in a European immigrant community and English-speaking, male-dominated world. These experiences and insights would contribute to Castillo's articulation of a Chicana identity, a politically conscious Mexican-American woman.

Castillo attended Chicago City College for two years and Northeastern Illinois University, where she received a B.A. in 1975. She taught ethnic studies at Santa Rosa College in California from 1975 to 1976 and was a graduate fellow at the University of Chicago, eventually earning an M.A. in Latin American and Caribbean studies in 1979. She served as a dissertation fellow in Chicano studies at the University of California, Santa Barbara from 1989 to 1990. Castillo earned a Ph.D. in American studies from the University of Bremen, in Germany, in 1991 and was awarded an National Endowment for the Arts fellowship for creative writing in 1995. She has taught at Mills College in Oakland, California, and at Mount Holyoke in South Hadley, Massachusetts. Castillo currently teaches in the English Department of DePaul University in her native Chicago.

Since the appearance of her initial chapbook of poetry, Castillo has published six volumes of poetry, four novels, one short story collection, and one collection of critical essays and has edited or coedited three Latino literary anthologies. Her collections of poetry are *Otro Canto* (1977, Another song), *The Invitation* (1979), *Women Are Not Roses* (1984), *My Father Was a Toltec* (1988), *My Father Was a Toltec and Selected Poems, 1973–1988* (1995), and *I Ask the Impossible* (2001). Her fiction includes the epistolary novel *The Mixquia-huala Letters* (1986), the epic *Sapogonia* (1990), the episodic novel *So Far from God* (1993), and the romance *Peel My Love Like an Onion* (1999). Her single collection of short stories appears under the title *Loverboys* (1996), and her single

collection of critical essays was published as *Massacre of the Dreamers: Essays on Xicanisma* (1994). Castillo also has published a children's book, *My Daughter, My Son, the Eagle, the Dove: An Aztec Chant* (2000).

In addition to her own work Castillo cotranslated (with Norma Alarcón) Gloria Anzaldúa and Cherríe Moraga's anthology *This Bridge Called My Back* (*Esta Puente, Mi Espalda,* 1988). She coedited (with Norma Alarcón and Cherríe Moraga) a collection of essays entitled *The Sexuality of Latinas* (1991). Finally, Castillo edited and introduced a collection of writings by various Latino authors on the figure of the Virgin of Guadalupe, entitled *Goddess of the Americas/La Diosa de las Américas: Writings on the Virgin of Guadalupe* (1996).

Castillo's first novel, *The Mixquiahuala Letters,* was awarded the Before Columbus Foundation's American Book Award in 1987. It relates the story of two women who meet in Mexico. Teresa, a Chicana, and Alicia, a gringa, have come to a language institute to study Spanish and the culture of Mexico. Because Teresa is in Mexico to reconnect with her cultural past, she becomes disenchanted with the Americans who seek an exotic summer experience. Teresa and Alicia try to make the connection on their own through their travels around Mexico; their experiences, however, remind them that they are equally at risk in the patriarchal culture of Mexico as they are in the United States.

Castillo's second novel, *Sapogonia,* takes its name from the Spanish word *sapo* (toad), which is sometimes used to refer to those who cross the border from Mexico to the United States. The novel focuses on two such *sapogones,* Máximo Madrigal and Pastora Velásquez Aké. While both have come to the United States, they have followed very different paths and have very different goals. Máximo, a modern-day version of the Spanish conquistador, sets out to conquer the United States, the art world, and every woman he meets. Pastora, on the other hand, is a singer, songwriter, and activist who wants to transform society; she resists Máximo's attempts to conquer her. The novel illustrates Máximo's and Pastora's precarious position in mainstream society, as well as the power struggles and violence in male-female relationships.

Castillo's third novel, *So Far from God*, was awarded both the Carl Sandburg Literary Award, in 1993, and the Mountains and Plains Bookseller Award, in 1994. *So Far from God* takes place in New Mexico and features the story of Sofía (which means "Wisdom") and her four daughters, Esperanza (hope), Fe (faith), Caridad (charity), and the youngest, La Loca (the crazy one). By surveying each of the daughter's lives, the novel represents the often negative and destructive nature of female-male relationships. Abandoned by her husband, Sofía manages to keep herself together and helps to change her community for the better. At the same time she also witnesses the catastrophic effects upon her daughters as they move away from the community. In this regard Castillo illustrates her concern for the balance between the material and spiritual elements of life, and she emphasizes the importance of remaining in touch with one's family and heritage.

While Castillo uses these themes in her fiction, she also examines them in her essays compiled in *Massacre of the Dreamers*. In the 10 essays assembled between 1987 and 1993 she investigates the origins of gender relations, as in "The Ancient Roots of Machismo" and "In the Beginning There Was Eva." She also discusses aspects of Chicana feminism, which she calls Xicanisma, in "A Countryless Woman" and "Un tapiz" (A tapestry). She examines female-female relationships in "Toward the Mother-Bond Principle." Her essays contribute to an ongoing conversation about the border in regard to gender relations and effects of patriarchal history on women. As such, her work can be read within the context of Chicano literature, border literature and Latina lesbian literature.

Bibliography

Castillo, Ana. "A Chicana from Chicago." *Essence* 24, no. 2 (June 1993): 42, 130.
———. *The Guardian: A Novel.* New York: Random House, 2007.
———. *Massacre of the Dreamers: Essays on Xicanisma.* New York: Plume, 1995.
———. *The Mixquiahuala Letters.* New York: Anchor, 1992.
———. *Peel My Love Like an Onion.* New York: Anchor, 2000.
———. *Sapogonia.* New York: Anchor, 1994.
———. *So Far from God.* New York: W. W. Norton, 2005.
———, ed. *Goddess of the Americas.* New York: Riverhead, 1997.
"Guide to the Papers of Ana Castillo, 1953–1990." California Ethnic and Multicultural Archives. Available online. URL: http://cemaweb.library.ucsb.edu/Castillo_toc.html.
Milligan, Bryce. "An Interview with Ana Castillo." *South Central Review* 16, no. 1 (Spring 1999): 19–29.
Saeta, Elsa. "A *MELUS* Interview: Ana Castillo." *MELUS: The Journal of the Society for the Study of the Multi-Ethnic Literature of the United States* 22, no. 3 (Fall 1997): 133–150.

Ritch Calvin

Castro, Fidel (Fidel Alejandro Castro Ruz) (1926–) *(Former president of Cuba, essayist, revolutionary)*

An enigmatic and controversial political figure, Fidel Castro was a Cuban revolutionary leader in the 1950s and premier from 1959 to 1976. From 1976 to 2008 he was president of Cuba. His rule is widely considered to be a dictatorship. At the same time many Latin Americans, such as Venezuelan president Hugo Chávez, tout Castro as an anti-imperialist hero who rid Cuba of the U.S. presence. After taking power, Castro appropriated privately owned land and distributed it among the peasantry (though it belongs to the state); he also nationalized privately owned businesses, many of which, such as Westinghouse, were American. His enemies decry Castro's suppression of democracy and civil rights; his supporters point out that although a poor country, and despite the crippling economic conditions of the U.S. embargo, Cuba enjoys a universal health care system and one of the highest literacy rates in the world.

Castro was born the fifth of nine children on August 13, 1926, at Finca Manacas, his family's sugar plantation, in Oriente Province. Castro was a child prodigy, excelling in sports and in his studies at the Belén Jesuit school in Havana. In October 1945 Castro enrolled in the University of Havana's Faculty of Law, where he immediately plunged into politics and became a student leader. In 1947 Castro joined the Ortodoxo, a social-democrat party rising rapidly to the limelight as an outspoken critic of the government of Ramón Grau. His political involvement and activism led him to leave law school to dedicate himself to activism. He spoke out against gangsterism under President Carlos Prío Socarrás and subsequently fled to the United States in fear for his life. He returned four months later to study for his degree, and in September 1950 Castro graduated with the title of Doctor of Law. He then began a law practice in 1950 in Havana, working mostly pro bono.

As a young lawyer Castro continued to be an outspoken political activist, and in 1952 he intended to campaign for parliament. These plans came to a halt when General Fulgencio Batista staged a coup d'état and overthrew the Prío government. Batista canceled the impending elections, declaring himself chief of state and suspending all rights guaranteed in the 1940 constitution. Castro criticized the government of Batista, going so far as to petition the courts and decrying the violation of the Cuban constitution by Batista's regime. The petition was denied, and seeing no further legal recourse available, Castro met with other rebel leaders to plan an attack on the Batista government. On July 26, 1953, Castro led insurrectionists in an attack on the Moncada Barracks. After the failed coup Castro and other rebels were imprisoned. Of those who were not killed in the initial attack, many were tortured and executed. Castro was tried separately from the other conspirators and in secret. He served as his own attorney, and it was during this trial on October 16, 1953, that he made his most famous speech, "HISTORY WILL ABSOLVE ME." After serving 19 months in prison on the Isle of Pines, Castro was released through Batista's general amnesty. He went into exile in Mexico, where he regrouped with revolutionaries, who called themselves the Twenty-sixth of July movement, to plan and organize a new attack on the Batista dictatorship.

On November 25, 1956, Castro and the other revolutionaries set sail for Cuba from Tuxpán, Mexico. Crossing 1,235 miles of ocean in tumultuous weather in an overburdened yacht named the *Granma*, the revolutionaries were delayed two days in their arrival, running aground on December 2 just south of the planned landing site, at Playa las Coloradas. The group sought safety from Batista's armed forces in the Sierra Maestra, from which they launched their revolutionary fight. From the mountains Castro and his rebels carried out guerrilla raids and beat off attacks by Batista's superiorly armed troops. By mid-1957 violence became endemic, especially in Santiago and Oriente Provinces, where daily life was interrupted by terrorism and strikes. Batista's use of bombers and other military equipment to crush the revolt alienated him from his supporters in the United States. In March 1958 the United States suspended arms shipments to the Cuban government, turning the tide decisively against Batista. On January 1, 1959, Batista fled to Miami with his closest aides, and the revolutionary party took control of Cuba.

During the first four years of power (1959–62), Castro began moving the revolution toward the left in order to accomplish some of his goals, such as socializing the economy and establishing a new pattern of foreign relations. Castro took advantage of the cold war to align Cuba with the Soviet Union, and Cuba became the first Communist state in the Western Hemisphere. This strategy moved Cuba out of the United States orbit while gaining substantial social and economic gains from the Soviet Union, as well as China and Vietnam.

Tensions between the United States and Cuba grew, rising to crisis levels in 1960 and 1961. As relations between the two nations eroded, the U.S. Central Intelligence Agency (CIA) began training Cuban exiles to invade the island. On April 15, 1961, the exile expeditionary force landed at the Bay of Pigs. The unsuccessful invasion was quickly crushed, and the fiasco increased Castro's prestige and gave new impetus for further reforms of Cuba's society and economy. In the wake of the Bay of Pigs invasion the Soviet Union pledged military support to Cuba in the event of an attack by the United States. The Soviets supplied aircraft and weapons, including missiles, to Cuba. The United States claimed that these were offensive weapons, whereas Cuba and the Soviet Union argued that they were for Cuba's defense. In October 1962 the tension came to a head, and the world came close to nuclear war. A compromise was reached by which the Soviet Union agreed to remove its missiles from Cuba in return for a pledge from the United States not to invade Cuba and to remove its own missiles from Turkey. Efforts by the United States to subvert and harass the Cuban government continued, however, including an economic embargo that continues to the present and unsuccessful assassination attempts against Castro.

Although initially supported by many Cubans, Castro alienated the middle and upper classes through enforced nationalization, suppression of opposing political parties, and suppression of emigration. Hundreds of thousands of Cubans have fled Cuba during the Castro regime. He has been accused of numerous human rights violations, including the unjustifiable deaths and imprisonment of thousands labeled as "counterrevolutionaries," "fascists," or "CIA operatives."

Supporters of Castro cite the increased nation's literacy rate and instituted universal health care as examples of the progress made under the Castro regime. Many supporters look to the history of U.S. hostility against Cuba to justify Castro's often harsh measures as a means of preventing the United States from presumably installing a puppet leader in his place. Castro's opposition, however, maintains that his use of the United States is only an excuse to justify his continuing political control. On July 31, 2006, Castro delegated authority to his brother, Raúl Castro, temporarily while he recovered from surgery. However, on February 18, 2008, Castro announced his retirement, and on February 24, 2008, Raúl was chosen as president.

Fidel Castro's speech "History Will Absolve Me" and his revolutionary activities are referenced throughout CUBAN-AMERICAN LITERATURE and SPANISH-AMERICAN CARIBBEAN LITERATURE more broadly.

Bibliography
Brenner, Phillip, et al., eds. *The Cuba Reader: The Making of a Revolutionary Society.* New York: Grove Press, 1989.
"Fidel Castro." Wikipedia. Available online. URL: http://en.wikipedia.org/wiki/Fidel_Castro#Bay_of_Pigs. Accessed July 10, 2005.
Keen, Benjamin. *A History of Latin America.* 5th ed. Boston: Houghton Mifflin, 1996.
Pérez, Louis A., Jr. *Cuba: Between Reform & Revolution.* Oxford: Oxford University Press, 1995.
Quirk, Robert E. *Fidel Castro.* New York: W. W. Norton, 1993.
Ruiz, Ramon Eduardo. *Cuba: The Making of a Revolution.* New York: W. W. Norton, 1968.

Khamla Dhouti

Cervantes, Lorna Dee (1954–) *(poet)*

Born in 1954 in San Francisco, California, Lorna Dee Cervantes is a poet and associate professor of English at the University of Colorado. Growing up in the "welfare class," Cervantes accompanied her mother to cleaning jobs and found herself immersed in the world of books she found in various households. A love of language developed, and Cervantes burst on the poetry scene in 1974 as a young writer. At a festival in Mexico she read her poetry during her brother's band performance. Encouraged by the praise she received, she devoted herself to writing full time, publishing the work of Chicano writers in her own literary journal, *Mango.* She earned her B.A. from San Jose State University in 1984.

EMPLUMADA (Feathered), her first collection of poetry, was published in 1981 and won the American Book Award. Of Native American and Mexican ancestry, Cervantes has seen firsthand how class and cultural identity are inescapable forces that shape those around her. Poems such as "Uncle's First Rabbit" and "Cannery Town in August" represent the theme of determinism in Cervantes's poetry. In both poems the characters are a product of their environment (gender, social status, ethnicity, etc.) and cannot escape their circumstances.

In "Uncle's First Rabbit," the character referred to only as "he" vows to be the gentle man his father was not. But the character's suppressed rage surfaces in domestic violence when he beats his own wife. This reveals an inherited rage as we learn that the speaker's mother was beaten by her husband. Cervantes does not judge the characters of her poetry. They are what they are because of who and where they are: immigrants in a country that places little value on their contributions. "Cannery Town in August" shows the lines of tired women leaving their shift at the vegetable cannery. Men in trucks wait to take them home. The women are indistinguishable from one another, bound in a sisterhood of drudgery familiar to those workers with limited proficiency in English and with limited educational backgrounds or prospects.

Much of Cervantes's poetry is written in the first person, and many poems rely on Native American motifs, connecting the speaker to her ancient heritage as a source of female strength. Her "Self-Portrait" begins with the words "I melt." The speaker is changed by her environment as she attempts to assimilate to mainstream culture without losing herself along the way. "Caribou Girl," meanwhile, represents the wisdom that a woman gathers from her female ancestors. The way to survival lies in the acceptance and internalization of the wisdom of our ancestors.

Her collection FROM THE CABLES OF GENOCIDE: POEMS ON LOVE AND HUNGER (1991) won the Paterson Poetry Prize. Historical and autobiographical details and poetic expressions mix in Cervantes's poems—often to startling effect. Cervantes's mother was murdered in 1982, and the loss seems to resonate in this volume. Loss, death, and hardship shape poems about men at sea, the finite pleasure of sex, and unexpected pregnancy.

The cyclical nature of history, man's inhumanity and his inability to learn from his past, is evoked by images of food and hunger. In "On Love and Hunger," the speaker cannot be satisfied until her lover's hunger is satisfied, knowing that the hunger, once fed, will come again and again. In "Raisins" the speaker tells her lover that he is the only food she has had all day; eating and loving are reciprocal: The speaker buys love with food, and feeds on love.

Cervantes's most recent book of poetry is entitled *Drive: The First Quartet* (2005). The volume contains five complete works: "How Far's the War?," "BIRD AVE," "Letters to David," "Play," and "Hard Drive." Cervantes also publishes the literary journal *Red Dirt*. Recognizing the heritage that makes her who she is—the Chicana, the Native American, and the Anglo—Cervantes offers in her poetry a compelling voice. Her work can be read within the context of CHICANO LITERATURE.

Bibliography

Cervantes, Lorna Dee. *Drive: The First Quartet*. San Antonio, Tex.: Wings Press, 2005.

———. *Emplumada*. Pittsburgh: University of Pittsburgh Press, 1981.

———. *From the Cables of Genocide: Poems on Love and Hunger*. Houston, Tex.: Arte Público Press, 1991.

McKenna, Teresa. "'An Utterance More Pure Than Word': Gender and the *Corrido* Tradition in Two Contemporary Chicano Poems." In *Feminist Measures: Soundings in Poetry and Theory*, edited by Lynn Keller and Cristianne Miller. Ann Arbor: University of Michigan Press, 1994, 184–207.

Rodriguez y Gibson, Eliza. "Love, Hunger, and Grace: Loss and Belonging in the Poetry of Lorna Dee Cervantes and Joy Harjo." *Legacy: A Journal of American Women Writers* 19, no. 1 (January 2002): 106–115.

Seator, Lynette. "*Emplumada*: Chicana Rites-of-Passage." *MELUS* 11, no. 2 (Summer 1984): 23–38.

Whyatt, Frances. "*Emplumada*." *American Book Review* 4, no. 5 (July–August 1982): 11–12.

Patricia Bostian

Chacón, Daniel (1962–) *(fiction writer)*

Daniel Chacón is a Mexican-American writer and educator born in 1962. He has published two major works, *Chicano Chicanery: Short Stories*

(2000) and *And the Shadows Took Him: A Novel* (2004). Chacón was raised in Pinedale, a working-class neighborhood in the agricultural outskirts of Fresno, California. His father was a welder, and his mother, a cashier at Kmart. As a youth, Chacón enjoyed visits to his grandparents and cousins, who lived nearby; the theme of family, therefore, is an important one in his fiction. He later attended California State University at Fresno and earned an undergraduate degree in political science and then an M.A. in English. He also completed an M.F.A. in fiction writing at the University of Oregon. Chacón's first language was English, not Spanish, because his parents wanted to keep their conversations private; however, he learned Spanish by studying the language and traveling to Mexico, Cuba, Argentina, and Spain.

In 2000 Chacón published *Chicano Chicanery: Short Stories,* which is divided into 13 sections. With titles such as "Andy the Office Boy" and "Too White" readers learn to recognize Chacón's playfulness and wit and to appreciate the resourcefulness of Mexican Americans living among their English-speaking "white" counterparts. Whether the setting is urban or rural, Mexican or American, Chacón's figures find ingenious and sometimes disturbing solutions to their problems. Although his characters initially appear as stereotypes, by the end of the narratives they often outsmart their opponents or upset audience expectations.

In the story "Godoy Lives" an illegal immigrant (Godoy) faces the same kind of humiliation and anxiety experienced by thousands of Mexicans when crossing the U.S. border. Godoy reflects on the advice he had been given before his crossing, namely that

> . . . the worst immigration officers in the U.S. were the ones of Mexican descent. Pick a white officer, he had heard, because the Mexican-American, the Chicano INS officers had to prove to the white people that they were no longer Mexicans. He had heard in the mountains that they would beat people up or sic vicious dogs on them, laughing as the bloody flesh would fly in all directions (7).

In this passage and elsewhere in the collection Chacón challenges the idea of a unified Mexican-American identity. By using different terms such as *Chicano* (a Mexican American who takes ethnic and political pride in his identity), *Mexican American, Pocho* (one who has become white), and *Mexican,* Chacón demonstrates that lines of nationality, culture, and language intersect in perplexing ways. "Godoy Lives" paints an interesting picture of how some Mexicans in Mexico view Mexicans in the United States, as in how they recognize that Mexican-American border officials may be more racist than their white colleagues. Godoy knows that many Mexican Americans aspire to integrate within the mainstream culture. Chacón docs not criticize his characters directly; instead, he lets the reader make connections between the characters and the choices they make under repressive conditions. Ultimately the reader is compelled to reflect on the economic and cultural issues affecting the lives of Mexican Americans, especially as they move away from labor-intensive agricultural work and into the U.S. middle class. In this regard Chacón's work can be read alongside that of ROLANDO HINOJOSA SMITH and NORMA CANTÚ.

Chicano Chicanery often relies on the wisdom and rhythms of oral traditions to create a sense of immediacy for the audience. Within a broader cultural context we can find parallels between *Chicano Chicanery* and the trickster figure in Native American legends, as well as in the eighth-century Arabian work *El Sendabar,* which praised shrewdness and survival over morality. His fiction tells entertaining and ironic stories about ordinary Mexican Americans whose image might otherwise remain one dimensional.

By 2004 Chacón had continued to draw his portrait of Mexican Americans, this time in novel form. *And the Shadows Took Him* features the story of the Medina family (William, Rachel, and their children, Vero, Billy, and Joey) and their experiences moving from a Californian barrio to Medford, Oregon. William Medina's pursuit of the American dream and a new job opportunity brings about the move. The protagonist is Joey

Medina, a Mexican-American boy whose Oregonian schoolmates expect him to be in a gang. This impression is based on the fact that he is an urban Latino from Northern California. Rather than disabuse his peers of this stereotype, Joey, who likes to act, starts to make up stories about his dangerous life in the barrio and goes on to found his own gang in Medford.

Chacón pays attention to issues of language and class in Joey's new circumstances and to the growing breach between father and son. In a scene between William and Joey, Chacón addresses the differences that exist even within the Medina family:

> "¡Piensas que tú eres mejor que yo, ese?" ["Do you think that you are better than me?"] his father said, as if he were a hoodlum ready to fight. "Just because you take Spanish classes at school, taught by some *gabacha* [non-Latina woman]?"

> "Please, Dad, your Spanish is horrible. Mom's the only one in the family who speaks it decently" (179).

Joey recognizes his father's derogatory use of the word *gabacha,* and this allows Chacón to address differences between family members. Through this story and others, Chacón opens a space where Mexican Americans can fruitfully argue about their identities and the choices they make in terms of their appearance, their use of language, and their associations. The tragic ending of the story, however, does not provide any easy resolution to these debates. The title, *And the Shadows Took Him,* prepares us for this kind of ending and, in fact, seems to reference another Mexican-American narrative, TOMÁS RIVERA's . . . *And the Earth Did Not Devour Him* (otherwise known as *THIS MIGRANT EARTH*), in which the protagonist reclaims a lost year of his youth. Chacón's work can be read within the context of CHICANO LITERATURE.

Bibliography

Chacón, Daniel. *And the Shadows Took Him: A Novel.* New York: Atria Books, 2004.

———. *Chicano Chicanery: Short Stories.* Houston, Tex.: Arte Público Press, 2000.

Selfa Chew

Chavez, Cesar (Cesar Estrada Chavez) (1927–1993) *(migrant farmworker, civil rights activist, labor leader)*

Chavez was born in 1927 on a farm near Yuma, Arizona. When he was 10 years old, his father lost the family home, and Chavez entered a life of migrant farming that would eventually lead him to the valleys of California. During these early years Chavez saw fieldworkers suffer many injustices. The idea that those who toiled in the fields and vineyards needed a voice to represent them began to grow. It was an idea that he would harvest later as a man.

Cesar Estrada Chavez cofounded the National Farm Workers Association (NFWA), an organization that later became known as United Farm Workers and (UFW), worked tirelessly for the rights of migrant laborers. An important figure in the civil rights movement, Chavez helped to expose the discrimination against and harsh treatment of farmworkers, especially Mexican Americans.

Chavez had a difficult time in school because of his migrant status. He attended almost 40 different schools and contended with the fact that speaking Spanish was prohibited in these settings. Despite the language barrier and the interruptions in his education, Chavez graduated from the eighth grade in 1942. Because his father had suffered an accident and his son was needed in the fields, Chavez did not finish his education—though he never gave up on his desire to learn.

From 1944 to 1946 Chavez served in the U.S. Navy. After his tenure in the military Chavez returned to California, where he met and married Helen Fabela. He and his wife settled in the East San Jose barrio of Sal Si Puedes, which means "Get out if you can." Cesar and Helen Chavez raised eight children together and eventually their family expanded to include 31 grandchildren.

As a fieldworker in the apricot orchards of San Jose, Chavez met Fred Ross, an organizer for the Community Service Organization (CSO), a social awareness group sponsored by the Industrial Areas Foundation. Chavez joined Ross's group, having reflected on the nonviolent protesters of history such as St. Francis and Mohandas Gandhi. Organizing new chapters of the CSO, launching voter registration drives, and speaking out against discrimination of fieldworkers, Chavez became the CSO's national director, a post he served in from the late 1950s to the early 1960s.

In 1962 Chavez resigned his post, after failing to convince the CSO to commit to help farmworkers organize. He and his family moved to Delano, California, where he founded the NFWA. Chavez advocated for fair wages, medical coverage, and a pension program for retired workers. By 1965 the NFWA had more than 1,200 member families. The NFWA joined with an AFL-CIO sponsored union to strike against the Delano-area table grape growers. The five-year boycott that followed drew support from millions of people. A national coalition of unions, churches, and students advanced their cause. The two unions eventually merged, becoming the United Farm Workers of America.

Over the next decades Chavez and his organization represented the rights of workers using peaceful protest and boycotts. In 1970 the California grape growers agreed to make contracts with the UFW on behalf of the fieldworkers, but later that year those same grape growers signed "sweetheart" deals with the Teamsters union in an effort to limit the UFW's power. More than 10,000 workers left the fields in response to this tactic.

Chavez called for a worldwide grape boycott, and eventually some 17 million Americans were boycotting grapes. California governor Jerry Brown signed the Agricultural Labor Relations Act into law in 1975. Chavez and the UFW had won the day, but Chavez did not cease his activities. In 1982, when the farm labor board seemed unresponsive to enforcing the laws, Chavez called for a boycott and held a 36-day Fast for Life to protest pesticide poisoning of fieldworkers and their families.

Chavez continued to work for the rights of migrant fieldworkers until he died in his sleep, on April 23, 1993, in San Luis, Arizona. More than 50,000 mourners attended his funeral. The Cesar E. Chavez Foundation was formed in his honor so others could learn from the life and work of this great Mexican American. In 1994 U.S. president Bill Clinton posthumously awarded Chavez the Presidential Medal of Freedom, the country's highest civilian honor. Chavez's motto was *"Sí se puede"* (It can be done). The life of this extraordinary man serves as a testament of what one person, with great heart and vision, can do for his fellow men and women. In 2003 renowned Chicano poet GARY SOTO published *César Chávez: A Hero for Everyone*, a biography of this important civil rights leader and labor organizer.

Bibliography

Fodell, Beverly. *Forty Acres: César Chávez and the Farm Workers.* New York: Praeger, 1971.

Goodwin, David. *Great Lives: César Chávez, Hope for the People.* New York: Fawcett, Columbine, 1991.

Levy, Jacques E., and César Chávez. *César Chávez: Autobiography of La Causa.* New York: Norton, 1975.

Matthiessen, Peter. *Sal Si Puedes: César Chávez and the New American Revolution.* New York: Random House, 1969.

Ross, Fred. *Conquering Goliath: César Chávez at the Beginning.* Keene, Calif.: United Farm Workers, 1989.

Soto, Gary. *César Chávez: A Hero for Everyone.* New York: Aladdin, 2003.

John P. Buentello

Chávez, Denise (Denise Elia Chávez)
(1948–   ) *(novelist, playwright, poet)*

Denise Elia Chávez was born in Las Cruces, New Mexico, on August 15, 1948. Chávez earned a B.A. in drama from New Mexico State University in 1971. She also was awarded an M.F.A. in drama from Trinity University in 1974 and an M.A. in creative writing from the University of New Mexico in 1982. Her papers are archived at the University of New Mexico.

Chávez has published several plays and has edited the collection, *Shattering the Myths: Plays by Hispanic Women.* Her published fiction includes two novels, FACE OF AN ANGEL (1994) and *Loving Pedro Infante* (2000), and one short story collection *The LAST OF THE MENU GIRLS* (1986). She has also had numerous stories, poetry, and plays anthologized, among them her *testimonio* "Heat and Rain." *The Last of the Menu Girls* won the Puerto del Sol Fiction Award, and *Face of An Angel* won the American Book Award in 1995.

When asked about her work, Chávez observes that her background in theater prepared her for a career in writing because of the ways that acting involves attention to gesture, color, intonation, silence, and rhythm (*Latina Self Portraits* 36). Her ability to represent intimate details constitutes one of the major successes in her writing. In her creation of Mexican-American characters she allows for multiple identities, instead of one static construction. Her complex characters are often endowed with a biting sense of humor to get them through life. She reflects that "With humor you can say some very deep things. Life has its sorrows and tragedies, but humor is something that tempers the bitterness, the hard edges of life. You keep surviving. That's the Mexican spirit" (*Latina Self Portraits* 37). Nowhere is the intermingling of representations of identity and humor more apparent than in *Face of an Angel* and *Loving Pedro Infante*.

In the latter Chávez tracks the development of local Pedro Infante Fan Club number 256, in Cabritoville, New Mexico. Pedro Infante club secretary Teresina (Tere) Ávila and her best friend, Irma (La Wirms), pay tribute to this Mexican celebrity in a desert town just outside El Paso. The career of singer-actor Pedro Infante (who died in a plane crash in 1957) provides a fantasy life through which Tere, La Wirms, and the fan club understand life, love, masculinity, femininity, and sexuality. The over-the-top romances and melodrama of the Pedro Infante movies parallel the turbulence of Tere's life as she carries on an affair with a married man and is forced to face the consequences of her actions. As a divorced, 30-something Chicana, Tere tries to discover what love means. As Chávez tells this funny tale of anguish, loss, and the recovery of self, she also

underscores the importance of Pedro Infante as a cultural icon along the U.S.-Mexico border, a kind of Mexican Elvis.

In *Face of an Angel* Chávez turns to another female narrator, Sovieda Dosamantes, to tell the story of her family in rural Agua Oscura (Dark Waters), New Mexico. Chávez uses service as a metaphor to define the relationships between people from different classes and ethnic backgrounds. Sovieda narrates stories about her family and her coworkers. Through these tales Sovieda eventually comes to understand herself as a Chicana who removes herself from hurtful or dead-end relationships. The novel ends with her as an expectant mother, in a state of grace within a community of women.

The Last of the Menu Girls is a series of interrelated vignettes that work as a short story cycle. Rocio Esquibel, who works a summer job at a hospital taking people's food orders, serves as the narrator. The story from which the title of the book is taken addresses sexuality through an odd combination of nudity and reverence. Rocio dances naked around the dry, dying body of her great-aunt Eutalia and the contrast between her young body and her aunt's (soon-to-be) corpse is striking. Other stories such as "Willow Game" address the loss of innocence, as Rocio's favorite tree is stripped bare and dies. The image of the dying tree suggests the absence of Rocio's father and perhaps, too, the lack of comfort from her mother. Ultimately Chávez's body of work touches on the problematic nature of what it means to be a Mexican-American woman living along the border. As such, her writing can be read within the context of BORDER LITERATURE and CHICANO LITERATURE.

Bibliography

Chávez, Denise. *Face of an Angel.* Farrar, Straus & Giroux, 1995.

———. *The Last of the Menu Girls.* Houston, Tex.: Arte Público Press, 1986.

———. *Loving Pedro Infante.* New York: Farrar, Straus & Giroux, 2001.

Feyder, Linda. *Shattering the Myths: Plays by Hispanic Women.* Houston, Tex.: Arte Público Press. 1992.

Horno-Delgado, Asunción, et al., eds. *Breaking Boundaries: Latina Writings and Critical Readings*. Amherst: University of Massachusetts Press, 1989.

Kevane, Briget, and Juanita Heredia. *Latina Self Portraits: Interviews with Contemporary Women Writers*. Albuquerque: University of New Mexico Press, 2000.

Mehaffy, Marilyn. "'Carrying the Message': Denise Chavez on the Politics of Chicana Becoming." *Aztlán: A Journal of Chicano Studies* 26 (2001): 127–156.

Nicole Guidotti-Hernández

Chicano literature

Chicano literature describes the writing of Mexican Americans from the 20th century to the present. People often use the word *Chicano* and *Mexican American* interchangeably, but the term *Chicano* generally refers to the ethnic pride and unique identity emerging from the civil rights movement among Mexican Americans (roughly from the 1940s to the present). The origins of Chicano literature date back to the 16th-century Spanish Conquest of Mexico and continue through the colonization of Mexico from the 16th to 19th centuries, including Mexico's independence and the later U.S. annexation of Mexican territory in 1848 under the TREATY OF GUADALUPE HIDALGO. The year 1848 is an important date because it marks the beginning of Mexican-American literature, when the Southwest region became part of the United States.

The word *Chicano* comes from *mexicano* and was first used in literature by Mario Suárez in his 1947 collection of short stories, *El hoyo* (The hole). Initially *Chicano* was meant as a pejorative word; however, Mexican Americans reclaimed the name as an assertive sign of their identity. Mexican Americans, particularly those who came of age during the civil rights movement, still use the word to signal their involvement in cultural and political activism. Because nouns agree in Spanish in gender (ending either in *o* or *a*), *Chicano* typically describes male writers or the corpus of Mexican-American literature since the 1940s, while *Chicana* refers to women writers and their writing.

The earliest form of Chicano literature consists of the 19th-century *corridos* (ballads sung in Spanish), the most popular being "The Ballad of Gregorio Cortez" from the 1850s. Nineteenth-century periodicals in the Southwest also published Mexican-American poetry and essays. The 20th century marks the emergence of such writers as JOSÉ ANTONIO VILLAREAL, JOSEPHINA NIGGLI, SABINE ULIBARRÍ, and AMÉRICO PAREDES. Niggli's *MEXICAN VILLAGE* was published in 1945, and Villareal's novel *POCHO* was published in 1959. The name *pocho* refers to an individual who has forgotten his Mexican roots and assimilated the values of a white, English-speaking establishment. Identity conflicts and assimilation problems occur as a theme in Chicano literature of the 1940s and 1950s.

Legitimization of Chicano identity through the use of Spanish and folklore drives much of the work written in the 1960s and 1970s. A clear sense of protest populates the literature of that period. Parallel to the African-American and Asian-American civil rights experiences, the Chicano movement looked to literary production as a vehicle for social protest and cultural affirmation. The revolutionary leader of the Crusade for Justice Rodolfo "Corky" Gonzales published his manifesto *Yo soy Joaquín/I AM JOAQUÍN* in 1967. The poem spread among Chicano activists and became an emblem of their struggle. It also introduced among a broad audience the concept of *AZTLÁN*, a reclaimed Chicano nation. After CESAR CHAVEZ founded the United Farm Workers (UFW) in 1965, a renaissance of Chicano letters developed. Inspired by the UFW and created to support the movement, LUIS VALDEZ's EL TEATRO CAMPESINO performed pieces highlighting poor working conditions and strike activities. Other protest theater groups established in the 1970s, such as Teatro de la Esperanza, still perform today. The 1970s also witnessed the rise of Chicana literature when the journal *El Grito*, owned by Quinto Sol Publications, edited an issue entitled *Chicanas en la literatura y el arte* (1973; Chicanas in literature and art).

Meanwhile, in the 1970s Quinto Sol established an annual prize for Chicano writers such as TOMÁS RIVERA and RUDOLFO ANAYA. Tomás Rivera's . . . Y no se lo tragó la tierra was awarded the Premio Quinto Sol, and the novel, although published first in Spanish, appeared soon after in a bilingual edition. In 1972 Rudolfo Anaya was honored with the Premio Quinto Sol for BLESS ME, ÚLTIMA (1972), a novel that became known internationally and continues to appear on high school and university reading lists. Both Rivera and Anaya's novels feature Mexican-American boys facing hostile environments along the border. Bless Me, Última is a Künstlerroman, an autobiography of an artist. Anaya narrates the story of how Antonio Márez comes of age in New Mexico. He seeks guidance in the figure of the CURANDERA (healer) Última, who teaches him about the power of nature and the ways to control it. Antonio and Última visit the realm of the supernatural, and after she dies, she continues to act as a voice of conscience. The novel has been interpreted within the context of MAGICAL REALISM, whereby the spirit realm and the material world meet. Also published in the 1970s were OSCAR ZETA ACOSTA's The AUTOBIOGRAPHY OF A BROWN BUFFALO (1972) and The Revolt of the Cockroach People (1973), in which Acosta, like Anaya and Rivera, used his own experiences for his work.

In 1973 Texas author Rolando Hinojosa Smith earned the Premio Quinto Sol for Estampas del valle y otras obras (1972; Sketches of the Valley and Other Works). Editorial Peregrinos continued to recognize distinguished writers by publishing Miguel Méndez's Peregrinos de Aztlán (1974) and Aristeo Brito's El Diablo en Texas (1974); like Hinojosa Smith and Rivera, both Méndez and Brito wrote in Spanish. Indeed, many early Chicano writers deliberately chose Spanish over English as their language of choice. ALEJANDRO MORALES, one of these Chicano writers who resisted publishing in English, found success with Caras viejas y vino nuevo (1975). In 1975 Ron Arias impressed readers with The ROAD TO TAMAZUNCHALE (1975), a novel that takes us through key events in Mexican history and inside Don Fausto's consciousness. These works portray life in the barrio, a Latino neighborhood that often intersects African-American and immigrant communities.

The tone of protest against discrimination, which characterizes these novels, continues in the 1980s; however, it becomes more nuanced, as in ARTURO ISLAS's border narrative The RAIN GOD, which appeared in 1984. Essayist RICHARD RODRIGUEZ launched a beautifully written and controversial trilogy of memoirs with Hunger of Memory: The Education of Richard Rodriguez (1982). He has since completed the trilogy with DAYS OF OBLIGATION: AN ARGUMENT WITH MY MEXICAN FATHER (1992) and BROWN: THE LAST DISCOVERY OF AMERICA (2002).

The 1970s and 1980s also gave rise to a new generation of women writers and editors who took the term Chicana as a source of pride. Margarita Cota Cárdenas founded Scorpion Press, and LORNA DEE CERVANTES, along with poets Orlando Ramírez and José Saldivar, founded Mango Publications. During this period vanguard writers such as Alma Villanueva, BERNICE ZAMORA, LUCHA CORPI, and Cervantes convinced the publishing houses to invest in Chicana writers. The 1980s, the "Decade of the Chicana," revealed a publishing frenzy with the literary output of HELENA MARÍA VIRAMONTES, SANDRA CISNEROS, CHERRÍE MORAGA, DENISE CHÁVEZ, PAT MORA, and GLORIA ANZALDÚA. Bilingual Press and Arte Público Press, for their part, advanced the critical literary production and creative writing of Chicanas. Years later the book lists of Aunt Lute Books and Third Woman Press featured Chicana authors.

In 1981, Anzaldúa and Moraga edited a critical volume of essays by women of color entitled This Bridge Called My Back. This collection, along with Anzaldúa's Borderlands/La frontera: The New Mestiza (1987), created a turning point not only in Mexican-American studies but also in American ethnic literature more broadly. In many ways Chicana writers have provided a foundation for discussions of race, language, class, and hybrid (mixed) identities that were somewhat lacking. Anzaldúa and Moraga are appreciated for their attempts to revamp feminine myths and to call attention to folkloric figures (such as La LLORONA and La MALINCHE). ANA CASTILLO continued this project with MASSACRE OF THE DREAMERS: ESSAYS ON XICANISMA (1994).

Chicano literature published in the 1990s approaches issues of gender and cultural affiliation with confidence and a sense of direction. Instead of the protest literature that characterized much of the writing of the civil rights era, "tropicalization" (hybridization of Hispanic and American culture) and technical experimentation dominate the literary scene. The decade's emerging writers are Graciela Limón, NORMA ELIA CANTÚ, and ALICIA GASPAR DE ALBA.

Contemporary Chicano writing comes in the form of fiction, poetry, and essays. It addresses themes as varied as immigration, assimilation, family life, and gay rights, but its essence has remained consistent over time—to validate the experiences of Mexican Americans.

Bibliography
Maciel, David R., Isidro D. Ortiz, and Maria Herrera-Sobeck, eds. *Chicano Renaissance: Contemporary Cultural Trends.* Tucson: University of Arizona Press, 2000.

Martín-Rodríguez, Manuel M. *Life in Search of Readers: Reading (in) Chicano/a Literature.* Albuquerque: University of New Mexico Press, 2003.

Novoa, Juan Bruce. *Retrospace: Collected Essays on Chicano Literature.* Houston, Tex.: Arte Público Press, 1990.

Rebolledo, Tey Diana. *Women Singing in the Snow: A Cultural Analysis of Chicana Literature.* Tucson: University of Arizona Press, 1995.

Imelda Martín-Junquera

Cisneros, Sandra (1954–) *(fiction writer, essayist)*

Sandra Cisneros is an important contributor to CHICANO LITERATURE. Cisneros was born in Chicago in 1954, the only girl in a family of seven children. Her Mexican father and her Mexican-American mother moved the family between Mexico and the United States a number of times, a phenomenon that drives much of her fiction. In 1976 she earned a B.A. from Loyola University in Chicago and an M.F.A. from the University of Iowa Writers' Workshop in 1978.

Cisneros was shy about sharing her writing until she recognized the significance of her heritage, thus her work focuses on issues that are related to her Mexican roots. She examines, for example, the conflict that Mexican Americans experience on the borderland between two very different cultures. She explores as well the frustration that Mexican and Mexican-American women encounter in a male-dominated culture that demands obedience from its women.

Cisneros's cultural concerns drive the plot of her first novel, *The HOUSE ON MANGO STREET* (1984), which takes place in contemporary Chicago and is told from the perspective of a first-person narrator, Esperanza Cordero. Cisneros examines the financial limitations of the Cordero family. While the Corderos have achieved the American Dream of owning a house, it is not the home of their dreams. Young Esperanza, whose name means "hope," is aware of this difference. Esperanza spends her free time in the streets of the barrio, where the children play in abandoned cars and spend what little money they have in junk stores. In addition, Cisneros explores the machismo of Mexican culture. Her fiction illustrates how women have limited choices and are often the victims of domestic abuse. Young Esperanza recognizes that she must fight her culture's sexism. At the same time, however, Cisneros reminds the reader of the importance of Esperanza's identity; an old lady, a neighbor of the Corderos, tells Esperanza, "You can't forget who you are." Through her protagonist Cisneros demonstrates that a woman (even a very young one) has the ability to empower herself.

Cisneros's collection of 22 short stories, *WOMAN HOLLERING CREEK AND OTHER STORIES* (1991), is set on the uneven cultural terrain of the Texas-Mexico border. The stories in the first section, "My Lucy Friend Who Smells Like Corn," are told from the perspective of a young narrator. While some are about the carefree life of a child, others, such as "Eleven," illustrate the pain that a child feels when she is different from her peers. In the second section, "One Holy Night," the stories take on a decidedly serious tone and feature one narrative about a girl who shames her family by getting pregnant. In section three, the story "Woman Hollering Creek," the collection's title story, is about the abusive marriage of Cleófilas. Cleófilas's escape is aided by Felice, who is like no other woman that Cleófilas has met. Here, Cisneros shows the importance of a female community, one that can help women leave their oppressive homes.

In her collection of 60 poems, *My Wicked Wicked Ways* (1987), Cisneros writes about Chicago, traveling in Europe, and guilt that surfaces from her Catholic background. *Loose Woman* (1994) contemplates love from a female perspective and the complications of being a Mexican American and a woman in search of an integrated identity.

CARAMELO (2002) is far more complex than her earlier works. It is a lengthy novel that incorporates the history of the relationship between the United States and Mexico in the early to mid-1900s. It tells the story of the Reyes family, who every summer drive from Chicago to Mexico City to visit relatives. The narrative examines four generations of the Reyes family and the hardships (racism and poverty) that they face as they attempt to assimilate into American culture. Much of the novel focuses on the relationship between Lala Reyes and her grandmother, Soledad. Lala attempts to understand her grandmother and her Mexican culture, especially after the "Awful Grandmother" dies and takes away an irretrievable part of the past.

Cisneros has published in many periodicals, including the *Americas Review, Revista Chicano-Riqueña, Village Voice, New York Times, Los Angeles Times,* and *San Antonio Express News.* Cisneros has won a number of awards for her writing, such as the Lannan Literary Award, the American Book Award, and the Before Columbus Award, as well as two fellowships from the National Endowment for the Arts and a fellowship from the MacArthur Foundation. In addition to being a writer Cisneros worked as a college recruiter and she has a great deal of experience teaching. She taught high school dropouts, and was a guest lecturer at several universities, including the University of California, Berkeley; University of California, Irvine; University of Michigan, Ann Arbor; and the University of New Mexico, Albuquerque. Currently Cisneros resides in San Antonio, Texas.

Bibliography

Cisneros, Sandra. *Caramelo.* New York: Vintage, 2002.

———. *The House on Mango Street.* New York: Vintage, 1984.

———. *Loose Woman.* New York: Knopf, 1994.

———. *My Wicked Wicked Ways.* Bloomington, Ind.: Third Woman Press, 1987.

———. *Woman Hollering Creek and Other Stories.* New York: Vintage, 1991.

González-Berry, Erlinda, and Tey Diana Rebolledo. "Growing up Chicano: Tomás Rivera and Sandra Cisneros." *Revista Chicano-Riqueña* 13 (1985): 109–120.

Newman, Maria. "Sandra Cisneros: Her New Book, Her New Look." *Hispanic* 15 (2002): 44–47.

Payant, Katherine. "Borderland Themes in Sandra Cisneros's *Woman Hollering Creek.*" In *The Immigrant Experience in North American Literature: Carving Out a Niche,* edited by Katherine B. Payant and Toby Rose, 95. Westport, Conn.: Greenwood, 1999.

Thomson, Jeff. "'What Is Called Heaven': Identity in *Woman Hollering Creek.*" *Studies in Short Fiction* 31 (1994): 415–424.

Diane Todd Bucci

code switching

Code switching is a linguistic term that means to alternate between two or more languages while speaking or writing. We can find several reasons why Latino speakers may move back and forth between Spanish and English. One is that the speaker lacks knowledge or strategies to speak exclusively in English or to speak exclusively in Spanish. Another reason is that bilingual speakers alternate between two languages either because communication takes place in a bilingual community or because certain expressions and words are better expressed in one language over the other. Code switching takes place when translation is problematic or inaccurate.

Code switching is not merely a linguistic phenomenon; it also signals a hybrid identity. The hybrid condition of Latinos results from the convergence of American English–speaking and Spanish-speaking cultures. When Latinos code switch, they may find that communication between Spanish- and English-speaking communities impedes absolute identification with one or the other culture. Consequently, the expression of cultural identity, whether in Spanish, English, or both languages, is a major concern in Latino literature and especially CHICANO LITERATURE, which is often set on the U.S.-Mexico border. Latino authors may reconcile their experience of living in a multilingual society by code switching. The switching of codes can also imply a political act because its deliberate use is meant to reaffirm a Latino identity within the United States. For any of these reasons code switching is a distinctive rhetorical device used by Latino writers, although it also appears in Asian-American and African-American texts, as well as immigrant and dialectically hybrid narratives.

In Chicano literature we find authors alternate between the words *border* or *frontier, la frontera,* the Spanish equivalent. This is an example of code switching. The *frontier* refers to the border that Mexicans cross in order to pursue the American Dream, but it also refers to the political and cultural line drawn by the United States when the TREATY OF GUADALUPE HIDALGO was signed on February 2, 1848. When the United States appropriated much of the Southwest, the Mexican people living in this region became U.S. citizens under the treaty. GLORIA ANZALDÚA, in *BORDERLANDS/LA FRONTERA: THE NEW MESTIZA* (1987), addresses this complex and fascinating history of the border moving south; she observes, as so many writers have, that Mexicans did not cross the border, but rather the border crossed them. In her groundbreaking book Anzaldúa regards the switching of codes as a new language that captures the unique identity of Chicanos. In her dedication she writes: "THIS BOOK / is dedicated *a todos mexicanos* [to all Mexicans] / on both sides of the border." Moving back and forth between English and Spanish, code switching is one of Anzaldúa's most important literary tools.

Mexican-American authors have recognized the challenge that code switching can pose to English readers. Accordingly many authors will explain through the context the meaning of a Spanish word or phrase. American-born writers and intellectuals of Hispanic ancestry may instead opt to write or speak exclusively in Spanish in order to validate their Hispanic roots; the novelists ROLANDO HINOJOSA SMITH and TOMÁS RIVERA are two examples. Alternatively, other Mexican-American authors may write in English and translate a word or an expression within the text into Spanish. SANDRA CISNEROS, for example, relies on the narrative context to explain passages from *The HOUSE ON MANGO STREET: ". . . abuelito* [grandpa] is dead. . . . *Está muerto.*" [he is dead]. Another solution authors use is to restrict code switching to expressive words—*sí* (yes) and *¡por Dios!* (God!)—familiar words—*mamá* (mom) and *hermana* (sister)—and cultural loans—*hacienda* (ranch) and *frijoles* (beans)—whose meanings become apparent in the novel. Cisneros has taken translation one step further in her epic novel, *CARAMELO,* by providing footnotes for terms such as *rebozo* (shawl).

Because they speak both English and Spanish on the island, Puerto Ricans also rely on code switching. PUERTO RICAN LITERATURE reflects the political, social, and cultural tensions that surface when one language dominates the other. In the 19th and early 20th centuries Puerto Rican authors such as Manuel Zeno Gandia and ANA ROQUÉ wrote in Spanish because Spanish was the language of colonial culture. When the island became a U.S. Commonwealth in 1898 and later when Puerto Ricans migrated to the Northeast in the 20th century, Puerto Ricans continued to write in Spanish, but they also gravitated toward English. This kind of move between languages is one concern of ESMERALDA SANTIAGO's memoir, *WHEN I WAS PUERTO*

RICAN, and a tension in Nuyorican poetry. TATO LAVIERA and VICTOR HERNÁNDEZ CRUZ are two representative Nuyorican writers who convey their hybrid situation by alternating between English and Spanish.

Code switching reflects everyday speech in many Latino communities. It has become a device that links a writer to a specific audience, whether Mexican American, Puerto Rican, Cuban American, or Dominican American. Cuban-American and Dominican-American authors express themselves in both Spanish and English, though English dominates contemporary Dominican-American literature. In DROWN, JUNOT DÍAZ not only uses Spanish words in his novel, such as *tía* for "aunt," but also incorporates slang from African-American speech. On a more dramatic level Cuban-American author GUSTAVO PÉREZ FIRMAT literally parcels his work *BILINGUAL BLUES* into sections of Spanish and English. However, a writer's desire to reach a wider audience cannot restrict him or her to the bilingual community. Editors/publishers have tackled the challenge of code switching by presenting the original and a translation of the author's work so that the text appears entirely in two languages between the same covers. For example, Evangelina Vigil Piñón translated TOMÁS RIVERA's *. . . Y no se lo tragó la tierra* as *. . . And the Earth Did Not Devour Him*; the English translation appears after the Spanish edition so that readers can move back and forth, if so desired. Readers of Latino literature can expect code switching to play a role in contemporary and future production of Hispanic-American authors. As the Hispanic population increases, we can also expect translations of English works into Spanish, as with JULIA ALVAREZ's *IN THE TIME OF THE BUTTERFLIES*.

Bibliography

Callahan, Laura. *Spanish/English Codeswitching in a Written Corpus.* Philadelphia; Pa.: John Benjamins, 2004.

Mendieta-Lombardo, Eva, and Zaida A. Cintron. "Marked and Unmarked Choices of Code Switching in Bilingual Poetry." *Hispania* 78, no. 3 (1995): 565–572.

Morales, Ed. *Living in Spanglish: The Search for Latino Identity in America.* New York: St. Martin's Press, 2002.

Valdés-Fallis, Guadalupe. "Code-switching in Bilingual Chicano Poetry." *Hispania* 59, no. 4 (1976): 877–886.

Marian Pozo

Cofer, Judith Ortiz (1952–   ) *(essayist, fiction writer, poet)*

Judith Ortiz Cofer was born in Hormingueros, Puerto Rico, in 1952. Because her father was in the U.S. Navy, she spent her childhood moving between Puerto Rico and a Puerto Rican neighborhood in Paterson, New Jersey. She was, for the most part, educated in the United States, and she completed her final two years of high school in Georgia. She earned her B.A. in English at Augusta College and her master's in English at Florida Atlantic University; in addition, she was an English Speaking Union of America Fellow in a graduate summer program at Oxford University.

Cofer began her writing career as a poet, but she now uses a variety of genres in her writing, including stories and essays. She incorporates into her work autobiographical elements as well as details of the lives of the people she has encountered. She has been influenced by canonical literature (especially the work of Virginia Woolf) and by the *cuentos* (folk and fairy tales) of her Puerto Rican culture. While she is fluent in both languages, Cofer writes in English; but because speaking Spanish is part of her identity, she often utilizes CODE SWITCHING in her writing. Like many Latino authors, Cofer feels trapped between two cultures, and she sees her writing as a means of building a bridge between those cultures, thus enabling her to claim both as her own.

Cofer's work has appeared in a number of journals and anthologies, and she has won many fellowships, grants, and awards. *Peregrina* (1985; Pilgrim woman), a collection of poetry, won the Riverstone International Chapbook competition, and the novel *The LINE OF THE SUN* (1989) was nominated for the Pulitzer Prize. In 2005 *Call Me Maria*

(2004), a novel for young adults, was one of two works to receive honorable mention for the Americas Award. Currently Cofer is a professor of English and creative writing at the University of Georgia.

SILENT DANCING: A PARTIAL REMEMBRANCE OF A PUERTO RICAN CHILDHOOD (1990), a collection of poetry, stories, and essays, was awarded the 1991 PEN/Martha Albrand Special Citation in Nonfiction as well as a Pushcart Prize. In the preface Cofer recreates in her writing her family memories and her childhood experiences as she moved back and forth between Puerto Rico and the United States. She reflects, for example, on love for her grandmother, called Mamá, and the influence of her grandmother's passion for telling tales, called "cuentos."

The LATIN DELI (1993) won the Anisfield-Wolf Book Award and was included in the Georgia Top 25 Reading List in 2005. Like her other collections, the work combines poetry, stories, and essays to portray her childhood and the colorful lives of the Puerto Rican women living in El Building in Paterson, New Jersey. The pieces convey the often painful and lonely immigrant experience of translocated Puerto Ricans who yearn for the beauty of their island homeland.

An Island Like You: Stories of the Barrio (1996) also records impressions of the migrant experience. Short stories center on the lives of teenagers who live in El Building in Paterson. Like their adult counterparts, the young characters of *An Island Like You* feel the pull between the Puerto Rican community and mainstream ways of being.

In *Woman in Front of the Sun: On Becoming a Writer* (2000), which is autobiographical, Cofer traces her development into an artist of the written word. She opens the collection by describing how her love for literature was inspired by a rebellious nun named Rosetta. In "Woman in Front of the Sun" she explains that when she writes, she attempts to create art from the ordinary events and lessons in her own life. In "In Search of My Mentors' Gardens" she identifies herself as an apprentice of Flannery O'Connor and Alice Walker.

The MEANING OF CONSUELO (2003) is a coming-of-age story about a young Puerto Rican girl growing up near San Juan in the 1950s, a period when the island felt the influence and domination of the United Sates. The novel won the 2003 Americas Award and was included in the teen age list of the New York Public Library. The work of Cofer contributes both to the tradition of PUERTO RICAN LITERATURE and to the expressions of dislocation found in SPANISH-AMERICAN CARIBBEAN LITERATURE.

Bibliography

Acosta-Belén, Edna. "A *MELUS* Interview: Judith Ortiz Cofer." *MELUS* 18, no. 2 (Fall 1993): 83–98.

Bost, Suzanne. "Transgressing Borders: Puerto Rican and Latina Mestizaje." *MELUS* 25, no. 2 (Summer 2001): 187–209.

Cofer, Judith Ortiz. *The Latin Deli.* New York: Norton, 1993.

———. *The Line of the Sun.* Athens: University of Georgia Press, 1987.

———. *Peregrina.* Golden, Colo.: Riverstone Press, 1986.

———. *Reaching for the Mainland.* Tempe, Ariz.: Bilingual Review Press, 1987.

———. *Silent Dancing: A Partial Remembrance of a Puerto Rican Childhood.* Houston, Tex.: Arte Público Press, 1990.

———. *Terms of Survival.* Houston, Tex.: Arte Público Press, 1987.

———. *Woman in Front of the Sun: On Becoming a Writer.* Athens: University of Georgia Press, 2000.

Faymonville, Carmen. "New Transnational Identities in Judith Ortiz Cofer's Autobiographical Fiction." *MELUS* 26, no. 2 (Summer 2001): 129–157.

Ocasio, Rafael. "Puerto Rican Literature in Georgia: An Interview with Judith Ortiz Cofer." *Kenyon Review* 14, no. 4 (Fall 1992): 43–51.

Diane Todd Bucci

Corpi, Lucha (1945–) *(novelist, poet)*

Lucha "Luz" Corpi was born in Veracruz, Mexico, in 1945. She came to the United States at age 19 and settled in California. She earned a B.A. from the University of California, Berkeley, and an M.A. in comparative literature from San Francisco State University, and became active in the

Oakland Chicano arts scene. From 1979 to 1980 Corpi was awarded a writing fellowship from the National Endowment of the Arts. While launching her career as a poet, Corpi also earned tenure as a teacher in the Oakland Public Schools Neighborhood Centers Program. She has published two collections of poetry, *Palabras de mediodía/Noon Words* (1980) and *Variaciones sobre una tempsted/Variations on a Storm* (1990). Her novels include the semiautobiographical *Delia's Song* (1989), *Eulogy for a Brown Angel* (1992), *Cactus Blood* (1995), *Black Widow's Wardrobe* (1999), and *Crimson Moon* (2004). *Eulogy for a Brown Angel* won the 1992 PEN Oakland Josephine Miles Award and the 1992 Multicultural Publishers Exchange Book Award. Corpi is also the editor of *Máscaras* (Masks), a collection of Latina writing, and author of a children's book, *Where Fireflies Dance/Ahí, donde bailan las luciérnagas* (1997).

Corpi has made a name for herself in detective fiction, although reviews are sometimes mixed. Her first three detective novels—*Eulogy for a Brown Angel, Cactus Blood,* and *Black Widow's Wardrobe*—center on the investigations of Gloria Damasco. Corpi's creation of a Chicana detective in a genre that tends to focus on the white, male detective is groundbreaking. Her most recent novel, *Crimson Moon,* inaugurates the Brown Angel series, with characters introduced in the Damasco books, although Damasco herself plays a tangential role.

Corpi uses these detective novels, a genre generally understood to be for escape and entertainment value, to engage in social critique and to retell Mexican-American history. Although the general struggle for civil rights underpins all of these novels, in *Eulogy* and *Cactus Blood* Corpi invokes two pivotal moments in Mexican-American history, the antiwar protest of the 1970 National Chicano Moratorium and CESAR CHAVEZ's 1973 United Farm Workers' strike and ensuing grape boycott. In *Black Widow's Wardrobe* Corpi uses her character Licia Lecuona to revive the historical figure of La MALINCHE (Hernan Cortés's interpreter during the Spanish Conquest of Mexico). Because of her alliance with the Spanish against the Aztec, La Malinche often has been portrayed as a traitor to her people (most famously by OCTAVIO PAZ). Corpi, in the book, contends that Malinche "was surely the most maligned and misunderstood woman in the history of Mexico" (85). This novel highlights the conflicting stories that have been told about her. La Malinche appears in Corpi's poetry, as well, and is called, as she was by the Spanish, Marina.

While considering the impact the Spanish Conquest has had on Mexican Americans, Corpi also considers in her fiction the civil rights movement as it operates in a militant Chicano movement and among the Zapatistas of Chiapas, Mexico. *Crimson Moon* features the investigations of Justin Escobar and Dora Saldaña who have two cases on their hands involving a missing activist and a missing woman writer. The plot involves a serial rapist and the Federal Bureau of Investigation's infiltration of Chicano activist groups in the 1970s.

Taken together, Corpi's detective novels address a corrupt legal system, the mistreatment of Vietnam veterans, pesticide contamination, sexism in the Chicano nationalist movement, and violence against women. Corpi also stresses the importance of activism for social change.

One of the most interesting aspects of the Gloria Damasco series is the idea of psychic awareness. As Corpi incorporates this attention to intuition and extrasensory perception in her novels, she challenges the notion that logic and reason—the rational mind, so to speak—are the only legitimate ways to achieve knowledge. She does not argue that psychic ability is more important than reason but insists that they are each valuable ways of knowing and can be used effectively together.

In many detective novels the crime is solved when the criminal is brought to justice through the police and court system. Corpi's novels capture the ambivalence Mexican Americans feel about the U.S. justice system, since that system often has ignored their rights or has used ethnic profiling to control them. Corpi insists that "goodness, like justice, was only a relative notion, depending on who interpreted or administered it" (*Eulogy* 61). None of the criminals in her work is ever put on trial; they are either killed or commit suicide. Still, justice is served, as the guilty parties pay the consequences for their actions.

Identity is also an important theme in Corpi's work, as demonstrated by her characters and her reference to a variety of cultural traditions. The images of La LLORONA and Madame Butterfly, for example, may appear to be an odd combination of Mexican and Chinese figures, yet somehow in *Eulogy* they make sense in an increasingly multicultural society. In *Cactus Blood* the narrative looks at the Mexican CURANDERA, the Native American shaman, and the Western physician as practitioners of equal value. In all these situations Corpi observes how people from different cultures might coexist and benefit from one another. At the same time she recognizes her own conflicted position as a Mexican-American author. In an interview about her participation in a conference of writers from the border, she observed that "for the Mexican I am too Chicana, and for the Chicano I am too Mexican. For the white, the 'gringo,' I don't even exist!" (Caribi 51). Corpi's work seeks to negotiate this uneven cultural terrain and can be read within the rich corpus of CHICANO LITERATURE.

Bibliography

Carabi, Angels. "Interview with Lucha Corpi." *Belles Lettres* 7, no. 2 (1991): 48–52.

Corpi, Lucha. *Black Widow's Wardrobe*. Houston, Tex.: Arte Público Press, 1999.

———. *Cactus Blood*. Houston, Tex.: Arte Público Press, 1995.

———. *Crimson Moon*. Houston, Tex.: Arte Público Press, 2004.

———. *Delia's Song*. Houston, Tex.: Arte Público Press, 1989.

———. *Eulogy for a Brown Angel*. Houston, Tex.: Arte Público Press, 1992.

———. *Palabras de mediodía/Noon Words*. 1980. Reprint, Houston, Tex.: Arte Público Press, 2001.

———. *Variaciones sobre una tempsted/Variations on a Storm*. Berkeley, Calif.: Third Woman Press, 1990.

———. *Where Fireflies Dance/Ahí, donde bailan las luciérnagas*. 1997. Reprint, San Francisco, Calif.: Children's Book Press, 2002.

Corpi, Lucha, ed. *Máscaras*. Berkeley, Calif.: Third Woman Press, 1997.

Dilley, Kimberly J. *Busybodies, Meddlers, and Snoops: The Female Hero in Contemporary Women's Mysteries*. Westport, Conn.: Greenwood Press, 1998.

Gosselin, Adrienne Johnson, ed. *Multicultural Detective Fiction: Murder from the "Other" Side*. New York: Garland, 1999.

McCracken, Ellen. *New Latina Narrative: The Feminine Space of Postmodern Ethnicity*. Tucson: University of Arizona Press, 1999.

Donna Bickford

Cross and a Star: Memoirs of a Jewish Girl in Chile, A **Marjorie Agosín** (1995)

Chilean-American author MARJORIE AGOSÍN first published *A Cross and a Star: Memoirs of a Jewish Girl in Chile* in Spanish as *Sagrada memoria: Reminicencias de una niña judía en Chile* in 1994. Celeste Kostopulos-Cooperman then translated the narrative to English in 1995. The idea of writing a family history grew out of an offhand suggestion from Agosíin's mother, Frida. This suggestion later became an "obsessive necessity to recreate this narrative of my parents and my ancestors" ("Journey" 421). Her mother's stories about growing up Jewish in the mostly German town of Osorno, in Chile, where she attended an Indian school after being excluded from German, Catholic, and English schools, set the memoir in motion. "It was this little story," Agosín writes, "submerged in an immensely greater and collective story, that inspired me to write about my mother" ("Journey" 423).

The memoir reveals the act of gathering anecdotes of family history. Agosín explains that "remnants, fragments, collages" are "woven together delicately with words" ("Journey" 425). At the same time the accumulation of finely grained details opens out to broader historical contexts, as in Agosín's image of a woven map, in which "This warp and woof of threads slowly managed to form the cartography of a larger story, the story of my family, my mother and her parents, but also the story of the south of Chile" ("Journey" 424). As suggested by the memoir's title, the text explores the complications of Jewish identity in a Catholic country, a position further complicated by Frida's blond hair and blue eyes. *A Cross and a Star* is thus at once a significant contribution to the documentation of Latin American Jewish life (and its various U.S. afterlives) and a piece of experimental writing that pushes at the factual and historical limits of the memoir form into the imaginary terrain of poetry.

Agosín re-creates the texture of family life and Jewish community from sketches of relatives and friends. The narrative lingers on family habits and idiosyncrasies, including Frida's father, Joseph, effectively exiled to Chile from Vienna for having fallen in love with a cabaret dancer; Uncle Mordechai, the obsessive student of the Talmud; Aunt Lucha, chronically ill and continually undergoing surgery; and Aunt Luisa, who won a beauty pageant in her youth. In addition to displaced people, objects also accumulate significance in Agosín's dense prose. The narrative pauses, for example, on the image of a family samovar, a neighbor's gold teeth, funeral parlor coffins, a Leica camera, and an eiderdown comforter.

In her introduction to *A Cross and a Star* Kostopulos-Cooperman places the text in a line of Latin American Jewish memoirs by writers such as Isaac Golemberg, Rosa Nissan, Elena Poniatowska, and Margo Glantz (whom Agosín mentions as strong influences on her text). At the same time, Kostopulos-Cooperman writes, *A Cross and a Star* features Agosín's "voice and creative imagination of poet/writer/child." This narrator, we learn, "is not always able to determine if she tells what she invents or if she invents what she tells" (xiii). The space between individual experience and family continuity is similarly complicated as Agosín moves between her own voice and that of her mother throughout the text. The author describes this movement as "a lyrical rhythm, an intimacy of two women, mother and daughter; the language is characterized as being part of a dream . . . the narrative ends with the voice of the author/daughter united with the voice of the mother" ("Journey" 428).

A Cross and a Star can be read alongside Agosín's ALWAYS FROM SOMEWHERE ELSE: A MEMOIR OF MY CHILEAN JEWISH FATHER (1998), as well as her own story, *The Alphabet in My Hands* (2000). Within a broader context Agosín's work can be read as a response to the Latin American exile experience (though the author was born in the United States) and therefore shares literary terrain with ISABEL ALLENDE and ARIEL DORFMAN.

Bibliography

Agosín, Marjorie. *A Cross and a Star: Memoirs of a Jewish Girl in Chile.* Translated by and with an introduction by Celeste Kostopulos-Cooperman. Albuquerque: University of New Mexico Press, 1995.

———. "A Journey through Imagination and Memory: My Parent and I, Between the Cross and the Star." Translated by Roberta Gordenstein. *Judaism* 51, no. 4 (Fall 2002): 419–428.

Lindstrom, Naomi. Review of *A Cross and a Star: Memoirs of a Jewish Girl in Chile. World Literature Today* 72, no. 1 (Winter 1998): 110–111.

Scott, Nina. "Marjorie Agosín as Latina Writer." In *Breaking Boundaries: Latina Writings and Critical Readings,* edited by Asunción Horno-Delgado et al., 235–249. Amherst: University of Massachusetts Press, 1989.

Alex Feerst

Cruz, Victor Hernández (1949–) *(poet, short story writer, editor)*

Victor Hernández Cruz was born on February 6, 1949, in Aguas Buenas, a mountainous region of Puerto Rico. Due to harsh financial circumstances on the island, his family moved to Spanish Harlem in New York City in 1955. Cruz finished his first compilation of poems, *Papo Got His Gun! and Other Poems* (1966), at age 17. These poems use humor, repetition, and rhythm to explore such themes as anger, city life, and death; some of the poems appear in New York's *Evergreen Review.* With his literary career developing, Cruz quit high school and cocreated the East Harlem Gut Theater, a group of Puerto Rican actors, musicians, and writers. He also became an editor for *Umbra* magazine in 1967.

After moving to California in 1968, Cruz became a public school teacher. His work experience helped him to write "Doing Poetry," a poem printed as a booklet. Cruz returned to New York in the middle of 1968 and worked on his first major collection of poems, *Snaps* (1969). *Snaps* received critical acclaim for Cruz's balanced rhythms and for his street smart ruminations on life, death, and violence. In the summer of 1969 Cruz attended the Summer Institute on Black Excellence at Cazenovia College in New York; his participation brought to light how Puerto Rican artists benefit from their Spanish, West African, and Taino (the indigenous group of Puerto Rico) heritage.

By 1973, Cruz had published *Mainland,* a volume that records impressions of the poet's move from New York to California. Like his Latino counterparts, such as MIGUEL ALGARÍN and TATO LAVIERA, Cruz combines Spanish and English diction in this collection, a technique otherwise known as CODE SWITCHING. Critics praised *Mainland,* especially for its "soul," and its innovative use of language; the title refers, of course, to the cultural and geographical space between Puerto Rico and the "mainland," the continental United States.

Cruz returned to academic life in 1972 and taught poetry at the University of California, Berkeley, and ethnic studies at San Francisco State College. The literary journals *Confrontations* (1971), *Yardbird Reader* (1972), and *Mundus Atrium* (1973) featured Cruz's poetry, along with the anthologies *The Puerto Rican Poets* (1972) and *You Better Believe It* (1973). Throughout this period of the 1970s Cruz, along with Algarín, gained recognition as a member of the NUYORICAN POETS CAFE. The Nuyorican Poets are a group of Puerto Rican writers who came of age on the mainland and who record their experiences and observations about life in Loisaida (the Lower East Side), New York City.

In 1974 Cruz was awarded a Creative Artists Program Service (CAPS) grant to support his third collection of poetry, *Tropicalization* (1976). This collection experiments with abstract language and surreal imagery to capture the New York barrio and the speaker's Puerto Rican past. *Tropicalization* moves back and forth between English and Spanish, as with the poem "Plaseres." By alternating between Spanish and English words that share sounds (*plaseres/placeres/pleasures/places*) Cruz deliberately makes both languages simultaneously familiar and foreign to readers. But Cruz's use of English and Spanish has meaning deeper than the shared sounds of words; by talking about place, being, and pleasure, Cruz is reminding audiences of his memories of Puerto Rico while living in New York. The preoccupation with his island past and his life in the Northeast is one that surfaces in most of his work.

Along with publishing *Tropicalization* in 1976, Cruz married Elisa Ivette and had a son, Vitin Ajani. Cruz became a contributing editor of *Revista Chicano-Riqueña,* and two of his poems were selected to appear on New York City buses by the Poetry in Public Places contest.

Cruz received another CAPS grant in 1978 to compose fiction and published some of this work that same year in *New World Journal* and *Invisible City.* His short stories also appeared in *Mango* (1980), a journal of Hispanic literature. At this time Cruz had his second child, Rosa. In 1982 Cruz devoted his time to *By Lingual Wholes,* a combination of poetry and prose. The collection uses humor, narration, and code switching as a form of political speech (one preoccupation is whether Puerto Rico will ever become independent of the United States). Cruz similarly blends Spanish and English diction in *Red Beans* (1991), which won the *Publishers Weekly* Ten Best Books of the Year Award. In 1997 Cruz wrote *Panoramas,* a collection of poems, essays, and stories that emphasizes the speaker's displacement and bilingualism; this work also addresses Cruz's relocation to Puerto Rico. Other collections include *Rhythm, Content and Flavor: New and Selected Poems* (1988) and *Maraca: New and Selected Poems, 1966–2000* (2001). Cruz's poetry is best read aloud, and perhaps even as song, in order to appreciate the playfulness of his language and sometimes cryptic imagination.

Bibliography
Cruz, Víctor Hernández. *By Lingual Wholes.* San Francisco, Calif.: Momo's Press, 1982.

———. *Doing Poetry*. Berkeley, Calif.: Other Ways, 1968.

———. *Mainland*. New York: Random House, 1973.

———. *Maraca: New and Selected Poems, 1966–2000*. Minneapolis: Coffee House Press, 2001.

———. *Panoramas*. Minneapolis, Minn.: Coffee House Press, 1997.

———. *Papo Got His Gun! and Other Poems*. New York: Calle Once, 1966.

———. *Red Beans: Poems*. Minneapolis, Minn.: Coffee House Press, 1991.

———. *Rhythm, Content and Flavor: New and Selected Poems*. Houston, Tex.: Arte Público Press, 1988.

———. *Snaps*. New York: Random House, 1969.

———. *Tropicalization*. New York: Reed, Cannon and Johnson, 1976.

Dick, Bruce Allen. *A Poet's Truth: Conversations with Latino/Latina Poets*. Tucson: University of Arizona Press, 2003.

Turner, Faythe E., ed. *Puerto Rican Writers at Home in the U.S.A.: An Anthology*. Seattle, Wash.: Open Hand Publishing, 1991.

Dorsía Smith Silva

Cuban-American literature

Cuban-American literature has its roots in Spanish-American culture; in addition, it owes some of its images and rhythms to West African and indigenous Taino influences. It is heterogeneous in character because Cuban-American authors come from different classes, races, and geographical experiences. Cuban-American literature began with a generation of individuals advocating Cuba's independence in the 19th century. Successive waves of authors in the 20th and 21st centuries fall into two categories. Either they are part of families who went into exile after FIDEL CASTRO's CUBAN REVOLUTION of 1959, or they are Americans of Cuban descent.

Cuban-American literature started as a literature of exile written by Cuban writers forced to flee to the island in search of political asylum from the Spanish colonial authorities. Such authors took seriously the historical factors (slavery and a sugar economy) relating to the island's turbulent political scene. During the 19th century Cubans who lived in U.S. exile include essayist and poet JOSÉ MARTÍ, poet and journalist José María Heredia, and novelist Cirilo Villaverde. These writers published their work with an overtly political agenda (and Martí was jailed for his views), and they shared values about the abolition of slavery and support for Cuban independence from Spain, achieved in 1898.

The next major group of authors fled Cuba during and after Castro's revolution in 1959 and include Heberto Padilla, Antonio Benítez Rojo, and Guillermo Cabrera Infante. These writers tend to focus on civil rights and governmental instability under Castro's regime. They write about both the hopes and disillusions of the early years of the 1959 revolution, the exodus after Castro came to power, and the experience of exile.

Writers who grew up on the island and migrated to the United States from the 1960s to the 1980s include REINALDO ARENAS, Lino Novás Calvo, Matías Montes Huidobro, and José Sánchez-Boudy. Authors such as Arenas expressed hostility toward Castro's regime. They denounce communism and what Arenas refers to as the hypocrisy of the Cuban government. Arenas also criticizes the double-speak of his fellow writers on the island. For Arenas the hypocrisy stems from the government's adoption of the platform of Martí—the equality of all citizens—yet Arenas points out that gays, artists, and intellectuals struggle with governmental persecution. In any case Cuban-American writers often are motivated by an intense nostalgia for their beautiful island and by the troubling sense of displacement in the United States. Their works, especially those of Arenas, recount the horrors of immigration, the perceived lack of truth in Castro's government record, and the challenge of acculturation in cities such as New York and Los Angeles. They are also aware that Cubans back on the island may call them *gusanos* (worms), who have abandoned their home and relatives for the capitalist and anti-Castro United States. One perspective that has become more visible as restrictions between the two countries grow is that Cubans in Cuba lament the devastating impact of the U.S. embargo and travel restrictions. Some Cuban Americans want to maintain these restrictions as a form of retaliation against Castro's legacy; others would prefer to see more trade and more freedom of movement between the countries, the island being only 90 miles from Florida. Now that Raúl Castro is president (February 2008) some freedoms seem to be increasing for Cubans; the future of U.S.-Cuba relations is a question mark, but is almost definitely going to change.

Although contemporary Cuban-American authors often are distanced from their parents' experiences on the island (because of the last 50 years of travel restrictions and the ongoing embargo), their literature touches upon many of the same ideas. Cuban-American literature expresses the challenge of living in between two worlds, Cuba and the United States. This is a more striking phenomenon when we consider that many Cubans relocated to New York, which, unlike Miami, is nothing like Cuba. Like their Cuban exile predecessors, many Cuban-Americans authors express a need to reconcile their Cuban heritage with their identity and status as exiles or immigrants in the United States. Even authors who were born in Cuba and lived there as children, such as GUSTAVO PÉREZ FIRMAT, consider themselves in exile.

The Cuban-American experience of living in between two languages and two cultures raises concerns about self-definition and allegiance. Authors question the cultural expectations that society, whether in the Northeast, Los Angeles, or Miami, imposes on the individual. It is not surprising, therefore, that autobiographical writings and fictionalized autobiography prevail in Cuban-American literature. Since the 1990s there has been a Cuban-American literary boom, especially with works that capture the experience of living simultaneously in two cultures, such as the writings of Pérez Firmat and Lourdes Gil. Meanwhile, themes about Cuba's history of poverty and repression under Fulgencio Batista's and Castro's governments and the exile experience are found in the works of Pablo Medina, VIRGIL SUÁREZ, and Pérez Firmat. These authors consider the challenge of acculturation in the United States. Medina's *Ex-*

iled Memories: A Cuban Childhood (1990) deals with the issue of a divided family and a feeling of rootlessness as a Cuban exile. Pérez Firmat's *Next Year in Cuba: A Cubano's Coming-of-Age in America* (2000) maps out the author's childhood in Cuba, adolescence in Miami, and adulthood in North Carolina; he develops this trajectory, along with the bicultural life of his children, in his poetry collection BILINGUAL BLUES (1995). Pérez Firmat's *Next Year in Cuba* closely follows the Cuban exile discourse and examines the fragmentation of the family, which he attributes to Castro's dictatorship. Medina's fictional autobiography, *The Marks of Birth* (1994), describes the impact of the revolution on one Cuban family, while Suárez's *Going Under* (1996) and memoir *Spared Angola: Memories from a Cuban-American Childhood* (1997) portray the advantages and disadvantages of his Cuban childhood and his present life in the United States.

Racism and the cultural clash between Cuban and American values drive Roberto Fernandez's *Raining Backwards* (1988) and *Holy Radishes* (1995). He satirizes a Cuban community that has been changed by the materialism and popular culture of the United States. In the same vein ELÍAS MIGUEL MUÑOZ and ACHY OBEJAS explore the impact of immigration and exile in gay communities. The search for identity and the self is also a common denominator in the poetry of Ricardo Alonso, Lourdes Casal, Octavio Armand, Ricardo Pau-Llosa, and José Kozer. Their writing explores how to negotiate two cultures and two languages.

Perhaps the best-known Cuban-American novelists are OSCAR HIJUELOS (*The MAMBO KINGS PLAY SONGS OF LOVE* [1989], *A SIMPLE HABANA MELODY: FROM WHEN THE WORLD WAS GOOD* [2002]) and CRISTINA GARCÍA (*DREAMING IN CUBAN* [1992], *The AGÜERO SISTERS* [1997], and *MONKEY HUNTING* [2003]). Hijuelos was born in New York but is preoccupied with the postrevolution politics of 1959 and the impact the U.S. embargo has on family ties, as in *EMPRESS OF THE SPLENDID SEASON* (1999). García's *Dreaming in Cuban* and *The Agüero Sisters* engage with Cuban history, mysticism, and the reconstruction of identity in New York and Miami. Taken together, Hijuelos and García collect the memories of their Cuban communities in exile to reconstruct in literary form a U.S. identity without the loss of Cuban heritage.

The heterogeneity of Cuban-American literature is not just generational; it is also linguistic and gender specific. Depending on their view of the United States and their background, Cuban-American authors will publish in English, Spanish, or both languages. Writers in exile, such as Hilda Pereira, MARIA IRENE FORNES, Montes Huidobro, and Benítez Rojo, Padilla, Kozer, and Gil, write in Spanish as a mean of preserving their Cuban cultural roots. Cuban-American literature produced in English is common with writers such as Medina, Hijuelos, García, and Suárez as they move between Spanish-speaking and English-speaking cultures.

Cuban-American women writers such as Dolores Prida, Achy Obejas, Raquel Puig Zaldívar, Ruth Behar, and Eliana Rivero address the challenge of being Cuban American as a form of minority politics. Their literature differs at times from that of their male counterparts in the expression of their most intimate emotions and their particular position as women living in often sexist and consumerist societies. Lesbian writer Obejas, for instance, brings to her writings issues of tolerance, (sexual) identity, and self-definition in such novels as *Memory Mambo* (1996). The narratives and essays of Rivero and Behar, meanwhile, speak of the alienation of women in the United States and also refer to the crucial task of identity construction. Furthermore, they celebrate their heritage and ethnicity since this provides them with a variety of perspectives to rediscover the self.

Cuban-American literature describes the problems that affect the Cuban-American community in its entirety; nevertheless, it is the individual experiences of immigrants and their children and the different levels of assimilation within the United States that shape the diversity of Cuban-American literature. The memories of a past life (whether their own or that of their relatives) on the island and the defining of the self on the mainland vary depending on generation, class, race, gender, and education. These similarities and differences shape the identities of Cuban Americans, build bridges among Cuban communities in the United States, and propel a literature that continues to establish itself as a significant contribution to American ethnic literature and the U.S. canon.

Bibliography

Alvarez-Borland, Isabel. *Cuban-American Literature of Exile: From Person to Persona.* Charlottesville: University Press of Virginia, 1998.

Kanellos, Nicolás. *Hispanic Literature of the United States: A Comprehensive Reference.* Westport, Conn.: Greenwood Press, 2003.

Luis, William. *Dance Between Two Cultures: Latino Caribbean Literature Written in the United States.* London: Vanderbilt University Press, 1997.

———. "Latin American (Hispanic Caribbean) Literature Written in the United States." In *The Cambridge History of Latin America Literature,* vol. 2: *The Twentieth Century,* edited by Roberto González Echevarría and Enrique Pupo-Walker, 526–556. Cambridge: Cambridge University Press, 1996.

Swanson, Philip. "Latino US Literature: Cuban American." In *The Companion to Latin American Studies,* edited by Philip Swanson. 138–146. London: Arnold, 2003.

Yolanda Pampin Martinez

Cuban Revolution (1959)

The Cuban Revolution has its origins in the 19th-century conflicts between the Caribbean island and Spain. After hundreds of years of colonial rule, Cubans waged ongoing warfare from 1868 to 1889 against Spanish authorities to gain their independence. Their struggle was unsuccessful, but in 1895 the poet and revolutionary JOSÉ MARTÍ led a finally successful campaign to end Spanish colonial rule. Ironically, though, as soon as the island was free from Spanish control it faced U.S. domination.

The Spanish-American War involved the United States, Spain, and Cuba, as well as other Spanish colonies. Cubans fought for independence from Spain in the 1890s and, by 1898, the United States launched an invasion of the island after the USS *Maine* exploded and sank in Havana Harbor—an event that heated tensions between Spain and the

United States. As a result of the Spanish-American War in 1898, the United States took military control of Cuba and occupied the island until 1902. In 1898, after the war, the United States envisioned economic stability for Cuba. In 1901 the United States presented the Platt Amendment to the Cuban government. This amendment stated that the United States would protect Cuba's interests, but this protection came with a price: the island's loss of political autonomy. The Platt Amendment was ratified on May 22, 1903. As long as the Platt Amendment existed, Cuba could not achieve full independence. In December 1903 the United States leased Guantánamo Bay as a military station. To this day the U.S. military base on the island remains a point of intense debate.

Cuban and U.S. relations have, however, often been amicable. In the 1920s Cuba enjoyed a period of prosperity with U.S. investment and tourism; Cuban-American author OSCAR HIJUELOS uses the 1920s and 1930s as a setting for his 2002 novel, *A SIMPLE HABANA MELODY: FROM WHEN THE WORLD WAS GOOD*, which illustrates the artistic energy, wealth, and decadence of this period. Afterward, however, the island suffered a series of coups. In 1933 Gerardo Machado assumed control of Cuba and was eventually overthrown by military leader Fulgencio Batista in the Revolt of the Sergeants. From 1933 to 1934 Ramón Grau San Martín ruled Cuba and enjoyed during his administration the abolishment of the Platt Amendment under U.S. president Franklin D. Roosevelt's Good Neighbor policy. Batista soon forced Grau's resignation, followed by a series of presidents, including Batista himself (1940–44). With the election of Carlos Prío Socarrás (Grau's candidate) in 1948, the wheels were set in motion leading up to Batista's second coup and dictatorship (1952–59).

Lawyer and political activist FIDEL CASTRO charged Batista with violating the constitution and began to wage his own campaign to rid Batista of power. July 26, 1953, marks the beginning of the Cuban Revolution. When revolutionaries launched the first surprise attack on the Moncada Barracks, his operation was discovered by Batista's men and,

though unsuccessful in action, the Twenty-sixth of July movement was successful ideologically in rallying the Cuban people against Batista's government. Among those who were arrested during the attack were Fidel Castro and his brother Raúl, now president of Cuba. While in jail, Castro wrote his famous speech "HISTORY WILL ABSOLVE ME." Bowing to the demands of the people, Batista released the Castro brothers and the other Moncada prisoners on May 15, 1955. Upon their release, they traveled to Mexico, where Castro would meet Ernesto "Che" Guevara.

A year later, on November 25, 1956, Castro and his revolutionaries left Mexico and headed for Cuba aboard the boat called *Granma* for Cuba. After landing at Las Colonadas in the Oriente Province of Cuba, they were stopped on December 5 by Batista's men at Alegría de Pío. Fidel and Raúl Castro and Guevara were among the survivors who headed up into the hills of the Sierra Maestra. This time the rebels' plan would prove successful. On July 12, 1957, the Twenty-sixth of July movement published the *Manifesto of the Sierra Maestra* calling for all Cubans to unite against the oppression of Batista. Cubans did rally against Batista, but Castro had to contend with Batista's friendship with American gangster Meyer Lansky and the support of the United States. In 1958 the United States sent military aid to Batista.

When the rebel army marched out of the Sierra Maestra and began to gain the advantage in the struggle, the United States withdrew its military support to Batista. This development resulted in Batista's departure on January 1, 1959. On January 7 Castro entered Havana and in doing so brought hope to many of the islanders. (Other, less-hopeful Cubans feared, rightly so, the nationalization of their property.) Castro reinstated Cuba's constitution, signed the Agrarian Farm Bill, and launched general elections. On May 8, 1960, diplomatic relations between Cuba and the Soviet Union were formed, and Castro referred to Cuba as a Communist country.

For nearly five decades Castro maintained a dictatorship over Cuba, though as of 2006 he ceded provisional power to his brother Raúl. In February 2008, Raúl was sworn in as the new president of Cuba. Castro's regime has succeeded in providing widespread access to education and health care on the impoverished island but at the same time has denied to Cubans important civil and political liberties.

Bibliography

Angole-Freyre, Frank. *Fulgencio Batista: From Revolutionary to Strongman.* New Brunswick, N.J.: Rutgers University Press, 2006.

Draper, Theodore. *Castro's Revolution: Myths and Realities.* New York: Frederick A. Praeger, 1962.

Farber, Samuel. *The Origins of the Cuban Revolution Reconsidered.* Chapel Hill: University of North Carolina Press, 2006.

Garcia Luis, Julio., ed. *Cuban Revolution Reader: A Documentary History of 40 Key Moments of the Cuban Revolution.* New York: Ocean Press, 2001.

Gonzales, Edward. "Castro's Revolution, Cuban Communist Appeals and the Soviet Response." *World Politics* 21, no. 1 (October 1968): 39–68.

Gott, Richard. *Cuba: A New History.* New Haven, Conn.: Yale University Press, 2004.

Guevara, Ernesto "Che". *Reminiscences of the Cuban Revolutionary War.* New York: Ocean Press, 2006.

Karol, K. S. *Guerrillas in Power: The Course of the Cuban Revolution.* New York: Hill & Wang, 1970.

Paterson, Thomas G. *Contesting Castro: The United States and the Triumph of the Cuban Revolution.* New York: Oxford University Press, 1994.

Perez-Stable, Marifeli. *The Cuban Revolution: Origins, Course and Legacy.* New York: Oxford University Press, 1999.

Skierka, Volker. *Fidel Castro: A Biography.* Malden, Mass.: Polity Press, 2004.

Suarez, Andres. "The Cuban Revolution: The Road to Power." *Latin American Research Review* 7 (Fall) 1972): 5–29.

Sweig, Julia. *Inside the Cuban Revolution: Fidel Castro and the Urban Underground.* Cambridge, Mass.: Harvard University Press, 2002.

Szulc, Tad. *Fidel: A Critical Portrait.* New York: HarperCollins, 1986.

Karen Holleran

curandera

Curandera means a "woman healer" in Spanish. The term refers to a medicine woman who restores health to her community, competing in some ways with Western medicine. One of the traditional figures of Mexican culture, the *curandera* heals people by using natural methods. She works in communion with nature, providing a holistic (physical and psychological) cure. A *curandera* experienced in assisting births is called a *partera* and is akin to a midwife. A *yerbera* is a *curandera* who knows the healing power of herbs; she may also use extracts from animals in her remedies. The *curandera* expert with massage techniques is commonly called a *sobadera*.

The *curandera* represents a syncretism, a merging of cultures in a single personality. She combines indigenous knowledge with the West African practices brought to the Americas by slaves; she also may draw on Arab influences brought through the Spaniards, as well as on Eastern shamanistic practices. The *curandera* plays a central role in the community, as a healer of bodies and souls. In her work with the soul she is like a priest; the community often supports her and pays for her cures through bartering.

Although the *curandera* is usually regarded as a religious figure, who often invokes God's aid in her cures, her practices may arouse suspicion. Not surprisingly, the distinction between *curanderas* and *brujas* (witches) is not clear cut. We see this fine line in SANDRA CISNEROS's *The HOUSE ON MANGO STREET* (1984). In this novel readers meet Elena, who reads tarot cards and is in touch with the spirit world; the narrator calls her the "witch woman" because of her treatments:

> If you got a headache, rub a cold egg across your face. Need to forget an old romance? Take a chicken's foot, tie it with red string, spin it over your head three times, then burn it. Bad spirits keeping you awake? Sleep next to a holy candle for seven days, then on the eighth day, spit (64).

Here Cisneros reinforces the idea of the *bruja* by using the appellation "witch woman." At the same time, however, Cisneros validates Elena's work as a *curandera* when the fortune she tells the protagonist is proven correct.

Undoubtedly, a *curandera* holds not only the power of healing but also the power of destruction in her ability to direct curses. Even though they normally use their knowledge to combat evil and to lift curses laid by witches, *curanderas* might sometimes make use of evil forces to punish a person or to break spells. The *curandera* is required in times of calamity, when supernatural events take place or death is around the corner. This ambiguity between healer and witch attracts many Chicana writers because, without doubt, the *curandera* is an empowered woman. The *curandera* is independent and respected by men and women equally.

Because of her power to heal, the *curandera* has been identified with aspects of the Virgin of Guadalupe; both figures heal the soul and help to mediate between God and worshippers. The Virgin of Guadalupe and the *curandera* are also connected to two emblematic Mexican figures: La MALINCHE and La LLORONA. La Malinche was Hernán Cortés's interpreter and lover; she gave birth to one of the first mestizos in Mexico. La Llorona is the weeping woman in Mexican folktales who has lost (or killed) her children. Both are powerful women who, despite their controversial backgrounds, often become heroines in CHICANO LITERATURE.

Curanderas appear throughout Hispanic-American literature. It is important to add that Caribbean writers use the word *santera* rather than *curandera* to refer to their female healers, the priestesses of the Afro-Caribbean practice of SANTERÍA. The healer Última plays a critical role in RUDOLFO ANAYA's novel *BLESS ME, ÚLTIMA* (1972).

As a *curandera*, Última harnesses the power of nature together with the wisdom of her age. We learn from her that *curanderas* are normally women of advanced years who have learned the particulars of their job from their predecessors; they acquire knowledge that allows them to combat evil in the world. Última represents the image of female empowerment in a patriarchal society. Like Anaya, ANA CASTILLO creates a *curandera* character, Doña Felicia, in *SO FAR FROM GOD* (1993). Doña Felicia practices a special skill among *curanderas*; she is a bonesetter. In *A Place Where the Sea Remembers* (1993) SANDRA BENÍTEZ creates a *curandera* character named *Remedios*, who "knows" where to wait for the body of a young boy to wash ashore. The woman healer is also the subject of Carmen Tafolla's work *Curandera* (1983) and PAT MORA's poem "Curandera." Healer figures can likewise be found in the work of CRISTINA GARCÍA.

Bibliography

Anaya, Rudolfo. *Bless Me, Última*. Berkeley, Calif.: Quinto Sol Publications, 1972.

Castillo, Ana. *Massacre of the Dreamers: Essays on Xicanisma*. New York: Penguin Books, 1995.

———. *So Far from God*. London: Women's Press, 1993.

Cisneros, Sandra. *The House on Mango Street*. Houston, Tex.: Arte Público Press, 1985.

Rebolledo, Tey Diana. *Women Singing in the Snow: A Cultural Analysis of Chicana Literature*. Tucson: University of Arizona Press, 1995.

Tafolla, Carmen. *Curandera*. N.p.: M&A Editions, 1983.

Imelda Martín-Junquera

Dangerous Border Crossers: The Artist Talks Back Guillermo Gómez-Peña (2000)

Dangerous Border Crossers features 300 glossy pages about performance artist GUILLERMO GÓMEZ-PEÑA and his multiracial troupe La Pocha Nostra. The book details the artists' thoughts about their life and work as "migrant provocateurs." Like his earlier work, *Dangerous Border Crossers* reveals Gómez-Peña's political consciousness. It expresses many of the same concerns of the previous anthologies: the environmental and economic tolls of globalization; the nuances of cultural identities; and the continuing North/South culture wars in a racist United States. But *Dangerous Border Crossers* differs from earlier publications, however, in the way Gómez-Peña emphasizes the experiences of performance artists on the road.

What happens on the road—in particular what happens before and after performance shows—is for Gómez-Peña essential to his art. Noting that most performance historians and critics neglect to consider what goes on before and after a performance piece, Gómez-Peña explains how the very process of traveling informs his work and even his identity. Several pieces recall unplanned incidents that Gómez-Peña and his troupe experienced while on the road. "Returning to America (1997)," "From Chiapas to Wales," and "The 'Psycho' in the Lobby of the Theatre" document some of these chance misencounters. These pieces demonstrate Gómez-Peña's attempts to transform actual border encounters, whether geographical or cultural, into commentary about the ongoing culture wars between white English speakers and Mexican Americans.

Readers familiar with the author will be pleasantly surprised here by the addition of a new persona to Gómez-Peña's repertoire of performance identities, namely, the "ethnocyborg." Drawing from popular culture and Mexican stereotypes, the ethnocyborgs are fictionalized characters that come to embody the ways in which popular media depict Mexicans. Figures like the "Robo-gang member" and the "Mexterminator" represent Gómez-Peña's Chicano voice in a genre (science fiction) largely devoid of racial characters. They also give Gómez-Peña a chance to critique the way in which American media "engineers" Mexicans in often unflattering images.

Dangerous Border Crossers includes interviews of Gómez-Peña and of his colleagues in the section "Conversations Across the Border Fence," which sheds light on the motivations behind earlier publications, especially *The NEW WORLD BORDER: PROPHECIES, POEMS AND LOQUERAS FOR THE END OF THE CENTURY* (1996). The most comprehensive of Gómez-Peña's anthologies, *Dangerous Border Crossers* spans the period between 1994 and 1999 and provides behind-the-scenes glimpses of his artistic practice. The self-reflective nature of Gómez-

Peña's work is a common and important quality of CHICANO LITERATURE and BORDER LITERATURE.

Bibliography

Alaimo, Stacy. "Multiculturalism and Epistemic Rupture: The Vanishing Acts of Guillermo Gómez-Peña and Alfredo Véa Jr." *MELUS* 25, no. 2 (Summer 2000): 163–185.

Fusco, Coco. "The Other History of Intercultural Performance" *The Drama Review* 38, no. 1 (Spring 1994): 143–167.

Gómez-Peña, Guillermo. *Dangerous Border Crossers: The Artist Talks Back.* New York: Routledge, 2000.

———. *Friendly Cannibals.* San Francisco, Calif.: Artspace Books, 1996.

———. *New World Border: Prophecies, Poems, & Loqueras for the End of the Century.* San Francisco, Calif.: City Lights, 1996.

———. *Warrior for Gringostroika: Essays, Performance Texts, and Poetry.* St. Paul, Minn.: Graywolf Press, 1993.

Lysa Rivera

Daughter of Fortune Isabel Allende (1999)

In 1999 Chilean-American author ISABEL ALLENDE published *Hija de la fortuna* in Spanish and its English translation, *Daughter of Fortune.* Both this novel and *Retrato en sepia (Portrait in Sepia),* also published in 1999, form part of a trilogy initiated in 1982 with *La casa de los espíritus* (*The HOUSE OF THE SPIRITS*).

Allende sets *Daughter of Fortune* in Valparaíso, Chile, and San Francisco, California, during the mid-19th century. The plot follows the mining industry in Chile as well as the gold rush of 1849 and corresponding settlement of San Francisco. Allende performs an interesting research exercise that involves a detailed re-creation of Valparaíso during the period of British investment in Chile in the 19th century. The story chronicles the lives of the adventurous Chilean men and women who decided to try their luck in San Francisco and look for a better way of life.

Daughter of Fortune tells the story of Eliza Sommers, a mestiza, the daughter of an unknown woman (presumably Indian and Spanish) and Captain John Sommers. She is left at the Sommers' doorstep when still a baby, adopted by Miss Rose Sommers, and brought up as a Sommers although not explicitly as John Sommers's daughter. Eliza's story begins when she falls in love with a clerk in the family import company, Joaquín Andieta. Joaquín is below her social station, but despite the class (and ethnic) differences, Eliza decides to follow Joaquín to San Francisco to become his wife. Things become complicated, however, when the reader learns that Eliza is pregnant and that she loses Joaquín's child during her journey to San Francisco. Her life is saved by Tao Chi'en, a "medicine man" in the service of Captain John Sommers. *Daughter of Fortune* alternates in its chapters about Eliza and those about Tao Chi'en; these plotlines come together when Eliza and Tao meet again in the American West.

Eliza's journey to San Francisco and re-encounter with Tao are turning points in her life. Although she wants to find Joaquín, her journey becomes one of introspection: What began as a search for the beloved becomes a search for the self. This search will lead to Eliza's affirmation of her identity, of her place in the world, and of her love for Tao Chi'en. Despite obstacles and the loss of her intended, Eliza achieves happiness with Tao; in fact, at the end of the novel it is not clear to readers whether Eliza finds Joaquín, but it is perfectly clear that she finds Tao. When Eliza and Tao go to see the head of what is presumably the bandit Joaquín Murieta (also spelled Murrieta), the reader never knows whether it is Eliza's Joaquín, but it is obvious that Eliza has found another companion in Tao Chi'en.

Daughter of Fortune's variety of female characters offer its audience unique examples of self-realization; these women are clearly connected to other character types in Allende's fiction. Eliza is like Alba in *The House of the Spirits* and Irene in *Of Love and Shadows* (1984) in her attempts to integrate the private and the public spheres. Allende creates other female figures who, one way or another, challenge the patriarchal system; for example, Rose Sommers seems to be a proper Victorian spinster who takes care of the family home and her relations. As the narration progresses, however, we discover that Rose is in Valparaíso with her brothers and has never married because of a past affair with a married man. Rose's indiscretion has tarnished the family name; her Victorian austerity constitutes a kind of repentance after being brought home by her brother. Even so, and despite her submissive appearance, Rose knows how to manipulate men to an advantage; she tries to teach Eliza to marry well and secure a good future, although Eliza rebels.

Another interesting character is Paulina del Valle. Paulina has been educated, like the rest of her sisters, to become the compliant, gracious, and bourgeois wife and mother. She nevertheless challenges her father's authority by eloping with her beloved, Feliciano Rodríguez de Santa Cruz, and never submits to her father's will. In choosing her spouse Paulina makes it clear that she is not going to be a self-sacrificing wife and mother. Even though she is going to have children and fulfill her obligations as a wife, she will devote her time to other matters, namely, business, for which she has "uncommon intuition" (63).

Daughter of Fortune introduces a number of marginal characters, too, who exemplify the strength, wisdom, and loyalty of women in Allende's fiction. Some examples are Mama Fresia, the indigenous servant who helps raise Eliza and introduces her to the world of natural healing, and the street-smart prostitutes with whom Eliza lives for a period of time. The novel depends on the theme of the quest and in so doing, revives other themes in Allende's writing: rebellious women, memory, destiny, and solidarity between marginalized communities. *Daughter of Fortune* relies on an omniscient narration. The author also develops parallel stories that come together, as in Allende's *Eva Luna* (1987). *Daughter of Fortune* was a *New York Times* best seller.

Bibliography

Allende, Isabel. *Daughter of Fortune.* New York: HarperCollins, 1999.

———. *The House of the Spirits.* Translated by Magda Bogin. New York: Knopf, 1985.

———. *Portrait in Sepia: A Novel.* Translated by Margaret Sayers Peden. New York: HarperCollins, 2001.

Feal, Rosemary G., and Yvette E. Miller., eds. *Isabel Allende Today: An Anthology of Essays.* Pittsburgh, Pa.: Latin American Literary Review, 2002.

Levine, Linda G. *Isabel Allende.* New York: Twayne, 2002.

Ramblado-Minero, María de la Cinta. *Isabel Allende's Writing of the Self: Trespassing the Boundaries of Fiction and Autobiography.* Lewiston, N.Y.: Edwin Mellen Press, 2003.

María de la Cinta Ramblado-Minero

Days of Obligation: An Argument with My Mexican Father Richard Rodriguez (1992)

Cultural critic RICHARD RODRIGUEZ published *Days of Obligation: An Argument with My Mexican Father* in 1992. As a followup to his 1981 memoir, *Hunger of Memory, Days of Obligation* focuses on questions of ethnicity, nationality, and faith. Rodriguez is a Mexican-American, Catholic, gay author living in California. Each of the chapters of the book is thematically distinct, treating different elements of the author's relationship to self, family and community in 10 related essays.

In "India" Rodriguez explores the concept of "indigeneity," employing viewpoints both Mexican and American and filtered through his own appearance: "I used to stare at the Indian in the mirror" (1). He contemplates the concept of "the Indian" as a stoic entity belonging exclusively to the past, waiting to be discovered by the European, and interprets this view through the eyes of La MALINCHE, Hernán Cortés's interpreter and mistress during the conquest of Mexico. In explaining the story of the Virgin of Guadalupe to an American friend, he finds himself concluding that "Catholicism has become an Indian religion. By the twenty-first century . . . Catholicism itself will have assumed the aspect of the Virgin of Guadalupe. Brown skin" (20).

This observation prepares readers for his next essay, "Late Victorians," which centers on the gay and lesbian community of San Francisco. Rodriguez alerts his audience to the contrast between the culture of death prompted by the AIDS epidemic and what Rodriguez considers to be a youthful American optimism. The chapter's title is a play on words. On one level it refers to the 19th-century architecture of the district where Rodriguez lives, an area reclaimed by members of the city's 1970s gay movement. On another level the title expresses the grief of the district's inhabitants because of AIDS-related deaths (including that of Rodriguez's friend César).

The essay "Mexico's Children" treats one of Rodriguez's common themes: the Mexican residing in the United States. Here, the essayist recognizes the tension between *living* in the United States and *being* American. This tension results from the promise "I will send for you or I will come home rich" (52) of the immigrant worker and the less promising reality of the marginalized Mexican American. Rodriguez reads this identity in terms of Mexican and Mexican-American history, family memory, and a "mother figure" who calls all her children back to her. The U.S. culture, in contrast, seems unfixed and self-recomposing, a place where "with one swipe of the rag, the past has been obliterated" (55).

Rodriguez's trip to Tijuana during Holy Week is an example of the dual nature of a border town, as depicted in "In Athens Once." Tijuana is not "Mexico" in the same way that other, perhaps more quaint or colonial cities are; Rodriguez thus expresses his detachment from the city's itinerant population.

In "The Missions" Rodriguez reflects on the 21 California mission churches established by Fray Junípero Serra in the 18th century. Rodriguez considers how "California was the northernmost extension of a mission system that connected Mexico, with Europe, with Spain, with Rome" (155). During the course of this essay Rodriguez contemplates this mission system and observes how the church functions in California's past and present, in its faith and its identity.

The most commented-upon chapter by critics is "The Head of Joaquín Murrieta," in which the author

writes "a story about a human head in a jar" (133). The subject of the essay concerns the 19th-century California bandit Joaquín Murrieta. Motivated by a letter from a priest who vehemently argued that Murrieta's (allegedly) dismembered head be given a proper burial, Rodriguez follows the trail of the Murrieta legend. He visits an Old West museum in which a jar with a human head is rumored to be that of the infamous bandit—an odd artifact from the conflict between Mexicans and Anglos.

The seventh essay, "Sand," considers the image Rodriguez has in his memory and in the present of Los Angeles. He recalls the city through his eyes as a child growing up in Sacramento and as an adult who once lived in the city. He observes its changes and remarks that for all the childlike tawdriness of the city, "The attention that L.A. lavishes on a single face [on a movie screen] is as generous a metaphor as I can find for the love of God" (154). Here Rodriguez finds the connection between Hollywood and the intense attention one would expect from the divine.

"Asians," the eighth essay, focuses on California's other major immigrant group: Asian Americans. Rodriguez considers how Asian Americans react to the issue of assimilation of U.S. culture and values in the classroom and in their communities. Viewing the tension in mainstream society into which émigrés are incorporated, he thinks about assimilation in terms of the losses involved (language, values, beliefs).

The ninth essay, "The Latin American Novel," weaves together a variety of topics: Catholicism and Protestantism (specifically evangelicals) in Latin America and the United States, Shakespeare, Irish Americans, and Rodriguez's adolescent relationship with a friend from Catholic school. As he writes of the magnetism his rebellious friend holds over him, he observes: "I will always be attracted, for the same reason I will never become. Because I am Catholic" (179). Rodriguez concludes the piece by repeating parts of a speech he delivered to Catholic priests; the speech addresses the significance of Catholicism in America.

Finally, the essay "Nothing Lasts a Hundred Years" recounts the author's youth in Sacramento.

In this work he highlights the contrast between the flux of 1950s American society and the fixed concepts suggested by his parents of the country they had left behind. Rodriguez's essay ends by circling back to the beginning of the book and his father: "In Mexico my father had the freedom of the doves. He summoned the dawn" (230).

Overall, Rodriguez can be considered a public intellectual who asks uncomfortable questions about the traditions he was raised with, the role of the family, the role of the Catholic Church, the influence of mainstream society on the immigrant, and the challenges of being gay in a patriarchal Mexican-American culture. As such, his work can be read within the context of CHICANO LITERATURE and GAY LATINO LITERATURE.

Bibliography

Rodriguez, Richard. *Days of Obligation: An Argument with My Mexican Father.* New York: Viking, 1992.
———. *Hunger of Memory: The Education of Richard Rodriguez.* Boston: D. R. Godine, 1981.
Rivera, Tomás. "Richard Rodriguez' *Hunger of Memory* as Humanistic Antithesis." *MELUS* 11, no. 4 (Winter 1984): 5–13.
Staten, Henry. "Ethnic Authenticity, Class, and Autobiography: The Case of *Hunger of Memory.*" *PMLA* 113, no. 1 (January 1998): 103–116.

Anna M. Nogar

Death and the Maiden Ariel Dorfman
(1991)

ARIEL DORFMAN was born in Argentina in 1942. A Chilean citizen, he supported president Salvador Allende and was forced into exile after general Augosto Pinochet led a successful military coup in 1973. Award-winning playwright, poet, columnist and professor, Dorfman is perhaps best known for his drama *Death and the Maiden,* written in the summer of 1990 and premiering in Santiago, Chile, on March 10, 1991. In 1994 Roman Polanski directed a film version of the play starring Sigourney Weaver, Stuart Wilson, and Ben Kingsley.

Death and the Maiden was published in 1991 and won the Olivier Award for Best Play of the London season. The title of the play alludes to Franz Schubert's quartet, a musical number that the protagonist can no longer endure to hear because of the memories that she associates with it. The play is based on actual events and tells the story of Paulina Salas, a woman trying to put her life back together after being victimized by the Pinochet regime (1973–1990). Paulina's husband, Gerardo Escobar, is a lawyer who has recently been appointed to head up the Investigating Commission that is charged with looking into disappearances and torture under the dictatorship.

In 1990, when Patricio Aylwin became president of Chile, he centered his platform on truth, justice, addressing human-rights violations, and reparations. The Aylwin government formed a truth commission, commonly known as the Rettig Commission after its chairman, charged with investigating crimes that ended in death or the presumption of death under the Pinochet dictatorship. The commission was presented as a compromise to ease public demands for justice, while trying to avoid provoking supporters of Pinochet. As is portrayed in the play, the commission was given the primary tasks of establishing as complete a picture as possible of the human-rights violations under the Pinochet regime, gathering evidence to allow for victims to be identified, recommending reparations, and recommending legal and administrative measures to prevent future repetitions of past abuses. According to a 1978 amnesty law enacted by the Pinochet regime, prior crimes could not be prosecuted. This left the commission with little power; it was to collect information and evidence on crimes, but the crimes were not to be prosecuted.

Although the play is not set in a particular country, it is clear that Dorfman intended to write about Chile. The action begins with the country in the midst of adapting to democracy and trying not to upset the delicate political and social balance. *Death and the Maiden* portrays fictional characters who must confront a violent past of secrecy and intimidation (a reference to the Pinochet regime). Gerardo, a middle-aged lawyer, has been appointed to the truth commission. His wife, Paulina, a former medical student, was a victim of torture and rape under the dictatorship. Roberto Miranda, a middle-aged doctor, becomes a hostage to Paulina, as she believes that he is one of the men responsible for her imprisonment and torture.

The author shifts the role of victim and victimizer while focusing on the dilemma of the three characters. Paulina, a former victim, becomes victimizer after kidnapping Roberto and holding him hostage until he confesses to his past crimes. Although she never saw the face of the doctor who took part in her torture, she recognizes Roberto's voice and is convinced that he is the one. What further condemns him in her mind is a copy of Schubert's *Death and the Maiden* that she finds in his car, the music her torturer played throughout her torture sessions. Gerardo is conflicted as he is first horrified by his wife's actions, and then he becomes angry when Roberto refuses to help him diffuse the situation by falsely confessing to the crime. Roberto, tied to a chair and threatened by a gun-brandishing Paulina, must decide whether to confess to gain his freedom, knowing that there is a strong possibility that Paulina will use his confession against him and kill him. As Paulina sits outside with Gerardo, recounting in detail the horrors she suffered, Roberto, tied up in the kitchen, intermixes his version of the story, showing how he also was a victim to the regime. The position of power in which he found himself caused him to succumb to base desires that went against everything that he had ever learned about goodness and decency toward women.

The open ending leaves the reader to guess what has transpired. It is unclear whether Paulina forgives Roberto after his confession or if she kills him. In the final scene, all three characters are listening to a performance of Schubert's quartet. Roberto appears in a faint phantasmagoric light, and the audience must decide whether he is real or a specter. Paulina has regained control of her life and is finally able to listen to her favorite music without being haunted by the horrors of torture and rape.

In the afterword, Dorfman recounts his return to Chile after 17 years of exile, and how he is finally able to write the play, inspired by the actual events and climate of the new democratic era. As he states, it is his hope that the play will serve as a type of catharsis, allowing the underlying deep dramas, sorrows, and hopes of the populace to be expressed, and that by revisiting the horrors and tragedies, they will never be repeated (74). *Death and the Maiden* offers what the Rettig Commission could not, the capture and trial of one of those responsible for the rape, torture, and death of thousands of Chilean citizens. The universality of the play and its themes of victimization, power, truth, justice, and vengeance address problems that can be found all over the world that are by no means limited to the experience and history of Chile.

Bibliography
Barsky, Robert F. "Outside Law in Literature: Construction and Representation in Death and the Maiden." *Substance* 26, no. 3 (1997): 66–89.
Brahm, Eric. "The Chilean Truth and Reconciliation Commission." Beyond Intractability (July 2005). Available online URL: http://www.beyondintractability.org/case_studies/Chilean_Truth_Commission.jsp?nid=5 221. Accessed October 1, 2007.
Dorfman, Ariel. *Death and the Maiden.* New York: Penguin, 1992.
Dorfman, Rodrigo. "Ariel Dorfman." Melloweb. Available online. URL: http://www.adorfman.duke.edu. Accessed October 1, 2007.
Levinson, Sanford, ed. *Torture: A Collection.* New York: Oxford University Press, 2004.
Verdugo, Patricia. *Chile, Pinochet, and the Caravan of Death.* Coral Gables, Fla.: North-South Center Press, 2001.

Khamla Dhouti

de Burgos, Julia
See BURGOS, JULIA DE.

de Hoyos, Angela
See HOYOS, ANGELA DE.

Desert Blood: The Júarez Murders Alicia Gaspar de Alba (2005)

As its subtitle suggests, *Desert Blood,* by ALICIA GASPAR DE ALBA, is a mystery novel based on a true situation involving women in Ciudad Juárez, Mexico. Published in 2005, the novel takes place in Ciudad Juárez, directly across the Rio Grande from El Paso, Texas; this region has become the site of an epidemic of violence against women since 1993. Estimates of the number of women killed since then range as high as 4,000, although many of these women's bodies have not been found. These crimes are often referred to as the "maquiladora murders" since many of the victims worked in factories located in Mexico. Workers in maquiladoras are primarily women who assemble or help to create a finished product from materials and equipment imported from the United States. Mexican manufacturers then export the completed product back to the United States. Gaspar de Alba spent four years researching these murders, which were little noted in mainstream American journalism until years after they had begun. On October 31–November 2, 2003, she organized a seminar "The *Maquiladora* Murders, or, Who Is Killing the Women of Juárez?" cosponsored by the Chicano Studies Research Center of the University of California, Los Angeles and Amnesty International.

The central character of *Desert Blood* is Ivon Villa, a Chicana graduate student, who returns home to visit her extended family in El Paso and to adopt the baby of a maquiladora worker, Cecilia, in Juárez. As she is flying to El Paso, Ivon becomes aware of the epidemic of murders of women in Juárez from an article in *Ms.* magazine and wonders why they have received so little attention in the media. Shortly after her arrival in El Paso, two events occur that make the reality of the murders central to Ivon's life. First, Cecilia and her unborn child are brutally murdered. Second, Ivon's younger sister Irene is kidnapped, and the evidence suggests a sex crime, possibly involving a serial rapist/killer. The main action of the novel involves Ivon's attempts to solve two mysteries: What happened to Cecilia and to her little sister,

and how could hundreds of murders have taken place with so little official response?

Ivon finds the answer to the second question in her pursuit of the first. She finds the underlying cause of the sexual abuse and murder of these women to be the devaluation of women in general. The kidnappers and murderers treat these women as objects to be raped and disposed of; compounding this problem, Mexican law enforcement does not regard the epidemic of primary importance. The murder victims are further devalued because they are poor women of color, often migrants from rural areas in southern Mexico. Another contributing factor to the lack of official response to the murders is male backlash against female maquiladora workers: Many men in the area, including some politicians and law enforcement officials, are threatened by female wage earners and believe that women who disrupt the traditional social order deserve whatever fate befalls them. Official corruption also facilitates the continuing bloodshed: Ivon discovers that some of the people who should be investigating the murders are in fact profiting from them. Finally, the difficulties involved in police actions that cross national boundaries play a role, as does the common attitude that the Mexican side of the border is an appropriate area for Americans to take part in activities that would be illegal in the United States.

Desert Blood demonstrates Gaspar de Alba's familiarity with Mexican and Mexican-American culture and with the El Paso–Juárez region in particular. In this regard she is an important contributor to BORDER LITERATURE, especially for her CODE SWITCHING in the novel. Her untranslated Spanish words and phrases, many of them idiomatic or folk expressions, set *Desert Blood* unmistakably in El Paso–Juárez. Gaspar de Alba also emphasizes family relationships and expectations. Ivon's mother, for example, does not accept Ivon's lesbianism and would like her daughter to lead a conventional Catholic heterosexual life. Ivon tries to reconcile life in the "Anglo" world as a graduate student with a dissertation to finish and a female lover with whom she wishes to adopt a Mexican child. *Desert Blood* won the 2005 Lambda Literary Foundation Award for the best lesbian mystery and the 2006 International Latino Book Award for the best English-language mystery.

Bibliography

Burnett, John. "Chasing the Ghouls: The Juárez Serial Murders and a Reporter Who Won't Let Go." *Columbia Journalism Review* (March–April 2004). Available online. URL: http://www.cjr.org/issues/2004/2/burnett-mexico.asp. Accessed August 4, 2006.

Gaspar de Alba, Alicia. *Desert Blood: The Juárez Murders.* Houston, Tex.: Arte Público Press, 2005.

Portillo, Lourdes, dir. *Señorita Extraviada (Missing Young Woman).* Balcony Releasing, 2003.

Salzinger, Leslie. *Genders in Production: Making Workers in Mexico's Global Factories.* Berkeley: University of California Press, 2003.

Sarah Boslaugh

Devil's Highway: A True Story, The Luis Alberto Urrea (2004)

LUIS ALBERTO URREA was born in Tijuana, Mexico, to a Mexican father and an American mother, but grew up in San Diego and Los Angeles, California. Urrea has taught writing at several U.S. colleges and is currently a professor at the University of Illinois, Chicago. *The Devil's Highway,* a Pulitzer Prize finalist, tells the true story of 26 Mexicans (from 16 to 56 years of age) who in May 2001 attempted to enter into the United States through one of deadliest regions. The Devil's Highway is in southern Arizona, where temperatures can reach 120° Fahrenheit. Only 12 of the men survived; the rest died of hyperthermia.

Urrea consulted reports from the U.S. Border Patrol, the regional Mexican consulate, and the U.S. Justice Department and conducted interviews to reconstruct the journey of the "Yuma 14," as the victims came to be known. The end result of Urrea's efforts is a critical, balanced, and powerful examination of illegal immigration and its actors (the migrants, the smugglers, the Border Patrol, and the U.S. and Mexican governments).

The Devil's Highway is divided thematically into four sections. "Cutting the Drag," the first section, opens with four disoriented men stumbling out of a mountain pass. The sun and the 110° Fahrenheit heat have turned their skin black, cracked their lips, and soaked up all of their bodily fluids so the men can no longer bleed or sweat. They oscillate between hallucinations of "God and devils" and visions of their children, wives, and tropical homeland (3).

In "Man's Sign," the second section, Urrea puts a human face on these migrants: They were farmers, ranchers, and fishermen who could not afford to buy the basics. Mister Moises offered them a ticket out of poverty; he recruited *"pollos"* (chickens), as illegal migrants are known. He collected 20,000 pesos (about $2,000, or a year's salary in Mexico) from Reymundo Barrera, his son Reymundo Jr., and four others from the same town. They had humble dreams: Reymundo wanted "to reroof his small house"; Enrique wanted to buy shoes and a school uniform for his son (51). They made a 2,000-mile trip to the U.S. border in Arizona, where Jesús (also known as Méndez), a *guía* (guide), was to take them through the desert.

In the third section, "Desolation," Urrea centers on the men's three-day walk through the Devil's Highway. Because Jesús did not know the region well, he took a wrong turn. Upon realizing that they were lost, he collected money from the migrants and promised to bring water and help. He never returned. Here, as throughout the novel, Urrea resorts to religious imagery to frame the story. He aptly titles this part "Desolation" to describe the landscape and the fate of the walkers. He writes: "In many ancient religious texts, fallen angels are bound in chains and buried beneath a desert known only as Desolation" (4). Bautista, one of the survivors, offers the following testimony: "One of the boys went crazy and started jumping up and down. He started screaming, 'Mama! Mama! I don't want to die!' He ran up to a big cactus and started smashing his face against it" (166).

In the last section, "The Aftermath," Urrea denounces the hypocrisy and apathy of both the U.S. and Mexican governments. Moreover, he scorns the governor of Veracruz who spent more than $68,000 to give the surviving migrants a hero's welcome but continues to disregard the economic conditions that feed illegal immigration. Likewise, the writer chastises the United States for not recognizing the contributions of illegal migrants. He cites a study conducted by North American Integration and Development of the University of California, Los Angeles that confirms that undocumented immigrants add "at least $300 billion per year to the U.S. gross domestic product (GDP)" (217). One of the most interesting questions that Urrea poses toward the end of his narrative is Who is ultimately responsible for the death of the "Yuma 14"? In the words of a Mexican consul it "is the politics of stupidity that rules both sides of the border" (214–215). In his concern for the rights and fates of immigrant workers, Urrea makes an important contribution to CHICANO LITERATURE and BORDER LITERATURE.

Bibliography

Heide, Markus. "Learning from Fossils: Transcultural Space in Luis Alberto Urrea's *In Search of Snow.*" In *Literature and Ethnicity in the Cultural Borderlands,* edited by Jesus Benito and Ana Marìas Manzanas, 115–125. Amsterdam, Netherlands: Rodopi, 2002.

Urrea, Luis Alberto. *Across the Wire: Life and Hard Times on the Mexican Border.* New York: Random House, 1993.

———. *By the Lake of Sleeping Children: The Secret Life of the Mexican Border.* New York and London: Anchor Books, 1996.

———. *The Fever of Being.* Albuquerque, N.Mex.: West End, 1994.

———. *Ghost Sickness.* El Paso, Tex.: Cinco Puntos Press, 1997.

———. *In Search of Snow.* New York: Harper, 1994.

———. *Nobody's Son: Notes from an American Life.* Tucson: University of Arizona Press, 1998.

———. *Six Kinds of Sky: A Collection of Short Fiction.* El Paso, Tex.: Cinco Puntos Press, 2002.

———. *Wandering Time: Western Notebooks.* Tucson: Unversity of Arizona Press, 1999.

Sonia Gonzalez

Diary of an Undocumented Immigrant
Ramón "Tianguis" Pérez (1991)

Born of Zapotec ancestry in Macuiltianguis, a village in Oaxaca, Mexico, Rámon "Tianguis" Pérez is a memoirist. He has published in Spanish two autobiographical narratives that have been translated into English: *Diary of an Undocumented Immigrant* (1991) and *Diary of a Guerrilla* (1999). Chronologically the second book takes place before the first and recounts Pérez's involvement with Florencio "Güero" Medrano, a Marxist revolutionary who risked many lives, including his own, to reclaim the rights of the indigenous of Mexico. Once embroiled in the indigenous revolt against the authorities in Oaxaca, Pérez is compelled to leave the country.

Taking place in the early 1980s, *Diary of an Undocumented Immigrant,* chronicles the dangers inherent in crossing the border and living illegally in the United States. The 237 pages are divided into 74 chapters and in four parts: "From Oaxaca to the Río Grande," "From Houston to San Antonio," "From L.A. to Oregon," and "Going Home." The episodic chapters narrate unusual or interesting experiences: crossing the border, being caught and deported, crossing again, job hunting, acquaintances, women, travel, nightlife, a heavy metal concert, migrant work, an auto accident, and so on. Pérez provides the sort of insight into the lives of undocumented immigrants available only from a firsthand account of going back and forth over the U.S.-Mexico border in the 1980s.

Pérez ostensibly has come in search of a job, yet he continually exhibits wanderlust; he becomes bored or impatient with relatively good jobs; he travels frequently, seeks amusements, and spends money unnecessarily. Saving money is not his primary goal; instead, he desires experience. He wants to prove his abilities, see something of the world, and return to his village as one who has passed the acid-test of manhood through illegal immigration. Though the average English-speaking American may not esteem a wetback (the original title in Spanish, *Diario de un mojado,* is translated literally as "Diary of a wetback"), Pérez at home could be elevated to the status of hero.

He explains that his trip out of Mexico is a common trek in the chapter entitled "Heading North":

> It didn't take a lot of thinking for me to decide to make this trip. It was a matter of following the tradition of the village. One could even say that we're a village of wetbacks. A lot of people, nearly the majority, have gone, come back, and returned to the country to the north; almost all of them have held in their fingers the famous green bills that have jokingly been called "green cards"—immigration cards—for generations. For several decades, Macuiltianguis—that's the name of my village—has been an emigrant village, and our people have spread out like roots of a tree under the earth, looking for sustenance. My people have had to emigrate to survive. First they went to Oaxaca City, then to Mexico City, and for the past thirty years up to the present, the compass has always pointed towards the United States (12).

Many men from his village make the journey, and most eventually return, so emigration is not always permanent. Despite the distance, these young migrants are still part of the village: "From the day of their departure, the whole town followed the fate of those adventurers with great interest" (13). And there is always cause for celebration when these pilgrims return: "People came home with good haircuts, good clothes, and . . . they brought dollars in their pockets. In the *cantinas* they paid for beers without worrying much about the tab. When the alcohol rose to their heads, they'd begin saying words in English. It was natural for me to want to try my luck at earning dollars" (14).

The rite of passage for Pérez, and for other immigrants, involves several steps as enumerated by anthropologists and academics. For Pérez they include answering the call to adventure, borrowing money to make the trip, following in the footsteps of men from his village, crossing the border, living by his wits, obtaining identification, finding work, adapting to customs, learning English, buying a car, having sex with a white woman, traveling, and finally returning to his village with tools, money, clothes, and language skills, to be welcomed as one who has been initiated and transformed.

At the narrative's end Pérez states he has achieved the goals that impelled him to go to the United States. Though he arrived here by crossing the Rio Grande on an inner tube, he majestically returns to Mexico aboard an airplane. Once in Mexico he is forced to pay a 70,000 peso bribe in order to keep his tools, but even though he has little money left, he will still buy drinks for those in the village cantina, where he will tell his stories and where he will be given the hero's welcome.

Bibliography
Pérez, Ramón. "Tianguis." *Diary of a Guerrilla: A True Story from an Ongoing Struggle*. Houston, Tex.: Arte Público Press, 1999.
———. *Diary of an Undocumented Immigrant*. Houston, Tex.: Arte Público Press, 1991.

Paul Guajardo

Díaz, Junot (1968–   ) (fiction writer)

Junot Díaz was born in Santo Domingo, Dominican Republic, in 1968. While still a boy, he and his family moved to the U.S. Northeast. He earned his B.A. from Rutgers University and an M.F.A. from Cornell University. The author of much short fiction, he is chiefly known for the short story collection, DROWN (1996), and *The Brief Wondrous Life of Oscar Wao* (2007). In 2008, Diaz won the Pulitzer Prize for distinguished fiction for *Oscar Wao*, which crowns the many awards he has received for his writings. He was the recipient of the John Simon Guggenheim Memorial Foundation Fellowship, the Creative Artist Fellowship from the National Endowment for the Arts, the PEN/Malumud Award (2002), and the Eugene McDermott Award from Massachusetts Institute of Technology (MIT; 1998). The *New Yorker* declared Díaz one of the Top 20 Writers of the 21st Century. He teaches at MIT.

Díaz's work reflects on issues of exile, language, the experience of growing up in the Dominican Republic, the experience of migration, and the challenge of living in a bilingual community. Often incorporating Spanish expressions and terms into his English text, Díaz envelops his readers in a sense of place and familiarity as he explores the urban communities of the U.S. Northeast and the beauty of the land of both New Jersey and the Dominican Republic. He writes about the coming-of-age of young boys struggling with absent fathers and working mothers, boys who are raised in poverty, crime, and a generational feeling of angst and frustration. Díaz frequently credits authors Toni Morrison and SANDRA CISNEROS for having influenced and challenged his own work and beliefs. He also acknowledges science fiction, comic books, and children's stories as literature that has helped him to find his voice.

In 2004 Díaz published "Homecoming, with Turtle" in the *New Yorker.* This story follows the relationship of a young Dominican man and his girlfriend as they travel to Santo Domingo. The trip is supposed to be an opportunity to repair the couple's relationship while they help dentists serve underprivileged youth in the poorest barrios of La Romona; instead it becomes the catalyst for the narrator's self-discovery as he travels through his island homeland to reconnect with a history and a people. The narrator struggles with speaking Spanish and with the fact that other Dominicans question his identity. When he returns to New Jersey without the girlfriend, he begins to recognize that in order to come to terms with who he is, he has to appreciate his heritage, his language, and his people. He does so by returning often to the Dominican Republic, immersing himself in the politics and culture, and accepting that he is who he is—both Dominican and American, but not one more than the other.

These are themes that Díaz first explored in his celebrated work *Drown*: urban life, the difficult transition from childhood to adulthood, and the struggle to keep a connection with one's motherland. Considered a novel as well as a collection of fiction owing to several interconnected stories, *Drown* was chosen as a finalist for the National Magazine Award for Fiction. The collection, Díaz explains in the *Harvard Gazette*, "'is a how-to-guide of how a boy gets to be made. I didn't like my teenage years. I felt like I was drowning.' Hence, the title" (3). As a whole, these stories focus on the experiences of young male protagonists who struggle with their identities and masculinity, both in the Dominican Republic and in their lives in the U.S. Northeast.

One of the most graphic and widely read short stories in *Drown* is "Ysrael," which focuses on the nine-year-old narrator and his brother, who visit their uncle's *campo* (humble country home or little farm) in the Dominican Republic during the summers. The narrator, along with the rest of the town, spends much time speculating about what happened to a boy named Ysrael. Readers learn that Ysrael hides behind a mask because his face was eaten off by a pig when he was a baby. The plot develops when Rafa, the narrator's brother, cruelly rips off the mask in order to get a better look at the child's terribly scarred face. In this story and others, the truth is often something ugly and better hidden than exposed. Díaz's work can be read within the context of DOMINICAN-AMERICAN LITERATURE.

Bibliography

Díaz, Junot. *The Brief Wondrous Life of Oscar Wao.* New York: Riverhead Books, 2007.

———. *Drown.* New York: Riverhead Books, 1996.

———. "Homecoming, with Turtle." *New Yorker* (June 14, 2004). Available online. URL: http://www.newyorker.com/archive/2004/06/14/040614fa_fact1. Accessed November 27, 2007.

Diógenes Céspedes, Silvio Torres-Saillant, and Junot Díaz. "Fiction Is the Poor Man's Cinema: An Interview with Junot Díaz." *Callaloo* 23, no. 3 (Summer 2000): 892–907.

Lewis, Marina. "Interview with Junot Díaz." Other Voices. Available online. URL: http://www.webdelsol.com/Other_Voices/DiazInt.htm. Accessed February 22, 2007.

Suárez, Lucía. *The Tears of Hispaniola: Haitian and Dominican Diaspora Memory.* Gainesville: University Press of Florida, 2006.

Rosa Soto

Dominican-American literature

Dominican-American literature has its roots in Spanish writing of the colonial period. Dominican letters began with Christopher Columbus's journals of the 1490s and the colonization of the island in the 16th century. One of the most famous writers of the colonial period is BARTOLOMÉ DE LAS CASAS. Dominican letters were published by church and imperial authorities with the settlement of Hispaniola in the 16th and 17th centuries. During the wars of independence in the mid-19th century (1844 and 1865), writers were posing important questions about their national identity, and they began to register more formally the multiethnic (African, Taino, and Spanish) influences of the island.

By the 1920s several Dominican writers had taken up residence in New York. They included José M. Bernard, who wrote a volume of verse entitled *Renuevos* (1907; Renewals), Fabio Fiallo, who published short stories, *Cuentos frágiles* (1908; Fragile stories); and Manuel Florentino Cestero, who published the poems collected in *El canto del cisne* (1915; The song of the swan) and the novel *El amor en Nueva York* (1920; Love in New York).

Contemporary Dominican-American literature shares similarities with themes and approaches utilized by Cuban-American, Puerto Rican, as well as African-American authors. Dominican literature written in the United States took shape in the middle of the 20th century with the contributions of Pedro Henríquez Ureña, his sister Camila Henríquez Ureña, and Francisco J. Peynado, whose cultural weekly, *Las Novedades,* opened literary doors to many Dominicans living in the United States.

During the three decades of Rafael Trujillo's ruthless regime (1930–61) and the U.S. invasion of the Dominican Republic in 1965, many Dominicans were forced to leave their country. They settled in urban communities such as Miami and New York City. New York, in particular, became a Dominican center of operations, enabling writers to publish their work. Publications of this period include Andrés Requena's novel *Cementerio sin cruces* (1951; Cemetery without crosses) and Ángel Rafael Lamarche's short fiction collection *Los cuentos que Nueva York no sabe* (1949; The stories that New York does not know).

As a result of poor economic conditions and political instability, the number of unemployed and destitute Dominican immigrants in the second half of the 20th century increased in the United States, especially during Trujillo's and Joaquín Balaguer's administrations. The U.S. occupation of the island in the 1960s added to the isolation of Dominicans. Dominican-American writers share these concerns about immigration, poverty, political tyranny, and assimilation in their work.

During the significant exodus of Dominicans in the 1980s and 1990s, Dominican-American literature became more noticeable in Hispanic communities. By this point migration was open not only to intellectuals and middle-class families but to all classes and racial mixes (black, mulatto, and white). Accordingly, Dominican-American literature addresses such topics as Trujillo's regime, the trying immigrant experience, the difficulties of adjustment within mainstream society, and the construction and negotiation of Dominican identities between two worlds. Exile and immigration for Dominican-American writers constitute a political position that prevents them from completely assimilating into U.S. culture.

One well-known literary figure who illustrates the translocation of Dominican communities to the U.S. Northeast is JUNOT DÍAZ. Díaz's, *DROWN* (1996), portrays the lives of poverty, misery, and exile of Dominicans who live either in the Dominican Republic or the United States. In the same vein Tomás Rivera Martínez's poem "From Here" and Héctor Rivera's "The Emigrants of the Century" describe the immigrant experiences with the despair and suffering deriving from exile. Other works, as in Franklin Gutiérrez's "Helen," center on topics such as the loss of identity and the role of Hispanic women within U.S. culture. Guillermo Francisco Gutiérrez's *Condado con candado* (1986; County under lock) and "Unlicensed Doctor in New York" reflect the chaos of modern civilization in New York City and offer a view of the Dominican reality of living in the city aspiring to the American Dream. Other Dominican writers who have contributed to Dominican literature in the United States are Alan Cambeira, Leandro Morales, Alexis Gómez Rosa, Carlos Rodríguez, Juan Rivero, Miriam Ventura, Tomás Modesto Galán, Teonilda Madera and RHINA ESPAILLAT.

Along with the topics of exile and migration, race becomes a major concern of Dominican-American literature. Writers such as Rolling, Sherezada "Chiqui" Vicioso, and Miguel A. Vázquez confront in their work racial issues such as the prejudice toward Hispanic Caribbean culture that exists on the mainland and the mutilating strategies of the self through the whitening of skin color.

Dominican poetry is best represented by figures such as Vicioso and JULIA ALVAREZ, who offer a female interpretation of the immigrant experience. Vicioso's poem "Perspectives," for instance, has a tone of loneliness and tragedy as a result of the impossibility of returning to a Dominican past. Alvarez's poetry collections *Homecoming* (1984), *The Other Side/El otro lado* (1995), and *Homecoming: New and Collected Poems* (1996) combine narrative with lyrical verse as they explore the poetic voice's search for self-identity as a woman confronting solitude, sexual desire, and the passing of time. Alvarez's fiction also focuses on themes of exile during Trujillo's dictatorship and from family and childhood memories, putting special emphasis on the negotiation between Dominican heritage and American life. Her *HOW THE GARCÍA GIRLS LOST THEIR ACCENTS* (1991) recalls the experiences of four sisters who, fleeing Trujillo's regime to the United States, struggle with defining their identities as Americans and Dominicans. *How the García Girls Lost Their Accents* is followed by its sequel *¡YO!* (1996), which describes the García family from multiple perspectives; the text focuses on the development of Yolanda García as a student and a struggling writer. Alvarez's two historically based novels, *IN THE TIME OF THE BUTTERFLIES* (1994) and *IN THE NAME OF SALOMÉ* (2000), also depict Dominican life during Trujillo's regime. The novels bring women into the national history of the island as potential instruments for the construction of democracy. They build upon the idea that a people united by the desire for democracy cannot be defeated.

New 21st century writers such as LOIDA MARITZA PÉREZ, Angie Cruz, and Nelly Rosario follow Alvarez's thematic threads. Although, like Alvarez, they write in English, their works continue to promote Dominican-American literature in the United States by focusing on the experience of adaptation of Dominican families. Pérez's *GEOGRAPHIES OF HOME,* (1999), Cruz's *Soledad* (2001), and Rosario's *Song of the Water Saints* (2002) center on the racial and cultural construction of female identity in the United States.

Dominican-American authors may choose to write in Spanish as a way of preserving cultural inheritance; however, this choice is problematic since it limits their number of readers. It was not until 1945, for instance, that Pedro Henríquez Ureña's 1940–41 Charles Elliot North Lectures entered the U.S. market in translation under the title *Literary Currents of Hispanic America*. With the English translation of Dominican works written in Spanish, we can see a cultural bridge between the literature by Dominicans from the island with the literature produced by Dominican children of immigrants born or raised in the United States. Translated works that have entered the U.S. market are *The Cross and the Sword* (1954), an English version of the 1882 novel *Enriquillo* by Dominican writer Manuel de Jesús Galván; Pedro Mir published in 1993 a bilingual collection of verse entitled *Countersong to Walt Whitman and Other Poems*; a bilingual edition of the epic poem *Yani Tierra* was published by Aída Cartagena Portalatín; and more recently, Viriato Sención's work that deals with the Dominican Republic's social and political realities, especially referring to the Trujillo and Balaguer governments, has appeared. The publication of *They Forged the Signature of God* in 1995, for example, corresponds to the Spanish version that appeared in Santo Domingo in 1992 under the title *Los que falsificaron la firma de Dios*.

The translation into English of important Dominican works is mainly due to intellectuals' interest in disseminating knowledge about the Dominican experience. The most important contributions have been made by Daisy Cocco de Filippis. De Filippis has compiled anthologies concerning gender issues within Dominican literary history as presented in the writings of Dominican women from colonial times to the present. She has coedited two bilingual collections of the writings of Dominicans in the United States, *Poemas del exilio y de otras inqui-etudes/Poems of Exile and Other Concerns: A Bilingual Selection of the Poetry Written by Dominicans in the United States* (1988) and *Stories of Washington Heights and Other Corners of the World* (1994), as well as a compilation of poetry, short fiction, and essays written by Dominican and other Latina women, *Tertuliando/Hanging Out* (1997).

As the second-largest Hispanic group in New York, and with strong cultural roots, Dominicans emphasize their contributions to Latino culture in the United States by expressing themselves mainly in Spanish. Dominican-American literature is characterized by the same literary motifs as are found in CUBAN-AMERICAN LITERATURE and PUERTO RICAN LITERATURE. Dominican-American writers call into question issues such as heritage, generation, migration, displacement, and dislocation. Their work analyzes immigrant and exile experiences of belonging to two different cultures, the Spanish-speaking Caribbean and the United States.

Bibliography

Luis, William. *Dance Between Two Cultures: Latino Caribbean Literature Written in the United States.* London: Vanderbilt University Press, 1997.

Sørensen, Ninna Nyberg. "Narrating Identity across Dominican Worlds." In *Transnationalism from Below,* edited by Michael P. Smith and Luis E. Guarnizo, 241–269. New Brunswick, N.J.: Transaction Publishers, 1998.

Torres-Saillant, Silvio, and Ramona Hernández. *The Dominican Americans.* Westport, Conn.: Greenwood Press, 1998.

Yolanda P. Martinez

Dorfman, Ariel (Vladimiro Ariel Dorfman)
(1942–) *(essayist, playwright, poet, novelist)*

Ariel Dorfman writes in both English and Spanish. He was born Vladimiro Ariel Dorfman, the son of Adolfo Dorfman and Fanny Zelicovich Vaisman. His parents were of Russian-Jewish descent, living in Buenos Aires, Argentina, when their son was born. His family fled Argentina for the United States following a military coup that brought Juan Perón to power. Dorfman's father, a history professor and ardent Marxist, found a job as an economist with the United Nations. The family remained in New York for 10 years, until Senator Joseph McCarthy's anticommunist hearings forced the organization to transfer Adolfo Dorfman to its Santiago, Chile, office. Although Dorfman lived for many years as a child and adult in the United States and Europe, he considers himself Chilean. While studying at the Universidad de Chile, Dorfman developed an active interest in the economic and social circumstances of his Chile and joined the first (unsuccessful) presidential campaign of Unidad Popular candidate Salvador Allende. He fell in love with a fellow student and campaign volunteer, Angélica, and the couple married in 1966. Thereafter he supported his growing family—a son Rodrigo was born in 1967—and his graduate studies by teaching English language and literature in a variety of settings. From 1965 to 1973 Dorfman also took a job as professor at the Universidad de Chile, working in the areas of Spanish, Spanish-American literature, and journalism. He continued to be politically and socially active during these years, and the convictions that he developed figure prominently in his writing. During this time he wrote the first published essays of his career (though he had long privately written fiction and poetry in English): "*Men of Maize*: Myth as Time and Language" (1967) and "Borges and American Violence" (1968). He also wrote a series of essays on Harold Pinter's plays that would later be anthologized in *The Absurd Between Four Walls.*

Following Allende's victory in the 1970 presidential election, Dorfman accepted a post as cultural and media adviser in the new socialist administration. This was a prolific period, and his writing encompassed a wide variety of forms—essays, novels, screenplays, slogans, and commercials—much of it dedicated to the sweeping reforms under way. During this time he collaborated with sociologist Armand Mattelart to pen the book that first brought him international recognition and with which he was most closely associated for years. This was *Para leer al pato*

Donald (1971), later translated as *How to Read Donald Duck,* a political critique of the imperialist underpinnings of American popular culture icons such as the Disney character. Dorfman has suggested, in *Heading South, Looking North,* that this work was the first that really allowed him to be identified as a Chilean writer (251), an ironic proposition considering the book's origins in his childhood obsessions with U.S. culture. A military coup on September 11, 1973, toppled Allendes's struggling socialist government just as Dorfman's first novel, *Moros en la costa (Hard Rain)* appeared in print. The bloody overthrow brought with it a violent purge of left-wing elements in the country. Facing imminent arrest and the possibility of imprisonment without trial, even torture or disappearance and death, Dorfman fled Chile in 1974. He spent a year at the Sorbonne in Paris and then served as the head of scientific research at the University of Amsterdam, from 1976 to 1980.

Dorfman continued to write during these difficult days, producing essays, short stories, poetry, and long fiction including *Ensayos quemados en Chile* (Essays burned in Chile) and *Superman y sus amigos del alma* (Superman and his soul mates), written with Manuel Jofre, in 1974; *Cría ojos* (Raising eyes) and *Pruebas al canto* (Trials for song) in 1979; and *Viudas (Widows)* and *La última canción de Manuel Sendero (The Last Song of Manuel Sendero)* in 1981. Many of these exhibited the same preoccupations that had occupied the author during his fervent political years in Chile—class inequality and racial injustice—with the added poignancy of his own experience of exile. In 1983 Dorfman produced a collection of essays, *The Empire's Old Clothes,* dedicated to analyzing "the major cultural myths of our time" (ix) as they appeared in popular Western fiction, especially comic books, magazines, movies, and television. This was a continuation and expansion of the project that he had begun with *Donald Duck,* and Dorfman's attention in these new essays focused on exploring the underlying ideologies and values that have shaped literature and entertainment in the Americas. He followed

this with the 1984 collection *Hacia la liberación del lector americano* (Toward the liberation of the American reader).

Thereafter Dorfman relocated to the United States with his family for a visiting professorship at the University of Maryland; in 1985 he joined the faculty of Duke University. He continued to be a prolific essayist and became a frequent contributor of interviews, editorials, and topical essays to major newspapers and magazines. In addition, he produced a volume of poetry, *Last Waltz in Santiago* (1988), and several plays, including an adaptation of his novel *Widows* that was cowritten with Tony Kushner. Among these is Dorfman's best-known English-language work, *DEATH AND THE MAIDEN* (1991). Written shortly after Pinochet left office, during investigations of human rights abuses that characterized Chile's return to democracy, the play imagines a confrontation between Paulina Salas, who suffered torture at the hands of an authoritarian government, and Roberto Miranda, a doctor who she believes was a participant in her interrogation. Her husband, Gerardo Escobar, a lawyer appointed to the commission and charged with investigating reports of torture and execution, must negotiate between his wife's need to exorcise her own demons, her captive's protestations of his own innocence, and his own desire to handle the matter through appropriate channels. The narrative never clearly establishes Roberto's guilt but rather emphasizes life-changing effects of torture on both the victim and the perpetrator. The play won a *Time Out* award and an Olivier Award and had successful runs in both New York and London.

The end of the dictatorship permitted Dorfman and his family to return to Chile, and he would thereafter divide his time between Santiago and Durham, North Carolina. He continued to contribute to U.S. publications and to write in English as well as Spanish. His 1999 memoir, *Heading South, Looking North: A Bilingual Journey,* explores the author's complex relationship with both the United States and Latin America, using his development as a bilingual writer as a means of exploring his ongoing experience with exile.

Many of his early essays—especially his literary and cultural criticism of imperialism—have now been translated and anthologized, many in the collection *Some Write to the Future* (1991). He has collaborated with his sons on various projects, including documentary film and stage plays. The play *Picasso's Closet,* which had its world premiere in 2006, and the novel *Burning City* (2003), cowritten with his son Joaquín Dorfman, take up issues of human resistance to oppression and fascism. As a writer, literary critic, and social commentator, Dorfman has grappled with issues of language, identity, and equality. His preoccupation with social justice and advocacy for more just and economically equitable relations within society dominate many of his endeavors. He manifests a cultural ambidexterity, an ability to move fluidly between the cultural and political extremes of the United States and Latin America and between English and Spanish. For its interest in Latin American history, politics, and the self, Dorfman's work can be read alongside that of Isabel Allende and Marjorie Agosín.

Bibliography

Adams, Patrick. "Deadly Politics." *Duke Magazine* 91, no. 5 (September–October 2005): Ariel Dorfman Web site. Available online. URL: http://www.adorfman.duke.edu/.

Doloughan, Fiona J. "Translating the Self: Ariel Dorfman's Bilingual Journey." *Language and Intercultural Communication* 2, no. 2 (2002): 147–152.

Dorfman, Ariel. *Blake's Therapy.* New York: Seven Stories Press, 2002.

———. *Death and the Maiden.* New York: Penguin, 1992.

———. *The Empire's Old Clothes.* New York: Pantheon, 1983.

———. *Exorcising Terror: The Incredible On-going Trial of General Augusto Pinochet.* New York: Seven Stories Press, 2002.

———. *Hard Rain.* Translated by George Shivers. London: Readers International, 1990.

———. *Heading South, Looking North: A Bilingual Journey.* New York: Farrar, Straus & Giroux, 1999.

———. *In Case of Fire in a Foreign Land.* Durham, N.C.: Duke University Press, 1999.

———. *Konfidenz.* New York: Farrar, Straus & Giroux, 1995.

———. *The Last Song of Manuel Sendero.* Translated by George Shivers. New York: Viking, 1987.

———. *Last Waltz in Santiago.* New York: Viking-Penguin, 1988.

———. *Missing.* London: Amnesty International, 1982.

———. *My House Is on Fire.* New York: Viking-Penguin, 1991.

———. *The Nanny and the Iceberg.* New York: Farrar, Straus & Giroux, 1999.

———. *The Rabbit's Rebellion.* Calgary, Canada: Transworld Distribution, 2003.

———. *The Resistance Trilogy.* London: Nick Hern Books, 1997.

——— *Some Write to the Future.* Translated by George Shivers. Durham, N.C.: Duke University Press, 1991.

Dorfman, Ariel, and Joaquin Dorfman. *Burning City.* New York: Random House Children's Books, 2005.

Dorfman, Ariel, and Tony Kushner. *Widows.* New York: Pantheon, 1983.

Dorfman, Ariel, and Armand Mattelart. *How to Read Donald Duck.* London: International General, 1975.

McClennan, Sophia A. "Ariel Dorfman's Literary World." *World Literature Today* 78, nos. 3–4 (September–December 2004): 64–67.

Carolyn Roark

Down These Mean Streets Piri Thomas (1967)

In *Down These Mean Streets,* Piri Thomas provides an autobiographical account of his life from boyhood to young adulthood. From the beginning of the text the formative events of his life are defined by race. His father is a dark-skinned Puerto Rican, and his mother, a light-skinned Cuban. Although his younger siblings, two brothers and a sister, are blond and blue eyed like their mother, Piri is brown skinned and has African features and kinky hair like their father. So, the book is not just about a Puerto Rican growing up in Spanish Harlem and learning to deal with the ambiguities of not being clearly white in a racially divided society; it also about how Piri, as a black Puerto Rican, ultimately experiences an acute sense of alienation from his own family. In his case there is little ambiguity about whether he is more white or black, and yet his appearance does not make him an African American culturally, socially, or psychologically.

Down These Mean Streets is a coming-of-age story about one young man's experiences in Harlem, the suburbs of New York, the South, and prison. While they are in some ways atypical for one individual, they are nevertheless representative of the connections between poverty and race in mid-20th-century America. For, in Thomas's experience, class stratification and racial segregation are related. Identifying Spanish Harlem as one's home is tantamount to describing oneself as both poor and Puerto Rican. Thomas's father eventually moves the family from Spanish Harlem into a predominantly Italian neighborhood and then to a Long Island suburb because he is trying to escape somehow both poverty and the racial issues that threaten his own family as surely as they do the nation.

Down These Mean Streets consists of 35 chapters divided into sections arranged roughly by geography and chronology: The narrator tells us about his life in "Harlem" in "Suburbia," "Down South," in "Prison" and in "New York Town." These sections remind the reader of the differences between living in the Northeast and living in the South (where Thomas works as a merchant seaman so that he can discover what it's really like to be black in America).

The final chapter of the work also includes an author's afterword. We find just enough symmetry in the book's structure to suggest authorial control over the materials and just enough variation to emphasize the contours of Thomas's formative experiences. Thomas's narrative presents incidents that are inherently interesting, and the level of interest is enhanced by his deft shifts of tone between dark comedy and deep pathos, between streetwise insolence and poignant sentimentality, and between knowing irony and welling bitterness. As a reviewer for the *New York Times Book Review* has pointed out, the book is also a "linguistic event," a dexterous blending of Spanish expressions, street slang, pop-cultural references, eccentric figures of speech, and several levels of word play.

Nevertheless, the first four sections of the book may stay with the reader longer than the last four. Quite naturally, as he ages, Thomas becomes more consumed by and more analytical about the issues defining his identity and circumstances, and there is less sustained immediacy and more rhetoric in the telling of his story. The book opens with Thomas's decision to run away from home to punish his father with worry after his father has arbitrarily punished him. The father-son relationship is vexed, with ups and downs; after he runs away, Thomas enjoys his father's gift of a new pair of skates. In another episode the family moves to a Long Island suburb; Thomas begins to adjust to his white schoolmates when a painful incident forces him to recognize how little they have actually accepted him. Again the ironies on which the incident turns keep Thomas and the reader off balance, and yet it is surprising to the reader when Thomas savagely rejects the friendship of a white boy who seems genuinely to want to be his friend. Despite the sympathy for Thomas that the first-person narrative generates, the author regularly reminds the reader that there is a profound difference between being given an intimate glimpse of such a life and having lived it.

Down These Mean Streets can be read along with such urban coming-of-age narratives as Es-MERALDA SANTIAGO's *WHEN I WAS PUERTO RICAN* and JUNOT DÍAZ's *DROWN*.

Bibliography

Gonzalez, David. "After Loneliness of Prison, Poet of the Streets Finds an Embracing Audience." *New York Times,* June 22, 1996, p. 23.

Lane, James B. "Beating the Barrio: Piri Thomas and *Down These Mean Streets*." *English Journal* 61 (1972): 814–823.

Luis, William. "Black Latinos Speak: The Politics of Race in Piri Thomas's *Down These Mean Streets*."

Indiana Journal of Hispanic Literatures 12 (Spring 1998): 27–49.

Rodriguez, Joe E. "The Sense of *Mestizaje* in Two Latino Novels." *Revista Chicano-Riqueña* 12 (Spring 1984): 57–63.

Martin Kich

Dreaming in Cuban Cristina García (1992)

Cristina García published her first novel, *Dreaming in Cuban*, in 1992. Set in Cuba, New York, and briefly in Miami, *Dreaming in Cuban* traces the lives of three generations of the del Pino and del Puente families as they are affected by political circumstances in Cuba and the United States. Through the grandmother, Celia, her daughters, Lourdes and Felicia, and grandchildren, Pilar, Ivan, and the twins, Milagro and Luz, the novel provides a complex perspective on Cuban politics and cultural identity in the last few decades of the 20th century.

Celia, the grandmother, embraces wholeheartedly the ideals of the Communist revolution, serving as a community judge and scouting the seashore by her home for a possible incursion by the United States. Living by herself, Celia remembers her past in letters to her Spanish lover, Gustavo, and talks telepathically with her granddaughter, Pilar, who lives in New York City. Celia recalls her youth before the CUBAN REVOLUTION. Celia is intimately associated with the sea: The color blue is used to describe her, and it is the color Pilar uses to paint her portrait.

Celia's daughters, Lourdes and Felicia, go their separate ways. Lourdes moves to New York with her husband after she is raped by members of the revolutionary army while she is pregnant with her second child, a son whom she subsequently loses. As a result Lourdes absolutely rejects communism, becoming, rather, a United States patriot. Lourdes waves the American flag, joins the volunteer police force in Brooklyn, and celebrates U.S. capitalism. She maintains a spiritual connection with her father, who has passed away. She enjoys raising her daughter, Pilar.

Felicia also rejects communism, but unlike Lourdes, she stays on the island of Cuba and, after burning her husband's face with hot oil, is forced to train with the revolutionary forces in the mountains. In a violent refutation of communism, Felicia, a hairdresser, burns the hair of one of her clients with acid because she thinks she is a spy. In fact, Felicia's character is associated with burning: Her second husband dies in a grease fire, and she pushes her third husband from a rollercoaster to burn to death on the high voltage power lines below. After this murder Felicia is inducted officially as a *santera* but subsequently becomes ill and dies within the year. Felicia's twin daughters reject their mother and for a time are reunited with their father. Felicia's son, Ivanito, finally joins Pilar as the new forward-looking generation of Cuban Americans.

Pilar is perhaps the most important character of the novel because she unites the family. A feisty, independent adolescent at the beginning of the novel, Pilar attends art school in New York City, much to Lourdes's dismay. Her explosive relationship with her mother culminates in a painting her mother has commissioned for the bakery to mark the grand opening of the second store and the "200th Birthday of America" (143). She offers a punk rendition of the Statue of Liberty, complete with a safety pin through the nostril, an irreverent fluorescent blue background marked by black, barbed-wire-like stick figures, and topped off by the slogan "I'm a mess" at the bottom of the painting. Pilar challenges her mother's patriotic ideology as well as the personal respect between them. Lourdes's surprising and dramatic defense of her daughter's painting marks a turning point in their relationship, one that leads to Pilar's maturity.

Pilar has always longed to return to Cuba. After seeing her father with a lover in a department store when she is 13 years old, Pilar runs away to her family in Miami in the hopes of traveling farther down to Cuba to visit her grandmother, whom she has not seen since she was very little. When Pilar and Lourdes finally return to Cuba after the death of Felicia, Pilar, now 21, paints portraits of her grandmother in blue as a flamenco dancer clad in a red dress. In Cuba Pilar imagines her grandmother against a background that resembles her painting of the Statue of

Liberty: "I have this image of Abuela Celia underwater, standing on a reef with tiny chrome fish darting by her face like flashes of light" (220). With this contrast García questions the two political ideologies, capitalist and communist. Liberty and Celia serve as symbols for their respective nations.

Most significantly, Pilar becomes the voice of the family, a role that is confirmed in the final page of the novel, in which Celia declares that Pilar will now "remember everything" (245). The bridge between grandmother and granddaughter, suggested in the last name del Puente (of the bridge), is emphasized by the artistic abilities of these two women, Celia's music and Pilar's art and bass playing. Pilar seeks the truth in events, in the family story, and in the political situations. In Cuba she visits Felicia's best friend to understand better her aunt's life and death. Ivanito also possesses the gift of language; his penchant for dancing and for learning languages links him with Pilar as the future generation with communicative talents. Celia, Pilar, and Ivanito contrast starkly with the other characters who are constantly misinterpreting, misunderstanding, or ignoring one another's attempts to communicate.

The parallels between the characters' lives in Cuba and the United States are numerous and complex: Pilar, like her mother in Cuba, is sexually exploited by kids in Central Park. Rufino speaks to his daughter, Lourdes, after he dies, while Celia and Pilar speak to each other in their dreams; Felicia and Lourdes both adopt extreme reactions toward the political situations in their respective environments. By highlighting the similarities in circumstances, García underscores the circularity of time, the repetitions of characters and events within families. Like the ocean waves, the scenes circle around and repeat themselves. It is the role of the new generation to use their knowledge of the past to move forward. For its characters and themes the novel can be read within the context of CUBAN-AMERICAN LITERATURE and SPANISH-AMERICAN CARIBBEAN LITERATURE.

Bibliography

Davis, Rocío G. "Back to the Future: Mothers, Languages, and Homes in Cristina García's *Dreaming in Cuban*." *World Literature Today* 74, no. 1 (2000): 60–68.

García, Cristina. *Dreaming in Cuban.* New York: Ballantine Books, 1992.

López, Iraida H. "Cristina Garcia's *Dreaming in Cuban*: The Contested Domains of Politics, Family, and History." In *U.S. Latino Literature: A Critical Guide for Students and Teachers,* edited by Harold Augenbraum and Margarite Fernández Olmos, 153–162. Westport, Conn.: Greenwood Press, 2000.

O'Reilly Herrera, Andrea. "Cristina García, *Dreaming in Cuban*." In *Reading U.S. Latina Writers: Remapping American Literature,* edited by Alvina A. Quintana, 91–102. New York: Palgrave MacMillan, 2003.

Amanda Holmes

Drown Junot Díaz (1996)

Dominican-American writer JUNOT DÍAZ made his literary debut with *Drown,* which takes place in the barrios of the Dominican Republic and in the urban communities of New Jersey. Read as both a collection of short stories and a novel, *Drown* consists of 10 tales about brothers Yunior and Rafa and their adolescent counterparts. The teens hide behind an outwardly cool demeanor to cope with an alienating and cruel world. With their fathers gone and their overextended mothers unavailable, these Latino youths come of age trying to fit in as best they can, longing for a love they can neither express nor obtain. Surrounded by friends of questionable principles, they seem caught in a dead-end life of sex and drugs, unable to change the course of their lives.

Even as Díaz's stories focus on the dire circumstances and despair of immigrant inner-city youth, they are told in a remarkably spare and dispassionate language. Almost all of the chapters use the first-person narrative voice, a type of narration that traditionally aims at making us privy to the narrator's feelings and emotions. Yet, instead of the expected intimacy, Díaz manages to maintain a stoicism, restraint, and understatement. This is nowhere more evident than in the first story, "Ysrael," which sets the tone for the rest of the book with its matter-of-fact description of the beating two brothers inflict on a disfigured child for no other reason than they can. The most violent events are consistently related in the most straightforward and unemotional manner. In "Aurora" the narrator tells us about his violent relationship with his girlfriend with remarkable impassivity.

Throughout the book we feel as detached from the characters and their motivations as they themselves do from the disturbing events that make up their lives. Díaz creates in the reader an awareness of the ties that bind individuals to their families and communities—however vulnerable those ties are. With its cool, reserved narration, the writing downplays the impact of beatings, drug deals, absent fathers, and distant mothers; the audience can see the defense mechanisms of troubled teens who live in hostile surroundings. Though there is an impassivity to the author's writing, *Drown* nevertheless provides readers with a glimpse of the emotional turmoil brought on by poverty, drugs, and fraught relationships. Indeed, these stories illuminate one another in a way that makes visible the pathos of the characters' lives. In "No Face," for instance, we are given access to the perspective of the deformed boy Ysrael, whom the narrator and his brother gratuitously beat up in "Ysrael." The boy narrator's agonizing over the knowledge of his father's affair in "Fiesta 1980" is taken up again in "Negocios," a story whose plot centers on the aftermath of the father's abandonment and migration to the United States.

Drown powerfully exposes the machismo under whose yoke teenagers still struggle to figure out who they are in Dominican immigrant communities. The novel offers an unsentimental glimpse at the inhospitable contexts in which Dominican teenagers grow up, a space where shoplifting and drug dealing often constitute the only means of supplying material necessities. In its treatment of island life and the experience of moving from the Dominican Republic to the U.S. Northeast, Díaz's novel can be read alongside JULIA ALVAREZ's *HOW THE GARCÍA GIRLS LOST THEIR ACCENTS* (1991) and LOIDA MARITZA PÉREZ's *GEOGRAPHIES OF HOME* (1999). Díaz has made a singular contribution to DOMINICAN-AMERICAN LITERATURE.

Bibliography

Connor, Anne. "Desenmascarando a Ysarel: The Disfigured Face as Symbol of Identity in Three Latino Texts." *Cincinnati Romance Review* 21 (2002): 148–162.

Díaz, Junot. *Drown.* New York: Riverhead Books, 1996.

Carine Mardorossian

El Bronx Remembered: A Novella and Other Stories Nicholasa Mohr (1975)

In *El Bronx Remembered* NICHOLASA MOHR gathers together 11 short stories and a novella that take place after World War II, a period of great migration from Puerto Rico to the U.S. Northeast. As in other works by Mohr—such as *NILDA* (1973) and *In Nueva York* (1977)—the northeastern barrio, with its Latino and immigrant groups, is portrayed as a dynamic cultural space. Mohr explores the lives of Puerto Ricans who struggle to adjust to cultural clashes between Spanish-speaking and English-speaking groups as well as the poor conditions of concrete tenements. Mohr describes the sense of community among Puerto Ricans and the different strategies they develop to survive the problems of cultural adjustment and racial conflict. Each story allows the reader entry into the grim, harsh, yet thriving cityscape of the Bronx where there is racism and injustice, but where Puerto Rican families and neighbors enjoy a sense of familiarity and sometimes solidarity.

In one of the stories, "A Very Special Pet," a Puerto Rican family keeps a live chicken in their house in order to have fresh eggs every day. The story presents the travails of these family members who have arrived in New York and find themselves in straitened circumstances. They keep dreaming of going back to the island, but the family situation gets worse, and Graciela, the mother, decides to sacrifice the chicken to feed the children. However, the children, who consider Joncrofo a pet, convince her not to kill the chicken, and she finally tries to make it come to life again. For them the chicken has become a symbol of that heritage left behind, of those dreams about going back to Puerto Rico; killing the chicken would have meant killing their dreams. Meanwhile, "Shoes for Hector" tells the story of a young boy from a poor family who is given a pair of orange shoes for his graduation by his uncle. Though he is too embarrassed to wear them, ultimately he must because he has no other shoes. He hopes that nobody notices the orange shoes and after his graduation party he decides to spend gift money on a new pair of shoes to avoid any more mortifying situations.

In "Once Upon a Time" we learn about inner-city violence when two girls discover a young boy lying dead on a rooftop; he is the victim of gang violence.

But "Mr. Mendelson" is a more positive story about successful interethnic relations. Mohr describes the relationship between Mr. Mendelson, an old Jewish man living alone in a Bronx tenement, and the Suarez family. Mr. Mendelson spends every Sunday with the Suarez family until the day he is taken to a residential hotel. When members of the Suarez family come to visit him, a nurse thinks they are delivery people. The story reveals the friendship between the Jewish man and the Suarez family, who have become kin for him, thereby overcoming religious and ethnic difference.

The novella, *Herman and Alice,* tells the story of two people looking for love and understanding in a harsh social environment. Alice is a girl who gets pregnant and whose insensitive mother tells her to keep helping in the house since she is the oldest in the family. Her mother rejects her because her daughter has not been able to break the chain of unwanted pregnancies and a life of sacrifice. Alice has to help clean the house and take care of her brothers and sisters as always, and she feels tired and depressed. Alice falls in love with Herman, a middle-aged man who lives in the same apartment building and who helps her during her pregnancy, and they end up getting married. Eventually, however, they break up; Herman goes back to Puerto Rico, Alice returns to her old boyfriend, and she gets pregnant again. This is a story of characters trapped in their own familiar, though often destructive, patterns.

The promise of the island to give an individual a sense of home likewise surfaces in the story "Uncle Claudio." The clash between Puerto Rican and other cultures provokes Uncle Claudio's return to the island where he can "get respect." He cannot understand young people's behavior, and he "lives in another time"(139). Throughout this collection Mohr explores how Puerto Ricans adjust or fail to adjust to the Bronx, how they must take on a new identity to accommodate their new urban circumstances, and how they experience different gender expectations as well as ethnic conflicts. The distance between Puerto Ricans from the island and mainland Puerto Ricans becomes more visible through this collection of stories; Mohr invites readers to consider the challenges of migration to cold and sometimes hostile urban neighborhoods. In this regard her work contributes to the growing canon of PUERTO RICAN LITERATURE and anticipates the work of ESMERALDA SANTIAGO and other authors who deal with issues of acculturation.

The sense of realism in *El Bronx Remembered* creates a poignant portrait of Puerto Ricans living in the Bronx. Mohr's storytelling is accessible, especially to young readers, and she was finalist for the National Book Award for Children's Literature in 1976.

Bibliography

Flores, Juan. "Back Down These Mean Streets: Introducing Nicholasa Mohr and Louis Reyes Rivera." *Revista Chicano-Riqueña* 8, no. 2 (1980): 51–56.

Miller, John. "The Emigrant and New York City: A Consideration of Four Puerto Rican Writers." *MELUS* 5, no. 3 (1978): 82–99.

Mohr, Eugene V. *The Nuyorican Experience: Literature of the Puerto Rican Minority.* Westport, Conn.: Greenwood Press, 1982.

Mohr, Nicholasa. *El Bronx Remembered.* New York: Harper & Row, 1975.

Sánchez González, Lisa. *Boricua Literature: A Literary History of the Puerto Rican Diaspora.* New York: New York University Press, 2001.

Zarnowski, Myra. "An Interview with Author Nicholasa Mohr." *Reading Teacher* 45, no. 2 (October 1991): 100–106.

Antonia Domínguez Miguela

Empire of Dreams Giannina Braschi (1988)

Puerto Rican poet and novelist Giannina Braschi (1953–) wrote *El imperio de los sueños* in 1988. Translated into English and published as *Empire of Dreams* in 1994, this collection of poetry centers on the lives of Puerto Ricans in New York. The book is divided into three parts: "Assault on Time," "Profane Comedy," and "The Intimate Diary of Solitude." "Assault on Time" tells us about loneliness, love, and the limited capacity of language to express human emotion; Belli writes "Behind the word is silence" (9). The next section, "The Profane Comedy," with its allusion to Dante, pays homage to the grotesque mode in all its exaggeration and dramatic potential. Finally, "The Intimate Diary of Solitude" features *The Death of Poetry* and *Rosaries at Dawn* and reflects on the speaker's identity and gender. The author assumes the personae, both male and female, of various figures, including Russian actress Berta Singerman.

Braschi uses a Chinese box structure to make the narrative both interconnected and complex; the texts reflect one another in one way or another. Thus, although the unity of the text as a whole is fragmentary, the repetition strengthens the cohesion of the text. The overall effect of this technique, also called *mise-en-abîme,* is that of a mirror. The story is dispersed in fragments that are connected. The effect is an endless yet crafted multiplication of words and worlds. Braschi's texts are remarkably avant-garde: The letters sit on the living room couch; colons and semicolons are alive and mark relationships. Life and writing are inextricably linked.

As Carolyn Kuebler notes, the words are used for their form or their sound rather than to tell a story. Braschi's work is thus postmodern in its intertextuality. It is a fabric made up of fragments of a textual New York where all the elements of reality (including the linguistic ones) come alive and take part in the play. In this carnival, shepherds, clowns, and buffoons contribute to create a theatrical atmosphere as Braschi completely destroys any convention. Through her language play, she breaks down the boundaries between races, languages, and genders. The result is the creation of a hybrid identity and a postmodern urban language. Most of the work is performed by a first-person poetic persona. Self-reflective and self-mocking, as Alicia Ostriker perceptively notices in her introduction to the English edition of this book, Braschi's writing is irreverent and performative. Her writing does not reproduce typical Latino images but subverts them, showing a new face and set of realities. This portrait of New York Puerto Ricans is made in a collage-like fashion, where references to popular culture are mixed with intertextual allusions to Petrarch, Dante, and Shakespeare, among others, the Anglo culture with the Latino one. Such combinations make her work an original and contemporary contribution to PUERTO RICAN LITERATURE.

Bibliography

Braschi, Giannina. *Empire of Dreams.* Translated by Tess O'Dwyer. Introduction by Alicia Ostriker. New Haven, Conn.: Yale University Press, 1994.

Carrión, María M. "Geography, (M)Other Tongues and the Role of Translation in Giannina Braschi's *El imperio de los sentidos.*" *Studies in Twentieth Century Literature* 20, no. 1 (1996): 167–191.

Cristina Garrigos

Emplumada   Lorna Dee Cervantes   (1981)

LORNA DEE CERVANTES's first publication, *Emplumada* (1981), won her the American Book Award in 1982. *Emplumar* means "to feather," *pluma* means "feather," and *plumada* means "the flourish of a pen." Taken together, *Emplumada* makes reference to a bird's change in plumage and on a metaphorical level captures the action of creating poetry. *Emplumada* is a metaphor for the richness of Mexican-American culture as well as a symbol of the freedom of flight.

Cervantes incorporates bird imagery in her poetry to express flight and, therefore, female agency. The book is divided into three parts, with a glossary of Spanish words and phrases at the end. Like the corpus of CHICANO LITERATURE to which it belongs, Cervantes's poems deal with racism and poverty and the universal experiences of love and death. But her work is also intensely personal with poems about family memory, domestic abuse, hunger, and rape. The poems "Lots: I" and "Lots: II" are about women who are sexually abused, yet the female speakers triumph in their emotional strength. Cervantes emphasizes female strength in other poems such as "Crow" and "Caribou Girl."

Emplumada expresses different aspects of the poet's life while growing up in California. Most of the poems are written free of rhyme and differ in the number of stanzas. Among the remembrance poems are "Uncle's First Rabbit," "Meeting Mescalito at Oak Hill Cemetery," "For Edward Long," "Before You Go," and "Oranges." All these poems refer to a member of her family or a lover. "Uncle's First Rabbit" is about a man who since childhood has wanted to run away from life. As a child, he enjoys the violent action of hunting rabbits. As an adult, he survives World War II and comes back to live with a wife whom he abuses. After 50 years of life he realizes that nothing of what he had dreamed for has happened. Then, as he watches his wife dying, he realizes he has always run away from life.

The poem "For Edward Long" recollects the lessons of the speaker's grandfather. Despite being a drunkard, the grandfather teaches the speaker to read poetry, and he listens to her sing. The poem "Oranges" uses the passing of an old woman to prompt reflections about the speaker's grandmother. The sight of the old woman transports the speaker to her grandmother's room, where now the granddaughter feels protected. In these poems communication helps Cervantes to convey the experience of belonging to humanity. This experience of connecting to humanity—both living and dead—also is conveyed in "Meeting Mescalito at Oak Hill Cemetery." Here, we meet a 16-year-old girl who visits a cemetery. The tombstones, instead of inspiring morbid feelings, connect the audience with nature and everything that is alive: "The cemetery stones were neither erect / nor stonelike, but looked soft and harmless; / thousands of them rippling the meadows like overgrown daisies" (10). Another poem, "Before You Go," moves from the moments of joy with a lover to an expression of a sense of failure about the relationship. In the third strophe, the female persona explains the reasons for the couple's feeling of inadequacy and the memories she has of the two together.

Meanwhile, "Cannery Town in August" is a poem about loneliness and isolation. A cannery is a place where many immigrants and Mexican Americans work, but the reader meets not individuals but ". . . bodyless / uniforms and spinach specked shoes [that] drift in monochrome down the dark / moon-possessed streets" (6). The commentary here is political insofar as the poet exposes the deadening effect of working in a cannery, the terribly taxing labor that only immigrants will do.

Cervantes's work is often autobiographical. Three poems that deal explicitly with identity are "Refugee Ship," "Oaxaca, 1974," and "Visions of Mexico While at a Writing Symposium in Port Townsend, Washington." In "Refugee Ship" the speaker blames her grandmother for raising her without the ability to speak Spanish—a common lament in recent generations of Latinos. On a related note, in "Oaxaca, 1974" the speaker returns to Mexico looking for her roots but feels like an outsider because she does not speak the language. And in "Visions of Mexico While at a Writing Symposium in Port Townsend, Washington" the speaker conveys her understanding of what happens in Mexico's everyday life, but she nevertheless feels disconnection. In that moment she feels that there is neither knowledge nor appreciation for Mexican culture and history.

Along with the yearning that Cervantes has to return to her origins is an awareness of Californian history. Her poetry reflects on how California's indigenous people have been dispossessed of their motherland by U.S. highways. "Freeway 280" deals with the richness of the land before freeways were built, and in "Poema para los californios muertos" (Poem for the dead Californians) the speaker compares the construction of rich houses and restaurants in today's California to the raping of that land. Overall, Cervantes is a political poet and subjects such as poverty, hunger, and racism prevail in her work.

The last two topics the poet deals with in this collection are racism and death. In the frequently taught work "Poem for the Young White Man Who Asked Me How I, an Intelligent, Well-Read Person, Could Believe in the War Between Races," the speaker compares "her land," which is a safe and happy territory without hate, boundaries, or hunger with the hostile domain outside her door. This poem is like a prayer for reconciliation and a testimony of her own experience as a Chicana living in the United States.

Emplumada is a journey of remembrance of what is most important to Cervantes: the matriarchal and patriarchal figures who shaped her as a child, as well as her friends and lovers through whom she learned about the different kinds of love. She is a feminist writer whose poetry conveys her concerns about domestic abuse, poverty, hunger, racism, and death. Consciously valuing the Mexican culture, she attempts to recover through her poetry what Chicanas have lost. Cervantes's poetry makes an important contribution to CHICANO LITERATURE.

Bibliography
Cervantes, Lorna Dee. *Emplumada*. Pittsburgh, Pa.: University of Pittsburgh Press, 1981.
Monda, Bernadette. "Interview with Lorna Dee Cervantes." *Third Woman* 2, no. 1 (1984): 103–107.

Rodríguez y Gibson, Eliza. "Love, Hunger, and Grace: Loss and Belonging in the Poetry of Lorna Dee Cervantes and Joy Harjo." *Legacy: A Journal of American Women Writers* 19, no. 1 (2002): 106–114.

Yarbro-Bejarano, Yvonne. "Chicana Literature from a Chicana Feminist Perspective." *Americas Review* 15, nos. 3–4 (1987): 139–145.

Luz Consuelo Triana-Echeverría

Empress of the Splendid Season Oscar Hijuelos (1999)

OSCAR HIJUELOS's *Empress of the Splendid Season* details the lives of a Cuban-American family in New York City. Taking place from the 1940s to the 1990s, the novel focuses on the Latino immigrant working class who makes its living serving privileged members of high society.

Lydia Colón is the central figure of the novel; she is born in Cuba in the 1920s, comes of age in the late 1930s, leaves the island in the 1940s, and then works and raises a family in New York. Her father, Antonio Colón, is a businessman and mayor of a small Cuban town where she and her sisters have been living a pleasant life with the trappings of the Latin American middle class, including servants and a chauffeur. Because of her sexual indiscretion with a middle-aged composer, which has ostracized her from her well-to-do family, Lydia is forced to leave her home and Cuba in 1947. Upon arriving in New York, Lydia must find work, and she accepts a low-paying job in a sewing factory; despite her good looks and elegant bearing, her facility with the English language is not sufficient for the department stores she would like to work at. Cleaning houses, though beneath her aspiration, is the kind of employment she undertakes for the remainder of her life. So, though born into an aristocratic family in Cuba, Lydia falls dramatically in class when she settles in New York. She is poor and without connections, and she has difficulty reconciling her self-worth with the harsh social reality of the immigrant experience.

While adapting to her new circumstances as a young Cuban-American woman in New York, Lydia meets Raul España. Raul is an industrious and dapper waiter in one of the city's neighborhood restaurants. After a courtship that takes place on the floors of city ballrooms, the couple marries. Raul whispers into Lydia's ear: "Lydia, you are the queen of queens of beauty, / the Empress of my love, / and you preside over the splendidness / of my feelings for you, / Like the morning sun on the most glorious day / of the most beautiful and splendid season, / which is love" (21). With those words—from which Hijuelos derives the novel's title—Lydia embraces the promise of change.

The sense of play and romance ends by the late 1950s, however, when Raul has demonstrated symptoms of heart disease. Lydia's domestic life is upset by the fact that he cannot earn enough money to support his wife and two children, Rico and Alicia. Lydia is forced to find full-time employment. Another fellow pre-revolution émigré, learning of Lydia's difficult domestic situation, tells her about a professor at Columbia University who needs a maid. Swallowing her formidable pride, Lydia becomes a cleaning lady, glimpsing the type of life she left behind in Cuba. She reflects on her reduced circumstances; given her beauty, prospects, and status as a young woman, "she had not seen herself on her knees scrubbing the mildewed tiles walls of a bathroom" (16). A constant tension of the novel is Lydia's inability to accept the reality of her life in New York with the increasingly distant memories of privilege. This tension estranges Lydia from her own children who have been raised entirely in New York and cannot relate to class issues on a (relatively) distant Caribbean island. Rico and Alicia resent their mother's haughty demeanor because the family lives closer to poverty than privilege. Like the children of many first-generation immigrants, Rico and Alicia are forced to fulfill the promise of opportunity and social advancement, which remains the base for their mother's sometimes cold and authoritarian actions.

The novel compares the harsh circumstances of immigrant workers with wealthy New Yorkers such as Mr. Osprey, an international attorney. Lydia respects Osprey and his "love for the refinements of life and lordly good manners" and cleans the Osprey home the entirety of her career (73). Though secure in employment, she is unable to move outside of the "Society of the Nevers: Never go to Europe. Never buy a piece of property . . . Never stop adding up the price of things. Never stop saving your pennies . . . And: even if things were to change, never lose the *bitterness of the poor*" (247). Despite differences between maid and employer, Lydia's relationship with Mr. Osprey remains one of the strongest and most important in her émigré life. In addition to his kindness toward and respect for Lydia, Mr. Osprey comes to the family's aid when Rico falls into legal trouble during the turbulent student demonstrations of the 1960s. The attorney continues to act as Rico's benefactor, affording him the chance to attend college. Rico completes his undergraduate education and then earns a Ph.D. and eventually works as a psychologist. Rico becomes the emblem of success in the España family, though he feels uncomfortable in this role.

Several vignettes capture the España family's immigrant experiences, though these episodes do not adhere to a strict linear order in the text. Hijuelos subverts such organization by moving back and forth in time, a technique that imitates the recollection of memories. Each chapter, divided into subsections, presents the development of the novel in a way that blurs temporal lines, forcing the reader to notice the centrality of past memories in the construction of self.

Exploring themes central to the Cuban immigrant experience in the second half of the 20th century, *Empress of the Splendid Season* documents the España family's response to such pivotal historical developments as the Vietnam War and, of course, the CUBAN REVOLUTION (1959). Hijuelos gives voice to the schism between pre-Castro immigrants (those who came in the first part of the 20th century) and the political exiles coming to the United States in the wake of FIDEL CASTRO's 1959 revolution. Other immigrants who arrived earlier seem to resent the Cuban exiles' demand for attention and support. These immigrants view such support as selfish, having themselves made it through difficult financial times without receiving special treatment in the workforce. Though Cuban culture and the Spanish language link both groups, Hijuelos carefully charts the places where the two groups of immigrants differ. Yet, Hijuelos likewise hints at a certain universality in his treatment of immigrant experiences, as each culture, whether Cuban, Chinese, or Irish, has to contend with new legal, educational, and social codes. His characters try to deal (not always successfully) with the pressure to assimilate and the equal pressure to maintain their heritage. For these aspects of the narrative *Empress of the Splendid Season* can be read within the context of CUBAN-AMERICAN LITERATURE.

The narrative comes to a close after Lydia, now widowed, breaks a hip at the age of 64; she can no longer work without pain. The song lyrics, "empress of my love . . . of the most beautiful and splendid season" reappear at the end of the novel and come to symbolize Lydia's failed hopes. The nostalgia she attaches to the songs of Cuban orchestras of the 1940s and 1950s corresponds with the plot of Hijuelos's Pulitzer Prize–winning novel, *The MAMBO KINGS PLAY SONGS OF LOVE* (1989), as well as *A SIMPLE HABANA MELODY: FROM WHEN THE WORLD WAS GOOD* (2000).

Bibliography

Hijuelos, Oscar. *Empress of the Splendid Season.* New York: HarperFlamingo, 1999.

Hitchings, H. Review of *Empress of the Splendid Season. Times Literary Supplement* (February 19, 1999), 22.

Wilhelmos, T. Review of *Empress of the Splendid Season. Hudson Review* 52, no. 2 (Summer 1999): 339–345.

Zach Weir

Enclave Tato Laviera (1981)

TATO LAVIERA was born in Puerto Rico and moved to New York City with his family in 1960. He later became a regular performer at the NUYORICAN POETS CAFE. His poetry collection *Enclave* won the Before Columbus Foundation's American Book Award in 1981. Throughout this work Laviera brings to life a sense of New York's rich music and multi-cultural scene. The author uses the term *enclave* to represent the Spanish Caribbean rhythm of the clave instrument, as well as the English meaning, which here represents the multicultural communities of New York City. Laviera is widely known for his use of CODE SWITCHING between Spanish and English, his use of SPANGLISH, and his adoption of African-American urban speech. This mixture of languages mirrors the mixture of cultures that Laviera seeks to highlight in *Enclave*. He is keen on capturing the moments when Latino, African-American and Afro-Caribbean cultures overlap with one another. These moments are captured through detailed characterizations in such poems as "juana bochisme," "flutist," and "vaya carnal." The result is a poetry that evokes the sounds and images of Nuyorican culture—and all of its out-reaching branches and underlying roots—and in beat with the heart of its people. The book begins with an introduction by Juan Flores, an important critic of PUERTO RICAN LITERATURE. Flores observes that when Laviera "raps, he fingersnaps" and that the "new universalism" of Laviera's poetry creates "a friendly, curious sympathy with other people and their diverse cultures" (5).

The author begins his collection with the poem "jorge brandon," an homage to the first Nuyorican poet who recited his poetry on the streets of New York's Lower East Side in the 1940s. He then explores the idea of identity in what has been called Laviera's most important poem, "jesús papote" (Luis 1,025). Laviera combines imagery of the birth of Christ with the birth of the Puerto Rican:

> He was born star of peace church bells
> he was born busting out loud cry church bells
> he was born son grand son great grand son
> he was born generations america puerto rico
> he was born europe africa 7 generations before
> he was born latest legacy family tree inheritor
> he was born he was born 20th century
> urban story greatest told abandonment (13).

Here Laviera connects the cultures of Europe, Africa, the United States, and Puerto Rico through the idea of birth. The phrase "7 generations," which follows the reference to "europe africa," creates a connection between generations and across continents. While surveying the origins of Puerto Rican identity, the speaker recalls "loud cry church bells." In heralding the birth of the Puerto Rican in the poem, Laviera mimics a phrase often associated with the birth of Christianity's Jesus Christ. But as a postmodern poet who mixes register and tones, Laviera then attaches "urban" and "abandonment" to the event, which creates a complex picture. Overall, this poem can be read as the birth of the urban Puerto Rican, his inheritance of a mulatto and mestizo heritage, and the birth of the poet. The birth is miraculous, ending in song and dance and *bendiciones* (blessings).

In "tito Madera Smith" we can appreciate Laviera's reference to both African-American and black Puerto Rican culture. The result is one of fragmentation and cultural borrowing as the subject of the poem is seen "splitting his mother's santurce [a district of San Juan] talk, / twisting his father's south carolina soul, / adding new york scented blackest harlem / brown-eyes diddy bops, tú sabes mami [you know, mother]" (25). Laviera joins authors such as PIRI THOMAS (*DOWN THESE MEAN STREETS*) and WILLIE PERDOMO in their exploration of the intersection of Latino and African-American cultures.

Throughout *Enclave* Laviera incorporates urban imagery in poems such as "unemployment line," "abandoned building," and "familia." The term *bochisme* in the poem "juana bochisme" is a play on *bochinche* and *chisme*. *Chisme* means "gossip," and *bochinche* means both "dangerous gossip" and "a crazy brawl." The character described in the poem talks at supersonic code-switching speed and humorously wins the favor of the reader despite, and perhaps because of, her lack of sensitivity. Both "unemployment line" and "abandoned building" are placed on the page in a way to represent the architecturally dull entities but the rhythm of the wording does not echo that dullness. In fact, the beats that jump off the page give humanity to the unemployed man chanting "usted me puede atender [can you help me]?" (29). Such humanity is more clearly seen in Laviera's portrayal of the Latino family, which is represented as strong and unified instead of broken. Phrases like "moments when sacrifices find glory" can be read as a reference to the satisfaction that comes when one generation struggles to make a better life for the next (38).

Laviera pays tribute to important Puerto Rican women poets by bringing two Boricua poets together in solidarity over political conflicts. Of poets JULIA DE BURGOS and SANDRA MARÍA ESTEVES, he writes:

> julia de burgos watched in pain
> remembering her day she inspired
> sandra to combat to denounce to
> demand thorough examination, no
> more wasteful deaths, no more
> bullets from destitute society (51).

He celebrates women for their talent and bravery, and his work should be considered feminist, in this respect.

"Prendas" (jewels) is the final section of poetry, and here Laviera sings the words to the *gente* [people] that he feels are connected to the urban Latino life. His alliance with the Chicano movement is vividly expressed through the use of caló, Chicano English, and SPANGLISH in "vaya carnal."

Meanwhile, Beatle John Lennon, murdered in 1980, is immortalized in "john forever." In this poem, Laviera honors Lennon by repeating the word *peace* and, in fact, calling the former Beatle "john of peace." This has significance because *peace* is the word Lennon wanted to be associated with; he had made it a mission during the 1970s— and the Vietnam War—to repeat the word *peace* as much as possible in the public eye. Laviera was clearly sensitive to this tactic.

The collection ends with "bomba, para siempre," a poem that has been set to music when performed. Even when reading it off the page one can hear the rhythm with the phrases "se queda allí, se queda allí, se queda allí, es mi raíz" (68). Laviera uses references to jazz, merengue, rock, and even the fox trot in the hopes of getting everyone off their feet and happily dancing. However, the message is not simply to be happy; Laviera is giving a history lesson on how many diverse cultures come together in order to create beauty and uplifting rhythm. In the end we are all part of the enclave, whether we realize it or not.

Bibliography

Laviera, Tato. *Enclave.* Houston, Tex.: Arte Público Press, 1981.

Luis, William. "From New York to the World: An Interview with Tato Laviera." *Callaloo* 15, no. 4 (Autumn 1992): 1,022–1,033.

Grisel Y. Acosta

Engle, Margarita (1951–) *(fiction, writer, poet)*

On September 2, 1951, Margarita Engle was born to a Cuban mother and an American father in Pasadena, California. In 1974 she earned a B.S. from California State Polytechnic University and in 1977 an M.S. from Iowa State University. She began doctoral work in biology in 1983 at University of California, Riverside. Recipient of the prestigious CINTAS Fellow of Arts International Award (1994–95) and the San Diego Book Award for *Skywriting* (1996), Engle uses a variety of genres, including short stories, fairy tales, and poetry to explore bicultural identity. She has contributed to a number of celebrated journals, such as *Atlanta Review, Bilingual Review, California Quarterly,* and *Caribbean Writer.* Readers can see that the author has traced the "nearly indistinguishable line between fact and myth, between act and belief, creation and conjuring." This "nearly indistinguishable line" between fact and myth characterizes MAGICAL REALISM, a mode of writing that appears in many works of SPANISH-AMERICAN CARIBBEAN LITERATURE.

Through her two novels, *Singing to Cuba* (1993) and *Skywriting* (1995), she has sustained an important theme in Cuban-American prose: the search for freedom. In a number of interviews she has expressed the necessity for people to enjoy both personal and political freedoms. Engle notes that she has been "deeply influenced" by the suffering of the Cuban people on the island as well as by her relatives who suffer in exile. Much of her work exorcises these sufferings by creating narratives that explore the complexity of Cuban culture.

Singing to Cuba explores multiple Cuban histories by illustrating the difference between the revolutionary activity of the 1960s and the striking silences of the island's "special period" (*el período especial*) in the early 1990s after the dissolution of the Soviet Union. Engle's narrative, filtered through the experiences of a Cuban-American woman returning to the island after a three-decade absence, exposes readers to slave and indigenous stories. These stories become increasingly significant because they reveal a Cuban history liberated from a solely post-1959 revolutionary framework. That Cuba existed long before FIDEL CASTRO's regime is a central element to Engle's novel.

The novel's aim is to counter one of the main character's assertion that "God, having such a big world to keep track of, sometimes forgot about little places" (121). By assembling accounts of painful experiences of lives cut short by the CUBAN REVOLUTION or made exorbitantly long by incarceration, Engle testifies to the power of remembering.

Meanwhile, *Skywriting,* set during the early 1990s, involves the fate of a *balsero,* one of many Cubans who have attempted to flee the island via a makeshift raft. Families await news of the *balsero's* rescue or demise, and the novel comes to focus on the relationship of half siblings separated by national borders. Born in the "barren California desert" but "conceived in the Cuban jungle" (2), Carmen Peregrín longs to reconnect with Camilo Peregrín, the Cuban half brother she has never met. The morning after she finally does meet him on the island, he leaves behind a mysterious parcel and disappears on a homemade raft into the sea—a *balsero* taking his chances on treacherous Caribbean waters.

Contained within this parcel is the 500-year history of the Peregrín family—*The Chronicle of Antilia*—a text that amasses tales from the Inquisition, journeys across oceans, assassination attempts, and songs of love and freedom. In Engle's hands this document takes on almost mythical proportions as it becomes not only the historical narrative of one Cuban family but, in effect, the history of the island itself. These stories act as "solid packets of memory bundled up and hidden next to our hearts" (283) and can be read within the context of CUBAN-AMERICAN LITERATURE.

Having published a book of poems for children, Engle has recently turned her attention to works geared toward a young adult audience. She published in 2006 *The Poet-Slave of Cuba: A Biography of Juan Francisco Manzano.* Illustrated by Sean Quall, this novel is about the 19th-century childhood and youth of one of the first literate slaves of Cuba. Engle plans for this to be the first in a series of young adult historical books about the island.

Bibliography

Caminero-Santangelo, Marta. "Margarita Engle, Cuban American Conservatism, and the Construction of (Left) US Latino/a Ethnicity." *Lit: Literature Interpretation Theory* 13, no. 4 (October–December 2002): 249–267.

Engle, Margarita. *Dreaming Sunlight*. London: Feather Books, 2003.

———. *The Poet-Slave*. New York: Henry Holt, 2006.

———. *Singing to Cuba*. Houston, Tex.: Arte Público Press, 1993.

———. *Skywriting*. New York: Bantam Books, 1995.

———. *Smoketree*. Decatur, Ill.: High/Coo Press, 1983.

Gómez-Vega, Ibis. "Metaphors of Entrapment: Caribbean Women Writers Face the Wreckage of History." *Journal of Political and Military Sociology* 25, no. 2 (Winter 1997): 231–247.

Requena, Gisele M. "The Sounds of Silence: Remembering and Creating in Margarita Engle's *Singing to Cuba*." *MELUS* 23, no. 1 (Spring 1998): 147–157.

Vásquez, Mary S. "Contrapuntal Song: Celebration and Rage in Margarita Engle's *Singing to Cuba*." *Confluencia: Revista Hispánica de Cultura y Literatura* 12, no. 2 (Spring 1997): 128–141.

Rafael Montes

Erased Faces Graciela Limón (2001)

Erased Faces is the fifth novel by Graciela Limón (1938–), an important voice in CHICANO LITERATURE. An acclaimed Mexican-American writer born in Los Angeles, Limón taught U.S. Hispanic literature and chaired the Department of Chicano Studies at Loyola Marymount University before retiring. Her previous works include *The Day of the Moon* (1999), *The SONG OF THE HUMMINGBIRD* (1996), *The Memories of Ana Calderón* (1994), and *IN SEARCH OF BERNABÉ* (1993). Her ambitious *Erased Faces* further develops several thematic concerns already present in her earlier narratives. These include the historical interactions between the two Americas and the sociocultural struggles of U.S. Latino and Latin American peoples, including racial discrimination, gender inequalities, and sexual politics. In *Erased Faces* these concerns become inextricably intertwined as the main characters embark in complex processes of self-discovery that involve dealing with love, betrayal, and death, as well as with the reconfiguration of personal and communal identities.

The novel weaves individual and collective stories against the background of the 1994 Zapatista uprising in the state of Chiapas, in southern Mexico. The Ejército Zapatista de Liberación Nacional (Zapatista Army of National Liberation, or EZLN) is an insurgent group of Mexican, mainly Maya, people who have engaged in a long guerrilla struggle against the government. On January 1, 1994, the EZLN seized several towns in Chiapas and denounced the poverty and exploitation of indigenous communities, whose situation, they believed, would worsen further as a result of the North American Free Trade Agreement (NAFTA). The Zapatistas named themselves after the revolutionary Emiliano Zapata, who led the peasants of Morelos (central Mexico) in the 1910 uprising against dictator Porfirio Díaz, an uprising that resulted in the MEXICAN REVOLUTION.

The protagonist of *Erased Faces*, Adriana Mora, is a Latina photojournalist born in Los Angeles and haunted by her parents' death when she was a child. As a girl, she endures years of loneliness and abuse by foster families. As an adult, she travels to a small village in Chiapas to record the lives of the Lacandón women. There she meets Chan K'in, an old Lacandón shaman who helps her unravel the meaning of her nightmares. An indigenous woman, Juana Galván, invites Adriana to join the EZLN and record their way of life. As the two women get to know each other and become lovers, Juana narrates to Adriana her own story of rural poverty and abuse by the man she was forced to marry.

Adriana notices the active participation of women in the rebel army, who constitute one-third of the insurgents and many of whom hold important commanding roles (Rovira 2). The narrative illustrates how indigenous women in the EZLN have challenged the patriarchal social order, winning "the right to marry whomever they want and divorce at will, to use contraception, to become literate and learn Spanish, and even to command male insurgents, while chores such as cooking are shared by both sexes" (Rovira 7). The protagonist is also affected by the stories of other insurgents such as Orlando Flores, whose family was cruelly punished after he dared to cross social boundaries and become friends with his master's son. Rebels like Juana and Orlando react to class- and gender-related oppression by fighting for change not just for themselves but for others, too.

Adriana gradually comes to understand the struggle of the Chiapas people at the same time that she unravels the meaning of her own nightmares, in a process that blurs the boundaries between historical and mythical memory. The novel does not follow a linear chronological development but shows the interactions between past and present; history, myth, and dreams; the personal and the political. In the book's acknowledgments, Limón explains that she wrote the novel after traveling to Chiapas in 1999. Like many authors of Latino fiction, Limón uses history to shape the setting of the novel but the characters are fictional. Limón explores the construction of historical and mythical narratives, and in doing so the text examines the nature of art together with the role of the artist.

The novel ends with the massacre that took place in Acteal on December 22, 1997, when many innocent people, mainly women and children, were killed by paramilitary forces. Juana is one of the many who die that day, and the novel is left open ended, forcing readers to imagine what Adriana will do next. *Erased Faces* is a novel as socially conscious as it is creative in its efforts to portray a variety of communal, deep-rooted social conflicts from the point of view of individual Mexican and Mexican-American female characters.

Bibliography

Limón, Graciela. *Erased Faces*. Houston, Tex.: Arte Público Press, 2001.

Rovira, Guiomar. *Women of Maize: Indigenous Women and the Zapatista Rebellion*. London: Latin America Bureau, 2000.

Marta Vizcaya Echano

Espada, Martín (1957–) *(poet, editor)*

Born in 1957, Martín Espada grew up in Brooklyn. The son of an active Puerto Rican community organizer, Espada participated in many political demonstrations as a child. These early experiences instilled in him a sense of social justice that became a prevailing theme in his poetry. Espada began writing at the age of 15 and quickly learned to use every minute of the day to write or think about writing. He attended the University of Maryland for one year, dropping out after a professor criticized his writing as "too hostile" and another chastised him for admiring Allan Ginsberg. After receiving a copy of Roberto Marquez's anthology *Latin American Revolutionary Poetry*, Espada returned to school, emboldened with a new sense of identity and a new direction for his poetry. The volume allowed him to realize a place for himself among activist poets of the Hispanic tradition. At the University of Wisconsin, Madison, Espada majored in history, with a concentration in Latin America. During this time he traveled to Nicaragua to witness the Sandinista revolution; he worked in a bar, a ballpark, a gas station, a primate lab, and a transient hotel; and he published his first book, *The Immigrant Iceboy's Bolero*.

Espada next moved to Boston to study law at Northeastern University. Upon finishing his J.D.,

Espada worked as a tenant lawyer for Spanish-speaking immigrants in Chelsea, Massachusetts. He finished his second book in 1987, *Trumpets from the Islands of Their Eviction*, shortly after receiving his law degree. Espada continued to write in his spare time, publishing a third book of poetry in 1990, *Rebellion Is the Circle of a Lover's Hands*, which went on to win the Paterson Poetry Prize and the PEN/Revson Fellowship. In 1993 Espada secured a position as a professor of English literature at the University of Massachusetts, Amherst. That same year he published a fourth collection of poetry, *City of Coughing and Dead Radiators*, followed by *IMAGINE THE ANGELS OF BREAD* (1996) and *A Mayan Astronomer in Hell's Kitchen* (2000). An anthology of Espada's poems, *Alabanza: New and Selected Poems 1982–2002*, was published in 2003 won an American Library Association Notable Book of the Year, and was the recipient of the Paterson Award for Sustained Achievement. Espada's eighth book, *The Republic of Poetry*, appeared in 2006. He has also published a collection of essays, *Zapata's Disciple* (1998); edited two anthologies, *Poetry Like Bread: Poets of the Political Imagination from Curbstone Press* (1994) and *El Coro: A Chorus of Latino and Latina Poetry* (1997); and released an audiobook of poetry called *Now the Dead Will Dance the Mambo* (2004). He continues to teach, leading creative writing workshops and seminars on Pablo Neruda and Latino poetry.

Much of Espada's poetry focuses on the marginalized and on the communal, as opposed to the personal experience of the individual. Though political in nature, Espada avoids strident, didactic rhetoric in his poetry and instead emphasizes putting a human face to history and politics. *The Immigrant Iceboy's Bolero* places urban poems side by side with photos of dilapidated barrios, taken by Espada's father, highlighting the abuse and neglect immigrants suffer, but most of all pays tribute to the perseverance and dignity of these immigrants. *Trumpets from the Islands of Their Eviction* was published shortly after Espada's graduation from law school, and the subject matter of the poems reflects that experience. Throughout the poems Espada draws attention to the many legal obstacles and challenges that immigrants face, as well as the legal system's history of immigrant mistreatment.

Espada's third book, *Rebellion Is the Circle of a Lover's Hands,* brought him widespread recognition. The book opens with a series of historical poems on Puerto Rico, meant to underscore the need for a collective history of Puerto Rico, a history outside the superficial "souvenir" understanding of the island. Espada places a human face on history when he describes the Ponce massacre through the eyes of a woman who has lost her fiancé. He also challenges official canonical history in his celebration of new heroes, such as Clemente Soto Vélez, a poet jailed for advocating Puerto Rican independence. *City of Coughing and Dead Radiators* addresses the harsh realities faced by the disenfranchised Latino poor, from cockroaches to lead paint poisoning. *Imagine the Angels of Bread* (which won an American Book Award) and *A Mayan Astronomer in Hell's Kitchen* continue Espada's tradition of advocacy poetry. The anthology *Alabanza* explores new geopolitical spaces, such as Achill Island in Ireland, the Mexican city, heartland and borderland, and the Arab world, revealing cultural crossovers. Finally, *The Republic of Poetry* celebrates the art and power of poetry. For its subjects and characters Espada's work can be read within the context of PUERTO RICAN LITERATURE.

Bibliography

Crohan, Catherine. "On Poetry, War, Language, and Baseball: An Interview with Martín Espada" *MultiCultural Review* 13, no. 1 (Spring 2004): 55–58.

Espada, Martín. *Alabanza: New and Selected Poems, 1982–2002.* New York: W. W. Norton, 2003.

———. *City of Coughing and Dead Radiators.* New York: W. W. Norton, 1994.

———. *Imagine the Angels of Bread: Poems.* New York: W. W. Norton, 1997.

———. *The Immigrant Iceboy's Bolero.* Houston, Tex.: Arte Público Press, 1986.

———. *A Mayan Astronomer in Hell's Kitchen.* New York: W. W. Norton, 2001.

———. *Rebellion Is the Circle of a Lover's Hands.* Willimantic, Conn.: Curbstone Press, 1990.

———. *The Republic of Poetry.* New York: W. W. Norton, 2006.

———. *Trumpets from the Islands of Their Eviction, Expanded Edition.* Tempe, Ariz.: Bilingual Review Press, 1994.

Salgado, César. "About Martin Espada." *Ploughshares* 31, no. 1 (Spring 2005): 203–208.

Michelle Lin

Espaillat, Rhina (1932–) *(poet, translator, essayist)*

Rhina Espaillat was born in Santo Domingo, Dominican Republic, on January 20, 1932. The daughter of Homero Espaillat and Dulce María Batista de Espaillat, she left her native land in 1939 and came to permanently reside in the United States with her politically exiled parents. Her father was secretary of the Dominican delegation headed by Espaillat's great-uncle, Rafael Brache. In 1937, while serving in Washington D.C., her great-uncle repudiated Rafael Trujillo's brutal dictatorship (1930–61) and decried the massacre of several thousand Haitians on the Dominican-Haitian border. The entire delegation was exiled at once, and neither Espaillat's great-uncle nor her father returned to their country until after Trujillo's assassination in 1961. Her mother returned briefly in 1937 to leave Rhina with family members. This return was a desperate risk taken in order to provide Espaillat with a home while her parents established physical and financial stability in New York. Espaillat grew up in New York City surrounded by other immigrants from Polish, Jewish, Greek, Italian, Chinese, and Latino backgrounds. She earned a B.A. in English from Hunter College in 1953 and an M.S. in education from Queens College in 1964. For 15 years, Espaillat taught high school English in New York City.

Espaillat published her first poetry collection at the age of 60. She writes in both English and Spanish, and most of her work can be categorized as part of the new formalist movement. She has translated literary works from Spanish to English and from English to Spanish, including the writing of the 17th-century Mexican mystic Sor Juana Inés de la Cruz, U.S. poet Robert Frost, and the contemporary Dominican poet César Sánchez Beras.

Thematically her own works center on family, love, discovery, and loss. Several of her poems and essays address the exile experience, the straddling of two cultures (U.S. and Dominican American) and two languages (English and Spanish). Espaillat has seven poetry collections, including *Lapsing to Grace* (1992), *Where Horizons Go* (1998), *Rehearsing Absence* (2001), and *The Shadow I Dress In* (2004), winner of the 2003 Stanzas Prize. Her work appears in numerous literary magazines and reviews and in some three dozen anthologies, among them *Contemporary American Poetry* (2005), *100 Great Poets of the English Language* (2005), *In Other Words: Literature by Latinas of the United States* (1994), and *Twentieth Century American Poetry* (2004). The author has won several literary awards, including three yearly prizes from the Poetry Society of America, the 1998 T. S. Eliot Prize, the Der-Hovanessian Translation Prize, the Richard Wilbur Award, and the Tree at My Window Award from the Robert Frost Foundation. Her eighth collection, *Playing at Stillness,* which won the 2003 National Poetry Book Award, was published in 2005. She was one of the 80 writers invited to participate in the National Book Festival sponsored jointly by the Library of Congress and Barbara Bush, held in 2003. Her work can be read within the context of DOMINICAN-AMERICAN LITERATURE as well as SPANISH-AMERICAN CARIBBEAN LITERATURE.

Espaillat reads her poetry and conducts writing workshops at universities throughout the U.S. Northeast. She lives in Massachusetts and there coordinates the Newburyport Art Association's Annual Poetry Contest and the Powow River Poets monthly reading series. Espaillat has been instrumental in bringing about bilingual poetry readings and bilingual activities shared by high school students from Lawrence and Newburyport in Massachusetts.

Bibliography
Cruz-Hacker, Alba. "Re: Interview Questions." E-mail to Rhina Espaillat, July 9, 2004.

———. "Re: Reply to Your Questions." E-mail to Rhina Espaillat, January 5, 2005.

Espaillat, Rhina. *Lapsing to Grace.* East Lansing, Mich.: Bennett & Kitchel, 1992.

———. *Mundo y palabra/The World and the Word.* Durham, N.H.: Oyster River Press, 2001.

———. *Playing at Stillness.* Kirksville, Mo.: Truman State University Press, 2005.

———. *Rehearsing Absence.* Evansville, Ill.: University of Evansville Press, 2001.

———. *The Shadow I Dress In.* Cincinnati, Ohio: David Robert Books, 2004.

———. *The Story-teller's Hour.* Louisville, Ky.: Scienter Press, 2004.

———. *Where Horizons Go.* Kirksville, Mo.: Truman State University Press, 1998.

Gwyn, R. S., and April Lindner, eds. *Contemporary American Poetry.* New York: Pearson Longman, 2005.

Alba Cruz-Hacker

Esperanza Rising **Pam Muñoz Ryan** (2002)

PAM MUÑOZ RYAN's best-known novel, *Esperanza Rising*, explores questions of family, identity, and different kinds of wealth and poverty. The novel's prologue introduces readers to six-year-old Esperanza Ortega, the daughter of a wealthy Mexican landowner of Aguascalientes. The year is 1930. Esperanza's father teaches her to listen to the land and tells her that, when she is quiet enough, she will be able to hear its heartbeat. This scene will be repeated in various forms several times throughout the novel; Ryan immediately establishes the importance of nature and the land in the story.

The first chapter of the novel, entitled "Uvas" (grapes), picks up six years later; at the family's ranch, El Rancho de Las Rosas, the harvest and its attendant celebrations begin and Esperanza's 13th birthday approaches. Readers learn more about Esperanza's upper-class lifestyle; the family employs numerous servants, and Esperanza is sheltered from any kind of labor. On the eve of Esperanza's birthday her father is murdered; his two powerful and corrupt brothers immediately take steps to seize the land, house, and fields for themselves. Esperanza's mother realizes how dangerous the uncles are when a mysterious fire destroys the house and crops. Esperanza and her mother make secret plans to travel north to the United States (servants Alfonso and Miguel will join them). They must leave Abuelita, Esperanza's grandmother, who is injured in the fire and needs to recuperate before she can travel; they promise to send for her as soon as she is well.

Their journey is long, dirty, and full of surprises for Esperanza, who learns for the first time in her life what it is like to be neither privileged nor pampered. In her response to Esperanza's complaints about riding in a train car full of peasants, her mother observes, "It is all right, Esperanza, because now we are peasants, too" (77). Esperanza has two other notable experiences on the train; she and her mother meet Carmen, who sells eggs for a living and talks about her great wealth despite her material poverty. Esperanza is surprised by how her mama talks to this peasant woman as if she is an equal. When Carmen leaves the train, Esperanza sees a beggar woman asking for food; up to this point in her life, Esperanza has always been carefully shielded from unpleasant sights such as beggars. The old woman is ignored by a group of obviously wealthy, light-skinned people, but Carmen, who has so little herself, stops and shares her food with the woman. Shortly afterward Miguel explains the class system to Esperanza: "There is a Mexican saying: 'Full bellies & Spanish blood go hand in hand'" (79).

Esperanza and her extended family find work as pickers and settle in at a migrant camp. The class boundaries that made her life so insulated and comfortable in Mexico are meaningless in Esperanza's new environment; she and her former servants are now equals. Esperanza's awakening continues as she has to learn chores that are foreign to her such as sweeping, washing clothes, and taking care of babies. When Esperanza's mother becomes ill with fever, Esperanza takes over her mother's responsibilities and goes into the fields to pick. At night Esperanza sits with Mama and begins to crochet the blanket that Abuelita had started; the rise and fall of the stitches mirror the

struggles in Esperanza's life. She realizes she needs to bring Abuelita to the United States, or else Mama may not recover.

Ryan creates a realistic young protagonist who loses nearly everything she's ever known—her father, her comfortable life, all her possessions, her dreams of growing up to be a regal *patrona* (head of household) like her mother—and yet rises to each new challenge even if she makes a few missteps in the process. While Esperanza and her coming of age are the main focus of Ryan's narrative, the author includes some key subplots. The story takes place during the Great Depression, a time when desperate farmers from the Dust Bowl of Oklahoma and surrounding states were heading west to California. Esperanza gets a crash course in both economics and discrimination. There are so many workers that the companies have no incentive to raise workers' wages; workers are housed in separate camps according to ethnicity so that they will not mingle and organize. Esperanza also learns that being Mexican, especially a non-English-speaking Mexican, marks her and the people that she loves as inferior in the eyes of society. She witnesses immigration raids that deport American citizens and sees a young friend passed over for honors because she is Mexican. Her family uses what little power they have, however, and travel some distance to shop at a store run by a Japanese man because unlike many business owners, he welcomes Mexican customers.

Ryan uses several tropes throughout the novel, most notably her choice to name each chapter after the fruit or vegetable that is in season. The novel begins and ends with grapes; readers have experienced a year in Esperanza's life and a full cycle of harvests. Ryan also uses roses as symbols of survival and growth in the story. On the day before her birthday, Esperanza pricks her finger on a thorn in the rose garden, and Abuelita reminds her "No hay rosas sin espinas" (There are no roses without thorns) (14). Servants Alfonso and Miguel secretly bring rose bushes from the garden at El Rancho de Las Rosas to California, where they add beauty to the migrant camp and remind Esperanza of her father.

Esperanza Rising contains some elements of MAGICAL REALISM, a school of literature often explored by Central and South American writers in which seemingly magical events happen within a real landscape; this is best represented by Esperanza's various attempts at, and ultimate success in, levitation at the end of the novel.

The title can be read as a reference to Esperanza's literal rising from the earth, particularly at the end of the story, but it also refers to Esperanza's riches-to-rags story and her discovery of a different kind of security. Early in the story Abuelita reminds Esperanza of the phoenix, the mythical bird that is reborn from its own ashes (50). She and her family rise from the literal ashes of their destroyed home in Mexico; they also unite to counter the indignities of poverty, of immigration, and of second-class citizenship.

The power of creation appears throughout the novel as well. Abuelita's words as she teaches Esperanza to crochet, that life is full of mountains and valleys and it is always possible to start over, gains power as the narrative proceeds. The act of creating something beautiful out of nothing appears throughout the book on both literal and figurative levels. Miguel and Alfonso literally create beauty with their secret rose garden in a dusty migrant camp; Esperanza's mother and later Esperanza herself make simple dolls from yarn for the younger girls to play with; and Esperanza continues the blanket Abuelita started in Mexico so that she will have something beautiful to give to her mother. Figuratively speaking, Esperanza takes circumstances that appear to offer nothing—a life of poverty, dust, hard labor, and discrimination—and creates a life of close familial ties, integrity, and tremendous emotional and spiritual wealth. *Esperanza Rising* can be read within the context of CHICANO LITERATURE and BORDER LITERATURE.

Bibliography

Muñoz Ryan, Pam. *Esperanza Rising.* New York: Scholastic, 2001.

Pam Muñoz Ryan. Available online. URL: http://www.pammunozryan.com/arthorstudy.html. Accessed December 12, 2007.

Tropp, Tasha. Review of *Esperanza Rising* by Pam Muñoz Ryan. *Journal of Adolescent & Adult Literacy* 45, no. 4 (December 2001–January 2002): 334.

Gabrielle Halko

Esperanza's Box of Saints María Amparo Escandón (1999)

María Amparo Escandón was born in Mexico in 1957 and now lives in Los Angeles, where she teaches writing at the University of California, Los Angeles. She conceived the idea of her novel *Esperanza's Box of Saints* after publication of her award-winning short story, written in Spanish, "Santitos." The novel, based on this story, however, was written in English (her second language). Escandón also translated the novel into Spanish, as *Santitos.* In addition to the short story in Spanish, the novel in English, and the translation of the novel in Spanish, Escandón wrote the screenplay for the Mexican film *Santitos,* which won the 1999 Latin American Cinema Award at the Sundance Film Festival. Her work can be read within the context of both Mexican and CHICANO LITERATURE.

In *Esperanza's Box of Saints* Escandón introduces us to her lively and compelling protagonist, Esperanza Díaz, a deeply religious widow who works in a hardware store. Esperanza has been raising her teenage daughter, Blanca, and she lives with another widow, Soledad, in a village in Veracruz (in eastern Mexico). *Esperanza's Box of Saints* centers on what happens to Esperanza when she loses Blanca to an illness; as a mother, Esperanza finds comfort in her faith and in the spirit world, which appears to her as a series of apparitions (in mundane places, like the kitchen stove). The author uses many voices to advance her narrative: Esperanza's conversations and confessions, her letters, Father Salvador's prayers, Blanca's diaries, and an omniscient narrator.

The novel opens with Esperanza's confession to Father Salvador, whose name appropriately means "savior." Esperanza explains that she has had an apparition after the funeral of Blanca, who died after having her tonsils removed in a local hospital.

Overwhelmed by grief and with distrust of hospital authorities, Esperanza believes her daughter is still alive and starts a quixotic search for Blanca. St. Judas Tadeo had appeared to Esperanza in her greasy oven door and announced that Blanca is not dead. Esperanza then follows his instructions blindly, and upon the saint's request, she packs her wooden saints into a box (thus the novel's title). She resolves to uncover the plot of what she considers is her daughter's kidnapping by the doctor who treated her at the hospital. Convinced that Blanca has been abducted by a child prostitution ring, Esperanza opens her grave, knocks on the coffin, and decides it is empty. The search to find Blanca, under the protection of St. Judas Tadeo, the patron saint of desperate causes, takes the distraught mother across Mexico to Tijuana, where she thinks Blanca might have been sold into a prostitution ring.

Names are important in this novel because they indicate significant aspects of each character. The name Blanca (white) signifies purity and suggests the girl's potential as a saint. Soledad's name means "solitude." And, true to this appellation, Soledad reminds Esperanza (hope) of her loneliness and vulnerability. Soledad prevents Esperanza from moving on in her life because she compels Esperanza to remember everything they used to share, even Blanca. But Escandón makes Esperanza's character resilient, despite the fact that Blanca has been buried and mourned. Readers can see in Esperanza the image of a devoted mother who has faith her daughter can be found alive, that her death is not real. Despite her sense that people will think she is crazy, Esperanza believes in the advice of St. Judas Tadeo; she regularly seeks his guidance, and she sets the figure that represents him on an altar everywhere she goes.

Esperanza leaves Soledad in their *pueblo* in order to embark on an epic journey across Mexico. On her path toward independence she experiences many diversions and obstacles. In her travels from Veracruz to Tijuana to Los Angeles, Esperanza meets many interesting people who recognize her sincerity. One such individual is a wrestler named El Angel Justiciero (the Angel of Justice), or simply Angel. Angel respects Esperanza and her decisions to follow St. Judas Tadeo; he patiently gains Esperanza's love and shares her faith without interfering in her search for Blanca. This kind of support is lacking in Father Salvador because, despite her testimony about her daughter, he remains skeptical of his parishioner's apparitions.

Escandón conveys a sense of humor and drama in Esperanza's pilgrimage. The widowed and bereaved mother searches for apparitions in every grease stain on her quest. Determined and strong-willed, she crosses the border into California. She relies on the same method that illegal Mexicans have used to enter the United States: hiding in a car trunk. On the verge of losing hope and faith, Esperanza returns to Veracruz, only to find that Blanca awaited her there, as an apparition on a rusty leak in the bathroom wall. Ultimately, her journey changes from a search for her daughter into a search for self-realization. She finds what she had been denying herself in the years she raised Blanca.

In the last part of the novel Angel rescues Esperanza from her from solitude, sadness, and boredom. It initially appears to the reader that the reunion has failed, but the author (with a wink to the reader) shows Esperanza in Angel's pickup truck headed for California. In conveying Esperanza's faith and the immediacy of her visions, Escandón relies on the imaginative mode called MAGICAL REALISM, where the supernatural is accepted as part of everyday life. In this regard *Esperanza's Box of Saints* can be read within the broader context of Latin American works such as Laura Esquivel's *Como agua para chocolate* (*Like Water for Chocolate*) and Gabriel García Márquez's *Cien años de soledad* (*One Hundred Years of Solitude*).

Bibliography

Escandón, María Amparo. *Esperanza's Box of Saints.* New York: Scribner, 1999.

Hoffman, Joan M. "Hope Is the Last to Die: The Quixotic Adventure of *Esperanza's Box of Saints.*" *Bilingual Review/La Revista Bilingüe* 25, no. 2 (2000): 163–171.

Mujica, Barbara. "Hope and a Box of Saints." *Americas* 53, no. 6 (November–December 2001): 60–62.

Imelda Martín Junquera

Esteves, Sandra María (1948–) (poet, artist)

Sandra María Esteves was born in 1948, in the Bronx, New York City. Esteves commonly refers to herself as a Puerto Rican–Dominican–Borinqueña-Quisqueyana–Taino–African American. Her heritage stems from ancestors who were the subjects of slavery, colonization, and migration. Associated with the NUYORICAN POETS CAFE on Manhattan's Lower East Side, Esteves's writing represents a Latina experience in a diasporic context. More specifically, her poetics address the crossing of African, indigenous, and Spanish lineages through migration.

Her poetry illustrates the dynamic interplay between language and culture, whether writing in English, Spanish, or both. Indeed, in her CODE SWITCHING between Spanish and English, Esteves engages in the debate about language use among Puerto Ricans—both those on the mainland who do not speak their mother tongue and those Spanish-speaking Puerto Ricans living on the island who, while able to speak English, nevertheless reject it as a sign of U.S. domination. This debate reflects, too, the ambiguous position of Puerto Ricans of New York. They are not from the island and therefore have a different urban experience living in the wintry Northeast; at the same time they are Puerto Rican in heritage, which means their political situation is vague. Puerto Rico is a U.S. commonwealth; the island is neither a country nor a state.

Esteves's most famous collection of poetry is *Bluestown Mockingbird Mambo* (1990). In it her poetics affirm her rich cultural identity and work to counteract social and economic marginalization on the U.S. mainland. The poem "So Your Name Isn't Maria Cristina" deals with Puerto Rican identity as shaped by language choices, gender roles, and political engagements. In Esteves's vision, Puerto Rican women uphold the values of the Catholic family and yet attempt to contest those values (staying at home, obeying patriarchal authority, suffering in silence, etc.) by participating in the political arena. But the political arena, made clear by Esteves's reference to the Young Lords, also was rife with sexism, especially in the 1960s and 1970s.

Overall Esteves's poetry displays a preoccupation with space, both public and private, as it creates meaning. Poems such as "Not Neither," from *Tropical Rain: A Bilingual Downpour* (1984), reflect on the effects of migration from the island to the mainland. After World War II thousands of Puerto Ricans relocated to the barrios of New York City. One important fact to keep in mind in reading Esteves's work, and PUERTO RICAN LITERATURE more broadly, is that Puerto Ricans are migrants, not immigrants. Ultimately, Esteves identifies not with the Caribbean island or with the vast terrain of the United States but with the Bronx, a borough that has a history of long-standing Puerto Rican residency. As a woman from the Bronx, Esteves cannot claim intimacy with the *campos* (countryside) of Puerto Rico, the fields and farms of the Puerto Rican country girl (*jíbara*). Thus, the Bronx provides a regional identity that is just as powerful as her Caribbean identity.

Throughout her career Esteves has been awarded numerous honors and fellowships, including the Arts Review 2001 Honoree from the Bronx Council on the Arts, the 2000 Louis Reyes Rivera Lifetime Achievement Award from Amherst College, the 1992 Edgar Allan Poe Literary Award from the Bronx Historical Society, and a 1985 poetry fellowship from the New York Foundation for the Arts. She has published six collections of poetry: *Yerba Buena* (1981), *Tropical Rain* (1984), *Bluestown Mockingbird Mambo* (1990), *Undelivered Love Poems* (1997), *Contrapunto in the Open Field* (1998), and *Finding Your Way* (2001). *Yerba Buena* was selected as the best book from a small press in 1981 by the *Library Journal*. She continues creating visual art, teaching writing workshops, writing poetry, and lecturing throughout the United States.

Bibliography

Acosta-Belen, Edna. "Beyond Island Boundraries: Ethnicity, Gender, and Cultural Revitalization in Nuyorican Literature." *Callaloo* 15, no. 4 (Autumn 1992): 979–998.

Esteves, Sandra María. *Bluestown Mockingbird Mambo*. Houston, Tex.: Arte Público, 1990.

———. *Contrapunto in the Open Field*. New York: No Frills Publications, 1998.

———. *Finding Your Way: Poems for Young Folks*. New York: No Frills Publications, 1999.

———. *Tropical Rain: A Bilingual Downpour*. New York: African Caribbean Poetry, Theater, 1984.

———. *Undelivered Love Poems*. New York: No Frills Publications, 1997.

———. *Yerba Buena*. Greenfield Center, N.Y.: Greenfield Review Press, 1981.

Flores, Juan, and George Yudice. "Living Borders/Buscando América: Languages of Latino Self-Formation." *Social Text* 8, no. 24 (1990): 57–84.

Mindicta-Lombardo and Cintron, Zaida A. "Marked and Unmarked Choices of Code Switching in Bilingual Poetry." *Hispania* 78, no. 3 (September 1995): 565–572.

Scott, Nina M. "The Politics of Language: Latina Writers in United States Literature and Curricula." *MELUS* 19, no. 1 (Spring 1994): 57–71.

Nicole Guidotti-Hernández

Eyewitness: A Filmmaker's Memoir of the Chicano Movement Jesús Salvador Treviño (2001)

Eyewitness: A Filmmaker's Memoir of the Chicano Movement is JESÚS SALVADOR TREVIÑO's autobiographical account of the Chicano rights movement from 1968 to 1975. A childhood bout of rheumatic fever that kept him bedridden for 11 months proved fortunate because he spent much of his recovery time reading. Treviño improved his reading skill by six grade levels during this time, which enabled him to overcome the poor quality of education of his elementary school. Treviño's story is fraught with ironies and contradictions, which have been experienced by many Hispanic-Americans. A complexity of his life is that many of the people most important to him are Americans of European origin, including his stepfather and his wife, yet during the civil rights movement Treviño took part in rallies that proclaimed "Death to the *gabacho*!" (non-Hispanic person). Treviño spent much of his younger years trying to determine where he belonged in the United States. He alternated between trying to "be more American" by becoming an academic overachiever (when many of his Chicano friends were dropouts) and asking his friends to call him "Jess" rather than "Jesús," and retreating from the European-American world to seek out his Mexican roots. Treviño's ultimate reconciliation of these two worlds, which was necessary for his personal and professional success, is the underlying story of *Eyewitness*.

In September 1972 the Hispanic political organization La Raza Unida held its first national convention in El Paso, Texas, with Treviño acting as national media coordinator. He was successful in attracting television coverage from ABC, CBS, NBC, and PBS and newspaper coverage from the *Los Angeles Times* as well as a number of movement newspapers such as *El Grito del Norte, La Raza,* and *La Nueva Vida*. In addition, Treviño produced a half-hour film, *La Raza Unida,* about the convention, which was aired on KCET on January 4, 1973.

Treviño began producing the weekly program *Acción Chicano* for KCET in 1972 and also produced reports for the weekly news program *The L.A. Collective* during this time. He took a leave of absence from KCET in February and March 1973 to attend a theater workshop held by EL TEATRO CAMPESINO; this experience directed his interest away from journalism and towards documentary and feature filmmaking. In January 1974 Treviño gave up his job at KCET, and he and his wife relocated to San Juan Bautista, California, to work in the film component of Centro Campesino Cultural, headquarters for El Teatro Campesino. However, due to creative and organizational differences they left the Centro after a year and returned to Los Angeles. Treviño's next job as a television producer was on the PBS educational program *Infinity Factory,* a series similar to *Sesame Street* but focused on mathematics. He also produced several documentary programs but found it difficult to remain employed in this field and since 1988 has produced mainly episodes of popular television series.

Bibliography

Chavez, Ernesto. *"Mi raza primero!" (My people first!): Nationalism, Identity, and Insurgency in the Chicano Movement in Los Angeles, 1966–1978.* Berkeley: University of California Press, 2002.

Chuy Treviño Web site. Available online. URL: http://chuytrevino.com.

Oropeza, Lorena. *Raza sí!, guerra no!: Chicano Protest and Patriotism during the Viet Nam War Era.* Berkeley: University of California Press, 2005.

Treviño, Jesús Salvador. *Eyewitness: A Filmmaker's Memoir of the Chicano Movement.* Houston, Tex.: Arte Público Press, 2001.

Sarah Boslaugh

F

Face of an Angel **Denise Elia Chávez** (1994)
Novelist and playwright DENISE CHÁVEZ's novel
Face of an Angel brings to life the history of the
Dosamantes family, longtime Mexican Americans
of Agua Oscura, New Mexico. The family name,
Dosamantes, means "two lovers," and the novel
begins by telling the story of Luardo Dosamantes's
relationship with a 13-year-old named Dolores Loera, who has the "face of an angel." Luardo
marries Dolores, and she bears him two children,
Sovieda and Hector. Eventually the marriage fal-
ters; Luardo engages in affairs with other women,
and Dolores seeks comfort in her Catholic faith.
Luardo Dosamantes's ongoing fantasy, even as an
older man, is to find a young lover, one 16 years
of age or so. His surname reveals aspects of his
macho character and the conflict he feels between
his desire for other women and the expectation of
fidelity in married life.

Face of an Angel explores the point of view of
Sovieda Dosamantes, the daughter of Dolores and
Luardo, who tries to make sense of her family's
past. *Face of an Angel* depends on framing devices such as a family tree, which introduces the
book. The family tree provides a framework for
Sovieda to tell the stories of her mother, Dolores,
her father, Luardo, her grandfather Papa Profe, her
grandmother Lupe, her cousin Mara, and her husband, Ivan. *Face of an Angel,* which is 457 pages, is
encyclopedic in its scope because of Chávez's rich

sense of textuality. The author weaves subtexts
within the main text, including diary entries, autobiographical accounts, and assorted documents.
Perhaps the most important text within the novel
comes in the form of Sovieda's project, *The Book of
Service: A Handbook for Servers.*

In *The Book of Service,* which functions as a
narrative within a narrative, Chávez explores the
theme of service in the workplace. Sovieda's lifelong career as a waitress at El Farol Restaurant
prompts her to record the stories of her counterparts to incite a food strike for worker's rights and
to write this unique instruction manual. In *The
Book of Service* Sovieda uses writing as a form of
empowerment. The fragments of the text, which
appear throughout the novel, create a narrative
space that allows working-class women to define
their own identities, instead of having them defined by someone else.

Starting from Sovieda's childhood in the 1950s,
we come to understand why service is one of the
novel's main themes. Service is both a practice and
condition of women's experience, and as such it
poses challenges in everyday life. The context for
the theme of service begins in part with Sovieda's
great-grandfather Manuel Dosamantes Iturbide,
who leaves Mexico to seek work with a rancher in
Texas. Manuel later runs his own ranch in Agua
Oscura, in New Mexico. He marries Elena Harrell
in the 1880s, and they have five children, one of

which is Sovieda's grandfather Profe Dosamantes. Profe marries Guadalupe Castillo, and they have five children, one of whom is Luardo Dosamantes. For generations the Dosamantes women have been serving the Dosamantes men.

Along these lines, Sovieda also gets caught up in the expectation of service. In the following passage Sovieda visits her father and cleans his apartment for him before he moves out:

> My work was almost done. Luardo had felt he was in the way. Cleaning, scrubbing, all those cleansers. Knowledge of vacuum cleaners, washers, electrical appliances, household gadgets, anything having to do with house or yard or animal, anything living or non-living that required attention, care, and maintenance, was of no concern to Luardo Dosamantes.
>
> I'd like to move to Mexico and live with a sixteen year old girl.
>
> There. That was it. A dream (13).

This moment demonstrates how Luardo is a patriarchal figure, content to watch his daughter clean house for him. Chávez depicts him as an old man whose dream is somewhat disturbing. He imagines himself returning to his Mexico and seducing a Mexican teenager, one he might have "fixed" to avoid having more children. The punchy prose that reads "There. That was it. A dream" reveals the dark humor of Chávez's writing.

Chávez uses humor to discuss how women are torn between the responsibilities of their family, religion, and work. The author makes humor the vehicle for revealing the taboo, the stereotypical, and the violent, as Chávez explains in an interview with Theresa Delgadillo: "You can have a wicked sense of humor when you're down and out and in the mud. You can laugh at the absurdity of life and the craziness. I never want to leave humor behind. It's who I am (37). Chávez uses humor to temper the disturbing episodes of the text, as with Mara's exorcism. Mara, Sovieda's cousin, has become prone to inexplicable nightmares and seems possessed by demons. At the recommendation of the local priest the Dosamantes women invite Reverend Pentergrast to their home to investigate Mara's troubles and to perform an exorcism on her. However, as a victim of incest, Mara's pain is perhaps more psychological more than spiritual. The exorcism is ridiculous and brutal, but humor provides a medium to expose incest and the misdiagnosis of Mara's sickness.

Indeed, spiritual, psychological, and physiological sickness account for many of the women's problems in the narrative; for example, the novel associates Sovieda's incessant medical problems with her unfaithful husband, Ivan. *Face of an Angel* demonstrates how Sovieda has, in general, unfulfilling relationships with men. Moreover, the Dosamantes family is not healthy because of its secrets about incest, infidelity, and repression of female autonomy. In this regard Chávez uses Sovieda to pose questions to the reader about power, about service, and about how bodies betray themselves through illness and exposure to violence. The theme of service creates class hierarchies and unequal interactions between men and women, as seen in the chapter in which Sovieda cleans house for her father. As a narrator, Sovieda attempts to understand how class, gender, and race operate in her family and in her town. Since violence and repression are perpetuated by silence, Sovieda disrupts the opportunity for the patriarchy to protect itself by exposing that repression through her narrative. On the one hand, Chávez uses the female body to reinforce stereotypical images of women. Yet, even so, through Sovieda and the trials of the Dosamantes family Chávez imagines newly configured histories, stories that revisit the truth to expose the abusive relations between men and women in this Mexican-American family.

Within a broader literary context, Chávez's writing has much in common with other Mexican-American women writers such as HELEN MARÍA VIRAMONTES, ANA CASTILLO, and SANDRA CISNEROS; in fact, Chávez names one of her chapters "House on Manzanilla Street," an obvious reference to Cisneros's *THE HOUSE ON MANGO STREET*. *Face of an Angel* has been favorably reviewed in a number of mainstream publications such as The *Village Voice, Library Journal,* and *Newsweek.* In addition, a number of articles have been published on the novel, as well as the novel being referenced in a number of dissertations on CHICANO LITERATURE.

Bibliography

Chávez, Denise. *Face of an Angel.* New York: Farrar, Straus, & Giroux, 1994.

Kevane, Bridget, and Juanita Heredia. *Latina Self Portraits: Interviews with Contemporary Women Writers.* Albuquerque: University of New Mexico Press, 2000.

Socolovsky, Maya. "Narrative and Traumatic Memory in Denise Chávez's *Face of an Angel.*" MELUS 28 (2003): 187–205.

Nicole M. Guidotti-Hernández

Fernández Retamar, Roberto

See RETAMAR, ROBERTO FERNÁNDEZ.

Flaming Iguanas: An Illustrated All-Girl Road Novel Thing Erika Lopez (1997)

Erika Lopez (1967–   ) is a New York–born cartoonist, writer, and performing artist of Puerto Rican heritage. Lopez studied at the Pennsylvania Academy of the Fine Arts. Her literary alter ego is Jolene Gertrude Rodriguez (also known as Tomato "Mad Dog" Rodriguez). Mad Dog is the first-person narrator of the Tomato trilogy, which includes *Flaming Iguanas, They Call Me Mad Dog: A Story for Bitter, Lonely People* (1998), and *Hoochie Mama: The Other White Meat* (2001). In each work Mad Dog reflects on her situation as a struggling but fun-loving bisexual mestiza (a woman of racially mixed ancestry) on the fringes of society. As such, Lopez's work can be read within the context of LATINA LESBIAN LITERATURE.

Flaming Iguanas, Lopez's first book, "appropriates and revises the American male genre of literary road writing," (Laffrado 406) exemplified by the Beat generation's manifesto, *On the Road* (1957), by Jack Kerouac. Motivated by a feeling of loneliness and the need to boost her self-esteem,

Tomato decides to start a one-woman biker gang, the Flaming Iguanas, find a motorcycle, and ride cross-country. She is accompanied by her Puerto Rican friend Magdalena. At first, hesitation and doubtfulness overshadow her intention to "run, live, and have no regrets" (20). In her journey of self-exploration, she asks herself what she is trying to prove and she questions:

> . . . this myth that said you have to leave your job, your life, your tear-stained woman waving good-bye with a kitchen towel behind the screen door so you can ride all over the country with a sore ass, battling crosswinds, rain, arrogant Volvos, and minivans (26).

On the same page, however, she is convinced she must experience the typically American, mythical adventure of being on the road for herself. At this point in the book, Lopez dissociates Tomato's motivations from those of her male literary ancestors, Kerouac, Hunter S. Thompson, and Henry Miller; she "couldn't identify with the fact that they were guys who had women around to make the coffee and wash . . . their shorts" (27).

In this way, even before actually leaving home, Tomato is aware of the cultural baggage that comes with a cross-country motorcycle trip but defies any of these expectations not only by calling her plan an "embarrassingly cheesy-brown low-budget adventure" (130) but also by the fact that she is a woman, an ethnic and sexual hybrid (a person produced by the interaction or crossbreeding of two unlike cultures), and does not really know how to ride a motorbike. Identity categories such as "Latina," "lesbian," or "biker chick" do not apply to her:

> I wasn't a good blue-collar heterosexual in a trailer home, I wasn't a real Puerto Rican in the Bronx, I wasn't a good one-night stand lesbian. I wasn't a good alcoholic artist, and I wasn't a real biker chick because I didn't want the tattoos (241).

Throughout the book the protagonist recollects situations in which she wanted to belong to one of these groups. As a child, she tried to pluck her eyebrows like the Puerto Rican women she knew, although she does not speak Spanish (146; 29). In a conversation with her lesbian mother, a "real strong woman," Tomato wanted to find out if she was not lesbian herself (51; 172). Lopez attempts to explore identity in terms of language and appearance.

On the road from Philadelphia to California Tomato experiences a sense of community with truck drivers, travelers, and other bikers. More important, though, the protagonist appropriates the traditionally masculine space of the road as she gains the confidence of a female biker who unmasks the "culture of fear" used to keep women at home or on the back of motorcycles (191):

> There is this myth that if you're a woman traveling alone people will instantly want to kill you. This is an example of where you shouldn't listen to anybody. So much of the way we live and the decisions we make . . . are based on fear (111).

Tomato's credo is never to act vague and to "take up space because it's not a school dance" (112). This strategy finally makes her "feel alone in the best way," confident, strong, and invincible (185). Her performance on the road and her humorous account of it in what Lopez subtitles a "road novel thing," a bold defiance of stereotypical genre expectations in itself, actually produces this space of self-confidence. Like authors such as GLORIA ANZALDÚA, CHERRÍE MORAGA, and ANA CASTILLO, Lopez examines the influence of race, gender, sexuality, and class in her writing and in her performance art.

Bibliography

Brady, Mary Pat. *Extinct Lands, Temporal Geographies: Chicana Literature and the Urgency of Space.* Durham, N.C., and London: Duke University Press, 2002.

"The Kronicals of Kitten Lopez." Available online. URL: http://erikalopez.com.

Laffrado, Laura. "Postings from Hoochie Mama: Erika Lopez, Graphic Art, and Female Subjectivity." In *Interfaces: Women-Autobiography-Image-Performance,* edited by Sidonie Smith and Julia Watson, 406–429. Ann Arbor: University of Michigan Press, 2002.

Lopez, Erika. *Flaming Iguanas: An Illustrated All-Girl Road Novel Thing.* New York: Simon & Schuster, 1997.

Alexandra Ganser

Fontes, Montserrat (1940–) *(novelist, screenwriter)*

Born in Laredo, Texas, on September 5, 1940, Mexican-American writer Montserrat Fontes was raised in Nuevo Laredo until she was nine years old, when she moved to Los Angeles. She earned her B.A. in English from California State University, Los Angeles, in 1966 and her master's degree in 1967. Fontes began her career as a high school teacher in Los Angeles before she turned to novel and screenwriting. She is the author of *First Confession* (1991) and *Dreams of the Centaur* (1996), conceived as part of a trilogy, and the screenplay for *Dreams of the Centaur.* The final installment of the trilogy, *The General's Widow,* will be based on her grandmother, the widow of assassinated Mexican general Arnulfo Gómez.

As NORMA ELIA CANTÚ argues, Fontes sees the border as a region scarred by acts of brutality. Her novels suggest that violence is at the core of our understanding of Chicano, Mexican, and indigenous identities. *First Confession* (1991), set in a small Mexican town across the Texas border in 1947, explores how children understand power through race, class, and gender relations. The novel chronicles the coming of age of Andrea Durcal and Victor Escalante, two nine-year-olds of the upper class. They come to understand the journey into adulthood as a struggle for power and knowledge. In that summer before they make their first confession and take their first communion, they begin to spy on the town prostitute Armida and devise a plan to steal her money. They discover how sex and economies of exchange are connected to women's bodies. Andrea and Victor watch Armida and "Smelly Hands" as they go behind the curtain where she "sold her touches," but instead, the two children witness her rape. Andrea recalls that, "For some reason I felt terribly close to her . . . she stood there brushing some invisible stain off her dress" (17). The curiosity and repulsion are what allow Andrea to identify with Armida when she is raped; however, the children feel justified in stealing her money because she is a prostitute. After they steal Armida's money, the children are beaten up by the river kids because they do not understand just how privileged they are in comparison to their counterparts from the other side of the border. The money Armida earned through prostitution brings violence to bear on her body; her husband also beats her, and she commits suicide. The children's desire to talk about sex and to redistribute the prostitute's money in the name of good opens up their own bodies to violence as well. Their desire to speak about Armida in endlessly accumulated detail sets off a chain of violent events and incessant guilt for the children. The dramatic climax comes when Victor confesses his sins before first Communion and Andrea chooses not to. Secrecy and power dominate their adult lives, and they are, in the end, what kill Victor (he commits suicide).

The 1996 American Book Award–winning novel *Dreams of the Centaur* is the second part of the trilogy. With formalistic innovation marked by spatial breaks, italics, and time lapses, Fontes chronicles the history of the Mexican family Durcal and the Yaqui struggle in Sonora, Mexico, between 1885 and 1900. The novel maps a history over a 3,000-mile radius that goes as far north as into Arizona and as far south as to the henequen (hemp) plantations located in the Yucatán. In the opening scene Felipa Durcal sees the dead face of her husband and speculates that Jose has raped the Yaqui servant girl Rosario. Felipa's vision foreshadows Jose's murder, which his eldest son, Alejo, vows to avenge. Jose's death and the rape of the Yaqui servant girl provide the dramatic tension for the plot that follows. After shooting Esteban, Alejo is immediately sent to the *bartolinas* (the pits), a prison where he meets Charco, his illegitimate half brother. While in prison, they are tortured. Place and memory become modes of resistance for Alejo and Charco as they attempt to grapple with the pain. Fontes deftly imagines the unequal power relations produced when Alejo and Charco face public forms of bodily mutilation.

The second half of the novel reverses their roles as they become a part of the prisoner regiments under Porfirio Díaz's regime. They are forced to deport the Yaqui to the henequen plantations in the Yucatán during the height of Díaz's dictatorship. Opposing the harsh treatment of the Yaqui and their participation in this genocidal project, they desert the army, become enslaved, and finally escape. Bound by a political sense of solidarity, Alejo and Charco become involved in the bloody battle of Mazacoba in the Sierra Bacatete where Alejo is shot and badly wounded. Felipa comes to the sierra to look for Alejo and witnesses the slaughter of Yaqui men, women, and children. It is here that her consciousness is raised about the Yaqui struggle when she finds Alejo and Charco, amputates Alejo's leg, and facilitates their escape to the United States. The novel illustrates the strong bond between a mother and son, the forging of new families in the wake of genocide, and the violent national histories of the borderlands that are often ignored in conventional accounts of American history. As such Fontes's work can be read within the context of BORDER LITERATURE and CHICANO LITERATURE, more broadly.

Bibliography

Canfield, J. Douglas. "Crossing Laterally into Solidarity in Montserrat Fontes's *Dreams of the Centaur.*" *Studies in 20th Century Literature* 25, no. 1 (Winter 2001): 240–260.

Cantú, Norma. "Border Texts and Border Violence: The Novels of Montserrat Fontes." Paper presented at the Conference on Chicana/o Literature, University of Sevilla, May 2004.

Fontes, Montserrat. *Dreams of the Centaur*. New York: W. W. Norton, 1996.

——— *First Confession*. New York: W. W. Norton, 1991.

Nicole M. Guidotti-Hernández

Fornes, Maria Irene (1930–   )

(playwright, director, stage designer)

Maria Irene Fornes was born on May 14, 1930, in Havana, Cuba. Alongside such playwrights as Sam Shepard, Fornes was a founder of the off-off

Broadway movement in the 1960s and has helped shape the development of noncommercial theater in the United States. In 1972 she cofounded and for several years directed the alternative theater group, the New York Theatre Strategy. While teaching and lecturing in various workshops and universities, Fornes has also directed creative writing classes for Latino playwrights such as Migdalia Cruz and Luis Alfaro. The recipient of several grants, including an esteemed National Endowment for the Arts grant in 1974, and 10 Obie Awards, one of which is for sustained achievement in theater, Fornes was recognized as a master American dramatist in 2002 by the PEN/Laura Pels Foundation. In celebration of her work, the Signature Theatre Company devoted its 1999–2000 season to four plays by Fornes as its playwright in residence.

Fornes's interest in the arts started with painting, which she studied with Hans Hoffman in New York after immigrating to the United States in 1945. Later she went to Europe, in 1954, to foster her painting skills. Seeing the original Roger Blin production of *Waiting for Godot* in Paris was a life-changing experience for her. Although she came back to New York in 1957 as a textile designer, she took up writing soon and published her first play in 1961. *The Widow* was inspired by her experience of translating old family letters. *The Widow* has never been staged, though it launched the playwright's prolific career. Besides translating and adapting works by Federico García Lorca, Pedro Calderón de la Barca, Henrik Ibsen, and Anton Chekhov, Fornes has written some 40 plays, among which the most credited are *The Successful Life of 3* (1965), *Fefu and Her Friends* (1977), *The Danube* (1981), *Mud* (1983), *The Conduct of Life* (1985), *Abingdon Square* (1987), *What of the Night?* (1988), *Enter the Night* (1993), and *Letters from Cuba* (2000).

Fornes made her stage debut as a playwright in 1963 with an absurd exploration of a master-student relationship, *Tango Palace* (formerly entitled *There! You Died*). Her early plays, such as *Promenade* (1965), *The Successful Life of 3*, and *Dr. Kheal* (1968), are marked by vaudevillian characterizations, a sense of the absurd, and "nowhere" settings. From 1977 onward, Fornes's writing has become more political, and her characters, more three-dimensional.

Through its innovative staging and play-within-a-play structure, *Fefu and Her Friends* leads to the discovery of the unexposed truths behind the lives of eight women who come together in Fefu's country house in 1935. The second act of the play invites its audience from the auditorium to walk through the main stage and watch four scenes backstage acted simultaneously. A politically driven play, *The Danube* illustrates the perverse effects of nuclear war on daily life through 14 scenes. These scenes rely on the use of dialogue, the actors' physical occupation of space, the playing of language tapes, puppetry, and postcard backdrops. Likewise, *The Conduct of Life* exposes the ill effects of power by focusing on an army officer's desire for promotion that ends up in abuse, torture, and rape.

Fornes's Pulitzer Prize–nominated play *What of the Night?* develops the idea of social corruption in four episodes ("Nadine," "Springtime," "Lust," and "Hunger") that are finalized with an apocalyptic vision, evolving from the Great Depression era into the future. *Letters from Cuba* is a play of nostalgia staged in two physical spaces to represent a Cuban immigrant girl in the United States and her family back in Cuba. In her representation of a family separated by geography and politics, Fornes's work can be read within the context of CUBAN-AMERICAN LITERATURE.

Since 1968 Fornes has directed most productions of her plays as well as works by other writers. Fornes's painting legacy surfaces in her use of the detailed mise-en-scène. Her plays constitute a visual exploration wherein the characters' postures are as carefully staged as the other components of stage design. The language of her plays is pure, poetic, and innovative. What marks a Fornes play is a strong sense of lyricism overshadowed by decadence, desire for knowledge or power, and ambiguous finales. Although Fornes has been considered by critics as a feminist, absurdist, realist, and, in some cases, avant-garde writer, the playwright's dramas defy categorization. The effects of everyday life (such as language tapes, books, or dresses she randomly finds in open markets or garage sales) are usually mingled with a variety of literary traditions in an experimental concord in a Fornes play. Her artistic inspiration comes from writers such as Ibsen, Chekhov, Samuel Beckett, and Virgilio Piñera to Edward Hopper in painting and Olga Guillot and Patsy Cline in music. The playwright has recently been working on an adaptation of *The Autobiography of Alice B. Toklas* by Gertrude Stein.

Bibliography

Delgado, Maria M., and Caridad Svich, eds. *Conducting a Life*. New York: Smith & Kraus, 1999.

Fornes, Maria Irene. *Fefu and Her Friends*. New York: PAJ Publications, 1990.

———. *Plays: Mud, The Danube, The Conduct of Life, Sarita*. New York: PAJ Publications, 1986.

———. *Promenade and Other Plays*. New York: PAJ Publications, 1987.

Kent, Assunta Bartolomucci. *Maria Irene Fornes and Her Critics*. Westport, Conn.: Greenwood Press, 1996.

Moroff, Diane L. *Fornes: Theater in the Present Tense*. Ann Arbor: University of Michigan Press, 1996.

Robinson, Marc, ed. *The Theater of Maria Irene Fornes*. Baltimore, Md.: Johns Hopkins University Press, 1999.

Yeliz Biber Tilbe

Freak: A Semi-Demi-Quasi-Pseudo Autobiography **John Leguizamo** (1998)

Actor, comedian, writer, and director John Leguizamo was born in Colombia in July 1964. *Freak: A Semi-Demi-Quasi-Pseudo Autobiography* is Leguizamo's own coming-of-age story about growing up Puerto Rican and Colombian in Queens, New York. An adaptation of the one-man Broadway show he performed in under the direction of David Bar Katz, the paperback version includes additional material woven into the narrative. *Freak* conveys through humor aspects of the comedian's life and that of his family, while also exposing conventional views (and misconceptions) about Latinos. *Freak* delves into family dynamics between husbands and wives and between

parents and children; toward that end Leguizamo explores the male and female roles in the household. *Freak* reveals how people categorically lump him, a Colombian Puerto Rican, with the rest of Latinos in Queens, as if Latinos were an ethnically coherent group. (*Latinos* is a term that includes many cultures: Puerto Ricans, Mexican Americans, Cuban Americans, Dominican Americans, Colombian Americans, etc.)

One of the themes of *Freak* is his parents' relationship. His representation of the relationship between his mother and father sets up a binary between machismo (male pride and sense of strength by virtue of tradition) and *marianismo* (female suffering as the consequence of male pride). In this regard *Freak* can be read alongside works such as OCTAVIO PAZ's essay "MEXICAN MASKS." But while setting up macho and *marianista* tensions, *Freak* nevertheless departs from them. Leguizamo explains that while his father had extramarital relationships, his mother, while going to school, became "involved" in feminist ideology. In the Broadway performance of *Freak,* the audience watches Leguizamo perform Gloria Gaynor's famous 1970s self-liberating song "I Will Survive" as a validation of the mother's resilience. She tells Fausto, her husband, that she no longer needs him, admitting that she has been aware of his relationships with other women.

As expected of an autobiographical text, Leguizamo makes references to his own acting career by watching what happens when actors are cast to perform his script. The assistant director of the show has to decide whether to use Latino or non-Latino actors. When Latinos are cast as Latino characters, Leguizamo and other social critics have noted that the parts are often superficial ones, roles as maids and drug dealers.

In *Freak* the assistant director comments about the "reality" of show business and reveals a preference for non-Latinos acting Latino roles. Examples of non-Latinos acting in Latino roles date to the 1940s with Henry Fonda acting the role of a Mexican priest in *The Power and the Glory;* in the 1980s Al Pacino acted as the Cuban drug dealer in *Scarface.* This misalignment reflects the challenge that

Latino actors face in seeking parts: In soap operas, television dramas, and films it is commonplace to find non-Latino actors playing Latino roles. It is perhaps less common for Latino actors to play crossover characters, but Leguizamo has done this in avant-garde films, such as *Moulin Rouge* (1997) and in the animated movies *Ice Age* and *Ice Age 2,* where he plays Sid the Sloth.

In addition to *Freak* Leguizamo has published *Mambo Mouth* (1991), which focuses on both fictitious and real members of his family, and *Spic-o-rama* (1993), which touches on stereotypes that mainstream American society has about Latinos. His 2002 work, *Sexaholix: A Love Story,* discusses his life as a Latino living in the United States.

Bibliography

Brantley, Ben. "A One-Man Melting Pot Bubbling Over with Demons." *New York Times,* February 13, 1998, p. B-1.

Leguizamo, John. *Freak.* New York: Riverhead Books, 1997.

Vellela, Tony. "One-man Show Translates Latin Culture into Universal Appeal." *Christian Science Monitor* 3, March 20, 1989, p. B-5.

Enrique Morales-Díaz

Friendly Cannibals Guillermo Gómez-Peña (1996)

GUILLERMO GÓMEZ-PEÑA's *Friendly Cannibals* is a bilingual (Spanish and English) multimedia novella set in the late 1990s and illustrated by Chicano artist Enrique Chagoya. Gómez-Peña draws on the conventions of the cyberpunk genre (a genre known for its grim outlook on the future) to present a bleak vision of United States. The novella imitates the staples of the cyberpunk setting, with collapsed geopolitical borders replaced by fully borderized cities and governments replaced by transnational corporations. It is a politically charged work that relies heavily on satire and offers a scathing critique of current race relations, in particular between white, English-speaking Americans and Mexican Americans, in the United States. In *Friendly Cannibals* the near future of the United States is one in which Spanish speakers are the cultural mainstream; Anglos are the nation's new "minority," and the government is now controlled by a multiracial government, the "Chicano Intifada."

True to the cyberpunk genre's form, *Friendly Cannibals* takes place in cyberspace and is told in the form of e-mails written from one "ethnocyborg" to another. An obvious narrative voice for the author himself, the "ethnocyborg" reiterates many of Gómez-Peña's views on the place of race in our contemporary cyberculture. Lodging a critique, for instance, of the Internet utopianism that pervaded the early 1990s, the narrator insists in an e-mail to his cyber-lover that cyberspace is an open and dynamic space.

One obvious way of reading *Friendly Cannibals* is as a literary representation of Gómez-Peña's political consciousness, an endeavor that likewise shapes his book *The NEW WORLD BORDER: PROPHECIES, POEMS AND LOQUERAS FOR THE END OF THE CENTURY* (1996). *Friendly Cannibals* is a compelling literary companion to Gómez-Peña's other work, illustrating—literally, with the help of Chagoya—the fears and desires expressed elsewhere in his performance art and essays. Politically charged and parodic, *Friendly Cannibals* represents a rare moment in the science fiction genre, itself predominantly a white, English-speaking form, in which a Chicano perspective sheds light on tense relations between the United States and Mexico. Gómez-Peña's work can be read within the context of CHICANO LITERATURE as well as science fiction and performance art.

Bibliography

Gómez-Peña, Guillermo. *Dangerous Border Crossers: The Artist Talks Back.* New York: Routledge, 2000.

———. *Friendly Cannibals.* San Francisco, Calif.: Artspace Books, 1996.

———. *New World Border: Prophecies, Poems & Loqueras for the End of the Century.* San Francisco, Calif.: City Lights, 1996.

———. *Warrior for Gringostroika: Essays, Performance Texts, and Poetry.* St. Paul, Minn.: Graywolf Press, 1993.

Lysa Rivera

From the Cables of Genocide: Poems on Love and Hunger Lorna Dee Cervantes (1991)

The themes of loss, hunger, longing, and genocide are at the heart of *From the Cables of Genocide: Poems on Love and Hunger,* LORNA DEE CERVANTES's second collection of poetry. In her lyrical voice Cervantes struggles with issues of death, divorce, and the weight of her family history. *From the Cables of Genocide* is not just a narrative about loss or sundering; it is also a story of recovery. While denouncing the decimation of her indigenous ancestors, Cervantes also celebrates her Mexican-American heritage.

Using an alter ego and gripping imagery, Cervantes meditates on moments of loss, as in the opening poem, "Drawings: For John Who Said to Write about True Love." She writes: "My skill is losing" (62). In order to fill the ensuing void, the poetic persona in "Drawings" embarks on an emotional journey, attempting to recover the memories of people and places that at one time formed part of her life. Fittingly, the act of walking and the experience of the journey are metaphors for this quest: "I walk a steady mile" (51). "Walking" appears as a trope in other key poems, such as "On Touring Her Hometown," "Walking Around," and "Shooting the Wren." As is made evident in "Drawings," the speaker yearns for a complete past, which is embodied by a heart which is the collection's most important symbol, representing in their life and love, totality.

Hunger as in Cervantes's EMPLUMADA (1981), is a central theme in *From the Cables of Genocide.* Memory and love become synonymous for physical and emotional nourishment. Genocide and the salvaging of her culture and history are also chief concerns in this collection. The poet carries the responsibility of writing down her history; thus, in "Walking Around," the speaker professes: "I walk,/heavy with the towing of ancestors" (31–32).

Yet, what was in *Emplumada* a lament for the silencing of her Native American culture grows into outrage in *From the Cables of Genocide.* Cervantes condemns the colonization of Native Americans, which can be read as genocide. The prevalent image of a spectral figure embodies their annihilation. In "Flatirons," dedicated to the Ute and Arapaho, she writes of the past by reflecting: "She is there / in the silent baying, in the memory of a native " (25–26). The ghost epitomizes the persistence of memory, the symbolic presence of her ancestors that still inhabit their sacred places. In "Pleiades from the Cables of Genocide," which narrates the Chumash myth of creation identifying the Pleiades as their forebears, she shows the ghost of her grandmother repossessing her rightful lands: "She rides / Now through the Reagan Ranch her mother owned" (80–81).

From the Cables of Genocide won the Paterson Poetry Prize for Best Book of Poetry published in 1991 and the Latino Literature Prize in 1993. It was also nominated in 1992 for the National Book Award.

Bibliography

Binder, Wolfgang. *Partial Autobiographies.* Erlangen, Germany: Palm & Enke, 1985.

Candelaria, Cordelia. *Chicano Poetry: A Critical Introduction.* Westport, Conn.: Greenwood Press, 1986.

Cervantes, Lorna Dee. *Drive: The First Quartet.* San Antonio, Tex.: Wings Press, 2005.

———. *Emplumada.* Pittsburgh, Pa.: University of Pittsburgh Press, 1981.

———. *From the Cables of Genocide: Poems on Love and Hunger.* Houston, Tex.: Arte Público Press, 1991.

González, Ray. "I Trust Only What I Have Built with My Own Hands: An Interview with Lorna Dee Cervantes." *Bloomsbury Review* 17, no. 5 (September–October 1997): 3, 8.

G

García, Cristina (1958–) (novelist, journalist)

The daughter of Francisco M. García and Esperanza Lois García, Cristina García was born on July 4, 1958, in Havana, Cuba. Like many middle-class families, the Garcías left the island after FIDEL CASTRO took power in 1959. Settling in New York, they ran a family restaurant, and García attended the Dominican Academy. In 1979 she graduated with a bachelor's degree in political science from Barnard College. Intending to pursue a career in the U.S. Foreign Service, García continued her education and graduated from Johns Hopkins University's School of Advanced International Studies in Washington, D.C., earning a master's degree in European and Latin American studies.

García initiated her writing career as a reporter for the *Boston Globe, United Press International, Knoxville Journal,* and *New York Times.* The height of her journalism career came with her tenure at *Time,* where she served as Miami bureau chief from 1987 to 1988; she covered news and events in Florida and the Caribbean.

Like her literary counterparts OSCAR HIJUELOS and GUSTAVO PÉREZ FIRMAT, García considers the effect of the CUBAN REVOLUTION and Castro's regime on Cubans who left the island for the United States. Her 1992 novel *DREAMING IN CUBAN* takes place in New York and includes many autobiographical details. *Dreaming in Cuban* tells the story of three generations of del Piño women: Celia del Piño, living in Havana, Lourdes del Piño, living in Brooklyn, and Lourdes's rebellious daughter, Pilar. After flight from Cuba, Lourdes del Piño runs a bakery in Brooklyn and is determined to succeed, by working hard, in pursuit of the American dream. Her daughter, Pilar, feels acutely the rifts in the family caused by Castro's government, the U.S. embargo against Cuba, and the torn allegiances of family members on the island and in the United States. Thus she stands in opposition to her mother's anti-Castro views and seeks alliance, at least to some degree, with her grandmother who remains in Cuba. Overall, the novel functions as both a fictional autobiography and an interesting portrait of the immigrant experience of Cubans in New York.

In the 1990s García began her career as a novelist with the support of several prestigious fellowships. These included the Hodder fellowship at Princeton University and the Cintas fellowship for artists and writers of Cuban descent, as well as a Guggenheim Foundation fellowship. From 1992 until 1995, García taught creative writing at the Los Angeles and Santa Barbara campuses of University of California. She has since taught in the English Department at the University of Southern California in Los Angeles, where she lives with her daughter, Pilar.

She published her second level, *The AGÜERO SISTERS,* in 1997. Like *Dreaming in Cuban,* it centers on the flight from Cuba to New York and later to Miami. This novel continues to explore the lives of families who are torn apart in their allegiances to Cuba and the United States. The story follows the lives of two sisters, Constancia and Reina, who move apart both emotionally and psychologically as the plot of the novel unfolds. One tension in the story is the mysterious circumstances of Blanca Agüero's death (Constancia and Reina's mother). Each daughter has her own memories of Blanca, memories that set Constancia and Reina at odds. Moving in time between the 1920s and the present, with a few narrative stops in between, the novel has a tapestry-like quality that makes it difficult for some readers. Geographically, the story line moves between Cuba and Florida, but García brings together the disparate elements and characters by the end of the story in a tentative reconciliation between the two sisters. The reader is left with hope for the family—torn apart by violence, geography, and politics—with discovery of Reina's pregnancy. Her child, fathered by an American, will presumably live in a world of multitudinous allegiances but without the intense strife of Reina and Constancia's generation.

García's most recent novel is MONKEY HUNTING (2003), which explores the theme of immigration through a wide lens that includes the heritage of Chinese, African, and Cuban families. The novel tells the story of 19th-century Chinese adventurer Chen Pen and Lucrecia, the Afro-Cuban mother of his children, and the challenges that their children and grandchildren face in the United States and China.

Like other Latina authors, García employs in her fiction the use of MAGICAL REALISM, especially in The Agüero Sisters. For its themes and characterizations, García's work can be read within the context of SPANISH-AMERICAN CARIBBEAN LITERATURE as well as CUBAN-AMERICAN LITERATURE.

Bibliography

Davis, Rocío G. "Back to the Future: Mothers, Languages, and Homes in Cristina García's *Dreaming in Cuban*." *World Literature Today* 74 (Winter 2000): 60–68.

García, Cristina. *Dreaming in Cuban*. New York: Knopf, 1992.

———. *The Agüero Sisters*. New York: Knopf, 1997.

———. *Monkey Hunting*. New York: Knopf, 2003.

García Ramis, Magali (1946–   )
(journalist, short story writer, novelist)

Magali García Ramis was born in Santurce, Puerto Rico, in 1946. She studied at the University of Puerto Rico and then earned an M.S. from Columbia University, in New York City, in 1969; after living in Mexico for a number of years, she returned to the island and currently serves as faculty in the University of Puerto Rico's Department of Public Communication. While working as a journalist, García Ramis developed her creative writing career. Her story "Todos los domingos" (Every Sunday) won the 1971 first prize in short fiction awarded by the Ateneo Puertorriqueño. In 1974 García Ramis received an honorable mention for "La vida de Chencho el Loco" from Cuba's premier cultural institute and publishing house, CASA DE LAS AMÉRICAS. Her first short story collection, *La familia de todos nosotros* (The family of all of us), was published in 1976, a watershed year in PUERTO RICAN LITERATURE, given the publication of seminal works by such authors as Luis Rafael Sánchez and Manuel Ramos Otero. *La familia de todos nosotros* introduces the main characteristics of García Ramis's fiction: a lighthearted sense of humor, an incisive social critique, and an interest in middle-class Puerto Rican family values, all of which are present in the title story.

The title story, "La familia de todos nosotros" takes place on the island Puerto Rico and can be read as a family dialogue between 15-year-old Lydia and her uncle Geño. The plot centers on the inexplicable sickness of Ileana, Geño's sister and Lydia's aunt, who has given up the will to live. Although the family sends for Geño, who is living in New York, Aunt Ileana's malaise continues even after his arrival, and Geño and Lydia, the unofficial family historians, tackle the problem. They begin to look for antecedents in the family archives and discover a few cases of family members who have suddenly given up on life; however, they attribute these illnesses to different causes. University trained, Geño "objectively" explains that Ileana's depression reflects a defeatist attitude that is typical of Puerto Ricans; meanwhile, Lydia "subjectively" sees her aunt's melancholy as "sadness of the soul." They do agree that the solution lies (literally and metaphorically) in the soil. Every night they apply soil to Ileana's hands and feet but hide this activity from the rest of their relations. The application of garden soil is a way of connecting to nature, a gesture that reminds the reader of the earth to which we will return in the cycle of life; it is also a way for García Ramis to celebrate the island earth as a part of a Puerto Rican identity.

Various family members come up with their own treatments (pills, prayers, and talismans). After a couple of days, Aunt Ileana suddenly recovers the will to live, and each member takes credit for the recovery. When Geño and Lydia explain their diagnosis and treatment, the family unanimously rejects them. Lydia notes that even though family members reached a different conclusion about the illness, their interpretations share the same basic premise: To explain and cure current maladies, a family needs to look back into its histories. That thematic premise, the use of a female narrative voice, and the plot device of the uncle returning from New York are further developed by García Ramis in *Felices Días, Tío Sergio* (1986), translated into English as *HAPPY DAYS, UNCLE SERGIO*. A bittersweet coming-of-age novel, *Happy Days* is about growing up during a period of intense development and modernization on the island.

Along with her fiction, García Ramis has published urban commentary in the island's newspapers and journals. She is one of seven authors who, following an initiative by ANA LYDIA VEGA, contributed weekly columns in 1985 to the Puerto Rican nationalist newspaper *Claridad*. Those essays, including the controversial "No queremos a la Virgen" (We don't want the Virgin), were reprinted in *El tramo ancla* (1988; The anchor lap). García Ramis's essays have also been collected in *La ciudad que me habita* (1993; The city that inhabits me). *La ciudad que me habita* includes the piece "Los cerebros que se van y el corazón que se queda" (The brains that leave and the heart

that stays), which addresses the 1980s migration of young Puerto Rican professionals and college graduates to the mainland. In "La manteca que nos une" (The lard that joins us) the author refers to Puerto Rican eating habits, namely the preference for fattening foods, as a marker of national identity. In "La guagua uno (modelo para armar)" (The number one bus) the author considers the heavily trafficked public bus route in San Juan (the capital) and the bus as a microcosm of Puerto Rican metropolitan society.

In addition, García Ramis has written *La flor de piel* (1990, Skin deep), a teleplay about domestic violence; this play was coproduced by the governmental Division of Women Affairs and was broadcast on the island. Her latest collection of fiction is *Las noches del Riel de Oro* (1995; The nights of the Golden Rail), and she is working on a novel that, in its 19th-century setting, would anticipate the 1950s plot of *Happy Days*. She joins several women writers, including Rosario Ferré and Vega, whose work reveals a feminist movement in Puerto Rican literature from the 1970s to the present.

García Ramis's latest novel, *Las horas del sur* (San Juan: Ediciones Callejon, 2006), reflects the author's ongoing interest with genealogical research. García Ramis once again resorts to the device of two young cousins, Enrique and Lydia, who inquire into their family history. Told mostly from the point of view of an older woman they interview in San Juan, the novel follows the adventurous life of carpenter-turned-journalist Andrés Estelrich. Estelrich grows up in Puerto Rico and travels throughout New York, Europe, and Mexico while working for a science magazine. He eventually returns to Puerto Rico during the 1950 nationalist revolution. *Las horas del sur* got a lukewarm reception, unlike *Felices Dias, Tio Sergio,* which is mandatory reading at many Puerto Rican schools.

Bibliography

García Ramis, Magali. *La ciudad que me habita*. Río Piedras, P.R.: Ediciones Huracán, 1993.
———. "Every Sunday." Translated by Carmen C. Esteves. *Callaloo* 17, no. 3 (Summer 1994): 851–861.

———. *La familia de todos nosotros.* San Juan, P.R.: Instituto de Cultura Puertorriqueña, 1976.

———. *Happy Days, Uncle Sergio.* Translated by Carmen C. Esteves. Fredonia, N.Y.: White Pine Press, 1995.

Vega, Ana Lydia, ed. *El tramo ancla: Ensayos puertorriqueños de hoy.* Río Piedras, P.R.: Editorial de la Universidad de Puerto Rico, 1988.

Roberto Carlos Ortiz

Gaspar de Alba, Alicia (1958–)
(novelist, essayist)

A mystery writer and historian, Alicia Gaspar de Alba was born in El Paso, Texas, in 1958. She received a B.A. (1980) and an M.A. (1983) in English from the University of Texas, El Paso, and a Ph.D. in American studies from the University of New Mexico in 1994. Her dissertation, entitled "'*Mi Casa [No] Es Su Casa*': The Cultural Politics of the Chicano Art: Resistance and Affirmation, 1965–1985," won the 1994 Ralph Henry Gabriel Award for Best Dissertation in American Studies. Gaspar de Alba is currently a professor in the Department of Chicano and Chicana Studies at the University of California, Los Angeles. In addition to her award-winning novel *DESERT BLOOD: THE JÚAREZ MURDERS* (2005), she has published criticism, short stories, and poetry.

The work of Gaspar de Alba often focuses on the lives of women and incorporates figures of Mexican culture such as LA MALINCHE and LA LLORONA. Her work can be read within the context of LATINA LESBIAN LITERATURE, CHICANO LITERATURE, and BORDER LITERATURE.

Bibliography

Gaspar de Alba, Alicia. *Chicana Art Inside/Outside the Master's House: Cultural Politics and the CARA Exhibition.* Austin: University of Texas Press, 1999.

———. *Desert Blood: The Juárez Murders.* Houston, Tex.: Arte Público Press, 2005.

———. *La Llorona on the Longfellow Bridge: Poetry y Otras Movidas, 1985–2001.* Houston, Tex.: Arte Público Press, 2003.

———. *Sor Juana's Second Dream.* Albuquerque: University of New Mexico Press, 1999.

———. *The Mystery of Survival and Other Stories.* Tempe, Ariz.: Bilingual Press/Editorial Bilingüe, 1993.

"Alicia Gaspar de Alba." VG: Voices from the Gaps. Available online. URL: http://voices.cla.umn.edu/vg/Bios/entries/alba_alicia_gaspar_de.html. Accessed December 17, 2007.

Sarah Boslaugh

Geographies of Home Loida Maritza Pérez (1999)

LOIDA MARITZA PÉREZ was born in the Dominican Republic in 1963 and is a 1987 graduate of Cornell University. *Geographies of Home*, her debut novel, represents working-class Dominican immigrants arriving in New York during the 1970s and 1980s. The experiences in the novel stand in contrast to those represented by middle-class authors such as JULIA ALVAREZ, Chiqui Vicioso, and Manuel Mora Serrano in that Pérez seeks to imagine a more inclusive portrait of Dominican identity.

Geographies of Home is a striking depiction of an immigrant family from the Dominican Republic trying to survive their grim reality of life in East Brooklyn, New York. With *Geographies of Home*, Pérez joins a number of authors who have used the house as a focal point to express identity, as in ISABEL ALLENDE's *The HOUSE OF THE SPIRITS* (1982), MAGALI GARCÍA RAMIS's *HAPPY DAYS, UNCLE SERGIO* (1986), and SANDRA CISNEROS's *The HOUSE ON MANGO STREET* (1984). Allende, García Ramis, and Cisneros investigate the complicated dynamics of ethnicity and gender with characters living in isolating circumstances. Likewise, in Pérez's novel, "home" serves as an emotional as well as physical space. The home in her work cannot resist the brutal realities of the contemporary immigrant experience. Pérez combines the metaphor of the house with an array of distinctive characters—all within the same family unit—whose gender and racial roles shift. The author thus avoids the often unforeseen pitfalls of stereotypes.

In her rendering of the perplexities of one family Pérez investigates the proverbial promise of the American Dream. Iliana, one of 14 siblings, is the youngest daughter of Papito and Aurelia. The entire family is plunged into the nightmarish struggle for survival in New York City. Iliana is a student at an elite college located more than five hours away from the grime of her urban existence, but a sense of alienation and a series of family crises force her to leave school. After receiving what she believes are telepathic messages from her ailing mother, Iliana returns to the dysfunctional family setting. Through family members she is besieged by madness, domestic violence, suicide, sexual assault, religious fanaticism, and self-hatred. But, in the family there is also a shared sense of resilience in the immigrant experience.

Iliana's father, Papito, seeks redemption in the unbending ways of the Seventh-Day Adventist Church. The depiction of the family as Adventists is particularly well conceived since Latinos are generally seen as Catholic. The proselytizing of this Protestant faith offers the author a ready device for juxtaposing alternate forms of spirituality. Aurelia, for example, while Adventist like her husband, nevertheless retains a very strong connection to the beliefs, rituals, and superstitions of her island past. She hopes the family chaos will simply "disappear" if she merely pretends it does not exist.

The author's portrait of the present-day immigrant experience is so powerful that it is often difficult to distinguish what is real and what is not. Throughout the novel both the magical and the mundane coexist; for example, Iliana's intelligence and almost supernatural intuition chafe against her parents' authority. She experiences guilt as she tries to help her family and define a "home" for herself. The author shows us early that "reality" is forever shifting, and "home" subsequently becomes more evasive in her attempts to define it. Pérez demonstrates that survival, in the end, depends on erecting a home for oneself, not necessarily a geographical site.

One can read Pérez's novel within the context of Dominican history and society. The island society has, especially during Rafael Trujillo's regime, conceptualized its identity in terms of its Spanish heritage, while aggressively denying its African connections. The Dominican-American intellectual Silvio Torres-Saillant and other scholars have observed that though the island population has African roots, there is a denial about blackness. Dominicans of African descent, according to Torres-Saillant, have failed to assert pride in their heritage, especially given the "negrophobia" of the lighter-skinned elite. For her part, Pérez was born into a society where, historically, the small but powerful elite has secured its privileges by alienating women and a considerable majority of its Afro-Dominican citizenry. For the most part, Afro-Latino immigrants arrive in the United States with very little, if any, familiarity with a discourse of black affirmation. Afro-Dominicans learn quickly that race and cultural identity do indeed matter in the United States; there are dire implications impinging upon one's very survival in the new environment. The Afro-Dominican newcomer has entered a society that often sees only black and white, and little in between. But, for immigrants from the Caribbean there is a range of ethnic mixes: mulattoes (Spanish and African), *trequeños* (people with wheat-colored skin), *indios claros* (light-skinned Indians), and *indios oscuros* (dark-skinned Indians).

For writers such as Pérez, the novel becomes an imaginative space to bring to the fore the keen intuition of women and those other marginalized individuals in the complicated process of self-discovery. She tries to answer, through her collection of family characters, the torturous question, Who are you? Pérez reminds us that in the process of self-discovery, one can find meaning and a sense of authenticity in identity, family, and home.

Throughout her novel Pérez explores the theme of identity and home by offering the diverse memories of an immigrant Dominican family who, like so many other immigrant groups, were lured to this country by the promise of escape from fear, poverty, and pain. Although there is the anxious question common to nearly all newcomers—that of trying to reconcile honored traditions, customs, and beliefs with the challenging expectations in the new, often threatening environment—the author here defies convention as she grants authoritative voice to each of the novel's characters. For its themes and characterizations her novel can be read within the context of DOMINICAN-AMERICAN LITERATURE.

Bibliography

Boyce Davis, Carol. *Black Women, Writing and Identity: Migrations of the Subject.* New York: Routledge, 1994.

Cambeira, Alan. *Quisqueya la Bella: The Dominican Republic in Historical and Cultural Perspective.* Armonk, N.Y.: M. E. Sharpe Publishers, 1997.

Heredia, Aida. "The Journey Inward." In *Daughters of the Diaspora: Afra-Hispanic Writers*, edited by Miriam DeCosta-Willis, 326–334. Kingston, Jamaica: Ian Randle Publishers, 2003.

Ojito, Mirta. "Dominicans, Scrabbling for Hope." *New York Times,* December 16, 1997, B1, B7.

Pérez, Loida Maritza. *Geographies of Home.* New York: Penguin, 1999.

Torres-Saillant, Silvio, and Ramona Hernández. *The Dominican-Americans.* Westport, Conn.: Greenwood Press, 1998.

Alan Cambeira

Goddess of the Americas/La diosa de las Américas: Writings on the Virgin of Guadalupe Ana Castillo (1996)

Mexican-American author ANA CASTILLO is the editor of *Goddess of the Americas/ La Diosa de las Américas: Writings on the Virgin of Guadalupe.* This eclectic collection of essays focuses on Mexico's patron saint and includes contributors who are writers, performers, spiritual advisers, social activists, and teachers. The pieces reflect the beliefs of Catholics, Protestants, Jews, and practitioners of the Afro-Caribbean religion Yoruba Lucumí. In terms of cultural identity contributors write about the Virgin from Mexican, Mexican-American, African-American, Jewish, and European-American perspectives. Of the 27 contributors, 11 are men and 16 are women; gay and lesbian voices are also represented. The diversity of voices in this anthology is fitting because there are multiple symbols attached to the Virgin of Guadalupe.

Each writer recounts an important aspect of the first miraculous appearance of the brown-skinned Madonna. In 1531 Spanish conquistadores brought the image of the Madonna from Extremadura, Spain, to Tepeyac, Mexico. The story is as follows: The Virgin appears as an apparition to the recently converted Indian Juan Diego. She asks that a church be built for her on an ancient place of worship, the Hill of Tepeyac, a site connected with the Aztec goddess of fertility, Tonantzin. Juan Diego asks the Basque bishop Zumárraga for permission, but the bishop denies Diego's request. The Virgin instructs the Indian to fill his *tilma* (cloak made of maguey fibers) with roses that are blooming in the dead of winter and take them to the bishop as proof of her presence. When Juan Diego opens his robe, the miraculous flowers fall out, revealing the image of the Virgin on the inside of his cloak. We can see this image today in the Basilica of Our Lady of Guadalupe in Mexico City. Over the centuries this image remains incorruptible. Its colors are still vibrant and its rough fibers have survived a bombing, a spill of nitric acid, and 116 years of unprotected exposure to believers' hands. Scientific studies performed on the *tilma* reveal other startling details: Its colors consist of no known pigment; the stars on Mary's mantle form constellations positioned exactly as they were on the day of her apparition; the likenesses of recognizable people have been identified in Guadalupe's irises, as if permanently reflected there.

Writers explain how Guadalupe is associated with Tonantzin, an Aztec goddess of fertility, sexuality, and war. The Virgin has meaning for a wide range of viewers, writers, adherents of the Catholic faith, and civil rights activists. Her banner has been carried by Mexican rebels seeking independence from Spain as well as by participants in CESAR CHAVEZ's United Farm Workers' demonstrations. For Guatemalan-American author Francisco Goldman, the Virgin recalls other unorthodox spiritual icons such as Guatemala's pleasure-seeking saint, Maximón. GUILLERMO GÓMEZ-PEÑA notes that the image of the Virgin has been used by politically conservative groups in Mexico, yet Gómez-Peña employs the image of the Virgin of Guadalupe to reclaim his Spanish and Aztec heritage and to contest English-speaking and U.S. authorities that infringe on the expression of cultural identity.

The worship of the Virgin of Guadalupe within the context of the Spanish Conquest has promoted different kinds of readings, some contradicting others. Nobel Prize winner OCTAVIO PAZ views the Virgin of Guadalupe and La MALINCHE (Hernán Cortés's interpreter and concubine) as two possibilities for Mexican women: the faithful, consoling mother and the disloyal, violated mother. His controversial view of women as passive and comes from his famous book *The Labyrinth of Solitude* (1962); this is probably the most often cited work on Mexican machismo (exaggerated pride in being a man).

Chicana and Mexican feminists such as Rosario Castellanos and Jeanette Rodriguez read the figure of the Virgin in both historical and feminist terms. Rosario Castellanos considers the association of the Virgin with Sor Juana Inés de la Cruz, the famous educated nun and writer of Mexico. Castellanos explains how the 16th-century nun was misunderstood and mistrusted because of her genius and her desire for a cloistered life.

Jeanette Rodriguez explains that since its early history, Christianity has associated victory, power, and judgment with the male European God and the maternal, compassionate, unconditionally loving aspects of God with the Virgin Mary. In her study of religion, race, and gender she comes to the conclusion that many Mexican-American women need to identify with a "feminine face of God," a sentiment echoed throughout this volume. SANDRA CISNEROS views Guadalupe-Tonantzin as a liberating figure in the context of her upbringing that locked her in "a double chastity belt of ignorance and *vergüenza*, shame" (46).

Some writers highlight the Virgin's brown skin that makes her accessible to people of color and more representative of the Americas than the numerous pale-faced Virgins. New Orleans native Luisa Teish describes how Christian conversion was used to justify exploitation of native peoples and Africans. The prohibition of their religious practices forced them to create hybrid forms such as Guadalupe-Tonantzin and the pantheon of *Orishas* (African deities) worshipped secretly, each associated with a Catholic saint. She sees several nature goddesses in Guadalupe. Living in the United States, she feels neither she, as a woman of African heritage, nor her past are honored, and Teish finds comfort in Guadalupe. Teish notes theologians' tendency to claim that black Virgins found in Europe were not originally black, which she calls an "attempt on the part of the Vatican to deny Mother Africa and the dark races as the foreparents of humanity" (141). This would be a vain effort, according to RICHARD RODRIGUEZ. Rodriguez, the author of *Hunger of Memory* (1981), *DAYS OF OBLIGATION* (1992), and *BROWN: THE LAST DISCOVERY OF AMERICA* (2002), sees Guadalupe's as the face of Catholicism in the 20th century.

Our Lady of Guadalupe, patron of the suffering, proletariat, undocumented, and marginalized, allows herself to be transformed infinitely to reflect her devotees in political banners, religious tracts, all manner of kitsch, tattoos, and T-shirts. Just as contemplation on the Virgin led the writers of this anthology to recall their encounters with the divine, the mystery, such will be the experience of readers of Castillo's *Goddess of the Americas*.

Bibliography
Castillo, Ana, ed. *Goddess of the Americas/La diosa de las Américas: Writings on the Virgin of Guadalupe*. New York: Riverhead Books, 1996.

Rodriguez, Jeanette. *Our Lady of Guadalupe: Faith and Empowerment among Mexican-American Women*. Foreword by Virgilio Elizondo. Austin: University of Texas Press, 1994.

Paula Straile Costa

Gómez-Peña, Guillermo (1955–)
(essayist, multimedia performance artist)

Born in 1955 and raised in Mexico City, performance artist Guillermo Gómez-Peña came to the United States in 1978 to perform as a "border crosser." His mission is to make experimental yet accessible art, to perform in politically charged sites for multicultural audiences. He seeks to collaborate with other artists and, in so doing, to cross and rid performance art of gender, age, and race boundaries. Gomez-Peña founded the binational arts collective known as Border Arts Workshop/Taller de Arte Fronterizo (1985–90). He has participated in a vast number of exhibitions, biennials, and festivals, including the Sydney Biennial (1992), the Whitney Biennial (1993), Sonart (1999), and Made in California at the Los Angeles Museum of Contemporary Art (2000). In 1991 he became the first Chicano/Mexican artist to receive a MacArthur Fellowship. He has also won a number of awards, such as the New York Bessie Award (1989), the Viva Los Artists Award (1993), and the Cineaste Lifetime Achievement Award at Taos Talking Pictures Film Festival (2000). Gómez-Peña's performance and installation are a global affair, as he has worked in hundreds of pieces across the United States, Canada, Mexico, Europe, Australia, the former Soviet Union, Colombia, Puerto Rico, Cuba, Brazil, and Argentina. He is author of *Ethno-Techno: Writings on Performance, Activism, and Pedagogy* (2005), *Codex Espangliensis: From Columbus to the Border Patrol* (2000), WARRIOR FOR GRINGOSTROIKA: ESSAYS, PERFORMANCE TEXTS, AND POETRY (1993), *The NEW WORLD BORDER: PROPHECIES, POEMS AND LOQUERAS FOR THE END OF THE CENTURY* (1996), *FRIENDLY CANNIBALS* (1996), *Temple of Confessions* (1997), and *DANGEROUS BORDER CROSSERS: THE ARTIST TALKS BACK* (2000). His use of multimedia, such as film and radio, and his unique and dynamic vision allow Gómez-Peña to contribute to the worlds of science fiction and fantasy, as well as to the ever-evolving terrain of cyberspace. His writing can be read within the context of both CHICANO LITERATURE and BORDER LITERATURE.

Bibliography
Gómez-Peña, Guillermo. *Codex Espangliensis: From Columbus to the Border Patrol.* San Francisco, Calif.: City Lights Books, 2000.

———. *Dangerous Border Crossers: The Artist Talks Back.* New York: Routledge, 2000.

———. *Ethno-Techno: Writings on Performance, Activism, and Pedagogy.* New York: Routledge, 2005.

———. *Friendly Cannibals.* San Francisco, Calif.: Artspace Books, 1996.

———. *New World Border: Prophecies, Poems and Loqueras for the End of the Century.* San Francisco, Calif.: City Lights Books, 1996.

———. *Warrior for Gringostroika: Essays, Performance Texts, and Poetry.* St. Paul, Minn.: Graywolf Press, 1993.

Lysa Rivera

Gonzales, Rodolfo (Corky Gonzales)
(poet) (1928–2005)

Though famous for only one poem, Rodolfo Gonzales was one of the most important activists and poets of the civil rights movement. Gonzales was born in Denver in 1928, the son of Mexican-American migrant farmers. Reared under straightened circumstances, and equipped with a high school degree, Corky Gonzales sought a means out of the poverty of the Denver barrio. In his late teens and early twenties, he trained as a boxer and achieved success as a professional featherweight. By the late 1950s, however, he came to focus on politics at both the local level in Denver and on the national level with Viva Kennedy, a presidential campaign that sought the (Catholic) Latino vote.

Throughout his career as an activist and writer, Gonzales developed his own brand of grassroots politics and drew attention to important issues among Mexican-American communities: access to education, decent housing, and opportunities for gainful employment.

Gonzalez's epic poem *I AM JOAQUÍN* (1967) tells the history of Mexican Americans from pre-Columbian times, up to the time of Hernán Cortés and on to the 20th century. Using one lyrical voice that moves through the ages, the poem identifies both the complexity and value of the rich heritage of the Mexican-American people: Spanish, Indian, and MESTIZO. The poem explores what it means to be mestizo, protests colonization, and laments cultural loss. The poem can be considered a significant contribution not only to the literature of civil rights, but also to CHICANO LITERATURE and Latino literature more broadly. *I Am Joaquín* can also be read alongside poems such as Pedro Pietri's "PUERTO RICAN OBITUARY" for its call for cultural autonomy within an "Anglo" English-speaking society.

Working primarily with urban youth, Gonzales founded the Crusade for Justice in Denver (1966);

this initiative resulted in a cultural center for Mexican-American artists and dancers as well as a school. At this time—the height of the civil rights movement—Gonzales embraced "El Plan Espiritual de AZTLAN", a Mexican-American manifesto that imagines the reclaiming of the territory that was lost after the TREATY OF GUADALUPE HIDALGO. The basic idea behind the manifesto is that Mexican Americans ought to be able to claim what was lost after the Treaty of 1858 not merely because the land once belonged to Mexico (and thus to some degree to the ancestors of today's Mexican Americans), but also because Aztlán is the mystical homeland of the Mexican-American people.

Within a broad context, the work that Gonzales did for the Chicano civil rights movement helped to stimulate productive discussions about work and education conditions for Latinos of diverse backgrounds. His death in 2005 was mourned by many Latinos, not only for the equally critical and self-affirming vision he offers in *I Am Joaquín*, but also for the energy he committed to the civil rights movement.

González, José Luis (1926–1996) *(fiction writer)*

José Luis González was a key figure in the modernization of PUERTO RICAN LITERATURE. Born in the Dominican Republic to a Puerto Rican father and a Dominican mother, González moved to Puerto Rico with his family at age 11. He was a student at the University of Puerto Rico when he published *En la sombra* (1943; In the shadow), his first short story collection. It was followed by *Cinco cuentos de sangre* (1945; Five blood stories), *El hombre en la calle* (1945; The man on the street), and *En este lado* (1954; On this side). In addition he published *Paisa* (1950), a novella about a Puerto Rican family torn apart by migration to the United States. Short stories such as "La carta" (1948; The letter) and "En el fondo del caño hay un negrito" (1950; There is a little black boy at the bottom of the water) are notable in the corpus of SPANISH-AMERICAN CARIBBEAN LITERATURE.

González moved to Mexico and earned a doctorate in literature from the Universidad Nacional Autónoma de México, where he became a professor. He became a Mexican citizen in 1955. After a 20-year absence the author returned to the publishing scene with revised versions of his early fiction, regrouped as *La galería y otros cuentos* (1972; The gallery and other stories) and *En Nueva York y otras desgracias* (1973; In New York and other disgraces). He also published "La noche en que volvimos a ser gente" (1972; The night we became people again).

Like MAGALI GARCÍA RAMIS, González's fiction takes a critical look at the effects of industrialization in rural Puerto Rico. The author was also concerned with the mass migrations that took place as part of the modernization process from the turn of the 19th century to the 20th. Among the themes addressed are the helplessness of the rural class, the degeneration of family values, and racial prejudice. Most of his characters were members of the Puerto Rican rural and working classes, often leading historians of Latin American literature to classify him as a regionalist writer.

Mambrú se fue a la guerra (1972; Mambrú went to war) includes a number of his important works. It features González's novella about the Korean War (and thus the title of the collection) and the short stories "La tercera llamada" (The third call) and "La noche en que volvimos a ser gente." In the latter González addresses the theme of Puerto Ricans living in New York with a lighthearted sense of humor and a hopeful vision.

The story is told from the point of view of a Puerto Rican factory worker in New York. While drinking beers with a friend, he narrates his experiences during a blackout in the city. Most of the story humorously recounts his efforts to get home from a Brooklyn factory in order to be with his wife, who is in labor with their first child. His dim-witted neighborhood friend, Trompoloco (Crazy Top), accompanies him. Once at home the narrator hears music coming from the roof. He goes upstairs and finds his neighbors having a party in the middle of the blackout. The protagonist inquires about the reason for the party. In response, a neighbor asks him to look up at the sky. He immediately understands. After spending years living under a sky illuminated by electric lights, the neighbors are reminded of Puerto Rican nights, lit only by the stars. The story ends when, after noticing similar parties on other rooftops throughout the barrio, the narrator explains that this evening was the night they became people again.

González's later work includes *Balada de otro tiempo* (1978; Ballad of another time), a short novel set in rural Puerto Rico; *La llegada* (1980; The arrival), a "fictional chronicle" about the U.S. occupation of Puerto Rico; and *La luna no era de queso* (1988; The moon was not made of cheese), a memoir.

The most important of his later publications is "El país de cuatro pisos" (1980; The four-storied country), an influential analysis of Puerto Rican national identity. In this essay González describes the development of Puerto Rican culture. He uses the metaphor of a four-storied building in which an Afro-Antillean foundation, a Spanish second floor, and an American third floor have set the basis for the fourth floor: Puerto Rico's current status as a commonwealth of the United States.

Bibliography

González, José Luis. *Balada de otro tiempo.* Río Piedras, P.R.: Ediciones Huracán, 1978.

———. *En Nueva York y otras desgracias.* 1973 Reprint, Río Piedras, P.R.: Ediciones Huracán, 1981.

———. *La galería y otros cuentos.* México: Ediciones Era, 1972.

———. *Mambrú se fue a la guerra.* México: Joaquín Mortiz, 1972.

———. *El país de cuatro pisos.* Río Piedras, P.R.: Cultural, 1980.

Roberto Carlos Ortiz

Guadalupe Hidalgo, Treaty of (1848)

The Treaty of Guadalupe Hidalgo officially ended the hostilities between the United States and Mexico during the 1840s. It is one of the most important U.S. documents. Bill Tate observes in his preface to the published version of the treaty that for Mexican Americans the Treaty of Guadalupe Hidalgo belongs next to the "Declaration of Independence, the Constitution, and the Bill of Rights" because it guarantees "their full rights as Americans; securing their life, liberty, and property" (3).

Interpretation of the causes of the U.S.-Mexican War, the initiation of the conflict, and the resolution of it has been the subject of much debate. Official histories of Mexico and the United States interpret the war in very different ways. Although, within the United States, the war with Mexico has historically been regarded as a "relatively minor incident" (Mahin 1); within Mexico, it has a much greater historical significance.

According to Ramón Eduardo Ruiz, the common arguments surrounding the causes of war fall into five "schools" of thought. The first argues that the Southern "slavocracy" desired a territorial expansion westward. The second school argues that it was the Northern commercial interests that fostered the westward expansion and eventual conflict. The third focuses on the ideological nature and political strategy of Manifest Destiny and states that the United States was fulfilling its destiny to claim all the western land and civilize the "savages." The fourth train of thought is that President James K. Polk and his personal and political ambitions were at the root of the conflict. Finally, the fifth school grapples with the question of a "national war guilt," the much more general idea of whether the United States or Mexico was "answerable for the conflict" (2–6).

Regardless of the cause of the war, official hostilities broke out in 1846, and the "Treaty of Peace" ended them. Once again, however, the interpretations of the treaty vary depending on location. The United States has tended to view the Treaty of Guadalupe Hidalgo favorably, as the country gained a very large portion of its territory through the treaty. Mexicans and Mexican Americans have tended to look upon the treaty as a political failure or as a U.S. betrayal of their interests. The treaty was negotiated in Villa Guadalupe Hidalgo, just north of Mexico City (now part of the Mexican capital), between the dates of January 2 and February 2, 1848, by José Bernardo Couto, Luis G. Cuevas, and Miguel Atristaín for Mexico and by

Nicholas P. Trist for the United States. It was then signed by the negotiators at the shrine of Our Lady of Guadalupe Hidalgo (Mahin 163).

The treaty itself consists of 23 articles. The first four pertain to the cessation of hostilities, the declaration of peace between the two nations, the return of any and all prisoners taken during the war, and the evacuation of occupied properties and lands. Article V pertains to the creation of a new boundary between the nations. The boundary line was amended with the Gadsden Treaty of 1853, which expanded the territory to include present-day New Mexico and Arizona. Article V has been the subject of recent debate. Because much of the boundary is defined by the paths of rivers, and because rivers shift their paths over time, the boundary line has actually moved. Some recent discussions have centered on whether or not that means that the possession of land shifts along with the shifts in the river. Articles VI and VII pertain to the passage of vessels along the boundary rivers. As a result of the treaty, the United States took possession of what would become Texas, California, Nevada, and Utah, as well as portions of Arizona, New Mexico, Colorado, and Wyoming.

Articles VIII and IX both pertain to the rights of Mexicans living within the territories ceded to the United States. These articles secure the rights of approximately 100,000 individuals either to "elect" to continue to be Mexican citizens or become U.S. citizens and remain within the United States, or to leave and "repatriate" to Mexico (Griswold del Castillo 62). The conversion to U.S. citizen would occur automatically after one year, should they take no action on their own behalf. Article XI charges the United States with suppressing the "savage tribes" in the new territories and preventing them from carrying out raids into Mexico. Article X, which was stricken from the treaty by the U.S. Senate, would have protected the Spanish and Mexican land grants in territories ceded to the United States.

It is Article VIII, perhaps, that has received the most attention because it pertains directly to the rights of citizens. For one, it is the basis of the claim by GLORIA ANZALDÚA and other authors that the border has encroached upon their cultural space. For another, Article VIII directly confers full citizenship upon Mexican Americans and grants them the right to hold and maintain property claims. Nevertheless, the "inviolable" rights, as spelled out in the treaty, did not withstand judicial and political interpretation in the following years, and eventually "the U.S. application of the treaty to the realities of life in the Southwest violated its spirit" (Griswold del Castillo 63). As early as 1849 there was discussion of excluding Mexican Americans as full U.S. citizens. Some of these claims were based on a desire to exclude Mexican Americans from benefitting from the California gold rush. In addition, although Native Americans had been considered full Mexican citizens under the Mexican constitution, they were excluded from U.S. citizenship under the Treaty of Guadalupe Hidalgo (Griswold del Castillo 69). During the 1960s and 1970s, Chicanos turned to the Treaty of Guadalupe Hidalgo as a basis for claims for social justice. They argued for the U.S. government to uphold the treaty and recognize the political rights of Chicanos and recognize the lands claims granted under the terms of the treaty. Several works of CHICANO LITERATURE, such as Rodolfo Gonzales's poem *I AM JOAQUÍN*, make reference to the treaty. It is a significant document in BORDER LITERATURE.

Bibliography

Griswold del Castillo, Richard. *The Treaty of Guadalupe Hidalgo: A Legacy of Conflict.* Norman: University of Oklahoma Press, 1990.

Mahin, Dean B. *Olive Branch and Sword: The United States and Mexico, 1845–1848.* Jefferson, N.C.: McFarland, 1997.

Ruiz, Ramón Eduardo, ed. *The Mexican War: Was It Manifest Destiny?* New York: Holt, Rinehart & Winston, 1963.

Tate, Bill. Foreword to *Guadalupe Hidalgo, Treaty of Peace 1848 and the Gadsden Treaty with Mexico, 1853.* Truchas, N.Mex.: Tate Gallery, 1967.

"Treaty of Mexico." Available online. URL: http://www.azteca.net/aztec/guadhida.html. Accessed December 27, 2007.

Ritch Calvin

Happy Days, Uncle Sergio Magali García Ramis (1986)

MAGALI GARCÍA RAMIS was raised in Santurce, a garden district of San Juan, and came of age in the 1950s, when islanders split between those who accepted Puerto Rico's U.S. commonwealth status and those who urged nationhood.

Originally published as *Felices Días, Tío Sergio* in 1986, its English translation, *Happy Days, Uncle Sergio* (1995), was well received by the *New York Times* and the *Library Journal*. A novel especially popular for high school and college readers in Puerto Rico, with growing audiences on the mainland of the United States, *Happy Days* features the coming-of-age story of the curious, rebellious, and somewhat awkward Lidia Solis. The plot involves Lidia's well-to-do and overbearing family and her impressions as a young woman growing up in a two-story house in the garden district of San Juan, Puerto Rico's capital. Lidia Solis reflects on her teenage years by recalling conversations with her mother, her brother, her grandmother (Mamá Sara), her aunts, and her cousins. As narrator of the novel, Lidia looks back wistfully on the 1950s: "[W]e were islanders and the sea, on every side the sea, was our only frontier. We lived surrounded by water and submerged in family tradition" (14). The appearance of Sergio Solis, her father's brother, changes Lidia's life during an otherwise ordinary summer. Uncle Sergio seems to challenge every notion the women of her family hold dear: He is single, he is probably gay, he is a communist, he listens to the same music as the maids do, and he refuses to embrace the American Dream with a nine-to-five job. He is also thoughtful and worldly, and he has the same green eyes as Lidia.

Throughout the text Lidia struggles to fit in with her family and to understand her island's commonwealth status—hers are questions of identity. We learn telling details about the Solis family from Lidia's participation in lively and sometimes heated arguments. Her role in family activities reminds Lidia that "in our everyday world everything was organized, decided and carried out by women" (22). Although Lidia misses a father figure, she recognizes that her female relations serve as role models: Aunt Elena is a doctor, Sara Fernanda is a secretary, Nati Machado is a medical technician, and Lidia's own mother, María Angélica, worked as a nurse during World War II. Lidia is torn between her intense shyness and her desire to mirror the Solis women in their travels, their sophistication, and their understanding of Puerto Rican history.

García Ramis sets *Happy Days* during the administration of Luis Muñoz Marín, who served four terms as Puerto Rico's governor, in 1948, 1952, 1956, and 1960. It was under his governance that the island invited U.S. development. For its part, the mainland has regarded Puerto Rico as a market ripe for its manufactures and technology; these appear in the novel as large-scale infrastructural systems (dams, airports, and power stations), appliances (washing machines and air conditioners), and the replacement of a European salon culture with 1950s westerns and detective television shows. García Ramis's explicit mention of Muñoz Marín is purposeful in that he ultimately rethought his support of independence in favor of commonwealth status. The older Solis women seem to support the governor's views, although without compromising their Spanish-American identity.

Along with issues of U.S. influence and domination, *Happy Days* confronts the island's adoption of European styles. In the estimation of the Solis family European goods and habits are a sign of refinement and worldliness. It is to France, Spain, and Germany, and not the United States, that the Solis family looks for inspiration and knowledge. When given the opportunity, the Solis women criticize Americans from the mainland. The belief in Europe as the center of the world is reinforced when Uncle Sergio delivers a lesson on art to Lidia, her brother, Andrés, and her cousin Quique (Enrique). While flipping through various images in a calendar, Sergio identifies the paintings of Henri Matisse and Paul Gauguin. This impromptu lesson soon becomes a discussion about the inheritance of cultural traditions, and Andrés, the voice of the future generation, offers this analysis: "There are no famous Puerto Rican artists because Puerto Rico doesn't have much culture and this island is too small. Only now, as part of the U.S., as a commonwealth has Puerto Rico begun to progress . . ." (33–34). Because he can offer no resolution to the debate, Sergio does not directly answer Andrés's charge but rather changes the subject back to Matisse, the modern French painter.

Once an encyclopedia salesman, Sergio recognizes the impact of what can be tidily called Western civilization, but in doing so he does not reject the local, the familiar, or the *jíbara* (pertaining to the country folk of Puerto Rico). Sergio attempts to strike a balance between harvesting the fruits of Europe and the United States and maintaining a distinct Puerto Rican identity. It is through his character, an *independista* (one fighting for

the island's separation from the United States), that *Happy Days* parallels the arguments of many Latin American writers. García Ramis's concern with Puerto Rico's identity echoes Cuban revolutionary JOSÉ MARTÍ's "Our America" (1891). In this essay Martí insisted on a productive tension between creation and imitation—a combination that Lidia finds difficult to strike. The questions Lidia poses about the island's future also correspond with Ana Roqué's *LUZ Y SOMBRA* (1903) and with the novels of García Ramis's contemporary, ESMERALDA SANTIAGO. All of these thinkers regard the U.S. presence in the Caribbean as a source of both hope and agitation.

For her part Lidia inherits the attitudes and beliefs of her family, and she lists them into two camps of what is good and what is evil. On the "good side" Lidia lists such things as Catholicism, the United States, Dwight D. Eisenhower, white people, the military, Francisco Franco, and "everything Spanish" as well as "everything German and Swiss, from Rhine wines to Cuckoo clocks" (41). García Ramis does not pause in the narrative to defend this list but rather invites her readers to consider why, for example, Franco would be "good," even though he was Spain's fascist dictator from the 1930s to the 1970s. Likewise, the notion of "white people" in Puerto Rico is a social construction of the 1950s because, though there are white-skinned families, the population is made up of MESTIZOS (of Spanish and Indian blood) and mulattoes (Spanish and African blood). Correspondingly, the Solis regard as evil "Communists, atheists, Protestants, Nazis, newly formed black African nations, Puerto Rican Nationalists, and any Puerto Ricans in favor of independence," as well as "[Rafael] Trujillo [the dictator of the Dominican Republic], and [Fulgencio] Batista [the president of Cuba overthrown by Fidel Castro in 1959]" (41).

This kind of categorical thinking between good and evil does not help Lidia make sense of changes in her life as a young woman, nor do binaries help her to understand her own island history. She is left with a sense of confusion that extends to her identity as a Puerto Rican of the 1950s and 1960s. In a heartfelt letter to Uncle

Sergio she takes inventory of her own upbringing as a young girl sheltered by her family. Lidia admits she has had a very good education and of her Catholic high school she writes:

> They educated us well, Uncle, very well. Together with *Uncle Tom's Cabin* came an explanation of civil rights and racism in the United States. *Portrait of a Lady* [by Henry James] was accompanied by a lecture about women's liberation . . . They asked us to write an essay about [Henry Wadsworth] Longfellow's poem "Evangeline." We had to read about its poetic structure, cadence, cultural and historical contexts, and write a twelve-page essay over the Christmas vacation (149).

She values what she has learned from the nuns at her school, and she is thirsty for more knowledge. This is one of the many autobiographical moments in the novel; in an interview with Carmen Esteves, García Ramis's translator, the author affirms the positive influence American nuns had on her as a student at Perpétuo Socorro School. The nuns taught García Ramis that "You should strive for excellence and try many things until you can find what you are good at" (Esteves 864). In her search to find what she is good at, where her place is, Lidia asks her uncle for direction. She expresses to him a desire to learn more about the Inca and Aztec, the natives of the Americas who had great civilizations but whose cultures were (and to some extent still are) ignored in history curricula. Likewise, Lidia begins to rethink in her letter the blind worship of European ideas and knowledge.

Lidia's challenge throughout *Happy Days* is to negotiate feelings of gain and loss. The first major loss is the dismantling of Villa Aurora, her childhood home. It is in this house with its creaky wooden floors, garden, and dovecote that Lidia gets to know her benevolent, reticent, and unconventional uncle. Villa Aurora is demolished to make way for an apartment building—a sign of things to come in the growing suburbs of San Juan. The Solis family moves into a newly constructed home in a development with lawns, modern conveniences, and clear property lines.

The expression of loss and gain is further emphasized in the title of the novel. "Happy Days" is a reference to a Puerto Rican *danza* (a kind of song) by Morel Campos that laments, "the joyful days of love will never return to console my heart" (Esteves 867). This song rings true when Lidia learns that Uncle Sergio has died in New York: This is a major loss for the fatherless narrator. Her trip to New York to reclaim his body and her return to the island marks the final transition from Lidia's adolescence to a reluctant womanhood; she mourns the death of an uncle who gave her an outlet for her teenage curiosity and eagerness to learn. For its themes and setting *Happy Days* can be read within the context of both PUERTO RICAN LITERATURE and SPANISH-AMERICAN CARIBBEAN LITERATURE.

Bibliography
García Ramis, Magali. *Happy Days, Uncle Sergio.* Translated by Carmen Esteves. Fredonia, N.Y.: White Pine Press, 1995.

Esteves, Carmen. "The Frontier: An Interview with Magali García Ramis." *Callaloo* 17, no. 3 (Summer 1994): 862–869.

Luz Elena Ramirez

Hernández Cruz, Victor

See CRUZ, VICTOR HERNÁNDEZ.

Herrera, Andrea O'Reilly (1959–)
(writer, editor)
Born in Pennsylvania to a Cuban mother and an Irish-American father, in 1959, Andrea O'Reilly Herrera is a professor of literature at the University of Colorado, Colorado Springs, where she is also director of the Ethnic Studies Program. Her research interests include the contributions of Victorian novelist Charlotte Brontë, French modernist Marguerite Duras, and Latina authors CRISTINA GARCÍA and SANDRA CISNEROS. In 2001 Herrera published a memorable novel based on her Cuban-American heritage, *Pearl of the Antilles.*

In *Pearl of the Antilles* Herrera traces four generations of Cuban women, who narrate the story of their lives through diaries, letters, and anecdotes. The novel covers the period before FIDEL CASTRO's overthrow of Fulgencio Batista's regime in 1959 through to the 1980s. *Pearl of the Antilles* focuses on several Cuban women: Fina, her daughter-in-law Rosa, Rosa and Pedro's daughter Margarita (Daisy), and Daisy's daughter Lily. Herrera represents the roles of women on the island and in the United States as mothers, grandmothers, daughters, daughters-in-law, and wives. The author explores the differences between urban (Havana) and rural life (Cienfuegos) on the island, as well as the status of exiles in the United States. She creates complex characters that follow life's sometimes predictable, sometimes unpredictable trajectories. Herrera looks at Cuban women as they come of age before and during the 1940s and 1950s. Later she compares the Cuban children who leave the island after Castro's CUBAN REVOLUTION with the generation of Cuban Americans born in the United States. In doing so, *Pearl of the Antilles* explores the feelings of alienation, community, and memory. Most salient is Herrera's literary treatment of nostalgia for Cuba, felt by the Cuban exile and the Cuban American. Through the character of Margarita/Daisy and through the settings of the novel, readers can begin to understand the experiences of Cuban exile and assimilation. In this regard her writing has much in common with García's *DREAMING IN CUBAN* (1992) and can be placed within the context of both CUBAN-AMERICAN LITERATURE and SPANISH-AMERICAN CARIBBEAN LITERATURE.

In addition to *Pearl of the Antilles,* Herrera has edited *Remembering Cuba: The Legacy of a Diaspora* (2001), a collection of testimonials, both written and visual, by Cubans and Cuban Americans. Through diverse media these artists express their personal vision of Cuba, past and present. *Remembering Cuba* samples the varied testimonies of displacement, as the authors capture the traumatic effects of exile as well as the triumph of the individual spirit. Herrera's literary productions advance a critical insight about Cuban Americans and the plurality of voices in this extranational community. Her vision looks beyond conventional or "official" discourses, which have defined this community for decades.

Bibliography

Alonso Gallo, Laura P. *Guayaba Sweet: Literatura cubana en los Estados Unidos.* Cádiz, Spain: Editorial Aduana Vieja, 2003.

Alvarez-Borland, Isabel. *Cuban American Literature of Exile: From Person to Persona.* Charlottesville: University of Virginia Press, 1998.

Herrera, Andrea O'Reilly. *Pearl of the Antilles.* Bilingual/Review Press, 2001.

Raúl Rubio

Herrera, Juan Felipe (1948–) *(poet, children's writer, performance artist)*

Juan Felipe Herrera was born on December 27, 1948, in Fowler, California. The son of Mexican migrant workers, Herrera traveled from harvest to harvest with his parents through many small farming communities in California before finally settling down in San Diego's Barrio Logan, where he was the childhood friend of Chicano poet ALURISTA.

Herrera received his bachelor's degree in social anthropology from the University of California, Los Angeles, in 1972 and went on to receive his master's, also in social anthropology, from Stanford University in 1980. His research as a burgeoning scholar in the field of anthropology enabled him to travel extensively throughout Mexico and Central America, but it was his passion for capturing these experiences in words that led him to a career in poetry. Herrera subsequently enrolled in the prestigious Writers' Workshop at the University of Iowa, where he received his M.F.A. in creative writing in 1990.

A longtime educator, Herrera has taught creative writing at a number of distinguished universities, including his alma maters Stanford and Iowa and Fresno State University. In 2005 he was appointed to the Tomás Rivera Endowed Chair of Creative Writing, as well as Chair of the Creative Writing and Writing in the Department of Performing Arts at the University of California, Riverside.

Herrera's first book, a collection of poetry entitled *Rebozos of Love,* was published in 1974, followed by the poetry collections *Exiles of Desire* (1985), *Facegames* (1987), and *Akrílica* (1989). These books first present immigration and the trials of adolescence as themes that Herrera will further explore in later works of poetry as well as in his bilingual children's books. His children's book *Calling the Doves* (1995) won the 1997 Ezra Jack Keats Award for New Writers of Children's Literature. An autobiographical tale, *Calling the Doves* is the story of Herrera's migrant farmworker childhood in California. His lyrical narration recalls the old Mexican songs and stories that his family shared while living in the little trailer house that his father had built in California.

Herrera continued to publish a number of critically acclaimed collections of poetry—*Night Train to Tuxla* (1994), *Love After the Riots* (1996), and *Mayan Drifter* (1997). He won the 1999 Américas Award for Children's and Young Adult Literature for *Laughing Out Loud, I Fly* (1998), which also won the Pura Belpré Honor Award. His novel in verse *Crashboomlove* (1999) earned him the first of two Latino Hall of Fame Awards.

Herrera is an accomplished performance artist, whose love for music and theater can be seen through his verse. As a result of his spoken-word poetic style, a number of his works have been adapted for stage and screen. *The Upside Down Boy* (2000) has recently been turned into a New York City musical, and *Crashboomlove* has been included in the PBS television production of *American Family.* More recently Herrera received his second Latino Hall of Fame Award for *Giraffe on Fire* (2001) and another Américas Award for *Cinnamon Girl* in 2006. He is now completing a spoken-word collection entitled *187 Reasons Mexicanos Can't Cross the Border,* which will include poetry spanning his career from 1970 to 2006.

Whether it is in his poetry, bilingual picture books, or theatrical writing, one can always count on Herrera to fill the page with the savory images of cilantro and roasting chiles, the cool sounds of jazz and blues, and the exhilarating feeling of moving whimsically through space and time. Herrera currently lives in Redlands, California, with his lifelong partner and fellow poet Margarita Luna Robles. For its themes and images his work can be read within the context of CHICANO LITERATURE.

Bibliography

Arteaga, Alfred. *Chicano Poetic: Heterotexts and Hybridities.* New York: Cambridge University Press, 1997.

Cavallari, Héctor Mario. "La muerte y el deseo: Notas sobre la poesía de Juan Felipe Herrera." *La Palabra* (Fall 1982). Available online. URL: http://www.cervantesvirtual.com/servlet/ SirvcObras/chic/80 23951132091538410080/p0000012.htm#I_51_. Downloaded July 17, 2006.

Flores, Juan, and George Yudice. "Living Borders/Buscando América: Languages of Latino Self-Formation." *Social Text* 24 (1990): 57–84.

González, Ray. *Muy Macho: Latino Men Confront Their Manhood.* New York: Vintage, 1996.

Herrera, Juan Felipe. *Border-Crosser with a Lamborghini Dream.* Tucson: University of Arizona Press, 1999.

———. *Calling the Doves/Canto a las palomas.* San Francisco, Calif.: Children's Book Press, 1995.

———. *Cilantro Girl/La superniña del cilantro.* San Francisco, Calif.: Children's Book Press, 2003.

———. *Crashboomlove: A Novel in Verse.* Albuquerque: University of New Mexico Press, 1999.

———. *Downtown Boy.* New York: Scholastic Publishers, 2005.

———. *Exiles of Desire.* Houston, Tex.: Arte Público Press, 1985.

———. *Giraffe on Fire.* Tucson: University of Arizona Press, 2001.

———. *Grandma & Me at the Flea/Los meros meros remateros.* San Francisco, Calif.: Children's Book Press, 2002.

———. *Laughing Out Loud, I Fly/A carcajadas, yo vuelo.* New York: HarperCollins, 1998.

———. *Lotería Cards and Fortune Poems: A Book of Lives.* San Francisco, Calif.: City Lights Books, 1999.

————. *Love After the Riots.* Willimantic, Conn.: Curbstone Press, 1996.

————. *Mayan Drifter: Chicano Poet in the Lowlands of America.* Philadelphia: Temple University Press, 1997.

————. *Memoria(s) from an Exile's Notebook of the Future.* Santa Monica, Calif.: Santa Monica College Press, 1993.

————. *Night Train to Tuxtla: New Stories and Poems.* Tuscon: University of Arizona Press, 1994.

————. *Notebooks of a Chile Verde Smuggler.* Tucson: University of Arizona Press, 2002.

————. "Poetry Marauder: An Interview with Juan Felipe Herrera. *Bloomsbury Review* 20, no. 2 (2000 Mar/April.): 19–20.

————. *Thunderweavers: Tejedores de rayos.* Tucson: University of Arizona Press, 2000.

————. *The Upside Down Boy/El niño de cabeza.* San Francisco, Calif.: Children's Book Press, 2000.

Medrano, Michael Luis. "Learning to Not Write: An Interview with Juan Felipe Herrera." *Dislocate* (July 28, 2004). Available online. URL: http://english.cla.umn.edu/creativewriting/dislocate/fall04/Herrera_interview.html. Downloaded July 12, 2006.

Ethriam Brammer

Hijuelos, Oscar (1951–) (novelist)

Born on August 24, 1951, in New York City to immigrant parents Magdalena and Pascual Hijuelos, Oscar Hijuelos draws on his rich Cuban heritage to write fiction. He earned his undergraduate degree and M.A. in creative writing from the City College of the City University of New York.

In 1978 he was recognized by Pushcart Press as an Outstanding Writer for his story "Columbus Discovering America." Hijuelos also was awarded fellowships from the National Endowment for the Arts and the American Academy in Rome, both in 1985, in acknowledgment of his first novel, *Our House in the Last World* (1983). The author of six novels and numerous short stories, Hijuelos has the distinction of being the first Latino author to be awarded the Pulitzer Prize in fiction (1990). His winning novel, *The MAMBO KINGS PLAY SONGS OF LOVE* (1989), was nominated as a finalist for both the National Book Award and National Book Critics Circle Prize for fiction; it was also made into a popular film. Hijuelos is an important voice in American letters, especially CUBAN-AMERICAN LITERATURE.

Hijuelos's decision to write in English, as opposed to Spanish, demonstrates a constant tension throughout his work. Even when detailing issues pertaining to Cuban culture, Hijuelos does so through the lens of his U.S. identity. Though both pre-Castro and postrevolutionary Cuba receive Hijuelos's attention, neither dominates within the context of the immigrant experience. Hijuelos's characters simply cannot rely on the idealized Cuban past when faced with the day-to-day hardships of the immigrant experience. Born in urban New York, Hijuelos gained an intimate knowledge of immigrant life as a first-generation Cuban American born to immigrant parents. His characters often negotiate competing cultural identities as Cubans and Cuban Americans, though they belong completely to neither category.

Hijuelos's first novel, *Our House in the Last World,* the most autobiographical of his works, portrays the immigrant experience of Alejo and Mercedes Santinio. Alejo and Mercedes marry in Cuba and settle in Spanish Harlem in 1944, where their children, Horacio and Hector, are born. Hector, born in 1951 (like Hijuelos), functions as the novel's protagonist, as he tries to forge an identity distinct from the Cuban manhood embodied by his father and older brother. Hector battles with the sickness and alienation caused by his childhood illness. Confined to his home and separated from others, Hector never overcomes the effects of this isolation. One aspect of his isolation is that Hector is forced to speak English and only English. Moreover, although Hector outwardly looks much like his father and brother, he does not feel Cuban enough to adopt their example. The Santinio family faces many difficulties in their assimilation to U.S. culture: Alejo never rises above kitchen work in a local restaurant and becomes an alcoholic; Mercedes becomes increasingly bitter, retreating into mysticism; Horacio escapes the confines of family life, yet Hector cannot. Following the death of Alejo, the family's pressing poverty takes on an even greater imperative at the novel's tragic end.

After *Our House in the Last World* Hijuelos's subsequent novels can perhaps be considered portraits of Cuban communities, rather than a portrait of Hijuelos's own experiences. *The Mambo Kings Play Songs of Love* portrays the life of Cuban immigrants who have come to New York after World War II. This novel takes as its background the mambo (a partner dance and form of Latin music), the Latin orchestra, and dancehall scene of the 1950s. Two brothers, Cesar and Nestor Castillo, come to the States and perform as musicians; they forge immigrant identities and relationships, while also building their own families. Nestor's son Eugenio, following the death of his father, forms a strong, if sometimes antagonistic, relationship with his uncle Cesar. Eugenio's relationship with Cesar provides the framework for the novel's non-linear narrative, as Eugenio reflects on the lives of his uncle and father.

Hijuelos returns to the immigrant experience in *The Fourteen Sisters of Emilio Montez O'Brien* (1993). Irish immigrant Nelson O'Brien and Cuban immigrant Mariela Montez meet in the United States. Nelson and Mariela marry and settle in Pennsylvania as their Cuban-Irish family expands to include 15 children. Nelson, a photographer, finds consistent work and outlets for his talent. He assimilates more easily than Mariela, who increasingly returns to the bittersweet memories of her Cuban past, distancing herself from Nelson and her children. In addition to Nelson and Mariela, the novel primarily focuses on the couple's firstborn, Margarita, and only son, Emilio. The scope of the novel remains ambitious, covering much of 20th-century history, which provides the background for the trials and triumphs of the Montez-O'Brien family.

Hijuelos returns to the themes of class and ethnic identity in *The EMPRESS OF THE SPLENDID SEASON* (1999). In this novel the protagonist, Lydia España, attempts to reconcile her high-class Cuban heritage with the poverty of her immigrant life. Lydia

and Raul España never transcend their reduced economic circumstances, though they project their desires for social mobility and wealth upon their children. Rico, in particular, achieves financial success never known to his parents, yet not without experiencing considerable alienation from his Cuban heritage.

Hijuelos's *A SIMPLE HABANA MELODY: FROM WHEN THE WORLD WAS GOOD* (2002), revisits the Cuban music scene celebrated in *Mambo Kings,* but with a significant difference. Based loosely on the life of Cuban composer Moises Simons, the novel charts Israel Levis's development as a talented pianist and award-winning composer of the 1920s, 1930s, and 1940s. Raised in a traditional Catholic family that expects him to marry and have children, Israel Levis nevertheless recognizes at an early age that he loves both men and women. While living the bohemian life in Paris in the 1930s, he is mistaken for a Jew and taken to a concentration camp of Nazi Germany. This experience of survival leaves him a broken man, and the music that once gave him a sense of freedom and joy becomes instead a reminder of how he had to play his famous compositions for Nazi officers. Levis's character serves as an important counterpart to the Castillo brothers in *Mambo Kings*; taken together, *Simple Habana Melody* and *Mambo Kings* reveal the development of Cuban music from the late 19th to the second half of the 20th centuries.

With both his commercial and critical success, Hijuelos has assumed an important role in contemporary American literature. Hijuelos constantly, yet carefully, expands the particular to chart territory within the universality of the American immigrant experience.

Bibliography

Harman, A. G. "A Conversation with Oscar Hijuelos." *Image: A Journal of the Arts and Religion* 22 (Winter–Spring 1999): 43–57.

Haygood, Wil. "After the Hounds." *Boston Globe,* November 18, 1990. Available online. URL: http://www.princeton.edu/~howarth/557/mambo5.html. Downloaded December 14, 2007.

Hijuelos, Oscar. *The Empress of the Splendid Season.* New York: HarperPerennial, 1999.

———. *The Fourteen Sisters of Emilio Montez O'Brien.* New York: Farrar, Straus, & Giroux, 1993.

———. *The Mambo Kings Play Songs of Love.* New York: Farrar, Straus, & Giroux, 1989.

———. *Mr. Ives' Christmas.* New York: HarperCollins, 1995.

———. *A Simple Habana Melody: From When the World Was Good.* New York: HarperCollins, 2002.

———. *Our House in the Last World.* New York: Persea Books, 1983.

Zach Weir

Hinojosa Smith, Rolando (1929–)
(fiction, writer, translator, essayist)

Born in Mercedes, Texas, where the Rio Grande meets the Gulf of Mexico, Rolando Hinojosa Smith is a Mexican-American fiction writer. He has traced his lineage to Spanish colonial Mexico, when his great-grandfather Juan Nepomuceno Hinojosa Hinojosa settled on the north bank of the Rio Grande in 1750. His father, Manuel Guzmán Hinojosa, was the last of his ancestors born on the Campuacuás Ranch. His mother's family, the Smiths, arrived to the area when the first Anglo Americans settled in the area in 1887.

Like his mother, Carrie Effie Smith Phillips, Hinojosa Smith was raised in a bilingual household, speaking and writing in both Spanish and English. This meant many advantages for him in his Mexican-American community and in English-language schools. He enlisted in the army at the age of 17, in 1940, and served in Japan and, later, in Korea. This war experience left a deep imprint in his mind and in his writing. His two works about Korea demonstrate what the war experience meant for him personally and literarily: The book of poetry *Korean Love Songs* (1978) and the novel *The Useless Servants* (1993) deal with the Korean War, as do to a lesser extent *Estampas del valle y otras* (1972; *Sketches of the Valley and Other Works*) and *KLAIL CITY* (1976).

A prolific contributor to CHICANO LITERATURE, Hinojosa has published fiction, poetry, and literary criticism. He teaches in the Department of English at the University of Texas, Austin, where he earned his B.S. in 1953. After some years as a high school teacher, he earned his M.A. from New Mexico Highlands University in 1962 and married a year later. His children are Robert, Clarissa Elizabeth, and Karen Louise.

Hinojosa Smith graduated in 1965 with a Ph.D. from the University of Illinois and since then has taught and presented his work at various universities; he earned grants and scholarships from the University of Minnesota and from the Ford Foundation. In 1985 he won his current position as the Ellen Clayton Garwood Professor of English at the University of Texas, Austin. In both Europe and Latin America Hinojosa has proved an ambassador of Chicano literature and is widely acclaimed for his chronicles of Belken County in the Klail City Death Trip series. Among the many important prizes he has received, he was awarded the CASA DE LAS AMÉRICAS Prize in 1976 for his novel *Klail City y sus alrededores,* which he later translated into English and published in 1987 as *Klail City.*

Hinojosa has adopted the crime fiction mode in novels such as *Partners in Crime,* published in 1985, and *Ask a Policeman,* published in 1998 and dedicated to his father, a police officer. He visits Spain regularly to participate in the Semana Negra de Gijón, a festival devoted to detective and hard-boiled fiction. The origins of the 13 volumes of the Klail City Death Trip series date back to 1972, when Hinojosa was awarded the Quinto Sol Prize for *Estampas del valle y otras obras,* which he translated into English and then later reedited as *The Valley* (1983). Characters in these novels meet to tell their own stories, recuperating the memory of their ancestors and passing them on to young family members and friends living in the border community. The series, taken as a whole or as a set of separate volumes, can be considered one of the masterpieces of BORDER LITERATURE.

Humor plays a crucial role in Hinojosa's novels as well as his use of the sketch technique. Critics consider him a postmodern writer for the constant interruptions in the narrative reminding the reader that he (or one of his personae) is the writer. In imagining Belken County, Hinojosa has created a new universe for Mexican Americans in which a multiplicity of voices expresses their hopes and worries. The inhabitants of the valley interact with Jehu Malacara and Rafe Buenrostro, main characters of the series, around whose lives the plots of the novels are structured. Since the protagonists are men, the focus of the novels is mostly on the lives that men lead in the valley. Women are secondary figures in the fiction, appearing as a male character's wife, mother, daughter, or lover.

As a scholar, Hinojosa has written essays about the condition of the Chicano writer, claiming a space for Chicanos in both U.S. and Mexican literatures. Hinojosa's scholarship has focused on Chicano authors such as TOMÁS RIVERA. Hinojosa has translated into English Rivera's . . . *Y no se lo tragó la tierra* (1971), which was published in 1987 under the title of THIS MIGRANT EARTH.

Many critical works and dissertations have been published about Hinojosa's chronicles of Belken County. His most recent novel, *The Happy Few* (2005), continues the Belken County series.

Bibliography

Hinojosa Smith, Rolando. *Becky and Her Friends.* Houston, Tex.: Arte Público Press, 1990.

———. *Dear Rafe/Querido Rafe.* Houston, Tex.: Arte Público Press, 2005.

———. *Klail City.* Houston, Tex.: Arte Público Press, 1987.

———. *Partners in Crime.* Houston, Tex.: Arte Público Press, 1985.

———. *This Migrant Earth* by Rolando Hinojosa Smith and Tomas Rivera. Houston, Tex.: Arte Público Press, 1986.

———. *Useless Servants.* Houston, Tex.: Arte Público Press, 2005. 1993.

———. *We Happy Few.* Houston, Tex.: Arte Público Press, 2006.

Lee, Joyce Glover. *Rolando Hinojosa and the American Dream.* Denton: University of North Texas Press, 1997.

Saldivar, J. David, ed. *The Rolando Hinojosa Reader: Essays Historical and Critical.* Houston, Tex.: Arte Público Press, 1985.

West-Durán, Alan, María Herrera-Sobek, and Cesar A. Salgado, eds. *Latino and Latina Writers.* New York: Charles Scribner's Sons, 2004.

Zilles, Klaus. *Rolando Hinojosa: A Reader's Guide.* Albuquerque: University of New Mexico Press, 2001.

Imelda Martín-Junquera

Hispanic Condition: Reflections on Culture and Identity in America, The
Ilan Stavans (1995)

The prolific writer and energetic scholar ILAN STAVANS has published books on Latino and Latin American literature at an astonishing rate. Born in 1961 in Mexico to Jewish parents, Stavans's background is important to understanding his book *The Hispanic Condition: Reflections on Culture and Identity in America.*

Stavans moved to New York City in 1985 to study at the Jewish Theological Seminary and earned a Ph.D. in Spanish literature from Columbia University. He holds an endowed chair at Amherst College, where his diverse interests include language, Latin American writers, Jewish writers, and U.S. Hispanic writers. Though he defies categorization, his oeuvre is made up of autobiographical prose, criticism, and fiction, as well as translations, interviews, documentaries, cartoons, dictionaries, and encyclopedias. In *The Hispanic Condition* Stavans presents his unique insight on being Mexican, American, and Jewish. He observes, "A polyglot, of course, has as many loyalties as homes. Spanish, I thought, was my right eye, English my left eye, Yiddish my [Eastern European] background, and Hebrew my conscience" (198). He recognizes his affinity with Mexicans of color, but he knew that his Eastern European background set him apart from darker-skinned mestizos. He was outside of Mexican life, too, because ". . . as a Jew, I had always been a marginal citizen in Mexico, which means . . . that I knew very well my way around any alien nation" (194–195).

The Hispanic Condition begins with a prologue and ends with a letter to Stavans's young son. Sandwiched in between are seven chapters packed with history, quotes, and commentary. Stavans is a widely read, eclectic scholar who provides some 433 bibliographical sources and at least 688 different references to significant personages, everyone from Mexican revolutionary Emiliano Zapata and Chicano novelist Oscar Zeta Acosta to Cuban revolutionary FIDEL CASTRO and Colombian Nobel Prize–winning writer Gabriel García Márquez. At the end of the book Stavans provides a useful chronology of Latino and Latin American cultural and literary events.

The first chapter, "Life in the Hyphen," asserts that Latinos "will never be the owners of a pure, crystalline collective individuality because we are the product of a five-hundred-year-old fiesta of miscegenation that began with our first encounter with the gringo in 1492" (13). The second chapter, "Blood and Exile," focuses primarily on Caribbean cultures as a mix of Africans, "Spaniards, Indians, mulattos, and mestizos" (32). "At War with Anglos," chapter 3, comments on the development of CHICANO LITERATURE as a countermovement to the "Anglo establishment" (89). For those overly proud of their Spanish heritage at the expense of their Indian blood, Stavans writes, "The Iberians who came to conquer belonged to the worst segments of society: proud scoundrels, brutal criminals, greedy gold seekers, and ambitious military men whose awkward morality was still feudal" (92). "Our history," he adds, "is a mirage, an invention" (95). Chapter 5 is entitled "Sanavabiche, Or, the Art of Cantinflear." *Cantinflear* is a reference to the Mexican comic persona, Cantinflas, a creation of Mario Moreno Reyes. Stavans uses the Spanish verb *cantinflear* because it signifies, among other things, the ability to use language as a weapon (129). In this chapter Stavans notes that Spanish has become a kind of weapon of resistance, "the glue that keeps Hispanics together" (129).

Chapter 6, "Toward a Self-definition," states that "Latinos get lost somewhere in the entanglement between reality and the dream. Anarchic, irresponsible, lazy, untrustworthy, treacherous—these ste-

reotypes reach way back to Columbus's diaries, in which Indians are described as naïve and 'peaceful idolaters'" (147). In chapter 7, "Culture and Democracy," Stavans suggests that "Ethnicity, rather than class, is behind the proliferation of multiple constituencies in the United States society today. We are no longer Americans as such but hyphenated identities: Hispanic-Americans, Asian-Americans, African-Americans, and so forth—a divided people" (166). This chapter considers the connection between politics and literature, specifically by looking at right-wing censorship of Latin American writers (among others Nobel Prize–winning poet Pablo Neruda and Chilean American novelist ISABEL ALLENDE). In his discussion of Latino access to education Stavans states, "the new Latino promises to produce a shelf of classics, books that will become national treasures" (190). Delivering on that promise, Stavans himself has produced a shelf of books.

The Hispanic Condition presents a panoramic sweep of Latino literature, art, culture, and identity. Stavans's essays are illuminating for readers interested in U.S. history and the role of Hispanics in that history. He brings to his subject a cosmopolitan perspective, encyclopedic knowledge, and literary clarity.

Bibliography

Gutiérrez, David G. Review of *The Hispanic Condition,* by Ilan Stavans. *Journal of American Ethnic History* 17, no. 1 (Fall 1997): 99.

Goldman, Ilene. "A Chronicle of Hyphen-Land." *Studies in Latin American Popular Culture* 15 (1996): 311.

Stavans, Ilan. *The Essential Ilan Stavans.* New York: Routledge, 2000.

———. *The Hispanic Condition: Reflections on Culture and Identity in America.* New York: Harper-Collins, 1995.

———. *On Borrowed Words: A Memoir of Language.* New York: Penguin Books, 2001.

———. *The Riddle of Cantinflas: Essays on Hispanic Popular Culture.* Albuquerque: University of New Mexico Press, 1998.

Paul Guajardo

"History Will Absolve Me" Fidel Castro

(1953)

"History Will Absolve Me," FIDEL CASTRO's most famous speech, was delivered on October 16, 1953. It served as part of Castro's defense while being tried for his leadership role in the failed attack on the Moncada Barracks earlier in the year, on July 26. The assault on the barracks was in response to what Castro and others perceived as the unjust and unlawful government of Fulgencio Batista.

In 1952 General Batista staged a coup d'état and overthrew the government of President Carlos Prío Socarrás. Batista declared himself chief of state, terminated the congress, and suspended all rights guaranteed in the 1940 Cuban constitution. Castro strongly criticized the government of Batista and in a bold move went to court to decry the violation of the constitution by the Batista regime's military coup. The court rejected Castro's petition, and seeing no further possible legal recourse, Castro organized an armed attack by some 165 insurrectionists on the Moncada Barracks in Oriente Province on July 26, 1953 (figures for the total number of participants vary from 126 to 167). This attack and another on Bayamo Garrison failed, and approximately half of the insurrectionists were killed. Many fled, but Castro and his brother Raúl were taken prisoner along with other insurrectionists and were tried as conspirators. Most were given sentences of up to 13 years. Castro was tried separately and in secret, in the nurses' lounge of the Santiago Civil Hospital. He served as his own attorney, and it was during this trial, on October 16, that he made his famous speech. His conviction was a forgone conclusion, and he was sentenced 15 years' imprisonment on the Isle of Pines. His sentence was the longest ever given to an insurrectionist in Cuba.

While still in prison, Castro published a longer version of his statement given in court as a political document. The speech defines what Castro and the insurgents imagined as the revolutionary government that would replace the Batista regime. Throughout the document Castro attacks the regime, exposing Batista's lies about the rebels, many of whom were tortured and murdered after the failed attempt to capture the Moncada Barracks. Castro repeatedly looks back in history to the brave leaders of the independence movement who gave their lives in the fight to liberate Cuba from Spain. In particular, Castro continuously refers to JOSÉ MARTÍ, a 19th-century intellectual, poet, and leader who inspired many in the fight for independence and who gave his life in battle before he could see a free Cuba. Martí is looked upon as the father of Cuban independence, and Castro strategically uses the figure of Martí during his famous speech—as well as and also after having attained power with the triumph of the CUBAN REVOLUTION in 1959—to rally Cuban popular support.

The speech is divided into five parts, or topics: his address to the court, a description of the events during the insurgence, a description of the insurgents' political and social plans for Cuba had the insurrection succeeded, the decrial of the torture and massacre of the insurgents, and the justification of the rebellion. In the first section of the document Castro addresses the court, "Honorable Judges," and begins to explain why he, as a lawyer, is defending himself instead of being represented by counsel. In the speech he contends that there are a number of irregularities, the most striking of which, perhaps, is the fact that he was denied the right to see the indictment against him. Left incommunicado for 76 days in solitary confinement, Castro had been denied his basic human and legal rights. He is in fact, he states, a prisoner of war. He is not allowed to interact with a defense council, he is not allowed to attend the trials of the other insurgents, and he is being tried separately from his comrades. Castro portrays himself and his co-conspirators as self-sacrificing patriots who have justice, if not the courts, on their side. They are, he insists, fighting for the freedom and good of all Cubans against a corrupt military regime.

Castro protests the vagueness of the charges leveled against him; he cannot directly address any particular charge in his defense. He states to the court that the charges against him and his comrades are false and that lies are being told about the assault on the Moncada Barracks. In the speech Castro says he and his counterparts cannot be accused of uprising against the constitutional powers of the state because Batista is a dictator who has done away with the constitution. As he asserts, the insurrection was not aimed against the constitutional powers but rather against an illegal dictatorship. The first section ends with the condemnation of the Batista regime and its manipulation of the court and judicial system.

This attack on the regime leads to the second section, the description of the events leading up to and constituting the insurgence. Castro focuses on lies broadcast on the Cuban radio by Batista, who gloated over the defeat of the rebellion. Castro focuses on the humanity of the rebellion, as he relates various plans put aside for fear of causing too much bloodshed or of traumatizing the families of high officials, whom they had initially planned to kidnap. He emphasizes the popular support of the rebellion, something that the regime emphatically denies. The majority of section two of the document focuses on the Cuban soldiers, forced to serve a dictator and precariously caught between the regime they serve and the greater Cuban community. The soldiers are ill treated, as they are not allowed to be truly soldiers but are forced instead to act as bodyguards and chauffeurs. Castro confidently maintains that he would have won the support of the soldiers, due in great part to their respect for the feelings of the majority of the populace. Castro tactically aligns himself with the enlisted soldiers, stating that he has defended the armed forces when others criticized them and showing how they, too, suffer under the Batista regime just as does the general populace.

The third section outlines what the insurgents had imagined for Cuba after the fall of the regime, including five revolutionary laws that would have been proclaimed after the capture of the Moncada Barracks. The laws include the return of power to the people and the restoration of the 1940 constitution; the transfer of land ownership to tenant and subtenant farmers, sharecroppers and squatters, and the indemnification of the former owners; the distribution of profits (30 percent) among the workers and employees of large industrial,

mercantile, and mining enterprises; the right of sugar planters to share 55 percent of production and the establishment of a quota system for small tenant farmers; and the confiscation of all holdings and "ill-gotten" gains from those who had committed frauds during previous regimes. The insurgents also imagined the nationalization of utilities, agrarian reform, educational reform, and the collection of taxes from big industry and the wealthy, who had evaded payment in the past. These laws are seen as a necessity for what Castro terms the ills of Cuba: tenant farming, foreign possession of land and industry, lack of industrialization, housing problems and the monopoly of the utilities, a poor education system, the lack of proper health care, and unemployment. Castro goes on to detail and define the revolutionary government that would have replaced what he condemns as the corrupt, unconstitutional Batista regime.

In the fourth section Castro repeats and further details the torture and massacre of the rebels. He outlines the history of cruelty in Cuba, graphically detailing the recent atrocities committed against the captured insurgents, and he applauds the bravery shown by the survivors.

The last section of the document once again attempts to justify the rebellion, reiterating the illegality of the Batista regime and how the courts have refused to intervene on behalf of the Cuban people and the constitution. He describes the corruption and crimes of the regime and points out how the very constitution that Batista overthrew is the legal standing that gives the insurgents the right to rebel against dictators. Furthermore, the right to rebel against unlawful dictators is, he argues, a universal right as seen throughout history. He illustrates this point by quoting the famous French Declaration of the Rights of Man: "When the government violates the rights of the people, insurrection is for them the most sacred of rights and the most imperative of duties."

Castro closes by once again looking to the history of Cuba and to Cuban heroes and martyrs who fought for freedom, justice, and human rights, including Carlos Manuel Céspedes, Antonio Maceo, Juan Gualberto Gómez, and Martí, all of whom fought for Cuban independence from Spain. Castro calls on these heroes to remind Cuba that he, too, is fighting for the island's independence from tyranny and despotism. He concludes by stating that he knows that the judges have no alternative but to condemn him. They are, after all, subjected to the same tyranny as the rest of Cuba. His final words in the speech give rise to its title: "I know that imprisonment will be harder for me than it has ever been for anyone, filled with cowardly threats and hideous cruelty. But I do not fear prison, as I do not fear the fury of the miserable tyrant who took the lives of 70 of my comrades. Condemn me. It does not matter. History will absolve me" (123). At the time of this writing, Raúl Castro is president of Cuba. Fidel Castro is one of the most influential and controversial figures of Latin American history.

Bibliography

Brenner, Philip, et al., eds. *The Cuba Reader: The Making of a Revolutionary Society*. New York: Grove Press, 1989.

Castro, Fidel. *History Will Absolve Me*, edited by Pedro Alvarez Tabío and Guillermo Alonso Fiel. Havana: Editorial José Martí, 1993.

"Fidel Castro." Wikipedia. Available online. URL: http://en.wikipedia.org/wiki/Fidel_Castro#Bay_of_Pigs. Accessed July 10, 2005.

Keen, Benjamin. *A History of Latin America*. 5th ed. Boston: Houghton Mifflin, 1996.

Pérez, Louis A., Jr. *Cuba: Between Reform and Revolution*. 2nd ed. Oxford: Oxford University Press, 1995.

Quirk, Robert E. *Fidel Castro*. New York: W. W. Norton, 1993.

Ruiz, Ramon Eduardo. *Cuba: The Making of a Revolution*. New York: W. W. Norton, 1968.

Khamla Dhouti

House of Houses Pat Mora (1996)

Winner of the Premio Aztlán literary award of Chicano letters, *House of Houses* is a family memoir. In this memoir Mexican-American author PAT MORA rebuilds in her imagination the multiple houses that her relatives were forced to abandon for economic or political reasons. Both her paternal and maternal ancestors suffered different hardships during the depression era and lost or had to sell their property. By creating a dream house Mora invites all her relatives, dead and alive, to partake in the imaginative reconstruction of her family's past. The Mora family and the Delgados (her maternal ancestry) who crossed the border into the United States left a deep imprint in Mora's mind. In her writing she tries to make sense of her Mexican-American identity, an identity fragmented by a family heritage on both sides of the border. In this regard her memoir echoes the sentiment of ambivalence in GLORIA ANZALDÚA's *BORDERLANDS/LA FRONTERA: THE NEW MESTIZA* (1987).

Set in El Paso, Texas, Mora's narrative moves back and forth crosses the border in an attempt to rescue stories of a traditional Mexican past. In order to offer an alternative view of official history, Mora shares intensely personal stories from her family "archive," and she makes appeals to the reader throughout the narrative.

In order to highlight her sense of a true account of events Mora provides several pictures of her ancestors with captions. These pictures represent the fragmented memories the author keeps about her family. As a collector of stories and family photos, she becomes the novel's healer: She listens to stories and testimonies that are a literary and cultural inheritance. At the same time Mora involves the audience in identity construction as it is manifest in the memoir.

A multiplicity of storytellers meet, including grandmothers, aunts, and mothers, who explain traditions from a time now long past. Mora lets her relatives decide when they want to talk and waits patiently, always ready to receive the precious gift of their oral accounts. Like the narrator, Aunt Lobo keeps a diary about the Delgado family, pages expressing her own truth, sometimes differing from the memories of other members of the family.

The structure follows the order of a whole year, each chapter representing a month, plus a first chapter that functions as an introduction to the characters. During the 12 chapters, from January to December, the reader learns about Catholic celebrations taking place each month. Mora correlates the months to incidents that have taken place in the family history. For example, it is during Lent, in April, that Raúl Mora falls mentally ill and suffers his own Calvary, a painful road to death like the one Christ had to take. The foundations of the house, that is to say, the history of the most distant ancestors named in the narrative, are set in January. Meanwhile, November brings the conclusion of the construction of the house of houses, which all the relatives populate at once in December. This last month represents a joyful time, when Mora has finally gathered the different points of view of the narrative to fill the "rooms" of the house.

This chronological organization gets disrupted when the reader discovers that time is one among the many barriers that Mora crosses in the narrative. The events narrated take the reader on a constant time travel from a past to a present time and back to the past where all the relatives who have already passed away are alive and willing to tell her their personal stories. With this strategy Mora attempts to create a timeless space to reunite all her loved ones in an animated dialogue crossing the fine line between life and death.

A metaphor for the process of writing the memoir itself, the garden is alluded to in every chapter, and its changes in every season. This garden embodies the space where members of generation after generation blossom and give fruits until they return to this same soil of the desert, which, far from dry and arid, proves fertile, a true barrier against the hostile environment surrounding it.

Bibliography

Mora, Pat. *House of Houses.* Boston: Beacon Press, 1997.

———. *Nepantla.* Albuquerque: University of New Mexico Press, 1993.

Oliver-Rotger, María Antonia. *Battlegrounds and Crossroads: Social and Imaginary Space in Writings by Chicanas.* Amsterdam and New York: Rodopi, 2003.

Imelda Martín-Junquera

House of the Spirits, The   Isabel Allende (1982)

ISABEL ALLENDE's *The House of the Spirits* (1985), originally published in Spanish as *La casa de los espíritus* 1982, recounts the experiences of several generations in the del Valle Trueba family. Nívea del Valle, an aristocratic suffragist in an unnamed South American country at the turn of the century, favors her youngest child, Clara, a precocious girl with psychic and telekinetic abilities. The closeness of these two figures sets a precedent for mother-daughter relationships that continues for several generations. After marrying Esteban Trueba, the fiancé of her deceased older sister, Clara becomes pregnant with her first child, a daughter she decides to name Blanca and with whom she converses while the baby is still in the womb. Blanca in turn gives birth to a daughter, Alba, who is cherished by mother and grandmother and schooled in the family lore. Even at a level above the plot, at the level of authorial construction, it is clear that these women share an unusual bond, because these characters' names are all variants of a theme: *Nívea* is a derivative of the Spanish word for snow, with its associations of whiteness; *Clara* suggests clearness or clarity; *Blanca* is the Spanish word for white; and *Alba* evokes the light of dawn. *The House of the Spirits,* then, is a matrilineal history of this rather eccentric family.

What makes this novel so incredibly rich, however, is the way it resonates with its personal, political, and literary contexts. In interviews and public appearances Allende has stated that there is far less fiction in this story than most readers assume. Her 2003 memoir, *My Invented Country,* for example, mentions a default marriage of her grandfather to the sister of his beloved after the beautiful girl died prematurely, a clairvoyant grandmother who communed with the dead, a pet named Barrabas, and an impossibly convoluted family home with a most impractical floor plan. All of these autobiographical details play prominent roles in *The House of the Spirits,* including the sprawling home, which, according to Allende in *My Invented Country,* functions as the novel's "protagonist" (19). But, for Allende the biographical and personal are unavoidably political; her family, after all, was specifically targeted in Chile's coup d'état. The last 100 pages or so of *The House of the Spirits* document, in careful journalistic detail, the dissolution of a democracy and the totalitarian military regime that replaces it. Writing a family history helps both Alba and Allende make sense of the chaos and terror. In Allende's world view, moreover, machismo and male prerogative are primarily to blame for the atrocities and violence recounted in the novel—violence that is far too often directed against women. Through her character Alba, Allende praises women for their ability to match male violence with quiet strength and resolve while simultaneously imagining a life free from bloodshed and terror when feminine principles are given equal footing. And it is in this aspect, finally, where *The House of the Spirits* responds to its literary precursors. Numerous critics have commented on the similarities between Allende's novel and *One Hundred Years of Solitude* (1967) by Gabriel García Márquez. Though she does employ the elements of MAGICAL REALISM, Allende's novel is far more than a mere recasting of García Márquez's work. Although she tells the history of the del Valle Truebas in a manner whereby the borders between the fantastic and the realistic blur or even disappear, much as García Márquez had done with the Buendía family, Allende introduces a female perspective in Latin American literature. For its historical perspective her work can be read alongside that of Chilean-American authors MARJORIE AGOSÍN and ARIEL DORFMAN.

Bibliography

Allende, Isabel. *The House of the Spirits*. Translated by Magda Bogin. New York: Bantam Books, 1993.

———. *My Invented Country: A Nostalgic Journey through Chile*. Translated by Margaret Sayers Peden. New York: HarperCollins, 2003.

Castellucci Cox, Karen. *Isabel Allende: A Critical Companion*. Westport, Conn.: Greenwood Press, 2003.

Feal, Rosemary G., and Yvette E. Miller. *Isabel Allende Today: An Anthology of Essays*. Pittsburgh, Pa.: Latin American Literary Review Press, 2002.

Frick, Susan R. "Memory and Retelling: The Role of Women in *La casa de los espíritus*." *Journal of Iberian and Latin American Studies* 7, no. 1 (2001): 27–41.

Hart, Stephen. "*The House of the Spirits* by Isabel Allende." In *The Cambridge Companion to the Latin American Novel*, edited by Efraín Kristal, 270–282. Cambridge: Cambridge University Press, 2005.

———. "Magical Realism in the Americas: Politicised Ghosts in *One Hundred Years of Solitude, The House of the Spirits*, and *Beloved*." *Journal of Iberian and Latin American Studies* 9, no. 2 (2003): 115–123.

Timothy K. Nixon

House on Mango Street, The   Sandra Cisneros (1984)

SANDRA CISNEROS's *The House on Mango Street* centers on the life of Esperanza Cordero, a Mexican-American girl growing up in a Chicago barrio. The 44 vignettes in the novella are so rich in metaphor and pattern that they could also be regarded as prose poems. No matter the genre, *The House on Mango Street* is a coming-of-age story, for Esperanza Cordero is on a quest—for self-knowledge, self-definition, and self-acceptance within her working-class community of Latinos, blacks, and immigrants. While this work conveys the anger, frustration, and embarrassment of its young narrator, more important, it portrays the power of Esperanza's spirit and her ability to overcome obstacles erected through patriarchal and socioeconomic forces.

Esperanza lives in both English-speaking and Spanish-speaking communities and explains that her name in Spanish "means too many letters," but in English it means "hope" (10). Cisneros prepares the reader for the interplay between Spanish and English in the dedication of her book, which reads "A las Mujeres/To Women." In writing about Esperanza's maturation Cisneros includes the collective stories of women in Esperanza's distressed neighborhood, a barrio filled with dilapidated buildings. We see the unfulfilled hopes of so many women around her who are thwarted by economic and gender barriers and dead-end futures. These very women inspire assertiveness in Esperanza, who avows "not to grow up tame like the others who lay their head on the threshold waiting for the ball and chain" (88). The women in her life influence her, including her mother who sighs, "I could have been somebody, you know" (90); her unhappily married grandmother, for whom Esperanza was named, "She looked out the window her whole life, the way so many women sit their sadness on an elbow" (11); Mamacita, who speaks no English and "sits all day by the window and plays Spanish radio shows and sings all the homesick songs about her country in a voice that sounds like a seagull" (77); and her close friend Sally, who flees her abusive father by marrying a man who forbids her to talk on the phone or look out the window (102).

One of the most important women in Esperanza's life is her Aunt Lupe, a powerful athlete blinded and wasted by disease, who tells her, "You just remember to keep writing, Esperanza. You must keep writing. It will keep you free" (61). Writing becomes a strategy in Esperanza's quest of self-expression. It is the transformational nature of writing that empowers her to represent the constraints of her poor neighborhood and its potential to nourish her imagination. Her growing consciousness is a direct result of her storytelling, as is her will to escape being a victim of her environment while simultaneously accepting the barrio as her own space.

Conflicts abound in this book: between the real and the ideal, aspirations and restrictions, freedom and confinement, innocence and experience, boys and girls, men and women, the haves and the have-nots, transience and stability, as well as belonging and alienation. Crafted with simple language and a conversational tone, this work is energized by these binaries and Esperanza's negotiation of them.

Esperanza's house, a major symbol in the book, is "small and red with tight steps in front and windows so small you'd think they were holding their breath" (4). This house represents the vari-

ous forces that stymie Esperanza, yet it also represents the catalyst for her imagination, fueling her vision of the ideal house she desires: "not a man's house . . . a house quiet as snow, a space for myself to go, clean as paper before the poem" (108). She embraces Mango Street, and that embrace is, as the final vignette implies, largely through the arms of her stories: "I like to tell stories . . . I make a story for my life, for each step my brown shoe takes. . . . I like to tell stories. I am going to tell you a story about a girl who didn't want to belong. . . . I put it down on paper and then the ghost does not ache so much" (109–110).

Esperanza imagines her departure and her return to Mango Street in the book's last lines, "I have gone away to come back. For the ones I left behind. For the ones who cannot out" (110). For readers young and old Esperanza Cordero personifies the saying that what does not kill us will make us stronger. In this regard Cisneros's story shares literary terrain with other Latino coming-of-age stories, namely ESMERALDA SANTIAGO's WHEN I WAS PUERTO RICAN (1993) and JULIA ALVAREZ's HOW THE GARCÍA GIRLS LOST THEIR ACCENTS (1991). Within a broader context Cisneros's novella can be read as one of the most popular contributions to CHICANO LITERATURE.

Bibliography
Brunk, Beth L. "En otras voces: Multiple Voices in Sandra Cisneros' *The House on Mango Street.*" *Hispanófila* 133 (2001): 137–150.
Cisneros, Sandra. *The House on Mango Street.* New York: Vintage, 1991.
Cruz, Felicia J. "On the 'Simplicity' of Sandra Cisneros's *House on Mango Street.*" *Modern Fiction Studies* 47 (2001): 910–946.
Doyle, Jacqueline. "More Room of Her Own: Sandra Cisneros's *The House on Mango Street.*" *MELUS* 19 (1994): 6–35.
Sandra Cisneros Web site. Available online. URL: http://www.sandracisneros.com/home.html.
Sloboda, Nicholas. "A Home in the Heart: Sandra Cisneros's *The House on Mango Street.*" *Aztlán* 22 (1997): 89–106.

G. Douglas Meyers

How the García Girls Lost Their Accents
Julia Alvarez (1991)

How the García Girls Lost Their Accents is the first novel published by Dominican-American writer JULIA ALVAREZ. An essayist, poet, and novelist, Alvarez is arguably the most prominent writer in DOMINICAN-AMERICAN LITERATURE. *How the García Girls Lost Their Accents* describes the experience of the García family after they move to New York from the Dominican Republic. This story of immigration involves the daughters' adaptation to life in the U.S. Northeast while trying to honor their Dominican roots.

The novel features Carlos and Laura García, and their four daughters, Carla, Sandra, Yolanda, and Sofia, from oldest to youngest. Alvarez focuses on the difficult process self-discovery that comes through the assimilation, sexual awareness, and moving between two languages and cultures. Like many Latino authors, Alvarez utilizes CODE SWITCHING by incorporating Spanish phrases into her English text. Alvarez also translates Dominican sayings into English to give the reader a sense of what it means for the García girls to "lose" their accents; of course, much meaning is lost in the translation.

Each chapter reads like a short story and is told from the perspective of each sister and several family members. *How the García Girls Lost Their Accents* unfolds in three sections presented in reverse chronological order: The first section deals with the girls' adulthood and college years in the 1970s and 1980s; the second shows their adolescence and adjustment to American life in the 1960s; and the third takes place in the late 1950s, prior to the family departure from the island. This unconventional use of time and perspective characterizes Alvarez's fiction, especially *¡Yo!* (1996), a sequel of sorts to *How the García Girls Lost Their Accents*.

In the beginning of *How the García Girls Lost Their Accents* Alvarez introduces the reader to Carla, Sandra, Yolanda, and Sofia. While the daughters are often treated as a group, Alvarez reveals distinct personalities in each one. The first chapter is narrated by Yolanda, a character who is further developed in *¡Yo!* When Yolanda returns to the Dominican Republic after a five-year absence, her Dominican cousins see the difference in her appearance and speech. Yolanda has difficulty remembering Spanish, and when she dares to travel the countryside by herself, her cousins and *tías* (aunts) are shocked at the thought of a young woman venturing out alone. Yolanda struggles to find a sense of home and belonging despite the differences that mark her as an American. This insider/outsider duality appears in episodes taking place in both the Dominican Republic and the United States and adds depth to the characters' psychology. While the novel describes the girls' failed relationships, estrangement from their parents, and complexes about their bodies, there remains an overarching notion of survival and humor in spite of adversity. The sisters share a bond that helps carry them through difficult times.

The second section of the novel shows the family's earlier days in New York City. The girls are harassed by their peers while they are trying to learn English and fit in at school. They have to leave behind their upper-class lifestyle in the Dominican Republic in exchange for their uncomfortable immigrant status in the United States. But the departure from the island is not final. In one instance, Sofia, the youngest daughter, returns to the island as a form of punishment for hiding marijuana in her bedroom. Sofia settles into her life in the Dominican Republic; she starts wearing makeup and goes out on dates with her boyfriend. Carla, Yolanda, and Sandy visit and discover that Sofia has a macho (protective and overbearing) boyfriend. Though previously the sisters had been lamenting their move from the island to the United States, the sisters nevertheless conspire to bring Sofia back to New York. They accomplish this task by indirectly revealing to their mother that Sofia has spent unchaperoned time with her boyfriend. While the girls generally agree with the American idea of sexual freedom for women, they disagree with the Latin American notion that a man controls a relationship. In exposing Sofia the García girls deploy both American and Dominican values to their advantage (even if they do not agree with them).

The last section of the novel depicts the childhood of the García girls and their father's involvement in an underground revolutionary movement to overthrow Rafael Trujillo's regime (1930–61). Carlos García's activities will eventually drive the family into exile, as mapped out in the earlier chapters. Alvarez's IN THE TIME OF THE BUTTERFLIES (1994) details the impact of Trujillo regime's on the Mirabal sisters—Las Mariposas, or "butterflies"—and on the Dominican people more broadly.

The last part of *How the García Girls Lost Their Accents* describes the relationship between the García family and their housemaids. While the relationship is generally amicable, in one case, Carla, the oldest daughter, inadvertently gets one of the housemaids fired. Alvarez's use of the maids reveals the importance of themes regarding class and race in the Dominican Republic. As background for the novel, it is worth noting that the Dominican Republic in the 20th century engaged in the process called *blancamiento*, "whitening" oneself through skin bleaches, hair straightening, or the change of other indicators of ethnicity.

How the García Girls Lost Their Accents unfolds as a coming-of-age story in the midst of the immigration experience. While it is a story of a particular Dominican family, ultimately Alvarez incorporates themes about finding the self in a new country that have universal appeal.

Bibliography

Alvarez, Julia. *How the García Girls Lost Their Accents.* New York: Plume, 1991.

———. *In the Time of the Butterflies.* Chapel Hill, N.C.: Algonquin Books, 1994.

———. *¡Yo!* Chapel Hill, N.C.: Algonquin Books, 1997.

Julia Alvarez Web site. Available online. URL: http://www.alvarezjulia.com.

Jo-Anne Suriel

Hoyos, Angela de (1940–   ) (poet)

Angela de Hoyos was born in Coahuila, Mexico, in 1940. Her father owned a dry-cleaners and her mother was a homemaker. When a young girl, de Hoyos suffered an accident in which she was burned and had to convalesce in bed for many months. She began to think of rhymes in order to occupy her time, and this influenced her later work as a poet. Her family immigrated to San Antonio, Texas, when de Hoyos was young, and it was in San Antonio that she began to pursue her interest in art and writing. During the civil rights movement, de Hoyos began publishing poetry and submitting her work to international competitions. Especially well received in Europe, she has won a number of a wards from the Centro Studii e Scambi Internazionle, including the Bronze Medal of Honor (1966), the Silver Medal of Honor for literature (1967), and the Diploma di Benemerenza (1968, 1969, and 1970).

Her interests in literature and desire to create a venue for the work of Chicano writers led her to establish M & A Editions, a small press, in San Antonio. M & A Editions printed de Hoyos's work as well as that of authors such as Evangelina Vigil-Piñón. By the 1980s de Hoyos founded the periodical entitled *Huehuetitlan* and developed a successful career as a painter, producing works inspired by Mexican-American culture.

In her free-verse conversational poetry de Hoyos places cultural and feminist issues within a larger philosophical framework. Her work is both multifaceted and revisionist as it engages with problems such as poverty, racism, and the disenfranchisement of children and women. Her imagined dialogue between the Spanish conquistador Hernán Cortés and his mistress and interpreter, La MALINCHE, reveals de Hoyos's wit and historical perspective.

Her book *Woman, Woman* focuses on the conventional roles for women and speaks of the female struggle to overcome the limits of those roles. She surveys history from the Aztec days to the present as she contests myths and archetypes and rereads the image of women in fairy tales, as in her poem "Fairy-Tale: Cuento de Hadas." In this erotically and politically charged poem she sustains the dynamic tension between men and women. She does so in her poem "Lesson in Semantics," too. In her books she mixes English and Spanish and takes the issue of language to a philosophical level as well.

De Hoyos's contributions to Mexican-American literature have proven to be influential to Latino culture in general.

Bibliography

Aguilar-Henson, Marcella. *The Multi-Faceted Poetic World of Angela de Hoyos*. Austin, Tex.: Relampago, 1982.

Hoyos, Angela de. *Chicano Poems for the Barrio*. San Antonio, Tex.: M & A Editions, 1979.

———. *Selected Poems: Selecciones*. Corpus Christi, Tex.: Dezkalzo Press/Arte Público Press, 1979.

———. *Woman, Woman*. Houston, Tex.: Arte Público Press, 1985.

Hoyos, Angela de, and Teresinha Alves Pereira. *While Spring Sleeps*. San Antonio, Tex.: Editorial Azteca, 1975.

Hoyos, Angela de, and Rámon Vásquez y Sánchez. *Will Not Harm the Ozone*. San Antonio, Tex.: Editorial Azteca, 1979.

Ramos, Luis Arturo. *Angela de Hoyos: A Critical Look/ Lo Heroico y Antiheroico en su poesia*. Albuquerque, N.Mex.: Pajarito, 1979.

Gabriela Baeza Ventura

I Am Joaquín Rodolfo "Corky" Gonzales
(1967)

Mexican-American poet and activist RODOLFO GONZALES (1928–2005) published *I Am Joaquín/Yo Soy Joaquín* in 1967. The epic poem represents a cultural affirmation of the Mexican-American heritage and an articulation of a Chicano consciousness about civil rights. It is considered a foundational text in CHICANO LITERATURE. Gonzales was very much dedicated to the struggle for civil rights, as demonstrated by Gonzales's founding of the Crusade for Justice in the 1960s and his ongoing outreach to Latino youths. In many ways *I Am Joaquín* expresses Gonzales's own fight for equality in a white, English-speaking culture. As a Mexican-American youth, Gonzales faced many financial obstacles at the University of Denver. He quit the school shortly after he had entered and instead took to boxing—a career that offered a path out of the poverty of the barrio.

Structurally *I Am Joaquín* is made up of 502 lines freely arranged. According to critic Juan Bruce-Novoa, the poem revolves around three sections. Lines 1–37 (Part 1) reflect on the social position of the Mexican American in the United States. Lines 38–462 (Part 2) rehearse the history of Mexican Americans, while the final lines, 463–502 (Part 3), call for action on the part of each and every Chicano and Chicana.

One of the first things about the poem that readily springs to mind regards the title and the significance of the name *Joaquín*. It has been suggested that the name derives from the 19th-century revolutionary figure Joaquín Murrieta, known as the Californio and mentioned in the poem itself (224, 245). Regardless of the origins of this proper name, *Joaquín* is metaphorically meant to allude to a collective Chicano identity. This goal is achieved through the constant repetition of the parallel structure "I am," by which Joaquín identifies himself with his own people as well as with a wide range of mythical, political, social, and historical referents. He assumes the identity of figures such as the Aztec prince Cuauhtémoc (38), the revolutionary Emiliano Zapata (164), and the artist Diego Rivera (406). His use of CODE SWITCHING also reveals a shifting identity between English-speaking and Spanish-speaking worlds.

In Part 1 Joaquín reveals his cultural conflict. He sees himself as a misfit within the Anglo society because he is at a crossroad between progress and civilization, leading to emptiness on the one hand and his self-fulfillment on the other. Part 2 is the longest section of the poem. It represents a mythical and historical tableau where prominent Mexican figures justify a persistent Mexican/Chicano struggle for freedom. Part 2 is bound together by the continuous fluctuation of past and present. This flux dates back to pre-Columbian times, then interrupted by the arrival of the Spanish conqueror Hernán Cortés. From this moment on Joaquín is defined by his hybrid nature as a MESTIZO, the result of cultural interactions between colonizer and colonized. Joaquín is at the same time "the Maya prince" (46) and "the sword and flame of Cortés" (49). The time line leaps to the 1800s, when Joaquín takes part in the fight for the independence of Mexico and the 1821 deliverance from the Spanish yoke. Next Joaquín embodies or accompanies a series of historical figures, ranging from President Benito Juárez and MEXICAN REVOLUTION leaders Pancho Villa to Emiliano Zapata. These figures exemplify the unyielding fight against tyranny. It is significant to note that this world re-created in the poem is not only occupied by men figures. Women characters also have their role in the poem, though confined to the domestic and religious spheres. The allusions to the "black shawled faithful women" (207–209), the Virgin of Guadalupe (217), and the Aztec goddess Tonantzin (218) illustrate this idea.

Joaquín returns to the present in lines 253–287, where he reflects again about how his cultural identity has been compromised. In rejecting his own origins and becoming part of the melting part, part of Joaquín feels ashamed.

Episodes from the past come back to the foreground again (288–334) when the speaker recounts a bloody history of betrayal and conquest in Mexico and abroad. The speaker takes the reader from "the altars of Moctezuma" (290) to the wars of Korea and Vietnam (332–334), where Joaquín bleeds. Joaquín's blood is a reference to the fact that many Latinos served on the front line of U.S. wars in the 20th century. With reference to the Treaty of GUADALUPE HIDALGO the speaker reminds the audience of broken promises made by the United States to Mexican citizens living in the Southwest (356). This reflection leads to the clash between Chicanos and white English-speaking culture (360–406). In the following sec-

tion (407–462) Joaquín expresses his refusal to accept assimilation by the Anglo society; after all he has survived all the calamities of history and society (442–462).

The last lines of the poem (Part 3) represent a call for immediate action, a call for a change that has already begun. His culture is still part of him, so he refuses to be absorbed into the U.S. mainstream. Joaquín represents all labels that society imposes on him while still being made up of the same hybrid cultural nature.

I Am Joaquín has enjoyed enormous popular attention. Shortly after its publication in 1967 it was recited at rallies and strikes. It was also taken to the big screen by EL TEATRO CAMPESINO in 1969. It soon became a referent for Chicana writings, as in the case of La ChrisX's poem "La Loca de la Raza Cósmica," which responds to *I Am Joaquín* in both form and argument, though with a Chicana perspective. Nowadays this epic masterpiece is regarded as the literary output that forged a Chicano consciousness and encouraged other writers to follow its path.

Bibliography

Bruce-Novoa, Juan. *Chicano Poetry: A Response to Chaos.* Austin: University of Texas Press, 1982.

Gonzales, Rodolfo. *I Am Joaquín/Yo soy Joaquín: An Epic Poem.* Toronto, Canada, and New York: Bantam Books, 1972.

Pérez Torres, Rafael. *Movements in Chicano Poetry: Against Myths, Against Margins.* Cambridge and New York: Cambridge University Press, 1995.

Alberto Zambrana and Marian Pozo

Imagine the Angels of Bread Martín Espada (1996)

MARTÍN ESPADA won the American Book Award for *Imagine the Angels of Bread.* Earl Shorris notes in *Latinos: A Biography of the People,* that Espada "is well on his way to becoming *the* Latino poet of his generation" (394). Espada's poetry in *Imagine the Angels of Bread* is chock full of vivid images and memorable figures, most drawing on his

Puerto Rican heritage and personal experiences. His jobs have ranged from digging latrines in Nicaragua and working as an attorney to writing poetry and teaching creative writing at the University of Massachusetts at Amherst. The political nature of much of his work has been deeply influenced by his father, who was an important early figure in the New York Puerto Rican community and a photographer, with whom he collaborated on his first published book in 1982.

In his interview with Espada, Steven Ratiner identifies three themes that permeate the poet's work: the human dimension of history, anger about social injustice, and "a sense of transcendence, that something exists which carries us beyond the bitterness of personal trials and the burden of history—and that always seems to involve the family, the redemption possible in the deepest human relationships" (n.p.). These themes drive *Imagine the Angels of Bread* and are often presented through pairings or groups of poems which share viewpoints, locations, or time frames.

In the title poem, "Imagine the Angels of Bread," Espada calls us to believe in the power to effect change so that the vision of a more just world may be realized. Through frequent repetition in the poem of the declaration "this is the year," Espada creates images of empowered squatters, immigrants, and adolescent mothers. The second stanza reinforces this notion with a series of "if-then" propositions that show the liberating effect of group will at crucial moments, such as the abolition of slavery and the victory over the Nazis in World War II. The poem concludes with a reference to the encounter between the indigenous of Mexico and conquistador Hernán Cortés and his Spanish counterparts, an encounter retold by Indian witnesses in Fray BERNARDINO DE SAHAGÚN's *Florentine Codex*. In this account the Indians perceive the Spanish arrival as the manifestation of their prophecies as they struggle to make sense of Spanish horses, attire, and weaponry. Initially the indigenous groups of the Americas perceived the Spanish and the horse as one animal, thus the line "many-legged gods."

Although the last lines of the poem abound in religious imagery of gods and of angels, the onus is on humanity to rise to the challenges of human suffering. This need for human will and action is reinforced in the poem "Thieves of Light," in which Espada, a locksmith, and an electrician from the local power company overcome the tyrannical behavior of the landlord Gus, who bullies and evicts his impoverished tenants. Luisa, a tenant, has endured her cold, rodent-infested apartment for three months, with only the light and warmth of her candles to try to keep her persistent cough from worsening. On her behalf the three men work to restore to her the bare comforts of life. Not divine intervention but human determination and ingenuity resolve the dilemma.

The undercurrent of anger in some of his poems is often deflected through the poet's use of humor or irony. In "My Native Costume," the title poem of the first section of the book, a suburban teacher tells Espada repeatedly to wear something distinctive for show and tell. When Espada attempts to tell her that, as a lawyer, his "costume" is a pinstriped suit, she reasserts that she wants him to come dressed in something Puerto Rican. As a compromise he dresses in a short-sleeved, embroidered guayabera shirt over a turtleneck (it is February and cold) as a gesture to his Caribbean roots. Espada's legal career is revisited in the poem "Offerings to an Ulcerated God." Here we see the determination of a Spanish-speaking defendant and the embarrassment of her volunteer interpreter in court; her evidence is not even considered before the judge renders his unjust verdict.

Meanwhile, in "My Cockroach Lover" the speaker recounts sharing an infested apartment with his acquaintance JC and lists several horrors of cohabitating with vermin. In a scene reminiscent of Kafka's Gregor Samsa, he dreams one night of a giant roach who strokes his face with antennae. He awakes already slapping himself, and it is humorously ambiguous to the audience whether the speaker is more distressed by the dream or by his realization that even the cockroaches do not love him. Yet other poems in the volume convey more outrage at deplorable circumstances. In "Do Not Put Dead Monkeys in the Freezer" the speaker recounts the inhumane treatment of monkeys in a laboratory; the speaker and the other lab assistants collect data until one panicked monkey escaped from a cage.

Although some of the poems, such as "Rednecks," "The Foreman's Wallet," or "The Hearse Driver," highlight the poor judgment of humankind, many of the poems focus on the need for human action to alleviate society's ills. "The Sign in My Father's Hands" recounts the bravery of Frank Espada, a civil rights activist who faced police brutality at the Schaefer Beer pavilion at the 1964 New York World's Fair; people were protesting the brewery's reluctance to hire blacks or Puerto Ricans. Virtually all of the poems in the second section of the book, "Hands Without Irons Become Dragonflies," valorize those who stand up to injustice, particularly poets, whose words as well as their actions inspire others. The Mexican-American poet DEMETRIA MARTÍNEZ, who was prosecuted for aiding Salvadoran refugees, is honored in "Sing in the Voice of a God Even Atheists Can Hear." The final poem of the collection, "Hands Without Irons Become Butterflies," commemorates the life of revolutionary poet Clemente Soto Vélez. Throughout the collection Espada employs the traditional imagery of the faithful to reveal the interconnectedness of each of us with the survival and improvement of the human community.

Bibliography

Espada, Martín. *Imagine the Angels of Bread.* New York: W. W. Norton, 1996.

"Martin Espada." Norton Poets Online. 2001. Available online. URL: http://www.nortonpoets.com/espadam.htm. Downloaded December 18, 2007.

Ratiner, Steven. "Poetry and the Burden of History: An Interview with Martin Espada." 2000. "Modern American Poetry." Available online. URL: http://www.english.uiuc.edu/maps/poets/a_f/espada/interview.htm. Downloaded April 27, 2008.

Shorris, Earl. *Latinos: A Biography of the People.* New York: W. W. Norton, 2001.

Rebekah Hamilton

In Cuba I Was a German Shepherd Ana Menéndez (2001)

Ana Menéndez was born in 1970, the daughter of Cuban exiles, and educated in New York. She earned a degree in creative writing from New York University, worked as a journalist, and published her debut work of fiction, *In Cuba I Was A German Shepherd,* in 2001. In this lyrical work Menéndez brings to life Miami's Cuban exile community during the administration of Bill Clinton in the 1990s. Consisting of 11 interrelated vignettes set in Miami, the collection of stories lays bare the unease and forced cohesiveness of the exilic experience.

The challenge of living in exile sets the Miami Cubans in Menéndez's stories apart from both their island and the United States—even though only 90 miles separate the two countries. Her characters, both men and women and from several generations, romanticize the past in the midst of their unsettled present. Each vignette captures the sounds, feelings, and images of life in Cuba; character memories inform the imperatives of the present.

In the collection's title story, "In Cuba I Was a German Shepherd"—featured in the 2001 Pushcart Prize anthology—Menéndez introduces the reader to four domino-playing immigrants, two of whom are political exiles from the early days of the CUBAN REVOLUTION, led by FIDEL CASTRO. Through the central character, Máximo, the reader gains insight into his experience as a Cuban exile and former life as a professor at the University of Havana. Beneath the facade of Máximo's comic demeanor, his jokes betray a second layer of meaning that exposes the pain wrought by memories of his Cuban past. The punch line of one such joke, used in the title of both the collection and this particular story itself, is telling: "Here in America, I may be a short, insignificant mutt, but in Cuba I was a German Shepherd" (28). Readers learn that his skills and degrees could not be used in the United States; thus, as an immigrant, he takes on the labor of preparing food for agricultural workers. His joke tempers the melancholy that pervades the collection.

Another theme broached by Menéndez includes the depiction of first- and second-generation Cuban Americans and their relation to the island. As many such children's only connection to Cuba is through the stories and recollections passed down from their parents, Menéndez observes that collective memory helps to shape one's individual identity. In the story "Her Mother's House," the main character, Lisette, travels to Cuba and hopes to visit the places painted so vividly in her mother's familial fiction. Upon arrival Lisette finds only the faintest trace of her mother's version of the family house, learning that her mother had greatly embellished the details of their wealth and social stature in Cuba. When she returns to Miami and answers the questions posed by eager cousins, Lisette responds: "Everything was the same . . . Somehow, it had made it through the revolution" (228). Though fundamentally inaccurate, Lisette's response is typical of the Cuban exiles who go to the island and then return; certain stories about family circumstances are shown to have a mythic quality. Menéndez's characters rely upon the malleability of the past, if only to deal with their inability to change the present circumstances of exile.

A detailed chronicle of both Cuban Miami and the unrest of political exile, *In Cuba I Was a German Shepherd* is a compelling contribution to CUBAN-AMERICAN LITERATURE.

Bibliography

Kakutani, Michiko. "As the Day Wanes, Missing the Cuban Sun." *New York Times,* June 19, 2001, p. E8.

Menéndez, Ana. *In Cuba I Was a German Shepherd.* New York: Grove Press, 2001.

Whitfield, Esther. "Umbilical Cords." *Women's Review of Books* 18, nos. 10–11 (July 2001): 31–32.

Zach Weir

Infinite Plan, The Isabel Allende (1991)

ISABEL ALLENDE was born in Peru, raised in Chile, educated in Bolivia and Beirut, and worked as a journalist in Venezuela. She now lives in California with her second husband, William Gordon. Originally published in Spanish as *El plan infinito* (1991), with the English translation appearing in 1993, *The Infinite Plan* is a fictionalized account of the life of Gordon. The author combines her perspectives of life in the United States with aspects of Gordon's own past to develop the character of Gregory Reeves. Allende divides the novel into four parts. Part 1 focuses on the Reeves and Morales family; Part 2 deals with Gregory's marriage to Samantha Ernst and the birth of his daughter; Part 3 centers on his life as an attorney and the collapse of his marriage with Samantha; and Part 4 tells the story of his marriage to Shannon and the birth of his son.

In Part 1 Allende introduces us to Gregory Reeves, a boy of Australian and Jewish extraction whose nomadic family travels through the United States during the 1940s. Charles Reeves, Gregory's father, preaches the ways of an alternative spirituality called "the Infinite Plan." While in Los Angeles, Charles Reeves falls ill, and the family is given shelter by Pedro Morales, a first-generation Mexican-American factory worker. Pedro Morales shares the home with his wife, Inmaculada, and his six children. Morales has completed instruction in the Infinite Plan and considers Charles Reeves his spiritual *maestro,* "master." Carmen and Juan José Morales are two of the Morales children who are roughly the same age as Gregory; he comes of age in their company. His youth and adulthood are marked by historical events such as the Vietnam War, the hippie movement, by his failed marriages, and professional difficulties as a lawyer. By the end of the novel Gregory seems to come to terms with his father's death, the idea of incest in his family, and the importance of the Moraleses in his life, as well as his own shortcomings; meanwhile, the omniscient narrator is revealed to be Gregory's lover and mate in life.

Through its account of Reeves, the novel chronicles key events of U.S. history during the second half of the 20th century. The critical vision presented in the text covers a number of issues, the most interesting being those related to minorities in the United States. The Morales family brings to the fore the struggles of Mexican Americans during the civil rights movement, a sign of the political commitment that characterizes much of Allende's writing. Allende keeps in mind the hardship of Mexican immigrants who go to the United States—the "Promised Land"—in order to see their dreams of prosperity come true. This vision begins when the Reeves family move in with the Morales and when Gregory forms lasting relationships with Carmen and Juan José Morales. Allende uses Gregory's experiences and those of the Moraleses to describe the traditions and conflicts of the barrio.

Aspects of the novel correlate with aspects of El Plan Espiritual de AZTLÁN (The spiritual plan of Aztláná), with its elevation of male power and pride (machismo) at the expense of female autonomy (Pratt 861). Pedro and his wife, Inmaculada, represent, respectively, machismo and *marianismo.* Pedro occupies the head of the household, and Inmaculada represents *marianismo,* as she is always helping Pedro, always "one step behind her husband" (43). She is the sacred mother figure, exemplifying tradition and supporting the patriarchy.

In contrast to her father's machismo and her mother's near sainthood, Carmen Morales is the epitome of *malinchismo. Malinchismo* refers to the indigenous woman La Malinche; it applies to those individuals, influenced by foreign culture and values, who reject Mexican traditions. Although she assimilates, Carmen becomes a successful, independent woman who earns her living by mixing her cultural heritage with other traditions in her "Tamar" jewelry line. The conclusion to the novel is optimistic, as the American Dream is fulfilled for all the characters: Gregory comes to terms with his decisions and his past; Pedro Morales dies after living an exemplary life; and Carmen has become a successful businesswoman. With its multicultural perspective and resolution of plot *The Infinite Plan* explores the idea of a pan-American identity, which makes possible understanding between different Latin American communities in the United States.

Bibliography

Allende, Isabel. *The Infinite Plan.* Translated by Margaret Sayers Peden. London: Flamingo, 1994.

Levine, Linda G. *Isabel Allende.* New York: Twayne, 2002.

Pratt, Mary Louise. "'Yo soy La Malinche': Chicana Writers and the Poetics of Ethnonationalism." *Callaloo* 16, no. 4 (1993): 859–873.

Ramblado-Minero, María de la Cinta. *Isabel Allende's Writing of the Self: Trespassing the Boundaries of Fiction and Autobiography.* Lewiston, N.Y.: Edwin Mellen Press, 2003.

María de la Cinta Ramblado-Minero

In Search of Bernabé Graciela Limón (1993)

In her celebrated debut novel, *In Search of Bernabé,* Chicana author Graciela Limón (1938–) explores the effects of El Salvador's military uprising in the 1980s on the poor and working classes of the country. How investment practices of individuals in the United States can negatively affect the lives of Central Americans is but one of the messages of the novel. The novel recounts the literal and personal journeys taken by several characters, among them Luz Delcano, who searches for her son, Bernabé, a Catholic seminarian. Limón mixes real and fictional characters with Bernabé, who is a funeral attendant at the mass for Archbishop Oscar A. Romero; Romero's life ended tragically after a real assassination. Through the course of the novel Bernabé gravitates toward the revolutionary activities to challenge the right-wing military government; meanwhile, Bernabé's half brother, Colonel Lucio Delcano, privately searches for his biological mother and discovers that she is Luz Delcano. Also in the narrative, Father Hugh Joyce, an American priest who prospered from the trafficking of contraband weapons, now confronts his own culpability in El Salvador's war.

At the center of the novel is Luz Delcano, a young woman named after her grandfather, Lucio. Luz is Lucio's illegitimate granddaughter, the product of Lucio's son having his way with a servant. At 13, Luz is raped by her grandfather and gives birth to a son, also named Lucio. Dismissed by the family upon the death of her grandfather, Luz goes to San Salvador, where she finds a job as a domestic. Her son, Lucio, has remained behind with the family.

An affair with her employer leaves Luz pregnant with Bernabé and unemployed. She settles in a small town on the El Salvador–Guatemala border, where she makes a living selling food. Determined to give her son a chance at a better future, Luz moves back to San Salvador.

As a result of the bombing and chaos at the archbishop's funeral, Luz is separated from Bernabé. Befriending a young man whose family is killed by the military, Luz embarks on a search for Bernabé that takes her to Mexico City and Los Angeles. When the young man is killed, Luz is deported back to war-torn San Salvador. While hiding in a bunker from gunfire, Luz meets Father Hugh Joyce, a former administrator at an American university. The priest is haunted by the voice of Augustín Sinclaire, an ex-seminarian who lures Joyce into investing the university's money in Sinclaire's company, a company that sells contraband weapons, including arms to Colonel Delcano and the military death squads. When this information is revealed, Joyce is dismissed from his position and transferred to El Salvador.

Luz's sons, Lucio and Bernabé, come to represent the two sides of El Salvador's complicated civil war. Raised by his father's powerful family, Lucio joins the military, is promoted to the rank of colonel, and becomes the chief of military intelligence, overseeing the death squads responsible for the murders of hundreds of Salvadorans. When he discovers that Luz is his biological mother, Lucio refuses to confront her and instead keeps surveillance over her and Bernabé. Following his separation from his mother at the archbishop's funeral, Bernabé becomes a guerrilla fighter against the military, finding himself to be "less human" with each killing. This path leads Bernabé to confront his half brother, Lucio.

In writing this novel Limón was influenced by her own work with Salvadoran immigrants in Los Angeles and her role in the delegation that traveled to El Salvador to investigate the 1989 murder of three Jesuit priests. The novel made an immediate impact on the literary world, earning the 1994 Before Columbus Foundation American Book Award and the University of California at Irvine Award for Chicano literature, as well as being named a Critic's Choice for the *New York Times Book Review* and a finalist for *Los Angeles Times*'s Art Siedenbaum Award for First Fiction. *In Search of Bernabé* was one of the first texts in Hispanic-American literature to address the violence in Central America. Limón's later novels also focus on the struggles of women in Mexico and Central America. Her second novel, *The SONG OF THE HUMMINGBIRD* (1996), centers on the first contact between Europeans and the native peoples of Mexico.

Bibliography

Limón, Graciela. *The Day of the Moon.* Houston, Tex.: Arte Público Press, 1999.

———. *Erased Faces.* Houston, Tex.: Arte Público Press, 2001.

———. *In Search of Bernabé.* Houston, Tex.: Arte Público Press, 1993.

———. *The Memories of Ana Calderón.* Houston, Tex.: Arte Público Press, 1994.

———. *Song of the Hummingbird.* Houston, Tex.: Arte Público Press, 1996.

Rodriguez, Ana Patricia. "Refugees of the South: Central Americans in U.S. Latino Imaginary." *American Literature* 73 (2001): 387–412.

Arlene Rodríguez

Intaglio: A Novel in Six Stories Roberta Fernández (1990)

Roberta Fernández is a Mexican-American fiction writer. *Intaglio: A Novel in Six Stories* recounts episodes from the lives of the narrator's Mexican and Mexican-American family. The title of the work, as Roberta Fernández explains in *Máscaras*, was carefully chosen. Intaglio, an art form of imprinting, is symbolic of how the narrator, Nenita, is imprinted upon by the women in her life. Their stories connect her to a long line of Mexican women living in the Southwest. Her home is in a region that is simultaneously American and Mexican, a borderland rich in history and dynamic in its bicultural communities. The borderland is the designation given to the area of the Southwest annexed by the United States from Mexico in 1848, creating a U.S. region inhabited by Mexicans.

The stories in *Intaglio* focus on women in this borderland region, specifically, Texas. Fernández says that the theme of transformation links the stories, which unfold in a nonchronological order. The lives of the women on both sides of Nenita's family are examined. As Nenita sifts through the *cuentos* (stories) she listens to and the events she witnesses, she comes to contemplate her own life and her future. The narration shifts between the perspectives of a young girl and a woman; men are often background figures or negatively portrayed.

Nenita seeks her own identity, looking backward to her ancestors for answers about it. Her creativity is simultaneously encouraged by Amanda and discouraged by her mother and others as they sway her from making a career of dance. Nenita sends Andrea the book of photos of her early career that she cherished in childhood, and she is devastated when Consuelo destroys them. More disheartening is that Andrea is not bothered by her sister's act. Nenita is left to piece together a history of her own, moving, as Fernández has indicated, from a visual to a textual representation of the lives of the community of women who make up her family. In between, the *cuentos* are explored and committed to memory. At the end of the novel Nenita has re-created Zulema's story, and in some ways her own, by filling the journal she received from her great-aunt with the tales she and Zulema shared, a journal that is rejected by her sister Patricia.

The novel opens with the story "Andrea," which focuses on the life of creativity that is both nurtured and stifled in the Chicano culture. "Amanda" is another story of a creative woman, a dress designer who nurtures the incipient creativity in Nenita by creating for her a cape that the daughter of a *bruja*, a "witch," would wear. Spirituality is at the heart of "Filomena." Filomena shares with Nenita the Tarascan indigenous traditions associated with the Roman Catholic celebration of All Saints' Day (Día de los Muertos), thereby forging a link for both to their Mexican ancestors. The novel continues the exploration of the roles of Mexican women, focusing on the role of the CURANDERA in "Esmeralda." The story "Leonor" likewise expresses Fernández's interest in healing and Mexican spirituality. The story "Zulema" concludes the novel and is told from the perspective of Nenita as a young adult woman, who has become distanced from her culture and seeks to reconnect to Mexican-American traditions.

In his reading of Fernández's work, John Sumanth Muthyala discusses the context of the MEXICAN REVOLUTION in the Southwest. After Mexicans fled their country to escape the turmoil of the revolution, those families living on the border faced the challenge of assimilation. The struggles with Americanization are seen in Consuelo, a character who was raised in Mexico, unlike her sister Andrea, who came of age in the United States. When Consuelo visits San Luis Potosí in Mexico, she finds it is not the city of her youth that she remembers. Similarly, Filomena returns to Michoacán but is unable to stay with her children there as her life is in the United States. Meanwhile Nenita, born and raised in Texas, learns nothing in school of the contributions of Mexican Americans in shaping her region, and as a graduate student she feels alienated in reading the work of European existentialists.

Mexican Americans in the borderland cling to their native cultural practices, especially those involving spirituality and the healer figure of the *curandera*. In *Intaglio*, the Day of the Dead celebrations, the *milagros* (tiny figurines or charms) sewn into Zulema's coffin lining, and the Christian faith of characters such as Filomena are all integral to understanding the Mexican-American way of life. After the rape of Veronica the women gather as unofficial *curanderas*, bringing herbs, lotions, and remedies of every sort to relieve Veronica of her suffering.

Finally, the work intertwines female archetypes and mythology from the Mexican culture—such as La LLORONA, the Weeping Woman; the *curandera*, the healer of the body; and the *bruja,* the witch/fortune-teller—that tie immigrants to their Mexican past. Zulema and other women in the novel attempt to shatter these archetypes. In her retelling of Sleeping Beauty, for example, the prince, situated in the time period of the Mexican Revolution, is unable to rescue the sleeping princess.

Intaglio was the winner of the 1991 Multicultural Publisher's Exchange and was published in a Spanish version in 2001. For its characterizations and themes *Intaglio* can be read within the context of CHICANO LITERATURE and BORDER LITERATURE.

Bibliography

Carbonell, Ana Maria. "From Llorona to Gritona: Coatlicue in Feminist Tales by Viramontes and Cisneros." *MELUS* 24, no. 2 (1999): 53–94.

Fernández, Roberta. "'The Cariboo Café': Helena Maria Viramontes' Discourses with Her Social and Cultural Contexts." *Women's Studies: An Interdisciplinary Journal* 17, nos. 1–2 (1989): 71–85.

———. "Depicting Women's Culture in *Intaglio: A Novel in Six Stories.*" In *Máscaras,* edited by Lucha Corpi, 73–98. Berkeley. Calif.: Third Woman Press, 1997.

———. *Intanglio: A Novel in Six Stories.* Houston, Tex.: Arte Público Press, 1990.

Muthyala, John Sumanth. "Roberta Fernández's *Intaglio*: Border Crossings and Mestiza Feminism in the Borderlands." *Canadian Review of American Studies* 30, no. 1 (2000): 92–111.

Patricia Bostian

In the Name of Salomé Julia Alvarez (2000)

The title of JULIA ALVAREZ's *In the Name of Salomé* refers to the legacy of Dominican poet Salomé Ureña de Henríquez. The author looks at Salomé's marriage to Francisco Henríquez, the birth of their three children in the late 19th century, and the road to self-discovery that the youngest child, Camila, embarks upon. The saga of the Henríquez-Ureña family incorporates aspects of U.S., Cuban, and Dominican history. In this regard *Salomé* corresponds with the use of history in IN THE TIME OF THE BUTTERFLIES (1994).

In both novels Alvarez employs narrative techniques that characterize her fiction: constant shifts backward and forward in time, multiple narrators, and CODE SWITCHING. Code switching in *Salomé* takes place when Alvarez quotes Dominican expressions in Spanish or translates their meaning in English.

Salomé is set in the Dominican Republic, the United States, and Cuba, spanning the period from 1856 to 1973. It tells the stories of Salomé Ureña de Henríquez and her daughter Salomé Camila Henríquez Ureña. Born in 1850, six years after the Dominican Republic's independence from Spain, Salomé starts writing at an early age and develops her own poetic voice as a young woman. Her poetry inspires fellow Dominicans and offers them hope during the many changes of government during the late 1800s. She becomes the national poet, giving voice to the divisions in the island between the rural and the urban, the rich and the poor, the elite and the folk. Salomé dies of consumption in 1897, when Camila is three years old.

Salomé's husband, Francisco Henríquez, maintains his political aspirations and is elected president of the Dominican Republic in 1916. He is ousted by U.S. forces shortly thereafter. Salomé and Francisco's second son, Pedro Henríquez Ureña, grows up to be a prominent poet, literary critic, and a Norton Lecturer at Harvard. Their third son, Maximiliano, remains in the Dominican Republic as ambassador during Rafael Trujillo's regime. Meanwhile, Camila struggles to deal with the weight of her family history as well as the precious, but scarce memories of her mother, Salomé. Although she initially seems withdrawn, Camila develops an inner strength. While living in Cuba she fights for civil liberties and spends a brief spell in prison during the regime of Fulgencio Batista. She then moves to the United States, where she becomes a lecturer at Vassar College in New York. After her retirement in 1960 she decides to return to Cuba to work for FIDEL CASTRO's revolution as a teacher.

The prologue recounts aspects of Salomé's life and Camila's own story to explain this decision to leave New York. The following 16 chapters are all named after poems by Salomé and are grouped in eight pairs. The first chapter in each pair has a Spanish title and deals with Salomé, whereas the second one in each has an English title and deals with Camila. In a twist adding further complexity to the narrative structure, the first chapter, about Salomé, shares its title with the 16th, about Camila; the second, about Salomé, has the same title as the 15th, about Camila, and so on. Salomé's life is narrated in chronological order and pauses with Camila's birth in 1894 and the three years that they share before the poet's death in 1897. Camila's story is told from her adult years and goes back in years to the short time that mother and daughter enjoy together. After this symbolic reunion of mother and daughter, the epilogue presents an elderly Camila, who has come to terms with the effects of Salomé's fame and early death.

Along with the theme of self-discovery Alvarez portrays the importance of family bonds and the homeland. Her novel also examines how patriarchal societies restrict women's life choices and condone male infidelity while repressing female sexuality. We learn that Camila's brothers disapprove of her lifelong attraction to her friend and companion Marion. As it interweaves these thematic strands, *Salomé* provides a poignant study of how personal lives, political developments, and literature are connected.

In the acknowledgments Alvarez explains that she undertook the project of writing *Salomé* thanks to the suggestions of fellow Dominican-American writer Chiqui Vicioso. She also states that she had access to Pedro Henríquez Ureña's diary, as well as to several editions of Salomé's poems. However, Alvarez stresses that the work is not a biographical or historical account but rather a creative interpretation of historical figures of the Dominican Republic, characters born of Alvarez's desire to explore the meaning of love and the formation of individual and collective identities. For its plot and themes *Salomé* can be read within the context of DOMINICAN-AMERICAN LITERATURE as well as SPANISH-AMERICAN CARIBBEAN LITERATURE.

Bibliography
Alvarez, Julia. *In the Name of Salomé*. Chapel Hill, N.C.: Algonquin Books, 2000.
Sirias, Silvio. *Julia Alvarez: A Critical Companion*. Westport, Conn., and London: Greenwood Press, 2001.

Marta Vizcaya Echano

In the Time of the Butterflies   Julia Alvarez (1994)

The Book of the Month Club designated JULIA ALVAREZ's *In the Time of the Butterflies,* a beautifully crafted and compelling narrative, as its choice for readers in 1994. The novel is arguably Alvarez's most daring work, depicting the lives of the Mirabal sisters, who fought against the regime of Rafael Trujillo (1930–61). To this day mere mention of Trujillo's name on the island elicits discomfort, despite the fact that he has been dead since 1961, when he was assassinated by his own men.

In the postscript to *In the Time of the Butterflies* Alvarez insists on the fictional aspect of her vision of the Mirabals. She remarks: "So what you will find here are the real Mirabals of my creation, made up, but, I hope, true to the spirit of the real Mirabals" (324). Likewise, in her portrait of Trujillo's regime she notes: "I sometimes took liberties—by changing dates, by reconstructing events, and by collapsing characters or incidents" (324). One example of poetic license can be found when Minerva Mirabal is dancing with Trujillo during a Columbus Day celebration; when he draws too close, she slaps him across the face. Such effrontery by a woman would not have been realistic in Trujillo's regime, nor in the Dominican Republic's Catholic and conservative culture of the 1950s. It is true historically, however, that Minerva and her sisters worked in an underground movement to unseat one of the worst dictators of the Caribbean and that they tested the patience of the SIM (Servicio Inteligencia Militar), Trujillo's secret police.

Alvarez dedicates multiple sections of her novel to each of the four Mirabal sisters: Patria, Dedé, Minerva, and María Teresa (Mate). Each one of them talks or writes about their childhood, their adolescence, their religious beliefs, and their growing and ultimately catastrophic involvement in the rebellion against Trujillo. Patria, Mariposa #3, whose name in Spanish means "country," is the eldest of the four daughters. She goes by the code name Mariposa #3. *Mariposa* means "butterfly" in Spanish, hence the title of the book. Comfortable with life in the country and devoted to the Catholic Church, Patria is educated at the Inmaculada Concepción convent and prepares to takes her orders there. At the age of 16, she has a change of heart and marries Pedrito González, whose farm is his livelihood and a key part of his identity.

Initially the Mirabal sisters are safe by virtue of their class and their father's accommodation of "el Jefe," a term that means "chief" or "leader" and in this context refers to Trujillo; however, certain events set the Mirabals on to their path of resistance. Patria experiences a crisis of faith after the loss of her newborn son, and though she does not abandon the Catholic Church, she does reconsider what her new role might be in her community. She takes decisive action when she witnesses the brutal shooting of a young peasant in Constanza. She begins to regard all young men as her own children, and this image of a common cause helps her to rebuild her lost faith. After joining the Acción Clero-Cultural, she names another son, born late in her marriage, Raul Ernesto in honor of Argentine revolutionary Ernesto "Che" Guevara and Raúl Castro (Che Guevara helped Raul and FIDEL CASTRO overthrow Cuba's dictator, Fulgencio Batista, in 1959).

The González home, an emblem of Pedro's ancestral roots and a source of pride, becomes a site of ammunition and weaponry for the Fourteenth of June movement (to overthrow the Trujillo regime). Patria makes the bold decision to hold meetings on the González property without her husband's consent. This move creates conflict in their 18-year marriage because Pedro knows the movement will jeopardize his patrimony and that of his sons. Nevertheless, Patria justifies her decision to help unseat Trujillo. Alvarez combines biblical language and the ideas of liberation theology (a Catholic movement that opposes right-wing government and fights for basic rights of Latin American peasantry, including access to food and shelter) when Patria declares: "The time was now, for the Lord said I come with the sword as well as the plow to set at liberty them that are bruised" (163). Pedro reconciles himself to the movement to overthrow Trujillo; he also wants to protect his eldest son, Nelson, who has gravitated toward his rebellious aunts and uncles.

A complex character in many ways, at the same time that Patria plots against the regime she also defies reader expectations by praying for the enemy. When members of her family are jailed for their subversive activities, Patria prays to the image of "el Jefe" and places fresh flowers under his picture as a way of tempering his repressive measures. Likewise, she offers to pray for Captain Peña, the local police authority, since that is the only thing she has left to give him. Her prayers, save one, have little effect, because the SIM destroy Patria's home, going so far as to dismantle the wood supports that bear the mark of each González generation. The one prayer that seems to work is when Patria offers herself up to God if Trujillo lets Nelson free—"Let me be your sacrificial lamb" (206). Nelson is released from prison, and by the end of the novel Patria's life is taken, as is Minerva's and Mate's.

Minerva Mirabal, Mariposa #1, represents the heart and energy of the Fourteenth of June movement; she is opinionated, intelligent, generous, and brave. She becomes one of the few women of her generation to complete an undergraduate degree and to obtain a law degree. This is a detail true to history, for the real Minerva Mirabal did earn a doctorate in jurisprudence. It is through Minerva's exposure to the revolutionary ideas of JOSÉ MARTÍ and Fidel Castro (author of the famous speech, "HISTORY WILL ABSOLVE ME") that Minerva envisions change for the island. When imprisoned, she shares her food with other inmates and creates a regimen in order to structure everyone's time. Minerva uses the experience of Castro at the Isle of Pines to build morale and to unify female inmates. These women are held for both political (revolutionary) and nonpolitical (prostitution, murder) crimes; regardless of their offenses, they become a kind of family and learn basic skills under Minerva and Mate's tutelage.

Although she devises strategies to cope with imprisonment, Minerva is vulnerable. After her release from prison she puts on a brave face because she knows that everyone expects optimism and dedication from Mariposa #1. But Minerva is, in fact, burnt out from her incarceration, sick from what is probably tuberculosis, and separated from Manolo, her husband, who is in prison. She feels the burden of a disintegrating revolutionary movement. She understands that she represents hope for her compatriots, so she continues the struggle, but with resignation. At this period in her life what she desires most is a stable home for her young children and the release of Manolo. On the last trip the Mariposas take together Minerva is warned by the cashier from El Gallo to avoid a certain road. She ignores his note and continues with Patria and Mate homeward until they are ambushed, murdered, and dumped in their jeep over a precipice.

Mate, Mariposa #2, is the youngest of the Mirabal sisters, and from an early age she uses her diary to make sense of her world. As a girl she writes about her First Communion, her flirtations, and her growing political awareness. Her diaries are vehicles for reflection, but when Mate includes Minerva's activities, the reader feels agitation that the diary will fall into the wrong hands. In the course of the novel Mate appears as a sweet-natured adolescent, an adoring wife and mother, and an industrious, though vulnerable revolutionary. She eventually becomes a target of Trujillo's secret police, and when she and Minerva are taken into custody, her charmed life begins to crumble.

Mate is physically tortured while in the chamber called "La 40" (la Cuarenta, "the Forty"), and she miscarries there. Trusted by both her prison guards and her cellmates, Mate nevertheless testifies about the treatment of women prisoners to the U.S. and Latin American journalists who have taken an interest in the human rights violations of Trujillo's regime. In its various forms—diaries, letters, notes, even sketches of bombs—Mate's writing reinforces Alvarez's concern with censorship.

Dedé Mirabal, the second eldest of the Mirabals, is the archetypal "middle child." She undertakes the accounting of farming business, stays close to her parents, forgoes a university education, and instead marries her cousin Jaime. She gives birth to three sons, tries to keep her marriage going, and watches as her sisters get more deeply entrenched in revolutionary activity. Throughout the text she functions as the reluctant repository of her sisters' memories. She is not with them on the fateful day that they die, November 25, 1960, but she is there to bury all of them and their driver, Rufino de la Cruz. The children of the three murdered Mirabal sisters are taken in by Dedé and Mercedes Mirabal (the mother). In these children Dedé sees the future of the island and its transformation as a site of tourism. She takes inventory of the construction of new homes in the mountains where her sisters were killed; she meets women who have decorative undergraduate degrees, and she watches them trivialize revolution in the Caribbean. She asks: "Was it for this, the sacrifice of the butterflies?" (318). Alvarez leaves the reader to consider that question.

Although it is tempting to take Alvarez's fiction as fact, to do so would be an error in interpretation. One can read the text as fictional biography, one combining true and imagined episodes of life in the Dominican Republic from the 1920s to the 1990s. Another approach to the text would be, as Ilan Stavans points out, to read *In the Time of the Butterflies* as a portrait of a Latin American dictator. In this regard we can read Alvarez's novel alongside Miguel Asturias's *El Señor Presidente* (Guatemala) and Augusto Roa Basto's *I, the Supreme* (Paraguay), as well as Mario Vargas Llosa's novel about Trujillo, *The Feast of the Goat*. With its political and historical plots Alvarez's work can be read within the context of both Dominican-American literature and Spanish-American Caribbean literature.

Bibliography

Alvarez, Julia. *In the Time of the Butterflies*. New York: Plume, 1994.

Ciria, Concepción Bados. "*In the Time of the Butterflies* by Julia Alvarez: History, Fiction, Testimonio and the Dominican Republic." *Monographic Review/Revista Monográfica* 13 (1997): 406–416.

Puleo, Gus. "Remembering and Reconstructing the Mirabal Sisters in Julia Alvarez's *In the Time of the Butterflies.*" *Bilingual Review/Revista Bilingüe* 23, no. 1 (January–April 1998): 11–20.

Stavans, Ilan. "Las Mariposas." *Nation* (November 7, 1994), 552–556.

Luz Elena Ramirez

Islas, Arturo (Arturo Islas La Farga)
(1938–1991) *(novelist, critic, scholar)*

Arturo Islas is the author of *The RAIN GOD* (1984), *MIGRANT SOULS* (1990), and *LA MOLLIE AND THE KING OF TEARS* (1996). Islas was born in El Paso, Texas, on May 25, 1938, the son of a working-class Mexican-American family. He survived polio at the age of eight, but the virus impeded the development of his left leg and foot, and he walked with a noticeable limp for the rest of his life. In 1969 Islas nearly died from gastrointestinal problems and underwent several drastic surgeries, one of which left him with a permanent colostomy. When coupled with his limp, the colostomy further exacerbated Islas's feelings of deformity. For Islas the pain of being handicapped was that it caused him to feel different from his schoolmates, his friends, even his family. He wrestled with these feelings of alienation throughout his life, returning to them through his fiction. Along these lines he wrote about the strain also of being a Mexican American in a prejudiced English-speaking, white culture and the challenge of being gay in a homophobic society.

Islas was an introspective, bookish child who did well in school. His studiousness paid off, and upon graduating from high school he earned a scholarship to attend Stanford University. When he enrolled at Stanford in 1956, Islas became the first member of his family to attend college. Islas graduated with a B.A. in 1960 and immediately entered Stanford's Ph.D. program in English, the first Mexican American ever to do so. Islas completed his doctorate in 1971 and was hired by Stanford's English Department for a tenure-track position. At Stanford, Islas was trained in the English and European canon and literary criticism. In his teaching and research Islas championed the works of Latin American authors, such as Colombian Nobel Prize–winning author Gabriel García Márquez and Mexican essayist OCTAVIO PAZ. In his own writing Islas represents the lives of Mexican Americans, emphasizing their Spanish and Indian heritage in the American Southwest.

Islas is best known for his novel *The Rain God*, which is the first book in a planned trilogy about the Angel clan, an extended Mexican-American family in the fictitious equivalent of El Paso. While recovering from a serious illness, Miguel Chico Angel, the narrator, recalls his past and the decisions his family made in their lives. The Angel clan includes Mama Chona, his grandmother, who left San Miguel de Allende, Mexico, and immigrated to the United States; his father, who commits adultery with a family friend; his aunt, who mourns her son's suicide; and his uncle, who is brutally murdered when he makes a pass at a homophobic young soldier. The writing in the novel is lyrical and compelling, telling as it does the story of three generations of the Angels and their Mexican-American communities.

Migrant Souls is Islas's second novel and focuses on Miguel Chico Angel and his cousin Josie Salazar. They both belong to the family's third generation, and not surprisingly, they rebel against the strictures and values of the Angel clan. Josie is a divorcée trying to raise her two daughters alone, and Miguel Chico is a closeted gay man grieving the end of a homosexual relationship.

Along with *The Rain God* and *Migrant Souls*, Islas wrote *La Mollie and the King of Tears*. This novel was published after the author's death and is set in San Francisco in the 1970s. Its protagonist, Louie Mendoza, and his girlfriend, Mollie, are referred to briefly in *Migrant Souls*. Among other things, *La Mollie and the King of Tears* explores the challenge of determining the truthfulness of what people say through its narrator-musician Louie Mendoza. Louie claims to love his brother Tomás, but his homophobia keeps him from being a part of Tomás's life. Since the entire novel is a monologue by Louie, readers must evaluate whether the story they are being told is credible. In this way Islas appears to have been continuing the experimentation with narrative techniques that he began in *The Rain God*.

Functioning as an intermediary between the Anglo and Chicano/a cultures was not an easy thing for Islas. While trying to introduce Latin American and Mexican-American literature to U.S. classrooms, Islas was unwilling to promote that which he viewed as lacking in artistry and excellence. He would not compromise his aesthetic standards for the sake of political expediency. For him, JOSÉ ANTONIO VILLARREAL's *Pocho* (1959), Oscar Zeta Acosta's The AUTOBIOGRAPHY OF A BROWN BUFFALO (1972), and RUDOLFO ALFONSO ANAYA's BLESS ME, ÚLTIMA (1972), texts that many consider the cornerstones of Chicano literature, are noteworthy for their historical value as opposed to their artistic merit. Islas was critical of RICHARD RODRIGUEZ. In Islas's mind Rodriguez was wrong to denounce affirmative action policies and bilingual education programs in his autobiography *Hunger of Memory* (1982); however, the logic of Rodriguez's own views about learning English and succeeding in school accords with Islas's own standards.

Beyond these political and philosophical stances, there was the added complication of Islas's sexuality. In his fiction he illustrated how both white and Mexican-American cultures marginalize gays. Islas died of AIDS in 1991 before he could finish his Angel trilogy. The last novel was to depict Miguel Chico coming out to his family. For its characters and themes Islas's work can be read within the context of LATINO GAY LITERATURE.

Bibliography

Aldama, Frederick Luis. *Dancing with Ghosts: A Critical Biography of Arturo Islas*. Berkeley: University of California Press, 2004.

Islas, Arturo. *La Mollie and the King of Tears*. Edited by Paul Skenazy. Albuquerque: University of New Mexico Press, 1996.

———. *Migrant Souls*. New York: Avon, 1991.

———. *The Rain God*. New York: Avon, 1991.

———. *The Uncollected Works*. Edited by Frederick Luis Aldama. Houston, Tex.: Arte Público Press, 2003.

Skenazy, Paul. "The Long Walk Home." Afterword to *La Mollie and the King of Tears*, by Arturo Islas. Albuquerque: University of New Mexico Press, 1996.

Timothy K. Nixon

Jaramillo, Cleofas Martinez

(1878–1956) *(folklorist, memoirist)*

Cleofas Martinez Jaramillo was born on December 6, 1878, in Arroyo Hondo, New Mexico, daughter of Marina Lucero Martinez and Julian Antonio Martinez. At the age of 20 she married Venceslao Jaramillo, a cousin and wealthy businessman and political aide to New Mexican governor M. A. Otero. This marriage thrust Cleofas Jaramillo into the elite New Mexican political society characterized by travel and comfort. Yet, Jaramillo also experienced tragedy as two of her children died young, while a third child, Angelina, was murdered at the age of 17. When her husband died, she faced the challenges of managing his estate, but she became an astute businesswoman. His death, along with the several political and social changes taking place in the 1920s and 1930s, led Jaramillo to record her Hispanic culture and history in several texts. These include *Cuentos del hogar/Spanish Fairy Tales* (1939), a translation of her mother's stories into English; *Genuine New Mexico Tasty Recipes* (1939), a collection of traditional recipes; *Sombras del Pasado/Shadows of the Past* (1941), an autobiography dedicated to the memory of her daughter Angelina; and *Romance of a Little Village Girl* (1955), her penultimate autobiography and more widely known text.

In addition to preserving Hispanic culture in her writing, Jaramillo founded the Sociedad Folklorica (Folkloric Society), a group of Hispanic women dedicated to sustaining Mexican-American cultural traditions and making them visible to New Mexican audiences. Jaramillo, similar to other New Mexican women writers of this period, such as Fabiola Cabeza de Baca and Nina Otero-Warren, preserved Mexican culture by collecting and publishing stories, poems, and recipes. It is remarkable that Jaramillo and her counterparts were successful as Mexican-American writers given the dominance of a patriarchal and English-speaking mainstream culture.

Romance of a Little Village Girl, a combination of personal experiences and folklore, records Jaramillo's maturation from her childhood in Arroyo Hondo to adulthood in 20th-century American society. The text documents the Mexican-American perspective of New Mexico's transition from a Mexican province to an American territory in 1848 with the TREATY OF GUADALUPE HIDALGO. The autobiography documents Jaramillo's personal history and the social struggles of her family and community. Each chapter begins with a Spanish romantic ballad, which helps readers to place her narrative within a tradition of Spanish epic poetry. This combination of poetry and narrative, romance and family history, cultural history and creative autobiography was common in Hispanic storytelling. Jaramillo's use of various genres within her autobiography parallels the collective ways of her community.

The Genuine New Mexico Tasty Recipes, a collection of traditional Hispanic recipes, also records Mexican-American culture and history by documenting native foods. Her text was inspired by an erroneous 1935 article in *Holland Magazine* that listed incorrect ingredients for the making of flour tortillas. Jaramillo decided to write a cookbook to document Mexican culture from her native perspective. Because the text values Hispanic cultural traditions, the cookbook can be read as a narrative of resistance to the Americanization projects of the 1930s and 1950s. By recording her knowledge of Hispanic food and customs, Jaramillo establishes herself as an authority on her culture.

Shadows of the Past, Jaramillo's first autobiography and similar to *Romance,* narrates both family and Hispanic New Mexican history. She writes this autobiography in order to preserve Hispanic folklore for future generations of Mexican Americans who may not be familiar with Hispanic customs. The text provides a glimpse into the lives of Mexican-American women living in the 19th century. Jaramillo details Hispanic feast days, weddings, wakes, games, and sports and brings to the foreground the participation of women within these events. The text offers contemporary readers insight into the various jobs and professions held by women who were CURANDERAS (healers), weavers, bakers, innkeepers, ranchers, and laundresses.

Jaramillo's concern with documenting Hispanic heritage and making it available to wider audiences suggest that she was conscious of the importance of her Mexican-American identity and culture. She records and publishes her history in response to the Anglo-American view that Mexican Americans should assimilate their identity and heritage. Jaramillo records Mexican-American history from a female perspective and thus offers an important perspective in CHICANO LITERATURE.

Bibliography

Goodman, Anne. "'I Yam What I Yam': Cooking, Culture and Colonialism." In *De/Colonizing the Subject: The Politics of Gender in Women's Autobiography,* edited by Sidonie Smith and Julia Watson, 169–195. Minneapolis: University of Minnesota Press, 1992.

Jaramillo, Cleofas Martinez. *Cuentos del hogar/Spanish Fairy Tales.* El Campo, Tex.: Citizens Press, 1939.

———. *The Genuine New Mexico Tasty Recipes: Potajes sabrosos.* Santa Fe, N.Mex.: Ancient City Press, 1971.

———. *Romance of a Little Village Girl.* San Antonio, Tex.: Naylor Co., 1955.

———. *Sombras del pasado/Shadows of the Past.* Santa Fe, N.Mex.: Ancient City Press, 1972.

Padilla, Genaro M. *My History, Not Yours: The Formation of Mexican American Autobiography.* Madison: University of Wisconsin Press, 1993.

Rebolledo, Tey Diana. "Tradition and Mythology: Signatures of Landscape in Chicana Literature." In *The Desert Is No Lady: Southwestern Landscapes in Women's Writing and Art,* edited by Vera Norwood and Janice Monk, 96–124. New Haven, Conn.: Yale University Press, 1987.

———. *Women Singing in the Snow: A Cultural Analysis of Chicana Literature.* Tucson: University of Arizona Press, 1995.

Rebolledo, Tey Diana, and Eliana S. Rivero, eds *Infinite Divisions: An Anthology of Chicana Literature.* Tucson: University of Arizona Press, 1993.

Marci R. McMahon

K

Klail City **Rolando Hinojosa Smith** (1976)

ROLANDO HINOJOSA SMITH originally published *Klail City* (1987) under the title *Klail City y sus alrededores* in 1976. The Spanish original won the prestigious Premio CASA DE LAS AMÉRICAS. *Klail City* continues Hinojosa's Klail City Death Trip series inaugurated with *Estampas del valle y otras obras* (1972; *Sketches of the Valley and Other Works*). His second book tells the story of a community through a series of vignettes set from the MEXICAN REVOLUTION (1910–20) to the 1960s. Given this span of time, we meet several generations of Texas Mexicans in *Klail City*. The three narrators are P. Galindo (a pseudonym for Hinojosa) and two cousins who come of age in the 1950s, Jehu Malacara and Rafe Buenrostro. *Malacara* means "bad face," and *Buenrostro*, "good face" in Spanish; however, one should not read these names literally because Hinojosa is not so obvious. Malacara and Buenrostro are ordinary individuals with their weaknesses and their strengths. Because they are orphans and move from one odd job to another, they form attachments to a variety of personalities, and their experiences widen the scope of the narrative. Both young men finish high school and graduate from college to become high school teachers.

Hinojosa relies on a cast of characters to record the imprint of life in a segregated city of Texas Mexicans and Texas Anglos. The setting of *Klail City* includes K. C. Park, where the old timers sit and tell stories, a whorehouse, cattle ranches (where land tenure is disputed), churches (Protestant and Catholic), bars and cantinas, the Oasis gambling house, and a J. C. Penney. Each vignette features commentary about the passions and foibles of life in the Rio Grande valley.

The author attends to questions of birth, marriage, and death with a sense of humor and often with irreverence. The prologue explains that folks of the evangelical spirit "go around asking why they were put on this earth" (8). The prologue uses this observation to poke a little fun at Texans who are reborn, as when the narrator observes, "My father had heard of a neighbor who claimed to have been reborn, and he went out to see this real, substantial, first class, genuine miracle and came back with the following report: 'I liked the old one better; he didn't talk as much'" (8). So much of *Klail City* depends on the reader's recognition of understatement. The prologue takes time to warn the audience:

> one should not expect to find legendary heroes here . . . although the reader suspects that there are certain and definite ways of being heroic. Showing up for work (and doing it) then putting up with whatever fool happens to come bobbing along is no laughing matter. Thus, by

refusing to break, by working hard at living and letting live, and neither quitting nor faltering, the mexicano folk know, in great part, what life is like and about (9–10).

As testament to "what life is like," Hinojosa begins his novel with gossipy news of Jovita de Anda's pregnancy and her hasty marriage to Joaquín Tamez. This rushed ceremony—there is no family of the bride in attendance, no flowers, no gown, and no formal celebration—allows the reader entry into the intrigues of Klail City. The justice of the peace is ushered into the Tamez home to make the wedding official, while Jovita de Anda's father sits reluctantly at home. There is a scandal, but time passes and the hullabaloo subsides; Jovita gives birth to a daughter, and in the coming years the Tamez family grows. This episode is important because it points to the union of the Tamez and de Anda families without much conflict. Hinojosa's Texas Mexicans have their family feuds and are divided by their fence posts and beliefs; nevertheless, on the whole they tend to accept and often enjoy each other's company.

The Klail City Death Trip series features Texas Mexicans who are like other individuals pursuing the American Dream. They are involved in war, career changes, marital affairs; perhaps because of migrant farming they have their greater share of accidents and acts of violence. Hinojosa's voice is tempered and ironic, especially in regard to the Texas Rangers, the police force, and local politicians, as well as military, school, and library personnel. These authorities tend to crack down, often arbitrarily, on the Mexican-American citizenry of Belken County. About 100 characters come and go in *Klail City*; they die in train wrecks, they die from gun shot wounds, they die from heart attacks while having sex or prospecting for treasure, they die in war (Mexican Revolution, World War II, and Korean War).

The author's style is concise and colloquial; we can see parallels between Hinojosa Smith's work and the crafted brevity of Ernest Hemingway, the imagined genealogies of William Faulkner, and the persistence of an individual and community spirit of TOMÁS RIVERA, author of THIS MIGRANT EARTH. Likewise, Klail City's treatment of migrant farming has much in common with the American classic John Steinbeck's *Grapes of Wrath.*

Hinojosa's work, usually written in Spanish and then translated into English, invites several lines of critical inquiry, especially within the context of CHICANO LITERATURE. Juan Bruce-Novoa notes how Hinojosa's ancestry and his experiences growing up have influenced his writing. José Saldívar examines the Klail City Death Trip series to consider Hinojosa's representation of people from the Texas-Mexican border.

Bibliography

Bruce-Novoa, Juan. *Chicano Authors: Inquiry by Interview.* Austin: University of Texas Press, 1980.

Glover, Joyce Lee. *Rolando Hinojosa and the American Dream.* Denton: University of North Texas Press, 1997.

Hinojosa Smith, Rolando. *Klail City.* Houston, Tex.: Arte Público Press, 1987.

———. *Becky and Her Friends.* Houston: Arte Público Press, 1990.

———. *Dear Rate/Querido Rate.* Houston: Arte Público Press, 2005.

Riles and Witnesses. Houston: Arte Público Press, 1982.

Saldívar, José David, ed. *The Rolando Hinojosa Reader: Essays Historical and Critical.* Houston, Tex.: Arte Público Press, 1985.

Zilles, Klaus. *Rolando Hinojosa: A Reader's Guide.* Albuquerque: University of New Mexico Press, 2001.

Luz Elena Ramirez

Lamazares, Ivonne (1962–) (novelist)

Ivonne Lamazares was born in 1962 in Cuba. Her mother died when she was three years old, and she went to live with her grandparents in Old Havana. When Lamazares was 14 years old, she moved to Florida. In 1984 she received her B.A. in English from Barry University, Miami Shores, Florida. In 1985 she received her M.S. degree in TESOL (Teacher of English to Speakers of Other Languages) from Florida International University, and in 1991 she received her Ed.D. in higher education from the University of Miami, Winter Park. Currently Lamazares teaches creative writing at the University of Central Florida and resides in Miami with her husband, Steve Kronen, a poet, and her daughter.

In 1995 Lamazares was the recipient of a Florida Arts Council Grant. She achieved literary recognition with her novel *The Sugar Island* (2000), which has been translated into seven languages. In December 2003 she was awarded a grant from the National Endowment for the Arts to work on her second novel, which will be entitled *Some Realms I Owned*.

The Sugar Island evolved from a 1996 short story entitled "Storm Captains." Tanya del Carmen Casals Villalta has been raised by Mirella in the midst of the CUBAN REVOLUTION. Mirella had left Tanya to join up with FIDEL CASTRO's army, only to return home pregnant by a rebel cook; she gives birth to Emmanuel. This coming-of-age novel focuses on Tanya's observations (representing the new generation of Cubans in contrast with older generations) and experiences of life and the totally dysfunctional environment around her. She lives in a country of extremes (militarism and SANTERÍA), and oppression (via the Committees for the Defense of the Revolution, CDR). Whereas the Cuban Revolution was the inspiration for Tanya's mother to follow Castro, Tanya finds her loyalties split between having a real mother/daughter relationship, stability, and finding her own identity amid turmoil. Everyone is just trying to survive.

In the search for freedom, Mirella designs a plan of escape but is caught and imprisoned. Tanya and her brother, Emmanuel, are sent to live with relatives. Upon her mother's release from prison, or "rehabilitation," Tanya is once again faced with attempting to understand and accept her mother's actions. Mirella decides that the only way to give her daughter a good life is for her and her daughter to leave Cuba and send for Emmanuel when they are settled in America.

The journey to the United States is fraught with horrific challenges and conflicts, where the consistently unreliable Mirella plays the role of the maternal hero. When Tanya and Mirella finally end up in America, they become resilient to the questions and fears of living in a foreign country. Acclimating herself to American customs and learning how to live in the States, Tanya is told that "to collect things was very American" (181). Watching her mother take numerous jobs, only to be fired and become increasingly discouraged, Tanya begins to realize that in order for her to face her own uncertainties and the future, she and her mother will have to face and resolve any conflicts if they want to succeed.

After a devastating visit from Tanya's father she finally realizes "the impulse of all things was to keep being themselves" (189). Tanya knew that trying to change someone into what she wanted or expected was futile. Constantly disappointed and having feelings of abandonment by her mother, her father, and her friends, Tanya tries to take illogical situations and make them logical. According to Lamazares, "the themes of the book are abandonment and betrayal." For its characterizations and themes her work can be read within the context of CUBAN-AMERICAN LITERATURE. With increased immigration to the United States since 1959, Lamazares represents a generation of authors who has sought intellectual and political freedom. Writing of their travails, experiences, and memories of the Cuban culture, Cuban writers keep their heritage alive.

Bibliography
Lamazares, Ivonne.
———. "Cousin Sarita." In *A Century of Cuban Writers in Florida*, edited by Carolina Hospital and Jorge Cantera, 219–224. Sarasota, Fla.: Pineapple Press, 1997.
———. *The Sugar Island*. Boston: Houghton Mifflin, 2000.
Smith, Dinitia. "In Summer, Some Literary Lions Pause to Offer Guidance to the Cubs." *New York Times*, August 7, 1997, pp. C11, C12.

Karen E. Holleran

La Mollie and the King of Tears Arturo Islas (1996)

ARTURO ISLAS is best known for his two novels about the Angel family, *The RAIN GOD* (1984) and *MIGRANT SOULS* (1990). His posthumously published novel *La Mollie and the King of Tears,* though lesser known, is a stylistically rich and significant contribution to CHICANO LITERATURE.

In 1986 Islas returned to his native Texas from California to teach creative writing at the University of Texas, El Paso. It was here that he began drafting a short story called "The Lame," which would eventually become the manuscript for *La Mollie.* Though Islas submitted the manuscript, the New York publishing industry was uninterested in the novel. Islas died in 1991. Ten years after the author had first drafted the novel, Paul Skenazy (who made minor editing changes to the manuscript) found a willing publisher, University of New Mexico Press.

La Mollie takes place in San Francisco in 1973 and is narrated by Louie Mendoza, a Mexican-American musician from El Paso. Louie's immediate audience is a professor who records the jazz musician's story so that he can study Louie's "accent." This professor is unnamed, works at a junior college, and is presumably white. He records episodes of Louie's life: "At the Movies," "Trees," "That Old Black Magic," and "Just Like Romeo and Juliet." In the first chapter, "At the Movies," Louie waits in a rundown San Francisco hospital to find out if his girlfriend, la Mollie, will live or die. Louie tells the professor the story of how the previous night he broke his leg and went to the hospital after a jazz gig. He had to hobble home from the hospital, across the Castro and the Mission Districts, only to surprise la Mollie, who thought he was dead. She faints, suffers a serious head injury, and has to be admitted to the same hospital. Interspersed into this narrative are the details of Louie's past life in El Paso, his move to San Francisco, and his love affair with la Mollie, a rich Anglo woman whose "family goes way back, all the way to the Mayflower" (5).

La Mollie, while retaining themes of Chicano identity, U.S. nationality, and sexuality present in *The Rain God* and *Migrant Souls,* diverges significantly in its content and style from these works. Unlike Islas's other work, *La Mollie* does not directly address family issues, nor does it engage as much with Catholicism or Aztec mythology. *La Mollie* is notably different from his earlier works because it presents the potential of a coming together of mainstream and Chicano communities.

It does this through Louie's hybrid identity; the narrator describes himself as a child of the border, and speaks proudly of his Yaqui Indian and Spanish heritage. Louie's complex storytelling couches his own "Chicano" narrative in the plot lines of Hollywood movies, Shakespearean plays, and such jazz songs as "That Old Black Magic," the title of chapter 3. Louie uses the movies he loves and the Shakespearean drama he was taught in school to construct his own love story. He imagines access to the dominant canon that, as a Mexican American from the barrio, he has been denied. In this way he is able to become both "a giant Mexican mural of Hollywood" (149) and "Chakespeare Louie, the baddest actor alive!" (166).

As the author, Islas remains ambivalent about Louie's "hybrid" combinations of Chicano experiences and Western cultural forms. Through references to movies such as *A Duel in the Sun* (the story of a Spanish and Indian "half-breed") and *Down to Earth* (starring Rita Hayworth, born Margarita Carmen Casino, and "whitened" for Hollywood with hair dye and eyebrow plucking), Islas reminds the reader of Hollywood's ethnic stereotypes. Additionally, all the narrative models Louie uses are tragedies, indicating that although Louie can momentarily "star" in any role, as a poor Chicano he is ultimately "the King of Tears."

Though he recognizes the challenges Louie faces as a Mexican American, Islas critiques Louie's homophobia and sexism. Islas addresses homosexuality in this novel not by focusing on a gay character but by setting the novel in San Francisco, the gay metropolis covered in a beautifying layer of "fairy dust" (53). Louie cannot contain his reactions to the gay men he knows, including his brother, Tomás. Islas similarly highlights Louie's objectification of women during his movie watching: "Imagine touching Betty Grable's legs or Ava Gardner's hair," he says, "I get turned on just thinking about it" (20). Here Islas reveals the way in which Louie and the Hollywood movies he loves take pleasure in objectifying women's bodies.

It is not only Louie, however, who is the subject of Islas's critique. Islas chooses an unnamed academic to record Louie's story for his own purposes.

In this way Islas makes readers aware of our own desire to "consume" Louie's story, looking for ways that he might fit our image of Chicano men. Indeed, Islas often complained of the publishing industry's inability to read the texts of Chicano writers as anything other than "authentic" representations of Chicano life. At the end of *La Mollie*, Islas leaves readers to question their motivations in wanting to hear Louie's "Chicano tragedy." Islas exposes the reader's impulse to search for "authenticity" in a character.

Bibliography
Aldama, Frederick Luis. "Ethnoqueer Rearchitexturing of Metropolitan Space." *Nepantla: Views from South* 1, no. 3 (2000): 581–604.

Islas, Arturo. *La Mollie and the King of Tears.* Edited by Paul Skenazy. Albuquerque: University of New Mexico Press, 1996.

Skenazy, Paul. "The Long Walk Home." Afterword to *La Mollie and the King of Tears,* by Arturo Islas. Albuquerque: University of New Mexico Press, 1996.

Megan Obourn

Lapsing to Grace Rhina Espaillat (1992)

The Dominican-American poet RHINA ESPAILLAT began her public literary career at the age of 60 with the publication of her first full-length collection of poems, *Lapsing to Grace*. Thematically, she covers a wide range of subjects, addressing matters of love, loss, and the experience of living between two cultures. *Lapsing to Grace* also includes poems that express the familiar experience of countless of U.S. immigrants (particularly Latin Americans) who maintain cultural ties to their respective native lands. Throughout her verses Espaillat explores some of the dual allegiances and the individual differences experienced in the acculturation process.

Given the fact that Espaillat has lived in the Northeast most of her life, many of her poems rely on this region's topography as a setting. Although some of the poems in this collection present nature as a source of comfort and physical and/or spiritual renewal, others portray the natural environment and its elements as antagonists—appropriately so, given the distinctive seasonality of the region. In "A Winter Walk" Espaillat shows her signature control of the craft and her revealing understatement as the speaker confronts nature's violence when she finds the carcass of a possum "on the page of snow" (2) that is "torn beyond all sorrow" (7). Yet, the poem also suggests a parallelism with humanity, demonstrating Espaillat's consistent ability to address multiple levels of meaning. Throughout this collection she explores pertinent issues of general human interest by utilizing vivid imagery, precise and striking language, and effective metaphors. The universally shared experiences of human grief and troubled family dynamics are portrayed in poems such as "Recollection," "Parable," "Miscarried," and "Cuttings." She also provides social commentary on our apathy toward the poor and destitute of society in "Incident," in which the speaker chooses to ignore the plight of a needy stranger in the subway and later feels guilt for her inaction and lack of charity.

These universals are juxtaposed with poems depicting some of the particulars ascribed to the immigrant experience. As an evident acknowledgment of her Dominican heritage, Espaillat includes verses written in Spanish, such as "Nosotros" (We), "Resignación" (Resignation), and "Quise Olvidarte, Dios" (I Wished to Forget You, God). She also includes poems that illustrate the realities of biculturalism and bilingualism, touching on the duality felt by many immigrants who are willing participants and contributors in the American experience yet also remain firmly attached to their ethnic roots and language. For instance, in "Learning Bones" Espaillat highlights individual differences in the process of acculturation as the speaker contrasts herself with her father. This poem offers insightful reflections on the transition from an ancestral vehicle of communication (the Spanish language) and a worldview based on tradition—symbolized by the father—to the speaker's acquisition of a new language (English) and a modern worldview based on utility and function. She begins the poem by stating: "I'm learning bones to please

my father's ghost" (1). This declaration implies the speaker's desire for some form of reconciliation with her father and with what her father represents—in this case, the fierce adherence to ancestral culture and customs. She is memorizing the human skeleton by its Latin nomenclature in the same manner that her father knew and recited its parts—a symbolic way in which he held on to his ethnic roots since he is portrayed as being very proud of his Latino heritage. The father, unwilling to forgo his cultural identity, was rigid like "stone" and would not call the "Sternum" a "breastbone" (10, 12). He held on to propriety and tradition and could not adapt to a new environment and time: "He didn't like my century" (19). In contrast, the speaker, "gospelled by [her] own time[,] . . . worshipped use," the utility and "function" of things (that is, "glands"), and embraced the modernity of a new land rather than retaining ancestral traditions exclusively (13, 16). The speaker is portrayed as looking toward the future and adapting to the new language and culture, whereas the father looks toward the past and is unable to effectively negotiate the changes that occur around him. This generational contrast is a useful approach to understanding the various responses to acculturation, as differences in age and maturity are likely to play an important role in this process: The young are usually more flexible, adapting more rapidly to new environments, whereas adults are more cemented in their own identity because they have already defined personalities and belief systems. The final lines of the poem address the father's decline in health and his eventual death, years after the initial setting of the poem. It concludes with a reiteration of the speaker's resolution to learn the human bones by their Latin lexicon in an attempt to celebrate her late father's unyielding grasp of his cultural identity, because, as the speaker declares, "we make amends in any way we can" (39).

Espaillat also explores some of the dual allegiances experienced by many immigrants (and some of their immediate descendants) even years after their full participation in U.S. society. "You Call Me by Old Names" explores the complexities of biculturalism by portraying the ambivalence and frustration that many immigrant minorities feel at times. The poem also denotes understanding of immigrants' reality: how many are perceived and thought of by a considerable portion of the mainstream culture. In the first stanza the speaker affirms her ties to the Dominican Republic, her ethnic roots of "family" and "blood" (2). The poem's winter setting, "walking through flakes, up to the knees / in cold and democratic mud," (3–4) highlights the speaker's complex experience at several levels. She finds it "strange" to hear her "old [ethnic] names" called while walking through a cold and barren place where her ancestors would never be since they are from a tropical island, and they would "never [know] the dubious miracle of snow" (7–8). The implied comparison between the snow in the United States and the perpetual summer of the island is evident. Standing there, surrounded by snowflakes, the speaker appears to symbolically embody her foreignness; however, this comparison does not necessarily have negative connotations toward the winter weather or the United States itself. The pairing of "mud" with "democratic," on the other hand, could suggest deeper issues than the fact that the snow has created literal mud on the ground since the United States houses the most ethnically diverse population on the planet, under the banner of democracy, and therefore holds a vast ethnic mud/mixture. After commanding the addressed subject in the poem, "Don't say my names, you seem to mock / their charming, foolish Old World touch," the speaker asserts her U.S. cultural identity (9–10). She wants to be called ". . . immigrant, Social / Security card such-and-such / or future citizen. . . ," which suggests a possible distancing from her ancestral ethnic identity in order to re-create a generalized human being, a generic American "who boasts / two eyes, two ears, a nose, a mouth" (11–14). The poem concludes by declaring that the old names belong to ". . . another life, / a long time back, a long way south" (15–16). The tone shifts throughout from frustration to acceptance, intermingled with hints of regret. The speaker displays ambiguous thoughts and emotions about her country of origin and her "old names" versus her new adopted country and her current "immigrant" status. The duality portrayed in this poem accentuates the continuous negotiation that bicultural and bilingual individuals must undergo while living in the United States, serving as an effective tool of identification for those with a similar background or as a point that requires consideration for those in the mainstream culture.

Lapsing to Grace is a powerful collection that brings to mind the universals of life, regardless of ethnic or linguistic backgrounds. The volume conveys the immigrant experience with the intent of disseminating a message of inclusion and acceptance. Espaillat delivers a beautifully crafted poetic text that simultaneously delights and instructs. Her work can be read within the context of DOMINICAN-AMERICAN LITERATURE as well as New Formalism.

Bibliography
Espaillat, Rhina. *Lapsing to Grace*. East Lansing, Mich.: Bennett & Kitchel, 1992.
———. *Where Horizons Go*. Kirksville, Mo.: Truman State University Press, 1998.

Alba Cruz-Hacker

Las Casas, Bartolomé de (1484–1566)

Born in Seville, Spain, Bartolomé de Las Casas was a Catholic priest, a historian, and a polemicist. A Dominican friar, Las Casas devoted much of his life to denouncing the cruel methods of conquest during the Spanish exploration and settlement of the Americas. His literary legacy includes cornerstone pieces of the early colonial period such as *Historia de las Indias* (c. 1606; *History of the Indies*), *Brevísima relación de la destrucción de las Indias* (1552; The Devastation of the Indies: A Brief Account), and *Apologetica historia sumaria* (c. 1552). From a historical standpoint Las Casas is of great significance, as he was the editor of Christopher Columbus's published journal and an eyewitness to the Spanish entry into the Caribbean, Mexico, Nicaragua, and Peru.

Las Casas was educated in Seville, where he studied Latin, and Salamanca, where he studied canon law in preparation for the priesthood. On April 15, 1502, he arrived in Santo Domingo, where he first became acquainted with Spanish aggression against the Indians. He witnessed the methods of conquest and religious conversion of the natives that would later constitute the main thread of his denunciatory writings.

This first trip to the Americas ended in 1506. By 1507 he had headed to Rome to be ordained a priest. While in Rome, Las Casas visited Pope Julius II and took the opportunity to inform the pontiff about the state of affairs in the colonies of the New World and about the fertile ground for the conversion of the natives (principally Taino). Las Casas then sailed back to the Americas, where he assumed his role of Indian *doctrinero* (religious counselor to the Indians). Paradoxically, Las Casas held Indians and properties himself, though this was not unusual for the time. The year 1510 saw the arrival of the first Dominican order to the island of Hispaniola, what is now Haiti and the Dominican Republic. By 1514 Las Casas had officially renounced ownership of Indians and planned a series of legal reforms. He emphasized the wrongs of the feudal-like *encomienda* system under which a group of Indians paid an annual tribute to the *encomendero* (the person in charge) in exchange for protection and religious education. Las Casas denounced slavery and established his reputation as a fierce defender of the oppressed.

Soon after his early protest against slavery Las Casas entered the Dominican Order, in 1522. It was probably around this time that he started to gather material for his monumental *Historia de las Indias*, an ambitious work never published during his lifetime but one that proved to be an essential source of information about the early colonization period. His *Apologetica historia sumaria* was partially taken from this work and continues his campaign to defend the Indians.

The year 1537 marked a turning point in the life of Las Casas, as the papal bull Sublimis Deus created a foundation for human rights in the Americas. According to Pope Paul III's Sublimis Deus, Indians were ratified as human beings (keeping in mind that the Christian world looked at non-Christians as barbarians) and, once converted to the Christian faith, deserved the church's protection against harm. In Las Casas's view Indians should not be deprived of their liberty, but this was a difficult argument to maintain in the colonial order because natives were used as slave labor.

From 1540 to 1545 Las Casas spent his time mainly on Spanish soil. His experience in the Americas and his ongoing fight for human justice made him a reliable repository of knowledge about the intricacies of life in the New World. In 1542 the New Laws were enacted, according to which both slavery and the *encomienda* system were abolished. Before heading back to the New World, Las Casas was consecrated bishop in Seville on March 31, 1544; he accepted the diocese of Chiapas, in what is now southern Mexico. He did not stay long in the Americas this time, and while preparing for what would be his final trip to Spain, he composed in secrecy *Aviso y reglas para confesores* to serve as guidelines for confession during his absence from Chiapas.

Upon his arrival in Spain in 1547, Las Casas found heated opposition to his now public (and renamed) Confesionario, which reached a climax point with the debates he held against the humanist Juan Ginés Sepúlveda (1490–1573). The dialectic between Las Casas and Sepúlveda produced an outburst of replies from each contender. The publication of *De justis belli causis apud indios* by Sepúlveda and *Treinta proposiciones muy jurídicas* by Las Casas led to the celebration of a meeting in Valladolid, Spain, in 1550 to solve the dispute. Domingo de Soto, Bartolomé Carranza, and Pedro de la Gasca took part in the meeting. Sepúlveda sustained the position that the Indians were inferior human beings and advocated the necessity for war against them due to their natural inclination to idolatry and sin. Unfortunately, the meeting ended with no apparent final resolution.

The final years of Las Casas's literary career were marked by two events. First, he resumed his monumental project known as *Historia de las Indias*, which he would work on until the very end of his life. Second, in 1552 he finally managed to bring to light his now widely read *Brevísima relación de la destrucción de las Indias.* The text seems to have been finished by 1542, but its publication was delayed by innumerable obstacles. When it finally came out in print, *Brevísima relación* enjoyed wide popularity not only in the Spanish-Indian context but also for completely different social and cultural realities. It can be read alongside the work of ÁLVAR NUÑEZ CABEZA DE VACA.

Because they were imperial rivals of Spain in the New World, countries such as England and France were attracted to Las Casas's catalog of atrocities committed by the Spaniards. English readers benefited from the translations that surfaced during the 16th and 17th centuries. The imperialistic aims of 16th-century Spain constituted a constant threat to Protestant Elizabethan England; therefore, it comes as no surprise that England felt attracted to such a negative description of the Spaniards, hence the proliferation of English translations of Las Casas's *Brevísima relación.* The first translation appeared in 1583 as *The Spanish Colonie, or Briefe Chronicle of the Acts and Gestes of the Spaniardes in the West Indies, And Nowe First Translated into English,* printed by Thomas Dawson for William Broome. In 1656 appeared another translation entitled *The Tears of the Indians, Being an Historical Account of the Cruel Massacres and Slaughters Committed by the Spaniards in the Islands of the West Indies, Mexico, Peru Etc. An Eye-witness Account written by Bartolome de Las Casas.* The edition, accompanied by illustrations depicting massacres by the Spaniards, was dedicated to Oliver Cromwell. It was translated into English by J. Phillips and printed for Nathaniel Brook. Finally, in 1689 came out a vivid catalog of Spanish misbehavior printed by R. Hewson under the title *Popery Truly Display'd in its Bloody Colours, Being a Faithful Narrative of the Horrid and Unexampled Massacres, Butcheries, and all Manner of Cruelties, that Hell and Malice could invent, Committed by the Popish Spanish Party on the Inhabitants of West-India.* Because of the availability of his work in English and other languages, Las Casas has been accused of being the driving force behind the "Black Legend." The Black Legend is associated with the Spanish and their exploits in the New World, especially during the Inquisition.

Las Casas's last two literary achievements, *Los tesoros del Perú* and *Las doce dudas,* were published near the very end of his life. Las Casas reacted against the intention of Peruvian slaveholders to buy a number of Indians from the Spanish Crown. As in most of his previous literary efforts Las Casas set himself up as a strong defender of the rights of the indigenous (the great Inca among them).

Las Casas made his final trip within Spain in July 1566, when he died at the Dominican convent of Nuestra Señora de Atocha in Madrid at the age of 82. Along with his literary legacy he bequeathed a life devoted to the public denunciation of the methods of the Spanish Conquest in the New World. Controversy nevertheless remains when we reflect upon the fact that along with condemning Indian servitude, Las Casas tolerated enslavement of West Africans; this reading of his views counts as an unhappy inconsistency in the annals of history. Within a literary context, Las Casas appears as a character in Manuel de Jesús Galván's novel *Enriquillo* (1879; *The Cross and the Sword*), and he is the subject of a growing body of criticism about the encounter between Spain and the Americas.

Bibliography

Hanke, Lewis. *Bartolomé de las Casas, Historian: An Essay in Spanish Historiography.* Gainesville: University of Florida Press, 1952.

Las Casas, Bartolomé de. *The Destruction of the Indies: A Brief Account.* Translated by Herma Briffault. Baltimore, Md.: Johns Hopkins University Press, 1992.

———. *In Defense of the Indians.* Translated by Stafford Poole. DeKalb: Northern Illinois University Press, 1992.

———. *Witness: Writings of Bartolomé de las Casas.* Edited by George Sanderlin. Maryknoll, N.Y.: Orbis Books, 1992.

Alberto Zambrana

Last of the Menu Girls, The   Denise Chávez (1986)

DENISE CHÁVEZ published *The Last of the Menu Girls* in 1986. Set in New Mexico, *Last of the Menu*

Girls features seven vignettes that function as a short story cycle or as a composite novel. Narrated by Rocío Esquibel and taking place in the 1960s, these vignettes are entitled "The Last of the Menu Girls," "Willow Game," "Shooting Stars," "Evening in Paris," "The Closet," "Space Is a Solid," and "Compadre." Rocío Esquibel is a 17-year-old Mexican American who takes food orders for patients at the Altavista Memorial Hospital. As the summer progresses, her responsibilities increase at the hospital, but her work is only seasonal, thus she is "the last of the menu girls."

While working, Rocío envisions a life outside menial labor: "I want to be someone else, somewhere else, someone important and responsible and sexy. I want to be sexy" (34). The desire to transcend a mundane existence bound by gender, racial, and class constraints is at the heart of the narratives that make up the book. Rocío observes in the opening story, "The Last of the Menu Girls," that "I never wanted to be a nurse. Never. The smells. The pain. What was I to do then, working in a hospital, in that place of white women, whiter men with square faces . . . Mr. Smith handed me a pile of green forms. They were menus. In the center of the menu was listed the day of the week, and to the left and coming down were the three meals, breakfast, lunch and dinner" (17, 19). In this passage Chávez sets up the narrative tension between having to work in a hospital with the aged and the sick and Rocío's realization that her youth and freedom are outside its walls. With each story we learn more about Rocío, her work, and her family, and we learn to recognize how she has been in the role of caretaker before. She has tended to her mother after surgery and to her great-aunt Eutalia on her deathbed.

One aspect of Rocío's desire for freedom is manifest in her nascent sexuality. "Shooting Stars" develops the idea of Rocío's longing for same-sex relations. In her desire to know womanhood intimately, Rocío muses on the beauty of women in her life and seeks a way to find love for herself. The conclusion of "Shooting Stars" reads like a spiritual chant to illustrate the regenerative powers of women's bodies.

As a point of contrast to the beauty of women in "Shooting Stars," we see the deformity of bodies in "Space Is a Solid." This chapter expresses the emptiness that Rocío feels and the effects of poverty and racism on her life. Rocío teaches a drama appreciation class to sick and handicapped students, one of whom is Kari Lee Wembley. Rocío falls on hard times and needs a cheap place to live, so she rents a property from a wealthy Texan, Mrs. Wembley, Kari Lee's mother. Chávez demands of the reader that we fill in the gaps of the narrative to account for Rocío's mental and emotional collapse when she is confronted by Mrs. Wembley. These gaps are represented through section breaks and the stream-of-consciousness technique. Not only is "space" a concept that Rocío teaches her theater students, it is also a hole for Rocío, a place where her broken spirit resides.

Last of the Menu Girls finds resolution in the fact that the world will only understand Rocío once she expresses herself as a Chicana writer in the final story, "Compadre."

Within the broader context of CHICANO LITERATURE Chávez's work can be read alongside TOMÁS RIVERA'S . . . *Y no se lo tragó la tierra* (*THIS MIGRANT EARTH*) for the ways in which both Chávez and Rivera employ multiple voices and fragmented narratives and for the ways the authors envision the triumph of the individual spirit.

Bibliography
Chávez, Denise. *Last of the Menu Girls*. Houston, Tex.: Arte Público Press, 1986.

Keating, Ana Louise. "Towards a New Politics of Representation? Absence and Desire in Denise Chávez's *The Last of the Menu Girls*." In *We Who Love to Be Astonished: Experimental Women's Writing and Performance Poetics*, edited by Laura Hinton, Cynthia Hogue, 71–80. Tuscaloosa: University of Alabama Press, 2002.

Rivera, Tomás. . . . *Y no se lo tragó la tierra/ . . . And the Earth Did Not Devour Him*. Translated by Evangelina Vigil-Piñón. Houston, Tex.: Arte Público Press, 1990.

Nicole M. Guidotti-Hernández

Latina lesbian literature

Writing by Latina lesbians reflects a rich cultural history of migration from the Caribbean, Mexico, and all of Latin America. Such writing uses a variety of languages and dialects and is further marked by differences in education, class, citizenship status, ethnic identity, and sexuality. Despite its complex origins, however, the work of writers who are both lesbians and Latinas has come to form a distinctive strand within U.S. literary production. The early Latina and Chicana lesbian texts were characterized by autobiography and politicized writing that integrated sexuality and ethnicity, often mixing genres and languages. Primarily published by small presses, these texts remained marginalized both from the Latino heterosexual community and the Anglo gay and lesbian community until the year 2000, when several Latina lesbian books were published by mainstream editors. By then writings had become more literary in nature and less based on identity politics.

Latina lesbian literature first emerged after the politicized fusion of race, ethnicity, and sexuality of the early 1980s. Influenced by social movements in civil rights, women's liberation, gay rights, and the Mexican labor struggle, women of color and lesbians of color joined forces in declarative statements of identity. Books such as the anthology *This Bridge Called My Back: Writings by Radical Women of Color* (1981), coedited by GLORIA ANZALDÚA and CHERRÍE MORAGA, Michelle Cliff's *Claiming an Identity They Taught Me to Despise* (1980), and Moraga's *Loving in the War Years: Lo que nunca pasó por sus labios* (1983) celebrated sexual identity and challenged racism, sexism, and homophobia. The model of identity politics established in these books was crucial for this first phase of the development of Latina lesbian literature. And while Spanish-language writings by lesbians in Spain, Latin America, and the Caribbean were available in a limited way to U.S. readers, writings by Latina lesbians were mostly a reflection and a product of the realities of living in the United States.

Two seminal books of the 1980s, both of them autobiographical writings by Chicana writers, are Moraga's *Loving in the War Years* (1983) and Anzaldúa's *BORDERLANDS/LA FRONTERA: THE NEW MESTIZA* (1987), both of which have remained in print since their first publication. Using a bilingual blend of creative nonfiction, short stories, and poetry, Moraga explores the link between sexuality and cultural identity and aligns herself with the strategies against sexual oppression proposed by Third World feminism. Moraga writes about her family, friends, and lovers in graphic detail and places her personal life within a larger political and cultural context. Similarly Anzaldúa's *Borderlands* blends prose and poetry in English, Spanish, and Nahuatl. Drawing on the details of her childhood in Texas along the U.S.-Mexico border, she emphasizes indigenous history and mythology as part of a poetic futuristic vision. Highly influential in feminist studies, cultural theory, and studies of ethnicity, these books were reality-based literary explorations rooted in the fusion of sexual and cultural identity. Both women continued to make significant contributions to the literature. Anzaldúa later published several children's books and edited further women-of-color anthologies such as *This Bridge We Call Home: Radical Visions for Transformation* (2002), which brought the grassroots ideology of her earlier work to the academy. Moraga went on to blend autobiography with poetry, prose, and social commentary in books such as *The Last Generation* (1993) and *Waiting in the Wings* (1997). While never straying from her Chicana lesbian roots, Moraga was also a social critic who took her writing to the stage with works such as *Heroes and Saints and Other Plays* (1994) and the *Hungry Woman: A Mexican Medea* (2000).

While other Latina lesbian books were published in the 1980s, they were not all clearly integral to the literature. For instance, Sheila Ortiz Taylor's novel *Faultline* (1982) had lesbian content but lacked references to Chicana/Latina culture. The anthology *Cuentos: Stories by Latinas* (1983) was coedited by Latina lesbians, but the content does not prioritize lesbianism (and the contributors are not all lesbians). ANA CASTILLO has lesbian and gay characters in several of her novels, but she does not identify as a lesbian (and lesbianism is absent from most of her work). In other cases the lesbian content is subtle or inferred. For example, friendships among women are central to Carmen de Monteflores's *Singing Softly/Cantando bajito* (1989), but the novel lacks overt lesbianism. Luz María Umpierre's poetry evokes the female erotic in *The Margarita Poems* (1987) and in her other poetry collections without declarative lesbian statements.

An early collection of writings by and about Latina lesbians is *Compañeras: Latina Lesbians, an Anthology* (1987). A combination of art, interviews, autobiographies, oral histories, and creative writings in Spanish, English, and SPANGLISH, it featured 63 Latina lesbians born in 14 different countries (including the United States). While not a literary collection, *Compañeras*'s value lies in its documentation and diverse representation. The anthology *Chicana Lesbians: The Girls Our Mothers Warned Us About* (1991) followed and featured poetry, fiction, essays, and artwork in English, Spanish, and Spanglish by 25 contributors. Again, part of the value of this collection is its varied representation of language, economic class, education, color, and culture. Both anthologies also underscore the politicized identity inherent in Latina lesbian literature from this period. For instance, the writings of Chicana lesbians are organized into sections titled "The Life," "The Desire," "The Color," and "The Struggle." Juanita Ramos, editor of *Compañeras,* dedicates the book to "For Latina lesbians everywhere. With much love and the conviction that one day we will be able to live our lives to our fullest potential without anyone to oppress us," making explicit the connection between Latina lesbian existence and politics.

A significant body of work emerged in the 1990s. Ibis Gómez Vega's *Send My Roots Rain* (1991), for example, set in a town on the Texas border, is a religious Mexican-American mystery with a romantic link between two women. A coming-out story with a Chicana lesbian protagonist is at the center of Terri de la Peña's first novel, *Margins* (1992). As in her subsequent novels (*Latin Satins* [1994] and *Faults* [1999]), de la Peña's characterization of Chicana lesbians is as rich in cultural heritage and family issues as in lesbian identity. In Kleya Forte Escamilla's *Mada* (1993), the Chicana graduate student protagonist becomes erotically fixated with a German actress. ALICIA GASPAR DE ALBA's *The Mystery of Survival and Other Stories* (1993) explores the clash of Mexican-American and Anglo cultures with a lesbian sensibility; some of the stories are written in English and others in Spanish. *Sor Juana's Second Dream* (1999), a historical novel also by Gaspar de Alba, re-creates Sor Juana's life in a definitive lesbian light. ACHY OBEJAS's collection of short stories *We Came All the Way from Cuba So You Could Dress Like This?* (1994) personifies a cast of characters that includes lesbians and gays and reflects the realities of Latina/o immigrants' lives. Her novel *Memory Mambo* (1996) portrays a young Cuban lesbian within the complexity of her close-knit family. Set on the Texas gulf coast, Emma Pérez's *Gulf Dreams* (1996) features a Chicana lesbian protagonist who tells her story of yearning for a young woman in a dream diary format. In Mariana Romo-Carmona's first novel, *Living at Night* (1997), the main character is a young Puerto Rican lesbian who works as a nurse's aide while she sorts out her life. Academic analysis of Latina lesbian writing also emerged in this period, with Elena M. Martínez's *Lesbian Voices from Latin America* (1996), which examines writings by Magaly Alabau, Nancy Cárdenas, Sylvia Molloy, Rosamaria Roffiel, and Umpierre.

It was during the time of this initial boom for Latina lesbian literature that the magazine *Esto no tiene nombre* (1991–94) came into being. Published by a Latina lesbian collective in Miami, *Esto no tiene nombre* (This has no name) started out as a newsletter for the group Las Salamandras de Ambiente and became a national magazine, with the stated mission of publishing materials by Latina lesbians. The magazine published poetry, fiction, essays, reviews, news, interviews, comics, and artwork by Latina lesbians from the United States and abroad, with the writings alternating in Spanish, English, and Spanglish. The contributors included established writers along with first-time authors. Nine editions were published in the four years that the magazine circulated. Afterward several members of the editorial collective continued with *Conmoción* (1995–96), its title having the double meaning of "commotion" and "in motion." Eighty-four contributors from 38 cities made *Conmoción* a dynamic Latina lesbian forum. The editors of *Conmoción* also created La Telaraña (The Spiderweb), a Latina lesbian writers' web, and published a newsletter that supported writers. Although regional periodicals such as the Chicana lesbian *Jota* (meaning "iota" or "jot," as well as "queer") and the women of color *Tongues* (both produced in Los Angeles) appear occasionally, there has not yet been a national Latina lesbian magazine to replace *Esto no tiene nombre* and *Conmoción*.

By the time *Conmoción* had stopped circulating, a new publishing climate was emerging. Up until then, most books by Latina lesbians had been published by small presses that offered minimal print runs and limited distribution and whose tiny operating budgets prevented them from promoting their publications in a significant way. The combination of lesbianism with the patriarchal aspects of Latino culture kept the books out of both Latino heterosexual and the white, English-speaking lesbian literary marketplaces; such books circulated largely as a result of word of mouth within the Latina lesbian community, with sales typically limited to alternative bookstores and special gatherings. However, in the late 1990s, as a result of the increasing Latina/o population, the pervasiveness of gay and lesbian issues in popular culture, and the increased visibility for all cultural products that the Internet provided, publishing opportunities opened up and the work of Latina lesbians and bisexuals began to be published by mainstream presses. Simon & Schuster published Erika Lopez's humorous autobiographical illustrated novel *FLAMING IGUANAS* (1997); Seven Stories published Spanish and English editions of Sonia Rivera Valdés's intimate tales, *Las historias prohibidas de Marta Veneranda/ The Forbidden Stories of Marta Veneranda* (2000); Beacon published Alina Troyano's performance scripts in *I, Carmelita Tropicana* (2000); Ballantine published Obejas's *Days of Awe* (2001); and

Farrar, Straus & Giroux published Felicia Luna Lemus's queer hipster punk novel, *Trace Elements of Random Tea Parties* (2003). While there is no indication that the mainstream publishing world is taking over Latina lesbian literary production, it is notable that these books were promoted to the U.S. market at large rather than solely to a niche audience.

The nature of Latina lesbian identity and the difficulties encountered in publishing in the age of multinational corporate takeovers shows that this literature will continue to develop largely on the margins, as it has since its beginnings. But, it is no longer the product of a politicized identity; instead, these contemporary writings first and foremost present themselves as literary artifacts with their Latina lesbian identity taken for granted. Authors continue to publish poetry and prose with both small and mainstream presses, adding to a body of work that is still coming into its own.

Bibliography

Anzaldúa, Gloria. *Borderlands/La frontera: The New Mestiza.* San Francisco, Calif.: Aunt Lute Books, 1987.

Costa, María Dolores. "Latina Lesbian Writers and Performers: An Overview." *Journal of Lesbian Studies* 7, no. 3 (2003): 5–26.

de la Tierra, Tatiana. "Activist Latina Lesbian Publishing: *Esto no tiene nombre* and *Conmoción*." In *I Am Aztlán: The Personal Essay in Chicano Studies,* edited by Chon A. Noriega and Wendy Belcher, 141–176. Los Angeles: UCLA Chicano Studies Research Center Press, 2004.

Martinez, Elena M. *Lesbian Voices from Latin America: Breaking Ground.* New York: Garland, 1996.

Moraga, Cherríe. *Loving in the War Years: Lo que nunca pasó por sus labios.* Boston: South End Press, 1983.

Ramos, Juanita. *Compañeras: Latina Lesbians.* New York: Latina Lesbian History Project, 1987.

Trujillo, Carla. *Chicana Lesbians: The Girls Our Mothers Warned Us About.* Berkeley, Calif.: Third Woman Press, 1991.

tatiana de la tierra

Latin Deli, The Judith Ortiz Cofer (1993)

This collection of poems, stories, and essays highlights Judith Ortiz Cofer's interest in identity formation and exile. The fractured content of mixed genres mirrors the fractured existence of the immigrants whose lives are broken across two lands, two languages. Having made frequent sojourns between the island and the mainland, Cofer writes about translocation with a sense of immediacy and a critical sense of distance.

The Latin Deli collects 39 poems and 15 prose narratives, most of which appeared previously in literary journals. A parallel to Cofer's collection can be seen in Jean Toomer's *Cane* (1923), which presents the lives of African Americans as a composite portrait of communities in the urban North and the rural South during the early 20th century.

In *The Latin Deli* Cofer's method expands our focus from the view of one central character to a variety of characters. In this regard the use of multiple voices in *The Latin Deli* is akin to the rich perspectives of Esperanza and her female counterparts in Sandra Cisneros's *The House on Mango Street* (1984). Cofer dramatizes the sense of alienation that comes through translocation (keeping in mind that Puerto Ricans are U.S. citizens; they can enter and leave the mainland freely). Through both poetry and prose the author captures the breadth of the Puerto Rican family, from nostalgic mothers and distant fathers to a younger generation who are caught between tradition and assimilation. All of Cofer's characters live in El Building, an apartment complex in Paterson, New Jersey. The opening prose selections introduce Cofer's method, for there we meet a series of protagonist-narrators, adolescent girls who could be a single character but for irreconcilable details among their situations: Elena, who lives on the second floor and whose father works in a blue jeans factory; Eva, on the third floor, whose father is El Building's wandering janitor by day and nightclub master of ceremonies by night; and an anonymous 16-year-old on the fifth floor whose father is a factory night watchman.

In the essay "The Myth of the Latin Woman," Cofer explains her objective as a writer: "My personal goal in my public life is to try to replace the old pervasive stereotypes and myths about Latinas with a much more interesting set of realities" (154). The concentration on younger protagonists and their conflicts with parents, especially mothers, is a theme in *The Latin Deli*. Rites of passage are doubly complex for young migrants, who must navigate the path to maturity in a land in which they feel themselves to be outsiders, despite the fact that they enjoy U.S. citizenship as Puerto Ricans.

Cofer's work marks an important contribution to both Puerto Rican literature and Spanish-American Caribbean literature, particularly to the literature of migration and translocation. Cofer's characters are economic refugees whose motive for flight to the mainland arises not from politics or violence; rather, they leave the island in pursuit of that happiness enshrined in the Constitution and labeled the "American Dream." This divergence of motive, however, in no way lessens the struggles of assimilation that her characters must endure.

Bibliography

Acosta-Belen, Edna. "A MELUS Interview: Judith Ortiz Cofer." *MELUS* 18, no. 3 (1993): 83–97.

Cofer, Judith Ortiz. *The Latin Deli*. Athens: University of Georgia Press, 1993.

———. *Reaching for the Mainland and Selected New Poems*. Phoenix, Ariz.: Bilingual Press, 1995.

———. *Woman in Front of the Sun: On Becoming a Writer*. Athens: University of Georgia Press, 2000.

McConnell, Thomas. "Assimilation and Fragmentation in Judith Ortiz Cofer's *Latin Deli* and *Year of Our Revolution*." *Atenea* 23, nos. 1–2 (2002): 57–63.

Thomas McConnell

Latino gay literature

Latino male homosexuality, bisexuality, and transvestism have been portrayed in numerous ways in works in English and Spanish by Latino authors in the United States. Gay figures are characterized at times sympathetically, other times with disapproval and contempt. It is important to acknowledge this wide range of depictions, ranging from homophobic to positive, in order to grasp fully the centrality (and controversial nature) of issues of sexual orientation for Latino/a culture.

Similar to many Latin American and Mediterranean societies, U.S. Latinos have historically constructed or defined masculinity in opposition to effeminateness. Words such as *maricón, pato, joto,* and *pájaro* are used to identify effeminate men, while masculine-acting men who have sex with men (and are generally not considered "homosexuals") are called *bugarrones* or *mayates*. Profound social transformations during the 20th century, including modernization and industrialization, urban migration, civil rights struggles, feminism, and the lesbian and gay liberation movement, have dramatically affected these ideas, and currently there is a turn toward what has been described as an "equal partners" model, in which (mostly) masculine-acting men interact with each other.

Among Chicano writers JOHN RECHY has been one of the most recognized for exploring issues of male homosexuality. His autobiographical novels and experimental texts *City of Night* (1963), *Numbers* (1967) and *The Sexual Outlaw* (1977) have documented the shifts that American and Latino sexualities have undergone. In *City of Night* a Texas-born protagonist of Irish and Mexican ancestry (much like the author) travels to New York, then Los Angeles, and on to New Orleans, working as a male hustler, or prostitute. For many years Chicano literary critics refused to recognize Rechy as a Chicano author; it was only thanks to the pioneering efforts of scholars such as Juan Bruce-Novoa that Rechy's contribution to CHICANO LITERATURE was finally acknowledged.

Not all Latino writers are as bold as Rechy. The well-known conservative essayist RICHARD RODRIGUEZ's discussion of his own homosexuality did not appear in early works such as *Hunger of Memory* (1982), and, in fact, it was not until *DAYS OF OBLIGATION: AN ARGUMENT WITH MY MEXICAN FATHER* (1992) that he wrote about his sexual orientation. More recently, the performance artist and playwright Luis Alfaro, famous for his drag AIDS activism as part of *Teatro Viva!* in Los An-

geles, has infused a strong dose of humor to gay Chicano letters. Other notable gay Chicano authors include the novelists ARTURO ISLAS, Michael Nava, and Erasmo Guerra; the poets Francisco X. Alarcón and Rigoberto González; the playwright Ricardo Bracho; and the short story writers Adán Griego, Al Luján, and James Cortez, the last two also being visual artists. Another Chicano novelist who makes reference to male homosexuality is Oscar Zeta Acosta, whose *The AUTOBIOGRAPHY OF A BROWN BUFFALO* (1972) and *The Revolt of the Cockroach People* (1973) are notoriously homophobic.

Puerto Rican and Nuyorican writers in the United States have also addressed issues of queer male sexualities. Homophobic concerns appear in foundational texts such as Bernardo Vega's *Memoirs* (1977), where the tobacco worker and labor leader describes throwing his watch overboard in 1917 as his ship approached the Statue of Liberty after being told that such timepieces were only worn by effeminate men. PIRI THOMAS's well-known memoir or autobiographical novel *DOWN THESE MEAN STREETS* (1967) also includes a famous passage about the protagonist's visit to an effeminate homosexual's apartment, where young men would go to obtain sexual favors. In his prize-winning play *SHORT EYES* (1974), which was later made into a Hollywood film, MIGUEL PIÑERO (who was widely reputed to have relationships with both men and women) described the dynamics among prisoners after a man convicted of child sexual abuse is incarcerated among them. In his moving volume of poetry *Love Is Hard Work: Memorias de Loisaida* (1997), MIGUEL ALGARÍN, one of the founding members of the NUYORICAN POETS CAFE, discusses his own bisexuality and his experiences living with HIV/AIDS, a topic other Puerto Rican and Nuyorican authors have also explored from a personal perspective, including the playwright and literary critic Alberto Sandoval-Sánchez and the poets Moisés Agosto and Alfredo Villanueva Collado. HIV/AIDS has also been addressed by the poet and scholar Carlos Rodríguez-Matos, who also edited an important anthology called *Poesída* (1995), and by the Chicano author Gil Cuadros in *City of God* (1994).

The first complex or gay-positive portrayals of male homosexuality by openly gay Puerto Rican writers occurred in the late 1960s and early 1970s in New York in the work of Manuel Ramos Otero and Víctor Fernández Fragoso, two authors who wrote in Spanish and died of AIDS; to this day, Ramos Otero's poetry and short stories, such as those in *El cuento de la mujer del mar* (1979; The story of the woman from the sea) and *Página en blanco y staccato* (1987; Blank page and staccato), continue to be highly influential. Other Puerto Rican and Nuyorican (also known as Diasporican) authors include the Chicago-born poet Rane Arroyo; the novelists Daniel Torres and Angel Lozada; the performance poet and novelist Emanuel Xavier (who is Ecuadorean–Puerto Rican); the playwright and cultural promoter Charles Rice-González, who founded the Bronx Academy of Arts and Dance together with his partner, the renowned Nuyorican dancer Arthur Avilés; the playwright Edwin Sánchez; and the short story authors Robert Vázquez-Pacheco and ALDO ALVAREZ, who is the editor of the online gay literary journal *Blithe House Quarterly*.

Cuban and Cuban-American authors who have explored gay Latino life include the novelists REINALDO ARENAS and ELÍAS MIGUEL MUÑOZ, the playwrights Jorge Ignacio Cortiñas and Nilo Cruz, the cultural critics José Esteban Muñoz and José Quiroga (who was raised in Puerto Rico), and the poet Rafael Campo. Dominican-American authors who have written about the topic include the poet Jimmy Lam and the writer JUNOT DÍAZ, whose book *DROWN* (1996) includes an eponymous short story about the negative effects of homophobia and how it serves to distance former childhood friends in a New Jersey housing project after one of them goes to college.

Gay U.S.–Central American authors include Horacio Roque Ramírez (El Salvador), Juan Rubio (Honduras), and Carlo Baldi (Costa Rica). Gay South American authors who live or have lived and written about the United States include Jaime Manrique (Colombia), Miguel Fálquez-Certain (Colombia), Alejandro Varderi (Venezuela), Silviano Santiago (Brazil), and Guillermo Reyes (Chile). Of all these Manrique is by far the best known, having published important works such as the novel *Latin Moon in Manhattan* (1992) and the book of essays *Eminent Maricones: Arenas, Lorca, Puig and Me* (1999). Finally, it is worth noting the important role that anthologies such as *Bésame mucho* (1999) and *Virgins, Guerrillas, and Locas* (1999) have played in disseminating the work of gay Latino writers and the efforts of scholars such as Arnaldo Cruz Malavé, David William Foster, and David Román to document and analyze gay Latino literary production.

Bibliography

Almaguer, Tomás. "Chicano Men: A Cartography of Homosexual Identity and Behavior." In *The Lesbian and Gay Studies Reader*, edited by Henry Abelove et al., 255–273. New York: Routledge, 1993.

Bruce-Novoa, Juan. *Retrospace: Collected Essays on Chicano Literature*. Houston, Tex.: Arte Público Press, 1990.

Cortez, Jaime, ed. *Virgins, Guerrillas, and Locas: Gay Latinos Writing about Love*. San Francisco, Calif.: Cleis, 1999.

Cruz Malavé, Arnaldo. "'What a Tangled Web!': Masculinity, Abjection, and the Foundations of Puerto Rican Literature in the United States." In *Sex and Sexuality in Latin America*, edited by Daniel Balderston and Donna J. Guy, 234–249. New York: New York University Press, 1997.

Foster, David William, ed. *Latin American Writers on Gay and Lesbian Themes: A Bio-Critical Sourcebook*. Westport, Conn.: Greenwood Press, 1995.

Manrique, Jaime, and Jesse Dorris, eds. *Bésame mucho: New Gay Latino Fiction*. New York: Painted Leaf Press, 1999.

Román, David. "Latino Literature." In *The Gay and Lesbian Literary Heritage*, edited by Claude J. Summers, 435–437. New York: Henry Holt, 1995.

Lawrence La Fountain–Stokes

Laviera, Tato (Jesús Abraham Laviera)
(1951–) *(poet)*

Tato Laviera was born Jesús Abraham Laviera in Santurce, Puerto Rico, in 1951. Like many Puerto

Ricans of the post–World War II period, Laviera and his family relocated from the island to New York in 1960. A Nuyorican writer, Laviera has demonstrated a commitment to his Afro-Caribbean heritage through his work in social services and through his career as a poet. Like his literary counterpart MIGUEL ALGARÍN, Laviera came of age on New York City's Lower East Side (Loisaida), where, as a black Spanish speaker, he faced language and cultural barriers. While working in social services, Laviera published his first book; he then dedicated himself full time to writing. His works include *La Carreta Made a U-turn* (1979), *Enclave* (1981), *AmeRícan* (1981), and *Mainstream Ethics* (1988). *Enclave* garnered him the Before Columbus American Book Award. Throughout his writing career he has taught creative writing and toured the country performing his poetry, directing plays, and organizing cultural events.

The major themes of Laviera's poetry are identity, the contestation of authority, and the expression of the self and community through the spoken word. Writing from a black Puerto Rican perspective, Laviera's poetry often criticizes social institutions such as schools, government, and the Catholic Church. The context of his work centers on issues of migration rather than immigration because Puerto Ricans are U.S. citizens by birth.

His first publication was *La Carreta Made a U-Turn*. Nicolás Kanellos observes in his foreword to the collection of poems that Laviera's title is a clever play on RENÉ MARQUÉS's 1956 play *La Carreta* (*The Oxcart*). The title is also an index of Laviera's CODE SWITCHING between Spanish (*La Carreta*) and English (*Made a U-Turn*). *La Carreta Made a U-Turn* focuses on the rhythms of *el barrio* (the neighborhood) to bring to life Nuyorican experiences. Laviera observes the role that two languages play in Nuyorican life and how Puerto Ricans move back and forth between English and Spanish.

Enclave, Laviera's second volume of poetry, was published in 1981. *Enclave* uses individual perspectives as a way to consider life in *el barrio*. Juan Flores explains that Laviera's poetic vision in *Enclave* depends on the concept of being "en clave," or "in key." Flores considers how, through his poetry, Laviera "activates"

[a]ll the various strains of the native Puerto Rican oral tradition: Afro–Puerto Rican poetry (Luis Pales Matos) and music (*la bomba* and *la plena*), Spanish declamatory rhetoric (Juan Borgia and Jorge Brandon), the *danza* ("Maria borinquen"), the canción jibara [the folk song]; from reminiscences of the indigenous, Taino legacy [the natives of Puerto Rico] to salsa and the Latin Hustle.

Flores rightly points out the complexity of Laviera's cultural roots, intertwined as they are in their Taino, West African, and Spanish lines. Through various personae Laviera revives in his writing and performance the rhythms of Afro-Caribbean music, most especially jazz and salsa sounds.

Laviera's poetry bears comparison to music because of the rhythms he creates in the fusion of Spanish, English, SPANGLISH (a mixture of the two languages), and African-American slang. These combinations help the poet convey an American identity that crosses regional, ethnic, and linguistic lines. In this regard his poetry breaks with the formality of the English canon. Instead, he fuses popular culture, street language, and Afro-Caribbean musical sensibilities to construct poetry based on raw experience. Laviera's poems remind us that in ancient times poetry was meant to be sung and heard.

Laviera's third collection, *AmeRícan*, conveys the tension between Puerto Rican and Nuyorican cultures through memorable scenes and events. Laviera coined the term *AmeRícan* to acknowledge the emergence of the Puerto Rican identity on the U.S. mainland. The specific spelling of the title represents a spin on the pronunciation of *American*.

Finally, *Mainstream Ethics* imagines a redirection of mainstream impulses to celebrate each unique American culture. At the same time Laviera considers the notion of a common civilization and places the converging mix of ethnic identities in New York City. Within a broad literary context Laviera's work can be read as part of the Nuyorican Poets Cafe phenomenon, as well as within the voices of resistance in Hispanic-American literature.

Bibliography

Aparicio, Frances. "Tato Laviera." *The Heath Anthology of American Literature.* 4th ed. Available online. URL: http://college.hmco.com/english/lauter/heath/4e/students/author_pages/contemporary/laviera_ta. html. Downloaded August 6, 2004.

Benson, Sonia G., ed. *The Hispanic-American Almanac.* New York: Gale, 2003.

Laviera, Tato. *AmeRícan.* Houston, Tex.: Arte Público Press, 1985.

———. *Enclave.* Houston, Tex.: Arte Público Press, 1985.

———. *La Carreta Made a U-Turn.* Houston, Tex.: Arte Público Press, 1979.

———. *Mainstream Ethics/Ética corriente.* Houston, Tex.: Arte Público Press, 1988.

Anne Marie Fowler

Levins Morales, Aurora (1954–) *(poet, essayist)*

Aurora Levins Morales was born in Indiera, Puerto Rico, to a Puerto Rican mother and a Jewish father. In 1967 the Levins-Morales family moved to the U.S. mainland, and since then the author has lived in Chicago, Minneapolis, and Berkeley. Levins Morales is a lecturer and activist deeply concerned with issues affecting Third World communities, especially the lives of women. Themes in her works include sexual abuse and racial discrimination, as well as ecology and social justice. She switches between prose and poetry in her work and combines both personal and collective narrative voices; in her writing Levins Morales seeks to express the female ethnic voice.

Her first and most acclaimed work, *Getting Home Alive* (1986), was written in collaboration with her mother, Rosario Morales. It is a project in which both women pay homage to a rich heritage, in which they find refuge from discrimination. Important themes in *Getting Home Alive* include female Puerto Rican identity, Third World and working-class feminism, women's relationships, Puerto Rican multiple identity (Latin American, African, Jewish, North American), memory as a means of recovering a past heritage, and writing as a means of self-discovery. *Getting Home Alive* is a hybrid collection of stories, poems, and personal essays in which the authors' Puerto Rican identity is formally described as mestizo, a mixture of Spanish and Indian blood. This multiple identity surfaces most notably in the poem "Child of the Américas":

> *I am not African. Africa is in me, but I cannot return.*
> *I am not taína. Taíno is in me, but there is no way back.*
> *I am not European. Europe lives in me, but I have no home there.*
> *I am new. History made me. My first language was spanglish.*
> *I was born at the crossroads*
> *And I am whole* (50).

For the speaker in this passage ethnic diversity is a source of power, and home is a place that can be found in many regions of the world. Hybridity is described as a heritage recovered by means of stories of female ancestors, island landscapes, sounds, and smells; it is also described formally through the mixture of voices and genres, prose and poetry. In her discussion of hybridity in the Americas Levins Morales enters into a literary conversation with authors such as Cuban revolutionary JOSÉ MARTÍ and Mexican essayist José Vasconcelos.

Levins Morales published both *Remedios: Stories of Earth and Iron from the History of Puertorriqueñas* and *Medicine Stories: History, Culture and the Politics of Integrity* in 1998. *Remedios* is a fascinating collection of prose and poetry that retells the history of Puerto Rican people through the lives of female ancestors from the Old and the New World. Commentary on healing herbs are accompanied by stories that rewrite history, telling the lives of a long line of women who have been silenced for centuries. Some of the stories tell about suffering and abuse, but most of them recount stories of strength and resistance.

Medicine Stories is a collection of personal essays grouped in five sections. The section "Historian as CURANDERA" deals with history and the struggle over who has the authority to tell the story of other people; "Speaking in Tongues" concentrates on the power of language and how it is used to silence other people's authentic stories; "Raíces" explores the realities and myths of identity politics and the complexity of Puerto Rican identity; "Privilege and Loss" discusses different aspects of privilege and the costs of accepting it. The final section, "Integrity," is about living a politics of integrity, about commitment, activism, and the integration of collective and individual liberation. The collection calls for a revision of personal and collective memories and history as a way to heal all wounds. Given its themes and settings Levins Morales's poetry can be read within the context of PUERTO RICAN LITERATURE.

Bibliography

Benmayor, Rina. "*Getting Home Alive*: The Politics of Multiple Identity." *Americas Review* 17, nos. 3–4: 71–77.

Levins Morales, Aurora. *Medicine Stories: History, Culture and the Politics of Integrity.* Cambridge, Mass.: South End Press, 1998.

———. *Remedios: Stories of Earth and Iron from the History of Puertorriqueñas.* Boston: Beacon Press, 1998.

Levins Morales, Aurora, and Rosario Morales. *Getting Home Alive.* New York: Firebrand Books, 1986.

López Springfield, Consuelo. "Mestizaje in the Mother-Daughter Autobiography of Rosario Morales and Aurora Levins Morales." *A/b: Auto/biography Studies* 8, no. 2 (Fall 1993): 303–315.

McCracken, Ellen. *New Latina Narrative: The Feminine Space of Postmodern Ethnicity.* Tucson: University of Arizona Press, 1999.

Rojas, Lourdes. "Latinas at the Crossroads: An Affirmation of Life in Rosario Morales and Aurora Levins Morales's *Getting Home Alive.*" In *Breaking Boundaries: Latina Writing and Critical Reading,* edited by A. Horno-Delgado, E. Ortega, N. Scott, and N. Saporta-Sternbach, 166–177. Amherst: University of Massachusetts Press, 1989.

Antonia Domínguez Miguela

Line of the Sun, The   Judith Ortiz Cofer
(1989)

JUDITH ORTIZ COFER spent her childhood shuttling back and forth between Paterson, New Jersey, and her grandmother's home in Puerto Rico. Though not associated with Puerto Rican writers living in New York, Cofer nevertheless shares their preoccupation with the experience of translocation, which is commonly depicted in PUERTO RICAN LITERATURE. Cofer's *Line of the Sun* was nominated for the Pulitzer Prize.

The Line of the Sun centers on the story of the author's uncle, Guzmán. Cofer bases her writings on memories of life in Puerto Rico and the stories of her relatives and ancestors. She cites English author Virginia Woolf as an influence in re-creating personal memories and family stories and imbuing them with a fictive life of their own. In first writing autobiographical works about her family, Cofer worried about the disconnect between her vision and the memories of family members. She now seems to accept—at least in her writing—the unreliable nature of memory as well as the key role it plays in the act of storytelling.

Cofer has been criticized for the novel's shifts in point of view; however, the multivoiced novel allows the reader to see a story unfold in the depth that an adolescent first-person narrator would be unable to achieve. The story begins with the narrator, Marisol, recalling the story of Mamá Cielo, her grandmother, and her sons, Carmelo and Guzmán. Her voice then fades away as others take up the story, or as it is told from a more omniscient point of view. Marisol imagines her parents' life in Puerto Rico based on bits and pieces of overheard conversations and creatively tries to fill in the gaps of her knowledge about events in the lives of her relatives before she was born.

The story is set in Salud, which means "health" in Spanish and which corresponds literarily with García Márquez's idyllic Macondo in *One Hundred*

Years of Solitude. Cofer says that Salud is patterned on Hormigueros, the village in western Puerto Rico where she was born and where her family still lives.

Much of the novel, both in the Salud section, and later in El Building in Paterson, is concerned with female relationships. Cofer declares that she had many strong women in her family, that their world was governed more by women than men (Ocasio, "Infinite Variety"). *The Line of the Sun* examines the spectrum of female identities that were possible in Puerto Rican culture in the 1950s. The female system of friendship between *comadres* (relationship of a godmother to the child's mother) developed into a community-centered way of child-drearing on the island and in the barrios of the mainland. There are five roles available to women in the novel: the long-suffering mother, the virgin or good daughter who is her mother's helper, the whore, the spinster, and the matrons who establish the town's moral center (Faymonville 139–140). Marisol realizes through her experiences in El Building and in the Catholic schools in Paterson that none is right for her.

Through the story of Guzmán these roles are played out. Cofer says, "I wanted Guzman to be a creation of Marisol so that when he shows up, the real Guzman [is] nothing like the Puerto Rican Indiana Jones that she has imagined him to be . . . , but who has a heart bigger than she can comprehend" (Lopez). Marisol says, "As long as he lived strictly in our imaginations, Guzmán could be given any dimensions we wanted" (177). She tells the story of Guzmán's wild childhood and his seduction by Rosa, the local practitioner of *espiritismo* (spiritualism). Known to the upstanding women of Salud as La Cabra (she-goat or whore), Rosa occupies a marginal, yet important role in the community because she offers remedies for spiritual calamity. Although Guzmán later comes to know what Rosa is, he cannot find another woman to take her place after she is run out of town by the matrons of the Holy Rosary Society. In later years, wounded and chastened, he returns to Salud and marries Rosa's daughter, Sarita, as despised for her piousness as her mother was for her carnality.

Both Guzmán and his brother, Carmelo, leave Salud—Carmelo for the Korean War where he is killed, and Guzmán for the mainland. When Guzmán finally reunites with his sister Ramona and her family in New Jersey, he fills in the gaps in Marisol's tale. A troublemaker in his youth, Guzmán has matured. It is his sister who needs saving as she proceeds with a *espiritismo* meeting in El Building. When a fire from the meeting spreads through the building, Guzmán rescues his nephew, Gabriel, from the flames. The physical demands of the rescue aggravate a knife wound that has not healed properly. As he recovers in the hospital, he decides to return to Salud. Marisol's father determines that Ramona should return to *la isla* as well, to recover with her family.

Unlike Guzmán, Ramona returns to Paterson to the house in the suburbs that her husband and Marisol have bought. Unlike her mother, Marisol feels safe in the suburbs away from the restrictions of El Building and the world of Puerto Ricans. Before the spiritualist meeting, Marisol had her palm read. The *espiritista* explains that Marisol has the line of the sun running across her hand, an indicator that she has an "artist's soul" (253). The novel ends with Marisol acknowledging that "the only way to understand life is to write it as a story" (290).

Bibliography

Cofer, Judith Ortiz. *The Line of the Sun.* Athens: University of Georgia Press, 1989.

Faymonville, Carmen. "New Transnational Identities in Judith Ortiz Cofer's Autobiographical Fiction." *MELUS* 26, no. 2 (Summer 2001): 129–158.

Lopez, Lorraine M. "Possibilities for Salsa Music in the Mainstream: An Interview with Judith Ortiz Cofer." *Bilingual Review* 17, no. 2 (May–August 1992): 143–147.

Ocasio, Raphael. "The Infinite Variety of the Puerto Rican Reality: An Interview with Judith Ortiz Cofer." *Callaloo* 17, no. 3 (Summer 1994): 730–743.

———. "Puerto Rican Literature in Georgia? An Interview with Judith Ortiz Cofer." *Kenyon Review* 14, no. 4 (Fall 1992): 43–51.

Patricia Bostian

Llorona, La (The Weeping Woman)

A female figure of Chicano and Mexican folklore, La Llorona has traditionally been used as a threat by mothers to frighten their children. Different tales have been created to explain the existence of this figure, but the most frequently heard version is about a woman who drowns her children because her lover will not accept them. Later on she regrets what she has done and starts her search for them; she gravitates to places where there is water, condemned to wander eternally, crying for her children. For this reason she often appears to people by riverbanks, lakes, lagoons, and so on. Represented as the "bogey man" of Chicano culture, some Chicana poets have placed her in front of windows, scratching with her nails, trying to get into homes. Having been scared as children, writers such as Cordelia Candelaria now treat her with resentment and tell her to 'Go 'Way from My Window.'

An image in Mexican and CHICANO LITERATURE, La Llorona has also continuously appeared in song. La Llorona has been recently transformed as an empowering icon for Chicana women, and her legend has acquired different meanings in women's writing. She is the mother who cries because her children have been taken away by Anglo-Saxon culture; Tey Diana Rebolledo observes: "La Llorona is also symbolic of Chicano culture, whose children are lost because of their assimilation to the dominant culture or because of violence and prejudice" (77). In this sense she is identified with La MALINCHE, an Indian interpreter and mistress of the Spanish conquistador Hernán Cortés and mother of his son. Compared to the Virgin of Guadalupe, La Llorona and La Malinche share the condition of embodying the opposite of what a good mother is supposed to be. La Llorona has also been pictured as a temptress for young men, appearing to them as a beautiful woman "but when they approach her (with sexual intent in mind), she shows herself to be a hag or a terrible image of death personified" (63).

ANA CASTILLO in SO FAR FROM GOD (1993) addresses this female figure in her characterization of La Loca, who is isolated from society in her novel. Another allusion is made when Fe, La Loca's sister, becomes "La Gritona" (the woman who yells), crying nonstop about the loss of her boyfriend. Similarly SANDRA CISNEROS in WOMAN HOLLERING CREEK AND OTHER STORIES (1991) describes the stream called "La Llorona" where a woman hollers at the top of her lungs; through her yelling she is liberating herself from the dominance of her husband. They both represent a more radical vision of La Llorona, whose sharp cries serve as a protest against patriarchal dominance. They deliberately express their feelings of anger or triumph by hollering.

Portrayed in serious or humorous ways, La Llorona surfaces frequently in CHICANO LITERATURE and BORDER LITERATURE.

Bibliography

Candelaria, Cordelia. *Ojo de la cueva/Cave Springs.* Colorado Springs, Colo.: Maize Press, 1984.

Castillo, Ana. *Massacre of the Dreamers: Essays on Xicanisma.* New York: Penguin Books, 1995.

———. *So Far from God.* London: Women's Press, 1993.

Cisneros, Sandra. *Woman Hollering Creek and Other Stories.* New York: Random House, 1991.

The Cry: La Llorona Web site. Available online. URL: http://www.lallorona.com. Accessed May 27, 2008.

Rebolledo, Tey Diana. *Women Singing in the Snow: A Cultural Analysis of Chicana Literature.* Tucson: University of Arizona Press, 1995.

Imelda Martín-Junquera

Long Night of White Chickens, The
Francisco Goldman (1992)

Francisco Goldman is the son of a Guatemalan mother and a Jewish father. He was born in 1954 and raised in a Boston suburb, as well as in Guatemala. His short fiction has appeared in several magazines including *Harper's,* the *New Yorker, Esquire,* and *Sí.* During the 1980s Goldman wrote journalistic pieces that focused on the civil wars in Central America. Goldman made his debut as a novelist with *The Long Night of White Chickens,* followed by his second novel, *The ORDINARY*

SEAMAN (1997). In 2004 Goldman published his third novel, *The Divine Husband.*

The Long Night of White Chickens is one of the first novels by a writer of Guatemalan descent written and published in English in the United States. The plot involves a Guatemalan girl, Flor de Mayo Puac, who works for and is taken in by the Graetz family. Roger Graetz, who is Flor's age, grows up in Massachusetts with his Guatemalan mother and Jewish father; he narrates the novel. As an adult, Roger comes to investigate how Flor was killed in Guatemala. Goldman relies on use of the flashback to tell Flor de Mayo's story. While in Massachusetts, Flor learns English, attends school, and graduates from the prestigious Wellesley College. She later returns to Guatemala and comes to direct an orphanage.

In *The Long Night of White Chickens,* Roger explains how his mother has recently met Moya, a well-to-do Guatemalan who was both Roger's schoolmate in a Guatemalan private school and Flor's lover. The narrative follows Roger in his futile attempts to uncover the mystery of Flor's death; Goldman incorporates Moya's own flashbacks about his relationship with Flor into the novel. We learn more about her through Roger and Moya and come to appreciate the political circumstances of her death at an orphanage that facilitated U.S. adoptions at the expense of Guatemalan families. Yanes Gómez has commended Goldman for making Flor a three-dimensional character, as opposed to the stereotypical one-dimensional female characters prevalent in Central American literature (642).

The Long Night of White Chickens uses Flor's story to expose the actual massacres of the peasantry by Guatemala's right-wing dictatorships of the 1980s, regimes funded in part by the United States. While the novel is fiction, Goldman has gone to extremes to make the correlation between realities that the characters live in and Guatemalan history. For example, Goldman calls the newspaper that Moya works for *El Minuto* (The Minute), the fictional equivalent of the real newspaper in Guatemala called *La Hora* (The Hour). In this way the author moves between the world of fiction and the reality of Guatemalan life during the 1980s. It can also be argued that these details, as well as the novel's first section entitled "Guate no existe" (Guatemala does not exist), play with the customary disclaimer that the characters and situations described in the text are purely fictional.

The title *The Long Night of White Chickens* makes reference to the brutal repressive war that many Guatemalans refer to as "La Violencia" (the violence) or "La Noche Larga" (the long night). The "long night" of the novel is when Moya and Flor meet for dinner at a Chinese restaurant; in preparation for the evening the restaurant staff is killing several white chickens. Goldman uses this title and this scene to strike a parallel between the chickens to be slaughtered and the poor of Guatemala.

The Long Night of White Chickens is significant in Latino literature for the way it characterizes people of mixed heritage, not just Spanish and Indian, but Eastern European as well. Goldman and his protagonist, Roger Graetz, share the same ethnic background, and Goldman observes that *The Long Night of White Chickens* reflects aspects of his own identity.

Aside from providing inspiration to U.S.-based artists such as John Sayles for his movie *Men with Guns, The Long Night of White Chickens* also contributes to the emerging literature of Central Americans reared in the United States and Latino literature in general. Within a Latin American context, Goldman's work can be read alongside such books as *I, Rigoberta Menchú: An Indian Woman in Guatemala* (1987), Graciela Limón's *IN SEARCH OF BERNABÉ* (1993), and Manlio Argueta's *One Day of Life* (1991) about the peasantry of El Salvador who are caught in the cross-fire of civil war.

Bibliography

Birnbaum, Robert. "Francisco Goldman, Author of The Divine Husband converses with Robert Birnbaum." Available online. URL: http://www.identitytheory.com/interviews/birnbaum154.php. Downloaded March 18, 2005.

Goldman, Francisco. *The Divine Husband.* New York: Atlantic Monthly Press, 2004.

———. *The Long Night of White Chickens*. London: Faber & Faber, 1992.

———. *The Ordinary Seaman*. New York: Atlantic Monthly Press, 1997.

Gustavo Adolfo Guerra Vásquez

Loving Che Ana Menéndez (2004)

Loving Che, Ana Menéndez's first novel, revisits a number of themes explored in her collection of short stories *In Cuba I Was a German Shepherd* (2001). Menéndez (1970–), the daughter of Cuban political exiles, has an intimate relationship with the exile community of Miami. In her work she attempts to record personal and political voices that sound in response to the Cuban Revolution and Fidel Castro's rise to power in 1959.

The novel's narrator provides both the introduction and the conclusion, which surrounds the epistolary form of the middle section. Raised by her grandfather in Miami's Cuban exile community, the narrator has known neither her mother nor her father, who is rumored to have died in a Cuban prison. Though she has questioned her grandfather repeatedly about the family's life in Cuba, the narrator gets no concrete answers and develops a somewhat critical view of the exile community, noting: "This endless pining for the past seemed to me a kind of madness; everyone living in an asylum, exiled from the living, and no one daring to say it plainly" (2). After the death of her grandfather the narrator travels to Cuba in hopes of finding some trace of her past.

Though the narrator never meets her mother during her travels to the island, after her last trip a package arrives addressed to her, postmarked from Spain. The package, wrapped tightly and well sealed, contains a number of handwritten letters and several photographs. The letters, though out of chronological order, appear to be written by the narrator's mother, Teresa de la Landre. The narrator "hoped, at first, that by arranging the notes and recollections in some sort of order, [she] might be able to make sense of them" (12). The packet, which is presented to the reader directly without the narrator's commentary, documents Teresa's life before, during, and after the revolution, forming a fragmented and impressionistic account of her past. The reader and narrator learn that Teresa was a painter and that through her husband, Calixto, she met and befriended a central figure of the revolution, Ernesto "Che" Guevara.

In addition to her poignant musings on memory, art, politics, marriage, and history, Teresa's letters reveal that she and Che Guevara conducted a clandestine love affair. With no official documentation outside of the letters in the narrator's possession, the packet suggests the difficulty of establishing identity for those Cubans exiled from their culture. The reader tends to agree with Teresa, who says that history may be no more than "another way of saying an idea about ourselves" (17).

Taking the letters and photographs to members of the Miami exile community, the narrator learns that the affair and her reconstructed past do not find a hospitable audience with those who have personally felt the effects of the revolution, living their lives in exile. The narrator consults a history professor who denies the authenticity of the letters, remarking, "I can understand how in the absence of a past, one might be tempted to invent history . . . But it was difficult for me to read about that man as a lover; it was difficult to see his photograph" (173–174). Yet, as Menéndez argues, all attempts to make sense of the past, all writing of history, involve such interpretation.

Through Teresa's letters Menéndez documents revolutionary Cuba and the subsequent introduction of socialism. From looted stores and expropriated homes and businesses to the murder of political prisoners, Menéndez does not overlook the cruelty of Castro's regime; However, Teresa's letters humanize Che Guevara, the Argentinean-born revolutionary who has become a Cuban hero and a Latin American Marxist icon. The content of the letters allows Menéndez to question the ability to navigate between the personal and the political for all Cubans, not simply those in exile. Photographs, letters, and personal interviews appear to be equally suspect in their distortion of the past, as each betrays "a certainty that is not given to actual life" (130). *Loving Che* muses on both art and memory in equal stride, establishing the importance of each in Teresa's life and, therefore, also in the narrator's search for her familial roots and history. *Loving Che* makes an argument for the inseparability between Cuban history and the present reality for both the exile population and those Cubans living on the island, having never left. As such Menéndez makes a compelling contribution to both CUBAN-AMERICAN LITERATURE and SPANISH-AMERICAN CARIBBEAN LITERATURE.

Bibliography

Kakutani, Michiko. "Lust, and Other Revolutionary Sensations." *New York Times,* February 24, 2004, p. E8ff.

Marquez, Sandra. "Recapturing a Cataclysmic Era." *Hispanic* 16, no. 12 (December 2003): 68.

Menéndez, Ana. *Loving Che.* New York: Atlantic Monthly Press, 2004.

Zach Weir

Luz y sombra Ana Roqué (1903)

A writer, editor, and advocate of women's rights, Ana Roqué was born on April 18, 1853, in Aguadilla, Puerto Rico, to Cristina Géigel de Roqué and Ricardo Roqué. As a young woman, Roqué pursued her studies of the natural sciences with Agustín Stahl, and she soon established herself as a teacher and writer. In 1872 Roqué married Luis E. Duprey and later bore five children, three of whom survived into adulthood; their marriage ended in divorce. In addition to *Luz y sombra* (1903; Light and shadow), her fictional works include several short stories, *Sara la obrera* (1895; Sara, the worker), and *Un ruso en Puerto Rico* (1919; A Russian in Puerto Rico). She also authored instructional texts on Spanish literature and grammar and on the fundamentals of world geography. Roqué's contributions to PUERTO RICAN LITERATURE are notable because she wrote at an important time in Puerto Rico's history, a period in which the island changed hands from Spanish colonialists to U.S. imperialists. She died in 1933.

Luz y sombra is a turn-of-the-century text that reveals the importance of letter writing for women in Puerto Rico. The main characters are Matilde and her husband, Paco; Julia and her husband, Sevastel; Rafael, Julia's lover; and Dr. Bernard, who seeks a cure for Julia's depression and anxiety. In its contrast of Matilde's country existence and Julia's urban life, the novel explores the island's Spanish colonial past and its more industrialized future as a U.S. commonwealth. In 1898, five years before Roqué published *Luz y sombra,* the United States expelled Spain from Puerto Rico and established military rule on the island. From 1899 to 1939 the United States introduced disease-resistant plants, created transportation systems, and brought industrial technologies that increased sugar harvesting, manufacturing, and exportation.

Roqué sets *Luz y sombra* in San Juan (the capital) and Riveras de la Plata (the country) in order to compare the fates of two women who write to each other about their engagements, marriages, and heartaches. Though Matilde and Julia share the same convent education, one to prepare them to be good wives, they differ in their intellectual pursuits and views on love. Due to their unique dispositions and values, Matilde gravitates toward lightness (*luz*), and Julia ultimately falls into shadow (*sombra*). Matilde remarks in her opening letter, "Cuan distintos son nuestros destinos!" ("How divergent our destinies are!") (26). The title, *Luz y sombra*, invites the reader to consider other kinds of binaries in the novel. Matilde revels in nature, while Julia indulges in the comforts of urbanity; Matilde is sentimental, and her best friend is a self-declared positivist (one who adheres to the observable rather than the ethereal). Matilde works hard with her husband to maintain their tobacco plantation; Julia circulates in exclusive social circles, well dressed, dutiful, but also repressed. The exchanges between Matilde and Julia reveal their dual perspectives on domestic life; their roles, in turn, say a great deal about Puerto Rico's negotiation of European (particularly Spanish) and U.S. influences.

In her book entitled *Foundational Fictions* (1991) DORIS SOMMER explains how women writers have been ignored as part of the 19th- and

20th-century project of "nation building" in Latin America. Within the Latin American context nation building refers to the transition between colony and independent country. This project tended to be dominated by the male writer-stateman and his vision. But in *Luz y sombra* we see a female world in which letter writing becomes an imaginative outlet for considering one's past, present, and future; in this regard the novel contributes to the project of nation building.

Along with the novel's binaries about the past and future, we see in the narrative the split between light (*luz*) and shadow (*sombra*), between Puerto Rico and Spain, Puerto Rico and the United States, tradition and modernism, the country and the city, and, on a smaller scale, the rich and the poor, the educated and the illiterate. These binaries operate within what Sommer calls a "foundational fiction." Sommer argues that fictional writing enables newly liberated countries or recently liberated colonies (like Puerto Rico) to perceive themselves as emerging nations. Traditionally, foundational fictions are "stories of star-crossed lovers who represent particular regions, races, parties, economic interests, and the like" (Sommer 5). Female characters typically secure political alliances and bridge schisms between classes. The novels and epic poems, which constitute this genre, are full of racial and economic paradoxes and overly romanticized plot lines, all of which require suppression or amplification of historical facts. Roqué's writing negotiates Puerto Rico's colonial past and modern present, and in this way follows general characteristics of the national romance. The characters of *Luz y sombra* bear an allegorical relationship to Puerto Rican society at the turn of the century, a society moving away from arranged marriages and toward autonomy though the mixed-class marriage.

In *Luz y sombra* marriage is the central issue because it is through marriage that women have a clearly defined role in society. At the beginning of the novel Matilde writes to her best friend about her prospects:

Dear Julia, my parents assuredly are thinking of marrying me off . . . they intend for my husband a gentleman twice my age . . . They say that he is quite an excellent person, and with a great deal of money. Imagine! What will the money matter to me? What I want is to be happy, living with my intended . . . they are marrying me to an older man who will only be able to talk to me of business, of numbers, and all that is crude and ordinary of life (25).

Matilde disparages a union based on expediency and instead argues for marrying for love. She confesses to Julia that she is attracted to Paco, her penniless, but earnest cousin. Matilde and Paco are two halves of a platonic whole (the idea that our ideal mate exists and we spend our lives looking for that partner). Julia, by means of contrast, reconciles herself to an arranged marriage to Sevastel, an austere man of 50 and of good birth. Theirs is a union based not on mutual affection—as with Matilde and Paco—but rather on convenience and money. Julia initially dismisses Matilde's romantic notions, and she regards matrimony to a man twice her age as the normal course of events in high society. Julia also lacks the kind of imaginative and spiritual outlets that Matilde finds in Riveras de la Plata. She explains to Matilde that "Nature, which you have always found so beautiful, says nothing to my heart, which does not know how to be enthusiastic about the ideal, with the impalpable and the elusive" (40).

Luz y sombra dwells on Julia's struggle and failure to stay true to her marital vows to Sevastel. When Julia falls in love with Rafael, Sevastel's friend, she discovers a passion within that she cannot control. Right before her wedding she looks out at a tempestuous sky and discovers her own profound longing for the young, handsome, and charming Rafael. Shedding a torrent of tears because of the decision she has made, Julia realizes she is to be trapped in a marriage without love or understanding. Julia's ensuing letters expose the emotional dead ends of the arranged marriage and the costs that daughters pay for family alliances. *Luz y sombra* dramatizes the psychological alienation and physical repugnance that can arise from two strangers living together.

Though too late, Julia ultimately endorses Matilde's views on love. She writes about her husband's dead eyes, his empty soul, and cold, statue-like body; these dramatize the physical and temperamental differences between the couple. Egocentric by nature, Sevastel cannot fathom his wife having emotional needs, much less her falling in love with Rafael. When he discovers the affair, his first impulse is to kill Julia; his second impulse is to kill Rafael and protect his honor with a duel. In this bloody resolution to Julia's affair Roqué upsets the notion that, in a patriarchal society, fathers and husbands attend to the needs of daughters and wives. Sevastel explains to Matilde that only blood will clean his good name. The duel, a misplaced ritual of the courtly past, has become terribly devoid of meaning, but in Julia's world there is nothing to replace it. This absence is where the idea of nation building is significant in *Luz y sombra*.

Matilde and Paco's wholesome marriage, although between cousins, poses an alternative to the socially parasitic relationship of the Sevastels. Matilde's union with Paco suggests that wealth and economic opportunity might be more evenly distributed by marrying across class lines. Roqué meaningfully juxtaposes the Sevastels' useless wealth with Matilde and Paco's industriousness on their plantation (one which no longer depends on slave labor). The Sevastels are consumers of foreign goods and ideas that do not make them happy; however, their marriage maintains the status quo.

Roqué critiques the Sevastel marriage and their worship of foreign things (clothing, art) and ideas (positivism, industrialism). Like José Martí, who in "Nuestra América" chides Spanish Americans for blindly copying European forms, Roqué calls for a strong self-identity and a moral basis. Julia is a young wife so utterly invested in the styles of her day that she forgets about the natural beauty around her. She has been trained to be her husband's ornament. Julia discovers that she needs more in life than money, but despite the attention of Dr. Bernard, who has counseled her after Rafael's death, she falls into a long depression until she finally dies. For Roqué, Julia serves as an example of why Puerto Rico must not mindlessly copy European or antiquated colonial forms, for these forms do not suit it wholly. It is an island whose contrasts define its essence, an island whose history must be recorded if we are to understand the complexities of being neither a nation nor a state. *Luz y sombra* reflects these complexities and illustrates that the experiences of women, whether wealthy like Julia or middle class like Matilde, are an index of psychological, social, and economic change.

Lizabeth Paravisini-Gebert has written an insightful introduction to the novel, which places *Luz y sombra* within Caribbean literature and, more broadly, within the English novel of manners. She rightly points out that Roqué's novel can be read alongside such authors as Jane Austen and George Eliot, who also criticize through fiction 19th-century social conventions that worked at a woman's disadvantage; added to this list should be Henry James's *Portrait of a Lady*. Roqué's focus on issues of Puerto Rican identity also anticipates MAGALI GARCÍA RAMIS's novel *HAPPY DAYS, UNCLE SERGIO* (1986), as well as ESMERALDA SANTIAGO's memoir, *WHEN I WAS PUERTO RICAN* (1993).

Bibliography

Roqué, Ana. *Luz y sombra*. Río Piedras, P. R.: Editorial Universidad de Puerto Rico, 1994.

Sommer, Doris. *Foundational Fictions: The National Romances of Latin America*. Berkeley: University of California Press, 1991.

Luz Elena Ramirez

magical realism

Magical realism, or magic realism, is a style of writing in which the author mixes fantastic elements with realistic ones. Though writers from a variety of cultural backgrounds rely on magical realism as a means of expression, the term is applied primarily to fiction by 20th-century Latin American writers such as Jorge Luis Borges (Argentina), Gabriel García Márquez (Colombia), Juan Rulfo (Mexico), Alejo Carpentier (Cuba), and José Donoso (Chile). For these and other authors magical realism is a mode that captures the supernatural aspects of Latin American life.

In Carpentier's influential prologue to his novel *El reino de este mundo* (1949; *The Kingdom of This World*), the Cuban author differentiates *"lo real maravilloso"* (the marvelous real), his version of the magical real, from the European movements of surrealism and the fantastic. The marvelous real is inherent in the culture of the New World; the inhabitants understand reality as containing elements of what from a European perspective would be termed fantasy. Carpentier claims that in Latin America the cultural belief system differs from other parts of the world in that people of Latin America have faith that supernatural events compose a part of everyday life. *El reino de este mundo,* which puts to practice the theoretical ideas, describes the Haitian revolution from the perspective of the Haitian inhabitants. In it the main charac-

ter, a runaway slave, transforms into a variety of animals to escape capture by the authorities. Carpentier argues that, unlike European surrealism in which the elements of fantasy are artificial, during the Haitian revolution the events he describes actually happened, reflecting a unique Latin American perspective of what constitutes real experience.

Other classic magical real works include Rulfo's *Pedro Páramo* (1955), which recounts the abuses of a landowner in a small village in rural Mexico. In the middle of this novella the reader discovers that the characters who are speaking are dead, speaking from the grave, including one of the main figures, Juan Preciado. However, the most commonly cited magical realist novel is *Cien años de soledad* (1967; *One Hundred Years of Solitude*) by García Márquez. In this novel García Márquez tells the story of Latin America through the generations of the Buendía family. Constantly introducing supernatural elements into otherwise historically accurate events, *Cien años* gives a political function to the magical real. One important example is the scene of the banana massacre, in which the mistreated workers on the plantation are collectively killed while protesting the abuses of the foreign owners. Thousands of dead bodies are loaded on the train and transported to the sea, all of this a reflection of real events that occurred in the banana republics of Central America and Colombia. On the following day, in the novel, the supernatural element is introduced: Nobody remembers what has occurred. Even the townspeople and the relatives of the victims deny that this ever took place. By framing the event in the magical realist context of the novel, García Márquez underscores the irregularity of the collective amnesia that stunts meaningful progress in Latin America and the rest of the world.

Magical realism therefore seeks to define the rich cultural identity of Latin America, while in some forms it is used to critique oppressive political actions. The Latin American employment of this style seems far removed from the first usage of the term by the German art historian Franz Roh in 1925. Roh coined the term when classifying the art form of New Objectivity in which the core of the represented object was revealed through fantasy; for example, in the painting by Christian Schad "Portrait of Dr. Haustein" (1928), the figure of a strange alien-like shadow hovers behind the crisp realist representation of a formally dressed man. When the term was first applied to Latin American literature in 1948, the Venezuelan author and critic Arturo Uslar Pietri defined magical realism as a "poetic negation of reality," a characterization that contradicts later ideas of magical realism, which identify it as an accurate portrayal of Latin American reality. For literary theorist Angel Flores the term refers simply to the unique mixture of realism and fantasy in Latin American writing, while some analysts since Flores have noted the connection between the "magical" part of the term and the myth and superstition of the indigenous roots of the New World.

With all the debate around the definition of this term, magical realism has come to signify such a wide array of artistic and literary creation that it has been denounced as unhelpful on more than one occasion. One of the most outspoken critics was Emir Rodríguez Monegal in his opening paper at the 1973 conference dedicated to magical realism, in which he compares the term with a labyrinth that lacks a center. Since then two dominant opposing viewpoints have developed surrounding the term: Magical realism either labels literature as primitivist or elevates it by characterizing a unique

form of cultural expression. The former takes offense from the definition of this particular New World reality as "magical," claiming that this term serves to continue the colonial European perception of the Americas as exotic. The latter observes the benefit of this category for the construction of a common cultural project.

Prominent authors in Latino literature have turned to magical realism in their works, most frequently to underscore political divisions between past and present. In particular, ISABEL ALLENDE, CRISTINA GARCÍA, and LOIDA MARITZA PÉREZ have all used magical realism to juxtapose often painful memories of the past in their Latin American homelands with current struggles in the United States. Allende, a Chilean author now residing in California, incorporates elements of fantasy into her novels such as *The HOUSE OF THE SPIRITS* (1982) in much the same way as García Márquez. The supernatural abilities of some of the characters reacting to chilling historical events effectively conveys a cold political reality during the early 1970s in Chile. Family portraits characterize many magical realist works in Hispanic America. As in *The House of the Spirits,* in *DREAMING IN CUBAN* (1992) Cuban-American author García infuses her tale of the del Piño family, divided between Cuba and the United States after the CUBAN REVOLUTION, with magical elements. Both Allende and García choose a strong female protagonist as the storyteller in their novels; both authors give these characters telepathic and supernatural powers, underlining the strength and tenacity of these women. Pérez from the Dominican Republic also makes use of the style of the magical real in *GEOGRAPHIES OF HOME* (1999). In this first work by Pérez, the author juxtaposes the nightmarish memories of the dictatorship of Rafael Trujillo with the present dynamics of the family living and working in the United States. The magical real that defines cultural expression for some mid-century Latin American authors becomes a signal of a cultural memory defined by a Latin American past for these Hispanic-American authors. The divided or hyphenated family identities are clearly marked by the hybridity of the style of the magical real.

Bibliography

Faris, Wendy B. *Ordinary Enchantments: Magical Realism and the Remystification of Narrative*. Nashville, Tenn.: Vanderbilt University Press, 2004.

Parkinson Zamora, Lois, and Wendy B. Faris, eds. *Magical Realism: Theory, History, Community.* Durham, N.C.: Duke University Press, 1995.

Reiss, Timothy J., ed. *Sisyphus and Eldorado: Magical and Other Realisms in Caribbean Literature*. Trenton, N.J.: African World Press, 2002.

Amanda Holmes

Malinche, La (c. 1500–1527/1530)

Known under various names, La Malinche, a historical figure in the Spanish conquest of Mexico, has evolved into a national myth. As Hernán Cortés's interpreter, lover, and mother to his mestizo son, she is probably the most controversial female symbol of Mexican identity. It is nearly impossible to retrieve the historical figure born of Indian nobility from the cultural images into which she has been packaged and repackaged over the years. The salient fact that emerges is that of Malinche's importance in the collective imagination of Mexico.

When she was baptized *Marina* by the Spaniards in 1519, her age was not recorded. Her year of birth is placed somewhere between 1500 and 1505. Her name offers a wide spectrum of meanings. Also known as Malinalli, Indians called her *Malintzin,* and it may be that she was called *Marina* because of some phonetic resemblance to this name. *Malinche* is a Spanish corruption of the Nahuatl word *Malintzin,* which in turn may have come from a Nahuatl mispronunciation of Marina plus the reverential *-tzin* suffix. The variety of names by which she is known reflects the different lights in which Mexicans have viewed her over time. For the sake of consistency, the name *La Malinche* is used here.

Although she played an important role in Cortés's conquest of Mexico, it is interesting to note that La Malinche is scarcely mentioned in Cortés's own account of the conquest, his *Cartas de relación* (*Letters from Mexico*). In his second letter to Carlos V he only makes reference to her on two occasions when he refers to her as the Indian interpreter from Pochontán (44). He speaks of Malinche's loyalty as well as how she saved him and his solders from an attack by Cholula Indians. He also mentioned her as the interpreter who always accompanied him, and he is explicit in informing the king that she was among the group of 20 Indians who were given to him (242).

Historians agree that there is evidence that Malinche was of noble origin. Francisco López de Gómara wrote in *The Life of Conqueror by His Secretary* that she was "the daughter of wealthy parents, who were related to the Lord of that country" (56).

There are different accounts to explain how the young girl was separated from her noble origins. According to some historians, when Malinche's father died, her mother remarried another cacique (chief), by whom she had a son. To protect the son's inheritance and right to rule Malinche was sold as a slave "to some indians from Xicalango" (López de Gómara 56). The majority of historians agree that she was in the group of 20 Indian women who were given to Cortés and his solders when they arrived in Tabasco from Cuba. Also beyond dispute is the fact that she became interpreter to Cortés, either along with Jerónimo de Aguilar or in succession to him.

After the Mexican conquest Malinche bore Cortés a son, Martín, who was taken from her and sent to Spain. This move was in keeping with the Spanish patriarchal norms of the time. As a slave, Malinche had already been trained to obey her masters, and submissiveness was a characteristic of the role of women both in Amerindian and in European societies. At the same time, however, Fray BERNARDINO DE SAHAGÚN's account of the conquest, the Florentine Codex, depicts Malinche as a cultural facilitator, not as a mere pawn, in the conquest.

In 1524 Cortes called again on Malinche during his campaign in Honduras, where she served as guide, interpreter, and strategist. During this campaign Cortés arranged for her to be married to Juan Jaramillo, one of his trusted soldiers. After that campaign Malinche disappears from the records; it is not known when and where she died, but it is believed she died young, in about 1530.

During the colonial period Malinche was on the whole considered as a valuable and faithful interpreter of Cortés, but Mexico's independence from Spain occasioned a totally different interpretation of Malinche. Elizabeth Salas states: "[H]er status as a great *conquistadora* declined at exactly the same time that the Mexicans threw out the Spaniards in 1821. From that time onward, her reputation dwindled to that of a traitor" (14).

After independence Mexican intellectuals searched for a national identity, an effort that gave rise to *indigenismo*. As its name suggests, *indigenismo* is an ideology that stands for everything native to Mexico, rejecting the Spanish. OCTAVIO PAZ, in his essay "The Sons of Malinche," saw the conquest initiate an inferiority complex based on the rejection of the indigenous. Paz's essay has been instrumental in the construction of Malinche as a negative symbol of treachery to the race and as a passive object of the conquest. Paz also strengthened this view with the notion of Malinche as *La Chingada*, which literally means she is "screwed," a term that one can still hear today in relation to Malinche. She is the woman who, from an Indian perspective, betrayed her people by being with Cortés sexually, and thus she is considered the first actor in the process of race mixing that gave rise to MESTIZAJE. The term *malinchismo* is derived from Malinche; a *malinchista* is a person who rejects all that is Mexican in favor of the foreign. These terms were in keeping with the nationalist fervor to forge a new identity that elevated the indigenous and criticized the Spanish colonial.

For a more modern feminist perspective on Malinche, see Laura Esquivel's recent novel *Malinche,* in which the traditional version of the indigenous woman is retold in light of recent historical research that has shown the complexity of her role as the mediator between two cultures, Hispanic and Native American, and two languages, Spanish and Náhuatl.

From whatever perspective she is regarded, Malinche emerges as a prominent protagonist at an important juncture in her country's history and, perhaps more important, as a national myth and Latin American female archetype, earthy counterpart to the Virgin of Guadalupe and the subject of several works of creative writing in recent years.

Bibliography
Cortés, Hernán. *Cartas de Relación.* 7th ed. México: Editorial Porrúa, 1973.
Cypess, Sandra Messinger. *La Malinche in Mexican Literature, from History to Myth.* Austin: University of Texas Press, 1991.
Esquivel, Laura. *Malinche: A Novel.* Translated by Ernesto Mestre-Reed. New York: Atria, 2006.
Leal, Luis. "Female Archetype in Mexican Literature." In *Women in Hispanic Literature: Icons and Fallen Idols,* edited by Beth Miller, 227–241. Berkeley: University of California Press, 1983.
López de Gómara, Francisco. *The Life of Conqueror by His Secretary.* Translated by Lesley Byrd Simpson. Berkeley: University of California Press, 1964.
Paz, Octavio. *The Labrynth of Solitude.* Translated by Lysander Kemp. New York: Grove Press, 1961.
Phillips, Rachel. "Marina/Malinche." In *Women in Hispanic Literature: Icons and Fallen Idols,* edited by Beth Miller, 97–114. Berkeley: University of California Press, 1983.
Salas, Elizabeth. *Soldaderas in the Mexican Military: Myth and History.* Austin: University of Texas Press, 1990
Taylor, John. "Reinterpreting Malinche." Available online. URL: http://userwww.sfsu.edu/~epf/2000/jt.html. Downloaded December 18, 2007.

Amparo Marmolejo-McWatt

Mambo Kings Play Songs of Love, The
Oscar Hijuelos (1989)

With *The Mambo Kings Play Songs of Love* Cuban-American novelist OSCAR HIJUELOS achieved critical and popular success and was awarded the 1990 Pulitzer Prize in fiction. The novel, set primarily after World War II in New York, relates the successes and failures of two brothers, Cesar and Nestor Castillo, as they attempt to achieve their particular version of the American Dream. Cesar and Nestor Castillo aspire to become famous and to prosper by performing and recording Cuban music with their orchestra, the Mambo Kings.

Finding it difficult to establish themselves as performers in the thriving dancehall scene of Havana, Cesar and Nestor Castillo leave Cuba for the United States in 1949. The narrator explains that "the scene might be better in New York . . . Cesar heard rumors about money, dance halls, recording contracts, good weekly salaries, women, and friendly Cubans everywhere" (33). To realize their ambitions Cesar leaves his young daughter, Mariella, on the island, and Nestor leaves behind his unrequited love. But, the brothers quickly join the vibrant Cuban immigrant community of New York; they find a place to live and day jobs with their cousin Pablo. Cesar and Nestor start new lives and begin to immerse themselves in the dancehall culture of the 1950s, the musical context in which mambo and other forms of Latin music gained popularity with an American audience.

Cesar and Nestor have to deal with many particularities of the immigrant experience, including loneliness, poverty, and the xenophobia that surfaced during and after World War II. In this age of the cold war, with its distrust of strangers, the brothers learn "which streets to avoid," and they recognize their vulnerability on the docks at night (36). While detailing the lives of the brothers during this period, the novel describes a diversity of cultural groups who are meaningful to Nestor and Cesar: the immigrant community, the musician/performer subculture, and the larger dancehall social scene, with its dancing, drinking, and dress codes. In this climate Cesar and Nestor achieve modest success and recognition, playing shows with the Mambo Kings in New York's top venues and befriending performers and clubowners.

The Mambo Kings' biggest break, and one the novel circles back to a number of times, comes when Desi Arnaz champions the Castillo brothers. The most famous Cuban immigrant in American entertainment, Arnaz has heard the bolero (ballad) called "Beautiful María of My Soul," or "Bella María de mi alma," written by Nestor in response to his unrequited love in Havana. The pinnacle of their fame and recognition comes with their appearance on the *I Love Lucy* television show. The

brothers perform as the Cuban cousins of Ricky Ricardo (played by Arnaz).

In top form by 1956 Cesar and Nestor have recorded a number of records and toured both coasts. The brothers appear to have made it; however, tragedy strikes when Nestor dies in a car crash following a late night of performing and hard drinking. Nestor's death leaves his wife, Delores, widowed and his children, Leticia and Eugenio, without a father. Mourning the loss of his brother and fellow performer, Cesar "lost his feeling for music and his soul withered" (202). Cesar blames himself for Nestor's death and adopts the younger brother's melancholy, from which he never fully escapes. Continuing to drink heavily during the years following Nestor's death, Cesar begins to play music once again to supplement his income as superintendent of the apartment building in which he lives. Largely indifferent to politics for most of his life, Cesar now needs the extra income to send to Cuba in order to alleviate his family's increasing poverty in the aftermath of the CUBAN REVOLUTION of 1959. Sponsoring two of his brothers in their flight from Cuba to Miami, Cesar will never again visit his native Cuba. He will never see his parents nor his young daughter. FIDEL CASTRO's rise to power and the U.S. embargo against the island will change family relations dramatically; this is a theme not just in Hijuelos's work but in CUBAN-AMERICAN LITERATURE more broadly.

Hijuelos charts the rise and fall of urban prosperity in New York through the lens of Cesar Castillo. With the influx of exiles fleeing Castro's Cuba Cesar takes on a type of paternal obligation to the young musicians coming to the city in need of work and friendship. Yet, never does Castillo find mooring for his restlessness, neither from his lascivious sexual relationships with numerous women nor from the consoling memory of times past when he and his brother "played jobs and were on a stage, or went out dancing" making them "Stars for a Night" (22).

Stylistically the novel relies heavily on memory, both personal and collective. The novel opens with a vignette in which Cesar reflects upon his life during a singular day in 1980. He has checked into the Hotel Splendour. Aware that his body cannot process alcohol, he nevertheless decides to drink himself to death while listening to recordings of the Mambo Kings and recalling various episodes of his life. Hijuelos structures the novel with a prologue and epilogue by Eugenio, Nestor's son and Cesar's nephew. In his attempt to record the Castillo brothers' lives and make sense of their youth and unrealized hopes, Eugenio provides the vehicle for the novel's meandering path.

Exploring larger issues such as domestic violence, sexuality, machismo, the Cuban Revolution, and the immigrant response to the influx of political exiles, Hijuelos takes on a plethora of themes central to the Cuban immigrant experience in the second half of the 20th century. Writing with a sensitive eye to both musical form and cultural specificity, Hijuelos mimics the musicality and rhythm of the times he documents. The author punctuates his narrative with Spanish words and phrases, which sound against the larger English-speaking New York backdrop. An elegy to both music and memory, *The Mambo Kings Play Songs of Love* documents a unique Cuban-American verse to supplement the chorus of the larger, always hopeful American dream. The novel helps to anticipate the subject of Hijuelos's *A SIMPLE HABANA MELODY: FROM WHEN THE WORLD WAS GOOD* (2002) and is a compelling and entertaining contribution to the growing corpus of Cuban-American literature.

Bibliography

Hijuelos, Oscar. *The Mambo Kings Play Songs of Love.* New York: Harper & Row Perennial Library, 1990.

Patteson, Richard F. "Oscar Hijuelos: 'Eternal Homesickness' and the Music of Memory." *Critique* 44, no. 1 (Fall 2002): 38–47.

Pérez Firmat, Gustavo. "Rum, Rump, and Rumba: Cuban Contexts for *The Mambo Kings Play Songs of Love.*" *Disposito* 41 (1991): 75–86.

Zach Weir

Marqués, René (1919–1979) *(playwright)*

Born in Arecibo, Puerto Rico, René Marqués was one of the most important Puerto Rican authors of the 20th century. Raised by his grandparents on the island, he inherited a traditional vision of the world. Marqués learned to combine his passion for literature with his education as an agronomist that led to work at the U.S. Department of Agriculture in the mid-1940s. He began publishing stories in 1941. *Peregrinación* (Pilgrimage), his only poetry collection, was published in 1944. Two years later Marqués studied Spanish theater at the University of Madrid. Back in Puerto Rico, he founded a small theater group and began publishing cultural criticism.

In 1949, with a grant from the Rockefeller Foundation, Marqués traveled to New York City to study playwriting at Columbia University. Upon return to Puerto Rico Marqués joined the governmental Division of Community Education. While working on the film *Una voz en la montaña* (1951; A voice in the mountain), the author was inspired to write *La carreta* (1956; The Oxcart). *La carreta* established Marqués's reputation among Latin American playwrights.

La carreta traces the moral disintegration of a Puerto Rican family that moves from the country to San Juan, the capital, to New York, and finally back to the island in search of a better life. The play is divided in three sketches. "El campo" refers to the countryside of Puerto Rico; "El arrabal" is the name for the slums of San Juan; and "La metrópoli" refers to the Bronx. The first sketch, or act, features the arrival of the oxcart that will take the family to San Juan, leaving behind their old farm and their grandfather. The grandfather loves the island and his land and resists the "call" of modernity that his children follow.

The second act takes place one year later in the San Juan slums. Luis, the older son, moves from job to job and finds out that his girlfriend is really her uncle's mistress. Chaguito, the younger son, becomes a thief in the city. He gets arrested and ends up in reform school. Juanita, the daughter, gets raped. She terminates her pregnancy and then attempts suicide. In the meantime, Doña Gabriela, the mother, can only helplessly watch the moral disintegration of her children.

The third act takes place a year later in the Bronx. Luis and Juanita now make enough money to buy luxury items; however, Luis has become a slave of factory work, and Juanita's morals have been compromised. Luis becomes a casualty of working with the factory's dangerous machines and is "eaten" by one of them. Juanita and Doña Gabriela decide to return to Puerto Rico. Juanita has the opportunity to marry her childhood sweetheart and live a simpler life. The title of the play, *La carreta,* refers not only to the oxcart of the first act but also to Juanita's oxcart. Her oxcart functions throughout the play as a symbol of a rural life on the island.

The symbolism in *La carreta* works on many levels. We see the absent father, resilient mother, and pure country girl who becomes a loose city woman. *La carreta* is often performed on the island and has arguably become Puerto Rico's quintessential migration melodrama. It is rivaled in popularity perhaps only by Rafael Hernández's song "Lamento borincano" (The Puerto Rican lament). Overall, Marqués offers an idyllic vision of rural life and a call for a return to the island. This vision has been deconstructed by a new generation of Puerto Rican writers that emerged in the 1970s. Poet TATO LAVIERA, for example, named his first poetry collection *La Carreta Made a U-Turn,* an ironic response to the "back to the land" movement of Marqués. The point for Laviera seems to be that once Puerto Ricans adjust to life in New York, there is no real return to the land, though the nostalgia remains.

During the 1950s and 1960s, Marqués became a major figure in the Puerto Rican cultural scene, with multiple theatrical productions, publications, and awards to his credit. Another important play was *Los soles truncos* (1958; *Fanlights*). This drama tells the tale of three spinsters (two living, one dead) who try to prevent the passing of time inside their old colonial home.

In 1959 Marqués founded the publishing house Club del Libro (Book Club), which published his novel *La víspera del hombre* (1959; The dawn of man). *La víspera del hombre* is the coming-of-age story of a young laborer in a coffee plantation who turns out to be the landowner's son. This is a common theme in Latin American literature: the discovery of a powerful or landowning father as the child of a single mother, mistress, or slave. In 1959 Marqués also edited the anthology *Cuentos puertorriqueños de hoy* (Puerto Rican short stories of today), which established the aesthetic principles of Puerto Rican writers from the generation of the 1940s.

As an essayist, Marqués's masterpiece is "El puertorriqueño dócil" (1960; "The Docile Puerto Rican"), a controversial analysis of the negative effects that the colonial system has had on the psychology of Puerto Rican men. According to Marqués, instead of fighting for their ideals Puerto Ricans have an inherent docility that impedes their progress and leads them to failure or death. Marqués's work can be read within the context of PUERTO RICAN LITERATURE as well as SPANISH-AMERICAN CARIBBEAN LITERATURE.

Bibliography

Marqués, René. *The Docile Puerto Rican: A Collection of Essays.* Philadelphia: Temple University Press, 1976.

———. *The Oxcart/La carreta.* Translated by Charles Pilditch. New York: Charles Scribner's Sons, 1983.

———. *La víspera del hombre.* Río Piedras, P.R.: Editorial Cultural, 2000.

Reynolds, Bonnie M. *Space, Time and Crisis: The Theatre of René Marqués.* York, S.C.: Spanish Literature Pub. Co., 1988.

Roberto Carlos Ortiz

Martí, José (1853–1895) *(essayist, poet, revolutionary)*

José Martí was born on January 28, 1853, in Cuba. His published work consists of more than 70 volumes, including three volumes of poetry. He lived much of his life in exile, studying and working in Europe, the United States, and throughout Latin America, and in all those places he spoke out for the rights of the disenfranchised and the poor. He died on May 19, 1895, in Dos Ríos, Cuba, while fighting for Cuba's independence from Spain.

Martí's parents emigrated from Spain to Cuba. His father, Mariano Martí y Navarro, was a soldier and policeman. His mother was Leonor Pérez y Cabera, and today, the street on which Martí was born bears her name. Martí was educated first in the local public school and later at the private Colegio de San Pablo, where its director, Rafael María de Mendive, fostered in his students a respect for democracy, an appreciation of workers rights, and a passion for Cuban freedom. He led by example, and the Spanish authorities imprisoned and later sentenced Mendive to exile. The young Martí visited his teacher in prison. That visit made an indelible impression on the young man, so much so that Martí also began to advocate Cuban independence. He too was imprisoned, forced into a labor camp, and, through the intervention of his father's friends, granted exile to Spain. He lived and studied in Spain for just four years but in that time earned a doctorate in philosophy and humanities. For the next two years Martí worked as a journalist in Mexico and as a college professor in Guatemala, and in 1878 he returned to Cuba, thinking to make a life there with his wife and son. After only a year, however, Martí once again faced deportation. After a brief time in Spain he immigrated to Venezuela, where he worked as a professor and where his agitation for democratic reforms forced his immigration to the United States. Taking up residence in New York City, he published there the famous essay "Nuestra América," or "Our America," in 1891. Throughout his career he earned a small income as a journalist and as publisher of a children's magazine; he also served as consul for Argentina and Uruguay. He was living in the United States when Cuba's revolution broke out in February 1895. Martí arrived in Cuba in April and insisted on being on the front lines of the battle; he died in an ambush, fighting for Cuba's freedom.

Martí's prose works speak eloquently to his commitment to an end not only of Spanish colonialism in Cuba but of all forms of expansionism. He was not, however, in favor of a complete rejection of the cultural inheritance from Europe. He recognized that Cuba was a product of Spanish influence, but he also saw that Cuba owed much of its cultural heritage to Africa and to the Taino people who inhabited the island before Christopher Columbus's arrival. He noted that Cuban identity incorporated these influences in a unique way and that the other island nations of the Caribbean and regions of Central and South America each transformed their influences to produce a multiplicity of cultures. This, indeed, is one of tenets of "Our America." He also writes of the necessary end to the subjugation of the poor and of racism against people of indigenous and African heritages. Recognizing U.S. dominance in the Western Hemisphere, he advocated an appreciation of Latin American ways and a rejection of foreign habits and beliefs if those beliefs clashed with what is "American" (Latin American). He wrote of worker's rights, speaking with admiration of some of Karl Marx's ideas, but it would be incorrect to ascribe the label "socialist" to Martí. He was very much in favor of individual and family ownership of the wealth they produced but envisioned a society of mutual responsibility and partnership, in which the community worked together to protect the rights of its members against racism and economic exploitation.

Martí's poetry is collected in three volumes, but its significance for Spanish-language literature is immeasurable, standing at a crossroads in European literature between romanticism and modernism. Martí introduced new rhythms in verse and used metaphors in ways that represent a departure from the formulaic rules of Spanish romantic literature. Martí published his first poem, "Abdalá," when he was 15; it celebrates the struggle for Cuban independence. However, he confessed that his real poetic career began with the work contained in *Ismaelillo* (1882). The volume's 15 poems are, on the surface, very much in the tradition of classical Spanish writers and describe emotional longing, in the tradition of Spanish romanticism. These poems convey the yearning for reunion with his son and the desire to see Cuba liberated.

Martí's second volume of verse, *Versos libres* (Free verses), was published posthumously but contains some of the poet's most skilled work. It ranges widely in subject from personal longing and depression to exile and longing for the freedom of oppressed peoples. Correspondingly, the poetry's form is free verse combined with the traditional form of the 11-syllable line, symbolizing the yearning and struggle for freedom but also the prison of oppression. *Versos sencillos* (1891; Simple verses) represents Martí's final complete volume of poetry, combining romantic and revolutionary themes and forms. Its subjects focus on Martí's personal inheritance, his parents, and his son. In his revolutionary use of language Martí stands with the Nicaraguan poet Rubén Darío at the vanguard of the modernist movement. Martí has been a major influence in SPANISH-AMERICAN CARIBBEAN LITERATURE and CUBAN-AMERICAN LITERATURE, as well as a political inspiration to leaders such as FIDEL CASTRO.

Bibliography

Belnap, Jeffrey Grant, and Raul Fernandez. *José Martí's "Our America": From National to Hemispheric Studies.* Durham, N.C.: Duke University Press, 1998.

Guerra, Lillian. *The Myth of José Martí: Conflicting Nationalisms in Early Twentieth-Century Cuba.* Chapel Hill: University of North Carolina Press, 2005.

Kirk, John. *José Martí: Mentor of the Cuban Nation.* Tampa: University Presses of Florida, 1983.

Martí, José. *Inside the Monster: Writings on the United States and American Imperialism.* Translated by Philip Sheldon Foner. New York: Monthly Review Press, 1975.

———. *José Martí: Major Poems, a Bilingual Tradition.* Translated by Elinor Randall and Philip Sheldon Foner. New York: Holmes & Meier, 1982.

———. *On Art and Literature: Critical Writings.* Translated by Philip Sheldon Foner. New York: Monthly Review Press, 1982.

———. *Our America: Writings on the Latin American Struggle for Independence.* Translated by Philip Sheldon Foner. New York: Monthly Review Press, 1977.

Rotker, Susana. *The American Chronicles of José Martí: Journalism and Modernity in Spanish America.* Hanover, N.H.: University Presses of New England, 2000.

West, Alan. *José Martí: Man of Poetry/Soldier of Freedom.* Brookfield, Conn.: Millbrook Press, 1994.

Bernard McKenna

Martín and Meditations on the South Valley　Jimmy Santiago Baca　(1986)

Jimmy Santiago Baca was born in Santa Fe, New Mexico, on January 5, 1952. At various times throughout his childhood and young adulthood Baca lived with his grandmother, in orphanages, and on the streets. In *Martín and Meditations on the South Valley*, Baca emphasizes the importance of the mother figure and the protagonist's Mexican-American heritage. Martín avows to his family: "I promised you and all living things / I would never abandon you" (49). In addition to his experience in orphanages and on the streets, Baca was shaped as a young adult by his time in prison. While incarcerated, Baca learned to read and write and developed a passion for expressive writing; it was in prison where first he honed his poetry skills. It is with this knowledge that one begins to see connections between Baca and his semiautobiographical persona/narrator in *Martín* (part 1) and *Meditations on the South Valley* (part 2).

Consisting of two long narrative poems, *Martín & Meditations on the South Valley* was published in 1986 and won the 1988 Before Columbus Foundation American Book Award. In *Martín* the central character-narrator (Martín) sets out on a mission of self-discovery, one that necessarily involves a search to uncover his heritage and his history. In the beginning Martín lives with his grandmother but soon moves to an orphanage. During his time in the orphanage he splits visits with affluent relatives (the Chávezes) and with relatives in rural Albuquerque (the Luceros). During the time spent with his different relatives Martín recognizes class differences and becomes aware of racial and ethnic tensions in the Southwest. Mostly, though, Baca focuses on the individual experiences of young Martín and his efforts to break the cycle of tragedy in his family.

When Martín leaves his barrio in Albuquerque ("Burque") and begins roaming around cities to the west and north, he experiences a disconnect from *la gente* (the people), both spiritually and psychically:

> Everything hoped for in my life
> was a rock closed road,
> where I had left my identity,
> and my family (9).

Martín's journey from the barrio to the cities and back is one fraught with anxiety, depression, confusion, and ultimately happiness. What we also encounter are the various landscapes of the narrator's journey—the mesas, *los llanos* (the plains), the cityscapes, and the barrios. Baca makes it clear that understanding one's heritage is to understand one's ancestors and native land, which in this case is AZTLÁN.

The ancient grounds of Aztlán work both literally and metaphorically in Baca's poetry. Literally, Aztlán's earth (*la tierra*) is the home of New Mexico's people and therefore the source of sustenance and shelter; metaphorically, Aztlán symbolizes the past as well as a potential future in its connection to Baca's heritage and identity. Baca is interested in Aztlán as the legend of an ancient and beloved land of the Native Americans and Mexicans; it represents a time before the European conquest and is a space that can be re-imagined if not reclaimed. Baca's modern imagining of Aztlán represents a borderland, where identity and national allegiance are vexed ideas. Baca imagines Aztlán as a holy and ancient space that has unified the peoples of New Mexico and the Southwest in general.

The second part of the book, *Meditations on the South Valley*, can stand on its own, but it is probably more beneficial to the reader to see it as a sequel to *Martín*. In *Meditations* the more predominant first-person narration of *Martín* gives way to an omniscient third person (though a narrator does speak often in first and second person). The purpose of this shift is to allow the reader a glimpse of the various personalities that make up the South Valley barrio. Readers of the poems can appreciate an intimacy with and affinity for the people of the South Valley, their struggles and loves, sense of home and safety. For Baca the South Valley figures as a place of communion and the genesis of his identity.

Baca makes multiple allusions to borderlands, to the sharp divides of class and race separating the barrios from areas like the Heights. In poem 16 Baca's narrator addresses his father, speaking about the difficulties the father faced during his lifetime in regard to race; in poem 6 a Heights resident identifies the narrator as a "gardener" because of the old truck he drives, upon which the narrator then reflects, "Funny how in the Valley / an old truck symbolizes prestige / and in the Heights poverty" (59). In poem 2 Baca shows us the narrator's sense of alienation and distaste in the face of the affluent Heights residents. The world of well-coiffed poodles and shiny cars the narrator sees in the Heights is the catalyst for his appreciation of the South Valley. The narrator finds comfort in what is familiar and begins to understand the importance of the barrio and the role it has played in the formation of his identity.

Above all, the connection the narrator has with the earth and the sense of rebirth he experiences when rebuilding his house underscore the overall theme of reconstruction. Throughout *Martín* and continued in *Meditations on the South Valley* is the idea that one must put together the pieces of one's past and identity. The metaphor of building (and rebuilding) both the house and the poems shows the reader that there is an important architecture involved in making meaning—that is, to fully understand one's self, one must construct identity based on the materials of the past and present. For its themes and images Baca's work can be read within the context of CHICANO LITERATURE and BORDER LITERATURE.

Bibliography

Baca, Jimmy Santiago. *Black Mesa Poems*. New York: New Directions Publishing, 1989.

———. *C-train (Dream Boy's Story) and Thirteen Mexicans: Poems.* New York: Grove Press, 2002.

———. *Healing Earthquakes: Poems.* New York: Grove Press, 2001.

———. *Martín and Meditations on the South Valley.* New York: New Directions Publishing, 1986.

———. *A Place to Stand: The Making of a Poet.* New York: Grove Press, 2001.

———. *Working in the Dark: Reflections of a Poet of the Barrio.* Santa Fe, N.Mex.: Red Crane Books, 1992.

Cochran, Stuart. "The Ethnic Implications of Stories, Spirits, and the Land in Native American Pueblo and Aztlán Writing." *MELUS* 20, no. 2 (1995): 69–91.

Gish, Robert Franklin. *Beyond Bounds: Cross-Cultural Essays on Anglo, American Indian and Chicano Literature.* Albuquerque: University of New Mexico Press, 1996.

Bryan Peters

Martínez, Demetria (1960–) (essayist, novelist)

Demetria Martínez was born in Albuquerque, New Mexico, in 1960, the daughter of Dolores Martínez, a schoolteacher, and Ted Martínez, an educator and the first Chicano to be elected to the Albuquerque School Board. Given her upbringing and her parents' work, Martínez describes her family as very political, and she is likewise a politically conscious writer. Much of Martínez's work centers on creating an identity as a Chicana woman in the Southwest; as a middle-class woman she consciously moves to create kinship between herself and the many immigrant, working-class, and poor Latinas of her community.

Martínez earned a B.A. from Princeton University's Woodrow Wilson School of Public and International Affairs, and she teaches at the annual June writing workshop at the William Joiner Center for the Study of War and Social Consequences at the University of Massachusetts. In New Mexico she is active with Enlace Comunitario, an immigrants' rights group. Her most recent book of autobiographical essays, *Confessions*

of a *Berlitz-Tape Chicana* (2005), won the 2006 International Latino Book Award in the category of Best Biography. Her other publications include the novel, *MOTHER TONGUE* (1994), which won a Western States Book Award for Fiction, and two books of poetry, *Breathing Between the Lines* (1997) and *The Devil's Workshop* (2002). She coauthored, with ALICIA GASPAR DE ALBA and Maria Herrera-Sobek, a book of poetry entitled *Three Times a Woman* (1989). Martínez also publishes short stories and writes a column for the *National Catholic Reporter,* an independent progressive newsweekly.

Martínez's novel and first widely available work, *Mother Tongue,* is based in part on Martínez's 1988 trial for conspiracy against the U.S. government in connection with transporting Salvadoran refugees into the country, a charge that, with others, carried a 25-year prison sentence. Martínez maintained she was covering the movement as a reporter and that therefore the First Amendment protected her from prosecution. She was found not guilty after a publicly contentious trial.

Mother Tongue tells the story of Mary, a young woman involved with the sanctuary movement who meets Jose Luis, a political refugee she eventually shelters. She becomes pregnant by Jose Luis and will give birth not to just a son but to a new political consciousness. Her political coming of age is closely identified with Jose Luis's political activities and his command of the "mother tongue," Spanish. Throughout the novel Mary seeks to reclaim her language and culture through love and activism.

Martínez's two books of poetry, *Breathing Between the Lines* and *The Devil's Workshop,* are both composed in the style of the personal lyric, but like much contemporary poetry written by members of ethnically centered communities, the poems often interrogate cultural and social issues, such as racism, poverty, identity, and abuse. Included with the intimately conversational poems in *Breathing Between the Lines* is an afterword that traces the poet's identity formation. Meanwhile, *The Devil's Workshop* interweaves images of disaster and resistance with those of personal and communal relationships; in her writing Martínez borrows from the practice of healing called *curanderismo,* a kind of folk medicine.

In her collection of autobiographical essays, *Confessions of a Berlitz-Tape Chicana,* Martínez continues to explore issues of identity and culture. In the titular essay Martínez focuses on Latino/as who, like her, did not grow up speaking Spanish. While in recognizing the loss of her Spanish language, the various indigenous languages of Latin America are the "mother tongues." Ultimately Martínez imagines a future in which Chicanos enjoy a cultural and linguistic fluency, moving between English and Spanish.

In essays ranging in topic from the war in Iraq to the "beauty trap" and gun ownership, Martínez raises questions about violence, spirituality, and the construction of difference. She suggests that the ideological barriers we erect prevent us from enjoying humanity. Other important writings include her column in the *National Catholic Reporter,* where she explores issues ranging from war to abortion in Latin American countries. In her 2004 essay published in the *Progressive,* entitled "Divided World," Martínez reveals her battle with bipolar disorder; true to her activist beliefs, however, Martínez uses the opportunity not to elicit sympathy for herself but to decry the state of medical care in the United States, specifically in its disenfranchisement of the working class and poor. Her work can be read within the context of CHICANO LITERATURE as well as the general context of Latino literature.

Bibliography

Demetria Martínez Web site. Available online. URL: "Home Page." 1 May 2006. http://www.demetria-martinez.com.

Dick, Bruce Allen. *A Poet's Truth: Conversations with Latino/Latina Poets.* Tucson: University of Arizona Press, 2003.

Ikas, Karin Rosa. *Chicana Ways: Conversations with Ten Chicana Writers.* Reno: University of Nevada Press, 2002.

Iverson, Kristen. "Poetry, Politics, and the Drama of the Unseen: An Interview with Demetria Mar-

tínez." *Bloomsbury Review* 18, no. 2 (March–April 1988): 11–12.

Manolis, Argie J. "The Writer As Witness: An Interview with Demetria Martínez." *Hayden's Ferry Review* 24 (1999): 37–51.

Martínez, Demetria. *Breathing Between the Lines.* Tucson: University of Arizona Press, 1997.

———. *Confessions of a Berlitz-Tape Chicana.* Norman: University Oklahoma Press, 2005.

———. *The Devil's Workshop.* Tucson: University of Arizona Press, 2002.

———. *Mother Tongue.* New York: Ballantine, 1996.

Jeanetta Calhoun Mish

Massacre of the Dreamers: Essays on Xicanisma Ana Castillo (1994)

ANA CASTILLO published *Massacre of the Dreamers: Essays on Xicanisma* in 1994 after writing her dissertation. The 10 essays emerged from Castillo's research for her Ph.D., which she completed in American studies at the University of Bremen, in Germany. Academic and interdisciplinary in nature, the essays include perspectives from the social sciences and cultural criticism; the writing is also autobiographical and creative, thereby blurring the boundaries between nonfiction and fiction.

Castillo states that her purpose in publishing these essays is to generate further intellectual discussion" (ix). Throughout the collection Castillo employs the terms *Xicanisma* and *Xicanista,* which are pronounced "Chicanisma" and "Chicanista." The use of the *x* from Nahuatl (the language of the Aztec) makes a political statement regarding her indigenous heritage (Milligan 29). Castillo observes that the "academic community" has taken the term *Chicana feminism* and converted it into something abstract, dull, and powerless. Castillo introduces the term *Xicanisma* to refer to a Mexican-American and even more specifically Chicana feminism. For the author Xicanisma can be taken out of the classroom and set into action at work, home, and society at large (11). The Xicanista, then, is anyone who adheres to and practices the ideology of Xicanisma. Castillo's conceptualization of Xicanisma is rooted in her understanding of the educator Paulo Freire's concept of *conscientización* (consciousness raising). *Conscientización* brings about empowerment through an understanding of social conditions, in this case those related to Mexican-American experiences. Through these essays Castillo attempts to raise the consciousness of Chicanas regarding their past and present, thereby motivating them toward action.

These 10 essays examine the interplay between binaries: American and Mexican, woman and man, spirituality and religion, mother and father, feminism and the Chicano movement. Castillo considers the history of the terms and argues that they are not in opposition but rather parts of a whole. In chapter 1, "A Countryless Woman: The Early Feminista," Castillo analyzes the relationship between Chicanas and white women. While white women can often declare themselves citizens of the world, the Chicana is usually confronted with the choice of assimilating into dominant culture, settling for a second-class status, or even becoming "invisible." Furthermore, while white feminists have often viewed themselves as separate from men, Xicanistas look at gender as a continuum.

In chapter 5, "In the Beginning There Was Eva," Castillo looks to indigenous beliefs of Mexico for insight. She seeks to find understanding of both the masculine and the feminine in her study of creative power. While Western civilization acknowledged the female in creation up until roughly the 11th century, this belief was supplanted by the split gender roles of the Judeo-Christian tradition. For Castillo the Aztec earth goddess Coatlicue provides an example of non-binary thinking because she represents both life and death.

The essay "Brujas and Curanderas: A Lived Spirituality" examines the relationship of Chicanas to the Catholic Church and indigenous practices. White feminists have challenged Christianity as sexist in its practice and have resurrected white goddesses to replace Jesus as a male god. Chicanas, on the other hand, look to the *india* (the Indian woman) for guidance, especially the CURANDERA

(healer). Castillo suggests that the remedies of the *curandera* are akin to the treatments of gynecologists and psychologists (153).

As a writer, Castillo also turns her critical eye to CHICANO LITERATURE in "Un Tapiz: The Poetics of *Conscientización*." Every literature has a tradition from which it draws and upon which it builds. The problem for Chicana writers has been that they have been compared to Western literary traditions. Chicana authors either have to conform to European or U.S. literary standards or else risk invisibility or denigration. Chicana writers, for Castillo, must draw upon their own traditions and cultural elements to make them their own. But, even within Mexican-American culture many feminine figures are seen in a negative light; therefore, the Chicana writer must reinterpret the meaning of these figures for themselves. For example, the figure of La MALINCHE has traditionally been interpreted as a traitor of indigenous Mexicans because she interpreted for Hernán Cortés and then became his mistress. As Castillo points out, Chicana writers have reinterpreted Malinche as, all at once, everything "[from] slave victim, heroine, and mother of the mestizo race to genius linguist and military strategist" (166). The reason that Malinche is often maligned is that she betrayed Mexican Indians by aligning herself with the Spanish in the early 1500s.

Ultimately Castillo wants to celebrate the feminine. Historically, she argues, both patriarchal society and mainstream feminism have devalued the female characteristics of "patience, perseverance, industriousness, loyalty to one's clan, and commitment to our children" (40). Xicanisma rejects nationalistic politics as well as binary divisions; instead Xicanisma requires the recovery and reintegration of the whole self, for women and for men. *Massacre of the Dreamers* stands firmly alongside Castillo's other works, such as *The* MIXQUIAHUALA LETTERS (1986), SAPOGONIA (1990), and SO FAR FROM GOD (1993). Castillo also edited the 1996 volume GODDESS OF THE AMERICAS/LA DIOSA DE LAS AMÉRICAS: WRITINGS ON THE VIRGIN OF GUADALUPE.

Bibliography

Castillo, Ana. *Massacre of the Dreamers: Essays on Xicanisma.* New York: Plume, 1995.

Gann, Randall L. Book review of *Massacre of the Dreamers. Educational Studies* 34, no. 2 (2003): 257–261.

Milligan, Bryce. "An Interview with Ana Castillo." *South Central Review* 16, no. 1 (Spring 1999): 19–29.

Moraga, Cherríe, and Gloria Anzaldúa, eds. *This Bridge Called My Back: Writings by Radical Women of Color.* Watertown, Mass.: Persephone Press, 1981.

Saeta, Elsa. "A *MELUS* Interview: Ana Castillo." *MELUS: The Journal of the Society for the Study of Multi-Ethnic Literature of the United States* 22, no. 3 (Fall 1997): 133–150.

Ritch Calvin

Meaning of Consuelo, The Judith Ortiz Cofer (2003)

JUDITH ORTIZ COFER expresses a hard-won love for her native Puerto Rico in the coming-of-age novel *The Meaning of Consuelo.* The semiautobiographical novel was published in 2003 and was selected for the Américas Award for Children's and Young Adult Literature. Born in Hormigueros, a town on the western end of Puerto Rico, Cofer grew up on the island, as well as in Paterson, New Jersey, depending on her father's naval schedule. The theme of identity, both Puerto Rican and American, is one that advances the narrative. Cofer recalls in many of her works that as a child, she never fit in, whether she was living on the island or on the mainland. The author's feelings of being an outsider allow her to represent her characters with depth and compassion. These characters include Consuelo; her father; her sister, Milagros (Mili); Abuelo, her grandfather; Isadora, her grandmother; her cousin Patricio; and Wilhelm, the teen to whom Consuelo loses her virginity.

In terms of setting the *autopista* (highway) that cuts through the island becomes a metaphor for *The Meaning of Consuelo.* The novel is organized into binaries that both complicate and simplify issues of identity. Cofer contrasts, for example, *gente decente* (decent people) with *la fulana* (outsiders). The novel is about the search for identity of Puerto Ricans in general and of Consuelo in particular. As such, Cofer tackles the generational tug of war between modernity and tradition.

In the 1950s Operation Bootstrap, a program of economic reform, was launched in Puerto Rico. Cofer explores through her characters the impact of U.S. industrialization on the island and the emergence of American merchandise in the Puerto Rican home. Consuelo's father believes in American technology; but Abuelo appreciates precolonial Puerto Rico, its Taino (Indian) history and oral traditions. Abuelo believes Puerto Rico is losing its cultural identity, while Consuelo's father looks to U.S. technology to save the islanders, to bring them up to a 20th-century standard of living. Consuelo's father constantly brings home new gadgets for his wife, such as unbreakable melamine dishes and a vacuum cleaner.

In addition to modernity and tradition the novel is concerned with mental instability, deviance, and sexuality. We see this at play with Mili's schizophrenia, Patricio's homosexuality, and Consuelo's sexual encounter with Wilhelm. All of these are family *tragedias* (tragedies), the name given to any cross that a family must bear; mental illness, premarital sex, and homosexuality are all things that compromise the family's status as *gente decente.*.

Consuelo is caught up in the family dramas and acts as the "comforter." As the good, studious daughter, Consuelo listens to the stories passed down from her grandmother. Indeed, as in Cofer's SILENT DANCING: A PARTIAL REMEMBRANCE OF A PUERTO RICAN CHILDHOOD (1990), long-held beliefs in *The Meaning of Consuelo* come from the family matriarch. Isadora is a strong female character, and generations later, the women in the family still base their decisions and actions on what Isadora would do in a given situation. Consuelo loves Abuelo's tales of Puerto Rico history, but the *cuentos,* the cautionary tales told by the women, oppress her.

Consuelo finally rebels against the identity imposed on her. She is weary of the role of consoler and the long-suffering martyrdom expected by family and Puerto Rican culture. Consuelo struggles to create an identity that is separate from how others define her. When her family fails to celebrate Consuelo's *quinceañera* (a birthday celebration marking a 15-year-old's entrance into womanhood), Consuelo decides to mark the event by having sex with Wilhelm, a military brat and "outsider." Consuelo's decision to have sex (a fall from grace) gives her the strength to move beyond her identity as *la niña seria*, "the serious child."

Another family *tragedia* is the burgeoning homosexuality of Patricio, Consuelo's cousin. Patricio's father relocates Patricio to New Jersey in order to remove him from the influence of such bad people as the local transvestite, Maria Serena. He does not want his son to descend to the status of outsider. One of the ironies of the novel is that family "secrets" are not really secrets, but just facts that members try to hide from public view.

While coming of age and to terms with her sexuality, Consuelo also acts as the guardian of Mili (short for Milagros, or "miracles"). When Mili becomes unreachable and diagnosed with schizophrenia, her father makes the decision to move to New Jersey. He is convinced that on the mainland Mili will benefit from superior medical care to that of the island. Thus the family is torn apart by Mili's illness. In making her way in the world Consuelo becomes a strong woman like her mother, who confronts her husband's infidelity.

While her parents fight over her father's affair with a lounge singer, Consuelo is left to care for her increasingly unstable sister. She worries about the danger that Mili faces from men. Mili's voluptuous body and psychological vulnerability invite abuse. In a particularly chilling scene Mili kills a chicken and laughs wildly while covered in blood. She sets off warnings that cannot be ignored as easily as her meanderings and bizarre chattering— her "language of birds." Mili's suicide (intentional or not) pushes Consuelo to leave Puerto Rico as her parents stay behind. Her father searches endlessly for Mili's body, which has never been recovered from the ocean; her mother retreats into the arms of the family. Knowing that caring for Mili is

no longer her obligation, Consuelo is free to leave and forge her own identity on the mainland. The rite of passage is, as to be expected, both painful and liberating.

Like other Latino authors, Cofer is concerned with language choices, both Spanish (the language of the home) and English (the language of Americans, civic life, and the military). Ultimately, English for Consuelo becomes a powerful tool of communication and allows her to connect with her cousin Patricio when he escapes his father and moves to New York. Through her voracious reading of Patricio's encyclopedia, she becomes comfortable with English. Thus the novel is a tribute to Consuelo's sexual and linguistic freedom and her transcendence from family tragedies. For its themes and charcterizations *The Meaning of Consuelo* can be read within the context of Puerto Rican literature.

Bibliography

Cofer, Judith Ortiz. *The Meaning of Consuelo.* New York: Farrar, Straus, & Giroux, 2003.

Mujica, Barbara. "Review of *The Meaning of Consuelo.*" *Americas* 56, no. 4 (2004): 59–61.

Patricia Bostian

Medina, Rubén (1955–   ) (poet, activist, professor)

Rubén Medina was born in Mexico City in 1955. Educated in Minnesota and California, he now lives in Wisconsin. His poetic works available in English are *Amor de lejos/Fools' Love* (1986), which was a finalist for Cuba's Casa de las Américas prize for poetry, and *Nomadic Nation/Nación nómada* (2003). A professor of Spanish at the University of Wisconsin, Madison, Medina specializes in Mexican literature and Chicano literature. Medina has analyzed the work of Noble Prize recipient Octavio Paz, author of the famous essay "Mexican Masks."

From 1975 to 1977 Medina was a member of the infrarealist movement, a group of young Mexican and Chilean poets that advocated an experimental poetry focusing on details of everyday life. The infrarealists rejected the dominant currents in poetry—principally those associated with Paz—and the literary establishments in Mexico of the 1970s. Medina's works appeared in 1976 in the infrarealist collection *Pájaro de color* (Colored bird) and in an anthology of infrarrealist works published by the magazine *Plural*. In 1977 Medina and fellow poet José Peguero published the magazine *Correspondencia Infra* in Mexico City.

After moving to the United States in 1978, Medina published *Baílame este viento, Mariana* (1980; Dance for me this wind, Mariana), which won first prize at the University of California at Irvine's Chicano Literary Contest. Many of the poems in this collection are autobiographical. In "Sonecito," for example, Medina recounts childhood memories of his Mexican neighborhood, the relationship with his grandparents, and their connection to national events in Mexico. Likewise, in "Danzón" the poet remembers the pain of "Mother" when "Father" would leave to be with other women. Medina pays homage to the hard work and humanity of lower wage earners in "Day Off" and "Clasificados." And, in "Volver a Casa" he traces the odyssey of a Marxist idealist who travels the globe to "change the world" and ultimately returns home and organizes football teams and cockfights.

During his years in graduate school at the University of Minnesota in the 1980s, Medina served as an editor of *Visiones de la Raza*. While completing his Ph.D. in literature at the University of California, San Diego, he wrote poetry and participated in a variety of community and labor organizations. He now publishes the magazine *Zona de carga*.

Portions of Medina's second collection of poetry, *Amor de lejos/Fools' Love*, were written during the time of his National Endowment for the Arts writer's fellowship (1981–82). Originally written in Spanish, versions of several poems were printed in a number of publications including the Puerto Rican and Mexican-American journal *Revistsa Chicano-Riqueña*. Some of *Amor de lejos*'s poems had been previously published in *Baílame este viento, Mariana* and have also appeared in a variety of anthologies of Latino literature.

Amor de lejos is a bilingual work that focuses on Mexico and the United States; the poems emerge from the pain of leaving one's homeland, family, and friends and from searching for community in a new land. "Franklin Avenue" celebrates the sense of community created in dilapidated apartments in Minneapolis, Minnesota, by those who live in the same poverty-stricken circumstances. In "Priam" the poet addresses his relationship with his father by affirming his identity as a son and by inverting traditional father-son roles. The title poem of this collection—which discusses the tensions of tolerance, difference, and immigration in the United States—exemplifies Medina's clever use of language by quoting the Mexican saying *Amor de lejos, amor de pendejos* (Love from a distance, fool's love).

Nomadic Nation/Nación nómada addresses how Mexican communities living in the United States inhabit a kind of "third country" that combines aspects of both Mexican and U.S. life. *Nomadic Nation* is organized into two sections, "Arriving" and "Leaving," and includes poems written in English, Spanish, and SPANGLISH. Establishing the theme of movement in "Puntos Cardinals," Medina sets aside traditional directions to define his personal compass. The nomadic subject and the use of CODE SWITCHING also appear in "Mapa del día":

The poet also uses popular culture with humor and irony as evidenced by the poem "Pay Per View." For Medina the intersections of Mexican and U.S. cultures create a space that blurs political borders. In this regard Medina's work has much in common with GUILLERMO GÓMEZ-PEÑA's *The NEW WORLD BORDER: PROPHECIES, POEMS AND LOQUERAS FOR THE END OF THE CENTURY* (1996).

Bibliography

Gibbons, Reginald, ed. *New Writing from Mexico, a Tri-Quarterly Collection of Newly Translated Prose and Poetry.* Evanston, Ill.: Northwestern University Press, 1992.

Heide, Rick, ed. *Under the Fifth Sun: Latino Literature from California.* Berkeley, Calif.: Heyday Books, 2002.

Medina, Rubén. *Amor de lejos/Fool's Love.* Translated by Jennifer Sternbach and Robert Jones. Houston, Tex.: Arte Público Press, 1986.

———. *Nomadic Nation/Nación nómada.* Madison: University of Wisconsin, 2003.

Analisa DeGrave

Mercado, Nancy (1959–) *(poet, dramatist, editor)*

Nancy Mercado was born and raised in Atlantic City, New Jersey. She majored in art history and Puerto Rican studies at Rutgers, then moved to New York City to earn an M.A. at New York University in liberal studies, with a focus on script writing and cinema studies. Mercado completed her Ph.D. in English at the State University of New York at Binghamton, with a concentration in creative writing. Her love for New York City is a theme throughout her work and is the subject of her manuscript *Rooms for the Living: New York Poems.* Because of shared urban experiences and themes, Mercado identifies with Nuyorican authors such as MIGUEL ALGARÍN and Pedro Pietri. As a spoken word artist, she has performed at the NUYORICAN POETS CAFE, which was founded by Algarín, and has been a featured artist on television and radio. Her poetry readings have taken her from the Northeast to the West Coast, as well as to Germany, France, and Canada.

Like many contributors of PUERTO RICAN LITERATURE, Mercado gathers family anecdotes and experiences about life in Puerto Rico and incorporates them into her poetry. Mercado has mixed feelings about the commonwealth status of the island, which is neither a state nor a country. The turn of the 19th to the 20th century marked Puerto Rico's transformation from a Spanish colony to a U.S. territory. Luis Muñoz Marín, the governor of Puerto Rico in the 1950s and early 1960s, invited U.S. development, which changed the traditional ways of life on the island. The subjects of Mercado's poetry include aspects of her grandmothers' lives in Puerto Rico, the travails of sugarcane workers there, and the transition between traditional habits and more modern ways

of being. Her volume *It Concerns the Madness* (2000) captures Mercado's poetic vision, a vision that moves back and forth from the island to the Northeast. Some poems in the collection deal blatantly with political themes and world events in such places as Somalia, Kosovo, and Iraq. It is in the politics of lived experience that Mercado truly shines.

Mercado's work has been widely anthologized, appearing in such groundbreaking collections as *From Totems to Hip-Hop: A Multicultural Anthology of Poetry across the Americas, Poetry after 9/11: An Anthology of New York Poets, Role Call: A Generational Anthology of Social and Political Black Literature and Art, Identity Lessons: Contemporary Writing about Learning to Be American,* and *Aloud: Voices from the Nuyorican Poets Cafe.* Her work also appears regularly in magazines and journals such as *Brownstone, Centro Journal, City Magazine, Gallatin Review,* and *Gare Maritime.* For 12 years Mercado worked as an editor and then editor-in-chief of *Long Shot Magazine.*

Mercado's work in the theater is varied, ranging from writing plays for children, producing plays for young audiences, and directing theater festivals. During her tenure as founding director of the Lola Rodríguez de Tío Cultural Institute in New Jersey, she wrote, produced, or directed several plays. These include *Palm Trees in the Snow, Chillin', Forever Earth, Planet Earth,* and *Alicia in Projectland* (coauthored with Pietri). She also staged *Away,* a piece about AIDS commissioned by the Centers for Disease Control and produced in the Northeast and Puerto Rico.

Mercado also works tirelessly to promote other artists and their work. She has organized the Latina Writers Coffeehouse series for the Brooklyn Public Library and the Word Power Literary series for the New Jersey Performing Arts Center. She recently edited the youth anthology *If the World Was Mine* for the New Jersey Performing Arts Center. In addition, Mercado does programming for gallery openings and other cultural events throughout New York's five boroughs. Mercado is currently a professor at Boricua College, specializing in Puerto Rican and Nuyorican literature.

Bibliography

Algarín, Miguel, and Bob Holman, eds. *Aloud: Voices from the Nuyorican Poets Cafe.* New York: Henry Holt, 1994.

Mercado, Nancy. *It Concerns the Madness.* Hoboken, N.J.: Long Shot Press, 2000.

Mercado, Nancy, ed. *Tripping over the Lunch Lady and Other School Stories.* New York: Dial Books, 2004.

Skiff, Paul. "The Balance of Understanding." September 23, 2001. Available online. URL: http://www.tribes.org/reviews/itconcerns.html. Downloaded December 18, 2007.

Marilyn Kiss

mestizaje/mestizo

In the Tlatelolco neighborhood of Mexico City is the Plaza de las Tres Culturas (Plaza of the Three Cultures). In it, the ruins of Aztec temples coexist with a colonial Catholic church and a massive housing project from the 1960s. This combination of architectural styles and social histories epitomizes the complexity of the notion of *mestizaje* (mixing of bloodlines). The Plaza de las Tres Culturas reveals the masonry of pre-Columbian culture, the religious iconography of Spanish imperial rule, and the emergence of a mixed-race, "mestizo," independent Mexico.

Mestizaje, the Spanish word referring to the mixing of "bloods" or "races," reveals the often forced relations between Spanish men and Indian or African women. A person of Spanish and Indian blood is called a mestizo (man) or mestiza (woman). But, the terms also signify on a broader level the encounter of peoples from Europe, America, Africa, and Asia, an encounter marked by oppression, resistance, destruction, and creation.

Mestizaje is associated with the complex process of social stratification in Latin America since the colonial period, and its consequences have remained well into the present. Colonial powers attempted to regulate the mixing of "races" through a policy based on social distinctions imported from Europe; these distinctions were fundamental in justifying and enforcing rule over exploited peoples. In short, the lighter the skin, the more accepted the person was in an ethnically diverse society. The 18th-century Mexican caste paintings illustrate vividly the social hierarchies in the New World. In a series of portraits, the results of race mixing are represented on a continuum that approaches or is distanced from "whiteness." The paintings illustrate a taxonomy that included classifications such as the "Spaniard and Indian produced a Mestizo," "Spaniard and Mestiza, Castiza," "Spaniard and Castiza, Spaniard," and "Black and Spaniard, Mulatto."

The 19th century marked a turning point in race relations in Latin America, especially as this was the time that most countries became independent from Spanish colonial rule. Authors such as Cuban revolutionary JOSÉ MARTÍ celebrated racial mixing as the emblem of Latin American identity. In postrevolutionary Mexico (early 20th century), philosopher José Vasconcelos (1882–1959) wrote *The Cosmic Race* (1925). *The Cosmic Race* imagines how the mixing of races and assimilation of indigenous and African descendants would yield a new historical force: a superior culture/"race" in Latin America. In considering the term *mestizaje* it is also important to mention the work of Cuban ethnologist Fernando Ortiz (1881–1969), who developed the concept of "transculturation." Transculturation explains the result of culture clashes generated by colonial encounters. This new concept moved the discussion from the realm of the biological to the realm of the cultural, while still responding to the same forces present in *mestizaje*.

More recently authors have developed a critical approach to colonial history that emphasizes the elements of violence already acknowledged by Ortiz in the 1940s. One key issue within this discussion is whether assimilation is a form of cultural violence. In this case assimilation is viewed as a tool for the eventual absorption of cultural and ethnic differences and the eventual "whitening" of those who are considered inferior by Eurocentric standards.

The experience and the concept of *mestizaje* has had a different development in the context of Latin America and the United States. In Latin America race mixing led to system of stratification with varied shades of color that made classifications difficult; one adage in Latin America is that money, not skin color, makes one white. In Latin America race mixing has been generally embraced within the nation-building project as in the national romances analyzed by Doris Sommer.

In the United States, meanwhile, especially in the South, the "one drop of blood" rule suggested that a mixed-race or black identity was undesirable, although in cities such as New Orleans even this rule was repeatedly tested and sometimes ignored if beauty or social connections ruled the day. Black/white categorizations have lost their explanatory power with the increasing number of Asians and Latinos in the United States. Not surprisingly then, many Latino writers have taken the idea of race mixing to describe the identities born by the experience of crossing back and forth the U.S.-Mexico border. Chicana writer and activist Gloria Anzaldúa advanced a radical revision of the mestiza in Borderlands/La frontera: The New Mestiza (1987). She introduced U.S. audiences to the term mestizaje, a heterogeneous identity borne of linguistic and ethnic mixing. Anzaldúa advanced new ways to conceptualize the world, writing that

> Living on borders and in margins, keeping intact one's shifting and multiple identity and integrity, is like trying to swim in a new element, an "alien" element. There is an exhilaration in being a participant in the further evolution of humankind, in being "worked" on. I have the sense that certain "faculties"—not just in me but in every border resident, colored or non-colored—and dormant areas of consciousness are being activated, awakened (iii).

The notion of mestizaje is thus varied and has been rewritten across history. While the colonial society sought to control indigenous and African populations according to the social dynamics of European rule, 19th- and 20th-century intellectuals conceptualized an ethnically diverse population that was to be integrated into new national projects. In the context of a globalized world, where national boundaries and identities are seen

as fluid, the notion of mestizaje has been displaced by such concepts as "heterogeneity" and "hybridity." Nevertheless, mestizaje directs the plots and characterizations of Chicano literature and Latino literature more broadly.

Bibliography

Anzaldúa, Gloria. Borderlands/La frontera: The New Mestiza. San Francisco, Calif.: Aunt Lute Books, 1987.

Duno-Gottberg, Luis. Solventar las diferencias: La ideología del mestizaje en Cuba. Frankfurt, Germany, and Madrid: Vervuert/Iberoamericana, 2003.

Kaup, Monika, and Debra J. Rosenthal, eds. Mixing Race, Mixing Culture. Austin: University of Texas Press, 2002.

Miller, Marilyn Grace. Rise and Fall of the Cosmic Race: The Cult of Mestizaje in Latin America. Austin: University of Texas Press, 2004.

Mörner, Magnus. Race Mixture in the History of Latin America. Boston: Little, Brown, 1967.

Ortiz, Fernando. Cuban Counterpoint: Tobacco and Sugar. Durham, N.C.: Duke University Press, 1995.

Wade, Peter. Race and Ethnicity in Latin America. London: Pluto Press, 1997.

Luis Duno

Mexican-American literature
See Chicano literature.

Mexican Folk Plays   Josephina Niggli   (1938)
Born in Monterrey, Mexico, Josephina Niggli was of Swiss, Alsatian, and Irish descent. Because of her experiences in Mexico and her perspective of village life there, Niggli's work, including Mexican Folk Plays and the novel Mexican Village (1945), has enriched the Latino literary tradition.

Mexican Folk Plays includes Tooth or Shave, Soldadera (Soldier woman), The Velvet Goat, Azteca, and Sunday Costs Five Pesos, all of which belong to the Mexican tradition of costumbrismo (folk literature). Niggli's plays enact the legends and customs of the Mexican people. Some of today's critics find her plays highly romanticized, while other readers praise Niggli for the realism of her characters and her skill as a playwright. For scholars William Orchard and Yolanda Padilla, Niggli's work demonstrates a deep understanding of the political realties of postrevolutionary Mexico, as it presents the everyday lives of the people of Mexico in order to challenge prevailing stereotypes regarding Latin American life.

Set in the early part of the 20th century, *Mexican Folk Plays* includes two comedies, *Tooth or Shave* and *Sunday Costs Five Pesos*; one tragedy, *Azteca*; one play about the MEXICAN REVOLUTION, *Soldadera*; and, in the author's own words, "a tragedy of laughter and a comedy of tears," *The Red Velvet Goat*. All the plays feature lively dialogue as well as various sets of oppositions: male/female, rich/poor, realism/idealism, kindness/cruelty. In them Niggli offers strong women characters that usually triumph over male discourse and logic.

Both *Tooth or Shave* and *The Red Velvet Goat* tackle issues regarding the gap between rich and poor in the rigid social order of Mexican life. Through her Mexican folk plays Niggli uses the opposition between wit and brawn to shed light on the social customs and hierarchies of the village. These two plays feature such customs and rites of passage as drawing water from the plaza fountain, attending baptisms, and learning the unspoken rules of courtship. Using elements of farce and slapstick, both plays include female characters that possess the intellectual sharpness and verbal nimbleness to outsmart their husbands. Although Maria (*Tooth or Shave*) and Mariana (*Red Velvet Goat*) do indeed prevail, neither woman overtly challenges male authority and tradition, as do some of Niggli's other characters.

Soldadera, meanwhile, deals with loss and heroism and, like Niggli's other plays, investigates binary oppositions. More specifically, Niggli uses the Mexican Revolution to explore conflicts between men and women, political ideals and reality, rich and poor. The play, set in spring 1914, takes place in a pass in the Sierra Madre in the northern Mexican state of Coahuila. A group of *soldaderas* guard a male prisoner, the Rich One, as they transport ammunition to Hilario. The name Hilario is perhaps a reference to Hilario C. Salas, a revolutionary leader in the Mexican Revolution. Rather than present the women in the play as mere camp followers, and by implication prostitutes, Niggli makes them full participants in the revolution.

In *Soldadera* Niggli offers a range of female personalities rather than one-dimensional stereotypes. *Soldadera* allows for female heroism. Adelita, the youngest of the *soldaderas,* symbolizes the hopes of revolutionaries, though hers is a naive and pure view. Within a broader context, according to Alicia Arrizón, "among women in both México and the U.S., Adelita is a symbol of action and inspiration, and her name is used to mean any woman who struggles and fights for her rights"; she "became a metaphor for love in times of war" (91). The title of one of the most popular songs of the Revolution, "La Adelita" represents both male vulnerability and stoicism in the face of death.

As the play unfolds, Adelita must confront the realism of war—the loss of lives, and her own innocent view of political change and confronts her misapprehensions about war, including her relationship with her compatriots. She now sees only hardness where before she saw goodness and sweetness. Ultimately, though, it is Adelita, who embodies revolutionary ideals, who offers her life so that *las soldaderas* can succeed. *Soldaderas* and the other plays in *Mexican Folk Plays* attest to Niggli's desire to provide American audiences with a compelling rendering of Mexican people and to her belief in the power and agency of women.

Bibliography

Arrizon, Alicia. "*Soldaderas* and the staging of the Mexican Revolution." *The Drama Review* 42, no. 1 (Spring 1998): 90–112.

Herrera-Sobek, María. *Beyond Stereotypes: The Critical Analysis of Chicana Literature.* Binghamton, N.Y.: Bilingual Review Press, 1985.

Hicks, Emily D. *Border Writing: The Multidimensional Text.* Minneapolis: University of Minnesota Press, 1991.

Niggli, Josephina. *Mexican Folk Plays.* With Introduction by Frederick H. Kockh. Chapel Hill: University of North Carolina Press, 1938.

———. *Mexican Village.* Chapel Hill: University of North Carolina Press, 1945.

———. *Pointers on Playwriting.* Boston: Writer, 1945.

———. *Step Down, Elder Brother.* New York: Rinehart, 1947.

Orchard, William, and Yolanda Padilla. "Lost in Adaptation: Chicana History, the Cold War, and the Case of Josephina Niggli." *Women's Studies Quarterly* 33 (2005): 95.

Usigli, Roldolfo. Foreword to *Mexican Folk Plays,* by Josephina Niggli. New York: Arno Press, 1976.

Catherine Cucinella

"Mexican Masks" Octavio Paz (1950)

"Mexican Masks" is the second essay in OCTAVIO PAZ's landmark collection of essays on Mexican culture, *The Labyrinth of Solitude* (1950). A poet and commentator on Mexican history and culture, Paz won the Nobel Prize in literature in 1990. In *The Labyrinth of Solitude,* Paz presents a bold and controversial commentary on the origins and development of Mexican identity. Unlike historians who attempt to provide statistical evidence to support their claims, Paz approaches his analysis in *The Labyrinth* from a "poetic" perspective; that is, he blends observation with metaphor and generalizations to explain the relationship between history and Mexican identity. Paz makes clear what he sees as the essential loneliness and alienation of the Mexican. According to Paz in "The Pachuco and Other Extremes," Mexican identity speaks to a peculiar, marked sense of alienation, a solitude that is ultimately a result of a country in constant search of its origins and parentage.

"Mexican Masks" is a complex essay that requires several readings. Paz discusses the construction of Mexican masculine identity and feminine identity. All Mexicans, he contends, wear various kinds of masks for various reasons, but ultimately they do so in order to conceal their true identity. Paz first addresses masculine identity. According

to Paz, the Mexican male wears a mask in order to conceal his interior self—his psychological, emotional, and spiritual self—because the Mexican male must never appear to be weak. To expose one's interior life—to a friend, a spouse, a business partner, whoever—is to divulge one's true identity and thus to render oneself vulnerable. In this respect the Mexican male regards every aspect of life as potentially dangerous and therefore resorts to what Paz calls "hermeticism." The hermit and Mexican macho are one and the same: In constructing a mask that conceals his identity, the Mexican male becomes invulnerable and impervious to suffering and danger.

According to Paz, the construction of male identity determines the construction of female identity and has unfortunate implications for Mexican women. Mexican female identity emerges as a result of pre-Columbian and Spanish conceptions of women. In pre-Columbian terms woman is a nature goddess, naked and open in her sexuality; she is the object of male desire. The Spanish conception of woman is that she is wild and unpredictable and must be "domesticated" in the home and by the church. She is deprived of her own free will in that she is relegated to a world of either/or: Either she is goddess or servant, saint or sinner, virgin or whore. Ultimately, writes Paz, the Mexican woman is mythologized. Perceived as frail to things that men perceive themselves impervious to, the Mexican woman assumes the image of the sufferer. Thus she, too, in her own way joins the Mexican male in wearing the mask of stoic solitude.

Essentially Mexican men and women wear the same mask. Paz calls this common mask the mask of dissimulation. Dissembling is more than merely lying; it occurs when one disguises one's true identity by acting. The difference between the actor and the dissembler is that the actor momentarily forgets himself then sheds this identity for his true identity. (Paz uses the metaphor of a snake shedding its skin.) Not so with the dissembler, who never forgets but is always concealing his true identity. Paz contends that the Mexican has transformed dissembling from a mere "fabric of invention" to an art form that defines every aspect of human interaction.

Paz suggests that these sensibilities originate in Mexico's colonial period, when the Indian and MESTIZO—a silent, invisible majority—would have naturally resorted to wearing a mask of compliance in the face of Spanish authority. (Silence is another theme Paz pursues in *The Labyrinth*.) Today the fear and suspicion linger on and fuel dissimulation.

Mexicans dissemble to such a degree that, for Paz, one's true identity can never be known. Paz points to Roldolfo Usigili's famous play *The Gesticulator,* in which gesticulation, like dissembling, conceals the true identity of characters. In *The Gesticulator* Paz sees a similar metaphor that describes the tensions in Mexican identity. The Mexican has transformed the act of gesticulation and dissembling into an art form, constructing truth and reality by masking identity.

In the end the Mexican mask is a grand negation of individuality, transforming every Mexican into what Paz calls Don No One, a collective nobody. Mexicans are born into a limbo of identity—are they Indian, Spanish, mestizo? They construct elaborate masks to conceal their true identities and fabricate new ones, become Nobody, and then fall into silence and solitude. Paz's often cited essay helps to create a context for the representation of gender roles in CHICANO LITERATURE and Latin American literature more broadly.

Bibliography

Paz, Octavio. *The Labyrinth of Solitude and Other Writings.* Translated by Lysander Kemp, Yara Milos, and Rachel Philips Belash. New York: Grove Press, 1985.

Quiroga, José. *Understanding Octavio Paz.* Columbia: University of South Carolina Press, 1999.

Kevin L. Cole

Mexican Revolution (1910–1920)

Beginning in 1910 with Francisco Madero's call to arms, the Mexican Revolution was one of the most important events in 20th-century Latin American history because, among other things, it mobilized the peasantry and resulted, ultimately, in the nationalization of foreign-held property—two factors that challenged the racial hierarchies of the status quo. The revolt against longtime dictator Porfirio Díaz reflected a challenge to the race-based social order that had, more or less, been in place since Spanish colonization. Madero, with the support of Emiliano Zapata, who represented the Mexican peasantry, was successful in unseating Díaz, who was known for inviting both European and U.S. investment, manufactures, and ideas into Mexico. Nevertheless, Madero's presidency ended with General Victoriano Huerta's coup d'état; Madero and his vice president were executed. Under Venustiano Carranza's disputed government, a new constitution in 1917 established laws for working conditions for the peasantry, though it would be years before these laws were actually enforced. Though some historians date the end of the civil war to 1920, discord and violence persisted up to the late 1920s.

The Mexican Revolution features as a theme or subject in BORDER LITERATURE and CHICANO LITERATURE, notably in JOSEPHINA NIGGLI's play *Soldadera* (1938), NELLI CAMPOBELLO's stories in *Cartucho* (1931) and, more recently, JOSÉ ANTONIO VILLARREAL's *The Fifth Horseman: A Novel of the Mexican Revolution* (1974) and PAT MORA's *HOUSE OF HOUSES* (1997).

Luz Elena Ramirez

Mexican Village Josephina Niggli (1945)

Born in Monterrey, Nuevo León, Mexico, JOSEPHINA NIGGLI spent her early years in Mexico; however, at age 15 she moved to San Antonio, Texas. Her father was a Texan of Swiss and Alsatian descent, and her mother, a Virginian of French and German ancestry. Niggli's bicultural and bilingual upbringing combined with her life in Texas to mark her as culturally Mexican American. Niggli began her writing career in the 1930s. In 1945 she published the first of her three novels, *Mexican Village*. Ten chapters make up this episodic novel that includes 80 plus characters. Through these characters Niggli presents a comprehensive look at the people of Hidalgo, a village in northern Mexico, and the folks in the surrounding region. Her characters include Nacho, the mayor of Hidalgo; Nemba, the herb woman and town witch; Tia Magdalena, a witch, or *bruja*; Bob Webster, an outlander and quarry master; and Father Zacaya, the village priest. The outlander, Bob Webster, functions as the link among the various stories in the novel.

Bob Webster, as well as the novel's setting—a border town—embodies one of *Mexican Village*'s main thematic concerns: the investigation of bicultural identity. This investigation reveals the oppositions that towns on the border between the United States and Mexico often generate: Spanish aristocrat/Indian peasant, insider/outsider, and "pure"/"mixed" blood. As Webster travels through Mexico and settles into the village life of Hidalgo, he moves closer to his Mexican heritage. In order to understand his "Mexicanness" Webster must listen to the stories of his family and legends of Mexico; thus Niggli stresses the importance both of an individual and collective memory. For example, Webster often "hears" the voice of his Mexican grandmother. Italicized passages signal this move to his childhood memories. The voice reminds him of Mexican legends: *So the great winds, Hurikán, transformed his horse into a mountain to guard his favorite valley* (6). It also tells him how to act appropriately Mexican: *When meeting strangers it is polite to speak your name* (14). And, it guides him toward behavior worthy of his heritage: *And always the patrón, the master, must ride with the least fear, throw the longest rope, climb the highest mountain. For is he not the patrón?* (22).

The significance of cultural memory enters the text in the form of stories and in the presence of the *bruja*, Tia Magdalena. In chapter 1, "The Quarry," Niggli introduces the legend of El Caballo Blanco, (The white horse; this is a reference to bandit Daniel Menéndez and his white horse). Webster, who wishes to name his white horse *El Blanco,* remembers the stories of his grandmother regarding El Caballo Blanco, and he also hears the story recounted by the leaders of Hidalgo. When Tia Magdalena proclaims that the only name for

Webster's horse is *El Blanco,* the gap between Mexican legends and Webster's personal memories closes. Tia Magdalena tells Don Nacho, the mayor and one of the four rulers of the village, "Don Bob, because he bought the horse, is obviously not afraid of ghosts. It is good for the people to witness bravery . . . And surely only a very brave man would ride a white horse in this valley" (42). This alignment between El Caballo Blanco and Bob Webster foreshadows Webster's ultimate position in Hidalgo. Through the use of Mexican history and folklore and their connection to Webster's character, Niggli addresses the complexity of bicultural identity.

In addition, to her concern with issues of identity, Niggli also possessed a desire to present an "authentic" picture of Mexicans to American readers and audiences. *Mexican Village* exemplifies this commitment in its carefully crafted characters. Although the novel does indeed include stereotypes, it also reconfigures or challenges those stereotypes. Stereotypes work on the level of the general or universal, thus by crafting particular characters with specific stories and experiences, a writer creates individuals. This move from the general to the particular occurs throughout *Mexican Village*. For example, Porfirio, the wood carver, appears in "The Quarry" as a typical, stocky Mexican. In this story he seems a mere decoration; however, in the following chapter, "The Street on the Three Crosses," Porfirio emerges as the subject of the narrative, moving from a mere background character to an individual. Through this move Niggli challenges her readers' expectations regarding Mexican people. The novel depicts people struggling to define their lives in the face of momentous changes in traditions, class hierarchies, and gender roles.

In *Mexican Village* Niggli intermingles the simple with the complex, the romantic with the realistic, the culturally "pure" with the "hybrid," and in so doing, she reveals the dilemma of rendering a "Mexican" agreeable to an American readership without resorting to demeaning characterizations. This tension marks the work of many authors of BORDER LITERATURE.

Bibliography

Niggli, Josephina. *Mexican Village*. Albuquerque: University of New Mexico Press, 1994.

Orchard, William, and Yolanda Padilla. "Lost in Adaptation: Chicana History, The Cold War and the Case of Josephina Niggli." *Women's Studies Quarterly*. 33, nos. 1–4 (Fall/Winter 2005): 90–113.

Catherine Cucinella

Migrant Souls Arturo Islas (1990)

Migrant Souls, by ARTURO ISLAS, takes place during the late 20th century in west Texas and along the Mexican border. The novel centers on the Angel clan, a Mexican-American family living in Del Sapo, a fictionalized version of El Paso. *Migrant Souls* can therefore be read within the context of BORDER LITERATURE. The novel grew out of a short story, "The Blind," which was published in *Zyzzyva* in 1986. *Migrant Soul's* working title, *A Perfectly Happy Family,* was far too obvious for Islas's dark sense of irony; the published title appropriately emphasizes the historical experience of Mexican Americans in Texas. The narrator observes of these settlers: "They had not sailed across an ocean or ridden in wagons and trains across half a continent in search of a new life. They were migrant, not immigrant, souls. They simply and naturally went from one bloody side of the river to the other and into a land that just a few decades earlier had been Mexico" (41–42).

The plot and characters of *Migrant Souls* follow Islas's highly acclaimed novel *The RAIN GOD* (1984), which focuses on the elders of the Angel family. With figures such as Mama Chona *The Rain God* critiques racial prejudice, machismo, and class-based pretension. It is important to read both *Migrant Souls* and *The Rain God* as a continuum in order to appreciate Islas's creative vision. The author had planned, though never realized, a trilogy; he died before he could write the last installment.

In *The Rain God* the Angel family celebrates their Spanish heritage, while denying their dark-skinned Indian ancestry. *Migrant Souls* does not pick up the narrative at the chronological point where *The Rain God* ends. Rather, *Migrant Souls* presents a fuller picture of the family's third generation: Miguel Chico, his cousin Josie Salazar, and their siblings and cousins. Readers learn how Miguel Chico and Josie's generation are affected by the values and strictures of the elders in the Angel clan.

Josie Salazar lives in California with her daughters but returns home to Texas when her marriage falls apart. Dark-skinned and rebellious, Josie stands in opposition to her aunt, Jesus Maria Angel Chavez, who has adopted the values of the Angel matriarch, Mama Chona. In *The Rain God* Mama Chona tries to "elevate" the MESTIZO lineage by privileging the Spanish blood over the Indian blood. Mama Chona, along with her female counterparts, in many ways perpetuates the abuse of male authority in the Angel family because she favors tradition and the keeping of appearances over emotional or physical well-being.

Mama Chona's two daughters, Eduviges Angel Salazar and Jesus Maria Angel Chavez, adopt the family myths and mistruths in *Migrant Souls.* These women deny their mestizo (Spanish and indigenous) heritage and pretend to be Spaniards of pure blood. Mama Chona believes, and tries to get her children and grandchildren to believe, that "the Angels discovered and claimed their portion of Mexico after surveying it with pure Castilian and Catholic eyes" (9). To Mama Chona and Eduviges, indians are uncouth, uncultured, and despicable. Josie is Eduviges's youngest daughter, and she rejects this attitude and embraces her Indian heritage. Josie's own father, Sancho Salazar, felt "his Indian blood came to life" whenever he was able to hunt and fish in northernmost Mexico (4); Josie is her father's daughter. Islas describes her as having "Apache eyes" (110). When grown and married and living in San Francisco, Josie is drawn into an adulterous affair. Islas clearly indicates that part of what attracts Josie to her lover is that he is Cherokee. After her divorce Josie returns to Del Sapo with her two daughters and spends the rest of her life challenging Eduviges's prejudice. In this effort Josie (and Islas through her) is espousing a key aspect of early Chicano activism: the reconnection with the indigenous half of the self.

The third generation of Angels feels the pressures of their elders' expectations, each in their own way. For his part, Miguel Chico struggles with a failed homosexual relationship in *Migrant Souls*. Miguel Chico's queerness places him at odds with the heterosexist, if not homophobic, Catholic values of his family, and he remains aloof and isolated from the family. Josie's sister Serena, a peacemaker between the generations, lives in a long-term lesbian relationship, but she does not insist the elder Angels recognize her relationship for what it is. Their cousin Rudy Chavez has a realistic view of racism in the United States: Mexican Americans face similar kinds of discrimination as African Americans. Rudy calls into question the faith capitalism and the American Dream that his cousin Ricardo Angel maintains. Thus each member of the third generation has diverging views on sexuality, tradition, work, and family.

Amazingly, Islas managed to complete *Migrant Souls* while quite ill with AIDS-related diseases and while working on La Mollie and the King of Tears. *La Mollie* was published posthumously, in 1996, and it shares a few characters with *Migrant Souls*. Mollie is the lover of Louis Mendoza, the narrator and protagonist of *La Mollie* and a character in *Migrant Souls*, Josie Salazar, meets Mollie, a wealthy *gringa* who attends a party in San Francisco. Likewise, *Migrant Soul*'s Miguel Chico appears briefly as an English teacher in a San Francisco Veterans Administration Hospital in *La Mollie*. Still, *La Mollie* is not to be considered the completion of the Angel clan trilogy because its focus is more on Louis Mendoza, his music, and his life in San Francisco. *Migrant Souls, The Rain God,* and *La Mollie* are contributors to Chicano literature and within a broader context to American literature, with the theme of searching for the self in the 20th century.

Bibliography

Aldama, Frederick Luis. Introduction to *The Uncollected Works,* by Arturo Islas. Houston, Tex.: Arte Público Press, 2003.

Islas, Arturo. *Migrant Souls.* New York: Avon, 1991.

Márquez, Antonio C. "The Historical Imagination in Arturo Islas's *The Rain God* and *Migrant Souls.*" *MELUS* 19, no. 2 (1994): 3–16.

Skenazy, Paul. "The Long Walk Home." Afterword to *La Mollie and the King of Tears,* by Arturo Islas. Albuquerque: University of New Mexico Press, 1996.

Timothy K. Nixon

Miraculous Day of Amalia Gómez, The
John Rechy (1991)

Novelist and essayist John Rechy published *The Miraculous Day of Amalia Gómez* in 1991. Told in vignettes and switching between past and present, Rechy's novel tells the story of a Mexican-American woman, Amalia Gómez, who seeks to discovery meaning in her life and in doing so, faces the troubles of her past. *Miraculous Day* is about female survival of domestic abuse and the complications of being Mexican American in Texas and California. In a series of episodes, Rechy focuses on Amalia's roles as a mother, wife, lover, and woman making her way in an unjust and ever-changing world. Amalia faces the death of one son, Manny, who gets caught up in gang warfare and is killed in prison. She laments the fact that she has lost touch with her other children, Juan and Gloria. Rechy leaves no aspect of Amalia's life unexamined on this ordinary Saturday that becomes "miraculous" when a cross appears to her in the sky as a sign of faith, reconciliation with loved ones, and forgiveness.

The reader follows Amalia as she walks around her Los Angeles neighborhood, trying to understand her childhood fears that have grown into adult realizations, the legacy of a mother who hated her, and abuse from two husbands. She considers the exploitative treatment of labor in the factory where she works, her lack of education, the friends she has discovered and lost, and the idea that she will punished by God for mistakes that she has made in her life.

The story begins with a silver cross that appears before Amalia in the morning sun. The plot develops as we follow Amalia around her neighborhood. It is there that she examines new graffiti on barrio walls; she fears that the writing will bring new gangs to mark their territory. Also on these walls is a mural that depicts revolutionaries fighting for Mexican-American liberation. The message of the mural is to bring Mexicans to the "promised land of justice"—AZTLÁN, a place where women are an important part of the struggle for freedom and part of Mexican folklore. Amalia then enters a local restaurant that becomes a metaphor for all that she has ventured and all that she has lost. Soon she meets her friend who works at the same sweatshop, Rosario, and the two discuss politics, *telenovelas* (soap operas), and life on the border. Rosario is on the run from local police for sheltering a friend who killed an immigration official.

Throughout the course of the novel, we learn that Amalia had an awful marriage to the man who raped her when she was 15. She bore a son from that rape, Manny. In her marriage to Gabriel she bore two children but the relationship ended. She has a relationship with Reynaldo in Los Angeles and hopes that she has not compromised herself after a night spent carousing with a young man named Angel. When she takes inventory of her past and confesses to a priest, Amalia is looking for forgiveness. What she suffers is a question of faith, and she does not get the forgiveness she expects. At the same time Amalia has signs of hope: A rose blooms on a dead bush, and a discussion with her children promises forgiveness. At the end of the novel Amalia is held hostage in a shopping mall, and she blesses the man who threatens to end her life. At that moment, with recriminations behind her, Amalia stares up at the sky, where she first saw the silver cross. Now she sees the Virgin reaching out to her, and Amalia is resurrected, hoping for a new life; her journey on this "miraculous day" is one of self-discovery. In this moment Rechy relies on the techniques of MAGICAL REALISM to combine the spiritual and material worlds.

Throughout the narrative Rechy incorporates aspects of Mexican and Mexican-American history ranging from the MEXICAN REVOLUTION of 1910 to the Zoot Suit Riots of the 1940s. In this regard Rechy's work can be read within the context of CHICANO LITERATURE.

Bibliography
Casillo, Charles. *Outlaw: The Lives and Careers of John Rechy*. Los Angeles: Alyson Publications, 2002.
Rechy, John. *The Miraculous Day of Amalia Gómez*. New York: Grove Press, 1991.
Rechy, John, Marsha Kinder, and Kristy H. K. Kang. *Mysteries and Desires: Searching the World of John Rechy*. CD-ROM. Los Angeles: Labyrinth Project, 2000.

Rosa Soto

Mixquiahuala Letters, The Ana Castillo (1986)

ANA CASTILLO's *The Mixquiahuala Letters* earned the Before Columbus Foundation's America Book Award in 1987. This work has been called "a post-modernist, Chicana feminist novel" and "a parody of modern ethnography and travel writing" (Quintana 72). *The Mixquiahuala Letters* consists of a series of letters written by two women who travel back and forth between Mexico and the U.S. Alicia is a lighter skinned woman than Teresa, though both are of Spanish ancestry. Forty letters recount the experiences of the two women while living in the United States and while traveling in Mexico. The letters are not, however, in chronological order. Instead, Castillo provides the reader with three different approaches to read the text. Castillo labels these strategies "for the conformist," "for the cynic," and "for the quixotic." In addition, each bundle of letters can each be read separately as a work of short fiction. Castillo's playfulness with the ordering of the letters is accompanied by new thematic terrain for the 1980s: the development of a Chicana consciousness.

The novel focuses on the correspondence between and relationship of Teresa and Alicia. The two women meet in Mexico at the North American Institute to study Mexican culture and language, but Teresa becomes disenchanted with her colleagues and while she is expecting to meet and study with Mexican "brothers and sisters," she instead finds herself in the company of blond Anglos. A politically conscious Chicana, Teresa seeks a connection with a culture that she believes constitutes a large part of her sense of self, but when she finds herself in the company of a group of Anglos who seek the "exotic," the experience at the institute is disillusioning and depressing. Teresa and Alicia travel around the country in an attempt to escape gender-bound roles; to this end they seek to reconnect with an indigenous (Aztec) past that validates the creative power of women. This escape is foiled repeatedly, as Teresa and Alicia are both objectified and threatened by a male authority. Although both Teresa and Alicia had hoped to find another way of being, had hoped to find some prepatriarchal model for society, had hoped to escape the dangers of living under the control of men within the United States, they do not find the answers or culture they seek.

Castillo's poetic aesthetic has come under scholarly scrutiny because, intentionally or not, her fiction follows the innovations of the Latin American "Boom" writers (especially, as critics have noted, Julio Cortázar and Juan Rulfo). The fractured narrative structure has several effects. For one, it actively draws the reader into the reading process, foregrounding the fact that meaning is produced in the act of reading. Perhaps more important, the fragmented structure of her novel reveals the complex subjectivity of the Chicana. While Chicano artists such as GUILLERMO GÓMEZ-PEÑA have represented the ways in which Chicano subjectivity breaks apart or "fragments" in Anglo society, Castillo represents the effects of a patriarchal, Anglo society on Mexican-American women. *The Mixquiahuala Letters* becomes the performance of a borderlands subjectivity and in this regard her work can be read alongside GLORIA ANZALDÚA's foundational work *BORDERLANDS/LA FRONTERA: THE NEW MESTIZA* (1987). Teresa exists in a dynamic space that involves multiple ethnic and linguistic identities: as an English-speaking American and a Catholic of Indian and Spanish ancestry. Her darker appearance and full plump figure sets her apart from the thinner and fairer-skinned Alicia. And, rather than rejecting her fragmentary identity, the novel validates Teresa's character by accepting her complex origins and

her linguistically dynamic letter writing. On the one hand, the novel's content argues that patriarchal society threatens and limits possibilities for Teresa and Alicia and that the ethnic and racial rifts prevent the two women from connecting in a meaningful way. On the other hand, the novel's form validates the complexity of Mexican-American identity. *The Mixquiahuala Letters* proposes a feminist approach to Mexican-American women's roles and can be read within the context of CHICANO LITERATURE.

Bibliography
Bus, Heiner. "'I too was of that small corner of the world': The Cross-Cultural Experience in Ana Castillo's *The Mixquiahuala Letters* (1986)." *Americas Review: A Review of Hispanic Literature and Art of the USA* 21, nos. 3–4 (Fall–Winter 1993): 128–138.

Castillo, Ana. *The Mixquiahuala Letters.* Tempe, Ariz.: Bilingual Press, 1986.

———. "Yes, Dear Critic, There Really Is an Alicia." In *Máscaras,* edited by Lucha Corpi, 153–160. Berkeley, Calif.: Third Woman, 1997.

Milligan, Bryce. "An Interview with Ana Castillo." *South Central Review* 16, no. 1 (Spring 1999): 19–29.

Quintana, Alvina E. "Ana Castillo's *The Mixquiahuala Letters:* The Novelist as Ethnographer." In *Criticism in the Borderlands: Studies in Chicano Literature, Culture, and Ideology,* edited by Héctor Calderón et al., 72–83. Durham, N.C.: Duke University Press, 1991.

Yarbro-Bejarano, Yvonne. "The Multiple Subject in the Writing of Ana Castillo." *Americas Review: A Review of Hispanic Literature and Art of the USA* 20, no. 1 (Spring 1992): 65–72.

Ritch Calvin

Mohr, Nicholasa (1935–   ) (novelist, short story writer, graphic artist)

Nicholasa Mohr is one of the best-known Latina writers in the United States. She was born in Spanish Harlem ("El Barrio") of Puerto Rican parents in 1935. After growing up in the Bronx, Mohr studied at the Brooklyn Museum of Art School. She became interested in writing when her art agent asked her to write about growing up Puerto Rican and female.

Mohr has written many books about youth and coming of age, including NILDA (1973), *Felita* (1979), *Going Home* (1986), *The Magic Shell* (1995), *The Song of El Coquí* (1995), and *Old Letivia and the Mountain of Sorrows* (1996). Her writing explores the Puerto Rican experience in the Northeast. Her other books include the short story collections EL BRONX REMEMBERED: A NOVELLA AND OTHER STORIES (1975), *In Nueva York* (1977), *Rituals of Survival: A Woman's Portfolio* (1985), and *A Matter of Pride and Other Stories* (1997). She has also published a memoir titled *Growing Up Inside the Sanctuary of My Imagination* (1994).

Her first book, *Nilda,* describes the Bronx through the eyes of a 10-year-old girl who is a second-generation Puerto Rican. Mohr's protagonist uses her imagination to help herself bear the hardships of her social and economic circumstances. Mohr departs from common depictions of barrio life in which Puerto Ricans figure primarily as gang members or criminals, as in, for example, the novels of PIRI THOMAS, which often focus on violence and drug dealing. Mohr prefers to tell the stories that were never told and that are not necessarily negative. Life affirming in their outlook, Mohr's characters are Puerto Rican women living in the barrio who, despite hardships, are a source of nurturing and even leaders of resistance. In Mohr's work familial relationships are often easily and freely described through the eyes of a young girl, such as Nilda.

Meanwhile, *Felita* and *Going Home* illustrate the character Felita's experiences growing up in El Barrio. As well, we see Felita on a return trip to Puerto Rico, where she discovers differences between the values of her family and community in New York and the values of her relatives and of Puerto Rican society at large.

Mohr's writing style is simple and direct involving plots of everyday people with everyday conflicts to overcome. Her storytelling emphasizes the humanity of her characters who are common people from northeastern neighborhoods. American women writers such as Carson McCullers and Katherine Anne Porter have inspired Mohr's writing, along with Puerto Rican poet JULIA DE BURGOS and Colombian Nobel Prize winner Gabriel García Márquez.

The stories in *El Bronx Remembered* and *In Nueva York* include bittersweet stories of survival under difficult circumstances. The northeastern barrio is again the predominant space where Mohr explores the experience of Puerto Ricans as they face interethnic clashes and poor living conditions. Characters in these collections, especially women, develop strategies to deal with negative circumstances. Each story adds a different human quality to the concrete landscape of the Bronx, where there is racism and injustice but also a sense of community and solidarity.

Rituals of Survival: A Woman's Portfolio consists of six vignettes about adult Puerto Rican women, each one representing various lifestyles, ages, and circumstances. Their common bond is their need to survive as individuals free from restricting social expectations. In *A Matter of Pride and Other Stories* Mohr again celebrates the beauty and resilience in her female Puerto Rican characters. Her prose has established a precedent for young Puerto Rican women writers to continue to question and critique their lives in an increasingly diverse urban landscape. An important contributor to PUERTO RICAN LITERATURE of the mainland, Mohr has earned the 1974 Jane Addams Children's Book Award and the *New York Times* Outstanding Book of the Year. She was also a National Book Award finalist. In 2001 Mohr moved from Park Slope, Brooklyn, to Spanish Harlem, where she was born.

Bibliography

Hernández, Carmen Dolores. *Puerto Rican Voices in English: Interview with Writers*. Westport, Conn.: Praeger, 1997.

Kevane, Bridget, and Juanita Heredia. *Latina Self-Portraits: Interviews with Contemporary Women Writers*. Albuquerque: University of New Mexico Press, 1999.

Mohr, Nicholasa. *El Bronx Remembered: A Novella and Other Stories.* New York: HarperKeypoint, 1975.

———. *Felita.* New York: Dial Press, 1979.

———. *Going Home.* New York: Dial Press, 1986.

———. *In My Own Words: Growing Up Inside the Sanctuary of My Imagination.* New York: Simon & Schuster, 1994.

———. *In Nueva York.* New York: Dial Press, 1977.

———. *The Magic Shell.* New York: Scholastic, 1995.

———. *A Matter of Pride and Other Stories.* Houston, Tex.: Arte Público Press, 1997.

———. *Nilda.* New York: Harper & Row, 1973.

———. *Old Letivia and the Mountain of Sorrows.* New York: Viking, 1996.

———. *Rituals of Survival: A Woman's Portfolio.* Houston, Texas: Arte Público Press, 1985.

———. *The Song of El Coquí.* New York: Viking, 1995.

Ocasio, Rafael. "From Nuyorican Barrio to Issues on Puerto Rican Literature Outside New York City: Nicholasa Mohr and Judith Ortiz Cofer." In *Literature and Ethnic Discrimination,* edited by Michael J. Meyer, 187–203. Amsterdam and Atlanta, Ga.: Rodopi, 1997.

Antonia Domínguez Miguela

Monkey Hunting Cristina García (2003)

CRISTINA GARCÍA's *Monkey Hunting* takes place during the 19th and 20th centuries in Cuba, China, and the United States. The protagonist, Chen Pan, is born in China in 1837. He willingly moves to Cuba at the age of 20, expecting a life of attractive women, plentiful food, and prosperity. He has been led to the island having heard myths about the Caribbean as a life of ease and by heeding the call of Westerners who seek cheap labor. However, Chen Pan has been tricked: The lengthy boat journey to Cuba is hellish, and on arrival he and the other Chinese are sold as slaves. By force he is made to cut vast amounts of sugarcane. Eventually Chen Pan finds freedom from grinding, unpaid labor and cramped squalor.

Chen Pan bears his privations with impressive stoicism and is presented as something of a hero

in that he channels his anger fruitfully. He kills one particularly brutal overseer and later fights for the Cubans against Spanish troops during the island's struggle for independence. He has no time for racism or misogyny. Unlike some Cuban and Chinese men, he has no hatred for blacks because he himself has lost freedom.

Chen Pan enters into a life-long companionship with a black slave, Lucrecia. He purchases her and her young child and fathers several mixed-race children with her. Chen Pan takes care of Lucrecia and forgoes the Chinese male attitude that women cause only trouble. Once he establishes himself as a trader, Chen Pan contributes much to Havana society, earning relative respect in his community. His one bitterness, however, is that Chinese immigration to Cuba has only a time-limited welcome, one that recedes with economic hardship. He feels betrayed by the immigration policies because of the contribution made by Chinese Cubans to the island's Ten Years' War against Spain and Cuban culture in general. We can read Chen Pan and his counterparts as productive citizens of Havana, a community of Chinese Cubans who have given their labor, money, and time to the economy. To this day this community produces a Chinese-language newspaper. With its attention to the island's rich cultural history, *Monkey Hunting* can be read within the context of CUBAN-AMERICAN LITERATURE.

Eventually, Chen Pan founds an ethnically mixed dynasty that spreads from New York to Havana and back to China. García interweaves the omniscient narration of Chen Pan's story with more fragmentary interludes about Chen Fang and Domingo Chen. His granddaughter Chen Fang recounts her sufferings caused by conservatives in Shanghai; as a woman, she recalls her flirtation with lesbianism, her teaching career, and then her imprisonment by intellectual-censoring functionaries of Mao Zedong's Cultural Revolution. She sees how the Communist Party controls the intellectual, familial, and financial lives of the Chinese. Her son, gripped by zealous admiration of communism, is, like all of the main characters, a product of a major political movement that requires the passage of time to evaluate.

Another descendant of Chen Pan, Domingo Chen, is raised in New York. His life is changed after fighting for the Americans in Vietnam. While stationed there, Domingo not only watches the bloody conflict between the Americans and Vietnamese; he also witnesses environmental destruction: fish shoals destroyed by chemicals, and vegetated hillsides burned to cinders by napalm. This theme of ecological damage links the imperialism of the Americans in Vietnam to the imperialism of the Spanish in Chen Pan's era. Chen Pan can remember a time when Cuba was covered with trees, before the Spaniards' agricultural vision flattened the landscapes. In *Monkey Hunting* Chen Pan and his relatives bear the burden of imperialism and authoritarian rule; they work in economies managed by powerful men or oligarchies (often foreign) who care only for profit, military might, or the pursuit of superiority over women and other races. In considering Chen Pan's 80 years of life, we can consider him a hero because he abhors these destructive urges.

Bibliography

García, Cristina. *Monkey Hunting.* New York: Knopf, 2003.

Lyon Johnson, Kelli. "Cristina Garcia." 2003. Voices from the Gaps: Women Writers of Color. Available online. URL: http://voices.cla.umn.edu/newsite/authors/GARCIAcristina.htm. Accessed May 26, 2008.

McCracken, Ellen. *New Latina Narrative: The Feminine Space of Postmodern Ethnicity.* Tucson: University of Arizona Press, 1999.

Kevin De Ornellas

Mora, Pat (1942–   ) *(fiction writer)*

Award-winning Mexican-American author Pat Mora was born on January 19, 1942 in El Paso, Texas. Growing up with bilingual parents, Mora was the granddaughter of immigrants who had fled to Texas during the MEXICAN REVOLUTION, the thrilling accounts of which can be read in her memoir *HOUSE OF HOUSES* (1996), winner of the Premio Aztlán in 1997.

In 1963 Mora received her bachelor's degree from Texas Western College and went on to receive her master's in 1967 from the University of Texas, El Paso. She was also awarded an honorary doctorate of letters from State University of New York, Buffalo, in 2006. As an educator, Mora has taught both children and adults, from secondary school to university, in addition to being named in 1999 the Garrey Carruthers Chair, Distinguished Visiting Professor at the University of New Mexico.

Mora began her writing career in 1981, publishing her work in literary journals. Her first collection of poetry, entitled *Chants,* was published in 1984 and won the Southwest Book Award. Just two years later Mora received her second of many Southwest Book Awards for *Borders* (1986), a poetry collection that builds on many of the same issues explored in her first book-length work. With the publication of *Communion* (1991) and *Agua santa/Holy Water* (1995) Mora solidified many of the major themes that she would examine throughout her career—the importance of family, living in Spanish- and English-speaking cultures, and desert life.

What is most striking about Mora's work is her tremendous sense of place, particularly her relationship with the desert border region surrounding her native El Paso. Whether in her poetry or prose, the desert border region springs forth in the reader's imagination with magical force. Full of radiant colors and deep dark contrasts, Mora's desert is a giver of life, a place where fragile blossoms grow sublimely in a wilderness where others might only see barrenness.

Indeed, Mora's work seems to spring from a spiritual relationship with the land where she lives. This spirituality takes many different forms in her work, recalling for the reader the mixture of indigenous and Catholic traditions that is such a large part of spiritual belief in many Mexican-American homes. Mayan folklore, for example, inspired her children's books *The Night the Moon Fell* (2000) and *The Race of Toad and Deer* (2001), while *Aunt Carmen's Book of Practical Saints* (1999), *A Library* for Juana: The World of Sor Juana Inés (2002), and *The Song of Francis and the Animals* (2005) reflect the writer's relationship with Catholicism. What one sees in most of Mora's work is a combination of indigenous and Western belief systems that emphasizes the loving connection one should have with the earth and humankind.

Womanhood in its various manifestations, such as motherhood, daughterhood, and sisterhood, is also a critical theme in Mora's writing. *Pablo's Tree* (1994), Mora's Américas Award–winning book about adoption, *Love to Mamá: A Celebration of Mothers* (2004), and *Doña Flor: A Tall Tale about a Giant Woman with a Great Big Heart* (2005) can all be read as celebrations of women and their intimate connections with family and with nature.

In addition to her career as educator and writer, Mora has also been recognized for her activism. Of particular note is her determination to establish "El Día de los Niños, El Día de los Libros" ("Children's Day, Books' Day") on April 30 of each year, a national day of celebration to commemorate language, cultural diversity, and bilingual literacy in the United States. Mora continues to write for adults and children and is a popular national speaker. For its subjects, settings, and characters, her work can be read within the context of CHICANO LITERATURE.

Bibliography

Barrera, Rosalinda B. "Profile: Pat Mora, Fiction/Nonfiction Writer and Poet." *Language Arts* 75, no. 3 (March 1998): 221–227.

Christian, B. Marie. *Belief in Dialogue: U.S. Latina Writers Confront Their Religious Heritage.* New York: Other Press, 2005.

Day, Frances Ann. *Latina and Latino Voices in Literature for Children and Teenagers.* Portsmouth, N.H.: Heinemann, 1997.

Fox, Linda. "From *Chants* to *Borders* to *Communion*: Pat Mora's Poetic Journey to Nepantla." *Bilingual Review/Revista Bilingüe* 21, no. 3 (September–December 1996): 219–230.

Mora, Pat. *Agua santa/Holy Water.* Boston: Beacon Press, 1995.

———. *Aunt Carmen's Book of Practical Saints.* Boston: Beacon Press, 1997.

———. *The Bakery Lady.* Houston, Tex.: Piñata Books, 2001.

———. *A Birthday Basket for Tía.* New York: Simon & Schuster Children's Publishing, 1992.

———. *Delicious Hullabaloo/Pachanga deliciosa.* Houston, Tex.: Piñata Books, 1998.

———. *The Desert Is My Mother/El desierto es mi madre.* Houston, Tex.: Piñata Books, 1994.

———. *Doña Flor: A Tale about a Giant Woman with a Big Heart.* New York: Dragonfly Books, 2005.

———. *House of Houses* Boston: Beacon Press, 1997.

———. *A Library for Juana: The World of Sor Juana Inés.* New York: Alfred A. Knopf, 2002.

———. *Love to Mamá: A Tribute to Mothers.* New York: Lee & Low Books, 2001.

———. *Maria Paints the Hills.* Santa Fe: Museum of New Mexico Press, 2002.

———. *My Own True Name: New and Selected Poems for Young Adults.* Houston, Tex.: Piñata Books, 2000.

———. *Nepantla: Essays from the Land in the Middle.* Albuquerque: University of New Mexico Press, 1993.

———. *The Night the Moon Fell: A Maya Myth Retold.* Toronto, Canada: Douglas & McIntyre, 2000.

———. *The Race of Toad and Deer.* Toronto, Canada: Groundwood Books, 2001.

———. *The Rainbow Tulip.* New York: Viking, 1999.

———. *The Song of Francis and the Animals.* Grand Rapids, Mich.: Eerdmans Books for Young Readers, 2005.

———. *This Big Sky.* New York: Scholastic, 1998.

———. *Tomás and the Library Lady.* New York: Knopf, 1997.

———. *Uno, Dos, Tres: 1, 2, 3.* New York: Clarion Books, 1996.

Mora, Pat, and Charles Ramirez Berg. *The Gift of the Poinsettia.* Houston, Tex.: Piñata Books, 1995.

Murphy, Patrick D. "Conserving Natural and Cultural Diversity: The Prose and Poetry of Pat Mora." *MELUS* 21 (1996): 59–69.

Rebolledo, Tey Diana. *The Chronicles of Panchita Villa and Other Guerrilleras: Essays on Chicana/Latina*

Literature and Criticism. Austin: University of Texas Press, 2005.

Torres, Lourdes. "Chicana Writers Explore the Land in the Middle." *Sojourner: The Women's Forum* 19 (1994): 10–12.

Ethriam Brammer

Moraga, Cherríe (1952–) *(poet, playwright, essayist)*

Cherríe Moraga was born in 1952 and raised in San Gabriel, California. Daughter of a Mexican mother and Irish-American father, Moraga earned a B.A. from Immaculate Heart College in Los Angeles (1974) and an M.A in literature at San Francisco State University (1980). She has since taught courses in women's studies, Latino literature, and creative writing at many prestigious institutions, including the University of California, Los Angeles, and University of California, Berkeley, San Francisco State University, and University of Massachusetts. Currently she is artist in residence at the Stanford University Departments of Drama and Spanish and Portuguese.

Moraga's work has earned international recognition, been widely anthologized, and won her several awards. Moraga's major works include two volumes of prose and poetry, *Loving in the War Years: Lo que nunca pasó por sus labios* (2000) and *The Last Generation* (1993). She coedited the classic volume entitled *This Bridge Called My Back: Writings by Radical Women of Color* (1983) with GLORIA ANZALDÚA; the book won the Before Columbus Foundation American Book Award in 1986. Her plays *Shadow of a Man* (1990) and *Watsonville: A Place Not Here* (1995) both won the Fund for New American Plays Award. In 1992 *Heroes and Saints* won the PEN West Award for Drama, the Critics Circle Award, and the Will Glickman Prize for the Best Play. Moraga also received the National Endowment for the Art's Theatre Playwrights' Fellowship in 1993. In addition she has written a memoir of her difficult process of becoming pregnant and having a baby in *Waiting in the Wings: Portrait of a Queer Motherhood* (1997). In *Waiting in the Wings* and others works about queer life Moraga makes an important contribution to LATINA LESBIAN LITERATURE.

Moraga blends different genres such as essay, poetry, and narrative. Like many Latino authors, she also utilizes CODE SWITCHING between Spanish and English in her writing. These techniques are tied to her identity politics and to her interest in social liberties. Moraga uses this blending of genres and languages to express her mestiza (mixed-blood), bicultural, and bilingual identity. Cultural concepts are uttered in Spanish in order to emphasize their Mexican-American context and meaning: She relies on terms such as *familia* (family), *comunidad* (community), *mujer* (woman), and *jota/joto* (queer) to challenge the English-speaking U.S. culture that encourages Mexican Americans to assimilate. Her writing resists self-erasure through assimilation and celebrates a specific Chicana reality. The writer also chooses to put her political analysis in everyday terms rather than those deliberately rarified terms of literary theory.

Moraga's *Loving in the War Years: Lo que no pasó por sus labios* explores various forms of oppression such as racism, sexism, and homophobia inside and outside the Mexican-American community. In this autobiographical collection of essays, poems, and stories she promotes an inclusive politics of coalition. She considers the internalized oppressions within the Mexican-American family. Affirming her Mexican heritage, Moraga finds herself identifying closely with her mother in spite of forces that would separate them. She critiques the Chicano nationalist movement of the 1960s and 1970s, which was created to empower and unify the Chicano community. Her concern is that despite being part of the civil rights movement, Chicano nationalism excluded and created a hostile environment for women and gays.

In *The Last Generation* Moraga reaffirms her commitment to the Chicano movement's goals of empowerment. *The Last Generation* considers the reformation of a Chicano tribe in "Queer Aztlán," an ancient land free of internal divisions and based on a respect for the earth. A touchstone for the Chicano nationalist struggle, AZTLÁN is associated with the U.S. Southwest and is the historical and mythological homeland of the Aztec before they migrated to central Mexico. *The Last Generation* extends across many borders, linking tribal movements within the United States, Canada, and Latin America, creating a global tribal consciousness. This work centers on themes of spirituality and ecology. Here Moraga aligns herself with pre-Columbian and modern traditions that honor both female and male ways of being.

Moraga's works examine the role of mythology in Chicano culture. She explores the unifying myths, such as those associated with Aztlán, as well as those that perpetuates male dominance and sexual control of women. One example of a controlling myth is that associated with the historical figure of La MALINCHE, Malintzin Tenepal, the indigenous translator and concubine of Hernán Cortés (Spanish conqueror of Mexico). Moraga and other Chicana feminist authors have reclaimed this mythical mother of the mestizo people who has been read as traitor to her people because she interpreted for Cortés. Moraga's drama delves deep into pre-Columbian mythology to juxtapose a Chicana lesbian reality with the goal of political enfranchisement.

In her play *The Hungry Woman: A Mexican Medea* (2000), Moraga appropriates the Greek mother-lover figure of Medea and transforms her into a dynamic Mexican character. *The Hungry Woman: A Mexican Medea* combines the Mexican legend of La LLORONA (the Weeping Woman), the Aztec moon goddess Coyolxauhqui, and the Aztec creation myth of the Hungry Woman. The Hungry Woman is a body covered with mouths crying out in hunger; the figure is broken in half by Aztec gods to create the earth and sky. The play, which Moraga ironically calls a "dyke story," depicts a postrevolutionary United States divided into ethnic nations. What these nations share is the practice of exiling homosexual members to the same place. Likewise, *Heart of the Earth: A Popol Vuh Story* (2001) is a feminist reinterpretation of the Quiché Maya creation myth. Using puppetry

to portray the primeval drama, Moraga comments on the dangers of patriarchy and racial creeds.

While Moraga has developed as an artist over the years, exploring new forms and motifs, her work has maintained the concerns of her earliest writings. Affirming the reality of lesbians of color, her universal message teaches one how to identify internalized forms of oppression, enabling individuals to be more empowered and accepting of difference.

Bibliography
Alarcón, Norma, Ana Castillo, and Cherríe Moraga, eds. *The Sexuality of Latinas.* Berkeley, Calif.: Third Woman Press, 1989.
Anzaldúa, Gloria, and Cherríe Moraga, eds. *The Bridge Called My Back: Writings by Radical Women of Color.* New York: Kitchen Table/Women of Color Press, 1983.
Hernández, Ellie. "The Gaze of the Other: An Interview with Cherríe Moraga." In *Latinas on Stage,* edited by Alicia Arrizón and Lillian Manzor, 192–200. Berkeley, Calif.: Third Woman Press, 2000.
Moraga, Cherríe. *Heroes and Saints and Other Plays (Giving Up the Ghost and Shadow of Man).* Albuquerque, N.Mex.: West End Press, 1994.
———. *The Hungry Woman: A Mexican Medea/Heart of the Earth: A Popul Vuh Story.* Albuquerque, N.Mex.: West End Press, 2003.
———. *The Last Generation.* Boston: South End Press, 1993.
———. *Loving in the War Years.* Cambridge, Mass.: South End Press, 2000.
———. *Waiting in the Wings: Portrait of a Queer Motherhood.* Ithaca, N.Y.: Firebrand Press, 1997.
———. *Watsonville/Circle in the Dirt.* Albuquerque, N.Mex.: West End Press, 2002.

Paula Straile-Costa

Morales, Alejandro (1944–) *(novelist, critic)*

Alejandro Morales was born in Montebello, California, in 1944 and is the son of Mexican parents, Morales began his education at the segregated elementary school in Simons, in the Los Angeles area. Simons is the site of the brickyard referred to in his novels *Caras viejas y vino nuevo* (1975; *Barrio on the Edge*), *Reto en el paraíso* (1983; Challenge in paradise), and *The Rag Doll Plagues* (1992). The Simons brickyard is also the center of activity in Morales's *The Brick People* (1988). After attending East Los Angeles Community College, Morales earned a B.A. in Spanish from California State University, Los Angeles. In 1971 he was awarded an M.A. in Spanish, and four years later he completed his Ph.D. at Rutgers University. Since 1975 he has taught in the Department of Spanish and Portuguese at the University of California, Irvine. His novel *La verdad sin voz* (1979; *Death of an Anglo*), is the true story of an Anglo doctor who was murdered in Mathis, Texas, after setting up a low-income clinic to treat Mexicans. Morales had difficulty publishing the novel, which takes place in the 1970s, because of the violence and hopelessness portrayed; it was finally published in Mexico in 1979. More recently Morales published *Nación pequeña* (2004; Small nation) and *Waiting to Happen* (2001), the first volume of the "Heterotopia" trilogy. His work can be read within the context of CHICANO LITERATURE.

Morales's work considers the intersections of urban life, manual labor, and immigration. His characters assume what can be called a commodity identity, one in which Mexican Americans are stripped of their individuality and dignity. He creates Mexican-American characters that are valued only for their labor; capitalism is often depicted as exploitative, especially in the manufacturing of bricks in *The Brick People. The Brick People* explores how some Mexicans can be coopted to help the Anglos in their utilization of Mexican labor. Mexicans and Mexican Americans made the bricks that built Los Angeles, but they ironically lack full access to civic life. The bricks from Simons were used to build Royce Hall at the University of California, Los Angeles, and helped to rebuild San Francisco after the 1906 earthquake. Simons Brickyard, the largest brickworks in the world in the 1920s, drew 90 percent or more of its workers from Guanajuato, Mexico. The story of the brickyard was forgotten until Morales researched, recorded, and remembered it.

Inspired by the history of the brickyard, *The Brick People* is deeply personal, recounting the contributions and travails of the author's family. Morales uses the name Revueltas as a pseudonym for his father's surname. At the age of 17, Morales's father (Octavio Revueltas in the novel) crossed the border from a Mexican ranch in 1918. At this time the MEXICAN REVOLUTION compelled many Mexicans to relocate and, appropriately, the appellation *Revueltas* means either "riots" or "mixed, scrambled" in Spanish. Morales thus invites his readers to imagine the autobiographical elements of his characters who cross cultural and political borders. Morales's own maternal grandparents emigrated from Guanajuato in 1912, when his mother (Nana in the novel) was six years old. Both sides of the author's family have roots in Mexico, but they planned a future in the United States and gave birth to Mexican-American children. Morales's father and grandparents lived and worked on the Simons site.

In *The Brick People,* Octavio Revueltas revolts against working conditions at Simons—the insecurity of employment during the Great Depression, the 12-hour workday, the hacienda-like system of the company town, and the low wages. He attempts to establish a union much in the way that agricultural workers of California sought better working conditions in the 1930s and 1940s. Octavio Revueltas refuses to be coopted by generous offers from the anti-union brickyard owner Walter Simons. For this he is exiled from the community. He revolts against the segregated city of Montebello by building his house on the border that divides the Mexican Americans from the white, English-speaking communities.

Among other devices *The Brick People* relies on an insect motif to bring out the racial tensions in the Los Angeles area. In the novel Mexicans and Mexican Americans are treated like cockroaches or vile insects. They are segregated, insulted, and dispossessed. But the characters maintain the vitality, adaptability, and regenerative powers of insects. For example, Doña Eulalia is robbed of her land and house. The oak tree symbolizing her ancestral roots is destroyed by the despoilers, and the tree is ultimately consumed by millions of insects. Yet, these insects are a symbol of energy, life, and regeneration. When the Simons brothers die, their corpses are invaded by insects—the metaphorical revenge of the *mexicano* against his oppressors. Morales traces this oppression back to one of the most important events in U.S. history: the 1848 Treaty of GUADALUPE HIDALGO. On paper the treaty guaranteed land tenure for Mexicans who became U.S. citizens at the end of the U.S.-Mexican War. In practice land rights were ignored, and family properties were appropriated by the United States. This theme is also explored in Morales's *Reto en el paraíso*.

Morales conveys an ambivalence about Simons that readers can see by comparing *Barrio on the Edge* with *The Brick People*. *The Brick People* deals with the brickyard at its height of production; it illustrates the positive and negative effects of the brickyard on the Mexican-American community. In *The Brick People* Simons offers its workers housing, a school, and a church; the general store where all the families buy their groceries recalls the haciendas of prerevolutionary Mexico, where all residents are expected to do their shopping and to which they enter into inescapable debt. Within the neighborhood diversions can be found in the founding of a baseball team, the hiring of a band, or other forms of Walter Simons's calculated benevolence. In this regard Morales models the character of Walter Simons on the paternalism of the early 20th-century Mexican dictator Porfirio Díaz.

Morales began writing *Caras viejas y vino nuevo* (*Barrio on the Edge*) while he was in high school, and he completed the book during his last year at Rutgers. *Caras viejas y vino nuevo* (which literally means "Old faces and new wine") deals with the closure of Simons Brickyard. The novel is about barrio youth who are plagued by unemployment, drug abuse, and gang warfare. The young men of the barrio, modeled on Morales's friends, acquaintances, and neighbors, come to represent Mexicans who are cast aside when they are no longer of use to capitalism.

Morales's *The Rag Doll Plagues* is, as its title suggests, both postmodern and apocalyptic. In this novel people come to live in and eat from contaminated garbage dumps in Mexico City, giving rise to blood mutation in a generation of garbage pickers. Ironically the blood of the garbage pickers becomes valuable in combatting the 21st-century plague. This plague threatens the human race, especially the Anglos who have little resistance. Anglo families adopt poor Mexican plague-resistant children who can be used for a blood transfusion to combat the contagion. Caught between the lines of medicine, disease, and management of ethnic population is Gabi Chung, a Chinese-American doctor. She has allowed one of her arms to be amputated at the elbow and has been fitted with a computerized prosthesis in order to perform instantaneous medical tests. Though helping to combat the plague, her character represents the height of detachment and functionality; in the name of science, she has lost some autonomy and individuality in the replacement of a human arm with a machine.

Morales's vision focuses on the community but extends to cover the major events of the 20th century. He depicts the discrimination against Mexicans during the deportations of the Great Depression, the enforcement of segregated neighborhoods, and the Zoot Suit Riots of World War II. In so doing Morales enters into a conversation with LUIS VALDEZ, author of the famous Chicano play *ZOOT SUIT* (1978), and offers his own commentary on the riots when U.S. soldiers entered Los Angeles barrios to threaten Mexican youth. With a multicultural perspective Morales also explores the mistreatment of the Chinese in several of his novels. In *The Brick People*, hundreds of Chinese are excavated from the clay on the Simons Brickyard; these laborers and immigrants had been massacred in the late 19th century. The massacre was dismissed as mere legend by the Anglo community, but the excavations reveal a historical reality. In this regard Morales has something in common with the Cuban Chinese characters of CRISTINA GARCÍA's *MONKEY HUNTING* (2003).

In his works Morales combines biography, autobiography, and fiction with attentiveness to the history of Mexican Americans in the United States;

his novels help to make the "invisible" individuals and laborers more visible.

Bibliography

Gurpegui, José Antonio, ed. *Alejandro Morales: Fiction Past, Present, Future Perfect.* Tempe, Ariz.: Bilingual Review Press, 1996.

Morales, Alejandro. *Barrio on the Edge.*

———. *The Brick People.* Houston, Tex.: Arte Público Press, 1988.

———. *Death of an Anglo.* Tempe, Ariz.: Bilingual Review Press, 1988.

———. *The Rag Doll Plagues.* Houston, Tex.: Arte Público Press, 1992.

———. *Waiting to Happen.* San Jose, Calif.: Chusma House Publications, 2001.

Tamar Diana Wilson

Mother Tongue Demetria Martínez (1994)

Mexican-American author DEMETRIA MARTÍNEZ published her first novel, *Mother Tongue,* in 1994. *Mother Tongue* portrays the relationship between Mary, a 19-year-old woman living alone in Albuquerque, New Mexico, and José Luis, an activist and liberation theologist from El Salvador. José Luis has had to flee his country due to the civil war. Mary's grandmother Soledad is involved with the sanctuary movement, a faith-based movement assisting refugees from El Salvador and Guatemala. Soledad asks her granddaughter to go to Albuquerque International Airport to welcome José Luis, who has been smuggled to the United States as an illegal refugee. Mary immediately falls in love with the man, but the differences in their age and background come in the way of their relationship. A decisive turning point is reached when José Luis beats Mary when they are having sex. Caught in a flashback and marked by the civil war in El Salvador, he takes Mary for a death squad soldier. This act of violence makes Mary remember, in turn, the sexual abuse suffered when she was seven.

The narrative, divided in five parts, spans 20 years; a 39-year-old Mary recalls how she met and fell in love with José Luis in 1982. She revisits the past in order to fulfill the promise she made to God

that she would tell their son the story of his parents; however, Mary's memories and impressions are both challenged and complemented by the intervention of other narrators. José Luis's version of events is interspersed throughout the novel, and one of his letters to Mary provides the epilogue. The narrative also conveys Soledad's voice through her letters, as well as the thoughts of Mary's son, also called José Luis. The characters' clashing standpoints appear in a wide array of eclectic materials. These materials include newspaper reports, journal entries, letters, poems by Salvadoran writer Claribel Alegría, quotations from the Salvadoran poet and revolutionary Roque Dalton and the American singer Paul Simon, horoscopes, recipes, and shopping lists. This rich use of textuality allows the author to convey effectively how ordinary people play an active part in international historical developments as their lives become linked with wider-reaching events. *Mother Tongue* reflects on the nature of love and spirituality, as well as on sociopolitical issues including immigration, activism, solidarity, and U.S. foreign policies.

The novel presents itself as a love story from its opening sentence, in which Mary announces that she knew she would make love to José Luis from the first time she saw him; however, its sociopolitical concerns are equally evident. Dedicated "to the memory of the disappeared," *Mother Tongue* advocates international solidarity and assistance to refugees, while criticizing U.S. policies in Central America. The story is partly based on Martínez's experiences in 1988, when she was indicted for smuggling two Salvadoran women into the United States together with other charges potentially leading to a 25-year sentence. As a reporter working on the sanctuary movement for the *Albuquerque Journal,* Martínez had accompanied a Lutheran minister as he helped the women enter the country. The government tried to use a poem by Martínez, "Nativity for Two Salvadoran Women," as evidence against her, but she was acquitted on First Amendment grounds. As the love theme becomes inextricably interlinked with the novel's sociopolitical concerns, the story of Mary and José Luis can be considered an allegory for the differences and connections between Latin American and U.S. Latino identities (Kandiyoti 421–446). *Mother Tongue,* which was awarded the 1994 Western States Award for fiction, was followed by the poetry collections *Breathing Between the Lines* (1997) and *The Devil's Workshop* (2002), and the essay collection *Confessions of a Berlitz-Tape Chicana* (2005). It can be read in the context of CHICANO LITERATURE as well as within the political framework of Latin American fiction.

Bibliography

Castillo, Debra A. "Barbed Wire Words: Demetria Martínez's *Mother Tongue.*" *Intertexts* 1, no. 1 (1997): 8–24.

Kandiyoti, Dalia. "Host and Guest in the 'Latino Contact Zone': Narrating Solidarity and Hospitality in *Mother Tongue.*" *Comparative American Studies* 2, no. 4 (2004): 421–446.

Manolis, Argie J. "The Writer as Witness: An Interview with Demetria Martinez." *Hayden's Ferry Review* 24 (1999): 37–51.

Martínez, Demetria. *Mother Tongue.* New York: Ballantine, 1996.

McCracken, Ellen. *New Latina Narrative: The Feminine Space of Postmodern Ethnicity.* Tucson: University of Arizona Press, 1999.

———. "Social Justice, Spirituality, and Chicana Writing: An Interview with Demetria Martínez." *Journal of American Studies of Turkey* 12 (2000): 59–74.

Marta Vizcaya Echano

Moya Luna, María Francisca

See CAMPOBELLO, NELLIE.

Muñoz, Elías Miguel (1954–   ) *(editor, poet)*

Elías Miguel Muñoz was born in Ciego de Avila, Camagüey, Cuba, on September 29, 1954. In 1969, at the age of 15, Muñoz immigrated with his family to the United States, settling in Canoga Park, California. He completed his high school education in Hawthorne and graduated from California State University, Dominguez Hills. He received his M.A. and Ph.D. in Spanish from the University of California, Irvine. In 1987 he revised his dissertation and published the book as *El discurso utópico de la sexualidad en Manuel Puig* (The Utopian discourse of sexuality in Manuel Puig). For four years Muñoz taught at Wichita State University and then became, with Tracy Terrell and Jeanne Egasse, an integral part of the *Dos mundos* textbook team (McGraw-Hill). He married the Latino literature critic Karen Christian and has two children, Aidan and Annika. After residence in New Mexico, he returned to California and to editorial work with McGraw-Hill.

Muñoz's poetry has been anthologized in such texts as *Hispanics in the U.S.* (1982), *9 poetas cubanos* (1984), *Cuban American Writers: Los atrevidos* (1988), and *Poesía cubana: La isla entera* (1995; Cuban poetry: The entire island). His first two collections of poetry, *No fue posible el sol* (1989; The sun was not possible) and *En estas tierras* (1989; In This Land), represent traditional themes of exile, loss, and nostalgia. Two poems in particular, "No fue posible el sol" and "Los niños de Newport Beach," consider the phenomenon of a Cuban family living among tanned, English-speaking southern Californians.

Muñoz's first novel, *Los viajes de Orlando Cachumbambe* (1984; The travels of Orlando Cachumbambe), depicts the autobiographical experiences of a graduate student immersed in Latino activism. Written in Spanish, *Los viajes de Orlando Cachumbambe* traces the mythic journey of Orlando's search of identity, a search that brings him face to face with anti-Cuban sentiment. His life seesaws between two cultures in his encounters with the university, his grandparents' home, and Union City, New Jersey, where Cubans live in exile. Caught between memory and actuality, the classroom and grandmother's kitchen, Muñoz ponders what GUSTAVO PÉREZ FIRMAT calls a "life on the hyphen," the condition of being Cuban American. Muñoz, like Pérez Firmat, lives both within and outside Cuban culture. After *Los viajes de Orlando Cachumbambe,* Muñoz edited a collection of poetry, *Desde esta orilla: Poesía cubana del exilio* (1989; From this shore: Cuban poetry of exile), which again deals with issues of being in exile from Cuba, a literary form of protest against FIDEL CASTRO's regime.

In 1989 Muñoz published *Crazy Love,* his first novel in English. Stylistically *Crazy Love* experiments with the expression of nostalgia and coming of age. Julian, the protagonist, is a Cuban-American bisexual rock musician whose crossover dreams traverse lines of ethnicity, sexuality, and family. Written in the first person, *Crazy Love* relies on multiple voices, letters, monologues, and songs. Because of the rich use of dialogue and mixing of modes, Muñoz transformed *Crazy Love* into a dramatic work, *The L.A. Scene,* which was produced in California and New York.

Especially notable in Muñoz's writing career is the publication of *The Greatest Performance* (1991), the first Latino novel to deal with AIDS and therefore an important contribution to LATINO GAY LITERATURE. *The Greatest Performance* represents a marginalized U.S. Cuban in a southern California setting. This novel is a jeremiad against machismo and the repression of gays in Latino (typically Catholic and traditional) culture. Mario, the gay protagonist, grows up in an environment of both physical and psychological abuse. Terribly sick, he suffers total rejection by his family as he lies dying. Only the friendship and loving care of Rosa, a Cuban-American lesbian teacher, affirms his existence. Muñoz uses raw emotion, humor, and sexuality in *The Greatest Performance* to confront homophobia, machismo, *marianismo* (elevating women to the level of the Virgin Mary), and AIDS within Latino community. He staged *The Last Guantanamera: A Performance,* based on themes of *The Greatest Performance.*

Meanwhile, his novel *Brand New Memory* (1998) features the story of Gina Domingo, a bright Cuban-American "princess" who lives in California. Gina Domingo is raised in an upper-class, suburban society by her hardworking florist father and her "French" mother, a social climber. As a high school student, Gina plans a career as a moviemaker. Fantasy dominates Gina's life as she imagines herself the mythical Taina (a woman of the indigenous group that peopled Puerto Rico and Cuba). Her grandmother's somewhat unexpected arrival from Cuba prompts Gina to explore her identity as a Cuban American. The reader must also acknowledge the elitism and racism of Cuban Americans who have "arrived." Identity becomes a construction that is at once familial, collective, and individual. *Brand New Memory* examines island and U.S. values, and it confronts stereotypes readily held by both Cubans and Americans. In *Brand New Memory* Muñoz brings to life Cuba, its history, its religious practices, and the diaspora. Not only does Gina Domingo acquire a "brand new memory"; so, too, does the reader through the reading experience. For its interest in identity and bicultural situations this work and others by Muñoz can be read within the context of CUBAN-AMERICAN LITERATURE.

Since the mid-1990s, Muñoz's work has been devoted to creative textbook development. He replaced the late Tracy Terrell as editor of the award-winning textbook *Dos mundos.* He has since published three readers in the McGraw-Hill Storytellers series. *Viajes fantásticos* features two of his short stories "Mi querida cuñada" (My dear sister-in-law) and El último sol" (The last sun), set respectively in Puerto Rico and Mexico. The literary reader *Ladrón de mente* (1999; Mind's thief) set in a postmodern vision of Spain, combines science fiction and history with particular attention to modernization and changing gender roles. *Isla de luz* (2001; Island of light) takes place on a fictional Caribbean island, Taina, incorporating events and personalities from the histories of Puerto Rico, Cuba, and the Dominican Republic. The journey allows the protagonist to travel from a floating spacecraft of the future to the mythical Taina of the past. The odyssey of Muñoz, which began in Camagüey, Cuba, now carries his readers to worlds beyond chronology, immersed always in Latino culture.

Bibliography
Mullins, Greg A. "Seeking Asylum: Literary Reflections on Sexuality, Ethnicity and Human Rights." *MELUS* 28, no. 1 (Spring 2003): 145–171.

Muñoz, Elías Miguel. *Brand New Memory.* Houston, Tex.: Arte Público Press, 1988.

———. *Crazy Love.* Houston, Tex.: Arte Público Press, 1988.

———. *El discurso utópico de la sexualidad en Manuel Puig.* Madrid: Editorial Pliegos, 1987.

———. *En estas tierras/In This Land.* Tempe, Ariz.: Bilingual Press, 1989.

———. *The Greatest Performance.* Houston, Tex.: Arte Público Press, 1991.

———. *Isla de luz.* New York: McGraw-Hill, 2001.

———. *Ladrón de mente.* New York: McGraw-Hill, 1999.

———. *Viajes fantásticos.* New York: McGraw-Hill, 1999.

John Charles Miller

Natural Man, A Gary Soto (1999)

GARY SOTO grew up in the Mexican-American culture of the San Joaquin Valley. To this day childhood experiences dominate his writing. Soto's work includes more than 40 books, three short films, and an opera libretto; Soto therefore is rightly praised as one of the country's foremost contributors to CHICANO LITERATURE and one of the most accomplished American writers of his generation, regardless of ethnic heritage. While his work arises from the specific complexities and details of Mexican-American life, Soto renders a moving portrayal of the human condition that is accessible to a variety of audiences. As he writes in the poem "Late Confession," there is no race of intrinsic preeminence, no ethnicity of superior being.

Soto's eleventh full-length collection of adult poetry, *A Natural Man* (1999), exemplifies this belief in the precariousness of identity. The collection depicts with humor and heartbreak the period between Soto's childhood to his late 40s; these depictions arrive in such clear, inclusive language and metaphor that they quickly transcend the personal to become universal evocations. Throughout these 44 narrative poems, Soto neither praises nor disdains his position on the margins of society; instead, he uses it as a strategic vantage point from which to observe, think, and communicate about life.

Driving these poems is Soto's wonderment with life, even in moments of frailty, boredom, and misery. Thus, in *A Natural Man*'s most self-consciously despondent (and least ironic) poem, "A Young Man's Belief in Dark Moods," Soto's language remains vibrant and his metaphors invigorating. For example, although melancholy while wandering the woods in a daze and thinking of LA LLORONA, he cannot ignore the natural beauty around him. Likewise, in the poem "Inheritance," a tender elegy for his grandfather, Soto recalls that the old man, despite being split between national cultures and languages, simply sought the peace and calm of sunset.

Thus, the reasons for Soto's melancholic tone are understandably many, but none is more significant than his acute awareness of his Chicano heritage and identity. The book includes Soto's recognition of his status as a Mexican American, which comes in the poem "The Blue Cavalry and the Falling Indians," which was prompted by watching an old western film on television. In the poem "Where Were You When You First Heard of Air-Conditioning" Soto situates himself within the Chicano working class, suffering the summer heat without the luxury of air-conditioning.

The most urgent political issue of *A Natural Man* is Soto's portrayal of the conflict between the curiosity of natural man and the rigidity of the citizen who is trained to serve the state as labor. The poem "Seventh Grade Shoes" is a good example of this conflict. Speaking in the first person, Soto details his school's systematized training of the individual to exist as chattel, as well as the socially induced "shame" of poverty. More ominously, at the poem's conclusion, he comes across a dead pigeon in the street, and the bird becomes a metaphorical warning about the danger in being an outcast: The pigeon had died and no one cared. In using the citizen figure Soto draws on such classics as Plato's *The Republic*.

With his poetic vision, Soto contributes to a rich history of California poets including Robinson Jeffers and Philip Levine. And, because of the situations and images of his writing, Soto makes an important contribution to Chicano literature.

Seth Michelson

New World Border: Prophecies, Poems and Loqueras for the End of the Century, The Guillermo Gómez-Peña (1996)

In *The New World Border: Prophecies, Poems and Loqueras for the End of the Century*, GUILLERMO GÓMEZ-PEÑA presents an anthology of his performance art, poems, and essays. Published in 1996, the book imagines the not-so-distant future world where geographical and political borders collapse and give way to conceptual borders. Expressing many of the themes in WARRIOR FOR GRINGOSTROIKA: ESSAYS, PERFORMANCE TEXTS, AND POETRY (1993), the individual pieces collected here rely on various forms of media to understand "the border" in North-South relations and between the United States and Mexico in particular. Titles of the pieces include "Freefalling Toward a Borderless Future" and "Real Life Border Thriller." With the title's allusion to the First World–Third World rhetoric Gómez-Peña offers a chronology of his art from 1993 to 1995 and focuses on work that expresses his political opposition to the First World and Third World models. Offering instead the conception of a "Fourth World," Gómez-Peña emphasizes a land free of political violence, a place where art and ideas flourish. For the author the Fourth World is shaped by shared experiences and is therefore more flexible and subject to change than the traditional nation-state demarcations.

Gómez-Peña explains "that the border cannot be fixed in any one site; it is dynamic and ever changing and thus defies easy categorization." He finds that the more expansive his Chicano identity is, the stronger his art will become as an artist creating projects in a postnational culture. The longest piece in the collection, "The New World Border: Prophecies for the End of the Century," documents one of Gomez-Peña's best-known and longest-running performance installations, which toured for two years around the United States, Canada, Europe, and South America. The performance was often presented in collaboration with Cuban performance artist Coco Fusco and Chicano artist Roberto Sifuentes. The artists spoke in English, Spanish, and French, as well as SPANGLISH and several made up "robo-languages." Crucial to this anthology—and something that we do not see in his earlier work—is Gómez-Peña's use of high-tech images, ideas, and equipment to convey the aforementioned political views. He is particularly interested in the idea of cyberspace, which he uses to symbolize the conceptual borders make up the utopian Fourth World, shaped by the dimension of time rather than space or place. In many ways an extension of Gómez-Peña's days with the Border Arts Workshop, *The New World Border* is essential reading for anyone interested in understanding the shifts in Gomez-Peña's political consciousness during the high-tech and highly globalized period of the 1990s. This work can be read within the context of CHICANO LITERATURE and multimedia performance art.

Bibliography

Gómez-Peña, Guillermo. *Dangerous Border Crossers: The Artist Talks Back*. New York: Routledge, 2000.
———. *Friendly Cannibals*. San Francisco, Calif.: Artspace Books, 1996.

————. *New World Border: Prophecies, Poems and Loqueras for the End of the Century.* San Francisco, Calif.: City Lights Books, 1996.

————. *Warrior for Gringostroika: Essays, Performance Texts, and Poetry.* St. Paul, Minn.: Graywolf Press, 1993.

Lysa Rivera

Niggli, Josephina (1910–1983) *(playwright, poet, short story writer, novelist)*

Josephina Niggli was born July 13, 1910, in Monterrey, Mexico. Critics such as María Herrera-Sobek and Raymund Paredes identify her as an influential voice in Hispanic literature because her work recalls the history of Mexico and explores the complications of inhabiting more than one culture. Her father, Frederick Ferdinand Niggli, of Swiss and Alsatian descent hailed from Texas, and her mother, Goldie Morgan Niggli, a concert violinist, came from an Irish, French, and German background. Despite her Swiss, Alsatian, Irish, French, and German heritage, Niggli is culturally Mexican American. She grew up both bicultural and bilingual, and her work demonstrates a Mexican influence evident in her representation of Mexican village life.

Frederick Niggli moved from Texas in 1893 and managed a cement factory in Hidalgo, a town in central Mexico. Because of political turmoil in Mexico, Niggli's family sent three-year-old Josephina to San Antonio, Texas. Eventually the Niggli family spent seven years living in various places throughout the southwestern United States. In 1920 they returned to Mexico, where Niggli lived until age 15. Before returning to San Antonio in 1925 Niggli studied at home under the guidance of her mother. In San Antonio Niggli attended Main Avenue High School and then Incarnate Word College, where she earned a bachelor's degree. In college Niggli wrote both prose and poetry, winning prizes for both. She was awarded first and second prizes in the National Catholic Poetry Contest and second place in the *Ladies' Home Journal* short story contest. In 1928 she published her first collection of poems, *Mexican Silhouettes*, written during her years at Incarnate Word in San Antonio.

Before enrolling in the Carolina Playmakers program, one of the leading drama programs in the country, at the University of North Carolina (where she received an M.A. in 1936), Niggli spent four years honing her playwriting skills with the San Antonio Little Theater. From 1935 to 1937 the Carolina Playmakers produced several of Niggli's plays including *Singing Valley* in 1936 and *The Cry of Dolores* and *The Fair-God* in 1937, as well as plays from her collection MEXICAN FOLK PLAYS, published in 1938. *Mexican Folk Plays* includes *Tooth or Shave, Soldadera* (Soldier woman), *The Velvet Goat, Azteca,* and SUNDAY COSTS FIVE PESOS. Also in this period Niggli worked in Mexican theater with the support of two Rockefeller fellowships (1935–36, 1937–38). In 1938 Niggli received the Fellowship of the Bureau of New Plays and moved to New York. The following year she accepted a position teaching English and drama at the University of North Carolina, Chapel Hill. For a brief time Niggli worked in Hollywood (1948) as a writer for MGM. She adapted her novel MEXICAN VILLAGE (1945) for film, and in so doing Niggli gained recognition as the first Mexican-American woman to earn writing credit for a major studio film. In 1956 Niggli began teaching English and drama at Western Carolina University, where she remained until 1975.

Best known as a playwright, Niggli also wrote three novels: *Mexican Village, Step Down, Elder Brother* (1947), and *A Miracle of Mexico* (1964). Her book on playwriting, *Pointers on Playwriting,* appeared in 1945 and in a revised edition in 1967.

Folklore and history are major concerns in Niggli's work, especially in her treatment of life in the village during and after the MEXICAN REVOLUTION (1910–20) and her interest in Mexican legends. For example, *Mexican Village* abounds with popular stories and songs of Mexico, and these elements allow the audience to gain insight about the various characters. Like other Latin American writers, Niggli also investigates racial boundaries, exposes hierarchies and class systems within Mexico, and questions accepted gender roles. In the historical drama, *Soldadera,* for example, Niggli depicts women as important participants in the Mexican Revolution rather than as mere camp followers.

Niggli does rely on Mexican and gender stereotypes, which, for some readers, made her work more palatable to her American audiences. Although Niggli includes stereotypes in her work, she also depicts fully developed and complicated characters who challenge those very stereotypes. For instance, alongside the swaggering macho, Niggli presents strong men who demonstrate sensitivity and vulnerability or women who refuse to conform to gender expectations (Paredes 90).

Niggli holds a fraught place in the canon of Hispanic-American literature. Niggli herself never comfortably identified as either Chicana or Mexican, yet her work both anticipates and provides a cultural context for CHICANO LITERATURE.

Bibliography

Herrera-Sobek, María. Introduction to *Mexican Village,* by Josephina Niggli. Albuquerque: University of New Mexico Press, 1994.

Niggli, Josephina. *Mexican Folk Plays.* New York: Arno Press, 1976.

———. *Mexican Village.* Albuquerque: University of New Mexico Press, 1994.

———. *Step Down, Elder Brother: A Novel.* New York: Rinehart, 1947.

Paredes, Raymund. "The Evolution of Chicano Literature." *MELUS* 5 (1978): 71–110.

Catherine Cucinella

Nilda Nicholasa Mohr (1973)

NICHOLASA MOHR lives in New York City, and much of her fiction is set in the Bronx. She started her artistic career as a graphic artist but soon discovered that writing was also a powerful way to express herself. Together with other Puerto Ricans who started writing in the 1960s and 1970s, such

as PIRI THOMAS, Mohr has become one of the most important literary voices within the Puerto Rican community in the United States. *Nilda,* published in 1973, is a novel about a girl growing up in a New York barrio in the 1940s, living in harsh circumstances. *Nilda* received the 1974 Jane Addams Children's Book Award.

In the novel Nilda has a brother who is a drug addict, a stepfather who is sick, and a mother who suffers trying to keep the family together. *Nilda* recounts the miseries of the barrio, its violence, drug dealing, and poverty, but it is a novel that also tells stories that need to be told, stories that are life affirming and positive despite adversity. In Mohr's work women act as the agents that previously had been almost absent in the literature about the Puerto Rican barrio. Mohr is especially interested in recovering women's stories while rejecting false stereotypes of Puerto Rican women. Nilda's mother is an example of a strong woman who in the end becomes a positive model for Nilda: "'I know you have something all yours. Keep it . . . hold on, guard it. Never give it to nobody . . . not to your lover, not to your kids, . . . it don't belong to them . . . and they have no right to take it'" (277). Important themes in *Nilda* are the female experience of growing up in New York, mother-daughter and familial relationships, art as a liberating force against oppressive social situations, and differences between Latin American and U.S. values, among others.

Nilda is a coming-of-age story but can also be considered partly autobiographical since the young protagonist (like the author herself) discovers art as an alternative way to cope with negative circumstances and as a mean of self-assertion. In *Nilda* life in the barrio is described from the female perspective of a young girl who is witness to all the violence that was present in Piri Thomas's neighborhood, but there are differences between both works due to the main character's gender. According to Mohr, when asked by a publisher to change her manuscript into a female version of Thomas's DOWN THESE MEAN STREETS (1967), she replied: "I have never been in jail. . . . Puerto Rican women in El Barrio have had to cope with other situations . . . In my works I have tried to capture the everyday richness and variety of a warm and vital community and my characters always try to overcome no matter what the circumstances" (Acosta-Belén 38–39).

The barrio is also seen as the source of nurturing and resistance, a refuge against "official" spaces like the school and the camp where Nilda does not feel at home and where she suffers humiliation and discrimination. The tragedy that awaits her in the outside world of the barrio is counteracted by the support she finds in her mother and stepfather. They represent the will to survive under unfavorable conditions, the warmth that such a threatened youth needs, and the resilience they need to advance in their future despite social stratification and segregation. Mohr seems to give examples of the positive human qualities that can also be found in the Latino barrio. The barrio can be a source of artistic creativity and a literary vocation: "The diagonal, horizontal and vertical cracks in the sidewalks became dividing regions stimulating her imagination. The different shapes of the worn-out surfaces of concrete and asphalt developed before her eyes into dragons, animals, oceans and planets of the universe" (35–36). Nilda frequently uses her imagination to transform an outside hostile world into a new, beautiful, but fictitious world.

Although the novel uses a third-person narrator, which facilitates a necessary distance from the character, the perspective of the young girl is still useful for Mohr to explore new possibilities to represent the wide Puerto Rican experience. Nilda's naive vision emphasizes the impact of some narrative events and helps the reader have a different perspective on personal and historical events. Mohr's language is concise and direct, making the novel an adolescent book; her realistic use of language makes her story appealing for young readers who recognize the street talk that accompanies standard literary English. For its themes and characterizations *Nilda* can be read within the context of PUERTO RICAN LITERATURE.

Bibliography

Acosta-Belén, Edna. "Conversations with Nicholasa Mohr." *Revista Chicano-Riqueña* 8, no. 2 (1980): 35–41.

Miller, John. "The Emigrant and New York City: A Consideration of Four Puerto Rican Writers." *MELUS* 5, no. 3 (1978): 82–99.

Mohr, Eugene V. *The Nuyorican Experience: Literature of the Puerto Rican Minority.* Westport, Conn., and London: Greenwood Press, 1982.

Mohr, Nicholasa. *Nilda.* New York: Harper & Row, 1973.

Ocasio, Rafael. "From Nuyorican Barrio to Issues on Puerto Rican Literature Outside New York City: Nicholasa Mohr and Judith Ortiz Cofer." In *Literature and Ethnic Discrimination,* edited by Michael J. Meyer, 187–203. Amsterdam and Atlanta, Ga.: Rodopi, 1997.

Sánchez González, Lisa. *Boricua Literatura: A Literary History of the Puerto Rican Diaspora.* New York: New York University Press, 2001.

Zarnowski, Myra. "Growing Up Puerto Rican: The Fiction of Nicholasa Mohr." *Dragon Lode* 9 (1991): 5–8.

Antonia Domínguez Miguela

Nuyorican Poets Cafe

The Nuyorican Poets Cafe is located at 236 East Third Street in Manhattan. Established by MIGUEL ALGARÍN, the Nuyorican Poets Cafe is listed as a "hot spot" in promotional materials about New York City, and heralded as a cultural center of the famed Lower East Side (Loisaida).

Now a New York City icon, the Cafe was originally founded in 1973 in the cramped East Village apartment of Puerto Rican poet Algarín. Gatherings included such authors as MIGUEL PIÑERO, Pedro Pietri, and Lucky Cienfuegos, and it provided a creative outlet for the streetwise and urgent voices of New York poets and artists. By the mid-1970s interest in the Cafe had spread because it offered a venue for avant-garde work by Latinos, especially Puerto Ricans living in New York (Nuyoricans). The success of the Cafe can be measured, in part, by the success of its performers and writers. By 1975 Piñero had received critical acclaim for his play SHORT EYES (1974), and Algarín had edited the anthology *Nuyorican Poetry: An Anthology of Puerto Rican Words and Feelings* (1975). The group thus moved to an Irish bar, the Sunshine Café, on East Sixth Street and renamed the site the Nuyorican Poets Cafe. Poetry readings evolved into the famed "poetry slams," theatrical pieces, musical performances, and art exhibitions. With increasing crowds the directors of the Cafe purchased and renovated its current site on East Third Street in 1980. Closed for a few years in the 1980s, it reopened in its renovated space with new vigor and with poet Bob Holman on the board of directors. In the 1990s the spectacular success of the Cafe as a hip cultural hangout became firmly established. Members of the surrounding working-class community could elbow their way to the bar and sit next to those who had arrived in a limousine. The Cafe was democratic, egalitarian, and "in."

According to the Nuyorican Poets Cafe's Web site, its mission is to "create a multi-cultural venue that both nurtures artists and exhibits a variety of artistic works." It is "dedicated to providing a stage for the arts with access for the widest public." Hundreds of poets received their start or at least a boost at the Cafe. Its "alums" are featured in a best-selling anthology that also received the 1994 American Book Award, *Aloud: Voices from the Nuyorican Poets Cafe* (1994), edited by Algarín and Holman. *Aloud* includes such notables as Algarín, cofounder Piñero, Pietri, WILLIE PERDOMO, NANCY MERCADO, Ntozake Shange, PIRI THOMAS, Tony Medina, Jessica Hagedorn, Edwin Torres, and Jimmy Santiago Baca. The list of performers at the Cafe reads like a "Who's Who" of late 20th and early 21st century spoken-word poetry.

The Nuyorican Poets Cafe holds the "Poetry Slam" every Friday night. With doors opening at 9 P.M., the small, brick-walled venue is packed by the time the slam starts at 10. Lines form in front of the Cafe and extend down the block. Winners of the slams are selected by the audience and can go on to national and international slam competitions. "Open Room" takes place after the slam.

Aspiring poets can bring a poem once they sign the list of the evening's performers. Many poets get their start in just this way.

Also renowned is the Cafe's openness to innovative theatrical projects. Some of these texts appear in the anthology *Action: The Nuyorican Poets Café Theater Festival* (1997), with works from such playwrights as Piñero, Ishmael Reed, and Amiri Baraka, as well as emerging figures, such as Frank Pérez, Gloria Feliciano, and Janice Astor del Valle. The theater has received more than 30 Audelco awards and an OBIE grant for excellence. Under the leadership of Rome Neal as theater artistic director, the Cafe has been praised for its poetry slams and performance.

With the rise of hip hop as a cultural phenomenon the Cafe responded with the "All That! Hip Hop, Poetry and Jazz" night hosted now by Flaco Navaja. In this space rap artists and emcees perform with one another. Another series entitled "Words" provides young writers and emcees a forum to perform to an audience of their peers.

Comedian, actor, and filmmaker John Leguizamo, author of *FREAK: A SEMI-DEMI-QUASI-PSEUDO AUTOBIOGRAPHY* (1998), is one of the many talents who appeared in the Cafe's "Fifth Night" screenplay reading and short film series. Of the hundreds of readings at the Cafe more than 40 have been made into films or are currently in production. Meanwhile, a comedy troupe, Nuyorican Rule, comments on Latino realities in its regular monthly appearances at the Cafe. Finally, live music is a constant at the Cafe. From hip hop to Latin jazz, rock to alternative, traditional to the most experimental, music keeps the place jumping until late in the evening. The Cafe's weekly "Latin Jazz Jam Session" has been a Critics Choice at *New York Press* for six consecutive years.

The Nuyorican Poets Cafe has been a staple of New York City nightlife for more than three decades. Its award-winning programs, its variety of productions and performances, and its singular "Poetry Slam" night have guaranteed it a special place in both New York and Latino cultural history. To attend one of its events it to experience

New York at its most vibrant; to participate in one of its events is to have "arrived."

Bibliography

Algarín, Miguel, and Lois Griffith, eds. *Action: The Nuyorican Poets Café Theater Festival.* New York: Simon & Schuster, 1997.

Algarín, Miguel, and Bob Holman, eds. *Aloud: Voices from the Nuyorican Poets Cafe.* New York: Henry Holt, 1994.

Nuyorican Poets Cafe Web site. Available online. URL: http://www.nuyorican.org. Accessed May 26, 2008.

Marilyn Kiss

Obejas, Achy (1956–) *(fiction writer, essayist)*

Achy Obejas was born in Havana, Cuba, in 1956. At the age of six she fled Cuba with her family on a raft that was picked up by an oil tanker, and they were taken to the United States. She first lived a year and a half in Miami, but Obejas grew up in Michigan City, Indiana. In 1979 she moved to Chicago, where she has worked as a journalist at the *Chicago Sun-Times,* the *Chicago Reader,* and, since 1992, the *Chicago Tribune.* She holds an M.F.A. in creative writing from Warren Wilson College, and has earned fellowships at Yaddo, Ragdale, and the Virginia Center for the Arts. Her work has appeared in the *Windy City Times,* the *Advocate,* the *Los Angeles Times, Ms.* magazine, the *Nation,* the *Village Voice,* and *Vogue.* Her fiction has appeared in numerous journals and anthologies including *Cubana* and *Cuba on the Verge;* her poetry has appeared in *Revista Chicano-Riqueña* and the *Beloit Poetry Journal.* Her awards include two Lambda book awards, a National Endowment for the Arts poetry fellowship (1986), the Peter Lisagor Award for team coverage of the 1998 Chicago mayoral elections, and the Pulitzer Prize in 2001 for contributions to the series Gateway to Gridlock. Obejas currently teaches writing at the University of Chicago and is at work on several projects, including an English translation of the work of Cuban poet Nicolás Guillén.

Her first book, a collection of short stories entitled *We Came All the Way from Cuba So You Could Dress Like This?* was published in 1994. The intimacy and candor with which its characters—gay men and women, Cuban exiles, drug addicts, and the HIV-positive—are portrayed earned Obejas critical praise by authors such as Dennis Cooper and scholars such as Nara Araujo and Jorjet Harper. The title story, which has been reprinted in several anthologies, tells from a young girl's perspective the story of her family's arrival in Miami after leaving Cuba on a boat. The narrative flashes forward to scenes of her life in the United States and speculations about the life in Cuba that would never unfold. Other stories feature such characters as a white HIV-positive man on a road trip to Santa Fe with his Mexican lover, who, despite being gay, has a wife and children. This situation speaks to the complicated nature of being gay while keeping up appearances in a conservative Catholic culture.

Obejas's first novel, *Memory Mambo* (1996), won the 1997 Lambda Award for lesbian fiction. It tells the story of Juani Casas, a 25-year-old Cuban-American lesbian who runs her family's laundromat. Other characters include Juani's macho husband, Jimmy, and Juani's Puerto Rican ex-girlfriend, Gina, whose dedication to Latino political activism has kept her in the closet. After her breakup with Gina, Juani hides her sexuality from her family and winds up chasing down her father's myriad fancies and fabrications. These mistruths include his claim of having invented duct tape and the CIA's subsequent theft of his formula. Her quest to ascertain what is true and false about her father leads to a surprising revelation about the memories and experiences of Cuban Americans who did not choose to leave the island but were taken from Cuba before they were old enough to understand their circumstances, making them at once privileged and blameless. Paul Allatson writes, "Juani also realizes that memory itself—elusive, unreliable, selective, contradictory, and always unsingular—poses identifactory difficulties for Cubans in the U.S.A., whether they live in Chicago like herself or in the huge Cuban enclave in Miami" (160).

Obejas's second novel, *Days of Awe* (2001), grew out of her own experience at a 1994 reading, at which she was approached by a several Latin American Jewish women who recognized her surname as common among crypto-Jews (also known as Marranos, or *conversos* in Spanish and in Hebrew as *Anusim*). *Days of Awe* weaves the story of a family of crypto-Jewish Cuban exiles in the United States into the broader history of Cuba over the 20th century. It is narrated by Alejandra San José, a Cuban-American interpreter of Catholic upbringing who uncovers (like Juani in *Memory Mambo*) a family secret. She discovers her parents' semi-hidden Jewish origins. The San Josés live in a Jewish neighborhood in Chicago, and her father affects the manners of an old-fashioned Spanish gentleman; at the same time, he surreptitiously dons tefillin (head garb for Jewish men) and prays in the basement. *Days of Awe* received a 2002 Lambda Award and was named Best Book of Year by the *Los Angeles Times* and *Chicago Tribune*.

In both *Memory Mambo* and *Days of Awe* Obejas writes about the experiences of gay, lesbian, and bisexual characters to question how such categories work across cultures. Obejas's work therefore reveals a parallel interest in Jewishness and Cuban identity while viewing cultural difference through the lens of sexuality. Obejas explores with verve the details of human relations that fall, often humorously, between categories, as she has remarked, "[W]hen I go [to Miami] with my girlfriend, it never fails. She says 'My god, you're so Cuban' whereas my mother, across the table, is saying in her head, "My god, you're so American" (Stovall 53). For its themes and characterizations Obejas's work can be read within the context of both CUBAN-AMERICAN LITERATURE and LATINA LESBIAN LITERATURE.

Bibliography

Allatson, Paul. *Latino Dreams: Transcultural Traffic and the U.S. National Imaginary.* New York: Rodopi, 2002.

Araujo, Nara. "I Came All the Way from Cuba So I Could Speak Like This? Cuban and Cuban-American Literatures in the U.S." In *Comparing Postcolonial Literatures: Dislocations,* edited by Ashok Bery and Patricia Murray, 93–103. New York: Palgrave, 2000.

Harper, Jorjet. "Dancing to a Different Beat: An Interview with Achy Obejas." *Lambda Book Report* 5, no. 3 (September 1996): 3.

Obejas, Achy. *Days of Awe.* New York: Ballantine, 2001.

———. *Memory Mambo.* Pittsburgh, Pa.: Cleis Press, 1996.

———. *We Came All the Way from Cuba So You Could Dress Like This?* Pittsburgh, Pa.: Cleis Press, 1994.

Shapiro, Gregg. "In 'Awe': Achy Obejas on Her New Novel." *La Vida* (September 2001): 20.

Stavans, Ilan. *La Plaza: Achy Obejas, Conversations with Ilan Stavans.* Directed by Les Blank. VHS. 30 min. WGBH, 2001.

Stovall, Natasha. "Achy Obejas's Tales of Exile." *Village Voice,* February 25, 1998, p. 53.

Alex Feerst

Occupied America: A History of Chicanos
Rodolfo Acuña (1972)

Occupied America, by renowned scholar, activist, and teacher RODOLFO ACUÑA, was first published in 1972 with the subtitle *The Chicano's Struggle toward Liberation* and has been reissued in four subsequent editions, most recently in 2003. A Spanish-language edition, *América ocupada:*

Los chicanos y su lucha de liberación, translated by Ana María Palos, was published in 1976. *Occupied America* has long been the preeminent textbook in Chicano/a studies courses taught at universities across the United States and has evolved with each edition, synthesizing the latest scholarship. Voluminously researched and meticulously documented, with well over 2,000 footnotes, the 2003 edition, *Occupied America: A History of Chicanos,* is a textbook that also serves, as Cynthia Orozco has observed, as a reference volume of Chicano studies.

The text proceeds chronologically from pre-Columbian civilizations to the Spanish Conquest. It moves on from Europe's encounter with the New World to the history of the United States, with in-depth coverage of events and experiences in Texas, New Mexico, Arizona, and California since the 1800s, including the impact of the Treaty of GUADALUPE HIDALGO in 1848 and the MEXICAN REVOLUTION, 1910–20. Acuña provides detailed analyses of the 20th century by surveying the effects of the Great Depression in the 1930s and World War II, as well as the upheaval during the 1960s civil rights movement. In later editions his book also discusses the entrenchment of conservative politics in the 1980s under Ronald Reagan and George H. W. Bush. *Occupied America* includes such divergent topics as archaeological evidence of Aztec society, the conditions of Mexican workers in the early 20th century, Latino barrios in Chicago, and ballot initiatives on immigration and education in 1990s California. Recurrent areas of focus include immigration law, labor conditions, demographic data, the Chicano/a experience and activism, electoral politics, and educational systems.

Since the fourth edition, the text has included a chapter on history before 1821, which marshals archaeological and paleographic evidence on pre-Columbian civilizations such as the Olmec, Maya, Toltec, and Aztec and discusses the divergent experiences of the Spanish Conquest in various regions of Latin America. The text's purview has also expanded to include feminist scholarship as well as commentary on the increasing presence of Central American communities in southern California and northern Virginia. Acuña relies on a range of disciplines—literature, history, sociology—to deepen the reader's understanding of Chicano/a studies as a field of research.

From the first edition an essential element of *Occupied America* has been Acuña's sustained resolution to "write directly for Chicanas/Chicanos" with an activist concept of history (Calderon 22). Reflecting on the research incorporated into recent editions of the work, Acuña contends: "The new generation [cares] less about activism, racism, or even Mexican identity. Some consider themselves scientists or postmodernists, which is fine, but the urgency of past generations may be missing from their work" (xiv). Acuña also urges fellow Chicano intellectuals to embrace the difficult burden of self-scrutiny, to "cut the umbilical cord with our own fantasy heritage and incorporate analysis of the flaws of our past and present" (xiv). Though it has changed somewhat in approach and style over successive versions, *Occupied America* continues, like all of Acuña's work, to flow from an activist notion of scholarship that is radical in the broadest sense, dealing, as he puts it, "more with the politics of social transformation than 'Chicano Power'—there is a subtle difference between achieving power within the system and changing the rules of the system" (xv). Three decades after its initial publication, *Occupied America* continues to be among the most taught texts in Chicano studies classrooms, standing not only as required reading in Chicano/a history but as a milestone in the now thriving paradigm it helped to establish. Together with *Occupied America,* Acuña's ANYTHING BUT MEXICAN: CHICANOS IN CONTEMPORARY LOS ANGELES (1996) provides a context for CHICANO LITERATURE.

Bibliography

Acuña, Rodolfo F. *Anything but Mexican: Chicanos in Contemporary Los Angeles.* New York: Verso, 1996.

———. *A Community Under Siege: A Chronicle of Chicanos East of the Los Angeles River, 1945–1975.* Los Angeles: University of California Chicano Studies Research Center, 1984.

———. *Occupied America: A History of Chicanos.* New York: Longman, 2003.

———. *Sometimes There Is No Other Side: Chicanos and the Myth of Equality.* Notre Dame, Ind.: University of Notre Dame Press, 1998.

———. *Sonoran Strongman: Ignacio Pesqueira and His Times.* Tucson: University of Arizona Press, 1974.

———. *U.S. Latino Issues.* Westport, Conn.: Greenwood Press, 2003.

Calderon, José. "We Have a Tiger by the Tail: An Interview with Rudy Acuña." *Color Lines: Race, Action, Culture* 2, no. 2 (Summer 1999): 21–23.

Alex Feerst

On Call Miguel Algarín (1980)

MIGUEL ALGARÍN, born in Santurce, Puerto Rico, is a poet, playwright, and cofounder of the NUYORICAN POETS CAFE in Manhattan. Algarín's collection of poetry, *On Call,* speaks to the blending of Puerto Rican culture within the confines of New York City, hence the term *Nuyorican. On Call* mixes Spanish and English (SPANGLISH) to reflect the bilingualism of his culture. This book of poems can be read as a treatise of identity and a reflection on the reality of life on the street. He speaks eloquently about death, hunger, and sexuality; he uses graphic imagery to confront the reader with the rawness of lived experiences. His poetic voice is edgy and dynamic.

In *On Call* Algarín captures the sights and sounds of life on New York's Lower East Side (Loisaida), a place pulsating with a mix of ethnicities: Puerto Rican, Dominican, African American, and many others. In "Sound Thread" Algarín creates a poetic voice that echoes the rhythm of jazz, with its undulations of bass and saxophone. This is Algarín's way of showcasing the connection between music and the spoken word. Algarín expounds on this musical syncopation in "Ray Barretto: December 4, 1976." The basis of the poem is the value of improvisation, the same concept used in performance and slam poetry. It is here that Algarín speaks to the artist's need to be recognized, much like the Nuyoricans in their adopted land.

On Call offers vignettes about Loisaida and takes a critical look at the people who struggle for every dime. Algarín points out that trying to make and save money can misdirect individual priorities—to the point where loved ones are tragically neglected. In "Baby Food" a woman who had recently given birth and just returned home from the hospital realizes she has forgotten money at the clinic. She leaves her baby with her German shepherd, who has not been fed in a week. Upon her return, she discovers that her baby has been mauled. Here Algarín does not use sentimentality; rather, he allows the facts to speak for themselves.

As a Nuyorican poet, Algarín addresses a community of writers, each with their own distinctive voice. For example, he pays tribute to TATO LAVIERA in his poem "Tato—Reading at the Nuyorican Poets' Cafe." He writes of how Laviera "sweats" words, how he uses language to overcome the darkness of being alone, electrifying poetry into something positive. In this regard Algarín expresses the desire of Nuyoricans to fit in and of their special attentiveness to the nuances of language, both in English and in Spanish. For his attention to language and imagery, Algarín's poetry can be read within the context of PUERTO RICAN LITERATURE.

Bibliography

Algarín, Miguel. *Body Bee Calling from the 21st Century.* Houston, Tex.: Arte Público Press, 1982.

———. *On Call.* Houston, Tex.: Arte Público Press, 1980.

———. *Time's Now/Ya es tiempo.* Houston, Tex.: Arte Público Press, 1985.

Esterrich, Carmelo. "Home and the Ruins of Language: Victor Hernandez Cruz and Miguel Algarín's Nuyorican Poetry." *MELUS* 23, no. 3 (Fall 1998): 43–56.

Anne Marie Fowler

Ordinary Seaman, The Francisco Goldman (1997)

Born in 1954, Francisco Goldman is a fiction writer of Jewish-Guatemalan descent. In *The Ordinary Seaman,* Goldman has created a spellbinding novel about the travails of 15 impoverished Central Americans: one Guatemalan, five Nicaraguans, and nine Hondurans. The author's acknowledgments provide details about the actual incident on which this novel is based, and his reasons for wanting to write about it.

The Central Americans are conned into using their savings to travel to New York City, employed as the crew of the freighter *Urus*. Hoping to return home with money from lucrative jobs at sea, the 15 men instead find themselves pawns in a get-rich-quick scheme of two deceitful North American entrepreneurs who call themselves the ship's captain and first mate. *The Ordinary Seaman* is a tale of adventure and despair; in this regard Goldman makes a gesture to Herman Melville's classic sea epic *Moby-Dick* (1851). In a powerful and compelling narrative, Goldman portrays the crew's life in a gutted, rat- and cockroach-infested, rusted-out wreck of a ship, the *Urus*, which remains immobile in a remote part of Brooklyn docks. Its Central American crew are virtually entombed and kept in the dark—without electricity and without access to news. The novel functions primarily as a narrative of their extended captivity trying (without wages) to make the ship seaworthy while they are marooned within sight of the Statue of Liberty. They fear violence as well as deportation if they leave the ship. They are the *Urus*'s only freight, abandoned and homeless human cargo.

The novel's protagonist is the ordinary seaman Esteban Gaitán, who seeks a better life in the United States. Esteban is a 19-year-old Nicaraguan, a former Sandinista guerrilla scarred by his experiences in the contra war and haunted by the death of his lover in that bloody confrontation between peasants and the military. A limited omniscient point of view allows the reader to know Esteban's thoughts and feelings; some of his shipmates's thoughts and feelings also emerge. For example, the elderly waiter Bernardo prophesies, "when that statue [of Liberty] walks, chavalos, this ship will sail" (45). Bernardo is severely burned in an accident onboard the ship and dumped by the ship's first mate at a local hospital. There, without family, he dies a needless death and he represents the novel's most poignant symbol of the exploitation of Third World workers in the United States. Goldman's storytelling also allows us some entry into the minds of the scheming "Captain" Elias and business partner, Mark, individuals with complex personal histories of their own. Though individuals with their own aspirations, Mark and Elias come to symbolize the heartlessness of U.S. capitalism.

In the course of the novel Esteban finds the courage to venture off the ship and investigate beyond Brooklyn's docks and warehouses. Initially he steals food to bring back to his shipmates, but eventually he forms alliances with residents of Brooklyn's Latino community and begins to make a life for himself there and to tell his shipmates about it. By the end of the novel he has embarked on a new life with a new love. Thanks to Bernardo's chance conversation with an elderly couple, to whom he tells about the crew's plight, the hitherto unnoticed Central Americans are discovered by maritime authorities. Ship visitor John, a member of the Seafarers' Institute, sets into motion plans for the amelioration of the crew's situation. In the last chapter, the ship visitor returns to find the freighter capsized and run aground, its muddy black propeller emerging from the gray-green harbor water. In an assertion of collective will the crew had hotwired the engine and made the ship move—finally. Freed from their floating prison, they, too, will finally be moving—some to be deported, penniless, to their old homes in Central America, and others, like Esteban, to create new lives in the United States, where they remain illegally.

At its heart *The Ordinary Seaman* is about displacement and survival, yet by the novel's end there is hope, for we see glimmers that, even under the most despicable circumstances, the triumph of the human heart is possible. Esteban appears to be headed for renewal as he forges community with other Latinos in his new Brooklyn neighborhood. A disturbing critique of injustice, *The Ordinary*

Seaman can be read as an allegory of a global and postmodern economy. The story reminds its reader that seemingly invisible, uprooted immigrants are everywhere in our midst and that we must not be complicit in profiting from their abuse. One need only consider the name of the ship, the *Urus,* to mine the political message here: *U-r-us, you are U.S., you are us.*

The Ordinary Seaman was a finalist for both the PEN/Faulkner Award and the IMPAC (Improved Management Productivity and Control) Dublin International Literary Prize. The novel was also named one of the Hungry Mind One Hundred Books of the Century.

Bibliography

Robert Birnbaum. "Interview: Francisco Goldman." Available online. URL: http://www.identitytheory.com/interviews/birnbaum154.php. Posted Dec. 8, 2004. Downloaded Dec. 20, 2007.

Goldman, Francisco. *The Ordinary Seaman.* New York: Atlantic Monthly Press, 1997.

Gruesz, Kirsten Silva. "Utopia Latina: The Ordinary Seaman in Extraordinary Times." *Modern Fiction Studies* 49 (2003): 54–83.

Rodriguez, Ana Patricia. "Refugees of the South: Central Americans in the U.S. Latino Imaginary." *American Literature* 73 (2001): 387–412.

G. Douglas Meyers

Paredes, Américo (1915–1999) *(fiction writer, poet)*

Américo Paredes was born and raised in Browns-ville, Texas. He was a descendant of settlers who moved north from the interior of colonial Mexico to what is now South Texas. These settlers brought with them a rich tradition of storytelling. The songs and legends of everyday life of the people in these border communities became Paredes's inspiration for his scholarly and literary works. In addition he drew directly from his own experiences growing up on the border for his poems such as "The Rio Grande" (1934), written when he was 18 years old:

Between 1945 and 1950 Paredes served in the U.S. military and wrote for *Stars and Stripes;* he also published in Spanish as a special features columnist for the Mexico City daily *El Universal.* After his experiences in Asia Paredes returned home to pursue an academic career and to return to the subject of the borderland. Paredes taught at the University of Texas, Austin, from 1956 to 1984. In addition to numerous scholarly writings, Paredes's works include two novels, a collection of poetry, a book of short fiction, and journal articles in both English and Spanish.

His best-known academic work is WITH HIS PISTOL IN HIS HAND: A BORDER BALLAD AND ITS HERO (1958), a study of ballads that record U.S.-Mexican border conflicts, with a concentration on the historical figure of Gregorio Cortez Lira. Cortez was a Mexican-American rancher who, on a summer day in 1901, became involved in a deadly pistol battle with a Texas sheriff. Although most of the ballads exonerate him of any crime, Cortez is chased, captured, and imprisoned; legends of the border region immortalize Cortez and have mesmerized audiences up to today. The story of Gregorio Cortez highlights the injustices committed against Mexican Texans, a theme in Paredes's novel *George Washington Gómez* (1990).

In *George Washington Gómez* the titular Mexican-Texan protagonist is born in the midst of the early 20th-century border wars. George Washington Gómez's father, Gumersindo, suffers an unjust attack by the Texas Rangers. As he lies dying, Gumersindo charges his brother-in-law, Feliciano, with the upbringing of his son. With its description of the border, the presence of white, English-speaking authorities, and the vulnerability of the Mexican-American family, *George Washington Gómez* is an absorbing and compelling novel.

In 1994 Paredes published *The Hammon and the Beans and Other Stories.* The book's title story, "The Hammon and the Beans," gives the reader a glimpse into the humorous but tragic world of a Mexican-Texan girl who lives in a border town populated by *americano* soldiers and Mexican Americans.

Between Two Worlds (1991) is a selection of poetry from the 1930s and 1940s. The poems touch on a myriad of subjects from the Rio Grande,

Africa, love, and war to Paredes's experiences as a journalist and aid worker in Asia. The poems read very much as if they were taken from his diary; for example, in 1935 he writes "Moonlight on the Rio Grande," which reads: "The moon is so bright it dazzles me / To look her in the eye, / She lies like a round, bright pebble / On the dark-blue velvet sky" (28). And, in a 1946 poem entitled "Song of the Gigolo," he writes: "Listen! / You are blonde, you are beautiful, / Cold arctic suns shine in you, / Let me darken you, warm you, envelop you whole." (89–90).

While a graduate student, Paredes had completed a novel entitled *The Shadow,* based on a prize-winning short story, but it remained unpublished until 1998. The protagonist, Antonio Cuítla, is president of an *ejido* (a collective agrarian colony). *Ejidos* were formed according to the postrevolutionary ideals of Mexico in the early part of the 20th century. The narrative centers on Cuítla and his strange illness, a *susto* (fright that causes sickness) he contracts when plotting the death of his troublemaking friend and comrade in arms, Jacinto Del Toro. Cuítla finds Del Toro already slain at the hands of Gerardo Salinas, an assassin from Mexico City hired by the disgruntled landowner Don José María, who had considered Del Toro's considerably violent disposition a threat to his remaining holdings. At the site of Del Toro's corpse, Cuítla encounters the shadow of death: "The shadow was just beyond the animal's head. It was a dense, shapeless mass of black rising out of the middle of the road, where no shadow should be. It made no movement or sound. It was just there in the silence of the noon" (10). Following this encounter Cuítla finds himself cursed with the *susto,* a malady that eats away at his body and soul. Even though he is offered the help of the local CURANDERA to cleanse him of this mysterious ailment, and though he senses that the ritual might indeed restore him, Cuítla refuses because he has embraced the identity of a rational, modern man—and has rejected the position of the superstitious *campesino* (peasant) subject to outmoded folkways established during the years of Spanish colonial rule. Paredes's

second novel thus becomes a work reflecting the tensions of developing border politics and culture in the process of modernization.

In his poetry and fiction Paredes clearly draws upon his folkloric heritage to carry on the ancient tradition of the bard. Bards compose and recite the ballads so that history can be remembered from generation to generation. A bard of the border, Paredes boldly records the trials of Mexican Americans in a white, English-speaking society. And, through his artistic vision and wisdom gained from a historical perspective he succeeds in entertaining and enlightening his readers. His work can be read as a context for discussions about BORDER LITERATURE as well as CHICANO LITERATURE.

Bibliography
Morín, José R. López. *The Legacy of Américo Paredes.* College Station: Texas A&M Press, 2006.
Paredes, Américo. *Between Two Worlds.* Houston, Tex.: Arte Público Press, 1991.
———. *George Washington Gómez.* Houston, Tex.: Arte Público Press, 1990.
———. *The Hammon and the Beans and Other Stories.* Houston, Tex.: Arte Público Press, 1994.
———. *The Shadow.* Houston, Tex.: Arte Público Press, 1998.
———. *With His Pistol in His Hand: A Border Ballad and Its Hero.* Austin: University of Texas Press, 1973.
Saldívar, Ramón. *The Borderlands of Culture: Américo Paredes and the Transnational Imaginary.* Durham, N.C.: Duke University Press, 2006.

Shimberlee King

Paula **Isabel Allende** (1994)
Paula (first published in Spanish in 1994, then in English in 1995) deals with a pivotal event in ISABEL ALLENDE's personal life: the sickness and death of her 28-year-old daughter. The novel is based on Allende's experience with her daughter's illness, her coma, and the suffering that a mother has for a daughter's untimely demise. More than that, and like Allende's previous novel, *The INFINITE PLAN* (1991), *Paula* presents itself as a family

portrait. But, while *The Infinite Plan* fictionalizes the story of her husband's life, *Paula* focuses on Allende's family history. In writing *Paula* Allende embarks on a genealogical journey that takes her back several generations. The book is divided into three parts. The first part, from December 1991 to May 1992, narrates the circumstances of Paula's illness. This section also recounts Allende's family history, including details of the author's youth until the coup d'état in Chile in 1973. The second part, from May to December 1992, is devoted to Paula's move from a Madrid hospital to Allende's home in California. It also tells the story of Allende's experience of exile, her transition from being a Latin American author to a U.S. Latina author, and her adaptation to a new life in California. The third part (the epilogue) describes Paula's final days once Isabel, the autobiographical narrator, has accepted the necessity of letting her daughter go. These final pages are marked by an evocation of feminine strength, characteristic of Allende's semiautobiographical novels.

The text creates a cathartic experience in which the narrator attempts to come to terms with her daughter's illness and death. At the same time Allende explores her own life up to the time of writing. The novel consists of two different stories: Allende's memoirs from the past to the moment of writing, and the narration of her daughter's illness from the first days of hospitalization in Madrid to her death in Allende's home in California. The two stories intertwine by means of a succession of fragments. Certain elements of the story told in the present bring the reader to a certain period in the past, and vice versa. The first pages are of great importance because they establish the nature of the book as a complex and fragmented double story: "Listen, Paula. I am going to tell you a story, so that when you wake up you will not feel so lost" (3). At this point the narrator tells Paula about the origins of the family, describing its most important members. The object of contemplation is an old family photograph, which features the narrator's mother, whose plenitude of life in the photograph seems similar to Paula's before she fell ill. In the photograph the grandmother is a young woman, happily married, with her whole life ahead of her. Thus, the theme about the plenitude of life and the desire to live connects the generations. The narrator thinks about how Paula was before her illness and wonders if all joy will be gone if Paula ever wakes up (and she does not). Through Paula's story Allende conveys a struggle to live, the importance of memory, and the race against time. The writing of the narrative is a race against time and forgetfulness in order to bring Paula back from an irreversible condition.

In the text Allende tells us of the writing process of all of her novels, making clear connections between fiction and real-life experience. In order to make sense of the terrible circumstances she faces as a mother the writer looks back on her family background and explains what was happening in Latin America before the time of her own birth in 1942. She explains to Paula and her audience about the origins of the Allende family in Chile and Peru (where Allende was born). Thus, she is not only concerned with herself and her experiences, but with the life of the members of her family who have influenced her.

It is also important to note that the narrator changes her addressee on multiple occasions. In the first part of the book the narrator addresses Paula; thus, the text is like a conversation between mother and daughter. In the second part and the epilogue the narrative voice addresses Allende's audience, although there is one moment before the epilogue in which the narrator addresses Paula to say good-bye to her. In the first part the narrator still has hope for Paula's cure, and that is why she is telling her the story; however, in the second part it seems that the writer-narrator is losing hope and feels there is no point in talking to Paula because she cannot hear her. This metaphorical usage of shifting point of view, symbolizing the gradual letting go experienced by the narrator, takes the reader through to the end of the third and final part of the book.

Allende's mission as a novelist is to pay tribute to the characters involved in the narration. Allende tries to communicate to the readers, and to Paula herself, her own experiences and family history.

The narration of the story becomes a way to survive the painful experience of her daughter's illness and death.

Bibliography

Allende, Isabel. *Paula.* Translated by Margaret Sayers Peden. London: Flamingo, 1996.

Levine, Linda G. *Isabel Allende.* New York: Twayne, 2002.

Ramblado-Minero, María de la Cinta. *Isabel Allende's Writing of the Self: Trespassing the Boundaries of Fiction and Autobiography.* Lewiston, N.Y.: Edwin Mellen Press, 2003.

María de la Cinta Ramblado Minero

Paz, Octavio (1914–1998) *(poet, essayist, editor, literary critic, publisher)*

The Nobel laureate Octavio Paz was born March 31, 1914 in Mexico City. One of the most influential Latin American authors of the 20th century, Paz wrote a wide variety of works, including *El laberinto de la soledad* (1950; *The Labyrinth of Solitude*), *¿Águila o sol?* (1951; *Eagle or Sun?*), *Piedra de sol* (1957; *The Sun Stone*), and *El mono gramático* (1974; *The Monkey Grammarian*). In addition to the Nobel Prize (1990), Paz received Spain's highest literary honor, the Cervantes Prize. He also earned a Guggenheim fellowship, the Belgium Grand Prix International de Poésie, the Jerusalem Prize, the Mexican National Prize for Letters, and the T. S. Eliot Award for Creative Writing.

On his mother's side, Paz was descended from Spanish nobility. Paz's father was an affluent Mexican lawyer and journalist who supported the peasantry led by Emiliano Zapata in the MEXICAN REVOLUTION (1910–20). The political upheaval of the decade forced many supporters of the revolution to flee Mexico, and the Paz family moved to Los Angeles, California, for several years. When the family returned to Mexico, their finances were so reduced that they had to move into a small house in Mixcoac, a town sufficiently close to Mexico City to allow Paz's father to continue his political work. Although the family was now poor, Paz had access to his grandfather's expansive library. The habit of voracious reading he developed at this time stayed with him the rest of his life. He reported that he first learned the craft of writing by immersing himself in the classics of Spanish literature and the great writers of Latin America who preceded him. Paz received his education from Marist brothers in local Catholic schools and then entered the National Autonomous University of Mexico.

By the time Paz began his university studies, he was already a published author, having had several poems and stories printed in regional magazines. At the age of 17 the ambitious Paz began his own literary journal called *Barandal* (Railing). Two years later Paz's first book of poetry, *Luna Silvestre* (1933; Forest Moon), was published. In order to concentrate on his writing Paz left the university without completing his degree.

Paz sent some of his poems to Chilean poet Pablo Neruda, whom he admired. Neruda was impressed with the aspiring poet and encouraged him to attend a meeting of leftist writers in Spain. While he was in Spain, Paz developed such sympathy for the Spanish civil war that he joined a unit fighting against the dictator Francisco Franco. Although he remained primarily a leftist for the rest of his life, Paz did not support FIDEL CASTRO and his revolutionary counterparts in Latin America. Paz was an outspoken and tireless defender of democracy and the freedom of expression, thereby sometimes angering both ends of the political spectrum.

In the 1930s Paz married fellow writer Elena Garro. Their marriage ended in the 1950s. By 1944 a Guggenheim fellowship allowed Paz to return to the United States. There he continued his education in poetry, reading Walt Whitman, T. S. Eliot, Ezra Pound, and William Carlos Williams. Following World War II Paz began a 25-year career as a diplomat by accepting a post in France. There he concentrated his reading on French authors, several of whom he translated into Spanish. He was particularly attracted to the surrealist poet André Breton's work, and Paz's own *Eagle or Sun?* is heavily influenced by surrealism. By uniting dissimilar images and blurring distinctions, Paz outlines Mexico's history, its present, and its future through a series of poems. The title is derived from the two sides of a Mexican coin, the equivalent of the expression "heads or tails," and represents two sides of a single entity.

In 1950 Paz published one of his most influential works, *The Labyrinth of Solitude,* about the nature of the Mexican character. *The Labyrinth of Solitude* is part autobiography, part Mexican history, and part philosophy, all played out against the MESTIZO heritage of Mexico. The volume is said to illuminate the Mexican character and has become a classic in the study of Latin American history, especially the essay entitled "MEXICAN MASKS."

After his years in France Paz served as a diplomat in Switzerland, the United States, and Japan. In the 1960s Paz became the Mexican ambassador to India, where he studied the country's literature and past. While in India Paz met his second wife, Maria-José Tramini. When 300 protesting Mexico City students were killed by the Mexican government in 1968, Paz resigned his diplomatic post in protest. The years he spent in India are reflected in *The Monkey Grammarian,* an examination of India. The work is variously called a narrative, an essay, and a poem, demonstrating Paz's ability to fuse the contradictory into a unified whole. The Far East continued to fascinate Paz, even though he never returned to India. In 1997 he published two works influenced by India: *A Tale of Two Gardens: Poems from India, 1952–1995* and a memoir, *In Light of India.*

After leaving India Paz and his wife lived in many places and Paz continued his writing, editing, and literary criticism. He founded a literary magazine *Vuelta* (Turn) that is credited with introducing many European writers to Latin American intellectuals. Paz also served as a visiting professor at several universities, including Harvard and Cambridge. In 1990 he published *Sor Juana: Or the Traps of Faith* about Mexican nun and poet Sor Juana Inez de la Cruz. [Originally published in Spanish in 1995 as *Sor Juana Inés de la Cruz o las trampas de la fé.*]

By 1998, Paz was suffering from cancer of the spine, and he succumbed to the illness. In spite of living outside the country for so much of his life,

Paz always considered himself a Mexican, and he was so beloved in his country that the public announcement of his death was made by the president of Mexico himself, Ernesto Zedillo. Through his more than 20 books, his essays, and political writings and in his devotion to human dignity and freedom, Paz became an individual of great influence not only in his native land but around the world. Paz's work creates a cultural context for both CHICANO LITERATURE and Latin American literature.

Bibliography

Fein, John M. *Toward Octavio Paz: A Reading of His Major Poems, 1957–1976.* Lexington: University Press of Kentucky, 1986.

Paz, Octavio. *The Labyrinth of Solitude: The Other Mexico, Return to the Labyrinth of Solitude, Mexico and the United States, the Philanthropic Ogre.* New York: Grove Press, 1994.

———. *Selected Poems of Octavio Paz.* Translated by Muriel Rukeyser. Bloomington: Indiana University Press, 1963.

Jean Hamm

Peel My Love Like an Onion Ana Castillo (1999)

As a novelist, essayist, and editor, ANA CASTILLO is perhaps best known for her novel *SO FAR FROM GOD* (1993). Her 1999 novel, *Peel My Love Like an Onion,* centers on the journey of self-discovery of Carmen Santos. As a girl growing up in Chicago, Carmen faces many obstacles. Her first language is Spanish, and thus she faces the process of assimilation that is thematically common in CHICANO LITERATURE. As a child, Carmen has polio, but her mother cannot afford proper medical attention, and Carmen suffers as a result. Known as "La Coja" ("The Cripple"), Carmen wears a brace on her left leg and must walk with crutches. She attends the School for the Handicapped, where she meets Miss Dorotea, a physical rehabilitation specialist and eighth-grade teacher of dance therapy. Miss Dorotea's job is to encourage her students to move with confidence, and she motivates Carmen to push herself beyond the basics. She inspires

Carmen to become a dancer and after five years of practice, Carmen is able to give up her crutches.

When Carmen is 18, Miss Dorotea introduces her to Agustín, the leader of a dance troupe. Agustín turns out to be an essential part of Carmen Santos's life. First he becomes Carmen's dance partner, and then he becomes her lover. Carmen develops a reputation as a respected dancer, a long way from when she wore crutches. She can dance, sing, and make her way in the world. Still, she knows her relationship with Agustín is complicated. Agustín is married and leaves Carmen every summer to return to his wife in Spain.

When she is 25, Carmen learns that she is pregnant with his child, and her mother kicks her out of their home. Carmen has a miscarriage, but she remains in her studio apartment at the Hollywood Hotel for 12 years. The hotel has roaches and the neighborhood is ridden with crime, but Carmen is pleased to have a space of her own and to be free of her overbearing mother.

Carmen and Agustín's union becomes even more troubled when, 17 years into their relationship, Carmen meets Agustín's godson, Manolo. Manolo is also a Spanish flamenco dancer, and he and Carmen have a year-long affair. Manolo and Agustín compete for Carmen's attention, but ultimately, the men demonstrate their loyalty to each other. Manolo chooses to leave her in order to travel to Spain with Agustín. Carmen, let down by the men in her life and discouraged by her returning polio, escapes to the New Mexican desert and lives completely alone for two years. The desert life fails to make her happy, and she returns to Chicago with the awareness that she has no skills: She's just a dancer whose "body . . . doesn't dance anymore" (166).

Upon her return to Chicago Carmen takes a job in a pizza shop, where she earns minimum wage. Her polio worsens, and she is no longer able to stand all day. In a disturbing moment of the narrative Carmen must quit a job that she does not want but needs. To support herself she takes on various unsatisfying jobs: She works as a shampoo girl, sells drinks in a movie theater, and sews bells onto acrylic sweaters. Woven throughout the novel is an awareness of the oppressed laborers throughout the world, those ethnic groups, women, and children who are "desperately poor" and grateful for even the most menial jobs. During this time Carmen returns to live with her mother and is determined to be a good daughter. She tries to be obedient and selfless, even though she admits that it is not always easy. The role of the Mexican-American daughter as a second-class citizen is a significant theme in the novel. While Mexican sons inherit the family's wealth, the dutiful daughters must learn to make money through marriage or through their labor; if unmarried they are a liability or an embarrassment.

Ultimately Carmen's polio is so crippling that she must be hospitalized. Just when things seem to be at their worst for Carmen, an old friend, Homero, asks her to sing at one of his concerts. Suddenly a singer with a recording contract, her success enables her to purchase a condominium. Because of the money that she is able to pass along, she eventually earns her mother's respect. During this time both Agustín and Manolo return. Carmen's most significant accomplishment is that by the end of the novel she is finally in control of all aspects of her life, especially her relationships with Agustín and Manolo. While she is once again involved with them both, it is on her terms. The novel contains an important lesson for women: Dignity is the sexiest thing a woman can learn.

Bibliography
Castillo, Ana. *Peel My Love Like an Onion.* New York: Doubleday, 1999.
Hampton Jones, Janet. "Ana Castillo: Painter of Palabras." *Americas* 52, no. 1 (2000): 48–53.

Diane Todd Bucci

Perdomo, Willie (1967–) (poet)
Willie Perdomo, a native of New York City, is a Puerto Rican poet and the author of *Smoking Lovely* (2003), *Postcards of El Barrio* (2002), and *Where a Nickel Costs a Dime* (1996). He was awarded the 2004 PEN America Beyond Margins Award for *Smoking Lovely* and the Coretta Scott

King Honor Book for Children for his book *Visiting Langston* (2002). His work has also been widely anthologized in such collections as *Aloud: Voices from the Nuyorican Poets Cafe, The Harlem Reader: Poems of New York,* and *Bum Rush the Page: A Def Poetry Jam.* In addition, Perdomo's poems have appeared in the *New York Times Magazine, One World Magazine,* and *PEN America: A Journal for Writers and Readers.* He has been featured in several PBS documentaries, including *Words in Your Face* and *The United States of Poetry.* Additionally, he has appeared on HBO's *Def Poetry Jam.* His play, *Please Do Not Feed the Pigeons,* was chosen as a finalist for the 2004 Heideman Award from the Actor's Theater of Louisville.

Perdomo grew up in El Barrio, the Spanish Harlem district of Manhattan. After a racist encounter at a Lower Manhattan prep school, the aspiring writer met his mentor Ed Randolph, who was the receptionist at his private school. Randolph gave Perdomo *The World of Apples* by John Cheever and *Leaf Storm* by Colombian Nobel Prize–winning author Gabriel García Márquez. After that Perdomo started dealing with all of the confusion of adolescence by writing. Perdomo continues to mine the sounds and images of his neighborhood, be they the music of the Caribbean or hip hop, the personalities of El Barrio, or the grittiness and diversity of the city.

As a spoken word artist, Perdomo has performed in Europe, Africa, the Caribbean, and throughout the United States. He reads his work at college campuses, libraries, coffeehouses, bookstores, and such fabled venues as New York City's Town Hall, Alice Tully Hall, Lincoln Center, the NUYORICAN POETS CAFE, Central Park Summerstage, and the John F. Kennedy Center for the Performing Arts in Washington, D.C. In addition to writing and performing Perdomo currently teaches at Friends Seminary. For its themes and images Perdomo's work can be read within the context of PUERTO RICAN LITERATURE.

Bibliography

Perdomo, Willie. *Postcards of El Barrio.* San Juan, P. R.: Isla Negra Press, 2002.

———. "Re: Encyclopedia Entry." E-mail to Marilyn Kiss, July 14, 2004.

———. *Smoking Lovely.* New York: Rattapallax Press, 2003.

———. *Visiting Langston.* Illustrated by Bryan Collier. New York: Henry Holt, 2002.

———. *Where a Nickel Costs a Dime.* New York: W. W. Norton, 1996.

"Willie Perdomo" Norton Poets Online. Available online. URL: http://www.nortonpoets.com/perdomow.htm. Accessed December 20, 2007.

Marilyn Kiss

Pérez, Loida Maritza (1963–) *(novelist, short story writer)*

Loida Maritza Pérez was born at a time when the Dominican Republic was awash in political and economic chaos caused by the dictatorship of General Rafael Trujillo. Although Trujillo was assassinated two years before Pérez's birth, the effects of his more than 31-year dictatorship (1930–61) were still being felt throughout this nation when she came of age and, to some extent, even now.

Due to the dire economic conditions on the island, Pérez's family moved to the United States when she was three years old. Later she graduated from Cornell University with a degree in English. While in college, Pérez read Gabriel Garcia Márquez's *100 Years of Solitude*—a novel known for its use of MAGICAL REALISM and its unique portrait of a Colombian community. Pérez perhaps felt captivated by the Garcia Marquez's techniques and vision, and she has sought in her writing to create her own portrait of a people.

Despite her American upbringing, she has remained acutely aware of the chronic poverty and repressive politics of Dominican life. Indeed, Pérez devotes her first novel, GEOGRAPHIES OF HOME, to explore the extreme conditions of life in the Dominican Republic as a consequence of Trujillo's authoritarian government, a reality her own family had suffered before immigrating to the United States.

Even though first conceived as a short story, *Geographies of Home* was finally published in 1999 in the form of a novel. In the latter, along with a vivid presentation of the hardships faced by immigrant families, Pérez addresses some of the landmark questions in the Caribbean debate, such as cultural identity, the problem of racism, the issue of gender, and individual difficulties in life as an immigrant.

Pérez has won numerous literary grants and awards prior to the publication of her first novel. In 1991 she was awarded a New York Foundation for the Arts grant, in 1994 a Ragdale Foundation grant, and in 1996 she was awarded a Pauline and Henry Gates fellowship. The same year of the publication of her début novel, she was acclaimed by *El Diario* as one of the 50 most important Latinas in the United States.

Geographies of Home met an overwhelmingly positive response by critics, particularly for Pérez's strong Caribbean influence in her narrative and the sensitive representation of the complexities of immigration. In the novel, she examines the way in which the sense of cultural and personal identity can shift depending on the location. In *Geographies of Home,* her characters experience different challenges in the United States versus the Caribbean, which forces them to reassess themselves.

Although undoubtedly it was after the publication of her novel that she became widely popular, Pérez has written a number of short stories appearing in *Bomb, Latina,* and *Callaloo.* Her work can be read within the context of SPANISH-AMERICAN CARIBBEAN LITERATURE as well as DOMINICAN-AMERICAN LITERATURE.

Bibliography

Loida Maritza Pérez. *Geographies of Home.* New York: Viking, 1999.
———. "*Prologue from* Geographies of Home." *Callaloo* 24, no. 2 (Spring 2001): 569–576.

Isabel M. Andrés Cuevas

Pérez Firmat, Gustavo (1949–)

(essayist, poet, cultural critic)

Gustavo Pérez Firmat was born in Havana, Cuba on March 9, 1949, and is one of today's most prolific and interesting cultural critics. The author of more than 50 articles, seven books of cultural criticism, four books of poetry, a novel, and a memoir, Pérez Firmat has bridged the traditional divide between academic and creative writing. An author and professor, Pérez Firmat deliberates on subjects such as Cuban literature and music, subjects that are, for him, both deeply cultural and personal.

At the age of 11 Pérez Firmat left Cuba with his family, escaping the CUBAN REVOLUTION (1959) and FIDEL CASTRO's regime. In 1979 he earned his Ph.D. in Spanish literature from the University of Michigan. Since then he has taught at Duke and Columbia Universities. At the latter he presently holds the prestigious position of David Feinson Professor of Humanities.

Pérez Firmat's first book, *Idle Fictions: The Hispanic Vanguard Novel, 1926–1934* (1983), was followed by *Literature and Liminality: Festive Readings in the Hispanic Tradition* (1986) and *The Cuban Condition: Translation and Identity in Modern Cuban Literature* (1988). In 1994 he published one of his best-known books on Cuban identity and U.S. popular culture, *Life on the Hyphen: The Cuban-American Way. Life on the Hyphen* earned both the Eugene M. Kayden University Press National Book Award and the Latin America Studies Association's Bryce Wood Book Award.

Pérez Firmat begins *Life on the Hyphen* with an incisive analysis of the 1950s television show *I Love Lucy.* After introducing the reader to Cuban performer Desi Arnaz, the author reflects on topics ranging from Cuban poet José Kozer to contemporary Cuban-American novelist OSCAR HIJUELOS and to the mainstreaming of Latin music with Gloria Estefan's band the Miami Sound Machine. Perhaps the most important aspect of the book is the author's understanding of what it means to be part of the "one-and-a-half generation," as Cuban sociologist Rubén Rumbaut has called it. The one-and-a-half generation refers to the children and adolescents who came to the United States in the 1960s and who in time have become *cubanglos,* "a word that has the advantage of imprecision, since one can't tell where the 'Cuban' ends and the 'Anglo' begins" (7), as Pérez Firmat points out. This is a hyphenated condition that many immigrants and exiles have come to inhabit, experience, and live.

By 1995 Pérez Firmat had published his memoir, *Next Year in Cuba: A Cubano's Coming of Age in America*. Nominated for a Pulitzer Prize in the nonfiction category, *Next Year in Cuba* is a beautifully written account of the experience of exile. The book begins on October 24, 1960, the day the author, along with his parents, siblings, and maternal grandmother, left Cuba indefinitely, perhaps never to return again. The family, of Spanish and Galician heritage, owned a successful *almacén*, or "packaging warehouse," in Cuba. Confiscated by the Castro regime 10 days before they left the island, the *almacén* would remain for many years after the business that Pérez Firmat's father hoped someday—after the end of Castro's regime—to recover. For nearly 30 years the author's father continued to believe in the future *regreso* (return) to Cuba and the recovery of his warehouse. Pérez Firmat writes in *Next Year in Cuba* that "Gustavo [senior] put his *alma* [soul] into his *almacén*. Take that away, and you unsoul him. Lose that, and you lose yourself" (117). *Next Year in Cuba* is as much a book about loss as it is about new beginnings, about what it is to be an exile. Contrary to what American readers might assume, the author does not write about the immigrant experience per se—a fact that Pérez Firmat has reiterated time and again. For Pérez Firmat Cubans are not immigrants, they are exiles: "Had we considered ourselves immigrants, we may have fared better in the long run. The exile and the immigrant go through life at different speeds. The immigrant is in a rush about everything—in a rush to get a job, learn the language, set down roots, become a citizen . . . Not so with the exile, whose life creeps forward an inch at a time. If the immigrant rushes, the exile waits" (121–122). And yet, uniting the exile and immigrant experience is a sense of loss. If *Next Year in Cuba* has continued to be praised over the years, it is because its author has told a story with compassion and understanding, at times with humor and at times with painful honesty.

In 1995 Pérez Firmat issued a collection of poetry, *Bilingual Blues*, that once again reflects on the experience of living in Spanish-speaking and English-speaking worlds. In 1999 he completed a collection of academic essays, *My Own Private Cuba: Essays on Cuban Literature and Culture*, followed in 2000 by a novel, *Anything but Love* (2000). *Anything but Love* reveals the author's love of language and word play. The semiautobiographical novel centers on the Cuban-American Frank Guerra, who leaves his Cuban wife, Marta. Guerra develops a relationship with an *americana* by the name of Catherine O'Neal. The narrative that follows spares us none of the graphic details of sex and divorce Cuban-American style.

Pérez Firmat's *Tongue Ties: Logo-Eroticism in Anglo-Hispanic Literature* (2003) considers what it means to be bilingual: linguistically, emotionally, and culturally. Meanwhile, *Scar Tissue* (2005) combines poetry and prose to reflect on the author's struggle with prostate cancer. With a curriculum vitae that includes the most important books on Cuban-American studies in the last 20 years, as well as a Pulitzer Prize nomination and an endowed professorship at Columbia, it is no wonder that *Newsweek* has included Pérez Firmat as one of the "100 Americans to watch for in the 21st century." His criticism provides an excellent context for Cuban-American literature as well as Spanish-American Caribbean literature.

Bibliography

Alvarez Borland, Isabel. *Cuban-American Literature of Exile: From Person to Persona*. Charlottesville: University Press of Virginia, 1998.

Gustavo Pérez Firmat Web site. Available online. URL: http://www.gustavoperezfirmat.com.

Pérez Firmat, Gustavo. *Anything but Love*. Houston, Tex.: Arte Público Press, 2000.

———. *Bilingual Blues: Poems, 1981–1994*. Tempe, Ariz.: Bilingual Press, 1995.

———. *The Cuban Condition: Translation and Identity in Modern Cuban Literature*. New York: Cambridge University Press, 1988.

———. *Idle Fictions: The Hispanic Vanguard Novel, 1926–1934.* Durham, N.C.: Duke University Press, 1993.

———. *Life on the Hyphen: The Cuban-American Way.* Austin: University of Texas Press, 1994.

———. *Literature and Liminality: Festive Readings in the Hispanic Tradition.* Durham, N.C.: Duke University Press, 1986.

———. *My Own Private Cuba: Essays on Cuban Literature and Culture.* Boulder, Colo.: Society of Spanish and Spanish-American Studies, 1999.

———. *Next Year in Cuba: A Cubano's Coming-of-Age in America.* Houston, Tex.: Scrivenery Press, 2000.

———. *Tongue Ties: Logo-Eroticism in Anglo-Hispanic Literature.* New York: Palgrave Macmillan, 2003.

Richmond, Carolyn. Review of *Idle Fictions: The Hispanic Vanguard Novel, 1926–1934. Hispania* 67, no. 2 (May 1984): 308.

Rolando Pérez

Piñero, Miguel (Miguel Gómez Piñero)
(1946–1988) *(poet, playwright)*

Born in the small town of Gurabo, Puerto Rico, in 1946, Miguel Gómez Piñero came to New York City at the age of eight. Piñero lived with his family on New York City's Lower East Side. After his father left the family, Piñero's mother, Adelina, had no source of income to support her children, and the family was forced out of their apartment. With no place to live, Adelina Piñero (then pregnant) slept with her three children in the hallways and bathrooms of tenement buildings.

With little or no income to buy food Piñero provided for his family in the best way he could, by stealing. Thus, without a father figure and while still only a child himself, Piñero took on the role of family provider.

After Piñero completed a year of junior high school, his mother moved the family to Brooklyn. There Piñero became involved in gang activity and petty street crime. Consequently, Adelina Piñero placed her son, around the age of 15, in the New York State Training School for Boys at Otisville,

where he stayed for one year. As a teenager, Piñero served time at Riker's Island Prison for both burglary and drug possession. The second time he was paroled, "Adelina committed him to Manhattan State Hospital where he earned his high school diploma" (Mercado 2). For a time Piñero successfully stayed away from drug use; however, he eventually returned to the habit, which he supported by stealing. In 1971 Piñero was sentenced to five years in Ossining Correctional Facility (Sing Sing Penitentiary) for armed burglary.

Piñero began to write in Sing Sing. He composed love letters for illiterate inmates in exchange for money, cigarettes, and favors. He later came to write poetry and drama and became involved with the Clay Stevenson Prison Workshop. At this workshop he met actor-director Marvin Felix Camillo. Camillo went on to direct Piñero's play SHORT EYES at Riverside Church in New York City. In 1974 *Short Eyes* was produced at the Shakespeare Public Theater and then at the Vivian Beaumont Theater in Lincoln Center, where it earned the prestigious New York Drama Critics Circle Award and the Obie Award for Best American Play of 1973–74. In 1977 *Short Eyes* was made into a Hollywood film directed by Robert Young.

Piñero established his career as a Nuyorican (New York Puerto Rican) writer and actor. He completed a book of poems, *La Bodega Sold Dreams* (1980), and two collections of plays: *The Sun Always Shines for the Cool; Midnight Moon at the Greasy Spoon; Eulogy for a Small Time Thief Plays* (1984) and *Outrageous One Act Plays* (1986).

The Sun Always Shines for the Cool is a play set in Justice's bar, a gathering place for pimps and prostitutes. Justice enforces the "laws" of his business, of his "community." Dramatic conflicts arise when these laws are broken. Despite being set in a world of criminals, the society Piñero creates in this play is a microcosm of mainstream society, complete with its own civil codes.

Eulogy for a Small Time Thief centers on a petty criminal who aspires to achieve the American Dream. The protagonist, David Dancer, looks forward to the day he can retire from crime and live on a farm, a pastoral vision in an urban setting.

In *Midnight Moon at the Greasy Spoon* Dominick, an illegal immigrant, argues with two American diner owners, Joe and Gerry. Ironically Dominick knows more about the history of the United States and what it means to be American than they do; this characterization tends to upset stereotypes about immigrants.

Piñero is best known for *Short Eyes,* and it is in this play that his satirical depiction of the New York underclass reaches its apex. Here prison life is complete with its leaders, followers, and outcasts; the hierarchy and the enforcement of roles and codes are managed by the inmates, often with the aid of the prison guards.

Piñero understood the criminal and underprivileged worlds because he belonged to the underclass as a youth. He depicted this life in his plays and poetry and relied on dichotomies (such as legal/illegal, good/bad, English/Spanish, Puerto Rico/New York) to give his work narrative tension. Piñero wrote about his ethnically and linguistically diverse community by CODE SWITCHING between Spanish and English. Similarly the author's use of SPANGLISH (an American dialect blending both English and Spanish) broadens the modes of poetic expression in American literature.

Along with plays and poetry Piñero wrote the *Miami Vice* episode "Smuggler's Blues" in 1984. He also made several guest appearances on *Miami Vice* as the character Esteban Calderone. Other television appearances included *Kojak* (1973), *Baretta* (1975), and *The Equalizer* (1985). Piñero acted in many films, among them *Fort Apache the Bronx* (1981) and *Breathless* (1983).

On June 16, 1988, Miguel Piñero died at 41 of liver disease brought on by his many years of heroin addiction. He has left his mark on the literary scene in New York with his involvement in the NUYORICAN POETS CAFE, his editing of *Nuyorican Poetry: An Anthology of Puerto Rican Words and Feelings* (1975) with MIGUEL ALGARÍN, and, of course, with his own writing and performances. In 2001 the poet and playwright became the subject of a film entitled *Piñero,* starring Benjamin Bratt.

Bibliography

Algarín, Miguel, and Miguel Piñero, eds. *Nuyorican Poetry: An Anthology of Puerto Rican Words and Feelings.* New York: William Morrow, 1975.

Gussow, Mel. "Stage: Piñero Evokes Hustlers' World." *New York Times,* September 28, 1979, p. C5.

Hart, Steven Edward. "The Family: A Theatre Company Working with Prison Inmates and Ex-inmates." Ph.D. dissertation, City University of New York, 1981.

Mercado, Nancy. "The Drama of Miguel Piñero." M.A. thesis, New York University, 1988.

Piñero, Miguel. *La Bodega Sold Dreams.* Houston, Tex.: Arte Público Press, 1980.

———. *Short Eyes.* New York: Hill & Wang, 1974.

———. *The Sun Always Shines for the Cool; Midnight Moon at the Greasy Spoon; Eulogy for a Small Time Thief Plays.* Houston, Tex.: Arte Público Press, 1984.

———. *Outrageous One Act Plays.* Houston, Tex.: Arte Público Press, 1986.

Nancy Mercado

Place Where the Sea Remembers, A
Sandra Benítez (1993)

SANDRA BENÍTEZ's heritage is "marcadamente mezclada" (thoroughly mixed) (Coonrod Martínez 110). She was born Sandy Ables in Washington, D.C., to an American father and a Puerto Rican mother. One year after her birth, her father was assigned to a diplomatic post in Mexico. Following a year in Mexico, Benítez's family moved to El Salvador, where Sandra spent the majority of her first 20 years. When she was a teenager, her parents sent her to live on a small dairy farm in Missouri with her paternal grandparents, though she returned to El Salvador every summer. She eventually earned a B.S. and an M.A. in Missouri. Although born to Anglo and Puerto Rican parents and raised between the United States and El Salvador, two of her novels have been set in El Salvador and two in Mexico.

Since its initial publication, *A Place Where the Sea Remembers* has garnered considerable critical and popular praise and has been awarded a number of prizes, including the Minnesota Book Award, and the Barnes and Noble Discover Award; it was a finalist for the *Los Angeles Times*'s First Fiction Award.

A Place Where the Sea Remembers features a series of individual stories that overlap and intertwine in order to craft a narration about some of the individuals who inhabit a small, seaside village in Mexico called Santiago. The novel is framed by the chapters about Remedios Elementales, the elderly CURANDERA, or healer. As the novel begins, Remedios waits by the sea for a body to wash ashore, though whose body it is does not become clear until the final chapter. In addition, true to her name, Remedio's chapters are constructed around the four elements: earth (21), fire (63), water (103), and air (141), which Remedios says "awakened her" as a young girl and "nurtured her" as a woman (142). These four chapters establish that Remedios is connected to the natural elements and signal that she—and the entire village—operates within a premodern conception of time.

The other eight chapters each focus on a different character, though within each chapter, the characters' lives and story lines are intertwined. These chapters include Candelario Marroquín (the salad-maker), Fulgencio Llanos (the photographer), Marta Rodríguez (the chambermaid), Rafael Beltrán (the teacher), César Burgos (the fisherman), Justo Flores (the birdman), Esperanza Clemente (the midwife), and Rosario "Chayo" Rodríguez de Marroquín (the flower girl). Benítez provides the profession and identity of each character at the beginning of the chapter, in Spanish and English. Benítez also utilizes the "yo soy" (I am) tradition of early Chicano literature. The "yo soy" poems of RODOLFO GONZÁLES, among others, were a means of asserting Chicano identity and individuality. In *A Place Where the Sea Remembers*, they operate less as assertions of individuality than as of identity. When Candelario Marroquín is promoted from waiter to salad-maker, it is matter of great pride to him (and signifies a pay raise, as well), and he tells everyone, "yo soy el ensaladero" ("I am the salad-maker") (9). When he loses his new job, he loses his identity, his pay raise, and his pride. While all the primary characters are known by, and identify themselves by, their professional titles, they also become individuals through the narrative.

In the novel Candelario and Chayo are married and childless. When Chayo's 15-year-old sister, Marta, becomes pregnant, she contemplates an abortion, until Candelario tells her that he and Chayo will take in and raise the child as their own. When Chayo becomes pregnant, however, she backs out of the promise, preferring to raise her own son. Since they will not take her baby, and since it is now too late for an abortion, Marta cannot fulfill her dream to go to El Paso, Texas, and so she has the local witch put a hex on Marta's son. When Chayo discovers what Marta has done, she disowns Marta.

Another chapter features Rafael, a teacher whom all of his colleagues think is too dedicated to his work. An *indígenista,* he is compiling a book of Indian legends, and when his mother, doña Lina, hires a young indigenous woman, Inés Calzada, to help around the house, he is angry because his mother belittles and dehumanizes her. Despite his mother's protests, he begins to teach Inés to read and write, but when she becomes pregnant and miscarries, doña Lina assumes that the child is her son's. In fact, Inés is married to a much older man who beats her, and so Rafael and Esperanza help her to escape Santiago. As she boards the bus to leave, Rafael gives her his prized leather satchel, and he watches his hopes ride off on the bus.

César Burgos is a fisherman who ekes out a living from the sea and supports his wife and three sons. However, when his wife, Concha, and two youngest sons travel to Oaxaca to attend to family, they are killed on the bus ride home. Following the accident, he and his oldest son, Beto, grow ever more estranged. Finally, feeling Beto slip away, César breaks down, though it proves to be the act that enables the rapprochement between the two men. They decide to build a roadside shrine for their loved ones and travel to where the bus crashed. At the crash site, César discovers that Beto blames himself for their deaths.

When doña Lina's rheumatism worsens, Rafael calls Esperanza for help. With Esperanza's care, doña Lina's condition improves, and she is able to go on her planned trip to Veracruz. In her absence, a relationship develops between Rafael and Esperanza, and they eventually wed. The wedding draws all the characters of the book together in the penultimate chapter. Although it appears to be a happily-ever-after story, tragedy strikes, leaving many of the characters forever changed.

The overriding theme of the novel seems to be that of loss: Candelario loses his job and his pride; Marta loses her dream of going to Texas; César loses his wife and two of his sons; Esperanza loses the opportunity to love after she is raped; Justo loses his wife, his daughter, his dog, and his favorite canary. But in the face of this loss, which is, at times, overwhelming, one can often find hope and possibility. When Marta loses her son, it opens up the possibility for her to finally leave Santiago and go to El Paso. When Rafael's mother finally goes to Veracruz, he is able to initiate a romance that culminates in a beautiful wedding. Although Esperanza (contrary to her name) has given up hope for ever opening her heart to someone, she finds Rafael who falls in love with her.

Bibliography

Benítez, Sandra. *A Place Where the Sea Remembers.* New York: Scribner, 1993.

Coonrod Martínez, Elizabeth. "Nuevas voces salvadoreñas: Sandra Benítez y Demetria Martínez." In *Reflexiones: Ensayos sobre escritoras hispanoamericans contemporáneas.* Vol. 1, edited by Piscilla Gac-Artigas, 109–119. Fair Haven: N.J.: Ediciones Nuevo Espacio, 2002.

Kendall, Robert. "A Place Where the Sea Remembers." *Hispanic Times Magazine* (May–June 1997). FindArticles.com. Available online. URL: http://findarticles.com/p/articles/mi_m0FWK/is_n3_v18/ai_20053498. Accessed September 26, 2007.

"Sandra Benítez (1941—)." In *Hispanic Literature of the United States: A Comprehensive Reference,* edited by Nicolás Kanellos, 78–79. Westport, Conn.: Greenwood, 2003.

"Sandra Benítez—About Sandra." Sandra Benítez (2006). Available online. URL: http://www.sandrabenitez.com/print_sandra.html. Accessed July 20, 2007.

Ritch Calvin

Pocho José Antonio Villarreal (1959)

Most critics agree that JOSÉ ANTONIO VILLARREALS first novel, *Pocho,* is the first Chicano novel. The fact that a Chicano novel was printed in 1959 by a major mainstream publisher (Doubleday) is equally significant. It demonstrates that Mexican-American writers, who have been marginalized in literary circles, could be represented by a mainstream press. And yet Villarreal and *Pocho* remain in an awkward literary space in CHICANO LITERATURE because Villarreal has consistently refused to identify as a Chicano writer, favoring instead to be called an "American writer" (Cantú 430).

Pocho is an autobiographical novel. Both the author and the protagonist are the sons of Mexicans who immigrated to the United States in the 1920s following the MEXICAN REVOLUTION. Both author and protagonist struggle with the violence exhibited by their fathers. Both eventually enter the military in order to find some space, knowing that there will be no return. And, finally, both the author and the protagonist embark upon a quest to become an artist, a writer. As Rosemary King and other critics have noted, then, *Pocho* is a bildungsroman, a novel of development, and furthermore the first Chicano bildungsroman. Still, the novel might more properly be called a *Kunstlerroman,* a novel of development of an artist. And, indeed, Villarreal has noted that he was very much aware of James Joyce's *A Portrait of the Artist As a Young Man* and modeled *Pocho* on Joyce's novel (Sedore, "'Everything'").

Pocho begins in Mexico, at the end of the Mexican Revolution. Juan Rubio is disillusioned by the revolution and makes the trip north to California, later joined by his wife, Consuelo. After settling in the Santa Clara area, Juan works as a farm laborer, though he never forgets his past and often dreams of returning to his homeland. In addition, Juan holds very traditional notions about the family and about being a man. As such, Juan is determined to rule over his family, even if by force. In many ways, then, Juan Rubio represents the conservative, patriarchal nature of Mexican culture (though Villarreal's depiction is based only upon a rural image).

As the novel progresses Richard finds himself attempting to reconcile his life in between two cultures, two sets of values, and two languages. His father represents one extreme in values and practices, which include machismo and community, while the local eccentric, Joe Pete, represents the other extreme, including isolation, individuality, and idiosyncrasy. Richard Rubio attempts to reconcile these two modes of being into a synthesis, or MESTIZAJE (Cantú 424). Richard's apparent assimilation leads him to think of himself as a *pocho,* one who has forgotten his cultural identity and his ties to Mexico. Richard seems to embrace his assimilated status, a position that runs against the ideology of the later Chicano movement.

While no one seems to doubt that *Pocho* was the first Chicano novel, and no one seems to doubt that it holds an important place in the history of Chicano letters, it nevertheless holds a very controversial position. Among the criticisms of the novel is that Villarreal shapes the narrative and the characters by using calques (loan translations), which leaves much of the dialogue sounding stilted and awkward (Myers). At the same time Villarreal's use of CODE SWITCHING in the novel became a technique well accepted and utilized by many Latino authors in their work.

Pocho is most often analyzed as social commentary, but with controversy because Villarreal is not readily read as a Chicano writer (Sedore, 240 Solace). On the one hand, much of the consciousness of the Chicano movement was predicated on the notion of solidarity and community. *Pocho* develops an argument against community and toward individuality. In so doing it conforms to a particular notion of assimilation. Although

Richard Rubio will be forever shaped by his Mexican heritage, he must leave his family and community in attempt to find himself. This search for self will be replayed in many Mexican-American texts, especially the autobiographical essays of RICHARD RODRIGUEZ. Rodriguez notes the loss that comes with assimilation into the English-speaking mainstream culture.

Bibliography
Cantú, Roberto. "Villarreal, José Antonio." In *Chicano Literature: A Reference Guide*, edited by Julio A. Martínez and Francisco A. Lomelí, 420–432. Westport, Conn.: Greenwood, 1985.

Carl, Shirley. "*Pocho*: Bildungsroman of a Chicano." *Revista Chicano-Riqueña* 7 (1979): 63–65.

Crane, Virginia M. "José Antonio Villarreal." In *American Ethnic Writers,* edited by David Peck, 470–472. Pasadena, Calif.: Salem, 2000.

King, Rosemary A. *Border Confluences: Borderland Narratives from the Mexican War to the Present.* Tucson: University of Arizona Press, 2004.

Luedtke, Luther. "*Pocho* and the American Dream." *Minority Voices* 1, no. 2 (1977): 1–16.

Myers, Inma Minoves. "Language and Style in *Pocho*." *Bilingual Review/ Revista Bilingüe* 16, nos. 2–3 (May–December 1991): 180–187.

Sedore, Timothy S. "'Everything I Wrote Was Truth': An Interview with José Antonio Villarreal." *Northwest Review* 39, no. 1 (2001): 77–89.

———. "Solace in Solitude: An American Adamic Alienation and José Antonio Villarreal's *Pocho*." *LIT* 11 (2001): 239–259.

Villarreal, José Antonio. *Pocho.* 1959. Reprint, New York: Doubleday, 1970.

Ritch Calvin

Puerto Rican literature

Spanish colonization of Puerto Rico accounts for the fact that much of Puerto Rican literature is written in Spanish. At the same time Puerto Rican literature has been deeply influenced by the massive migration that took place from the island to the U.S. mainland during the 20th century. The island is a commonwealth, which means that it is neither a state nor a nation. Not surprisingly, the development of a "national" identity in Puerto Rico involves contradictions that are reflected in its literature. Puerto Rican literature is split between two shores: literature written by island authors, and the more recent Puerto Rican literature written in the United States. Puerto Rican literature of the mainland (especially New York) is typically published by the children of the different migratory waves of the 20th century. Puerto Rican literature on the island has been characterized by the attempt to solve the contradiction of being a Latin American island and a U.S. commonwealth. Islanders have almost all the rights of U.S. citizens (except the right to vote in national elections), but Puerto Rico is not a state. As a former Spanish colony, Puerto Rico is culturally different from the U.S. mainland.

Under the Spanish colonial power, Puerto Rican literature did not emerge as such until the second half of the 19th century. In 1849 Manuel Alonso (1822–1889) published a distinct portrait of country folk in his collection of verses *El jíbaro*. Also at this time, when the island sought autonomy from Spain and European domination, the island became the beloved *patria* (country) in the nationalist poetry of José Gautier Benítez (1851–80). The year 1898 is significant Puerto Rican history and letters because it marks the arrival of U.S. troops and influences after the Spanish-American War. MANUEL ZENO GANDÍA lamented the "decline" of an island people under U.S. imperial power in his landmark 1890s quartet *Crónicas de un mundo enfermo* (Chronicles of a sick world).

Anti-assimilationist figures reaffirmed a distinct Puerto Rican heritage, culture, and language, among them José de Diego (1866–1918), Luis Llorens Torres (1878–1944), and the modernist Luis Palés Matos (1898–1959). Matos, in particular, celebrated the ethnic diversity of the island with his Afro-Caribbean poetry. These writers explore issues of cultural identity and the impact of migration on the people who leave the island for the mainland (usually New York) as well as the families who stay behind. The transformation of the island includes industrialization, the decline of a sugar-based economy, assimilation policies, migration to the mainland, and creation of the *estado libre asociado* (commonwealth). This transformation from rural and traditional ways to life as an American commonwealth became the subject of works by writers belonging to the 1940s generation.

The 1940s generation includes authors such as RENÉ MARQUÉS, JOSÉ LUIS GONZÁLEZ, and Pedro Juan Soto (author of *SPIKS*). The literary inheritors of this generation continued to write about changes in Puerto Rico from the 1960s to the present. Using new literary techniques, this new wave of authors often departed from the realist tradition of their predecessors and began to experiment in the same way that Latin American authors developed MAGICAL REALISM as a form of expression. Contemporary writers such as Rosario Ferré, ANA LYDIA VEGA, and MAGALI GARCÍA RAMIS in some ways demonstrate a compromising attitude about assimilation to U.S. values and ways of being. On one hand, these authors want to preserve what it means to be Puerto Rican (speaking Spanish, being part of Latin America, and celebrating a traditional, predominantly Catholic culture). On the other hand, they realize that speaking English and entering the American mainstream is a part of daily life.

With World War II we can draw a distinction between the literature that is written and published in Puerto Rico and the literature produced on the mainland. Two branches of the same tree have developed simultaneously and render visible the complex identities held by Puerto Ricans. Puerto Rican literature on the mainland can be traced back to such memoirs as PIRI THOMAS's *DOWN THESE MEAN STREETS* (1967). Thomas paved the way in many respects for Bernardo Vega's *Memoirs of Bernardo Vega* (1984), Jesús Colón's *Puerto Rican Sketches and Other Stories* (1982) and NICHOLASA MOHR's *In My Own Words: Growing Up Inside the Sanctuary of My Imagination* (1995). These works represent the experience of adapting to a new urban space and moving between English-speaking and Spanish-speaking communities.

These memoirs as well as autobiographical novels written in the 1980s and 1990s constitute a consolidated literature written by and about Puerto Ricans in the United States. Along with Nuyorican poetry these narratives convey a deep concern for the socioeconomic situation of Puerto Ricans, whether black, white, or mulatto, and about their multiethnic, urban communities.

At the same time that the memoir developed in the 1970s and 1980s, we see the emergence of Puerto Rican poetry and drama in the New York area. Connected to the NUYORICAN POETS CAFE and to the political movement of the African-American Young Lords, Puerto Rican mainland poets produced a socially aware literature. Established figures of this literary movement are TATO LAVIERA and MIGUEL ALGARÍN; NANCY MERCADO is among its emerging poets. Nuyorican poetry is especially remarkable for its originality as a new street poetry based on the spoken word and with strong ties to jazz and salsa music (as with the work of Laviera). It is a poetry that is created and read for the community (usually presented at the Nuyorican Poets Cafe). Nuyorican poetry seeks to express Puerto Rican experiences in the barrios, with particular attention to poverty, survival, and interethnic relationships. Nuyorican poets use street slang, rhythms from jazz and salsa music, and a combination of Spanish and English, which become vehicles for poetic expression. The authorial use of CODE SWITCHING and SPANGLISH give a kind of unity to a fragmented Puerto Rican identity.

One of the best-known Puerto Rican poets is VICTOR HERNÁNDEZ CRUZ. His poetry offers a striking contrast between Puerto Rican and American cultural forms. Each poem is characterized by rich symbolism, word play, and code switching between Spanish and English. His experimentation with words, images, and sounds from both cultures can be described as "tropicalization," also the title of his 1976 poetry collection. Tropicalization is a process by which different elements of Latin American culture penetrate the representation of U.S. urban life; it is a literary response to the mainstream by Latinos living in the United States.

The urban experience of Puerto Ricans is also represented in Puerto Rican theater. MIGUEL PIÑERO stands out as one of the best-known Puerto Rican playwrights. His work SHORT EYES, winner of the New York Drama Critics Award for Best American Play in 1974, is a dramatic representation of Puerto Rican survival in a U.S. prison. Other Puerto Rican playwrights in the Northeast area include Federico Fraguado, Cándido Tirado, Richard Irizarry, Ivette M. Ramírez, Alberto Sandoval, and Carmen Rivera. Puerto Rican theater in the 1980s and 1990s is especially concerned with the daily experience of racism, making a living, and the underworld. More contemporary plays explore the challenges of Puerto Ricans living among other ethnic groups.

During the last decades a growing number of Puerto Rican writers have composed narratives about growing up Puerto Rican in the barrios and about the development of a northeastern Puerto Rican identity. Some of these writers are ESMERALDA SANTIAGO (WHEN I WAS PUERTO RICAN, 1993), ED VEGA (Mendoza's Dreams, 1987), JUDITH ORTIZ COFER (The LINE OF THE SUN, 1989) and Abraham Rodriguez, Jr. (Tales of the South Bronx: The Boy Without a Flag, 1992). With the mixing of Latino communities we also find authors who are half Puerto Rican, including Ernesto Quiñonez (BODEGA DREAMS, 2000), John Leguizamo (Freak, 1997), and Erika Lopez (FLAMING IGUANAS, 1997).

For most Puerto Rican authors the island figures as an important element of their past and in the need to find a new "home" in the United States. Puerto Rican identity is for these writers something complex; they have to redefine their vision all the time because of the interaction of many ethnic groups on American soil. Recurrent themes in their work are ethnic stereotyping, isolation, and lack of respect and understanding by mainstream society.

Bibliography
Antush, John V., ed. *Nuestro New York: An Anthology of Puerto Rican Plays*. New York: Mentor, 1994.
Babín, María Teresa, ed. *Borinquen: An Anthology of Puerto Rican Literature*. New York: Vintage, 1974.

Hernández, Carmen Dolores. *Puerto Rican Voices in English: Interviews with Writers.* Westport, Conn.: Praeger, 1997.

Manrique Cabrera, Francisco. *Historia de la literatura puertorriqueña.* Río Piedras, P.R.: Editorial Cultural, 1969.

Sánchez González, Lisa. *Boricua Literature: A Literary History of the Puerto Rican Diaspora.* New York: New York University Press, 2001.

Santiago, Roberto, ed. *Boricuas: Influential Puerto Rican Writings, an Anthology.* New York: Ballantine, 1995.

Turner, Faythe, ed. *Puerto Rican Writers at Home in the USA.* Seattle, Wash.: Open Hand Publishing, 1991.

Antonia Domínguez Miguela

"Puerto Rican Obituary" Pedro Pietri
(1973)

Pedro Pietri was born in 1944 in Puerto Rico and was one of the founders of the NUYORICAN POETS CAFE. In 1973 he debuted on the literary scene with a memorable poem entitled "Puerto Rican Obituary." A satiric commentary about Puerto Ricans living in New York, the poem consists of troubling scenarios about men and women pursuing the American Dream, chasing fortune, facing discrimination, and dying a predictable death. The poem describes Puerto Ricans as people who "never spoke back / when they were insulted" (4–5). Their hard work is never rewarded; instead, "They worked / They worked / They worked / And they died / They died broke / They died owing" (14–19). Pietri develops this theme in his snapshot of five Puerto Ricans— Juan, Miguel, Milagros, Olga, and Manuel. The five Puerto Ricans living in New York assimilate, but their interactions with mainstream society are still marked by broken English and broken dreams.

Drawn to the city and its promises of wealth, "where mice live like millionaires" (60), Pietri's Puerto Ricans are "waiting for the garden of Eden" (33). Storekeepers, bosses, tax collectors, and bill assessors blight their hopes; each day passes with more failure and disappointment. The title of the poem centers on a community's dying spirit, a

people trudging along without the awareness of where they come from. Each individual is "born dead and dies dead."

As compensation for their frustrations, these lost souls seek comfort in lottery tickets and fortune-telling. The healer-seer figure, "sister lopez," can talk to the spirits of loved ones who have passed away; she provides a critical connection between the world of the living and that of the dead. Petitioners seek from their deceased loved ones the magic number that will win the lottery. Pietri refuses, however, to romanticize such communion between the living and the dead. He brings the reader back to the deaths—both literal and metaphysical—of Juan, Miguel, Milagros, Olga, and Manuel. They are dying, and their people are dying. The reason is that the people in the poem have lost sight of their roots, their origins, their communities, and they "will not return from the dead / until they stop neglecting / the art of their dialogue" (210–212). In place of Spanish Pietri's Puerto Ricans undertake "broken english lessons / to impress the mister goldsteins" (213–214). The pluralized name, "mister goldsteins," creates a type of the Jewish businessman who, with the speaker's reluctant recognition, keeps Puerto Ricans employed.

Coping with pressures from work and yielding cultural turf in the city to other ethnic groups, the Puerto Ricans in Pietri's poem begin to grow jealous of one another. Milagros hates Olga because she earns more money for the same job. Manuel resents Miguel, Milagros, Juan, and Olga because their broken English is better than his. Though bound by their heritage, Puerto Ricans are, like any group, prone to internal divisions over status symbols such as television sets, cars, and homes in white neighborhoods. As a conclusion to a list of grievances against American society, the speaker envisions a different world. He laments: "if only they / had turned off the television / and tuned into their own imagination" (274–276). Pietri's solution partakes in a broader literary conversation about the importance of creating one's own identity, shaped by a community's values and beliefs. His work corresponds with many arguments of Latino and Latin American authors; for example, he seems to echo José Martí's essay "Our America," which advises that the key to the future of the Americas is to create and not to imitate. Similarly, in its validation of the Puerto Rican people Pietri's poem validates José Vasconcelos's concept of a "cosmic race," one with many ethnicities and many bloodlines. Finally, in its bitter attitude toward assimilation, the poem corresponds with Rodolfo Gonzales's *I Am Joaquín* (1967), an epic poem that tells the story of Mexican-American origins, sacrifices, and aspirations in the United States. In these ways "Puerto Rican Obituary" offers many levels of meaning for audiences of Puerto Rican literature and Latino literature more broadly.

Bibliography

Gonzales, Rodolfo. *I Am Joaquín/Yo soy Joaquín: An Epic Poem.* New York: Bantam Books, 1972.

Marti, José. *José Martí Reader: Writings on the Americas.* Edited by Deborah Shnookal and Mirta Muniz. New York: Ocean Press, 1999.

Pietri, Pedro. "Puerto Rican Obituary." Mark Sullivan. Available online. URL: http://www.msu.edu/user/sullivan/PietriPoemObit.html. Accessed December 23, 2007.

Vasconcelos, José. *The Cosmic Race: A Bilingual Edition.* Baltimore, Md.: Johns Hopkins University Press, 1997.

Luz Elena Ramirez

Quinn, Anthony (1916–2001) *(actor, memoirist)*

Anthony Quinn was a Mexican-American actor who launched his film career in 1936. His career lasted several decades during which time he won two Academy Awards. Though married into Hollywood "royalty," Quinn played mostly supporting roles in all sorts of ethnic guises (Arab, Greek, Mexican). He was born in 1916 in Chihuahua to a Mexican Indian mother and an Irish-Mexican father. Lacking the suave good looks that turned fellow Mexican Ramón Novarro into a Latin lover of film, Quinn was relegated to small roles as ethnic villains.

In 1937 he married Katherine DeMille, daughter of legendary director Cecil B. DeMille. Quinn worked steadily, first at Paramount and then at Fox studios, and by the end of the 1940s had appeared in about 50 films. His best films of this period include the Bing Crosby and Bob Hope comedy *Road to Singapore* (1940), and the Tyrone Power Technicolor vehicles *Blood and Sand* (1941) and *The Black Swan* (1942). He starred opposite Henry Fonda in the western *The Ox-Bow Incident* (1943) and opposite John Wayne in *Back to Bataan* (1945).

In 1947 Quinn decided to broaden his repertoire on Broadway. After watching him onstage, director Elia Kazan chose him to star as Stanley Kowalski in the original American touring production of Tennessee Williams's *A Streetcar Named Desire*. Kazan then cast him as Emiliano Zapata's brother, Eufemio, in the 1952 film *Viva Zapata!* opposite Hollywood legend Marlon Brando. The role as a Mexican revolutionary earned Quinn the first of two Oscars as best supporting actor and revitalized his film career. He was cast in high-profile roles under the guidance of prestigious international directors. He appeared in Federico Fellini's *La Strada* in 1954, and he won an Academy Award in Vincente Minnelli's *Lust for Life* in 1956. In addition he was nominated for an Oscar in George Cukor's *Wild Is the Wind* in 1957. Contemporary audiences will recognize Quinn as an Arab in David Lean's classic epic, *Lawrence of Arabia* (1962). The actor's winning streak culminated with *Zorba the Greek* (1964). He played the title role of an exuberant Greek peasant who teaches a stuffy British writer to embrace life; this became Quinn's signature role and earned him his last Academy Award nomination.

After the success of *Zorba the Greek* Quinn continued to work steadily, and he wrote two memoirs. In 1972 Quinn published the memoir *The Original Sin: A Self-Portrait*. Dedicated to his mother, the memoir opens with the middle-aged Quinn feeling like a total failure despite being at the top of his professional career. He sees "the boy," a symbol of his childhood that will haunt and have imaginary conversations with him throughout the book.

In therapy sessions and a visit to see his mother, Quinn confronts his family history, especially the figure of his patriarchal father and the three women in his childhood: his mother, his paternal grandmother, and his younger sister. He then recalls his early days in Hollywood and his relationship with Katherine DeMille. The memoir ends with Quinn confronting "the boy," who finally stops haunting him when the actor admits loving himself as a child.

He wrote another memoir in 1995 entitled *One Man Tango,* which begins with the story of Quinn's parents. Whereas *Original Sin* ended with his early days as a film actor, *One Man Tango* recounts events in the author's old age. In the narrative Quinn spends most of the time relating backstage anecdotes about life in Hollywood, including the actor's affairs with several prominent leading ladies. In the 1990s Quinn garnered some media attention after an affair with his secretary resulted in two babies and a bitter divorce battle from second wife, Iolanda. Quinn's memoirs are interesting, if ideologically conventional, self-analyses of Mexican masculinity in which a Latino man comes to terms with his origins in order to find happiness. As explorations of masculinity by a Latino celebrity, they correspond with *A Book,* the memoir by Cuban entertainer Desi Arnaz. After a long acting career Quinn died from respiratory failure in 2001.

Bibliography

Quinn, Anthony. *The Original Sin: A Self-Portrait.* Boston: Little, Brown, 1972.

Quinn, Anthony, and Daniel Paisner. *One Man Tango.* New York: HarperCollins, 1995.

Roberto Carlos Ortiz

Rain God, The Arturo Islas (1984)

In the 1970s ARTURO ISLAS began trying to interest publishers in his first novel, *Día de los muertos/ The Day of the Dead*. Though Islas amassed a large number of rejections—many of them revealing a bias against CHICANO LITERATURE—he never gave up on the story. For almost a decade Islas continued to revise his novel and search for a publisher that could appreciate the "rich particularity" of the Mexican-American experience. Finally, a small publisher in northern California, the Alexandrian Press, published the novel in 1984 under a new name, *The Rain God*. Islas's novel, so long in the making, garnered positive critical attention. The Border Region Library Association, an organization of U.S. and Mexican libraries and librarians, awarded it the Southwest Book Award in January 1986. Since its release *The Rain God* has increased in popularity and has gained a wide readership. Many critics agree that this is Islas's finest work and a masterpiece of Chicano literature and LATINO GAY LITERATURE.

In *The Rain God* Islas weaves together elements of autobiography and Aztec mythology. The novel is set on the U.S.-Mexico border in a fictional Texas community that resembles Islas's own hometown of El Paso. Like Islas, who taught literature at Stanford University, the novel's narrator, Miguel Chico Angel, is an English professor at a university in northern California. In another autobiographical parallel with Islas's own illness, Miguel Chico undergoes a life-saving radical surgery that leaves him with a permanent colostomy. *The Rain God* opens with Miguel Chico slowly recovering from the surgery. Miguel Chico's near-death experience unleashes a series of recollections of his family. Throughout *The Rain God* Miguel Chico recounts some of the major events in the lives of the Angel clan, with particular attention to his grandmother Mama Chona; his nanny, Maria; his father, Miguel Grande; his uncle Felix; and his cousins JoEl and Lena.

In the first part of the narrative Miguel Chico recalls memories of his earliest childhood and the women who cared for him as a boy (in fact, his name means "little Miguel," as opposed to his father, "big Miguel"). Islas juxtaposes two female forces in Miguel Chico's early life. The first is his grandmother and the family matriarch Mama Chona. The second is Maria, an undocumented Mexican woman who cares for Miguel Chico while his mother works. Both women are described as having physical characteristics that reveal their Indian heritage, but their attitudes about that ancestry are drastically different. Maria—with her wide face, prominent cheekbones, and "skin the color and texture of dark parchment" (13)—is comfortable in her own body. Her playtime with the young Miguel Chico involves calling attention to her Indian-like features. For her part Mama Chona professes a bloodline more purely Spanish than it actually is, even though she has "enough Indian blood to give her those aristocratic cheekbones" (141). In this way Mama Chona is a foil to Maria. Mama Chona snubs Maria as a domestic worker, and she disapproves of her "uneducated Spanish" (13). The two women appear at key points in the text. Miguel Chico's memories of Maria and an account of her death open the novel; the story of Mama Chona's death closes *The Rain God*.

In another memory Miguel Grande discovers Maria and Miguel Chico playing with paper dolls. He complains that his son is being raised to be a *joto* (queer), and he is furious at her for allowing the boy to dress in a skirt. Andrew Rivera characterizes Miguel Grande's behavior as misguided machismo, "a form of Chicano masculinity" (48). Ultimately Miguel Grande's fixation with masculinity and privilege backfires on him. Though posing as a virile lover, Miguel Grande is emasculated after an adulterous affair because his wife and his lover remain friends, despite his infidelity. The women are both emotionally stronger than Miguel Grande and more committed to each other than either is to him.

Miguel Grande is at once the character who makes concessions too easily and the character who judges others. Felix, his brother, is a father and husband, but he also seeks sexual intimacy with men. Miguel Grande is embarrassed about his brother's bisexuality. Miguel Grande fears family and public disgrace because of Felix's increasing indiscretion with young men, indiscretion that results in Felix's murder. Miguel Grande's fear of exposure compels him to give into Anglo authorities who suggest that an investigation into the death of Felix Angel would be unwise, since he was killed after making a pass at a young soldier. To them Felix's murder is the unfortunate but unimportant death of a queer Mexican American. Miguel Grande, hoping that "the stigma of being *jotos* would not reach past his brother," agrees (87).

Islas portrays the brutal murder of Felix in graphically realistic detail. The author may have been working through some of the outrage he felt about his own uncle's death under similar circumstances in 1967. After Felix's murder, his son, JoEl, succumbs to drug use and instability. Felix's daughter, Lena, is outraged at Miguel Grande's willingness to allow her father's murderer to go unpunished. Lena grows contemptuous of the Angel family for its hypocritical attitudes, attitudes that hold that appearances are more important than family relations. Each Angel generation, therefore, must confront the past in order to accept the present, especially Miguel Chico, but also his cousins.

The Rain God was the first installment in what was to be a trilogy about the Angel family. In the second novel, MIGRANT SOULS (1990), Islas describes, in a manner that is highly reflective of his own experience, Miguel Chico's efforts at writing a novel. Miguel Chico (Mickie) writes a novel entitled *Tlaloc* (the Aztec name for the god of rain), which is "published by a small California press" *Tlaloc* "was an academic, if not commercial, success" (210).

Islas died of an AIDS-related illness before he could finish the third novel in the trilogy. He did however complete a manuscript entitled *LA MOLLIE AND THE KING OF TEARS*, PUBLISHED IN 1996.

Bibliography

Aldama, Frederick Luis. Introduction to *Arturo Islas: The Uncollected Works*. Houston, Tex.: Arte Público, 2003.

Islas, Arturo. *The Rain God*. New York: Avon, 1991.

———. *Migrant Souls*. New York: Avon, 1991.

Márquez, Antonio C. "The Historical Imagination in Arturo Islas's *The Rain God* and *Migrant Souls*." *MELUS* 19, no. 2 (1994): 3–16.

Rivera, Andrew. "Remembrance and Forgetting: Chicano Masculinity on the Border." *Latino Studies Journal* 8, no. 2 (1997): 35–55.

Timothy K. Nixon

Rechy, John (John Francisco Rechy) (1934–) (novelist)

John Francisco Rechy was born on March 10, 1934, in El Paso, Texas. His mother was Guadalupe Flores, a Mexican aristocrat, and his father was

Roberto Rechy, a Texan of Scottish origin. As soon as he could, Rechy with questions about sexuality and faith, left his family. As a young man, he studied journalism at Texas Western College (now the University of Texas, El Paso). He ultimately left the campus and joined the army. After a brief time in the military, and in order to survive, Rechy became a drifter and a hustler in New York City. Rechy published his semiautobiographical novel *City of Night* in 1963. Following the success of *City of Night,* Rechy continued to write and publish more than 12 books, including *The MIRACULOUS DAY OF AMALIA GÓMEZ* (1991).

He currently lives in Los Angeles and teaches film and creative writing at the University of Southern California. Rechy's novels focus much of their attention on issues of loneliness, self-discovery, and survival. His work can be read within the context of CHICANO LITERATURE, as well as LATINO GAY LITERATURE.

Bibliography

Casillo, Charles. *Outlaw: The Lives and Careers of John Rechy.* Los Angeles: Advocate Books, 2002.

Rechy, John. *Beneath the Skin: The Collected Essays of John Rechy.* New York: Carroll & Graf, 2004.

———. *City of Night.* New York: Grove Press, 1994.

———. *The Miraculous Day of Amalia Gómez.* New York: Grove Press, 1991.

Rechy, John, Marsha Kinder, and Kristy H. K. Kang. *Mysteries and Desires: Searching the World of John Rechy.* CD-ROM. Austin: University of Texas Press, 2000.

Rosa Soto

Remembering to Say "Mouth" or "Face"
Omar S. Castañeda (1993)

Omar S. Castañeda (1954–97), the son of philosopher Hector Neri Castañeda, was born in Guatemala in 1954. He moved to the United States at age three with his family; at 11 he became a naturalized U.S. citizen. After serving in the U.S. Air Force, he received a B.A. in 1980 and an M.F.A. in 1983, both from Indiana University, which now offers a scholarship in his name.

Castañeda spent several summers in the 1980s and 1990s in Guatemala researching folklore; two research trips were funded by Fulbright grants. He sought to find the living evidence for the *Popul Vuh*—the "Mayan Bible"—a line of inquiry that influenced his fiction writing. He taught at Beijing Teacher's College, Rollins College in Florida, and at Western Washington University from 1989 until his untimely death.

Remembering to Say "Mouth" or "Face" (1993), a collection of short stories, received the Nilon Award for Excellence in Minority Fiction. It is divided into three sections. The first, "On the Way Out," combines semiautobiographical stories, including an account of a Guatemalan immigrant's life in America, and sketches of a writer's introspective time in New York. The second section, "Crossing the Border," focuses on an American writer's experiences of life in a Guatemalan village. The third, "Remembering," retells stories drawn from the *Popul Vuh.*

The short story "On the Way Out" tells of a boy's assimilation into America and his subsequent struggles as an adult with drug addiction. Originally published in the *Kenyon Review,* "On the Way Out" generated some controversy over its detailed and aesthetic descriptions of shooting up and its surrealist rhapsodies of drug experiences, such as "When I'm off, my laughter feels like it is a tree blossoming out from my mouth, the branches full of birds and chattering squirrels . . . but what I enjoy most is that the laughter has roots that entwine their dendritic ends into every vein and capillary of my body" (14). The story concludes with his mother making a series of mystical sculptures in order to rid his body of demons and cure his addiction.

"Shell and Bone" is narrated by a midwestern boy whose enigmatic relationship to his Guatemalan roots is embodied in the fragments of bone and the seashell that "flowed freely from [his] pockets" (45). He writes, "The shell and bone came wherever I lived. Often I awakened, my room inundated by the myriad forms of brittle calcium-amassed during the night as if by dreams" (45). When he travels to Guatemala with his father to see his dying grandfather, their familial link is evident in the "Tears [that] fell to the ground with the clatter and clicking of obsidian teeth . . . exact miniatures of the shells that followed me through the streets of Indiana, Michigan, the United States" (53).

"Under an Ice Moon" narrates an American writer's travels in Guatemala. His lover and travel companion is an anthropologist who, despite her greater expertise, is passed up for the grant, while the narrator, with imperfect Spanish and scant historical knowledge, is chosen as a cultural emissary whose speculative representation of Guatemala has been authorized by the award. His lover reproaches him as a social scientist whose claims to truth are suspect: "When you write out your story, you'll just name the plants as if you always knew what they were. Isn't that the way with everything? The great faking of knowledge. Dazzle them with surfaces!" (61). Not surprisingly, their relationship falls apart, and as it does so, Castañeda brings to the audience's attention debates about authenticity and local knowledge gained by experience versus academic, knowledge gained by reading books and writing articles.

Jonathan Harrington describes Castañeda's style as "florid and unpredictable . . . ornate [and] luxuriant" (206). Though often departing from realism in favor of the meditative and the fabulous, Castañeda considered his work intensely political. Though not unusual now in Latino fiction, Castañeda incorporated elements of Guatemalan indigenous folklore to represent the diversity of the Latino experience. Castañeda explained his work's often radical stylistic experimentation as a kind of liberatory practice, finding it preferable for art to "err on the side of excess or disruption" (Harrington 210). For his characterizations and themes his work can be read within the context of Central American literature and Latino literature.

Bibliography

Bick, Suzann. Review of *Remembering to Say "Mouth" or "Face."* *Antioch Review* 54, no. 1 (Winter 1996): 110–114.

Castañeda, Omar S. *Cunuman.* Sarasota, Fla.: Pineapple Press, 1987.

———. *Naranjo the Muse: A Collection of Stories.* Houston, Tex.: Arte Público Press, 1997.

———. *Remembering to Say "Mouth" or "Face."* Boulder, Colo.: Fiction Collective Two, 1993.

Harrington, Jonathan. "A Truly Immense Journey: Profile of Omar S. Castañeda." *Americas Review* 23, nos. 3–4 (Winter 1995): 204–216.

Alex Feerst

Retamar, Roberto Fernández (1930–)
(poet, essayist, editor, scholar)

Roberto Fernández Retamar is one of Cuba's most renowned literary figures. He was born in Havana on June 9, 1930, and studied art and architecture in Cuba before turning to linguistics and literature, studying in Paris and London, respectively. Retamar discovered his vocation as a writer and a leftist intellectual during his first trip to New York in 1947, the same city that had had such a formative influence on Cuban revolutionary JOSÉ MARTÍ. He followed in Martí's footsteps as an engaged intellectual who actively participates in political and cultural life rather than merely writing about it.

Retamar was 28 years old when the CUBAN REVOLUTION broke out in 1959, and despite much criticism, he has remained loyal to FIDEL CASTRO ever since. He was a visiting professor at Yale University between 1957 and 1958, returned to Cuba to take up his post as a professor at Havana University in 1959, and served as a diplomat in Paris in 1960 before permanently moving back to Cuba in 1961. He took important trips to the Soviet Union in 1963, to Vietnam in 1970, and to nations such as Chile and Nicaragua, which, along with the United States, Mexico, and the Caribbean, constitute the Americas that Retamar and Martí write about.

Retamar is primarily known for his essays, especially for his landmark work "Caliban: Apuntes sobre la cultura en nuestra América" (1971; "Caliban, Notes Towards a Discussion of Culture in Our America"). "Caliban" is a manifesto that promotes a Latin American mixed identity as identified by Martí. The essay was conceived as a response to the Uruguayan José Enrique Rodó's famous pamphlet *Ariel* (1900). Retamar argues in response to Rodó that it is the slave CALIBAN, rather than the intellectual Ariel, in Shakespeare's *The Tempest* who is the most appropriate symbol of MESTIZAJE (the mixing of Spanish and Indian blood) in America. Retamar celebrates the racially and culturally mixed populations of the Americas in opposition to the Spanish rhetoric of purity, a purity that can be questioned based on the Moorish occupation and Jewish settlements of Spain.

In his later essays Retamar explores the relationship between Western and Spanish-American cultures rather than the opposition he sees in them in "Caliban." When asked in an interview whether these later writings might not contradict "Caliban's" earlier focus, Retamar explained that these later essays did not contradict so much as complement "Caliban." And indeed, his work as a whole testifies to his investment in challenging easy binaries. The importance of "Caliban" to Latin American and postcolonial criticism is further evidenced by the number of revisions and expanded versions of it that have appeared since its original publication.

As a poet Retamar has written more than a dozen books of verse, including his early volumes *Elegía como un himno* (1950; Elegy like a hymn) and *Patrias* (1952; Fatherlands) and later collections such as *Felices los normales* (2002; Happy the normal). His award-winning poems, which are often about everyday things and events, have been called "conversational" or "colloquial" as well as self-mocking and melancholy. Since 1965 Retamar has been editor of the official magazine of CASA DE LAS AMÉRICAS, a publishing house and humanities center in Havana. The significance of Casa de las Américas in Latin America cannot be overestimated. Since its inception, Casa de las Américas has functioned as the cultural epicenter of the region, hosting and supporting artistic, literary, musical, and theatrical events, awarding a series of annual prizes and awards, and establishing vital intellectual ties within the hemisphere.

Bibliography

Echevarria, Roberto Gonzalez. "Roberto Fernandez Retamar: An Introduction." *Diacritics* 8, no. 4 (Winter 1978): 70–75.

Monegal, Emir Rodriguez. "The Metamorphoses of Caliban." *Diacritics* 7, no. 3 (Autumn 1977): 78–83.

Retamar, Roberto Fernandez. *Aquí*. Santa Clara, Cuba: Ediciones Capiro, 2000.

———. *Caliban and Other Essays*. Translated by Edward Baker. Minneapolis: University of Minnesota Press, 1989.

———. *Ensayo de otro mundo*. Santiago, Chile: Editorial Universitaria, 1969.

———. "More Than a Bird's-eye View of My Labor: Essays and Occasional Pieces." *World Literature Today* 76, nos. 3–4 (2002): 5–12.

———. *La poesía, reino autónomo*. Havana: Editorial Letras Cubanas, 2000.

Carine M. Mardorossian

Return: Poems Collected and New
Alurista (1982)

ALURISTA is one of the trailblazers of CHICANO LITERATURE. He came to the United States from Mexico when he was 14, and came to prominence in the 1970s and early 1980s with a series of books that included *Floricanto en Aztlán* (1971), *Nationchild Plumaroja* (1972), *Timespace Huracán* (1976), *A'nque* (1979), and *Spik in Glyph?* (1981). As can be surmised from the titles of his books, Alurista works as much in Spanish as he does in English and occasionally moves into SPANGLISH. His is a poetry that demands its reader be equally at home in both languages. This was a key factor in developing what was beginning to surface as a Chicano identity.

Return was published in 1982; it brings together *Nationchild Plumaroja* and a collection titled *Dawn's Eye* (poems written between 1979 and 1981). As a whole the book provides a good introduction to the work of Alurista. Due to the span of time it covers (1969–82) the book allows the reader to get a sense of both the enduring concerns and also the evolution of Alurista's work.

His aim is to reach the "ascendant people" (76) of AZTLÁN: "our nación / our dwelling / our responsibility" (53). In this sense Alurista's enterprise can be seen as the construction of a subjective space that would allow someone to say something like "I am part of *la raza*," the "ascendant people" in question—or, in a more political tack, "I will fight for *la causa*." In the process we find that the space for neutrality is inhospitable at best. Since the reader cannot simply elect to be neutral in his/her reading, is that subjective space available to only one ethnicity, or, is it, instead, one that can be possible for all to occupy? Alurista's answer is not straightforward. It involves at least three moments.

First, there are constant references to "northamerikkka, yankeeland" (80) and "the power of the yanki" (87). This might appear as a blanket condemnation, but in fact it is only aimed at those who condone, enable, and/or participate in the "kill / for / markets / and / cheap / labor / pools" (97). Alurista's project is anticapitalist; capitalism creates an oppressive environment where "howling humans / freeze / in the fields of profit" (87). This is an ideological problem more than an issue of race.

Second, and this is the most prevalent aspect in all of *Return*, there are constant specifications of what Aztlán entails, which would make it into something like an idealized (and ahistorical) pre-Hispanic "amerindia . . . razared" (red Indian race; 53, 58, and passim). Alurista came under attack for what some critics saw as an all-too-simple mythological answer (one where tortillas and other clichés proliferate) to very material socioeconomic and political problems. And while this may seem to be asking too much of the poet, it was a critique that coincided with Alurista's own expectations of the poet as the creator of a culture, a figure who would "envision a concrete reality, . . . direct / resultant of our dreams" (52).

The most important tension at the heart of *Nationchild Plumaroja*, included in *Return*, is that which is produced between a criticism of the cultural, economic, and political situation of the Chicano, as the poetical voice sees it, and the proposed solution or way out of that predicament. This is a movement that is also carried out in three steps. First, there are the specific conditions that have to be voiced so as to escape from the silence of oppression (which allows for the problems to be ignored); second, there is a plea for organizational discipline and unity among Chicanos; third, there is the still-to-come nation of Aztlán, a mythical place that will provide the ultimate answer to united Chicanos. While the first two steps are absolutely concrete, the third presents a problem that can be seen as in contradiction with the underlying logic at work in the first two. But this idealized move only appears so in retrospect—perhaps because of the silence "history" has imposed on this period. During that time, however, the Chicano movement was actually engaged in trying to secure lands in New Mexico for a Chicano state. For example, Reies López Tijerina, a member of the group, was persecuted by federal officials for his involvement in this campaign.

Alurista's work is openly political, but he warns in the introduction to *Return* that this is a poetry that has to do with other areas as well: "I don't think that my work can be defined only as political," adding, "it's scientific, it's psychological, it's spiritual, it's cultural" (xiv). This is more apparent in the second book included in *Return*, titled *Dawn's Eye*, which includes later poetry. Thus, while we still find references to Lenin in "2 B Done" (132) and a call for an "unbending revolution" in "Return" (138), this is now more visibly blended with references to family, popular culture, love poems, and Alurista's travels.

Bibliography

Alurista. *Return: Poems Collected and New*. Ypsilanti, Mich.: Bilingual Press/Editorial Bilingüe, 1982.

Andouard-Labarthe, Elyette. "The Vicissitudes of Aztlán." *Confluencia: Revista Hispánica de Cultura y Literatura* 5, no. 2 (1990): 79–84.

Davis-Undiano, Robert Con. "The Emergence of New World Studies: Anaya, Aztlán, and the New Chicana." *Genre: Forms of Discourse and Culture* 32, nos. 1–2 (1999): 115–140.

Grandjeat, Yves-Charles. "Alurista's Flight to Aztlán: A Study of Poetic Effectiveness." In *Missions in Conflict: Essays on U.S.-Mexican Relations and Chicano Culture*, edited by Renate von Bardeleben et al., 123–131. Tübingen, Germany: Narr, 1986.

Keller, Gary D. Introduction to *Return: Poems Collected and New.* Ypsilanti, Mich.: Bilingual Press/Editorial Bilingüe, 1982.

Lomelí, Francisco A. "Alurista (1947–)." In *Latino and Latina Writers: Introductory Essays, Chicano and Chicana Authors,* edited by Alan West-Durán et al., 101–116. New York: Scribner's, 2004.

Rojas, Guillermo. "Alurista, Chicano Poet, Poet of Social Protest." In *Otros mundos, otros fuegos: Fantasía y realismo mágico en Iberoamérica,* edited by Donald A. Yates, 255–260. East Lansing: Michigan State University, Latin American Studies Center, 1975.

Jaime Rodríguez-Matos

Rio Grande Fall Rudolfo Anaya (1996)

RUDOLFO ANAYA's novel *Rio Grande Fall* was published in 1996 and is the second installment in Anaya's four novels featuring detective Sonny Baca. The others are *ZIA SUMMER* (1995), *SHAMAN WINTER* (1999), and *Jemez Spring* (2005). The four novels represent a complete seasonal cycle, which shapes the narrative structure. Anaya invents the detective genre by depicting the supernatural as an entry into the mythic-spiritual world rather than a device that camouflages evidence. *Rio Grande Fall* picks up where *Zia Summer* ended, with Sonny investigating the murder of his cousin, Gloria Dominic, and intensifying his struggle with Raven. *Rio Grande Fall* begins with the murder of Veronica Worthy, the key witness against Tamara Dubronsky, one of Raven's followers accused of murdering Gloria. Raven orchestrated the murders of Gloria and Veronica, but Sonny has difficulty tracking him. In many Indian cultures and in these novels Raven is a mythic "transforming trickster" who moves easily between the streets of Albuquerque and the spirit world.

In the novel fall marks the change of seasons, the end of the violent era of the Fifth Sun in the Mesoamerican time cycle, and the transformation of Sonny into a shape-shifting trickster with sufficient power to challenge Raven. Fall is the season of Day of the Dead, a time "of remembering the ancestors and celebrating the good they did on earth" (116). The novel uses New Mexican history in the narrative, especially regarding Elfego Baca, a real-life New Mexican lawman in the 1880s who is portrayed as the fictional Sonny's great-grandfather. Fall is a time of transformation. Lorenza Villa, a *CURANDERA* (folk healer) warns Sonny, "'Like all ages of transformation, this is the time when we are most vulnerable'" to Raven's chaos (299).

As Sonny works to unravel the details of Veronica's death, he discovers Raven's plan to blow up a truck loaded with nuclear waste. An irony that complicates the portrayal of Raven as purely evil is that Raven intends the violence to protest the ecological destruction posed by the nuclear Waste Isolation Pilot Plant (WIPP) in Carlsbad. If Raven bombs a WIPP truck the fallout will destroy Albuquerque. In addition to Raven's ecoterrorist plot the novel portrays the horrible harvest of the drug wars. Sonny's murder investigation uncovers a CIA-connected Colombian drug cartel operating a large-scale supply system in New Mexico, the profits from which fund secret, inhumane animal research on baboons as well as Raven's WIPP protests. All are connected to economic displacement and gentrification in Albuquerque that force people from their ancestral lands, many now homeless and "pushed to the edges of society, stripped of their dignity, made refugees" (64).

Sonny cannot solve any of these real-world crimes without venturing into the mytho-spiritual realm, but he does so somewhat reluctantly. Sonny's detective and intuitive abilities increase as he develops his power as a *brujo* (witch) and as he becomes more aware and in control of his *nagual* (animal spirit), the coyote. Yet, for much of the novel Sonny relies on "the power of the pistol" used by Elfego Baca and is unable to accept that it, like Raven, has a legacy of violence (300). Lorenza tells Sonny to "Trust your [coyote] medicine," but Sonny has difficulty trusting the unseen and "brujos who can transform themselves into their animal forms" (295). When Sonny finally assumes the role of Coyote, another "transforming trickster," he is guided and protected by Lorenza and Don Eliseo, a shaman. As Coyote, Sonny tries to disempower Raven and realizes that "in a world of violence it was impossible to retain inner harmony" (71).

Much of the novel's action takes place in the mythic domain where Sonny battles Raven for control of the human world as "this era of time is ending" (298). Sonny's quest for peace promised by Don Eliseo's Lords and Ladies of Light, the ancient Mesoamerican gods and goddesses, is thwarted by Raven who wants to capitalize on the unavoidable "'violence as the Fifth Sun dies. Raven is one of those who thrive on chaos'" (298). The fate of the novel's characters is determined by the actions of these tricksters. Who controls the fall or the transformation determines whether the next season, winter, the storytelling time, will be one of chaos or harmony.

Bibliography

Anaya, Rudolfo. *Jalamanta: A Message from the Desert.* New York: Warner Books, 1996.

———. *Jemez Spring.* Albuquerque: University of New Mexico Press, 2005.

———. *Rio Grande Fall.* New York: Warner Books, 1996.

———. *Shaman Winter.* New York: Warner Books, 1999.

———. *Zia Summer.* New York: Warner Books, 1995.

Davis-Undiano, Robert Con. "Mestizos Critique the New World: Vasconcelos, Anzaldúa, and Anaya." *LIT: Literature Interpretation Theory* 11, no. 2 (2000): 117–143.

Fernández Olmos, Margarite. *Rudolfo A. Anaya: A Critical Companion.* Westport, Conn.: Greenwood Press, 1999.

Flys-Junquera, Carmen. "Murder with an Ecological Message: Rudolfo Anaya and Lucha Corpi's Detective Fiction." *Revista Canaria de Estudios Ingleses* 42 (2001): 341–357.

Geuder, Ann-Catherine. "Marketing Mystical Mysteries: Rudolfo Anaya's Mystery Trilogy." In *Sleuthing Ethnicity: The Detective in Multiethnic Crime Fiction,* edited by Dorothea Fischer-Hornung and Monika Mueller, 81–94. Madison, N.J.: Fairleigh Dickinson University Press, 2003.

Ramos, Manuel. "The Postman and the Mex: From Hard-boiled to *Huevos Rancheros* in Detective Fiction." *Hopscotch: A Cultural Review* 2, no. 4 (2001): 160–167.

Sandra L. Dahlberg

Ríos, Alberto Alvaro (1952–) (poet, fiction writer)

Mexican-American writer Alberto Alvaro Ríos was born in 1952 in Nogales, Arizona, on the border with Mexico. His father was from Tapachula, Chiapas, in southern Mexico, and his mother was born in Warrington, Lancashire, England. After growing up in Nogales Ríos attended the University of Arizona, where he earned his degree in literature in 1974 and a second degree in psychology in 1975. In 1979 he earned a master's in creative writing, also from the University of Arizona. That same year he married Lupita Barron of Nogales, Sonora, Mexico.

A contributor to Chicano literature, Ríos writes in several genres, including poetry—Whispering to Fool the Wind: Poems (1982), *Five Indiscretions* (1985), *The Lime Orchard Woman* (1988), *Teodoro Luna's Two Kisses* (1990), and *The Smallest Muscle in the Human Body* (2002)—fiction—*The Iguana Killer* (1984), *Pig Cookies* (1995), and *The Curtain of Trees* (1999)—and memoir—*Capirotada* (1999).

His awards are numerous. *The Smallest Muscle in the Human Body* was a 2002 National Book Award finalist. He has received a Western Literature Association Distinguished Achievement Award, a Latino Literary Hall of Fame Award, the Arizona Governor's Arts Award, fellowships from the Guggenheim Foundation and the National Endowment for the Arts, the Walt Whitman Award, the Western States Book Award for Fiction, and six Pushcart Prizes in poetry and fiction.

Ríos's work can be placed within the context of border literature for its focus on regional and Mexican-American culture. His work challenges preconceived notions of boundaries. Past and present, self and other, near and far, internal and external, here and there, the body and the world, Ríos reveals how these seemingly separate spaces hold opportunities for connection, conversation, understanding, and multiple imaginative possibilities. The world Ríos creates in his books is a world characterized by MAGICAL REALISM. Ríos explores the pliability of dreams and material reality, where dreams inform and emerge from reality as much as reality emerges from and informs dreams. A writer of the heart and the mind, Ríos moves fluidly within and through the realms of both. Family stories are as strong as local legends. Great-aunts are like forces of nature, and forces of nature display human traits. Ríos's writing—whether poetry, fiction, or memoir—is a writing of place, community, and family. And as places, communities, and families are made up of friends, loners, outcasts, lovers, enemies, and any one of these disguised as any other, so too are Ríos's books multiply populated. And as places, communities, and families are held together by strands of tradition, understanding, secrets, and love, so too are Ríos's books held together.

Ríos's writing is expressive of a consciousness that embraces familial, historical, intellectual, stylistic, and spiritual nuances without quieting the contradictions that exist between these different facets of experience. Ríos writes of revolutions and of the "disappeared." He writes about victims of violence hung from telephone poles. He writes of aunts, of his Nani, and of other familial matriarchs and patriarchs. He writes of fortune-tellers and of science. He writes of the dead who speak through drain pipes and the creak of rocking chairs, of how many people happen to be airborne above the United States at any given time, of the dispossessed of a town, and of the homeless, the unwanted, and the mentally unique and thus feared. He writes in forms from many cultures. He skillfully and imaginatively weaves composites of ideas, of places, and of people that gain the power of all their component parts. Ríos writes about composites the way Aztec deities were composites—the plumed serpent, the were-jaguar—and, in writing such composites, he evokes a consciousness that spans multiple spaces and centuries.

Ríos currently teaches at Arizona State University where he is a distinguished Regents' Professor and the Katharine C. Turner Endowed Chair in English. He resides in Chandler, Arizona, with his wife and son, Joaquin.

Bibliography

Dunaway, David King, and Sara L. Spurgeon, eds. *Writing the Southwest.* New York: Plume/Penguin, 1995.

Praitis, Irena. "'He gathered to himself through the years / Something of everything he knew': Metaphor, Composites, and Multiplicity in the Poetry of Alberto Ríos." *Cultura, Lenguaje y Representación* 1, no. 1 (2004): 81–88.

Ríos, Alberto. *Capirotada.* Albuquerque: University of New Mexico Press, 1999.

———. *The Curtain of Trees.* Albuquerque: University of New Mexico Press, 1999.

———. *Five Indiscretions.* New York: Sheep Meadow Press, 1985.

———. *The Iguana Killer.* Lewiston, N.Y.: Blue Moon and Confluence Press, 1984.

———. *The Lime Orchard Woman.* New York: Sheep Meadow Press, 1988.

———. *Pig Cookies.* San Francisco, Calif.: Chronicle Books, 1995.

———. *The Smallest Muscle in the Human Body.* Port Townsend, Wash.: Copper Canyon Press, 2002.

———. *Teodoro Luna's Two Kisses.* New York: W. W. Norton, 1990.

———. *Whispering to Fool the Wind.* New York: Sheep Meadow Press, 1982.

Rosaldo, Renato. "Fables of the Fallen Guy." In *Criticism in the Borderlands,* edited by Héctor Calderón and José David Saldívar, 84–93. Durham, N.C.: Duke University Press, 1991.

Vela, Richard. "The Idea of Boundaries in the Work of Alberto Ríos." *Pembroke Magazine* 34 (2002): 115–121.

Irena Praitis

Rivera, Tomás (1935–1984) *(essayist, fiction writer)*

Mexican-American author Tomás Rivera was born in 1935 in Crystal City, Texas. His parents were migrant farmers who worked throughout the Midwest, so Rivera spent much of his childhood traveling with them. In the 1950s Rivera also worked as a farm laborer. He earned a bachelor's degree in English and a master's in educational administration, both from Texas State University, and a Ph.D. in Romance languages and literature from the University of Oklahoma.

Rivera worked as an administrator and a professor at several universities and was the chancellor at the University of California, Riverside, at the time of his death. In addition to being an academic and an author of poetry, fiction, and essays, Rivera served on a number of foundations and boards nationwide and was known for being a Chicano rights advocate. All of his work shared a common goal: to better the Chicano community. The Tomás Rivera Mexican American Children's Book Award is now given in his honor.

Rivera wrote in both Spanish and English about the hardships encountered by the working class. For the most part he focused on Mexican-American migrant workers, especially children. While one of his goals was to give voice to the oppressed, he also illustrated their strength of character and faith in God.

The Searchers: Collected Poetry (1990) contains poems published by Rivera during his lifetime as well as those discovered after his death. Both *The Searchers* and *The Harvest/La cosecha* (1988), a collection of short stories, were published posthumously. Rivera's short stories, poetry, and essays are now available in *Tomás Rivera: The Complete Works* (1992).

. . . Y no se lo tragó la tierra/ . . . And the Earth Did Not Devour Him (1971) is Rivera's most famous work and is considered a classic in CHICANO LITERATURE. It won the Premio Quinto Sol literary prize in 1970 and was originally written in Spanish. ROLANDO HINOJOSA SMITH offers an English rendition of Rivera's book called *THIS MIGRANT EARTH* (1987), which captures the south Texas rhythms of speech and colloquialisms of Rivera's Spanish. More recently, Evangelina Vigil-Piñón published a literal translation of Rivera's work called *. . . y no se lo tragó la tierra/ . . . and the earth did not devour him.*

. . . Y no se lo tragó la tierra consists of 14 short stories and 13 untitled vignettes. The collection is about post–World War II migrant workers from south Texas who spend most of their lives traveling or in the fields picking crops. Through the use of first-person, third-person, and omniscient narrators, the work is told from a variety of perspectives, but the emphasis is on the coming-of-age experiences of an unnamed boy and the frustration that he experiences as a result of being a poor Mexican American. Several themes, including poverty and racism, are woven throughout the pieces. While the migrant families value education, the Mexican-American children have only uneven access to public schooling; the migrant children are stereotyped as lice-ridden individuals who steal. The poverty experienced by the workers is so great that the children search for treasures in the local garbage dump. The young narrator shares a widespread frustration about migrant life, and his anger escalates when his father and nine-year-old brother suffer from heat stroke while working. Despite the importance of his family's Catholic beliefs, he dares to curse God, and this episode gives the book its title: Despite his cursing of God "the earth did not devour him." Ultimately the nameless narrator is empowered by the anger he feels. The work ends on a positive note because by remembering the events of the past, even the painful ones, the boy finds a sense of resolution: All the utterances of his neighbors, friends, and family members come to mind and are both familiar and somewhat comforting. In 1993 the text was adapted into a film titled *. . . And the Earth Did Not Swallow Him* by filmmaker Severo Perez.

Bibliography

Flores, Lauro H. "The Discourse of Silence in the Narrative of Tomás Rivera." *Revista Chicano-Riquena* 13, nos. 3–4 (1985): 96–106.

Gonzalez-T, César A. "Archetypes of Integration in Chicano Literature: Tomás Rivera's *Tierra*." *Confluencia* 5, no. 1 (Fall 1989): 85–90.

Grajeda, Ralph F. "Tomas Rivera's . . . *Y no se lo tragó la tierra*: Discovery and Appropriation of the Chicano Past." *Hispania* 62, no. 1 (1979): 71–81.

Rivera, Tomás. *The Harvest: Short Stories.* Edited by Julian Olivares. Houston, Tex.: Arte Público Press, 1988.

———. *The Searchers: Collected Poetry.* Houston, Tex.: Arte Público Press, 1990.

———. *Tomás Rivera: The Complete Works.* Edited by Julian Olivares. Houston, Tex.: Arte Público Press, 1998.

———. . . . *Y no se lo tragó la tierra/ . . . And the Earth Did Not Devour Him.* 3d ed. Revised and translated by Evangelina Vigil-Piñón. Houston, Tex.: Arte Público Press, 1990.

Urioste, Donaldo W. "The Child's Process of Alienation in Tomas Rivera's ". . . *Y no se lo tragó la tierra*." In *The Chicano Struggle: Analyses of Past and Present Efforts,* edited by John A. Garcia et al., 178–191. Binghamton, N.Y.: Bilingual Press, 1984.

Diane Todd Bucci

Road to Tamazunchale, The Ron Arias
(1975)

Ron Arias (1941–) belongs to the first generation of Chicano authors who emerged after the founding of the United Farm Workers by CESAR CHAVEZ in 1965. Arias's novella *Road to Tamazunchale* describes the physical and metaphysical journey of Fausto Tejada, the main character, who travels to Peru, Mexico, and Los Angeles. In telling his tale of adventure and discovery Arias incorporates elements from European chivalry narratives, the picaresque novel (with the influence of Miguel Cervantes), and the chronicles of the Spanish conquistadores. Fausto travels to Cuzco, Peru, to examine the roots of his indigenous heritage, which he has neglected. In his journey Fausto accepts the hospitality of the Spanish viceroy and dons the apparel of the conquistador, acknowledging his Spanish heritage. At the same time, and as an indio (an Indian), Fausto lacks fluency in the Spanish language, so he uncomfortably occupies this role as "colonizer."

Road to Tamazunchale plays with the line between reality and fiction and demonstrates Arias's interest in postmodern expression and play with plot. The novel depends on a rich sense of textuality signaled by Fausto's relationship with books: Fausto is a book salesman in his active life, and he takes books with him when he travels to Tamazunchale, Mexico. Every page is filled with metafictional references. The protagonist's name, Fausto, brings to mind Christopher Marlowe's and Johann Wolfgang von Goethe's Dr. Faustus. But unlike Marlowe and Goethe's characters, Arias's Fausto maintains a sharp irony about humanity. Fausto is clearly Arias's version of Cervantes's fictional character Don Quixote. Like Don Quijote, Fausto Tejada travels and learns through his experiences; however, instead of going to Spain, Fausto and his companions visit the underworld of Chicano reality in Los Angeles. There he experiences the problem of the *mojados* (wetbacks) coming illegally from Mexico into the United States, the unemployment Mexicans face, as well as the violence of gangs and the crushing aspects of urban poverty. Fausto's companions include the Peruvian shepherd Marcelino Huaca with his unruly alpacas and Mario and Carmela, who are pachucos (urban Mexican Americans who both adapt to and resist the U.S. mainstream). Fausto, Marcelino, Mario, and Carmela each represent an important aspect of Mexican, Mexican-American and Latin American history.

Arias uses the setting of Tamazunchale to bring together aspects of this history, a place where the dead and the living, the real and the imagined, meet on common ground. The world of the living gets intermingled with the world of the dead to form a unique reality, especially when Fausto Tejada visits the dead in his imagination. He engages in conversation with Evangelina, his deceased wife, and remembers or dreams about a journey with her to bring illegal workers into California. Mrs. Rentería, a spinster, enjoys for three days the company of David, a handsome drowned wetback found in the river. Instead of burying him, Fausto, Mario, and Carmela return him to the river, "where others can find him" (75). Every character is very alive in Arias's novel, even the ones who have died. Mortality becomes uncertain because Fausto transcends space and time in his nonlinear journeys. In this sense the novella is reminiscent of Juan Rulfo's Mexican surrealist novel, *Pedro Páramo* (1955), and the narrative mode called MAGICAL REALISM. Arias experiments with the narrative form in the way his stories interconnect and in the way that plays are performed within the main plot. Arias takes his characters out of the realm of literature when Fausto and Marcelino appear suddenly in a battlefield scene of a film about colonial times in Peru. Fausto's pilgrimage to Tamazunchale can be understood as the journey of life, a journey toward death. It is a metaphysical adventure that Fausto embarks upon as he lies on his deathbed. Prior to dying he not only reviews but, in reality, revises the path of his life. For its settings and thematic concerns Arias's work can be read within the context of CHICANO LITERATURE.

Bibliography

Arias, Ron. *The Road to Tamazunchale.* Tempe, Ariz.: Bilingual Press, 1997, 181–206.

Martin-Rodriguez, Manuel M. "Border Crisscrossing: *The* (Long and Winding) *Road to Tamazunchale.*" In *Cross-Addressing: Resistance Literature and Cultural Borders,* edited by John C. Hawley, Albany: State University of New York Press, 1996.

Walter, Roland. *Magical Realism in Contemporary Chicano Fiction.* Frankfurt, Germany: Vervuert Verlag, 1993.

Imelda Martín-Junquera

Rodríguez, Luis J. (1954–) *(poet, novelist, memoirist, journalist, children's author, social activist)*

Luis J. Rodríguez was born on July 9, 1954, in El Paso, Texas. The son of María Estela Jiménez, a Tarahumara Indian, and Alfonso Rodríguez, a former high school principal, he is the second of their four children. After living in Ciudad Juárez, Mexico, until age two, Rodríguez and his family moved to Los Angeles, specifically the Mexican section of Watts, then later to East Los Angeles. Both of these areas were segregated communities, a fact that resonates in Rodríguez's work as well as his life. Los Angeles was a city synonymous with glamour, but one in which the contributions and presence of Mexican Americans were and are undervalued. From his earliest writings to the most recent the question of American identity and the quest for social justice is central to this author.

Readers of Rodríguez's memoir, *Always Running: La Vida Loca, Gang Days in L.A.* (1993), feel this centrality. As the subtitle shows, this visceral account of growing up in America's mean streets focuses on "the crazy life" of Chicano gang culture. Rodríguez relates his conflict with a dominant society that has historically refused to accept Mexicans socially, economically, and politically. At the same time the author expresses his own sense of internal conflict, and he therefore presents a coming-of-age story, a special kind of education tale involving violence and desperation as the means to self-knowledge and the opening of new worlds.

Always Running describes the cumulative effect of gang life, which nearly destroyed Rodríguez. (The book was written as a cautionary tale for his son Ramiro.) Rodríguez was not just a troubled teen, however. His many guises—delinquent, boxer, student, protester, and so forth—were all many layers peeled away to reveal a thirst for wholeness and usefulness in life. Even while still in gangs Rodríguez began to understand the spiritual fulfillment as well as practical urgency of activism on behalf of the Mexican people of Los Angeles. Gradually Rodríguez transformed himself into an artist who wrote about what he knew, found healing in writing, and connected with countless individuals, many possessing the same desires as himself.

In the midst of his gang intervention, union organizing, and journalistic efforts, Rodríguez's first book, *Poems Across the Pavement,* was issued in

1989 by Tia Chucha Press, a publishing house he started after moving to Chicago in the mid-1980s. Winner of San Francisco State University's Poetry Center Book Award, *Poems Across the Pavement* launched an engaging literary career.

In 1991 *The Concrete River* was published by Curbstone Press. This collection of poems, like the first, deals to a great extent with Rodríguez's experience in the City of Angels, but the writing is richer, more vivid and nuanced in rendering life in the barrio. In this work Rodríguez realized a not-so-common balance of aesthetics and politics, producing a communal as well as private voice about Chicano urban realities. *The Concrete River* won the PEN West/Josephine Miles Award for Literary Excellence in 1992. That same year Rodríguez received a Lannan Fellowship for Poetry, joining a prestigious company of writers of exceptional work.

A leader in several areas, Rodríguez has received major awards for his work. He is the recipient of the Carl Sandburg Literary Award (1993), the Lila Wallace–Reader's Digest Writer's Award (1996), the Hispanic Heritage Award for Literature (1998), the Americas Award for Children's and Young Adult Literature (2000), the "Unsung Heroes of Compassion" Award (2001), presented by the Dalai Lama, and the Sundance Institute Arts Writing Fellowship (2002), among many others.

Originally based in Chicago, Rodríguez's Tia Chucha Press has relocated to Los Angeles with its founder. In 2001 Rodríguez and his family created Tia Chucha's Café and Centro Cultural—a bookstore, café, art gallery, performance center, cybercafe, and workshop space in Sylmar, California, northeast of Los Angeles in the San Fernando Valley. To date Tia Chucha Press has published nearly 40 books of poetry, including two anthologies showcasing its talent.

The work of Rodríguez has not been without controversy. *Always Running* is one of the most banned books in public schools and libraries. Nevertheless, Rodríguez has carved a niche for himself in American life and letters. Though his voice has often been a skeptical one regarding U.S. democracy, such skepticism is a fundamental part of the American poetic spirit. He has questioned the causes of homelessness, gangs, overcrowded prisons, discrimination toward immigrants, narrowness in American poetic subject matter, and so forth. And he has been on the front line, resisting authoritarianism and ignorance while writing out of an experience and consciousness that tries to humanize his subject matter.

Rodríguez's latest works, *My Nature Is Hunger: New and Selected Poems* and the novel *Music of the Mill,* both published in 2005, reveal a seriousness and exuberance that make him one of the more vital poets and storytellers in the United States today. There is conscience and passion as Rodríguez bridges political feeling with the complexities of language. Rodríguez has traveled a remarkable distance from the youth who was "always running" to the man of mature vision, one who has been shaped and not destroyed by his experiences. For its themes and characters Rodríguez's work can be read within the context of CHICANO LITERATURE.

Bibliography

Brown, Monica. *Gang Nation: Delinquent Citizens in Puerto Rican, Chicano, and Chicana Narratives.* Minneapolis: University of Minnesota Press, 2002.

Cohen, Aaron. "An Interview with Luis J. Rodríguez." *Poets and Writers* (January–February 1995): 50–55.

Foster, Sesshu. Review of *Poems Across the Pavement* and *The Concrete River. Americas Review* 22, nos. 1–2 (Spring–Summer 1994): 279–282.

Herrera-Sobek, María. "Geography of Despair: The Mean Streets of L.A. of Luis Rodríguez's *Always Running.*" *Latino Studies Journal* 8, no. 2 (Spring 1997): 56–67.

Perez, Vincent. "'Running' and Resistance: Nihilism and Cultural Memory in Chicano Urban Narratives." *MELUS* 25, no. 2 (Summer 2000): 133–146.

Rodríguez, Andrés. "Contemporary Chicano Poetry: The Work of Michael Sierra, Juan Felipe Herrera, and Luis J. Rodríguez." *Bilingual Review* 21, no. 3 (1996): 203–218.

Rodriguez, Luis J. *Always Running: La Vida Loca, Gang Days in L.A.* Willimantic, Conn.: Curbstone Press, 1993.

———. *The Concrete River.* Willimantic, Conn.: Curbstone Press, 1991.

———. *Hearts and Hands: Creating Community in Violent Times.* St. Paul, Minn.: Seven Stories Press, 2001.

———. *Music of the Mill.* New York: Rayo, 2005.

———. *My Nature Is Hunger: New and Selected Poems.* Willimantic, Conn.: Curbstone Press, 2005.

———. *Poems Across the Pavement.* Chicago: Tia Chucha Press, 1989.

———. *The Republic of East L.A.: Stories.* New York: Rayo, 2002.

———. *Trochemoche.* Willimantic, Conn.: Curbstone Press, 1998.

Andrés Rodríguez

Rodriguez, Richard (1944–   ) *(essayist, memoirist)*

Born in San Francisco, California, in 1944, Richard Rodriguez was raised in Sacramento, where he attended a Catholic school. Rodriguez earned a bachelor's degree at Stanford University, after which he spent two years at Union Theological Seminary studying with leading Protestant and Jewish theologians. He later spent time at London's Warburg Institute and Oxford before he began, but did not finish, his Ph.D. in English at the University of California, Berkeley.

Rodriguez is best known for his controversial opposition to affirmative action and bilingual education, two issues often championed by Chicano authors. In Rodriguez's opinion these attitudes are anti-assimilationist, alienating, and detrimental in their effects. He believes in the benefits of the mixing of cultural, racial, and ethnic identities in the United States, a phenomenon he has termed as the "browning of America." Central to his writing is his experience of separation from family, personal alienation, and finally assimilation into mainstream American society, as he left behind the Spanish-speaking household of his childhood and entered into the English-speaking American public sphere. Rodriguez argues passionately against bilingual education, stating that if he had not been forced to learn English, he would have never been able to attain a functional public identity and become a productive member of society, with all the benefits that entails. In addition the themes of ethnicity, personal pride, and U.S. immigrant culture and history dominate Rodriguez's writings.

An acknowledged prose stylist, Rodriguez has worked as a teacher, journalist, and educational consultant. He has worked as an editor for the Pacific News Service, *Harper's* magazine, and *U.S. New & World Report.* He also writes for a considerable number of periodicals, such as the *Los Angeles Times,* the *New York Times,* the *Wall Street Journal, American Scholar, College English, Time, Harper's,* and the *New Republic.* Rodriguez frequently appears on the PBS program *The NewsHour with Jim Lehrer.* Rodriguez has written two documentaries for the BBC and several books.

Hunger of Memory: The Education of Richard Rodriguez (1981) reflects, as its title suggests, on Rodriguez's education and experience of growing up as a Mexican American in California. He values his education despite some ambivalence and describes his decision not to finish his dissertation on Renaissance literature. His next work, Days of Obligation: An Argument with My Mexican Father (1992) reflects on the racial and religious makeup of ethnic communities in San Francisco. *Days of Obligation* was nominated for a National Book Award. In Brown: The Last Discovery of America (2002), Rodriguez explores issues of race, arguing that America has been brown since its inception, as he himself is. Brown, in his view, is not a color but a mixture, evidence of the blending of cultures that began the moment the African and European met within the Indian eye. In this regard Rodriguez focuses on the concept of mestizaje, the mixing of races in the Americas. For his reflection on what it means to be Latino in the U.S.—a perspective that has complicated notions about the black and white divide of American culture—Rodriguez earned in 2003 the Melcher Book Award.

In 1997, he received a George Foster Peabody Award, one of television's highest honors, for his *NewsHour* essays on American life. Rodriguez's awards also include the Frankel Medal from the National Endowment for the Humanities and the International Journalism Award from the World Affairs Council of California.

Bibliography

Gregorio, Eduardo de. "Language and Male Identity Construction in the Cultural Borderlands: Richard Rodriguez's *Hunger of Memory*" In *Literature and Ethnicity in the Cultural Borderlands,* edited by Jesús Benito and Anna María Manzanas, 127–134. Amsterdam: Rodopi, 2002.

Rodriguez, Richard. *Brown: The Last Discovery of America.* New York: Penguin, 2002.

———. *Days of Obligation: An Argument with My Mexican Father.* New York: Penguin, 1992.

———. *Hunger of Memory: The Education of Richard Rodriguez.* New York: Bantam, 1981.

Torres, Hector A.; "'I Don't Think I Exist': Interview with Richard Rodriguez." *MELUS* 28, no. 2 (summer 2003): 164–202.

Isabel M. Andrés Cuevas

Ruiz de Burton, María Amparo
(1832–1895) *(novelist, playwright)*

María Amparo Ruiz de Burton was born in Loreto, Baja California. She was the granddaughter of Baja California governor Don José Manuel Ruiz. While the Ruiz family could not be considered rich in terms of liquid assets, they were elite in terms of their family's prestigious position within *californio* society.

In 1847 Ruiz met her future husband, Captain Henry S. Burton. Serving in the U.S. Army, Burton was on an expedition to quell the armed resistance of *mexicanos* to the Treaty of GUADALUPE HIDALGO. In 1848, at the age of 16, she sailed to Monterey in Alta California (Upper California) to avoid the hostilities of the U.S. takeover of Mexican California. After their marriage in 1849 Ruiz and Captain Burton were stationed in Chicago, Philadelphia, and Washington, D.C.,

during a tumultuous period in U.S. history, including the Civil War. Her husband died in 1869 from malaria, and Ruiz de Burton immediately returned to San Diego to oversee her properties. She administered a cement factory and ranches north and south of the border. Ruiz de Burton assimilated into Californian English-speaking society, despite the fact that she would forever hold on to her Mexican identity.

Her bilingual correspondence, gathered into the 2001 book *Conflicts of Interest: The Letters of María Amparo Ruiz de Burton* by editors Beatriz Pita and Rosaura Sanchez, accounts for her desire to be a translator and mediator between *californios* and Anglos. In her correspondence she deploys sympathy as a political strategy to make people pay attention to her in a male-dominated world. While her critiques of U.S. imperialism are sometimes scathing, they still convey a serious amount of emotion, affect, and passion toward her subject that can in turn be understood as sympathetic representations of her subjects.

Ruiz de Burton gained social mobility through her marriage to Captain Burton. Yet, her correspondence indicates her frustration and desperation in finding U.S. government officials outside her access. In the 1870s several squatters challenged the title to her landholdings at Rancho Jamul. As historian Armando Alonzo has shown, the ownership and management of land are crucial to understanding the way 19th-century *mexicanos* understood their identities. Ruiz de Burton's legal squabbles with family and squatters alike remind us of the intense economic competition for land at the height of the period of U.S. expansionism, before and after the U.S.-Mexican War. *Californios* appealed to the courts to defend their land claims that were often taken by way of barbed wire fences. The different systems of designating land ownership and larger questions of language and fraud emerged as many *californios* were dispossessed from their lands. Alonzo argues that during the Mexican period the number of valid land grants claims totaled 588. In U.S. California the Land Grant Act of 1851 did not cover the three-year lag time between the signing of the Treaty of Guadalupe Hidalgo and the adjudication process for validating these land claims. Mexican land titles were not marked by acreage; instead physical features of the land were used to identify ownership. The lack of precise measurements hindered the appeals process. Many claims were denied by U.S. authorities, and many *californios* were forced to sell off their land in small tracts so as to have their cases heard in the courts. Lawyers were often paid with land if the claim came out in favor of the titleholder (Alonzo 263–264).

These struggles over citizenship, identity, and assets appear as themes in her first novel, *Who Would've Thought It?* (1872). Ruiz de Burton reveals anxieties of being lumped together with the lower-class mestizo (person of mixed Spanish and Indian blood). *Who Would've Thought It?* is set during the U.S. Civil War and can be read as a Latin American romance, a political satire, as well as a sentimental novel. This text relies on history and sentimentality because women are associated with the home and the frontier; the domestication of female bodies through marriage and the domestication of frontier spaces come to symbolize America. The novel partakes in an ongoing discussion that centers on the political nature of novels written by women in the mid- to late 19th century.

Set in New York, *Who Would've Thought It?* situates Mexican womanhood within the context of the so-called free and liberal North. The text depends on our ability to recognize Lola as the sentimental heroine. Lola is the figure that allows for a discussion of Mexican racial identity and womanhood. Through its domestic narrative the text critiques the violence of U.S. expansionism and hegemony. Ruiz de Burton's larger and contradictory project to assimilate upper-class *californios* like Lola Medina into the U.S. body politic fails because of the plot. Thrown into a staunchly Protestant and Anglo family in the land of Lincoln, Lola and Julian become symbols for a divided nation during the 1860s. The couple marry despite regional differences and move to the Mexican border. What this failed assimilationist project does accomplish

is to rupture a black-white racial binary in the American imagination, as in *Uncle Tom's Cabin* (1852). Similarly the union disrupts the North-South binary during the Civil War. Lola Medina compels us to recognize that Mexican Americans are part of the nation-state in the Southwest.

Ruiz de Burton's second novel, *The SQUATTER AND THE DON* (1885) takes up the conflicts over land between *californios* and squatters. Taking place before and after the Treaty of Guadalupe Hidalgo, *The Squatter and the Don* begins its domestic plot in California. Through marriage and alliances between the Alamar (Mexican) and Darrell (American) families the novel describes the decline of the *californios* as the ruling elite. The story is set at a time when California is still part of Mexico. Then the novel tracks the emergence of English-speaking landholding Americans as the new ruling elite, an elite aided by U.S. expansionism and capitalism. In her historical romance the author acknowledges the influence that railroad tycoons had on regional economies. She uses her character Leland Stanford to represent the abuse of railway managers and owners who, despite the possibility of great growth, deliberately ignored San Diego as a site for the expansion of the Texas Pacific Railroad. The novel argues that San Diego and the *californios*' gradual economic disenfranchisement (the economy shifted from agrarian to merchant capitalism and development) can be attributed to the absence of a railroad line. With the disputes over land ownership, the potential for economic growth, and the need for political alliances between *californios* and Anglos, Mexican women's bodies become the vehicle for the merging of *californio* landholdings and property. When the last Mexican don dies, we see the disappearance of the 19th-century California society. Don Mariano Alamar's daughters are married off to Anglo men. His death represents the end of one generation and the future of assimilation.

Little is known about her play *Don Quixote de la Mancha: A Comedy, in Five Acts, Taken from Cervantes' Novel of That Name* (1876). It is merely referenced in newspapers and her own personal correspondence: a copy of the text has yet to be found. Given her novels and correspondence, Ruiz de Burton has invited numerous debates about race, heritage, and citizenship in Latino literary and U.S. cultural studies. Considered the first U.S. Mexican novelist, scholars continue to debate her position in the formation of the literary canon, as a recovered author, and as a precursor to contemporary configurations of Mexican-American identity in CHICANO LITERATURE.

Bibliography

Alonzo, Armando. *Rancheros and Settlers in South Texas, 1734–1900.* Albuquerque: University of New Mexico Press, 1998.

Aranda, Jose. "Contradictory Impulses: María Amparo Ruiz de Burton, Resistance Theory and the Politics of Chicano/a Studies." *American Literature* 70, no. 3. (September 1998): 551–579.

Montes, Amelia Maria de la Luz, and Anne Goldman. *María Amparo Ruiz de Burton: Critical and Pedagogical Perspectives.* Lincoln: University of Nebraska Press, 2004.

Rivera, John-Michael. "Embodying Greater Mexico: María Amparo Ruiz de Burton and the Reconstruction of the Mexican Question." In *Look Away: The U.S. South in New World Studies,* edited by Jon Smith and Debra Cahn, 451–470. Durham, N.C.: Duke University Press, 2004.

Ruiz de Burton, María Amparo. *Conflicts of Interest: The Letters of María Amparo Ruiz de Burton.* Edited by Beatriz Pita and Rosaura Sanchez. Houston, Tex.: Arte Público Press, 2001.

———. *The Squatter and the Don: A Novel Descriptive of Contemporary Occurrences in California.* With an introduction by Beatriz Pita and Rosaura Sanchez. Houston, Tex.: Arte Público Press, 1992.

———. *Who Would've Thought It?* With an introduction by Beatriz Pita and Rosaura Sanchez. Houston, Tex.: Arte Público Press, 1995.

Nicole Guidotti Hernandez

Ryan, Pam Muñoz (1951–) *(fiction writer)*

Pam Muñoz Ryan was born in Bakersfield, California, on December 25, 1951 of Mexican and Italian heritage. She grew up in a large family. Her maternal grandmother, on whose life her novel ESPERANZA RISING (2002) is based, spoke only Spanish. Ryan grew up speaking both Spanish and English. She earned both bachelor's and master's degrees from San Diego State University. And she lives in southern California with her husband and four children.

Ryan has written more than 20 books for children and young adults, ranging from picture books to novels. She has won numerous awards for her writing including the Pura Belpre Award, the Willa Cather Award for Best Young Adult Novel, and the Jane Addams Children's Book Award. Her picture books include *When Marian Sang* (2002), the story of opera singer Marian Anderson's triumph over discrimination, and *Amelia and Eleanor Go for a Ride* (1999) about the friendship between First Lady Eleanor Roosevelt and pilot Amelia Earhart.

All of Ryan's novels focus on young female protagonists who are in the process of discovering themselves and their place in the world. Ryan's first novel, *Riding Freedom* (1998), focuses on a young woman named Charlotte Parkhurst who is a gifted horse handler. Charlotte lives in the 1860s and disguises herself as a man to live the life that she wants, a plot based on the real life of Charlotte Parkhurst. She becomes a well-known stagecoach driver despite the potentially career-ending loss of an eye; she travels from the East Coast to California, buys a farm, starts a way station for stagecoaches, and ultimately votes in a national election.

Esperanza Rising takes place during the Depression and centers on the protagonist's adjustment to life after leaving Mexico and working in the fields of California. *Becoming Naomi León* is a coming-of-age story involving border crossings between California and Mexico. Naomi and her brother are abandoned by their mother and come to live with their grandmother in the Lemon Tree trailer park. When Naomi is a teen, her mother tries to reclaim her, and the family is torn by a custody battle, one in which Naomi realizes who she is and what she wants. For its themes concerning border crossings, Muñoz Ryan's work can

be read within the context of both CHICANO LIT-
ERATURE and BORDER LITERATURE.

Bibliography

Carger, Chris Liska. "Crossing Borders, Finding Family." *Book Links* 16, no. 3 (January 2007): p. 36–38.
Pam Muñoz Ryan. Available online. URL: http://
www.pammunozryan.com/arthorstudy.html. Accessed December 12, 2007.

Ryan, Pam Muñoz. *Becoming Naomi León.* New York:
Scholastic, 2004.
———. *Esperanza Rising.* New York: Scholastic,
2001.
Tropp, Tasha. Review of *Esperanza Rising* by Pam
Muñoz Ryan. *Journal of Adolescent & Adult Lit-
eracy* 45, no. 4 (December 2001/January 2002):
p. 334.

Gabrielle Halko

S

Sáenz, Benjamín Alire (1954–) *(poet, fiction writer)*

The fourth of seven children, Benjamín Alire Sáenz was born in 1954 in Old Picacho, a farming village next to Las Cruces, New Mexico. Though Spanish was his first language, Sáenz learned English while attending public schools. Memories of a rural childhood, the loss of his family farmhouse, the pain brought to the family by his father's alcoholism, and his Catholic upbringing are present in many of his poems. The importance of family relationships drives two bilingual children's books, *A Gift from Papá Diego/ Un regalo de papá Diego* (1998) and *Grandma Fina and Her Wonderful Umbrella/Abuelita Fina y sus sombrillas maravillosas* (1999), which was chosen as the Best Children's Book of 1999 by the Texas Institute of Letters. These children's books are highly imaginative and recall Sáenz's love for his grandparents, as well as his respect for the knowledge and hard work of his elders.

By the time he graduated from Las Cruces High School Sáenz had already been employed as a janitor, wall painter, onion picker, and construction worker. Influenced by theologian Thomas Merton and by Mexican-American labor organizer CESAR CHAVEZ, Sáenz entered Saint Thomas Seminary in Denver, Colorado, in 1972. He earned a B.A. in humanities and philosophy and later moved to Belgium. By 1981 he had completed his theological training at the University of Louvain. In this period he traveled extensively throughout Europe; he also worked in a homeless shelter in north London. Besides his talent as a writer, Sáenz is also a painter, and he is currently working on the illustrations of Octavio Rivera's *Fantastic Dreams of Summer.*

Sáenz declares that his priesthood career reflected his interest in political issues more so than religious beliefs. At 26, Sáenz was ordained a Catholic priest and began to work for the barrio communities of El Paso, Texas, and Alamogordo, New Mexico. At the age of 29, he quit the Catholic priesthood with the intention to write his first novel, supporting his art by waiting tables. In 1984 he entered the Creative Writing Program at the University of Texas, El Paso, and received a fellowship for the University of Iowa, where he spent a year as a graduate student. In 1988 he received a Wallace E. Stegner Fellowship in poetry from Stanford University. His first book of poems, *Calendar of Dust* (1991), won an American Book Award. *Flowers for the Broken,* a collection of short stories, was published in the following year. He returned to El Paso in 1993 as a professor in the bilingual Master of Fine Arts program at the University of Texas. He was granted a poetry fellowship from the Lannan Foundation in 1995. During the same year *Carry Me Like Water* (1995), which draws on the conventions of MAGICAL REALISM, was translated into German and Dutch and sold with great success in Europe.

The border is a recurring image in Sáenz's work, which includes poetry, drama, fiction, and nonfictional prose. A continuous exploration of the links between his family in New Mexico and Texas and his family in Mexico takes his readers to mountains, rivers, cities, deserts, and bridges along the U.S.-Mexico border. In *Dark and Perfect Angels* (1995) Sáenz makes a poetic journey to trace his great-grandparents' legacy of strength and love:

> *From her, he learned*
> *About the mysteries of the corn, grew strong*
> *on her harvest.*
> *She blew into his mouth her gift of words*
> *until the language*
> *Of his birth had disappeared. After the first*
> *freeze*
> *They clung to each other's limbs like leaves*
> *refusing*
> *To fall, neither one aware when winter*
> *came and left (41).*

In this passage, Sáenz uses nature imagery to signal the teaching of a child by an elder. We can see through the references of the "the first freeze" and the arrival of winter the changes that take place in the speaker's life. Here, as elsewhere in Sáenz's writing, wisdom is passed on from one generation to another.

In 1997 Sáenz published the novel *The House of Forgetting*, which centers on ethnic identity, gender expectations, and class conflicts. In this novel Mexican American Gloria Santos has been "shaped" since her childhood to be the ideal woman that Thomas Blacker, a professor at the University of Chicago, imagines. But the cost of that shaping is the isolation that Santos experiences.

Given the range of themes covered in his poetry and prose, it is clear that Sáenz is committed to his political beliefs, expressing in his most recent books his concern about discrimination against Latinos in the United States. These books include *Elegies in Blue* (2002), which was nominated for the *Los Angeles Times* Book Award and *Sammy and Juliana in Hollywood* (2004), his first novel for young adults. The English and Spanish versions of his third novel, *In Perfect Light,* were published in 2005. For its themes and images Sáenz's work can be read within the context of BORDER LITERATURE and CHICANO LITERATURE.

Bibliography

Aldama, Frederick Luis. *Spilling the Beans in Chicano-landia: Conversations with Writers and Artists* Austin: University of Texas Press, 2006, 251–260.

Dick, Bruce Allen. *A Poet's Truth: Conversation with Latino/Latina Poets.* Tucson: University of Arizona Press, 2003.

Sáenz, Benjamín Alire. *Carry Me Like Water.* El Paso, Tex.: Cinco Puntos, 1995.

———. *Dark and Perfect Angels.* El Paso, Tex.: Cinco Puntos, 1995.

———. *Elegies in Blue.* El Paso, Tex.: Cinco Puntos, 2002.

———. *A Gift from Papá Diego/Un regalo de papá Diego.* El Paso, Tex.: Cinco Puntos, 1998.

———. *Grandma Fina and Her Wonderful Umbrellas/Abuelita Fina y sus sombrillas maravillosas.* El Paso, Tex.: Cinco Puntos, 1999.

———. *The House of Forgetting.* New York: HarperCollins, 1997.

———. *In Perfect Light.* New York: Rayo, 2005.

———. *Sammy and Juliana in Hollywood.* El Paso, Tex.: Cinco Puntos, 2004.

Selfa Chew

Sahagún, Bernardino de (c. 1499–1590)
(historian, theologian)

Fray (friar) Bernardino de Sahagún was born in Sahagún de Campos, a village belonging to the Spanish city of León in about 1499. Sahagún has found a solid place in Latino cultural history thanks to the creation of his masterpiece *Historia general de las cosas de la Nueva España (General History of the Things of New Spain),* an ambitious project which took most of his lifetime to complete. The book, also known as the Florentine Codex, describes Aztec ways of life and the encounter with the Spanish in the 1500s. It was written entirely in Nahuatl, the language spoken by the Aztec and other indigenous groups of Mexico. Not until 1829 was this monumental work first published in Spanish. As the compiler and editor of *Historia general de las cosas de la Nueva España*, Sahagún and his codex have been credited as the forerunners of modern anthropology and ethnography.

Sahagún, christened Bernardino Rivera, was born to a well-to-do family at the turn of the 15th century. The first 30 years of his life are not well documented in the annals of history. We do know, however, that he studied at the University of Salamanca, an important institution for the training of theologians and humanists. In Salamanca he responded to a religious calling and entered the Franciscan Order at about 20 years of age. When placing such a religious figure as Sahagún in his historical context, one should keep in mind the tremendous impact that the discovery of the New World had on contemporary minds. In this sense the post-discovery era became a dynamic time for priests, who saw their mission as one of converting the native inhabitants of the Americas to Catholicism. In this respect Sahagún was a man of his time; in 1528 he traveled to Cádiz, Spain, and left for the New World to help with the evangelizing of natives by the Franciscan Order. Sahagón never returned to Spain.

Upon his arrival in Mexico he alternated preaching and baptizing but soon realized that it would be a great advantage, with regard to his religious undertakings, to be able to speak the language of the native inhabitants. When one considers his modus operandi, one cannot deny that Sahagún was well ahead of his time, as he envisioned that the key to a complete understanding of "the other" rested upon linguistic grounds. It was therefore necessary for him to learn how to speak and write Nahuatl. Shortly after his arrival in New Spain Sahagún moved to Tlaltelolco, where teaching would rank first among his priorities at the College of Santa Cruz (inaugurated in 1536). From Tlaltelolco he moved to the valley of Puebla, where he devoted several years to preaching and doing research on the "heretical customs"

of the native indians. It is in this context that his compilation of sermons adapted to the Nahuatl language and entitled *Sermonario de dominicas y de santos en lengua mexicana* was first conceived. The collection was targeted toward the natives and was therefore written in a direct style.

The time span that stretches from 1545 to 1570 constitutes the most prolific period in the literary life of Sahagún. After struggling against the outbreak of plague among the indigenous population and to which he himself almost succumbed in 1546, Sahagún began an ambitious yet carefully planned project to collect all possible areas of knowledge related to the native way of life. This work developed from direct contact with the indigenous inhabitants and was written entirely in Nahuatl, with a Spanish translation. In 1547 he had already started his *Tratado de la retórica y teología de la gente mexicana*, written in Nahuatl. And, during his stay at the College of Santa Cruz, he had begun to write a work entitled *Postilla sobre las epístolas y evangelios de los domingos de todo el año*, which was meant to be a compilation of the Holy Scriptures adapted to the "Mexican tongue" (that is, Nahuatl).

In the 1550s Sahagún spent time preaching in Tepepulco and is reported to have paid several visits to Michoacán and Teotihuacán, where he had the chance to contemplate the beauty of native architecture. Between 1550 and 1555 the friar continued compiling information for his innovative project, the *Historia general de las cosas de la Nueva España*. Twenty-first-century readers are perhaps familiar with canonical versions of the Spanish Conquest such as Hernán Cortés's *Cartas de relación* (1519–26; *Letters from Mexico*) or Bernal Díaz del Castillo's *Historia verdadera de la conquista de la Nueva España* (1632; *The Conquest of New Spain*). The version of the conquest that we possess is generally the winners' version, but in book 12 of the *Historia general*, Sahagún gives a voice to the conquered, who describe the Spanish invasion of Mexico from the standpoint of the defeated. In this regard his work corresponds with that of his contemporary and fellow priest Bartolomé de Las Casas.

It was during the 1560s that Sahagún began to erect the methodological system that underlies the *Historia general*. As a rational man in his own time, his opus emerges for practical reasons—religious purposes. Sahagún appreciated that the traditional methods of conversion did not lead to the intended results. He saw that true conversion would be the direct result of immediate contact with the native population. In order for true conversion to have the desired effects, a system based on interviews with the natives was to be created; this is how the so-called *minutas,* the 16th-century version of our modern questionnaires, came to life. Along with the *minutas,* Sahagún laid the foundations of the *informantes* (informant), the basis of modern ethnological and anthropological processes. Natives were asked questions related to their social and religious environment, and their answers were copied down in Nahuatl. Results were compared and contrasted, and a group of trilingual peers from the College of Santa Cruz reviewed the entire process. It was Sahagún's task to come up with the final layout of the project, which would originally be made up of four books. Later this division would spawn a greater number of books, which would be finally rounded off to the 12 that we now possess.

Early in the 1560s Sahagún began to write *Psalmodia cristiana,* a number of religious songs translated into Nahuatl. In 1561 he also adapted to Nahuatl a work entitled *Coloquios y doctrina cristiana con que los doce frailes de San Francisco, enviados por el Papa Adriano VI y por el emperador Carlos V convirtieron a los indios de la Nueva España.* Late in the 1560s he wrote a Nahualt grammar book, *Arte de la lengua mexicana con su vocabulario apéndiz,* which unfortunately is not preserved today. By 1569 his *Historia general* was almost finished; however, economic problems in 1570 put his work to a stop, and so Sahagún was forced to come up with a process of synthesis. Part of his work was sent to both the Council of the Indies and the pope, Pius V, the latter part entitled *Breve compendio de los soles idolátricos que los indios desta Nueva España usaban en tiempos de su infidelidad.* Sahagún experienced much adversity but never ceased to write: In 1574 he finished his *Ejercicio cotidiano en lengua nahuatl* and completed *Vida de San Bernardino de Siena.* In 1577 the Spanish king, Philip II, had all versions of Sahagún's *Historia general* confiscated under the pretense that should the work be preserved, natives would always remain attached to their paganism. Sahagún Fray Bernardino handed the copies of his work to Fray Rodrigo de Sequera, who in turn took them to Europe with him in 1580.

Despite continuous adversities Sahagún continued to broaden his literary production. Curiously enough, in 1583 he completed his one published work during his lifetime, *Psalmodia cristiana y sermonario de los santos del año, en lengua mexicana, ordenada en cantares o psalmos para que canten los indios en los areytos que hacen en las iglesias.* Between 1583 and 1585 he wrote *Arte adivinatoria y calendario mexicano.* Known today as the writer of one of the most influential works about the colonial period and forerunner of modern anthropology and ethnography, Sahagún passed away on October 28, 1590. His histories create a critical context for the reading of CHICANO LITERATURE and Latin American literature more broadly.

Bibliography

Boruchoff, David A. "Sahagún and the Theology of Missionary Work." In *Sahagún at 500: Essays on the Quincentenary of the Birth of Fr. Bernardino de Sahagún,* edited by John Frederick Schwaller, 59–102. Berkeley, Calif.: Academy of American Franciscan History, 2003.

León Portilla, Miguel. *Bernardino de Sahagún: First Anthropologist.* Oklahoma City: University of Oklahoma Press, 2002.

Quiñones Keber, Eloise. *Representing Aztec Ritual: Performance, Text, and Image in the Work of Sahagún.* Boulder: University of Colorado Press, 2002.

Sahagún, Fray Bernardino de. *Bernardino de Sahagún's Psalmodia Cristiana.* Translated by Arthur J. O. Anderson. Salt Lake City: University of Utah Press, 1993.

———. *General History of the Things of New Spain: Florentine Codex.* Translated by Arthur J. O. Anderson. Salt Lake City: University of Utah, 1950–1982.

Alberto Zambrana

Salinas, Raúl (1934–2008) *(poet, essayist, political activist)*

Raúl Salinas was born in San Antonio, Texas, in 1934 and raised in the East Austin barrio. His education, partly in a Catholic primary school, ended in the 11th grade. After quitting school at age 17 he began educating himself in the black jazz and blues clubs adjacent to Mexican neighborhoods; it was in East Austin that he developed an appreciation for the mixture of jazz and poetry. Salinas later moved to California for work picking fruit; once settled in Los Angeles, Salinas, like many of his Mexican-American counterparts, adopted the streetwise 1950s pachuco persona. In 1957 the first of three incarcerations for drug offenses initiated his growing consciousness that resulted in a "poetry as activism" stance, one that prompted Salinas's involvement with prison reform. Salinas viewed the composing of poetry as therapy for minority issues—both inside the prison system and out. Many of his early poems are published in his first collection, *Un Trip through the Mind Jail y Otras Excursions* (1980).

Salinas became involved with a writing community of inmates by contributing to such prison newspapers as *The Echo* (Huntsville, Texas). Until his parole in 1965 Salinas wrote a "The Quartered Note," a monthly column enhanced by Salinas's knowledge of jazz and the saxophone. The monthly columns are included in the collected writings *raúlrsalinas and the Jail Machine: My Weapon Is My Pen* (2006), along with other journalistic pieces. The book reprints a Thanksgiving Day prison essay about President John F. Kennedy's drug regulations, entitled "So Much Mystery, So Much Misunderstanding" (1964). The prison essay was originally reprinted in the *Beaumont Enterprise* (Texas), making it the first article Salinas published on the outside. His prose and poetry are characterized by candor and his advocation of the rights of the disenfranchised.

During his sentence in Leavenworth (Kansas) after another drug arrest in 1967, Salinas wrote for the prison newspaper *Aztlán de Leavenworth*, first published in 1970. His best-known poem, "Un Trip through the Mind Jail," was published in the inaugural issue of the prison newspaper. The poem describes the experience as his soul leaves the confines of his prison cell and travels back to the early years of his youth in the East Austin barrio La Loma. The poem pays tribute to Mexican-American barrios, affirming a profound sense of culture and place.

His second collection of poems, *East of the Freeway: Reflections de mi pueblo* (1995), covering his experiences in the East Austin barrio, reveals an accomplished writer capable of utilizing *poetic gymnastics,* Salinas's term for his mature poetics. He left Marion federal penitentiary (Illinois) in 1972 as a leader of the prison reform movement. Salinas uses the term *Xicanindio* to describe the combination of a Mexican-Chicano-indigenous ethnicity. Upon his return to Austin, Salinas opened the Resistencia Bookstore, offering the most extensive collection of poetry and postcolonial writings in the region. The bookstore quickly became a community locus for touring and local poetry readings and for socially conscious political events. After *Freeway*'s publication, Salinas received the Windcall Award for writing dedicated to social justice issues.

Three recordings of Salinas performing his poetry—*Los Many Mundos of raúlrsalinas: Un Poetic Jazz Viaje Con Friends* (2000), *Beyond the Beaten Path* (2002), and *Red Arc: A Call for liberación con salsa and Cool* (2005)—follow the debut initiating of his recording work with music, *Intimacies: Austin Poets Audio Anthology Project, Volume I* (1985), taken from a radio broadcast of Texas poets. They reveal a self-assured voice that resonates with emotion while exposing tensions between marginalized individuals and mainstream society. The music clubs of La Loma barrio shaped his "inner rhythms"; blues, jazz, and traditional Mexican *corridos* (ballads) all became inspirations in his use of language. He mixes black English and standard English with Texas Spanish, along with street slang to form a singular textual expression that succeeds with brass instrumentation and jazz improvisation.

Salinas's writing can be viewed as an expression of dedication to prison and urban reform and in this regard can be read alongside the work of other Mexican-American writers, such as RICARDO SÁNCHEZ. Salinas's work is archived at Stanford University Special Collections. Louis Mendoza edited the Salinas collection for his 2006 publication *raúlrsalinas and the Jail Machine*. By his own accounts Salinas viewed himself as much a part of the international "family of poets" who express political and social concerns about the barrio and prison life. For its themes and images Salinas's work can be read within the context of CHICANO LITERATURE.

Bibliography

Mendoza, Louis. "The Re-education of Xicanindio: Raul Salinas and the Poetics of Pinto Transformation." *MELUS* 28, no. 1 (2003): 39–60.

Salinas, Raúl. *East of the Freeway: Reflections de mi pueblo*. Austin, Tex.: Red Salmon Press, 1995.

———. *Indio Trails: A Xicano Odyssey through Indian Country*. San Antonio, Tex.: Wings Press, 2006.

———. *Los Many Mundos of Raúl Salinas: Un Poetic Jazz Viaje con Friends*. San Diego, Calif.: Calaca Press, 2000.

———. *raúlrsalinas and the Jail Machine: My Weapon Is My Pen; The Unpublished Writings of Raúl Salinas, 1957–1972*. Edited by Louis Mendoza. Austin: University of Texas Press, 2006.

———. "Shame on the Shaman," "The Jewel Thing," and "Casting My Vote." In *Intimacies: Austin Poets Audio Anthology*, Vol. 1, directed by Hedwig Gorski. Audiocasette. Austin, Tex.: Perfection Productions, 1987.

———. *Un Trip through the Mind Jail y Otras Excursions*. Houston, Tex.: Arte Público Press, 1999.

Hedwig Gorski

Sánchez, Ricardo (1941–1995) *(poet, educator)*

Ricardo Sánchez was born in 1941, in El Paso, Texas, and grew up in the neighborhood known as El Barrio del Diablo (Devil's Barrio). He was the youngest of 13 children born to Pedro Lucero and Adelina Gallegos Sánchez. Like RAÚL SALINAS, Sánchez overcame the prejudice of the Texas educational system and a criminal past to become a respected writer and speaker. He earned a doctorate in American studies at the Union Graduate School in Cincinnati, Ohio, and published nine collections of poetry. Between 1985 and 1991 he also contributed weekly columns to the *San Antonio Express News* and the *El Paso Herald Post*.

Sánchez's writing exposes institutional hypocrisy and criticizes those who give way to inauthenticity or falseness in the recognition of self-identity. Early poetry collections include *Canto y grito mi liberación* (1971; I sing and shout my liberation) and *Hechizospells* (1976). These poems convey anger about the struggles in his life and the lives of Mexican Americans living in the Southwest. Sánchez enlisted in the army and would have started officer training if not for the deaths of his two brothers. Arrested for robbery on two occasions, he served prison terms in both Texas and California. Like Salinas, Sánchez served jail time and went on to educate youth about the stigma associated with prison and the obstacles posed by incarceration; he made clear from his own mistakes the costs to be paid for leading a gang life.

Sánchez used his poetry to describe the distinct qualities of the borderlands between Texas and Mexico. He tried to educate his people about the generalized abuses of power at all levels and the salvation that love provides. He vehemently criticized the use of the government term *Hispanic*, a generalized category for Spanish speakers in the United States. Sánchez, viewed each regional Chicano (and Latino) community as distinctive and unique, just as each Native American tribe is unique. Poetry collections such as *Eagle-Visioned/Feathered Adobes: Poems* (1996) and *Honey Madness: Alaskan Cruising Poems* (1982), which was written during a residency at the University of Alaska, describe his self-vision. He taught a creative writing course for the university at the Lemon Creek Alaska State Prison and edited the debut issue of the *Lemon Creek Gold: A Journal of Prison Literature* resulting from his course. His charismatic, larger-than-life personality gave voice to his celebration of life and love, as well as his concern for the welfare of border communities. Sánchez believed that true knowledge of a person's roots leads to valuing of the entire community, or *la raza* (literally, "the race"), and contributes to self-dignity. *The Loves of Ricardo* (1997) is a posthumous collection in which editors Roberto Barcena and Sue Hetherington bring together the love poems that Barcena had found in Sánchez's notebooks. The poems show a more intimate side of a man who was experienced in the harshness of barrio and prison life.

Sánchez returned to El Paso after resigning from Washington State University when he was diagnosed with cancer. After his death in 1995 the city inducted him into the El Paso Writers Hall of Fame preceded by a major celebration of his work by the University of Texas, El Paso, and the El Paso Public Library. Sánchez's voluminous archives are housed at Stanford University and in the Benson Latin American Collection at the University of Texas, Austin. For his subjects and images Sánchez's work can be read within the context of CHICANO LITERATURE.

Bibliography

Christensen, Paul. *West of the American Dream: An Encounter with Texas.* College Station: Texas A&M University Press, 2001.

Dr. Ricardo Sánchez Web site. Available online. URL: http://www.dr-ricardo-sanchez.com. Accessed June 20, 2008.

López, Miguel R. *Chicano Timespace: The Poetry and Politics of Ricardo Sánchez.* College Station: Texas A&M University Press, 2001.

Sánchez, Ricardo. *Brown Bear Honey Madness: Alaskan Cruising Poems.* Austin, Tex.: Slough Press, 1981.

———. *Eagle-Visioned/Feathered Adobes: Manito Sojourns and Pachuco Ramblings, October 4th to 24th, 1981.* El Paso, Tex.: Cinco Puntos, 1990.

———. *The Loves of Ricardo.* Edited by Roberto Barcena and Sue Hetherington. Chicago: Tia Chucha Press, 1997.

Vento, Arnoldo Carlos, ed. *The Ricardo Sánchez Reader.* La Vergne, Tenn.: Lightning Source Inc., 2000.

Hedwig Gorski

Santería

Santería has its origins in the religions of the Yoruban peoples of West Africa. It is still practiced in the Caribbean. Brought to the Americas by West Africans who would be later enslaved on plantations, Santería is practiced primarily in those areas where slave populations were predominantly Yoruban—Brazil, Cuba, Haiti, Puerto Rico, and Trinidad. The term *Santería* is actually the result of a European misinterpretation of Yoruban practices. Whereas Europeans thought that slaves had adopted Christianity and were celebrating the Christian saints (*santos,* in Spanish), the Africans were actually honoring their religious beliefs, which they had only superficially syncretized (blended) with Catholic rituals and beliefs; for example, the figure Elegguá (Elegúá) became St. Anthony, and the figure Oggun (Ogún) became St. Peter (Robinson n.p.). Santería has been preserved orally, with one generation passing down wisdom and practices to the next. Both men and women may officiate in Santería rituals; priests are *santeros,* and priestesses are *santeras.*

Santería is actually a generic term covering the variations known as *candomblé* practiced principally in Brazil, vodou in Haiti, and *espiritismo* in Puerto Rico. Contrary to popular belief Santería bears only a resemblance to its representations in popular films and fictions featuring vodou dolls and zombies. The main deity of Santería is Olorún, or Olodumare, from whom emanates *ashé,* the spiritual force that animates all life. Believers communicate with Olorún through *orishás,* who represent the spiritual energy available in animate creatures and inanimate natural forces. This energy can be used for noble or evil purposes. Santería rituals are supposed to facilitate access to the power of the *orishás*. These rituals involve achieving a trance state through rhythmic songs and dance, divination exercises, totemic offerings, and blood sacrifices; taken together, these demonstrate one's subservience to the power of the *Orishás*. In recent years adherents to Santería who live in the United States, especially in Florida, have clashed with animal rights activists because of the use of animal sacrifice.

Not surprisingly, Santería figures as an element of Spanish-American Caribbean literature, Cuban-American literature, Puerto Rican literature, and Dominican-American literature. In Cristina García's *The Agüero Sisters* (1997), for example, Constancia hires a *santero* to bless her Florida skin-cream factory. Ernesto Quiñonez's *Chango's Fire* (2004) features a friendship between the protagonist, Julio, and Papelito, a Spanish Harlem *santero*. Chango, also known as Shangó, is the deity of lightning, fire, and dance. In these works and others we see references to Santería that add an "exotic" spiritual dimension to the narrative. Santería appears as part of the plot or setting in many mystery-detective and thriller novels, such as Suzanne Proulx's *Declared Dead* (2002), John Lescroart's *Guilt* (1998), Lisa Miscione's *Angel Fire* (2002), Gary Indiana's *Gone Tomorrow* (1996), Mark Costello's *Big If* (2003), Colin Harrison's *Bodies Electric* (2002), Tim Wendell's *Castro's Curveball* (1999), Pete Hamill's *Forever: A Novel* (2002), and Alex Abella's *The Killing of the Saints* (1991), *Dead of Night* (1998), and *Final Acts* (2000). In some cases what began as an inventive experiment in bringing magical realism to the detective genre has succumbed to some of the most overworked stereotypes about Santería.

Bibliography

Brown, David H. *Santería Enthroned: Art, Ritual, and Innovation in an Afro-Cuban Religion.* Chicago: University of Chicago Press, 2003.

De La Torre, Miguel A. *Santería: The Beliefs and Rituals of a Growing Religion in America.* Grand Rapids, Mich.: W. B. Eerdmans, 2004.

Fernandez Olmos, Margarite, and Lizabeth Paravisini-Gebert. *Creole Religions of the Caribbean: An Introduction from Vodou and Santería to Obeah and Espiritismo.* New York: New York University Press, 2003.

Gonzalez-Wippler, Migene. *Legends of Santería.* St. Paul, Minn.: Llewellyn, 1994.

———. *Santería: The Religion: Faith, Rites, Magic.* St. Paul, Minn.: Llewellyn, 1994.

Mason, Michael Atwood. *Living Santería: Rituals and Experiences in an Afro-Cuban Religion.* Washington, D.C.: Smithsonian Institution, 2002.

Robinson, B. A. "Santería, a syncretistic Caribbean religion." Religious Tolerance.org. Available online. URL: http://www.religioustolerance.org/santeri.htm. Updated September 10, 2007.

Vega, Marta Moreno. *The Altar of My Soul: The Living Traditions of Santería.* New York: One World, 2001.

Wedel, Johan. *Santería Healing: A Journey into the Afro-Cuban World of Divinities, Spirits, and Sorcery.* Gainesville: University Press of Florida, 2004.

Martin Kich

Santiago, Esmeralda (1948–) *(novelist, memoirist)*

Esmeralda Santiago was born on May 17, 1948, in Macún, Santurce, Puerto Rico. Like many other Puerto Ricans, Santiago migrated with her family to the United States for economic reasons during the years of Operation Bootstrap in the 1950s and 1960s. Operation Bootstrap was the U.S. industrialization of Puerto Rico that often involved changes in business, education, and public health at the expense of island traditions and values.

As a Spanish-speaking teenager, Santiago faced a new life and a new set of challenges in Brooklyn. In *When I Was Puerto Rican* (1993), she describes these challenges and her success at the Performing Arts High School, where she excelled in drama and dance. In 1976, soon after she received a B.A. from Harvard University, graduating magna cum laude, she returned to Puerto Rico. She later earned an M.F.A in fiction writing from Sarah Lawrence College and today lives in Westchester County, New York, with her husband and two children. Santiago has written educational and documentary films for her husband's film and media production company, Cantomedia, founded in 1977. For her writing she has been awarded honorary doctorates of letters from Trinity University, Pace University, and Metropolitan College. She is actively involved in community-based programs for young people, particularly in organizations devoted to the arts and literature, and is highly committed to the problems of domestic violence and child abuse, some of the issues that arise in her memoirs and novels.

Santiago began to write personal essays in 1984 that focused on her experience of growing up in Puerto Rico, neither a state nor a country, but a U.S. commonwealth. Her nonfictional essays first appeared in 1985 in newspapers such as the *New York Times* and the *Boston Globe* and in magazines such as *House & Garden* and *Metropolitan Home*. These essays anticipate the themes of her books: identity, life in the barrios of New York, island politics, violent situations, and the experience of motherhood. To date she has published four novels and a children's book, *A Doll for Navidades* (2005), and coedited two anthologies *Las Christmas: Favorite Latino Authors Share Their Holiday Memories* (1998) and *Las Mamis: Favorite Latino Authors Remember Their Mothers* (2000). Santiago's international literary acclaim came with the publication of her first novel-memoir, *When I Was Puerto Rican*.

As with other contributions to SPANISH-AMERICAN CARIBBEAN LITERATURE, Santiago's works combine elements of history with episodes from family life. *When I Was Puerto Rican* focuses on Negi's (Santiago's alter ego) childhood on the island and the mainland and questions about her Puerto Rican identity at the familial and cultural level. The novel addresses a nostalgic vision of an independent Puerto Rico and the subtle and overt transformations of the island under U.S. domination. Furthermore, *When I Was Puerto Rican* deals with a wider thematic framework of Latina literature, such as the meaning of home and identity, dislocation and displacement, and the struggle of reconciling Puerto Rican traditions and the American way of life. It does this by describing Negi's early years on the island and then her adolescence and young womanhood in Brooklyn.

Santiago's second novel, *AMÉRICA'S DREAM*, first appeared in 1996 and was soon published in six languages. The novel narrates the journey of Puerto Rican hotel housekeeper, América González, who searches for a better life on the mainland. She seeks refuge from her alcoholic mother, her abusive boyfriend, and her unloving 14-year-old daughter. América's dream, however, remains unfulfilled in the land of freedom; she soon finds herself undervalued by her U.S. employer, Karen Leverett, and she is continuously haunted by her past. By making women employees the focal point of the narration, Santiago gives voice to those people who cannot speak for themselves and stresses class distinctions and social and cultural differences between employers and employees.

In 1998 Santiago decided to continue her chronicle of adolescence from the barrios of Brooklyn to the theaters of Manhattan in *ALMOST A WOMAN*, the sequel to her first novel. *Almost a Woman*, which, won three awards from the American Library Association and was adapted into a film for PBS Masterpiece Theatre, reveals a successful Negi in her progress toward womanhood. Once again Negi is faced with the dilemma of remaining true to confining, yet familiar aspects of her Puerto Rican culture. Challenged by her own yearning for independence on the mainland and determined to move away from her strict mother, her responsibilities with her many siblings, and her inquisitive grandmother, she begins her journey into adult life with her new lover, the Turkish filmmaker Ulvi, who provides the title to the novel's sequel, *The Turkish Lover* (2004).

Santiago recounts Negi's audacious voyage toward self-liberation through her relationship with the dominating Ulvi in *The Turkish Lover*.

Against all odds Negi emerges triumphant from Harvard in 1976. At the age of 28 and seven years after leaving her mother in Brooklyn to start her travels with Ulvi, she finally goes back to her Puerto Rican homeland.

Santiago's literary motifs render her part of a wider group of Latina writers, united by themes but also by personal experience. The plight of the migrant, the journey toward self-discovery, and the acceptance of his or her hybrid self shape both Puerto Rican literature and Latino literature more broadly.

Bibliography

Kevane, Bridget. "A Puerto Rican Existentialist in Brooklyn: An Interview with Esmeralda Santiago." In *Latina Self-Portraits: Interviews with Contemporary Women Writers,* edited by Juanita Heredia and Bridget Kevane, 125–140. Albuquerque: University of New Mexico Press, 2000.

Perivolaris, John D. "Travelling Voices of Caribbean Nationhood: Bilingualism, Translation and Diaspora in the Work of Julia Álvarez and Esmeralda Santiago." *Journal of Iberian and Latin American Studies* 3, no. 2 (1997): 117–125.

Santiago, Esmeralda. *Almost a Woman.* New York: First Vintage Books, 1999.

———. *América's Dream.* New York: HarperCollins, 1996.

———. *A Doll for Navidades.* New York: Scholastic Press, 2005.

———. *Las Christmas: Favorite Latino Authors Share Their Holiday Memories.* New York: Knopf, 1998.

———. *Las Mamis: Favorite Latino Authors Remember Their Mothers.* New York: Knopf, 2000.

———. *The Turkish Lover.* Cambridge: Da Capo Press, 2004.

———. *When I Was Puerto Rican.* New York: Vintage, 1993.

Vizcaya Echano, Marta. "'Somewhere between Puerto Rico and New York': The Representation of Individual and Collective Identities in Esmeralda Santiago's *When I Was Puerto Rican* and *Almost a Woman.*" *Prose Studies* 26, nos. 1–2 (2003): 112–130.

Yolanda P. Martínez

Sapogonia: An Anti-Romance in 3/8 Meter Ana Castillo (1990)

Ana Castillo published her second novel, *Sapogonia: An Anti-Romance in 3/8 Meter* in 1990. *Sapogonia* offers an exploration of "the geographic and psychic borderlands" of Mexico and the United States (Lynch 130). The title of the book refers to an imaginary place in the Americas that has no physical borders. It is the location of the Sapogones, a mestizo (mixed-race) people shaped by their European past and indigenous roots. Because of pressures from the north, they will attempt to assimilate, but because of their heritage, they will always stand apart from mainstream society. The term *Sapogón* derives from the Spanish word for toad, *sapo.* The metaphor of the toad has been used by Gloria Anzaldúa and Arturo Islas to describe those who reside in the borderlands.

Sapogonia describes the relationship and intrigues in the lives of artist Máximo Madrigal and singer and activist Pastora Velásquez Aké. The central character, Máximo Madrigal, leaves his family and homeland of Sapogonia to "conquer" new territory in the United States. He intends to conquer the art world with his sculptures, though along the way he also "conquers" a series of women, whom he dominates and then abandons.

One of the themes of the novel is indeterminacy. Máximo is trapped between Sapogonia and the United States, between conquerer and conquered, between Pastora, who is a Latina, and Laura, who is white. For her part Pastora is involved with a woman named Perla, although the women do not seem to establish intimacy. Pastora, like Máximo, is caught between cultures and the affections of two people. In order to reinforce the theme Castillo begins the novel with an epigraph: "This is the story of make-believe people in a real world, or, if you like, the story of real people in a make-believe world" (2). Likewise, Máximo states: "All my life has been divided into two realities: dreams of revelation and prophecy, and those dreams that manifest my present" (11). Both the epigraph and the statement leave the reader trapped in a space of indeterminacy, unable to determine the reliability of the narrators and the veracity of the ending.

As in her other novels, Castillo relies on multiple narrative voices to tell her story. At first glance it appears that the author employs a first-person, second-person, and third-person narrator, but careful reading reveals that there are actually several third-person narrators, and none of these multiple narrators is necessarily reliable. Elsa Saeta concludes that, for Ana Castillo, the "structure and narrative strategy of the novel thus serve to reinforce one of the novel's major themes: the tenuous relationship between the real and the unreal, between reality and illusion, between historical fact and narrative fiction" (71). While much of the novel progresses chronologically, the novel also introduces shifts in time; for example, the very first chapter occurs at the very end of the narrative chronology, and, in fact, the characters and circumstances involved in chapter 1 do not become clear until the very end. The narrative uncertainty of the opening chapter signals the narrative instability; it also corresponds with Castillo's The MIXQUIAHUALA LETTERS (1986).

The multiple narrative voices and the fractured chronology reinforce the multiplicity of perspectives and positions. For Castillo, as she explains in MASSACRE OF THE DREAMERS: ESSAYS ON XICANISMA (1994), the Chicana occupies an indeterminate space, and she cannot be reduced to a single subject position. For its themes and concerns Castillo's work can be read within the context of BORDER LITERATURE and CHICANO LITERATURE.

Bibliography

Alarcón, Norma. "The Sardonic Powers of the Erotic in the Work of Ana Castillo." In *Breaking Boundaries: Latina Writing and Critical Readings,* edited by Asunción Horno-Delgado, 94–107. Amherst: University of Massachusetts Press, 1989.

Castillo, Ana. *Sapogonia: An Anti-Romance in 3/8 Meter.* Tempe, Ariz.: Bilingual Press/Editorial Bilingüe, 1990.

Lynch, Joy. "'A Distinct Place in America Where All *Mestizos* Reside': Landscape and Identity in Ana Castillo's *Sapogonia* and Diana Chang's *The Frontiers of Love.*" *MELUS* 26, no. 3 (Fall 2001): 119–144.

Milligan, Bryce. "An Interview with Ana Castillo." *South Central Review* 16, no. 1 (Spring 1999): 19–29.

Saeta, Elsa. "Ana Castillo's *Sapogonia*: Narrative Point of View as a Study in Perception." *Confluencia: Revista Hispánica de Cultura y Literatura* 10, no. 1 (Fall 1994): 67–72.

Yarbro-Bejarano, Yvonne. "The Multiple Subject in the Writing of Ana Castillo." *Americas Review: A Review of Hispanic Literature and Art of the USA* 20, no. 1 (Spring 1992): 65–72.

Ritch Calvin

Seguín, Juan Nepomuceno (John N. Seguín) (1806–1890)

Juan Nepomuceno Seguín was born in San Antonio, Texas, on October 27, 1806. In 1858 he published *Personal Memoirs of John N. Seguín,* a work that helps place his military and political career with a historical context. Seguín's ancestors helped found San Antonio and were present in Texas from the mid-1720s. Seguín was the son of Erasmo Seguín, an important figure who held offices under three separate governments: the Spanish Crown, the Mexican republic, and the Texas republic. Seguín would follow in his father's footsteps and play a vital role in the Texas revolution and the Republic of Texas.

During the course of his military and political career Seguín held many important positions and played an active role in the transition of Texas from a Mexican state (with Coahuila) to a fledgling independent republic. He served as mayor of San Antonio in 1833 and was elected political chief for the Department of Bexar in 1834. Seguín served as captain of a military company in the Texas militia in the campaign against the Mexican army in 1835 and also led the only Tejano unit that fought in the Battle of San Jacinto during the Texas revolution. He personally accepted the Mexican surrender of San Antonio in 1835. Seguín served as the military commander of San Antonio until 1837 and was later elected to the Texas senate, serving as the only Texas-Mexican senator during the Republic of Texas, from 1837 to 1849. He was reelected as mayor of San Antonio and served from 1841 to 1842. During this tenure as mayor Seguín led failed military campaigns against Comanche Indians and participated in controversial land speculation business activities for which many citizens in San Antonio criticized him. His participation in General Antonio Canales's federalist campaign against the centralists in Mexico during this period led to more tension between himself and the citizens of San Antonio.

Seguín had placed himself in a difficult position in San Antonio in the early 1840s. He acted as intermediary between the Tejanos, longtime residents of Texas who had fought with their Anglo counterparts for Texas's independence, and the growing Anglo population. The arrival of new Anglos with the waves of immigration that followed the Battle of San Jacinto resulted in problems for the Tejano community. Seguín had the precarious position of being the most prominent Tejano leader, who was supported by powerful Anglos, such as Sam Houston, but had also become the personal enemy of other Anglos who looked to shatter his political career. As a result he was forced to flee to Mexico for his own (as well as his family's) personal safety. After arriving in Mexico he was forced to serve under General Adrián Woll in the Mexican invasion of Texas in 1842. This caused additional problems for him and led many Anglo Texans to accuse him of treason.

The *Personal Memoirs of John N. Seguín* deals specifically with the issues that contributed to the turmoil he endured in the later part of his life. The memoir was published in English in 1858. It consists of various documents that detail his "public life in relation to Texas" (102). Seguín wrote his memoir "in response to the attacks of scribblers and personal enemies who falsify historical fact with which they are but imperfectly acquainted" (73). In response to the attackers who sought to drive him from his homeland, he states that he "felt like a foreigner in my native land" (73). He provides the reasons for which he left Texas and explains "I had determined to free my family and friends from their continual misery on my account, and go and live peaceably in Mexico. . . . I resigned my office, with all my privileges and honors as a Texan" (97). To those who accused him of treasonous acts while serving in the Mexican army during their invasion of Texas, he retorts: "When I arrived in Laredo, the military commander of that place put me in prison. Santa Anna directed that I be sent to the City of Mexico, but [General] Arista . . . interceded with him on my behalf to have the order revoked . . . but on the condition that I should return to Texas with a company of explorers to attack its citizens and, by spilling my blood, vindicate myself" (97). Thus, he explains that "he had no alternative left but to linger in a loathsome condition in confinement or to accept military service" (74).

Seguín's *Personal Memoirs* did not serve to exonerate him in the minds of all Anglo Texans, but it did serve the purpose of presenting the reasoning behind his controversial actions during the later part of his career. Seguín returned to Texas in 1848, and by 1852 he had been elected as Bexar County justice of the peace. Texans never forgot his contribution to their state's history, and the town of Seguin (located 35 miles northeast of San Antonio) is named in his honor.

The *Personal Memoirs,* due to limited availability, has been examined only by those few historians and individuals overtly interested in Seguín's life. In 2002, however, Jesús F. de la Teja published a monograph on Seguín and his *Personal Memoirs*; the publication of this material has made these documents more widely available to all scholars and students interested in Texas history. In addition to compiling and editing the *Personal Memoirs,* de la Teja provides a 70-page biographical essay of Seguín titled "The Making of a Tejano." This essay focuses not only on Seguín, but also on his father, Erasmo, who played an important political role during the Mexican period of Texas history (1821–36). De la Teja acknowledges that this biography is incomplete, though the essay provides an excellent historical context for understanding the implications of Seguín's political, military, and economic activities, as well as others' reactions to them. The edited *Memoirs* follows this biographical essay. The contributions of

Tejanos such as Segín remain largely understudied in the areas of Texas and borderlands history. As de la Teja notes, the edited *Memoirs* "illustrate the possibilities for original research on early Tejano leaders" (x). Much work remains to be undertaken not only to complete the biography of Seguín but also to shed light on the contributions of other prominent Tejano leaders during this period. Seguín's work provides a historical context for BORDER LITERATURE.

Bibliography

de la Teja, Jesús F., ed. *A Revolution Remembered: The Memoirs and Selected Correspondence of Juan N. Seguín.* Austin: Texas State Historical Association, 2002.

Seguín, Juan N. *Personal Memoirs of John N. Seguín: From the Year 1834.* San Antonio, Tex.: Ledger Book & Job Office, 1858.

Deb Cunningham

Shaman Winter Rudolfo Anaya (1999)

RUDOLFO ANAYA's *Shaman Winter* is the final book in a quartet of novels about Albuquerque. Throughout the three Baca novels, *ZIA SUMMER,* (1995); *RIO GRANDE FALL* (1996), and *Shaman Winter,* Anaya departs from the format of the detective novel, emphasizing more and more the mystical, shamanistic elements of the narrative.

Sonny Baca, the great-grandson of colorful Old West lawman Elfego Baca, represents the college-educated, urban Chicano who has assimilated into the dominant, English-speaking culture. This series relates Sonny's return to his *nuevo mexicano* heritage with the help of Don Elisio, his aged neighbor, a benevolent *brujo* (sorcerer/shaman) who exemplifies the wisdom of Mexican-American and Pueblo Indian ways. To defeat the villain of the series, an evil *brujo* called Raven, who has battled Don Eliseo and Sonny in many previous incarnations, Sonny, still in a wheelchair from a murderous attack at the end of the previous book, *Rio Grande Fall,* must learn to access his own magical powers and take Don Eliseo's place as a guardian of the light on earth.

More than in any of Anaya's previous work since *BLESS ME, ÚLTIMA* (1972), *Shaman Winter* is concerned with Chicano mysticism and mythology, combining Aztec, Toltec, and Pueblo Indian beliefs with elements of traditional Hispanic Catholicism. In *Shaman Winter* much of the action takes place in magic duels between the two *brujos,* Sonny and Raven, with the help of their *naguals* (power animals), Raven's eponymous birds and Sonny's coyotes.

Shaman Winter's narrative thread moves in and out of the past and present through dreams of key moments in New Mexico's history of conquest and colonization. The reader enters into a supernatural world in which the antagonist, Raven, kidnaps four of Sonny's female Indian and Mexican-American ancestors, threatening thus to wipe out his bloodline and Sonny's existence. These dream passages remind the reader of the omission of these female and indigenous perspectives from the current history of New Mexico. In between the historic dream action, Raven kidnaps four teenage girls related to Sonny. A villain of both the past and the present, Raven is also masterminding the building of a nuclear bomb in the heart of the Los Alamos nuclear facility to wipe out much of the Southwest and to trigger a full-scale nuclear war. Characters who reflect the law enforcement of the FBI and CIA want Sonny to help catch Raven before he detonates the bomb or uses the vials of Ebola virus that they learn he has stolen. At the same time none of these agencies can be trusted as it becomes apparent that Raven has help at the highest levels. Meanwhile, the local police and the families of the missing girls appeal to Sonny for help in their safe return.

Anaya's mystical, lyrical style and concern with the sacredness of nature are taken to new heights in this book. Saving the environment from nuclear assault becomes critical and a way of pointing up the need to recognize and return the land itself to its sacred status and end the destruction of habitat and sacred places.

In *Shaman Winter* Anaya makes greater use of female characters than he has since *Bless Me,*

Última. Lorenza Villa is not only a CURANDERA (healer) but also a shaman. In the earlier books she has helped Sonny learn to access his spiritual power. In this final book of the series she guides Sonny's wheelchair and becomes a full partner in his otherworldly battles with Raven. Like his Chicano and Latin American counterparts, Anaya relies on the techniques of MAGICAL REALISM. Rita López is pregnant with Sonny's child, but she undergoes a black magic–induced miscarriage of Sonny's daughter; this episode then becomes a pivotal development in the narrative, especially in the last battle of *brujería* (sorcery) within the final dream.

Although *Shaman Winter* closes the series, Anaya fails to resolve the narrative with a happy ending; readers consider whether Raven is still alive and learn that another nuclear bomb and vials of Ebola virus are still missing. It is the spiritual narrative, rather than the detective plot, that is resolved in this final book. Don Eliseo dies to help defeat Raven and becomes one of the Lords of Light. For his part Sonny comes into his power completely, becoming a *brujo* guardian of his people to take Don Eliseo's place, marrying Rita, and working for the Chicano community to pass on to others the wisdom he has gained.

Anaya's work has received greater critical recognition than most Chicano writers, though it is only in the recent past that he has finally been published by a major trade publisher. Ann Catherine Geuder examines this decision as Anaya's strategy for getting his cultural and spiritual message to a wider audience. Carmen Flys Junquera situates the mysticism of Anaya's Alburquerque Quartet within a spectrum of mysteries by Latino and African-American authors. Within the context of BORDER LITERATURE we can read Anaya's mysteries alongside those of LUCHA CORPI and ALICIA GASPAR DE ALBA.

Bibliography

Anaya, Rudolfo. *Bless Me, Última.* New York: Warner Books, 1994.

———. *Shaman Winter.* New York: Warner Books, 1999.

Dick, Bruce, and Silvia Sirias, eds. *Conversations with Rudolfo Anaya.* Jackson: University Press of Mississippi, 1998.

Fernández Olmos, Margarite, ed. *Rudolfo A. Anaya: A Critical Companion.* Westport, Conn.: Greenwood, 1999.

Flys Junquera, Carmen. "Detectives, Hoodoo, and *Brujería*: Subverting the Dominant U.S. Cultural Ethos." In *Sleuthing Ethnicity: The Detective in Multiethnic Crime Fiction,* edited by Dorothea Fischer-Hornung and Monika Mueller, 97–113. Madison, N.J.: Fairleigh Dickinson University Press, 2003.

———. "Murder with an Ecological Message: Rudolfo Anaya and Lucha Corpi's Detective Fiction." *Revista Canaria de Estudios Ingleses.* 42 (2001): 341–357.

———. "Nature's Voice: Ecological Consciousness in Rudolfo Anaya's Alburquerque Quartet." *Aztlán* 27, no. 2 (2002): 119–138.

Geuder, Ann Catherine. "Marketing Mystical Mysteries: Rudolfo Anaya's Mystery Trilogy." In *Sleuthing Ethnicity: The Detective in Multiethnic Crime Fiction,* edited by Dorothea Fischer-Hornung and Monika Mueller, 81–94. Madison, N.J.: Fairleigh Dickinson University Press, 2003.

Vasallo, Paul, ed. *The Magic of Words: Rudolfo A. Anaya and His Writings.* Albuquerque: University of New Mexico Press, 1982.

Linda Rodríguez

Short Eyes Miguel Piñero (1974)

As a child, MIGUEL PIÑERO migrated with his family from Puerto Rico to New York City. Later, as a troubled youth, Piñero entered a world of crime by stealing and using drugs. While serving time in Sing Sing Penitentiary he began to write drama and worked with the Clay Stevenson Prison workshop. He became widely known when his play *Short Eyes* was a hit on off-Broadway and then on film.

Set in a house of detention, the play depicts a social structure complete with its own civil codes and distinct methods of communication. Whites are the minority in the prison system, and although the prison administration is also predominantly white, the rules of living are dictated by the ethnic breakdown of the inmates. The finest example of a social microcosm exhibited in Piñero's work is found in *Short Eyes*.

The society in *Short Eyes* is a subculture. Violence and death are acceptable methods of retribution for those who violate its "moral" codes. The prison officials—who are supposed to represent outside, or "normal," society—actually make up part of this subculture. They adhere to its civil codes as much as inmates do. In this "code of conduct," one of the biggest offenses anyone can commit is the sexual molestation of a child; therefore, when a new white inmate (Clark Davis) accused of this very offense is introduced into this society, dramatic conflict is explosive.

A white prison guard (Nett) knowledgeable of Davis's crime violently beats Davis before admitting him into the house of detention. He also informs the other inmates on the nature of Davis's crime. Although a prison official and, hence, a representative of "normal" society, Nett is actually an integral part of the prison subculture, as witnessed through his action. Clark Davis's character, on the other hand, is more indicative of "normal" society. His whiteness, respectful demeanor, use of language, and middle-class status all attest to this, despite his criminal endeavor. These elements set Davis apart from the other inmates including from the only other white inmate, Longshoe. Thus, Clark possesses none of the subcultural elements inherent in the other prisoners. Nett and Longshoe turn their backs on Clark to support the inmates' civil code instead. This ultimately spells Davis's demise.

These characters act in stark contrast to the character of Juan. Although also an integral part of the prison subculture, Juan is the voice of reason and the only one Clark can turn to for help. Piñero makes this especially clear when Clark confesses to Juan his sexual obsession with little girls. Although utterly appalled, Juan checks his desire to injure Clark; instead, he offers Clark good advice. The contrast between Juan's character and that of Clark, Longshoe, and the other inmates (including the prison guard, Nett) comes to a climax when Juan defies the prisoners' decision to kill Davis.

Juan even takes this to the extreme, threatening his fellow inmates with death should they go through with their plan to kill Davis. Outnumbered, Juan is unable to carry out his threat and in the end cannot save Clark.

In this way Piñero has inverted societal structure. Nett, the prison guard responsible for protecting the prisoners and for upholding law and order, becomes a criminal. Longshoe, a criminal who is in the white minority and who is expected to protect his fellow white inmate, Clark, turns against him and, instead, upholds the inmates' civil codes that ultimately result in Clark's death. And Juan, a convicted criminal who is Puerto Rican, is the only voice of reason and the only person Clark can turn to for help.

Piñero's play opened off-Broadway just before another Mexican-American play, Luis Valdez's *Zoot Suit*, hit theaters. Both were transformed into films. These critically acclaimed works, written by a Puerto Rican and a Chicano writer, respectively, depict a slice of life of their communities. Both Piñero and Valdez created the space in which urban U.S. Latino experiences could be enacted through drama.

Bibliography

Irizarry, Roberto. "The House of Pretension: Space and Performance in Miguel Piñero's Theatre" *Latin American Theatre Review* 37, no. 2 (Spring 2004): 77–94.

Piñero, Miguel. *Short Eyes*. New York: Hill and Wang, 1974.

Platizky, Roger S. "Humane Vision in Miguel Piñero's Short Eyes" *The Americas Review: A Review of Hispanic Literature and Art of the USA* 19, no. 1 (Spring 1991): 83–91.

Nancy Mercado

Silent Dancing: A Partial Remembrance of a Puerto Rican Childhood Judith Ortiz Cofer (1990)

JUDITH ORTIZ COFER's poetry, fiction, and essays draw on her experiences of life in Hormigueros, Puerto Rico, and her time spent in Paterson, New

Jersey. The title of *Silent Dancing: A Partial Remembrance of a Puerto Rican Childhood* comes from an essay in the collection that follows the panning of a video camera as a home movie is being made of a party. As the adults dance in a conga line, each has a moment on the screen, and Cofer is able to give their story as she knows it. Cofer explains in the preface to *Silent Dancing* that through her *ensayos* (essays)—the word in Spanish indicating practice or rehearsal—she is acknowledging that "the past is a creation of the imagination . . . although facts can be confirmed" (12). The collection is a combination of autobiographical selections followed by poems that comment on or respond to the theme of the essay.

Although she does feel a kinship with Latino writers as they struggle to assimilate into American culture while maintaining ties to their own (Ocasio 48), Cofer maintains a distance, both aesthetically and geographically, from Puerto Rican writers (especially those who got their start in the NUYORICAN POETS CAFE) who focus on urban experience in New York. Her experiences come from New Jersey and the South. She lives in Athens, Georgia, and teaches at the University of Georgia. Cofer writes in English, a choice for which she has been criticized. Puerto Ricans living on the island often argue that writers from Puerto Rico should write in Spanish. Cofer explains that having been educated in English, she speaks English with a Spanish accent and speaks Spanish with an American accent. She can read, speak, and dream in Spanish but cannot write in that language (Ocasio 44). Not surprisingly, she addresses the complexity of belonging to two cultures in all her writings.

Storytelling is at the heart of Cofer's work. The narrative tradition of her grandmother is celebrated in *Silent Dancing*. Women and young girls gather under the mango tree at the boundary of Mamá's property and hear *cuentos* (cautionary tales) about other women, their affairs, their losses, their joys, and their sorrows. That the stories sometimes vary in the details supports Cofer's belief that the past can be freely interpreted and re-created for the present. As she

matures, Cofer begins to understand the "subtext of sexual innuendo" that runs through the tales (142). The family stories, told by Mamá at her *casa* (house), and by her mother during their time in New Jersey, along with Cofer's memories of her life on *la isla* (the island) and in the United States form *Silent Dancing*.

One particular story about María Sabida made a strong impression on Cofer. Sabica was a legendary Puerto Rican figure who outsmarted the chief *ladrón* (outlaw or thief) to bring peace to her village. Cofer's first stories are extensions of the María Sabida story. Many of the women in Mamá's tales are strong women who serve as role models for young girls. Others are presented as cautionary examples of how life can go wrong if conventions and tradition are not followed: Felícita, her aunt, had eloped and gone to New York. Divorced, she returns home to be ostracized by her family and village. María la Loca contracts a fever after being left standing at the altar and never regains her sanity. The stories of these two women mingle with those Cofer witnesses herself in New Jersey: Providencia, the forever pregnant woman in El Building; Vida, the young girl who longs to be a movie star.

These stories offer conflicting guidance about how to negotiate adolescence and how to adapt to two cultures—the Spanish-speaking, Catholic home of her mother and the harsher, yet freer life outside El Building. *Silent Dancing* has been compared to both ESMERALDA SANTIAGO's *WHEN I WAS PUERTO RICAN* and Paule Marshall Brown's *Brown Girl, Brownstones* in its depictions of the difficulties of a young girl coming of age in the cultural mix of two worlds. Cofer is overwhelmed by the cultural clash as she nears her *quinceaños,* a rite of passage for 15-year-old girls after which they are treated as women. As a Puerto Rican girl, she is held to the strict standards demanded by her culture for modesty. As an American, she wants to be free to do what other teenage girls do—attend parties and date boys.

Cofer traces her development as a writer from those afternoons listening to Mamá to her struggle to adjust to life in the United States. For its themes and images Cofer's work can be read within the context of PUERTO RICAN LITERATURE.

Bibliography

Acosta-Belén, Edna. "A *MELUS* Interview: Judith Ortiz Cofer." *MELUS* 18, no. 3 (Fall 1993): 83–97.

Cofer, Judith Ortiz. *Silent Dancing: A Partial Remembrance of a Puerto Rican Childhood.* Houston, Tex.: Arte Público Press, 1991.

LeSeur, Geta. Review of *Silent Dancing. MELUS* 18, no. 2 (Summer 1993): 121–124.

Ocasio, Rafael. "Puerto Rican Literature in Georgia: An Interview with Judith Ortiz Cofer." *Kenyon Review* 14, no. 4 (Fall 1992): 43–50.

Patricia Bostian

Simple Habana Melody: From When the World Was Good, A Oscar Hijuelos (2002)

In *A Simple Habana Melody: From When the World Was Good,* OSCAR HIJUELOS offers a compelling portrayal of the life of Israel Levis and his love, mostly unrequited, for a famous Cuban singer, Rita Valladares. These two fictional characters are loosely based on, respectively, the popular Cuban conductor Moisés Simons and the famous Cuban entertainer Rita Montaner. In the novel Hijuelos uses music and Levis's compositions as ways to understand the island's independence from Spain, the energy of the roaring 1920s and bohemian 1930s, and the complicated years leading to, but not including, FIDEL CASTRO's revolution. The author explains that "having written *Mambo Kings,* I wanted to do something sort of like a prequel to that whole period" (González n.p.). Levis's character, born in 1890, uses music to express "Cuba's emerging national soul" (107). He finds inspiration everywhere around him, in

> The *tick tack* rapping of the shoemaker's hammer, brooms sweeping dust out of darkened entranceways, the cries of children playing in the gutter, the singsong chants of vendors selling newspapers . . . He heard music in the sonorous tinkle of water-splashed fountains, in

the clip clop of horse hooves, in the clanging of church bells, in the straining voices of divines preaching the *placitas* [little plazas] on Sunday mornings (109).

Though inspired by the rhythms of Havana, Levis flees the anti-intellectual Gerardo Machado regime for the "freedom" of Europe in the 1930s.

In Paris, Levis becomes intoxicated by the city's decadence and creative energy. Through his work he meets real celebrities such as Italian tenor Beniamino Gigli and New York composer George Gershwin; likewise, he corresponds with modern artists such as Maurice Ravel and Igor Stravinsky. Levis, however, realizes that he is a composer for the masses, and his serious opera, based on the fiction of French author Émile Zola, is never completed. His bohemian world completely falls apart when Nazi authorities occupy Paris and label the composer, despite his protests, Jewish. At the same time the narrator admits that the family name "originated with some distant Catalan ancestor, who may or may not have had some Jewish blood, but nothing was made of that, for, going back centuries to postmedieval Spain, as his father once explained, the peasants often derived their names from their masters—and there had been many prosperous Jews living in Spain before the inquisitions of Isabella forced them either to convert, to die or to flee her sacred kingdoms" (49). This passage refers to the *conversos,* Jews or Arabs who take on the outward appearance and habits of Catholics but nevertheless maintain their faith. As an unwitting *converso* and willfully oblivious to how he, Israel Levis, would be received in an anti-Semitic Europe, the composer finds himself deported to Buchenwald, Germany.

"El Maestro" suffers greatly in the Buchenwald concentration camp, but his pain is primarily associated with surviving, while others die terrifying deaths. By 1947 Levis returns to Cuba, a broken man recovering from diphtheria and hepatitis; his own compositions are intolerably bittersweet. "Rosas Puras," written especially for Rita Valladares, haunts him beyond measure, not only because it reflects a time when he was hopelessly in love with the singer but also because Levis was forced to perform the rumba for German officers. The novel ends with a tentative resolution as Levis trains the young and talented Pilar Blanca, who represents Cuba's next generation of musicians; this generation, however, will live and work outside the country. Indeed, it is notable that Hijuelos concludes his story in 1953; Levis dies in his sleep and anticipates little of the dramatic changes to come six years later, when Castro would launch a successful coup against Fulgencio Batista. For its themes and characters Hijuelos's work can be read within the context of CUBAN-AMERICAN LITERATURE.

Bibliography

Hijuelos, Oscar. *A Simple Habana Melody: From When the World Was Good.* New York: HarperCollins, 2002.

Santiago, Fabiola. "When the World Was Good." *Hispanic* 15, no. 6 (June 2002): 58.

Luz Elena Ramirez

Simple Plan, A   Gary Soto   (2007)

GARY SOTO's book of poems *A Simple Plan* is divided into two parts. Part 1 features 15 poems; part 2, 24. The poems of part 1 seem to dwell on a younger poet (as in most of Soto's poetry, the speaker and the poet seem to be the same), struggling with poverty and the alienation of growing up Chicano in white, English-speaking U.S. society. The persona of part 1 is tortured, furthermore, by an unusual poetic sensitivity that develops amid a bittersweet home life filled with nasty but amusing relatives. These poems evince a strong desire to escape the streets and cityscapes of Fresno, California, with its canals, junkyards, alleyways, and dirt lots. Characteristically, Soto refuses to dwell on the misery of growing up in such conditions; his poems are often humorous; the tone, reflective.

The persona of part 2 seems to be that of an older, "experienced" Soto, married and occasionally given to reflection on political issues, such as immigration, and on growing older as a poet. The younger dog abandoned by the restless narrator in part 1's "A Simple Plan" mellows into "The old stray" of part 2's "Old Dog Sniffing Air." The two parts taken together create the impression of a writer's life, through all stages of development. Poems are either syllabic compositions (such as "A Simple Plan") or free-verse poems that nonetheless display Soto's deft ear for rhythm (for example, the anapestic rhythm of "Earned and Unearned Pennies").

Anchoring this collection is a series of poems about growing up. In much of his poetry Soto looks to his childhood as the genesis of his art. One of the finest examples is "Bean Plants." Where in earshot of the highway, "the roar of the freeway," a young Mexican-American boy manages to coax a few bean plants to poke their fragile heads above the ground. Meanwhile, "Soap Opera" and "Earned and Unearned Pennies" center on the pain and beauty of entering adolescence, particularly challenging for an impoverished youth with artistic sensibilities growing up against the backdrop of industrial south Fresno.

Soto's love poems are often humorous and fraught with the pain of longing. "Teeth Marks," for example, is one of the funniest poems in the collection. The adolescent speaker tries to imagine the fate of a pencil he loaned to a girl in his class who has moved away. The narrative moves from the pencil to an imagined sexual encounter. As in the image of a stepfather with a shot glass, in part 2 of *A Simple Plan*, Soto reflects on mature love with "Thirty-Year Marriage" and "Life in a Small Apartment," which act as companion poems.

For this poet the promise of love and the possibility of poetry lie beyond the city limits represented in his poetry. In part 1, the poet yearns to escape Fresno. In "Escape from Town," the 17-year-old budding poet stares at furniture and garbage floating down one of Fresno's ubiquitous canals and imagines he sees his first love beckoning to him from one of the departing love seats. "Waiting at the Curb: Lynwood, California, 1967" is another escape poem in which a Latino family finds itself caught between cultures. As in some of Soto's prose fiction, for example, *Living Up the Street* (1985), American mass-mediated culture has imposed itself on the family, confounding its sense of identity. Cars, cut-offs, 45 records and the variety show *Laugh-In*, force a sense of class-consciousness and white middle-class values on family members.

The issue of acculturation surfaces in such works as "Hermanos," which recounts the tale of five brothers, four of whom move to the United States to take up labor typically associated with Mexican immigrants. The youngest stays behind in Mexico to work at a chicken farm in Zacatecas. Soon the older brothers send photos of their cars, symbols of their manly prowess and success; however, subsequent letters are appeals for money as the older brothers run afoul of the American Dream and their cars are stolen or impounded. The serene image that ends the poem is of the young brother, finally content with his simple life at home. The problem of negotiating two cultures in Soto's work is far from simple, but "Hermanos" points out the pitfalls along the path to success for Mexican immigrants and the possibility of finding peace within one's native culture, despite the hardship of poverty. Perhaps Soto has found peace in *A Simple Plan*, as well, adopting Pablo Neruda as a father poet and eulogizing his friend Ernesto Trejo, the great Mexican poet who died young. Soto's work can be read within the context of CHICANO LITERATURE.

Bibliography

Soto Gary. *Living up the Street*. New York: Bantam, 1985.

———. *Natural Man*. San Francisco: Chronicle Books, 1999.

———. *A Simple Plan*. San Francisco: Chronicle Books, 2007.

Tony Perrello

Smallest Muscle in the Human Body, The
Alberto Alvaro Ríos (2002)

ALBERTO ALVARO RÍOS's *The Smallest Muscle in the Human Body* was a finalist for the 2002 National Book Award. Like Ríos's WHISPERING TO FOOL THE WIND (1982), *The Smallest Muscle in the Human Body* draws from a tradition of MAGICAL REALISM to explore the "borderland" between Mexico and the United States. Ríos, who was born and grew up in Nogales, Arizona, writes about "The places in between places" that "are like little countries / Themselves" (5). As poems such as "Some Extensions on the Sovereignty of Science" attest, the people living within these poems balance carefully on an "edge in the middle" (102) so often established by a border. This "edge in the middle" is not only geographic. Borders exist between lovers, within families, within the body, and they also divide the heart. Borders emerge between words and concepts. These poems begin with a border place and explore, map, and remap the very idea of place, of the self, and of understanding. Through demarcations we attempt to establish distinctions, but these acts of separation often reveal dynamic connections. Ríos's poems enter "the places in between places" that defy our cartographic efforts.

The Smallest Muscle in the Human Body introduces people that celebrate the multiplicity of a border landscape. In "Day of the Refugios" we learn that the Fourth of July "meant more than just one thing" (5). Independence Day in the United States coincides with the name day for Saint Refugio in the Catholic calendar. The "fireworks" and "shrimp cocktails" that honor a declaration of freedom also pay tribute to the women named Refugio in the speaker's family. Meanwhile, figures like the "Birdman of Nogales" exist in conjunction with the landscape becoming a conglomeration of the flora and fauna of the world around them. Ríos's border people gather "something of everything" that they know in becoming who they are (7).

Ríos's poems present the body as a boundary between the interior self and the world. Throughout *The Smallest Muscle in the Human Body* the boundary between the self and the world emerges from a continual, reciprocal process. The chili in "My Chili" bites back with the intensity of its spice (41–45). The glass of water in the poem "The Nipple Button" enters like a sigh (51–52). The body, with pliability, shifts as it takes in the world around it. As the world remakes the self, so does the self remake the world. The process of naming and renaming continues, as the poem "The Venus Trombones" reveals, until we become uncertain as to which is stronger, "The names for things, / The things themselves" (39).

The poems "The Cities Inside Us" and "What We've Done to Each Other" explore relationships between people. A metaphoric cartography emerges from the desire to understand the world by mapping it. As the speakers in these poems attempt to explain and "map" those they love, Ríos reveals how much we can know and still not know when we create maps. These poems reveal that our dimensions are more infinite than the means we have for expressing them. Just as maps offer a two-dimensional representation of a three-dimensional reality, we use language in an attempt to represent the many levels of our emotions and experiences. Ríos's poems explore the extent to which we can know and not know each other through our efforts to codify. In "If I Leave You" no matter how much a father loves a son, he cannot accompany him or protect him from bad dreams (85–89); in "The Lemon Kind of Baseball" no matter how close brothers were growing up, they still strive to remember when they were "brother[s] every day" (92–93); in "Writing from Memory" no matter how much a family cares for one another, they still find that they now tell "some other family's story" when they reminisce (100–101).

Throughout this volume, as the characters speak, organize, and converge with the world around them, language itself remains a primary focus. Ríos explores language and invites us to journey with him. In the last poem of the volume, "Some Extensions on the Sovereignty of Science," we learn that "The smallest muscle in the human body is in the ear" (103). This volume asks us to stretch this small muscle and listen to the world. The careful crafting of the poems, their metaphors and imagery, and their sound reveal the extent to which Ríos tests the tensile strength of language. Even though such testing reveals that

"Words are our weakest hold on the world" (103), these poems reveal just how much is within our grasp. For its images and settings Ríos's work can be read within the context of BORDER LITERATURE and CHICANO LITERATURE.

Bibliography

Deters, Joseph. "Fireworks on the Borderlands: A Blending of Cultures in the Poetry of Alberto Ríos." *Confluencia* 15, no. 2 (2000): 28–35.

Ríos, Alberto. *The Smallest Muscle in the Human Body.* Port Townsend, Wash.: Copper Canyon Press, 2002.

———. *Whispering to Fool the Wind.* New York: Sheep Meadow Press, 1982.

Sedore, Timothy S. "An American Borderer: An Interview with Alberto Ríos." *South Carolina Review* 34, no. 1 (2001): 7–17.

Wooten, Leslie. "The Edge in the Middle: An Interview with Alberto Ríos." *World Literature Today* 3, no. 2 (2003): 57–60.

Irene Praitis

So Far from God   Ana Castillo (1993)

ANA CASTILLO is an important contributor to CHICANO LITERATURE. Her popular novel *So Far from God* takes place in Tome, New Mexico, and centers on the lives of Sofia and her four daughters: Esperanza, Fe, Caridad, and Loca. Early on in the narrative Sofia tells her husband, Domingo, to leave because of his gambling debts. Domingo leaves the family home for 20 years; during his absence the reader learns more about the complicated lives and losses of the four daughters. Castillo's choice of character names is important: Esperanza means "hope"; Fe means "faith"; Caridad means "charity"; and Loca means "crazy." Each episode about these daughters involves an incredible event or plot detail that will test the reader's beliefs about Castillo's family portrait. But, if we understand *So Far from God* within the context of both Chicano literature and Latin American literature, we can appreciate a narrative that relies on the use of MAGICAL REALISM and a strong feminist voice. The women figures in the novel live life, suffer, make changes, and sometimes triumph. Sometimes the losses outweigh the achievements, and in this regard Castillo's writing can be said to be harshly realistic.

Esperanza is the eldest and the only daughter who earns a college degree. At school Esperanza is an outspoken student who protests many things, including the lack of Chicano studies courses in the curriculum. When her boyfriend, Rubén, leaves her for a white woman, she returns to school to earn a master's degree in communications. Afterward, Esperanza obtains a job at a local television station and becomes a newscaster. When Rubén returns after being left by his wife, she refuses a job in Houston and they reunite. Ultimately, however, she realizes that she is not satisfied by their relationship. Thus, it is significant that Esperanza gains control over her life and ends her relationship with Rubén. Eventually she takes a job in Washington, D.C., and is sent to Saudi Arabia, where she is killed while covering the war in the Middle East.

Fe looks forward to the day when she can escape Sofia's home and Tome, their New Mexican town. She works in a bank and wants to marry and live the American Dream. Thus, she is devastated when she is jilted by her fiancé, Tom: She lets out a continuous scream that lasts for days and severely damages her vocal cords. Eventually she decides to marry her cousin, Casmiro, who has a degree in accounting. In her pursuit of material success Fe leaves the bank for a higher-paying job at an arms manufacturer. Fe's desire for a better life and her diligence as a worker become her downfall: She is promoted to a position where she must use, unbeknownst to her, illegal chemicals. Fe develops cancer and dies a painful death.

Like her sisters, Caridad also has problems with men. She is deserted by her husband, Memo, and she begins to lead a promiscuous life in the bars of Tome. One day she returns home, near death after having been raped and brutally beaten. After a miraculous recovery she rents a trailer from a local CURANDERA, Doña Felicia, and she becomes her apprentice. Eventually she falls in love with a Native American woman, Esmeralda. In one of many plot twists the two women jump off a cliff to their deaths.

The fourth sister, La Loca, is considered by locals to be a saint. When she is three, she has what turns out to be an epileptic seizure and is declared dead; thus, her "resurrection" at her funeral appears to be a miracle. She develops a phobia of people and never leaves the family home. La Loca is a recluse but mysteriously contracts AIDS, which eventually kills her. Although she appears to have had a very limited life, she does not regret not being a part of the society that disappointed and, ultimately, killed her sisters. Unlike her sisters, La Loca recognizes that her needs were met at home, and she dies feeling satisfied.

Despite the heartbreak that she experiences as a result of her daughters' tragedies, Sofia has an inner strength that enables her to survive many hardships. In addition to raising her daughters alone, she single-handedly runs the family business, a butcher shop, which includes raising and butchering livestock and managing the store's finances. She even develops a political consciousness. She grows tired of watching gringos come in and abuse the local land. She recognizes that to change things the community must come together. As a result of her determination the community starts a sheep-grazing and wool-weaving enterprise, develops a food co-op, fights the local drug problem, and establishes a low-interest loan fund for entrepreneurs. Over time, the morale of the residents of Tome improves significantly.

Clearly, Castillo tells a tale of female empowerment: Women must recognize that they have a voice and the power to change lives of loneliness and disenfranchisement. As well, the importance of home is an important theme: Leaving home does not always bring fulfillment, but staying there can be difficult.

Bibliography

Castillo, Ana. *So Far from God.* New York: Plume, 1993.

Delia Lanza, Carmela. "Hearing Voices: Women and Home and Ana Castillo's *So Far from God.*" *MELUS* 23, no. 1 (1998): 65–79.

Manríquez, B. J. "Ana Castillo's *So Far from God*: Intimations of the Absurd." *College Literature* 29, no. 2 (2002): 37–49.

Rodriguez, Ralph E. "Chicana/o Fiction from Resistance to Contestation: The Role of Creation in Ana Castillo's *So Far from God*." *MELUS* 25, no. 2 (2000): 63–82.

Diane Todd Bucci

Sommer, Doris (1947–) *(Latin American studies scholar, translator)*

Born in Ulm, Germany, Doris Sommer came to the United States in 1951. She earned her first B.A. in Spanish language and literature from Rutgers University (1968) and a second in English literature from Hebrew University of Jerusalem (1970). Her first M.A. is in English literature, from Hebrew University of Jerusalem (1970), and her second M.A. is in comparative literature, from Rutgers University (1975). Sommer also earned a Ph.D. from Rutgers in comparative literature (1977).

After completing her doctoral studies Sommer began teaching at Rutger's Livingston College, where she stayed until 1980. From 1980 to 1991 Sommer taught at Amherst College and then moved to Harvard University. Widely recognized for her work, Sommer has received many prestigious fellowships, including the John Simon Guggenheim Foundation Fellowship (1995), an American Express Grant (1992), a W. E. B. DuBois Institute Fellowship at Harvard University (1982–83), and a National Endowment for the Humanities Research Fellowship (1982–83). She is now the Ira Jewell Williams Professor of Romance Languages and Literatures at Harvard. In addition to her professorship, Sommer is also director of graduate studies for the Department of Romance Languages and Literatures.

From her first book, *One Master for Another* (1984), to her most recent, *Bilingual Aesthetics: A New Sentimental Education* (2004), Sommer examines the role of literature in nation formation. *One Master for Another: Populism as Patriarchal Rhetoric in Dominican Novels* (1984) focuses on six Dominican novels from the 19th and 20th centuries and analyzes their connection to populism. Among the novels discussed are the national novel *Enriquillo* (1882) by Manuel Jesús Galván, Juan Bosch's *La mañosa* (1936; The tricky one), *Over* by Ramón Marrero Ansty (1840), Freddy Prestol Castillo's *El masacre se pasa a pie* (1937; The massacre goes away on foot), Marcio Veloz Maggiolo's *En abril en adelante* (1975; In April and hereafter), and Pedro Mir's *Cuando amaban las tierras comuneras* (1975; When they loved the communal land).

Expanding her analysis to include 19th-century novels from several Latin American countries, Sommer elaborates on the relationship between literature and nationalism in her second book, *Foundational Fictions: The National Romances of Latin America* (1991). In *Foundational Fictions* Sommer argues that a direct connection between romance novels and nationalism exists. Throughout Latin America, Sommer explains, authors of romance novels were also "among the fathers of their countries, preparing national projects through prose fiction" (73). These novels explore "private passions with a public purpose" (7). Sommer asserts these author-leaders create consent among the literary characters and, by extension, consent between citizen and nation. She writes: "Love plots and political plotting keep overlapping with each other" (41). These "foundational fictions," as Sommer calls them, create "the desire for authoritative government from the apparently raw material of erotic love" (51). The impact of *Foundational Fictions* on cultural studies has been profound; it is one of the most frequently cited books on Latin American literary criticism.

Sommer published her third book, *Proceed with Caution, When Engaged by Minority Writing in the Americas,* in 1999. While 19th-century romances try to conceal differences to promote the concept of a unified nation, *Proceed with Caution* contends that minority writers may often prevent unity by trying to interrupt a reader's identification with a text. In a study that includes readings of Inca Garcilaso, Rigoberta Menchú, Toni Morrison, Cirilo Villaverde, and Mario Vargas Llosa, and others, Sommer claims a reader goes into a text with the goals of understanding it; however, minority writers may incorporate techniques to create "limits of intimacy" that disrupt this goal. Techniques such as CODE SWITCHING, withholding information, and deferring translation are intended strategies to challenge the code. This deliberate interruption emphasizes the imbalances of power and knowledge, an imbalance that often accords with the plot of the narratives. Scholars and critics, previously in control, are forced into an "un-learning" of learned reading strategies.

An invitation to "bilingual games" is extended to readers in *Bilingual Aesthetics: A New Sentimental Education* (2004). Code switching, one of the techniques discussed in *Proceed with Caution*, enriches language and its uses. "Part of bilingual gamesmanship," reasons Sommer, "is to train a predisposition toward feeling funny, or on edge, about language, the way that artists, activists, and philosophers are on edge about familiar or conventional uses" (xiii).

Sommer has edited several books, including *The Places of History: Regionalism Revisited in Latin America* (1999); *Nationalisms and Sexualities* (1991), along with Andrew Parker, Mary Russo, and Patricia Yaeger; and *Bilingual Games: Some Literary Investigations* (2003). In 2005 she edited *Cultural Agency in the America,* (2005) a collection of essays by prominent Latino and Latin American scholars who write about the intersections between creativity, the arts, and social change. In addition, she edited José Marmol's *Amalia* (2002). Her work provides a critical context for SPANISH-AMERICAN CARIBBEAN LITERATURE and Latin American literature more broadly.

Bibliography

Sommer, Doris. *Bilingual Aesthetics: A New Sentimental Education.* Durham, N.C.: Duke University Press, 2004.
———. *Foundational Fictions: The National Romances of Latin America.* Berkeley: University of California Press, 1991.
———. *Proceed with Caution, When Engaged by Minority Writing in the Americas.* Cambridge, Mass.: Harvard University Press, 1999.
———. *One Master for Another: Populism as Patriarchal Rhetoric in Dominican Novels.* Lanham, Md.: University Press of America, 1984.
Sommer, Doris, ed. *Bilingual Games: Some Literary Investigations.* New York: Palgrave Macmillan, 2003.
———, ed. *Cultural Agency in the Americas.* Durham, N.C.: Duke University Press, 2005.
———, ed. *The Places of History: Regionalism Revisited in Latin America.* Durham, N.C.: Duke University Press, 1999.

Arlene Rodríguez

Song of the Hummingbird, The Graciela Limón (1996)

Mexican-American writer Graciela Limón taught for 35 years at Loyola Marymount University in Los Angeles. As a professor and a novelist, she has continuously sought to dignify female historical figures who had been marginalized culturally. Limón, whose parents were Mexican immigrants, appreciates narratives about female historical figures, particularly those who have fought prejudice. *The Song of the Hummingbird,* one of the novels that made Limón an important figure in CHICANO LITERATURE, gives voice to the Mexica (Aztec) of Tenochtitlán (Mexico City) who were militarily and culturally overwhelmed by invading Spaniards in the 1500s.

Hummingbird is actually a rewrite of an earlier Limón novel, *María de Belén: The Autobiography of an Indian Woman* (1990). *María de Belén* is a complicated, scholarly, and highly self-reflexive novel. The fictional de Belén's complaints about the colonial rule of the disrespectful Spanish are presented in the form of a 16th-century manuscript. Professor Natalia Roldon, a fictional figure whose parallel with the author may be misleading to audiences, has provided endnotes to the manuscript, clarifying and elaborating on de Belén's account; however, the endnotes, which represent the dominant opinions about the benefits of European involvement in the Americas, often jar with the experiences recorded by de Belén. Although the novel is formally complex, Limón's polemic is straightforward: Official narratives often tell only an inadequate story, overlooking the suffering of the victims of the clash between foreign rulers and native subjects.

Like *María de Belén, The Song of the Hummingbird* insists on the value of counter-narratives— historical accounts written by history's losers. *Hummingbird*, however, has a much simpler narrative structure than *María de Belén*. Set in 1583, the novel describes the meetings between an elderly Mexica woman, Huitzitzilin (Hummingbird) and a young Spanish priest, Father Benito Lara. Father Lara believes that the old lady, facing death, needs to confess and repent her pagan life and customs; however, Huitzitzilin defends her Aztec heritage and refuses to confess to the priest because she does not share his religious views.

Lara is both appalled and compelled by Huitzitzilin's stirring account of her humiliation at the hands of the invading Spaniards. Despite his zealous Christian distaste for the Mexica's religious idolatry and supposedly lascivious lifestyles, he is moved to accept aspects of Huitzitzilin's story; he recognizes 'the difficulty of her circumstances and perceives how alien the Spanish are to the native Mexica. The priest gradually realizes the value of the old woman's account of the Spanish invasion, writing down much of it. He begins to view the Spanish Conquest through her eyes and even expresses some nostalgia for preinvasion Mexico, for Aztec life before the Spanish arrived. In this regard Limón's work can be read alongside Fray BERNARDINO DE SAHAGÚN's *General History of Things Related to New Spain*, especially book 12, the Florentine Codex. Sahagún records in Nahuatl the Aztec testimony about the Spanish-Indian encounter and Hernán Cortés's assault on Moctezuma's empire.

In *The Song of the Hummingbird* the Spanish invasion has serious consequences for Huitzitzilin. She describes the raping by Spaniards of indigenous women, which can be read as the Spanish male imperial power violating the female Mexica. It must be pointed out, though, that Huitzitzi-lin is also maltreated by her own tribe's males: Tetla's beating of her is particularly grueling. For Limón male violence, especially against defenseless women and peaceable communities, is the cause of much physical and psychological distress, whether it is perpetrated by indigenous oppressors or by invading outsiders.

Bibliography

Limón, Graciela. *María de Belén: The Autobiography of an Indian Woman*. New York: Vantage, 1990.

———. *The Song of the Hummingbird*. Houston, Tex.: Arte Público Press, 1996.

McCracken, Ellen. *New Latina Narrative: The Feminine Space of Postmodern Ethnicity*. Tucson: University of Arizona Press, 1999.

Kevin De Ornellas

Soto, Gary (1952–) *(poet, novelist, essayist)*

Gary Soto was born in 1952 in Fresno, California, to Mexican-American parents. Soto's early volumes of poetry have garnered great praise, including awards from the Guggenheim Foundation, the National Endowment for the Arts, and *Poetry*'s Levinson Award. Soto grew up in the San Joaquin Valley, where his grandparents and parents made their living in low-paying field and factory jobs. The conditions of these workers, along with the death of his father when Soto was five, are central themes in his poetry. After finishing college at California State University, he pursued his M.F.A., and began teaching at the University of California, Berkeley, in 1977.

In 1977 Soto published his first volume of poetry, *The Elements of San Joaquin*, which won the United States Award of the International Poetry Forum. The book offers the perspective of many narrators and enriches our understanding of Soto's youth in Fresno. The often hostile environment of Soto's Fresno is peopled with such characters as a robber waiting for his victim ("The Underground Parking") and a homeless factory worker ("San Fernando Road").

The second section focuses on the elements and the seasons of a year in the San Joaquin Valley. Ruminations on the sun, wind, earth, and rain join with descriptions of the physical activities of those who work in the fields to present a picture of the beauty of a land that is watered with the sweat and blood of Mexican-American laborers.

Critic Raymund A. Paredes observes that the characters in *The Elements of San Joaquin* are not just field-workers but include the urban poor of Soto's youth. In an essay about why he became a writer, Soto reflects on the people who lived around him: family, neighbors, classmates. It is the portraits of the lives of these people, as well as the lives of his grandparents and others who worked the San Joaquin Valley fields, that appear in the third section of the book. One of the most powerful poems in the collection, the closing poem, "Braly Street," introduces the themes that will be mined over and again in subsequent volumes. A return to the street of the narrator's childhood brings to mind the domestic details of everyday life (the momentous and the mundane); remnants of the past have been paved over and buried under industrial buildings. Death, in the form of violence and disease, poverty, and the helplessness and ultimately uselessness of the lives of the previous inhabitants of Braly Street, hangs like a miasma over the neighborhood.

Critic Patricia de la Fuentes points out the images of dust and dirt that mark many of Soto's poems in *The Elements*. The dust and wind are two of the primary elements from the book's title. They are forces that drive everything, reducing mortal inhabitants and their creations to oblivion. The images are often repeated in *Black Hair* (1985), where the themes of time and disintegration are central. "In August" involves layers of memory as the narrator remembers seeing a blimp as he and his siblings fish for pickles in a barrel, the memory stirring an even earlier one of his father stroking his hair. The final lines of the poem establish a consistent theme in the book, one where time does not heal so much as it allows entropy to collapse all that the poems' speakers know and hold dear. Acknowledgment of one's mortality is inescapable in Soto's poems, and there is often little joy in the lived moments.

Soto's second volume of poetry, *Tale of Sunlight*, published in 1978, uses conventions of MAGICAL REALISM. In a review of his early volumes Theresa Meléndez notes that Soto is drawn to many writers. In particular, one can recognize the influence on Soto of Gabriel García Márquez, to whom he dedicates the poem, "How an Uncle Became Gray."

By 1981 Soto had published *Where Sparrows Work Hard,* a move away from the personal, intimate voice of his earlier poems to a more sophisticated, distanced, and cynical one. In 1990 he released the collection *Who Will Know Us?* (1990). These poems are praised by reviewers for their strong sense of place, grounded in metaphors that have wide appeal. The poems are about earthly activities ("Friday Night Fish") and how they link one to one's place and culture. The volume has also been noted as a spiritual autobiography with the poet's poems about his father's death. Reflections on marriage and on the simple marks of domestic life combine with musings on the meaning of stained-glass windows in Catholic churches.

Soto's *Home Course in Religion* was published in 1991. The book is divided into two sections. The first includes poems that take the reader through the narrator's childhood and adolescent years, where he ponders his existence and his relationship to his god. The second section, for all its metaphysical searching for the meaning of existence, finds the narrator sure only of the practical elements of his life: marriage, career, and family.

Soto's children's collection, *A Fire in My Hands* (1991), introduces each of its 23 poems with a prefatory comment reflecting on the origins of the work. Soto here collects poems about his own childhood experiences and his observations about being the father of a young child. Two additional volumes of poems for children, *Neighborhood Odes* (1992) and *Canto familiar* (1994), are set in a Mexican-American neighborhood and create a sense of childhood innocence, echoing the rapid conversational tone of sing-song voices in the neighborhood. Soto follows his characters through their days, seeing the world from their eyes.

In *New and Selected Poems* (1995) Soto collects poems from six previous books, including *Tale of Sunlight* and *Home Course in Religion*. Recurrent images of his work as a laborer in California are filtered through a religious lens. Soto's 1997 *Junior College: Poems* returns to the San Joaquin Valley of the 1960s and addresses the issue of racism and stereotypes. Its poems emphasize the role that higher education plays in helping Mexican Americans achieve their goals. Soto's 11th full-length collection of adult poetry, *A NATURAL MAN* (1999), describes the period between Soto's childhood to his late 40s. His latest collection is *A SIMPLE PLAN* (2007).

Soto's poems about the Mexican-American experience, especially of migrant and factory workers in California, have earned him the distinction of one of the United States's foremost Chicano poets and a major contributor to CHICANO LITERATURE. The universality of his work has given him the distinction of a foremost American poet.

Bibliography

de la Fuentes, Patricia. "Ambiguity in the Poetry of Gary Soto." *Revista Chicano-Riqueña* 11, no. 2 (Summer 1983): 34–39.

———. "Mutability and Stasis: Images of Time in Gary Soto's *Black Hair*." *Americas Review* 17, no. 1 (Spring 1989): 100–107.

Meléndez, Theresa. Review of *Where Sparrows Work Hard*. MELUS 9, no. 4 (Winter 1982): 76–79.

Paredes, Raymund A. "The Childhood Worries, Or Why I Became a Writer." *Iowa Review* 25, no. 2 (Spring–Summer 1995): 104–115.

———. "Mexican American Authors and the American Dream." *MELUS* 8, no. 4 (1981): 71–80.

Soto, Gary. *Black Hair*. Pittsburgh, Pa.: University of Pittsburgh Press, 1985.

———. *Canto Familiar* San Diego: Harcourt Brace, 1995.

———. *Elements of San Joaquin*. Pittsburgh, Pa.: University of Pittsburgh Press, 1977.

———. *A Fire in My Hands*. Orlando, Fla.: Harcourt, 2006.

———. *Home Course in Religion: New Poems*. San Francisco: Chronicle Books, 1991.

———. *Junior College: Poems*. San Francisco: Chronicle Books, 1997.

———. *A Natural Man*. San Francisco Chronicle Books, 1999.

———. *Neighborhood Odes*. San Diego: Harcourt Brace Jovanovich, 1992.

———. *New and Selected Poems*. San Francisco: Chronicle Books, 1995.

———. *A Simple Plan*. San Francisco: Chronicle Books, 2007.

———. *Tale of Sunlight*. Pittsburgh, Pa.: University of Pittsburgh Press, 1978.

———. *Where Sparrows Work Hard*. Pittsburgh, Pa.: University of Pittsburgh Press, 1981.

———. *Who Will Know Us?* San Francisco: Chronicle Books, 1990.

Patricia Bostian

Soto, Pedro Juan (1928–2002) *(fiction writer)*

Pedro Juan Soto was born July 11, 1928, in Cataño, Puerto Rico. He migrated, along with his family, to New York City in 1946. There he worked as a reporter for various Spanish-language publications and received his bachelor's degree from Long Island University (1950) and master's degree from Columbia University (1953). Between 1950 and 1951 he served in the U.S. Army. In the late 1970s he earned a doctorate from the University of Toulouse, in France. His fiction won him awards from the Instituto de Literatura Puertorriqueña (1959) and the prestigious prize from CASA DE LAS AMÉRICAS in Cuba (1983). Perhaps because of his forced adjustment to an English-speaking culture, Soto has written about the pressures to assimilate in works such as SPIKS. *Spiks*, in addition to *Usmail* and *Ardiente suelo, fría estación*, has been translated into English. Soto's more recent publications include *La sombra lejana* (1999) and *Palabras al vuelo* (1990). A longtime fighter in the cause of Puerto Rican independence, Soto's work is a good example of what political commitment can produce fictionally and can be read within the context of both SPANISH-AMERICAN CARIBBEAN LITERATURE and PUERTO RICAN LITERATURE.

Bibliography

Simpson, Victor C. *Colonialism and Narrative in Puerto Rico: A Study of Characterization in the Novels of Pedro Juan Soto.* New York: P. Long, 2004.

Soto, Pedro Juan. *Hot land, cold season/Ardiente suelo, fría estación.* New York: Dell, 1973.

———. *Un oscuro pueblo sonriente: novela.* Havana: Casa de las Américas, 1982.

———. *Palabras al vuelo.* Havana: Casa de las Américas, 1990.

———. *La sombra lejana Guaynabo.* Puerto Rico: Editorial Plaza Mayor, 1999.

———. *Spiks.* Translated by Victoria Ortiz. New York: Monthly Review Press, 1973.

———. *Usmaíl.* Translated by Myrna Pagán and Charlie Connelly. St. John, Virgin Islands: Sombrero Publishing Co., 2007.

Soy la Avon Lady and Other Stories
Lorraine López (2002)

Lorraine López was born in 1956 in Los Angeles and lived much of her life in the San Fernando Valley. In 1993 she moved to Athens, Georgia, to pursue a graduate degree in English through the Creative Writing Program at the University of Georgia. She has two grown children and resides with her husband in Nashville, Tennessee, where she is an assistant professor at Vanderbilt University.

The distinctive flavor of her writing comes from her experiences growing up in California, both inside and outside Mexican-American culture. She explains to interviewer Jantje Tieken that "Spanish is not my native language. Neither my parents nor their parents were born in Mexico" (n.p.). Her first book, *Soy la Avon Lady and Other Stories,* published by Curbstone Press in 2002, was awarded the inaugural Miguel Mármol Prize and also received the Independent Publishers Book Award for Multicultural Fiction and the Latino Book Award for short stories awarded by the Latino Literary Hall of Fame. López has published poetry and prose in the *Prairie Schooner, New Letters: A Magazine of Writing and Art, US Latino Review,* and *Mammoth Anthology of Short Fiction.* Her second book, *Call Me Henri,* a novel for young adults, was published in 2006.

In *Soy la Avon Lady and Other Stories* López presents the reader with a collection of 11 short stories, all but one set in the U.S. Southwest. "Ivor's People" takes place in Antigua, best known to Americans as a tourist destination. "Ivor's People" examines the needs and desires of tourists on the one hand and those of the locals, hustling to make money off them, on the other. All the stories survey the strange, yet sometimes familiar space between cultures and languages. López's writing explores the conflicting dreams of contemporary America and the Latino heritage from which the characters are descended and of which they remain fiercely proud. Each of the characters emerges with his or her own idiosyncracies. In some stories the conflict between cultures manifests itself as that between generations ("Mother-in-Law's Tongue") and in others between young women of the same generation ("Love Can Make You Sick"). In other stories the conflict manifests itself in terms of the characters' uncertainty about sexual identity. This uncertainly is never something overt, and López never draws attention to it nor comments on it; it is simply there, in the peripheral vision of the reader, in at least four of the stories, adding to the sense of confusion as the characters strive to establish an identity in their hybrid worlds. In several stories there is an implicit contrast between the smaller southwestern communities where the characters live—particularly the real and curiously named town of Truth or Consequences—and the larger, easily recognizable southwestern cities, such as Albuquerque. López's writing also gestures toward the MAGICAL REALISM associated with Latin American fiction, as her characters face tragicomic situations and surreal moral compromises as they go about the ordinary business of everyday life.

In some of the stories the social acceptance of a character is an issue, as with "Sophia," where the eponymous main character is an overweight teenager who is isolated and tormented by her schoolmates. The theme of identity, and particularly sexual identity, is brought to the fore in "Frostbite," "A Tatting Man," and "To Control a Rabid Rodent."

In "Frostbite," for instance, the elderly protagonist, Rudy, is sought out by his grandson, who is on a quest for answers to his problems, particularly with regard to his sexual identity: "What if it turns out that I'm bisexual or even gay?" (29), he asks his grandfather. The answer never comes, and, as Rudy later says, "I didn't know what I should have said. I still don't know what it is that I should have said, but I felt kind of stiff and fake and the boy knew it. . . . But we both knew that I let him down pretty hard" (30).

In "A Tatting Man" the author presents Joaquin Benavides, who himself seems to undergo a subtle shift in sexual identity as he takes to wearing his recently deceased wife's clothes and makeup in the house and smoking her Virginia Slims cigarettes (he never smoked before her death). Joaquin even allows himself to be dragged by his wife's friend, Mrs. Padilla, into the sewing bee to which his wife used to belong, and he finds comfort in watching *Marimar*, the *telenovela*, or soap opera, to which his wife was addicted. There is a wry humor here, well managed by the author, who never allows the reader to think disparagingly of Mr. Benavides nor any of the other quirky characters, whose actions are always treated as perfectly normal. It is for the reader to discern behind it all the loneliness, grief, and striving to achieve human dignity.

The question of identity surfaces as well in the title story, featuring Molly the Avon Lady. The author explains that she used the title for this story—and the book—from the poem "La loca de la raza cósmica," "because it consists of a series of statements beginning with the word *soy*, which means 'I am' in English. This poem describes various roles Chicanas have assumed, ranging from methadone clinic patients to officers in the PTA" (Tielken n.p.).

In "Soy la Avon Lady" Molly tries to come to terms with her past and struggles to make sense of being mistaken for a transvestite. The search for identity in Molly is represented in the question "*¿Quién es?*" (Who are you?) (91) and links her to the memory of her dead grandmother. The phrase returns to haunt her at the end of the story after an attempted rape by the biker, Lowell, who was expecting a transvestite. This story about the quest for identity ends with no resolution.

In two stories, "The Crown on Prince" and "To Control a Rabid Rodent," the protagonists are teenage boys who get into trouble with the law because of their instincts to do the right thing. In the former the boy, Teddy, responds to an anonymous phone call in an effort to save a young baby from a violent father. When he intervenes, he is held by the cops, who find him rummaging for the child in a Dumpster. In the latter story Jonathan Escamilla shoots a rabid prairie dog with his new rifle but ends up killing the man next door as well. In both cases the mistake/accident is eventually acknowledged by the authorities, but the stories' interest centers on the child protagonist and their nonchalance in the face of what they propose to do or what results from their actions. There is a kind of redemptive innocence that seems closer here to the heart of the author's storytelling than the facts in the stories and the legal implications thereof. As in many of the other stories there are painful domestic situations and relationships that precipitate the actions ("The Crown on Prince") or that are revealed as a result of them ("To Control a Rabid Rodent"). Actions and consequences are transcended somehow by the focus on a kind of unconscious and understated grace and innocence that makes everything seem right at the end.

The last two short stories in the collection, "Mother in-Law's Tongue" and "Walking Cycles," are closely related. In these stories the young woman, Tina, impregnated by her boyfriend, who is now dead, becomes a link between her parents and her boyfriend's family and her dead boyfriend. The two families eye each other with suspicion, unsure of how—or how far—to assert the rights of parenthood and tradition, as they understand them. Given tensions between family members, the boyfriend's mother later finds herself excluded from the delivery room where her grandchild is being born. These are indications of worlds and cultures in (often uneasy) adjustment, as there occurs the inevitable interpenetration born of the desire to assert self and (cultural) identity and to stake a claim in the modern America.

Although López's book is a collection of separate stories, several of them are linked by settings (the town of Truth or Consequences), or by a significant defining event (such as the death of the grandmother in a car accident). In the last two stories, as the second is a continuation of the first, perhaps the reader can expect lengthier works of fiction from López in the future.

Bibliography

Bruce Novoa, Juan. *Retrospace: Collected Essays on Chicano Literature.* Houston, Tex.: Arte Público Press, 1990.

Herrera-Sobek, María, and Helena Viramontes, eds. *Chicana Creativity and Criticism: New Frontiers in American Literature.* Albuquerque: University of New Mexico, 1996.

López, Lorraine. *Soy la Avon Lady and Other Stories.* Willimantic, Conn.: Curbstone Press, 2002.

Quintana, Alvina A. *Home Girls: Chicana Literary Voices.* Philadelphia: Temple University Press, 1996.

Tieken, Jantje. "Interview with Lorraine López, author of *Soy la Avon Lady and Other Stories.*" Curbstone Press. Available online. URL: http://curbstone.org/ainterview.cfm?AuthID=117. Downloaded December 26, 2007.

Amparo Marmolejo-McWatt

Spanglish

Spanglish is a term coined from the blending of the words *Spanish* and *English*. Considered by some a new dialect or even a new language, Spanglish results from the mixing of Spanish and English sounds and words in oral and written communication. Spanglish is a worldwide phenomenon, and it may arise in any speaking community where Spanish and English coexist. Heterogeneous in origin, Spanglish is spoken in the United States a result of historical conditions and cultural borrowings. Words may differ depending on the state and the speaker's origin. The various forms of Spanglish include, among others, Cubonics, spoken by Cuban Americans, and Mexican-American Spanglish. ILAN STAVANS

has compiled the first dictionary of Spanglish, in which he defines about 6,000 words. Literary critic Juan Bruce-Novoa considers the synthesis of English and Spanish a third language called "interlingualism," which describes communication in border communities and in districts where two or three cultures may meet.

Spanglish surfaces in literature as a representation of real speech and as a social and political discourse. Spanglish is the linguistic product of Latinos. Though Latinos come from a number of ethnicities and geographies, the transference of Spanish into English and vice versa is part of the Latino identity. When writers decide to use Spanglish, they affirm the historical reality of a social group that is growing as fast as its code of communication. Literary Spanglish is the conscious or unconscious manifestation of its oral counterpart, thus reflecting the survival of the Spanish language and by extension of the Hispanic culture within the Anglo milieu.

Three main variants of Spanglish can be distinguished: CODE SWITCHING, borrowing, and direct translation. In code switching the speaker shifts back and forth, in this case, between English and Spanish. Borrowing implies either the complete assimilation of a foreign word or part of it, in which case the word is adapted to the morphology and phonetics of the other language. Finally, direct translation is to translate directly an expression from one language into another even though most of the times it lacks coherence. It only makes complete sense if it is used among bilinguals. The novel *POCHO* (1959), by JOSÉ ANTONIO VILLARREAL, for example, contains the expression *"Ésta es su casa,"* which has been translated literally as "This is your house"; however, a better way to translate this phrase is "Make yourself at home." Only a person familiar with both languages, English and Spanish, is able to understand the nuances involved in the translation of an expression or word. Thus, Spanglish may leave some readers at a disadvantage if they rely on a weak translation, but this is a minor casualty of the richness of fiction that incorporates Spanish and English words and phrases.

Spanglish is common in CHICANO LITERATURE, PUERTO RICAN LITERATURE, DOMINICAN-AMERICAN LITERATURE, and CUBAN-AMERICAN LITERATURE.

Bibliography

Morales, Ed. *Living in Spanglish: The Search for Latino Identity in America.* New York: LA Weekly Books, 2002.

Stavans, Ilan. *Spanglish: The Making of a New American Language.* New York: Rayo, 2003.

Marian Pozo Montano

Spanish-American Caribbean literature

The term *Spanish-American Caribbean literature* describes the literary production of the Spanish-speaking Caribbean (Puerto Rico, the Dominican Republic, and Cuba). It also includes literature by writers of the Caribbean diaspora (those people who leave their homelands) and Latinos of Caribbean heritage born or brought up in the United States.

Common threads such as the search for cultural roots and the politics of identity have been central concerns in Caribbean literary production since colonial times. Caribbean literature is particularly characterized by its heterogeneous nature in both urban and rural settings. Puerto Rican colonial literature is marked by the strong influence of Spanish culture and by a rich oral tradition brought by West African slaves to the island. Dominican literature dates back to Christopher Columbus's "discovery" writing of the 1490s and moves toward a concept of 19th-century nationhood with Manuel Jesús Galván's 1882 novel *Enriquillo* (about a Taino prince); writers have also had to reckon with the terror of Rafael Trujillo's 20th-century regime (1930–61).

In Cuba 19th-century authors such as JOSÉ MARTÍ celebrate the African, Spanish, and indigenous mixture of cultures; more recently, writers have responded, sometimes ambivalently, to FIDEL CASTRO's Communist regime. While the CUBAN REVOLUTION resulted in a high literacy rate on the island and accessible health care, the cost has been the insulation of the islanders who remain on the island and who face the economic hardship of a U.S. embargo.

From the beginning of the 19th century onward, expressions of nationalism appear in the fields of poetry and prose in the Spanish Caribbean. Puerto Rican Manuel Alonso published the classic *El Gíbaro* (The peasant) in 1849. In 1934 essayist Antonio Pedreira contemplated Puerto Rico's island consciousness with *Insularismo* (Insularism, or the keeping to oneself and keeping away from foreign influences). In 1891 Cuban independence figure Martí wrote about the hybrid nature of Caribbean cultures and the encroachment of the United States as an imperial influence in his famous essay, "Nuestra América" ("Our America"). Meanwhile, the first great Cuban woman writer, Gertrudis Gómez de Avellaneda, published her antislavery novel, *Sab,* in 1841. For her part, Salomé Ureña Henríquez (1850–97) was the first woman in the Dominican Republic to write nationalistic poetry; JULIA ALVAREZ's novel IN THE NAME OF SALOMÉ (2000) pays tribute to her.

After the Spanish-American War in 1898 and throughout the 20th century, the number of Spanish-speaking islanders in the United States increased considerably. During the 19th century many Cuban and Puerto Rican writers escaped from the Spanish colonial government to New York, seeking political asylum. This "literature of exile" was committed to the fight for Cuba's and Puerto Rico's independence and the search for national identity. Among the most notable exile writers in the United States are Cubans José María Heredia, Cirilo Villaverde, Martí, and essayist Fernando Ortiz and Puerto Ricans Eugenio María de Hostos, Manuel Zeno Gandía, and Francisco Gonzalo "Pachín" Marín, who also criticized the political situation of Puerto Rico under U.S. sovereignty. The "literature of exile" for Dominican writers surfaced, by means of contrast, in the 20th century. Dominicans, the newest arrivals in the United States among the Spanish-speaking Caribbeans, had left their country because of a declining economy after Trujillo's dictatorship in 1961 and the U.S. invasion in 1965; they formed communities throughout the United

States in the 1970s, 1980s, and 1990s, especially in the Northeast.

Puerto Ricans are not immigrants to the United States, but rather islanders who have a commonwealth relationship with the mainland. Large numbers of Puerto Ricans migrated to the mainland in the 1940s and 1950s as a result of Operation Bootstrap, the U.S. effort to industrialize Puerto Rico. Important figures of the generation of the 1940s, known as Nuyorican writers (Puerto Ricans living in New York), are Pedro Pietri. JULIA DE BURGOS, TATO LAVIERA, RENÉ MARQUÉS, and PEDRO JUAN SOTO. These writers consider the effect of displacement of Puerto Ricans living in New York.

Cubans, who left the island for political and economic reasons, arrived in the United States in three main migratory waves after the Cuban Revolution of 1959. The search for Cubanness and the roots of nationhood are central concerns in the literature of figures such as REINALDO ARENAS, Alejo Carpentier, Nicolás Guillén, José Lezama Lima, Heberto Padilla, and Antonio Benítez Rojo, whose works are also critical of Castro's government.

Like their exile counterparts, Latino writers in the United States contemplate the life of exile but usually from their parents' or grandparents' point of view. Latino authors describe the conflicts of identity that arise as a result of the clash that occurs when two languages and cultures come together. Topics such as isolation and alienation from mainstream society are ever present in CUBAN-AMERICAN LITERATURE, PUERTO RICAN LITERATURE, and DOMINICAN-AMERICAN LITERATURE. Cuban-American writers CRISTINA GARCÍA, GUSTAVO PÉREZ FIRMAT, and OSCAR HIJUELOS describe the effect of exile on families living on the island and in the United States. Puerto Rican authors NICHOLASA MOHR, JUDITH ORTIZ COFER, ESMERALDA SANTIAGO, PIRI THOMAS, and AURORA LEVINS MORALES focus on the problematics of Puerto Rican self-representation in contexts of ethnicity, gender, and nationhood. In the same vein Dominican Americans such as Julia Alvarez, JUNOT DÍAZ, and Sherezada "Chiqui" Vicioso write about their childhood memories and the difficulty in adapting to life in the United States. Other contemporary Domini-

can-American novelists are LOÍDA MARITZA PÉREZ, who published GEOGRAPHIES OF HOME (1999), and Alan Cambeira, who launched the Azúcar series with AZÚCAR! THE STORY OF SUGAR (2001).

The geographical, sociohistorical, and cultural forces of the Caribbean have created a rich literature written by both the immigrants and descendants of the diaspora experience.

Bibliography

Luis, William. "Latin American (Hispanic Caribbean) Literature Written in the United States." In *The Cambridge History of Latin America Literature*, Vol. 2: *The Twentieth Century,* edited by Roberto González Echevarría and Enrique Pupo-Walker, 526–556. Cambridge: Cambridge University Press, 1996.

Stabb, Martin S. "The Essay of Nineteenth-Century Mexico, Central America, and the Caribbean." In *The Cambridge History of Latin America Literature*, Vol. 1: *Discovery to Modernism,* edited by Roberto González Echevarría and Enrique Pupo-Walker, 590–607. Cambridge: Cambridge University Press, 1996.

Swanson, Philip, ed. *The Companion to Latin American Studies.* London: Arnold, 2003.

Yolanda P. Martinez

Spiks Pedro Juan Soto (1956)

PEDRO JUAN SOTO's fiction highlights the conflicts created by the commonwealth status of Puerto Rico and the island's relationship to the United States; in particular, his work reflects on the Spanish language as it is spoken by Puerto Ricans. As such readers can appreciate two central characteristics of Soto's writing: One is an emphasis on urban settings that serve as a reaction against the *costumbrista* movement (which centered on the speech and way of life of the rural areas of Puerto Rico); the second, a result of his time in New York and a formative literary education conducted in English, is that Soto felt less at ease writing in Spanish than some of his contemporaries, (such as RENÉ MARQUÉS and JOSÉ LUIS GONZALEZ). Soto published solely in Spanish but thought his Spanish sounded too much like a translation from English. This led him to experiment with a more economical and direct style.

His concise style is best evidenced in *Spiks* (1956). This book is made up of seven short stories and six "miniatures." Throughout, Soto reproduces the colloquial use of Spanish by the migrants in New York. Thematically, this is coupled with a grim depiction of the living environment. *Spik* stands here as a marker for the difficulty with speech of Soto's characters. This lack is also at work in the depiction of their economic and political circumstances. Soto, like most of the writers from his generation, is pessimistic concerning the conditions and possibilities of the Puerto Rican. His dim appraisal is reflected in the constant loss of hope of the characters. Among them we find a couple that is broken up because one of them has to move to New York, an unemployed painter who has to give up on his artistic aspirations because of lack of money, a man who dies as he asks the policeman who shot him for a job, a teenager whose idea of making it is being the king of the pool hall (whose dream is shattered by the violence of his male role models). In "God in Harlem," the most accomplished piece of the collection, Nena, the protagonist, explains that life for her is no "fandango" (72; translation modified). Like Nena, these characters seem to be "losing a world: [their] hope" (91). The difference between this loss and the despair portrayed in other depictions of the Puerto Rican (for example, Marqués's *La carreta*) is that this world is no longer directly tied to the island. Soto is not indicating that what is lost is their connection to their *isla del encanto* (island of enchantment). Rather than Puerto Ricans who have lost their way in New York, here we have a picture of the Puerto Ricans of New York who are there because of enduring political and economic problems on the island (as it turns out, of disenchantment).

The despair is all encompassing; even the idea of God seems to have suffered in the process. When Nena finds herself in the middle of a massive "culto" (Protestant service), the people around her are disappointed because the end of the world (promised in the flyers advertising the event) turned out to be a man with a Bible. One of the disappointed worshippers explains that the problem must be that the trip to New York is one for which "nobody'd sell the Lord a . . . ticket" (91). This is a crowd that might agree with poet Rubén Darío's claim, in his "To [Theodore] Roosevelt," that the United States may have everything, but it lacks God. Nena is convinced that God is with her. After this realization the narrator tells us: "She knew neither pain, nor hate, nor bitterness. She was being born" (92). In that sea of despair Nena appears as a dim but important ray of hope.

Bibliography

Miller, John C. "The Emigrant and New York City: A Consideration of Four Puerto Rican Writers." *MELUS* 5, no. 3 (1978): 82–99.

Simpson, Victor C. *Colonialism and Narrative in Puerto Rico: A Study of Characterization in the Novels of Pedro Juan Soto.* New York: Peter Lang, 2004.

Soto, Pedro Juan. *Spiks.* Translated by Victoria Ortiz. New York: Monthly Review Press, 1973.

Squatter and the Don, The María Amparo Ruiz de Burton (1885)

MARÍA AMPARO RUIZ DE BURTON was born in Mexico in 1832 and became a U.S. citizen through marriage and relocation. Her novel *The Squatter and the Don* has been identified as the first published English-language narrative to offer, via the author's unique perspective, a portrayal of the systematic disenfranchisement of those former citizens of Mexico who by circumstance or choice found themselves a part of the United States.

The second of two novels by Ruiz de Burton (the first novel, *Who Would Have Thought It?* was published anonymously in 1872), *The Squatter and the Don* is set in southern California in 1870. In the novel Ruiz de Burton writes of the Alamars, an old *californio* cattle ranch family living outside San Diego, an area that after the U.S.-Mexican War became part of the United States. Manifest Destiny (a policy of territorial expansion) and legislation that allowed Americans to stake their claim on so-called public lands for very little money enticed many families to migrate west. As a result the Alamars face the breakup of their ranch and of their traditional way of life. The "squatters," as the new arrivals were called, claim large portions of the Alamar's land. In addition business speculators further fuel an interest in the area, believing San Diego will be the end point of a new western railroad line.

Although the United States promised to protect the new citizens and their property under the TREATY OF GUADALUPE HIDALGO in 1848, laws passed shortly afterward required the former Mexican citizens to prove ownership of their ranches. Rumors that Don Mariano Alamar's claim was rejected encourage squatters to relocate and claim their allowance of 320 acres of the don's ranch. In an attempt to stem the ongoing killing of his cattle, Don Mariano proposes to introduce them to the traditional uses of the land—cattle ranching and fruit farming. The squatters reject the offer. Later, through the corruption of government officials, Don Mariano's title is rejected, giving the squatters the legal right to their claims.

Among those staking a claim on the don's property is William Darrell. Believing the don's claim to be rejected, Darrell nevertheless promises to pay for the land. Yet, unlike the others who have claimed property, Darrell is not technically a squatter. Acting on the moral advice of his mother and on his own conscience, Darrell's son Clarence has paid Don Mariano for the property in secret. While meeting with the don, Clarence meets the don's daughter, Mercedes. Although she returns his love, Mercedes believes Clarence is a squatter and therefore an inappropriate match for her. Clarence redeems himself by revealing that he paid for the land and is therefore not a squatter. In fact, through his own investment in the stock market, Clarence is a very wealthy man and therefore a good match for the aristocratic Alamars. With his new fortune Clarence proposes a partnership with the family to start a bank in San Diego, a promising venture in light of the anticipated boom the new railroad will generate in the city.

The narratives of the land rights disputes, railroad speculation, and romance continue until the novel's conclusion. By the novel's end Clarence and Mercedes are united, but with their reunion we see the rejection of the don's title, the rejection of San Diego as the terminus for the new railroad line, and Don Mariano's death. Ruiz de Burton, herself involved in a long litigation with the United States, documents in this novel the final days of the *californios* and the start of a new way of life in the area, one that marks the beginning of the social, political, and economic struggles of the new Americans.

Bibliography

Alemán, Jesse. "Historical Amnesia and the Vanishing Mestiza: The Problem of Race in *The Squatter and the Don* and *Ramona*." *Aztlán: A Journal of Chicano Studies* 27 (2002): 59–93.

de la Luz Montes, Amelia, and Anne Elizabeth Goldman, eds. *María Amparo Ruiz de Burton: Critical and Pedagogical Perspectives.* Lincoln: University of Nebraska Press, 2004.

Ruiz de Burton, María Amparo. *The Squatter and the Don.* Houston, Tex.: Arte Público Press, 1997.

———. *Who Would Have Thought It?* Houston, Tex.: Arte Público Press, 1995.

Sánchez, Rosaura, and Beatrice Pita, eds. *Conflicts of Interest: The Letters of María Amparo Ruiz de Burton.* Houston, Tex.: Arte Público Press, 2001.

Arlene Rodriguez

Stavans, Ilan (Ilán Stavans, Ilan) (1961–) (critic, essayist)

The son of Eastern European immigrants, Ilan Stavans was born on April 7, 1961, in Mexico City, Mexico. His father, Abraham Stavans, and his mother, Ofelia Slomiansky, raised him in a Jewish household. He attended the Universidad Nacional Autónoma de México until 1984. In 1985 he immigrated to the United States and graduated with an M.A. from the Jewish Theological Seminary in 1987. By 1990 he earned a Ph.D. in Spanish and Hispanic-American literature from Columbia University. Since then

Stavans has been a professor at Columbia University, Baruch College of the City University of New York, and Amherst College, where he holds the Lewis-Sebring Professor chair in Latin American and Latino culture. He was the editor of *Hopscotch: A Cultural Review* and is advisory member of several editorial boards, including that of *World Literature Today* and the *Bloomsbury Review*. Stavans was awarded the Bernard M. Baruch Excellence in Scholarship Award in 1993 for his book *Imagining Columbus: The Literary Voyage* (1993) and was nominated for a Pushcart Prize in 2000 for the short stories "On My Brother's Trail" and "Xerox Man."

Known primarily as a cultural critic, author of the controversial *The HISPANIC CONDITION: REFLECTIONS ON CULTURE AND IDENTITY IN AMERICA* (1995), Stavans has also written a memoir (*On Borrowed Words: A Memoir of Language,* 2001), short stories, and plays and has edited a number of important encyclopedias and anthologies, including the four-volume *Encyclopedia Latina* (2005), *Tropical Synagogues: Short Stories by Jewish–Latin American Writers* (1994), and the *Norton Anthology of Latino Literature* (2005).

Stavans offers a unique perspective on cultural studies because he, himself, enjoys and contends with a richly "hyphenated" condition. GUSTAVO PÉREZ FIRMAT has popularized this hyphenated condition in his work, *Life on the Hyphen: The Cuban-American Way.* We can apply the notion of hyphenation to Stavans's experience of growing up in Mexico, being raised in a Yiddish-speaking Jewish household, and moving to the United States. He writes in Spanish and English and has become interested in the work of Eastern European writers such as Franz Kafka and Bruno Schulz.

In 2001 Stavans published "Octavio Paz: A Meditation," an essay on the Mexican Nobel Prize–winning writer and a fitting subject for Stavans as OCTAVIO PAZ was perhaps one of the first critics to pave the way for cultural studies. *The Labyrinth of Solitude* (1950) was Paz's response to his experience of Mexican otherness; in his famous essay, "MEXICAN MASKS," he discusses how Mexican men and women are culturally trained to wear masks. This notion of masking accords with many plots of CHICANO LITERATURE. Yet, Paz's is one of the most articulate, beautifully written books on the question of "minority" identity within mainstream U.S.culture. By the time Stavans wrote *The Hispanic Condition,* however, the Mexican American or Chicano had been made part of two generic ethnic groupings: Hispanic and Latino. As Stavans writes, "Although these terms may seem interchangeable, an attentive ear senses a difference. Preferred by conservatives, the former [Hispanic] is used when the talk is demographics, urban development, drugs, and health; the latter [Latino], on the other hand, is the choice of liberals and is frequently used to refer to artists, musicians, and movie stars. Ana Castillo is Latina . . . former New York City Schools Chancellor Joseph Fernandez is Hispanic" (24). And yet, regardless of the labels used, "not since the abolition of slavery and the waves of the Jewish immigration from Eastern Europe has a group been so capable of turning everybody upside down," declares Stavans (19). The hundreds of millions of dollars generated in revenues from the Spanish-language television networks Telemundo and Univision are testament, if nothing else, to the unprecedented growth of Hispanic culture, which has pushed out to the margins the xenophobic critics of bilingual education and the supporters of the English-only movement.

Stavans's stories collected in *The One-Handed Pianist and Other Stories* (1996) were originally written in Spanish and have been translated into English by Amy Price, David Unger, and Harry Morales. In the collection, "Talia in Heaven" has been described as the most Kafkaeque of Stavan's work and the one most directly having to do with his Jewish heritage. "A literary debut is like a Bar Mitzvah," says Stavans in an interview with the *Literary Review.* "You're called to present yourself in front of the community" (Sokol 555). Steven More observes: "Stavans has already distinguished himself as a critic and essayist: this volume of his brooding, erudite fiction places him in that small circle of writers who are as accomplished at fiction as they are nonfiction" (157). In anticipation of Pablo Neruda's centenary, Stavans edited *The*

Poetry of Pablo Neruda (2003), an anthology of the Chilean's poetry, translated by MIGUEL ALGARÍN and other contemporary poets. This is one of numerous books Stavans has edited over the years, and one that captures his sense of what it means to be an editor. Referring to Reuben Staflovitch, the character of "Xerox Man," he says: "What he is is an editor . . . Every passionate reader is one" (Sokol 556). Perhaps one can say that Reuben, this passionate reader, is also the writer of essays and fiction, the translator, and the editor that we all know as the Ilan Stavans of Latino studies.

Bibliography

Grover, Mark L. Review of *The Hispanic Condition: The Power of a People. Library Journal* 126, no. 19 (November 15, 2001): 88.

Heller, Scott. "'Living in the Hyphen' Between Latin and American: Amherst College's Ilan Stavans explores Latino culture in his writing and in a new journal." *Chronicle of Higher Education,* January 9, 1998, p. A17.

More, Steven. Review of *The One-Handed Pianist and Other Stories. Review of Contemporary Fiction* 16, no. 2 (Summer 1996): 156–157.

Sokol, Neal. "Translation and Its Discontents: A Conversation with Ilan Stavans." *Literary Review* 45, no. 3 (Spring 2002): 554–571.

Stavans, Ilan. *The Hispanic Condition: The Power of a People.* 2d. ed. New York: Rayo, 2001.

———. *Imagining Columbus: The Literary Voyage.* New York: Twayne, 1993.

———. *Octavio Paz: A Meditation.* Tucson: University of Arizona Press, 2001.

———. *On Borrowed Words: A Memoir of Language.* New York: Viking, 2001.

———. *The One-Handed Pianist and Other Stories.* Albuquerque: University of New Mexico Press, 1996.

Stavans, Ilan, ed. *Encyclopedia Latina.* 4 vols. New York: Grolier, 2005.

———. *The Norton Anthology of Latino Literature.* New York: Norton, 2005.

———. *The Poetry of Pablo Neruda.* New York: Farrar, Straus & Giroux, 2003.

———. *Tropical Synagogues: Short Stories by Jewish-Latin American Writers.* New York: Holmes & Meier, 1994.

Rolando Pérez

Suárez, Virgil (1962–) *(writer, professor, editor)*

Virgil Suárez was born in 1962 in Cuba. As a contributor to CUBAN-AMERICAN LITERATURE, Suárez reflects on his exile and immigrant experience in the United States. The only son of a policeman father and seamstress mother, Suárez was born in Havana and moved to the United States after living for a brief period in Spain. In 1987 he received an M.F.A. from Louisiana State University and began his writing and editing career in earnest.

Suárez's work has been published in national and international journals and anthologized widely. Currently Suárez is a professor of creative writing at Florida State University. He has conducted readings, workshops, and lectures at universities, libraries, prisons, and community groups both nationally and internationally.

Suárez is an award-winning writer. He was awarded a National Endowment of the Arts fellowship in 2001 and the G. MacCarthur Poetry Prize in 2002. In 2004 his poetry appeared in *Best American Poetry.* His work has also been nominated five times for the Pushcart Prize. Of the generation of Cuban-American writers who look less to the past and conditions of exile in order to define themselves, Suárez instead focuses on the needs, both cultural and practical, of Latino communities. Toward that end he writes about different ethnic communities of which he has been part. Throughout his various works he contrasts island life with living in a new country, the need for family, the clashes that occur between cultures, and the search for personal identity among immigrants. In his poetry he uses form and metaphor to capture everyday objects and experiences. Themes such as exile, separation from one's family, and the need to connect with the past help Suárez's audience understand the life of immigrants in a U.S., often urban context.

His writing focuses on the voice of the immigrant and the uneasiness associated with new surroundings. Suárez's father is an imposing presence in much of his work, especially his poetry collections *Palm Crows* (2001) and *Banyan* (2001) and his memoir *Spared Angola: Memories from a Cuban American Childhood* (1997). His novels chronicle the experiences of fictional characters who seem to resemble closely Suárez's own experiences in attempting to preserve family ties in the midst of extreme risk.

Suárez has collaborated on a number of anthologies with such coeditors as Delia Poey, Ryan G. Van Cleave, VICTOR HERNÁNDEZ CRUZ, and Leroy V. Quintana. With these editors Suárez has made available to a broad audience some of the best Latino literary works. He has helped bring to the fore the work of American poets who write about freedom, democracy, patriotism, and religion. The works in these anthologies express a patience and defiance of mainstream ways that, taken together, come to signal a "Latino" spirit.

Bibliography
Benson, Sonia G., ed. *The Hispanic-American Almanac.* 3d ed. New York: Gale, 2003.

Cruz, Víctor Hernandez, Leroy V. Quintana, and Virgil Suárez, eds. *Paper Dance: 55 Latino Poets.* New York: Persea Books, 1995.

Gotera, Vince. "Synecdoche: Brief Poetry Notices." *North American Review* (January–February 2002): 44.

Kanellos, Nicolás. *Short Fiction by Hispanic Writers of the United States.* Houston, Tex.: Arte Público Press, 1990.

Manso, Leira Annette. "*Going Under* and *Spared Angola: Memories from a Cuban-American Childhood*: A Contrapunteo on Cultural Identity." *Bilingual Review* 24, no. 3 (1999): 295–298.

Suárez, Virgil. *Garabato Poems.* San Antonio, Tex.: Wings Press, 1999.

———. *Guide to the Blue Tongue.* Urbana: University of Illinois Press, 2002.

———. *Havana Thursdays.* Houston, Tex.: Arte Público Press, 1995.

———. *Landscape and Dream.* Hammond: Louisiana Literature Press, 2003.

———. *Latin Jazz.* New York: W. Morrow, 1989.

———. *90 Miles.* Pittsburgh, Pa.: University of Pittsburg Press, 2005.

———. *Palm Crows.* Tucson: University of Arizona Press, 2001.

———. *Spared Angola: Memories from a Cuban American Childhood.* Houston, Tex.: Arte Público Press, 1997.

———. *You Come Singing.* Chicago: Tía Chucha Press, 1998.

Suárez, Virgil, and Delia Poey, eds. *Little Havana Blues: A Cuban-American Literature Anthology.* Houston, Tex.: Arte Público Press, 1996.

Suárez, Virgil, and Ryan G. Van Cleave, eds. *American Diaspora: Poetry of Displacement.* Iowa City: University of Iowa Press, 2001.

———. *Red, White, and Blues: Poets on the Promise of America.* Iowa City: University of Iowa Press, 2004.

———. *Vespers: Contemporary American Poems of Religion and Spirituality.* Iowa City: University of Iowa Press, 2003.

"Virgil Suarez." *Notre Dame Review* (Summer 2000). Available online. URL: http://www.nd.edu/~ndr/issues/ndr10/suarez/suarez.html. Downloaded August 17, 2004.

Anne Marie Fowler

Sunday Costs Five Pesos Josephina Niggli (1938)

Niggli spent her childhood in Mexico and her high school and college years in San Antonio, Texas, before entering the well-known Carolina Playmakers, a graduate program at the University of North Carolina, Chapel Hill. Her father was of Swiss and Alsatian descent, and her mother was of French and German heritage; therefore, she is not ethnically Mexican. Nevertheless, readers of her plays see in them themes consistent with BORDER LITERATURE. Daily life in Mexico, the history and folklore of Mexico, and a commitment to make Mexicans visible as subjects all characterize her work. *Sunday*

Costs Five Pesos was published in her 1938 collection, MEXICAN FOLK PLAYS.

In the foreword to *Mexican Folk Plays* Roldolfo Usigli identifies Niggli's comedies as her best. He does not necessarily find "universally Mexican" elements in these plays, but Usigli does believe Niggli's "characters contain the essentials of any Mexican small-town folk attitude towards life" (xviii). Indeed this "attitude towards life" emerges as a key element in all the plays included in the tome. The play *Sunday Costs Five Pesos* uses humor to investigate the needs and dreams of Mexican women engaged in courtship and the daily business of living.

Sunday Costs Five Pesos, first produced in 1937, is one of the five plays in the collection and is set in the town of Las Cuatro Milpas (the Four Cornstalks) in northern Mexico in the afternoon. The title comes from an old Mexican law that imposes a fine of five pesos on any woman who starts a fight on a Sunday. The play opens with a quarrel between a couple, Fidel and Berta. Through a push-pull dialogue (Fidel attempting to get to the cause of Berta's anger, and Berta divulging just enough information to keep Fidel offguard), the source of the conflict emerges. Berta exposes Fidel's insensitivity: "Two times you walked around the plaza with the Celestina last night, and I sitting there on a bench having to watch you." Fidel responds: "But it was a matter of business" (185). This seemingly simple exchange hinges on social rituals and on how Mexican men and women interpret those rituals.

This male-female opposition propels the story. Fidel naively views his attention to Celestina as business. Celestina's father, Don Nimfo García, is going to decide who will carve the doors to a new church in a neighboring town; Fidel, a carver, hopes to get the job. For her part, Berta understands the codes of village life and walking publicly in the plaza with a man signals a woman's acceptance of his attention; it implies a public commitment. *Sunday Costs Five Pesos* provides several glimpses of the rules that define female behavior. When Fidel asks Berta to sit with him on the steps outside her house, she professes shock: "And have Salomé and Tonia say that I am a wicked, improper girl?" (186). Perhaps Berta acts more from

coyness than decorum, but her response does express a concern of unmarried girls and women: the importance of reputation, a concern which influences Berta's reaction to Fidel's public stroll with Celestina. Niggli uses the comedic (and time-tested) aspects of misunderstandings between the sexes to expose the consequences to women when gender expectations are flaunted. Berta will have to bear the public humiliation, not Fidel.

Contrary to his claims of innocence, Fidel's response to his own indiscretion indicates that he understands the rules of courtship. When asked if he explained his motivations to Celestina, Fidel admits: "Of course not! Does a girl help a man buy a trousseau for another girl? That was why it had to appear as though I were rolling the eye at her" (188). He goes on to tell Berta that although the world does not know his motivation, he, indeed, hopes to buy a house for "Berta, my queen" (188). Fidel then questions Berta's trust in him. Berta, like many of Niggli's female characters, possesses a sharp logic that allows her to challenge Fidel's assertions: "Does the rabbit doubt the snake? Does the tree doubt the lightning? Do I doubt that you are a teller of tremendous lies? . . . I know what my own eyes see, and I saw you flirting with the Celestina . . . and so did all the world!" (189). Berta's response suggests that the public aspect of Fidel's behavior demands that she save face and reject him.

As the quarrel between Fidel and Berta escalates, Fidel assumes an attitude of male prerogative. He tells Berta that she must accept his explanation. Berta, whom Niggli describes as very pretty but with a fiery temper, asks if she must obey Fidel as a dog does its master. Fidel does not deny the analogy; rather, he responds: "You are my future wife" (189). At this moment the play exposes patriarchal expectations: A wife will obey her master.

The "action" then shifts to Berta, Celestina, Salomé, and Tonia. Berta's friends devise a plan to bring Fidel back, but before the plan comes to fruition Celestina appears to challenge Berta to a fight. The fine (five pesos) for starting a fight on Sunday makes both women reluctant to initiate the contest. Salomé suggests that the two women play "fingers," and the loser must begin the brawl and pay the fine. Before Celestina or Berta completes this preliminary competition, Celestina discovers Salomé signaling to Berta. Celestina slaps Salomé, and the two women fight. Niggli's stage directions allow the audience insight into the nature of this fight: "*There is no man involved, nor a point of honor. Rather a matter of angry pride. So the two are not attempting to mutilate each other. They are simply gaining satisfaction*" (205). Women do not generally physically fight in order assuage a wounded ego; however, Niggli's women sometimes disregard accepted gender-specific behaviors. The focus of the play thus shifts away from Berta and Fidel's issues to female interaction and competition.

Sunday Costs Five Pesos reflects Niggli's desire to position Mexico, Mexicans, and Mexican women as subjects of drama and narrative. In this regard her work can be read as an early contribution to CHICANO LITERATURE.

Bibliography

Herrera-Sobek, María. *Beyond Stereotypes: The Critical Analysis of Chicana Literature.* Binghamton, N.Y.: Bilingual Review, 1985.

Niggli, Josephina. *Mexican Folk Plays.* Introduction by Frederick H. Kockh. Chapel Hill: University of North Carolina Press, 1945.

———. *Mexican Village.* Chapel Hill: University of North Carolina Press, 1945.

———. *New Pointers on Playwriting.* Boston: The Writer, 1967.

———. *Soldadera (Soldier-woman): A One-Act Play of the Mexican Revolution.* New York: S. French, 1936.

———. *Step Down, Elder Brother.* New York: Rinehart, 1947.

Usigli, Roldolfo. Foreword to *Mexican Folk Plays*, by Josephina Niggli. New York: Arno Press, 1976.

Catherine Cucinella

Tattered Paradise: Azúcar's Trilogy Ends!
Alan Cambeira (2007)

Dominican-American writer Alan Cambeira initiated his Caribbean trilogy of novels with *AZÚCAR! THE STORY OF SUGAR* (2001), its sequel, *AZÚCAR'S SWEET HOPE: HER STORY CONTINUES*, and the final installment, *Tattered Paradise* (2007). In this new episode in the narrative of Azúcar, the author continues to represent the harsh existence of the Caribbean people through his account, respectively of the exploitation of sugarcane workers and the unforeseen consequences of tourism.

Setting this new narrative and the circumstances surrounding tropical sweatshops, Cambeira offers realistic insight into the horrid conditions of workers from the assembly plants. In particular, the narrator brings to the fore the cycle of exploitation in the islands, along with the interest of political leaders in disguising this reality under the deceptive form of the garment industry.

On this occasion, Azúcar, the protagonist of the trilogy, learns that her tropical paradise, which she helped create upon becoming regional director of the luxury tourist resort expansion project, is, as the novel's title suggests, dangerously tattered. The results are grave, affecting not only her but the island's entire population. Azúcar had hoped that the historic cycle of economic, socio-political oppression had ended. Nevertheless, now she agonizes that her idyllic island has become North America's new garment district, with its abysmal working conditions. However beneficial the concept of globalization presents itself, the new assembly plants, with their massive labor force of underpaid and abused workers—mainly young uneducated women and vulnerable underaged girls—are simply sweatshops.

As in the case of the earlier novels in the saga, *Tattered Paradise* is rich in sensuous descriptions of the aromas and textures of the region's indigenous plants and flowers, which contribute to transport the reader to the very tropical scenario in which the novel is set. Furthermore, through its carefully constructed characters, the novel raises awareness of the deplorable abuses of human rights committed in the name of economic development and globalization in the 21st century.

Akin to works by African-American writes such as Toni Morrison or Octavia Butler, Cambeira's novel calls for the preservation of an identity continually menaced by Western greed. In this sense, *Tattered Paradise*'s intertextuality reveals that collective agency does provide a grounded resistance against socio-historical, economic, and cultural transgressions. Simultaneously, in the midst of that claim for identity, questions related to race, gender, class, sexuality, or the prevalence of tradition are likewise addressed to as paramount in the achievement of a true self-realization of the Caribbean community. Cambeira's novels can be read within the context of DOMINICAN-AMERICAN LITERATURE as well as SPANISH-AMERICAN CARIBBEAN LITERATURE.

Bibliography

Cambeira, Alan. *Azúcar's Sweet Hope: Her Story Continues.* Atlanta, Georgia: Belecam & Associates, 2004.

————. *Azúcar! The Story of Sugar.* Frederick, Maryland: Publish America, 2001.

————. *Tattered Paradise . . . Azúcar's Trilogy Ends!* Frederick, Maryland: Publish America, 2007.

Isabel M. Andrés Cuevas

Teatro Campesino, El

In 1962 activists CESAR CHAVEZ, Helen Chávez, and Dolores Huerta began to organize (mostly) Mexican-American farmworkers in California. Their goal was to expose worker and consumer abuse by large businesses and landowning groups in the United States. Historian Yolanda Broyles-González explains: "For farm labor, those abuses included exploitation by growers, crew leaders and parasitic labor contractors; the widespread use of child labor; pesticide and herbicide poisoning; substandard housing; generally inhumane working and living conditions. . . . For consumers, the struggle is against contaminated food and water supplies" (xi). One of the results of this civil rights struggle was the birth of a theatrical movement that took shape in large cities and on university campuses around the country; El Teatro Campesino was part of this movement. El Teatro Campesino presented aspects of Chicano culture to English- and Spanish-speaking audiences and dramatized the problems facing Mexican Americans (Broyles-González xii). According to scholar Nicolás Kanellos, the roots of this theater, known as *teatro campesino* (pleasant theater), can be traced to the *carpas* (tents) pitched by small theater companies visiting farms to perform for the workers. This theatrical tradition prompted Mexican-American laborers and communities to support El Teatro Campesino and the Chicano theater movement more broadly.

In order to understand the effects that this type of theater had on Chicano communities, it is important to note that El Teatro Campesino was part of a larger Hispanic theatrical tradition dating back to the conquest and colonization of the New World. According to Bruce McConahie and Daniel Friedman, there already existed a theater for the working classes during the 19th century that served as the prototype for LUIS VALDEZ's theatrical movement. The roots of Hispanic theater in general can be traced to the first dramatic performances in the New World in 1598 in El Paso, Texas. These roots can also be traced to California, specifically San Francisco and Los Angeles. Kanellos writes that by 1789 the Hispanic theatrical tradition was already taking shape in what would become the Golden State and by the 1800s, "an Hispano-Mexican professional stage survived Anglo-American immigration and take-over and this surviving theatrical tradition served as a foundation for the three decades of the twentieth century" (89).

Between 1920 and 1930 many dramatists in this tradition were expected to please an audience that wished to see itself represented onstage. In other words, the audience wanted performances that spoke not only to their condition as migrants and immigrants but also about political and social events that were affecting their lives in the United States. Theater became a way to both preserve one's culture and promote resistance against the dominant, English-speaking society.

Born during the apex of the civil rights movement, El Teatro Campesino sought an opportunity to express the struggles taking place. In 1965 Cesar Chavez and the United Farm Workers (UFW) union united thousands of agricultural workers in a strike against the Southwest landowners. According to Broyles-González, one of the most important goals in the Chicano movement was the struggle for the "right to have rights" as depicted in the confrontation between the UFW and the landowners in California and other states.

Valdez, a theater student in California and later a member of the San Francisco Mime Troupe, began to formulate the creation of a troupe of agricultural workers that would complement his life experience as the son of farmers and his theater training. He saw the need and opportunity for such an endeavor in Chávez's struggle. Theodore Shank writes that in order to convince other farmworkers to unite with the strikers, Valdez hung two signs around the necks of two volunteers that read "strikers" and a third that read "scab." This is how El Teatro Campesino's technique developed, with volunteers using signs and masks as their only costumes to develop their scenes. Valdez's technique became known as *actos* (acts) 15-minute bilingual dialogues in comedic form that represented the lives of farmworkers. These *actos* represented specific problems in symbolic ways; for example, the signs used did away with the idea of individuality and created a world that represented the struggle of the farmworkers against their employers. Since many of the audience members were either monolingual or bilingual, the use of both Spanish and English in performances was necessary so that everyone could understand the messages in the *actos*. This CODE SWITCHING became a useful practice once Valdez and El Teatro Campesino changed focus to concentrate on problems facing the broader Mexican-American community. Using masks and physical expressions in the spirit of the commedia dell'arte would serve to take Valdez's message to the public and, at the same time, entertain them.

Because Valdez worked mostly with performers with no formal theatrical training, he found it necessary to familiarize them with what he had learned. He worked with farmers who wanted to develop their declarations regarding their living and working conditions.

Valdez wanted to create dramatic pieces that would educate and entertain his audiences. For Valdez the *acto* was a political affirmation of dissatisfaction with the status quo. The *acto* was not part of a larger theatrical piece but a declaration in itself; its name was not important but rather its message. The *acto's* roots can be traced to the theater of Bertolt Brecht and his *Lehrstucke,* or "teaching pieces," and to the "agit-prop" of the Russian revolutionary theater that influenced political theater in the United States in the 1930s. Valdez believed that the *acto* was the quickest way of communicating the problems Chicanos faced. Valdez explained that there were five purposes to the *actos*: "inspire the audience to social action; illuminate specific points about social problems; satirize the opposition; show or hint at a solution; [and] express what people are thinking" (Huerta 16). The *actos* were represented through improvisation and created by the participants who based them on their own experiences. All the daily conflicts performed onstage had a solution: join the union. For Valdez the *acto* only needed two characters to improvise a conflict, and this conflict would be staged with basic information: Who they were, where they were, and what they were doing. In early performances *actos* centered on the lives of the farmworkers as well as the tribulations of Mexican-American communities throughout the United States. El Teatro Campesino's use of Mexican *mitos* (myths) brought to life religious beliefs, whether Catholic or indigenous in origin. Valdez and his groups, in fact, began studying Mayan philosophy to interpret reality. The content of the *mitos* was based on an indigenous vision that was religious, political, social, and cultural. What El Teatro Campesino was looking for was not a division among classes but a way to solve existing problems, and through a Mayan philosophical approach Valdez sought to find harmony and a universal truth. El Teatro Campesino looked for answers and solutions beyond their particular moment. Mary Denning Boland states: "[T]he *mito* attempts not only to represent universal harmony, but also to act as a ritual capable of affecting that harmony—a religious sacrament" (83).

By the third period of El Teatro Campesino's trajectory, many supporters and followers began to identify Valdez as a sellout because he seemed to have abandoned his original goals of representing the problems facing the Chicano community and looking for solutions. Accepting financial assistance from different U.S. organizations, Valdez began to study the pachuco and the events that took place in the 1940s between this group of young Mexican Americans and English-speaking, white sailors. This study by Valdez led to the creation of ZOOT SUIT in 1978. Not only did *Zoot Suit* become a Broadway show, but it also produced a feature film version of the same name. Valdez thus became the first Chicano in the history of the United States to take an original work to Broadway.

Although El Teatro Campesino and Valdez took a different path in the 1970s than originally intended, the impact that this group had on the Latino (not just Mexican-American) communities throughout the United States cannot be denied. This theatrical movement was created to fight against established order, against a status quo imposed on groups of people exploited by those who benefited from agribusiness. Valdez wished to educate his audiences, Chicanos and farmworkers, and the rest of the world of the mistreatment that many had to endure. The purpose of El Teatro Campesino's performances was to inform; with its *actos* and *mitos,* it was able to deliver its message. Audience members were able to see themselves and their lives in each performance, a reflection of themselves, and at the same time were able to find possibilities for change. Valdez was faithful in this way to his original goals of educating a public that was willing to listen and accept what was happening while simultaneously entertaining the audience.

Bibliography

Boland, Mary Denning. *An Analysis of the Theatre of Luis Valdez.* Ann Arbor, Mich.: University Microfilms International, 1983.

Broyles-González, Yolanda. *El Teatro Campesino: Theatre in the Chicano Movement.* Austin: University of Texas Press, 1994.

Huerta, Jorge A. *Chicano Theatre: Themes and Forms.* Ypsilanti, Mich.: Bilingual Press/Editorial Bilingüe, 1982.

Kanellos, Nicolás, ed. *Hispanic Theatre in the United States.* Houston, Tex.: Arte Público Press, 1984.

———. *Mexican American Theatre: Legacy and Reality.* Pittsburgh, Pa.: Latin American Literary Review Press, 1987.

McConachie, Bruce, and Daniel Friedman, eds. *Theatre of the Working Class Audiences in the United States: 1830–1980.* Westport, Conn.: Greenwood Press, 1985.

Oboler, Suzanne. *Ethnic Labels, Latino Lives: Identity and the Politics of (Re)Presentation in the United States.* Minneapolis: University of Minnesota Press, 1995.

Valdez, Luis. *Luis Valdez—Early Works: Actos, Bernabé and Pensamiento Serpentino.* Houston, Tex.: Arte Público, 1971.

Enrique Morales Diaz

This Migrant Earth Tomás Rivera (1987)

This Migrant Earth is ROLANDO HINOJOSA SMITH's English rendition of *Tomás Rivera's* Spanish novel *... Y no se lo tragó la tierra* (1971). Hinojosa rearranged each vignette and translated each word with a regard for the nuances and rhythms of the colloquial Texan Spanish of Rivera's novel. A more literal translation of Rivera's work can be found in Evangelina Vigil-Piñón's *... And the Earth Did Not Devour Him* (1987). *... Y no se lo tragó la tierra* was awarded the Premio Quinto Sol in 1970.

In *This Migrant Earth* a young Mexican-American boy offers primary perspective of the novel, and each chapter adds to the composite portrait of a Texan border community of the 1940s and 1950s. Two themes are important in the narrative. The first is the idea of time and the boy's "lost year," a period in which he retreats into his own world after witnessing many accidents, mishaps, and sicknesses. The second critical aspect of the novel is Rivera's attention to what constitutes a home, allowing the reader entry into the domestic and agricultural settings of the border region and the Midwest, where the migrant farmers go every year. "Home" is where the farmworkers live in any one picking season, and it is a vision of the community and its shared spaces. At least half of the episodes take place in a truck on its way "up North" or in cramped chicken coops that offer little shelter from the elements (cold, heat, rain, dirt) during the seven months out of every year that the migrant workers cultivate and harvest crops.

Within a historical context *This Migrant Earth* serves as a social commentary about the harsh living conditions of Mexican Americans who harvest cotton, fruit, vegetables, and grain. In one of the 27 episodes we see a boy thirsty for water and a calculating boss who will not let the child laborer refresh himself. When the Mexican-American boy sneaks a drink out of the cattle trough, the rancher shoots in his direction to scare him but kills him instead. In another vignette a father and son become violently ill because of heat stroke; while they recover, they are losing pay and the rest of the family is compelled to keep working in the fields. As in many other Chicano narratives the working of land and the ownership of land are contested issues and, therefore, the source of conflict between Anglo farmers and Mexican-American laborers.

Every now and then one member of the barrio tries to make the best of things, but this often ends in failure or catastrophe. In "Burnt Offerings" Doña Chona García submits to the confines of her shack, but her husband, Don Efraín, seeks diversion for his three young children. Efraín encourages his little girl and two boys to box with one another as a distraction from the daily tedium. In the absence of their parents the children take out the boxing gloves and the rubbing alcohol and begin playing around. They are trying to re-create the boxing matches they saw in a movie:

"Well what happened was that the oldest—Raulito—he started to fry himself some eggs at the same time the other two were goin' at it, and I think something must've happened and they the little guys burned up; caught fire, see?"

"Maybe he put on too much alcohol on them, you think that's it?"

"Who's to know? Those coops are so damned small, and you know how much stuff we have to keep in there. I don't know, but it could've been the kerosene tank atop the stove. Exploded or something; maybe that's what set them on fire, and the coop too" (14–15).

Today's readers might condemn the Garcías for leaving their children unsupervised, but Rivera (and NORMA ELIA CANTÚ, as well as a number of Chicano writers) make clear the occasional necessity of leaving the children at home. The youngest children fall under the care of the oldest child, while parents toil in the fields. Perhaps the parents might have done something different, but one community member observes: "[W]hat can you do? It's there, waiting for you, but you never know when. Or how" (15). The idea of something being out there is Rivera's acknowledgment of the hazards of migrant life. Whether migrant laborers and their families exercise caution, they are part of what Rivera calls a "cold, materialistic, and most inhuman system" (Olivares 365).

Because of the poverty of the barrio and the visibility of prosperity elsewhere, the children of the novel grow up with resentment, as seen in "And All Through the House." One young boy asks his mother why Santa Claus does not come to their house. Rivera makes the division between the migrant world and the town especially clear when the mother, in answer to the complaints of her children, tries to purchase some Christmas gifts. She is uncomfortable, however, with leaving her own home because she feels exposed and out of place. When she arrives, in a panic, at the local department store she manages to choose her purchases. But, in the midst of an agoraphobic attack she walks out without paying for them; her attack is misread as thievery because "these damn people [are] always stealing something, stealing" (27).

Not only are the novel's Mexican Americans regarded as thieves, their children are regarded as dirty, as in the chapter entitled "The Hurt." When the young boy (the main consciousness of the novel) is stripped and checked for lice, he feels humiliated by the school nurse. The boy recognizes that another source of shame comes from old women in his neighborhood who check each other's heads while Anglos drive by and gawk. In this episode the barrio becomes an ethnological "zoo" and the lice picking creates an "us and them" divide. Rivera's awareness of how others perceive migrant laborers helps him to create a complex picture of the boy's community. He does not romanticize the Mexican Americans of the novel, and this restraint gives his stories a hard-won honesty. Like any good storyteller, Rivera knows when to shock his audience.

The novel takes its most sinister turn in the episode called "With This Ring." In order to continue school a young boy stays with Don Laíto and Doña Bonny while his parents continue to work elsewhere in the fields. Don Laíto and Doña Bonny's house is a repository for all the canned foods, clothing, and junk that they sell or give away: "And you should've seen it! Well, you couldn't there being no light, see? It was jam-packed, tight, and close, on account of the smell. Full of all kinds of stuff, boxes of God-knows-what, and empty bottles, old calendars, piles of clothes" (87). The house becomes the scene of a crime when a Mexican worker falls into a sexual relationship with Doña Bonny. She and her husband call the Mexican "*mojado*" (wet back), and she figures out that he is alone in the area without family. The couple murder the Mexican, and they force the boy to dig his grave. Disgusted, lonely, and scared, the boy seeks the only comfort he has: "I wanted to go home" (87). Two months later the couple visit the boy and give him the Mexican's ring as a reminder to the boy to keep his mouth shut.

Despite the sordidness, the hardships in the fields, the alienation the boy feels at school, and the unending money worries, the Mexican-American barrio does offer some comforts to each family. It is in the barrio that members of the community gather, exchange stories, help one another, and celebrate the important events of life such as the wedding referred to in the following passage:

That back yard was all worked over; decked out in Texas Pecan branches, Indian paint brush, wild lilies, hollyhock; and then—careful,

now—the tamping down all around the tarp; smooth as glass it was. And water. They watered the dancing area first of all, and they watered it down some more. There. Hard, smooth, there, that'll hold the dust in time for the dance (53).

For one day, the land does not devour; it has yielded its flowers and fruits. The earth's hardness, ordinarily a burden to the laborer, now allows for communion, a place to dance, a place to celebrate. The image of the Mexican-American family dancing on top of the soil, instead of working it or being buried in it, signifies reclamation. The land is theirs as it was before the Treaty of GUADALUPE HIDALGO and before there was an enforceable border.

Rivera ends his novel with affirmation. The boy who has suffered a "lost year" revolts against the land by cursing God and kicking up the dirt. He had sought comfort under a neighbor's house, but then he emerges to climb a tree. This act counters the general movement of the workers, which is to drag themselves along the soil. At this new height, the boy extends his hand and waves to someone who is not actually there. Yet, whether there is anyone there is not as important as the fact that the boy has risen above the earth instead of being buried in it or broken by it through toil.

Literary critics offer several approaches to reading *This Migrant Earth* and the Spanish original, . . . *Y no se lo tragó la tierra*. Héctor Calderón looks at the parallel between Rivera's work and that of Miguel Cervantes's *Don Quixote de la Mancha* (1605), arguing that both writers participated in a rich oral culture relying on the "the storytelling ballads, legends, popular tales, sayings, and proverbs"; both authors also experimented with the short story form (100). Other scholars look at the autobiographical elements of Rivera's fiction, noting the parallel between his own experience of migrant farming as a child and the interconnectedness between his family and community living in the Rio Grande valley. For its themes and settings Rivera's work can be read within the context of BORDER LITERATURE and CHICANO LITERATURE.

Bibliography

Bruce-Novoa, Juan. *Chicano Authors: Inquiry by Interview.* Austin: University of Texas Press, 1980.

Calderón, Héctor. "The Novel and the Community of Readers: Rereading Tomás Rivera's . . . *Y no se lo tragó la tierra.*" In *Criticism in the Borderlands,* edited by Héctor Calderón and José Saldívar, 97–113. Durham, N.C.: Duke University Press, 1991.

Hinojosa Smith, Rolando, Gary Keller, and Vernon E. Lattin, eds. *Tomás Rivera, 1935–1984: The Man and His Work.* Tempe, Ariz.: Bilingual Press, 1988.

Olivares, Julián, ed. *Tomás Rivera: The Complete Works.* Houston, Tex.: Arte Público Press, 1991.

Rivera, Tomás. . . . *Y no se lo tragó la tierra/ . . . And the Earth Did Not Devour Him.* Translated by Evangelina Vigil-Piñón. Houston, Tex.: Arte Público Press, 1987.

Rivera, Tomás and Rolando Hinojosa Smith. *This Migrant Earth: An English Rendition of Tomás Rivera's . . . Y no se lo tragó la tierra.* Houston, Tex.: Arte Público Press, 1987.

Luz Elena Ramirez

Thomas, Piri (Juan Pedro Tomás)
(1928–   ) *(memoirist, novelist)*

Piri Thomas's first book, DOWN THESE MEAN STREETS (1967), created a sensation because of its frank treatment of the author's experiences as a dark-skinned Puerto Rican growing up in Spanish Harlem. Although he has subsequently written several autobiographical books and a collection of short stories, *Down These Mean Streets* remains the work with which he is most readily identified.

Thomas was born Juan Pedro Tomás on September 30, 1928, in New York City, his birth name later anglicized to John Peter Thomas. He grew up during World War II, and came of age in the 1950s. Drug addiction contributed to his transformation from street kid to desperate criminal. In 1950 he was convicted for his participation in an armed robbery and served seven years in prison. During his imprisonment Thomas used writing to make sense of what had brought him to such a seemingly dead end at such a young age. He produced a manuscript similar to the novel *Down These Mean Streets,* but that early manuscript was lost shortly after his release from prison. Ever since getting out of jail, Thomas has worked with drug addicts and prison inmates through a number of programs. In 1967 his efforts in this regard were formally recognized with a Levers Brother community service award.

In 1962 a grant from the Louis M. Rabinowitz Foundation enabled Thomas to reapproach the autobiographical manuscript that he had completed in prison but had then lost. *Down These Mean Streets,* which covers his life from boyhood to young adulthood, has been discussed as much for its style as for its content. It established Thomas as the preeminent chronicler of the Latino experience within the hard and blighted environments of urban America. It has marked out the territory subsequently explored not only in nonfictional works by other authors but also in novels such as Abraham Rodríguez's *Spidertown* (1993) and Díaz's DROWN (1996).

In *Saviour, Saviour, Hold My Hand* (1972) Thomas reflects on his experiences since his release from prison. As such, it can be read alongside the prison poetry and memoirs of RAÚL SALINAS and RICARDO SÁNCHEZ. *Saviour, Saviour, Hold My Hand* conveys Thomas's efforts to develop a more measured sense of his place in the world—an understanding of the process by which he has been transformed from a convicted violent criminal to a renowned author and a literary spokesperson for a previously ignored segment of the American experience.

In *Seven Long Times* (1974) Thomas describes his experiences as a prison inmate and is concerned with his psychological adjustment, moral development, and physical survival. Like that of *Down These Mean Streets, Seven Long Times* engages the reader on a very visceral level. The prison milieu is marked by an inescapable assault on the senses. Within this highly charged but stark environment each prisoner's dully repetitive daily routine is marked by the exhausting effort to anticipate the unexpected. The prisoner contends with violence that crackles under the surface of each remark, gesture, and movement—like electricity through failing wires.

Stories from El Barrio (1978) is a collection of stories for young adults. Thomas reworks some of the material of *Down These Mean Streets* into tales with a somewhat softened edginess and a more apparent didactic purpose. A poet of some distinction, Thomas is also the author of *The Golden Streets,* a play produced in New York in 1970. For its themes and images Thomas's work can be read within the context of PUERTO RICAN LITERATURE.

Bibliography

Arrillaga, Maria. "These Streets That Are Not Mean: To Piri Thomas, an Enduring Friend." *Confrontation: A Literary Journal* nos. 56–57 (Summer–Fall 1995): 47–55.

Binder, Wolfgang. "An Interview with Piri Thomas." *Minority Voices: An Interdisciplinary Journal of Literature and the Arts* 4 (Spring 1980): 63–78.

Cintron, Humberto. "An Interview with Piri Thomas." *Forkroads: A Journal of Ethnic-American Literature* 1, no. 1 (Fall 1995): 41–52.

Greenberg, Dorothee von Huene. "Piri Thomas: An Interview." *MELUS* 26 (Fall 2001): 71–100.

McGill, Lisa D. "A Conversation with Piri Thomas." *Bilingual Review/Revista Bilingüe* 25 (May–August 2000): 179–184.

Stavans, Ilan. "Race and Mercy: A Conversation with Piri Thomas." *Massachusetts Review* 37 (Autumn 1996): 344–354.

Thomas, Piri. *Down These Mean Streets.* 1967. Reprint, New York: Vintage Books, 1997.

———. *Saviour, Saviour, Hold My Hand.* Garden City, N.Y.: Doubleday, 1972.

———. *Seven Long Times.* Houston, Tex.: Arte Público Press, 1994.

———. *Stories from El Barrio.* New York: Knopf, 1978.

Martin Kich

Treasures in Heaven **Kathleen Alcalá** (2000)
Mexican-American author Kathleen Alcalá (1954–) published *Treasures in Heaven* in 2000. *Treasures in Heaven* is the third novel in a trilogy that began with *Spirits of the Ordinary* (1997), followed by *The Flower and the Skull* (1998).

All three novels center on the heroine, Estela. In *Treasures in Heaven* we find Estela seeking refuge in early 20th-century Mexico City during a tumultuous time under the rule of dictator Porfirio Díaz. She flees the tumultuous borderlands for the city because of the persecution of her Jewish husband. With her youngest child she finds an urban life where she can blend in as a Mexican woman living on her own. Upon arrival in Mexico City Estela soon discovers that she lacks the means to live respectably in the metropolis and quickly falls into desperate financial straits. She sets about finding her old love, Dr. Victor Carranza, who helps her through his connection to a woman known as Señorita Mejora de Gonga. Señorita Mejora de Gonga, referred to as La Señorita, proves to be one of the most important figures in Estela's life.

In her move to Mexico City Estela ponders the contradictions between what she wishes could be and what history and its circumstances press upon her as a woman living in troubled times: "[H]er heart ached for all of the happy conjunctions we all wish for, to live out our lives in the place of our choice with the person of our choice, perhaps to raise happy, healthy children, to hear the birds sing, and be greeted with respect by one's neighbors. But as with most of us, this was not to be" (5). Estela helps La Señorita establish a school for the *desafortunados* (unfortunate, disadvantaged) of Mexico City. Alcalá contrasts the social ills of Mexico with the city's turn-of-the-century debut as the "Paris" of Latin America; she looks at how capitalism and "modern growth" affect a nation and a people. The title, *Treasures in Heaven,* refers to the Catholic belief in the beatitudes in which Christ promises treasures in heaven for the *desafortunados.*

La Señorita is an eccentric woman of the social elite in Mexico City who uses her connections to help the downtrodden. Estela is shocked when she learns that she is educating the children of prostitutes, and she questions the morality of helping such women. La Señorita refuses to judge the poor women and explains the importance of the school, la Escuela de Pacienca (School of Patience):

The streets of Mexico teem with women who have been tasted, then abandoned, by men. Often they are brought into a household at twelve or thirteen to watch the children or to do the laundry. A pretty one is soon forced behind the cooking shed by the patron or oldest son. She is warned not to tell, or she will lose her position. But sooner or later her belly begins to swell, and she finds herself on the street with no more regard than an abandoned dog. These young women do what they have to in order to survive (27).

Treasures in Heaven shows how the classist ideas of the Porfirian oligarchy and the antipathy of the Catholic Church create an untenable position for the impoverished women of Mexico. They willingly work but find themselves in an era of modernization complicated by economic hardship. For example, clean water is available, but only La Señorita's good social connections make it possible to have it delivered; at the same time, the church serves the state, insisting that the poor submit to the exploitation of the wealthy: "'The Church merely promises treasures in heaven. . . . It does not promise what we are due in this life, nor does it show people how to attain it. Only the rich and the Church benefit from the present order'" (96), but the truly religious remain invisible—they labor among the untouchables.

Estela progresses in her duties and proposes that the school grow into an establishment to combat the growing problem of prostitution among the women: "We need to catch them before they become used to the street" (30), and for this reason, the children's refuge, La Pacienca, increases in scope. For the sake of the *desafortunados* La Señorita dedicates her fortune to creating an underground journal. The first publication, *Viajes,* caters to bourgeois sensibilities and leads to a more radical publication, *La Linterna. La Linterna* addresses the health and welfare of women and children who are compelled to live without the help and protection of a husband or father. *La Linterna* combats the public apathy that ignores the depressing conditions of early 20th-century Mexico.

The Porfirian regime that Alcalá depicts reveals a country dedicated to science, capitalist wealth, and a class system that correlates with racial divisions. Alcalá critiques Díaz's Eurocentric philosophies, revealing the bad fit with the Mexican national landscape and unmasking the refusal of the upper class to understand the real conditions of existence in Mexico. We learn that, "everything that happens in Paris is mimicked here. Many of these people do not feel secure in their own backgrounds, feel inferior, and so try to make themselves better through imitation" (145). Like so many Latin American countries, Mexico adopted foreign habits and ways of being at the expense of local ones.

For Alcalá, La Pacienca provides access to practical forms of knowledge that make it possible for the poor women to free themselves from the bonds of poverty and the degradation of prostitution. Through the school and the publications *Viajes* and *La Linterna* women from all walks of life learn to protect themselves and their children from disease, poverty, and degradation.

Kathleen Alcalá is a fiction writer and essayist born on August 29, 1954, in Compton, California, to Mexican parents. She has published a trilogy of novels taking place in 19th-century Mexico, as well as a collection of short stories, *Mrs. Vargas and the Dead Naturalist* (1992), and a book of essays, *The Desert Remembers My Name* (2007). For its concerns with the way political history (especially the Mexican Revolution) and family history overlap, her work can be read within the context of Chicano literature and border literature.

Bibliography
Alcalá, Kathleen. *The Desert Remembers My Name: On Family and Writing.* Tucson: University of Arizona Press, 2007.

———. *The Flower and the Skull.* San Francisco, Calif.: Chronicle Books, 1998.

———. *Spirits of the Ordinary: A Tale of Casas Grandes.* San Francisco, Calif.: Chronicle Books, 1997.

———. "To Tell the Counternarratives." In *Conversations with Contemporary Chicana and Chicano Writers*, edited by Hector Avalos Torres, 325–346. Albuquerque: University of New Mexico Press, 2007.

———. *Treasures in Heaven*. San Francisco, Calif.: Chronicle Books, 2000.

Johnson, Rob. "An Interview with Kathleen Alcalá." By Rob Johnson. The American Center for Artists. Available online. URL: http://www.americanartists. org/art/article_interview_with_kathleen_alcala. htm. Accessed December 27, 2007.

Kathleen Alcalá author's Web site: Available online. URL: http://www.kathleenalcala.com/bio.htm. Accessed December 27, 2007.

Shimberlee King

Treviño, Jesús Salvador (1946–)
(journalist, writer, director, producer)

Jesús Salvador Treviño was born in El Paso, Texas, in 1946, the son of Jesus Victor and Evangelina Mercado Treviño. He grew up in Los Angeles and graduated from Occidental College in 1968. A film director, producer, and writer, Treviño's work in television and film is characterized by a political consciousness while his fiction is shaped by the conventions of MAGICAL REALISM." He is author of *EYEWITNESS: A FILMMAKER'S MEMOIR OF THE CHICANO MOVEMENT* (2001), which chronicles his educational and professional career in a period that coincides with the Chicano civil rights movement. His first professional success was as writer, cohost, and producer for the Los Angeles–based television program *Ahora!*, the first Mexican-American public affairs program in the United States. His documentaries include *Yo Soy Chicano* (1972), *Raíces de Sangre* (1979), *Gangs* (1988), *Birthwrite* (1989), and *Chicano!* (1995). Treviño wrote the episode "Seguín" (about JUAN NEPOMUCENO SEGUÍN) for *American Playhouse* (1982) and has directed more than 50 episodes of popular television series including *Third Watch*, *Resurrection Blvd.*, *Babylon 5*, *Star Trek: Deep Space Nine*, and *Star Trek: Voyager*.

In 1968, while a senior at Occidental College in Los Angeles, Treviño became involved in the Educational Issues Coordinating Committee (EICC), a body organized after a series of walk-outs by Los Angeles Hispanic high school students protesting poor conditions in their schools. He then organized a chapter of the United Mexican-American Students (UMAS) at Occidental College and met CESAR CHAVEZ when UMAS became involved with farmworker's issues. These two experiences convinced him of the importance of the Chicano community's organizing around common goals and exerting influence on the American political system.

Treviño's breakthrough as a journalist and filmmaker came by way of a chance meeting with Frank Sifuentes, community adviser for the New Communicators program at the University of California, Los Angeles. Upon Sifuente's recommendation Treviño applied for and was accepted in the New Communicators program, which was created to train African Americans and Latinos for jobs in the motion picture industry. While a student at New Communicators, he was part of a film crew that covered the first National Youth Conference in Denver, Colorado. This youth conference—a critical moment in the civil rights movement—was attended by more than 1,500 Mexican-American young people who heard the speech the Plan de Aztlán, which asserted the need for Chicano self-determination.

The KCET (Los Angeles) Spanish-language television program *Ahora!* provided Treviño with his first professional news job. He began in 1969 as a production assistant but was soon promoted to writer, cohost, and producer. In 1971 he and KCET producer Sue Booker created the documentary *Soledad,* about conditions at California's Soledad prison; it won first prize and a special jury award at the Atlanta Film Festival. The same year KCET was awarded a grant from the Ford Foundation to produce a documentary film about Chicano history, which was written and directed by Treviño. Completed in 1972, this film, *Yo Soy Chicano,* combines standard documentary techniques such as interviews and narration with dramatic reenactments of historic events that trace Chicano history from pre-Columbian nations to the present. It was broadcast nationally on the Public Broadcasting System (PBS) on August 8, 1972.

Bibliography

Jesús Salvador Treviño Web site. Available online. URL: http://www.chuytrevino.com. Accessed May 26, 2008.

Treviño, Jesús Salvador. *Eyewitness: A Filmmaker's Memoir of the Chicano Movement.* Houston, Tex.: Arte Público Press, 2001.

———. *The Fabulous Sinkhole and Other Stories.* Houston, Tex.: Arte Público Press, 2001.

———. *The Skyscraper That Flew and Other Stories.* Houston, Tex.: Arte Público Press, 2005.

Sarah Boslaugh

Ulibarrí, Sabine (1919–2003) *(fiction writer, poet)*

Born in Santa Fe, New Mexico, on September 21, 1919, Sabine Ulibarrí is one of New Mexico's foremost fiction writers of the 20th century. His short stories and poetry have frequently been characterized as *costumbrista,* representative of rural New Mexican life, culture, and traditions, and the distinct New Mexican identity that suffuses Ulibarrí's work sets it apart from other contemporaneous Hispanic fiction. Ulibarrí considered his writing to be "a conversation, really, that I carry on with the Hispanic people" (García 189), a reflection of the geography and culture that surrounded him and informed his writing for nearly his entire life.

Raised in the villages of Las Nutrias and Tierra Amarilla, Ulibarrí began teaching at age 17 in the public schools located in the rural communities of Ranchitos, San Juan, and El Rito before moving to Washington, D.C., in 1942. Ulibarrí briefly enrolled at George Washington University while working as a translator until he enlisted in the military and served in active duty for three years. In recognition of his 35 flight combat missions during World War II Ulibarrí was awarded the Air Medal four times as well as the Distinguished Flying Cross.

After the war he returned to New Mexico, where he completed bachelor's degrees in English and Spanish, and a master's degree in Spanish at the University of New Mexico (UNM). In 1958 he received a Ph.D. in Spanish from the University of California, Los Angeles, for his dissertation on Juan Ramón Jiménez (published in Madrid in 1962). Ulibarrí was appointed to the UNM Spanish department in 1950 and retired in 1990, though he continued to teach into the 1990s. During his tenure at the university he opened the Center for Andean Studies in Quito, Ecuador, and conducted language-immersion institutes at UNM and in Spain.

As Ulibarrí considered teaching his profession, and writing fiction and poetry a pastime (García 187), the success that his writing achieved surprised and delighted him. His first published creative work was a collection of 50 poems entitled *Al cielo se sube a pie* (1961; One rises to heaven on foot); with it, his publishing career took flight. Aside from one other collection of poetry, *Amor y Ecuador* (1966; Love and Ecuador), and one book of traditional children's fairy tales, *Pupururú* (1987), Ulibarrí mainly wrote and was renowned for his works of short fiction.

He published seven short story collections, all self-translated: *Tierra Amarilla: Cuentos de Nuevo Mexico* (1964; *Tierra Amarilla: Stories of New Mexico/Cuentos de Nuevo México*), *Mi abuela fumaba puros/My Grandmother Smoked Cigars and Other Tales of Tierra Amarilla* (1977), *Primeros encuentros/First Encounters* (1982), *El Cóndor and Other*

Stories/El condor y otros cuentos (1988), *Governor Glu Glu and Other Stories/El gobernador Glu Glu y otros cuentos* (1988), *Sueños/Dreams* (1995), and *Mayhem Was Our Business/Memorias de un veterano* (1997). Though most of his stories have regional settings and themes, the most recent two collections depart from this trend, the former being based on Ulibarrí's dreamscapes and the latter on his experiences in World War II.

Many of Ulibarrí's stories, such as "Man Without a Name/Hombre sin nombre," address profoundly psychological and philosophical issues via the evolution of the narrative's structure and characters. In other stories Ulibarrí addresses concepts of identity, love, loss, growth, and change by constructing the narrative such that the reader is placed "in unusual positions so as to see the world, and, consequently, to judge it differently" (Ulibarrí xii). In stories with familiar or folkloric settings Ulibarrí uses this familiarity to challenge the reader's perception of quotidian elements of modern society by presenting a traditional, but dynamic, past environment in bold relief.

In an interview with folklorist Nasario García, Ulibarrí stated that Chicano writers did not generally label his writing "Chicano" because "they don't find in my fiction or in my poetry a political or social agenda. I don't carry any banners" (García 185). Ulibarrí instead attributed the unique posture of his work to his upbringing in New Mexico, asserting that it developed out of the bilingual environment in which he was raised and from the fact that he did not share the immigrant and minority experiences of other Hispanic authors (García 185).

Literary critic María Herrera-Sobek reads a recovery of modern Hispanic identity in Ulibarrí's writing, postulating that his work achieves the political ends "of reconstructing a collective memory, of recuperating and restoring a past that defines the present for the collectivity, for the community" (59). By re-creating and reflecting on the past Ulibarrí's evocative, psychologically engaging stories draw the modern reader to the questions they present and to the issues they compel him or her to confront.

Bibliography

García, Nasario. *Pláticas*. Lubbock: Texas Tech University Press, 2000.

Herrera-Sobek, María. "Memory, Folklore Reader's Response, and Community Construction in *Mi abuela fumaba puros/My Grandmother Smoked Cigars*." In *Sabine R. Ulibarrí: Critical Essays*, edited by María Duke Dos Santos and Patricia de la Fuente, 57–62. Albuquerque: University of New Mexico, 1995.

Ulibarrí, Sabine. *The Best of Sabine R. Ulibarrí*. Edited by Dick Gerdes. Albuquerque: University of New Mexico, 1993.

Anna Nogar

Under the Feet of Jesus   Helena María Viramontes (1995)

Chicana writer HELENA MARÍA VIRAMONTES's first novel, *Under the Feet of Jesus,* offers a realistic portrayal of the harsh working conditions of Mexican and Mexican-American migrant field-workers in California, a harshness compounded by the threat of toxic pesticides. The narrative follows a family of migrant workers, 37-year-old Petra and her five children and 73-year-old Perfecto, her male companion. As they move from farm to farm, they meet a number of people, one of whom is Alejo, a young worker exposed to a deadly dose of pesticides. The narrative follows the family's journey as they attempt to care for the sick Alejo despite their own hardships.

In its depiction of its characters' toxic working conditions the novel has much in common with ANA CASTILLO's SO FAR FROM GOD (1993) and LUCHA CORPI's *Cactus Blood* (1995). Works of Viramontes, Castillo, and Corpi, in terms of themes, can be read as CHICANO LITERATURE or environmental justice literature. Environmental justice literature protests the link between the poisoning of the natural environment and the communities in which poor people of color live and work. Viramontes's focus on the hardships of the California field laborers' experience—backbreaking work, poverty, and homelessness—has also prompted some critics to compare *Under the Feet of Jesus* with John

Steinbeck's 1939 Dustbowl classic, *The Grapes of Wrath*. Viramontes's novel shares important affinities, too, with such works as Raymond Barrio's *The Plum Pickers* (1969) and TOMÁS RIVERA's . . . *Y no se lo tragó la tierra* (1971; THIS MIGRANT EARTH) and their focus on migrant life.

Under the Feet of Jesus is notable for its postmodern style. The author's stream-of-consciousness narration reveals multiple perspectives, and the story unfolds in nonlinear episodes. This disorienting narrative mirrors the instability of the family's existence. Yet, the novel's fragmented narration is held together by lyrical prose and poetic metaphor; its characters are often associated with lush earth imagery. Petra's aching legs swell "with varicose veins" that rupture "like earthquake fault lines" (124). As one who loves "stones," Alejo believes "himself to be a solid mass of boulder thrust out of the earth" (52). The "white" hot sun blazing on the fields makes Estrella, Petra's 13-year-old daughter, feel as if her "eyes sting like onions" (50). This combination of bleak and poetic nature imagery provides vivid snapshots of the workers' connections to a landscape that is both cruel and beautiful.

The author also uses nature symbolism from Mexican indigenous tradition to empower her characters, especially the female protagonists. Petra (Greek for "rock") represents a Mother Earth figure. While she has limited resources, she relies on powerful natural remedies with which to heal and protect others. Her associations with earthly maternal strength contain traces of Cihuacoatl (Nahuatl for "snake woman"), goddess of motherhood and fertility in Aztec mythology. Her daughter Estrella (whose name means "star" in Spanish) represents redemption in the novel. As she fights to save Alejo, she develops a growing sense of social and spiritual consciousness. Estrella's celestial associations also hark back to Coatlicue (Nahuatl for "serpent skirt"), a goddess who gave birth to the stars. As rock and star, Petra and Estrella symbolize the dual embodiment of the terrestrial and celestial forces of nature identified within Mesoamerican indigenous oral tradition as female strength.

Although the protagonists are depicted as emotionally strong, they are never without physical hardships. The endless search for adequate food and shelter is a daily challenge for Petra's family due to their nomadic lifestyle. Themes of home and homelessness therefore take on potent significance. As Petra attempts to keep house in temporary shelters, Perfecto longs for his "native soil" (100) in Mexico. The "roar" of a train passing the fields reminds the field-workers of "arrivals and departures, of home and not of home" (55). Moreover, most workers live in dread of La Migra (U.S. Border Patrol) that hunts down illegal immigrants and returns them to Mexico. Because of language barriers and carelessness the Border Patrol often deports U.S. citizens in the process. This has been, in fact, a problem since the Bracero program of the 1940s; the Bracero program relied on Mexican labor to harvest crops with the understanding that workers would return after each harvesting season; however, legal migrant workers were often sent to Mexico, despite the fact that their homes were in such states as Texas, Arizona, and California. Petra, fearing La Migra, keeps the family's U.S. birth certificates tucked beneath the feet of her Jesucristo (Jesus Christ) statue hoping its power will protect her family. These references to home, deportation, and citizenship underscore the workers' need to feel a sense of belonging in a world that often treats them as invisible or as threats.

This world of anxiety is offset by expressions of hope through spiritual salvation, especially in the novel's allusions to the Virgen de Guadalupe (Virgin of Guadalupe), a powerful saint in Mexico. The Virgen de Guadalupe serves as a salvation figure who intervenes for social justice among indigenous people and contains special resonance for migrant workers. In the 1960s CESAR CHAVEZ used her image to inspire farmworkers to fight for their rights as laborers. By the end of *Under the Feet of Jesus* Estrella seems transformed into a version of this powerful icon. Climbing into the loft of a barn, surrounded by a "sparkle of stars" (like the stars that surround the image of the Virgen de Guadalupe), she believes her "heart powerful enough to summon home all those who strayed" (176). The novel's affirmation of the Virgin's powers within the young Estrella suggests that the workers' future salvation is rooted in the power of both social protest and spiritual faith.

Bibliography

Alarcón, Norma. "Making Familia from Scratch: Split Subjectivities in the Work of Helena María Viramontes and Cherríe Moraga." In *Contemporary American Women Writers: Gender, Class, Ethnicity,* edited by Lois Parkinson Zamora, 87–98. London: Longman, 1998.

Carbonell, Ana María. "From Llorona to Gritona: Coatlicue in Feminist Tales by Viramontes and Cisneros." *MELUS* (Summer 1999): 53–74.

Johannessen, Lene. "The Meaning of Place in Viramontes's *Under the Feet of Jesus.*" In *Holding Their Own: Perspectives on the Multi-Ethnic Literatures of the United States,* edited by Dorothea Fischer-Hornung and Heike Raphael-Hernández, 101–109. Tübingen, Germany: ZAA Studies, 2000.

Viramontes, Helena. *Moths and Other Stories.* Houston, Tex.: Arte Público Press, 1995.

———. *Their Dogs Came With Them: A Novel.* New York: Dutton, 2000.

———. *Under the Feet of Jesus.* New York: Dutton, 1995.

Kristina Wright

Urista, Alberto Baltazar

See ALURISTA.

Urrea, Luis Alberto (1955–) *(essayist, novelist, poet)*

Luis Alberto Urrea was born in 1955, in Tijuana, Mexico, to an American mother and a Mexican father. When he was three years old, the family moved to San Diego, California. After graduating from the University of California, San Diego, in 1977, he did relief work on the border for several years. In 1982 he started teaching expository writing at Harvard University and has since taught at different universities in the United States.

His fiction, nonfiction, and poetry concentrate on themes that are related to his upbringing in a binational, bilingual family and his work in northern Mexico. This autobiographical aspect is obvious in his critically acclaimed nonfictional trilogy that focuses on life along the U.S.-Mexico border. The first two volumes, *Across the Wire: Life and Hard Times of the Mexican Border* (1993) and *By the Lake of Sleeping Children: The Secret Life of the Mexican Border* (1996), combine documentary, vignettes, and portraits of persons living along or stranded at the border. The third volume, *Nobody's Son: Notes from an American Life* (1998), is more directly framed as a memoir.

The three books approach the border region, its social problems, and its cultural life in a personal tone. They confront the reader with the desperate situation of individuals and the brutal reality many have to face who are dreaming of a better life across the border. While sections of the book involve the *testimonio* (eyewitness account), in other sections Urrea gives a first-person account of his experiences among the poor on the Mexican side of the border. In the introduction to *By the Lake of Sleeping Children* he writes: "If, as some have suggested lately, I am some sort of 'voice of the border,' it is because the border runs down the middle of me. I have a barbed-wire fence neatly bisecting my heart" (4). In this passage Urrea employs characteristic Chicano enunciations of border subjectivity. He uses the border as a metaphor for being divided, for having two parts, for his hybrid identity. The words he chooses to express his border subjectivity seem to place him in the tradition of Chicano/a literary imagination. His imagery corresponds to such Chicana authors as GLORIA ANZALDÚA who, in her BORDERLANDS/LA FRONTERA: THE NEW MESTIZA (1987), similarly refers to the border as a "1,950 mile-long open wound . . . running down the length of my body" (3).

Urrea's two collections of poetry, *The Fever of Being* (1994) and *Ghost Sickness* (1997), contain poems, partly in Spanish, about his childhood experiences in a culturally and linguistically mixed family. His poetic voice is touching, sentimental, often tragic-comic. The childhood poems deal with the effect of living with a dominant father, family disputes, and economic hardship. The lyrical "I" leads the reader into intimate situations of his early youth in Mexico and California, as for example in "The Sunday Drive," the opening poem of *The Fever of Being*. *The Fever of Being* also features narrative poems, such as "Horses," that focus on the history of the American West. Taken together, his nonfiction books and poetry address issues such as poverty and despair at the border between the United States and Mexico.

The tone and character choices of his 1994 novel, *In Search of Snow*, meanwhile, might at first surprise the reader accustomed to his poetic and nonfiction works. Neither is the protagonist of *In Search of Snow* a Mexican American, nor does the narrator explicitly situate his voice as a Chicano. Moreover, in the first two of three parts of the novel Mexicans are represented in stereotypical outline as menacing to the white Anglo protagonist. Despite its themes and style, which are deliberately set apart from a "Chicano" voice, *In Search of Snow* is nevertheless a novel about the meeting of cultures between the United States and Mexico, a prominent topic in BORDER LITERATURE.

Set in the 1950s, the narrative focuses on the biographies of the protagonist, Mike McGurk, and his father, Turk McGurk, who own a Texaco station in the middle of a desolate desert valley near Tucson, Arizona. Although narrated in a humorous and satirical tone with laconic, farcical dialogues, the narrative is nevertheless built on very serious historical subtexts that once in a while enter the present of the fictional world and cause trouble. Contact histories of different ethnic groups (Native Americans, Mexican Americans, European Americans) are indirectly made part of the narrative. Thus, the novel, on a subtextual level, takes up conflicts that have affected the different cultures of the Southwest.

As a member of a younger generation that is more detached from the history of the Chicano movement, Urrea's work, as with DEVIL'S HIGHWAY, focuses on themes such as migration and life on the border. Urrea's contribution to different genres makes him an important voice in the Latino literary scene of the last decade of the 20th century and beginning of the 21st century.

Bibliography
Anzaldúa, Gloria. *Borderlands/La Frontera: The New Mestiza.* San Francisco, Calif.: Aunt Lute Books, 1987.
Heide, Markus. "Transcultural Space in Luis Alberto Urrea's *In Search of Snow.*" In *Literature and Ethnicity in the Cultural Borderlands,* edited by Jesús Benito and Ana María Manzanas, 115–126. Amsterdam and New York: Rodopi, 2002.
Urrea, Luis Alberto. *Across the Wire: Life and Hard Times on the Mexican Border.* New York, London: Anchor Books, 1993.
———. *By the Lake of Sleeping Children: The Secret Life of the Mexican Border.* New York and London: Anchor Books, 1996.
———. *The Fever of Being.* Albuquerque, N.Mex.: West End, 1994.
———. *Ghost Sickness.* El Paso, Tex.: Cinco Puntos Press, 1997.
———. *In Search of Snow.* New York: Harper, 1994.
———. *Nobody's Son: Notes from an American Life.* Tucson: University of Arizona Press, 1998.
———. *Six Kinds of Sky: A Collection of Short Fiction.* El Paso, Tex.: Cinco Puntos Press, 2002.
———. *Wandering Time: Western Notebooks.* Tucson: University of Arizona Press, 1999.

Markus Heide

Valdez, Luis (1940–) *(playwright, director, actor)*

Born in Delano, California, to migrant farmworker parents, Luis Valdez is a renowned Chicano playwright as well as actor and director in both theater and film. Recipient of the Presidential Medal in the Arts and six honorary doctorates, Valdez was a founding faculty member of California State University, Monterey Bay.

His first full-length play, *The Shrunken Head of Pancho Villa* (1964), was written while an English major at San José State University and expresses the resistance to assimilation characteristic of 1960s and early 1970s Chicano theater. Like the majority of his work, it is a bilingual reflection on the Chicano experience. In his "Notes on Chicano Theatre" Valdez articulates the importance of creating theater for *la raza*, the Chicano people.

After graduation Valdez spent a year with the San Francisco Mime Troupe before founding El Teatro Campesino (the Farmworkers Theater) in 1965. Valdez had approached Cesar Chavez with his idea of a theater to support the United Farm Workers and its strike for agricultural reforms. He was told it was a wonderful idea but there were no resources. Through innovation, hard work, and the use of whatever was available, El Teatro Campesino was nonetheless born on the picket line and the back of flatbed trucks. The *actos*, a form of theater designed to engage directly with social issues and pose a solution, focused initially on the strike. *Dos Caras del Patroncito* (1965; Little patron) demonstrates the arbitrariness of power as a way of questioning the growers, while *Quinta Temporada* (1966; Fifth season) explores the support of the churches and the union in the strike effort. The *actos*, created collectively, were agitprop theater that educated the workers and incorporated masks, signs, and aesthetic strategies from commedia dell'arte, Bertolt Brecht, and Mexican popular performance.

Later, Valdez and El Teatro Campesino moved away from a direct relationship with the union, addressing other social issues of importance to Chicanos, including education in *No saco nada de la escuela* (1969; I don't get anything out of school), the war in Vietnam in *Vietnam campesino* (1970; Peasant Vietnam) and *Soldado razo* (1971; Private), and social roles and stereotypes in *Los vendidos* (1967; The sold). The best known of these early works is *Los vendidos*, a comedic self-critique of the Chicano community, exploring what happens when Mrs. Jimenez, a secretary in the California governor's office, comes to Honest Sancho's Used Mexican Lot to buy a brown face to support the administration. The stereotypes for sale, supposedly robots, are the revolutionary, the farmworker, the pachuco and the Mexican American, but the play ends with a revelation that this is a grand scheme to manipulate the system.

Following his exploration of Mayan and Aztec philosophy as part of the indigenous elements of Chicano identity, Valdez composed the poem *Pensamiento serpentino* (1971; Serpentine thought) that illustrates his theatrical philosophy, insisting on the importance of spirituality to Chicano art and culture, manifest in the actor-training practices of El Teatro Compesino, the Theater of the Sphere, and currently the Vibrant Being. This investment also resulted in the creation of another genre of theater, the *mito,* which explores the spirituality and myths of the Chicano experience. *Bernabé* (1970), whose central character is a man with special needs who marries the Moon, asserts the importance of a sacred relationship with the land.

Valdez is best known for ZOOT SUIT (1978), a cultural phenomenon in Los Angeles before moving to Broadway and then to Hollywood as a film directed by Valdez himself. Set in Los Angeles during and after World War II, it explores the iconic figure of the pachuco through two historical events, the Sleepy Lagoon murder trial and the Zoot Suit Riots. *Zoot Suit* follows Henry Reyna and his alter ego, El Pachuco, who has power over the narrative and the stage, through the false accusation of murder, indictment by the press, and eventual vindication. Filming *Zoot Suit* provided Valdez access to contacts in Hollywood and television. He went on to create the Peabody Award–winning television version of his stage play *Corridos!* a collection of Mexican ballads, and the feature film *La Bamba* (1987), about singer Richie Valens.

He also continued as a playwright with *Bandido!* First performed in 1982, the play excavates the history of Tiburcio Vásquez, a romantic 19th-century figure considered a bandit by some and a revolutionary by others. Using careful historical research, the play foregrounds the way Vásquez's image has been shaped by history and narrative. In *I Don't Have to Show You No Stinking Badges!* (1986) Sonny Villa, the middle-class son of two bit-part actors, drops out of Harvard in order to come to grips with reality. This play engages directly with limited and stereotypical opportunities for Chicanos on television and in movies. Set in a farming community in California's Central Valley

in 1973, *Mundo Mata* (2001), a reworking of his 1974 play *El fin del Mundo,* traces Mundo's conversion from a sellout to the agricultural bosses to supporter of the farmworkers in their demands for reforms. Valdez's *Mummified Deer* (2000) recounts the history of Mama Chu, exploring the persecution of the Yaqui by the Mexican government and the powerful pull of family secrets.

Valdez's interest in the Mexican ballad tradition led to an update of *Corridos! Corridos Remix* (2005), which engages both contemporary ballads and other cultural traditions. His ongoing interest in spirituality produced *Earthquake Sun* (2004), which combines the Mayan story of two warrior brothers with a futuristic science fiction account of cloning and virtual reality. Valdez's commitment to political theater and to exploring the life of the Chicano family and farmworker, their indigenous roots, and their spiritual connection to the earth continue to remain central to his art. As such, his plays make an important contribution to CHICANO LITERATURE.

Bibliography

Broyles-González, Yolanda. *El Teatro Campesino: Theater in the Chicano Movement.* Austin: University of Texas Press, 1994.

Huerta, Jorge A. *Chicano Drama: Performance, Society and Myth.* Cambridge: Cambridge University Press, 2000.

———. *Chicano Theater: Themes and Forms.* Tempe, Ariz.: Bilingual Press, 1982.

Valdez, Luis. *Luis Valdez—Early Works: Actos, Bernabé and Pensamiento serpentino.* Houston, Tex.: Arte Público Press, 1990.

———. *Mummified Deer and Other Plays.* Houston, Tex.: Arte Público Press, 2005.

———. *Zoot Suit and Other Plays.* Houston, Tex.: Arte Público Press, 1992.

Jon D. Rossini

Vega, Ana Lydia (1946–) *(fiction writer)*

Ana Lydia Vega was born in 1946 in Puerto Rico and has become an important female voice in PUERTO RICAN LITERATURE. Like other island writers, she writes in Spanish. Upon publication, the short story collection *Vírgenes y mártires* (1982; Virgins and martyrs), by Vega and Carmen Lugo Filippi, unwittingly became a "feminist Bible" for Puerto Rican women. Vega and Filippi were professors of French at the University of Río Piedras, where they had previously collaborated on a French textbook aimed at Spanish speakers. *Vírgenes y mártires* became an influential literary collection and corresponds with the explosion of female writing on the island during the 1970s and 1980s. Vega's writing features what has become a trademark use of slang and a humorous vulgarity to parody social conventions, especially conventional notions of class, race, and gender. For example, in her story "Wilkins, o el enchule original" (Wilkins, or the original crush) she adopts the guise of a Latin pop star fan to expose the discourse of violence that pervades Latin American romantic music. Likewise, "Pollito Chicken" (a school rhyme used to teach English) uses themes of migration, sexuality, and Americanization. The protagonist, Suzie Bermudez, is a Puerto Rican woman living on the U.S. mainland. Ashamed of her cultural background, she nevertheless returns to the island lured by a government ad aimed at tourists Her nationalist pride is awakened by the sexual prowess of a dark-skinned hotel bartender who leads her to shout for Puerto Rican independence in the middle of orgasm.

In "Letra para salsa y tres soneos por encargo" (Lyrics for salsa and three *soneos* by request) a nameless young woman turns the tables on a man who harasses her in the street. On the third day she surprisingly picks him up, takes him to a motel, pays for a room, quickly undresses, sits down to watch him undress, and throws him a condom. Intimidated by her behavior, the guy hides in the bathroom, unable to get an erection. It then turns out that the sexually assertive woman is a dental assistant who has picked up the guy—short, overweight, black, and vulgar— just to lose her virginity.

Vega's book *Encancaranublado y otros cuentos de naufragio* (Encancaranublado and other shipwreck stories), published the same year as *Vírgenes y mártires,* won the 1982 CASA DE LAS AMÉRICAS prize

for short stories. Its general theme is Caribbean solidarity. In the title story, "Encancaranublado," a trio of castaways, from Haiti, the Dominican Republic, and Cuba, shares a small boat heading to Miami, but their animosities cause them to capsize. An American ship rescues them; however, the trio must accept the help of a Puerto Rican, who, in some ways, can be considered the Caribbean rival of or obstacle to the Hatitians, Dominicans, and Cubans, who undertake desperate measures to land on U.S. shores. With this plot Vega reminds readers that Puerto Ricans are citizens of the United States, though Puerto Rico is a commonwealth, not a state; they automatically enjoy the right to work, live, and seek an education on the mainland.

Following *Encancaranubladoct,* Vega cowrote, with director Marcos Zurinaga, the screenplay of *La gran fiesta* (1985; The great party), the first Puerto Rican movie to enter the international film festival circuit. Set against the takeover of the Puerto Rican casino by the U.S. military during World War II, the film uses the love triangle between the son of a Spanish merchant, the prim daughter of Puerto Rican landowners, and a "loose" nationalist woman as a metaphor of insular island relations.

Vega has regularly published essays of cultural commentary on the island's newspapers and journals. In 1985 she initiated a weekly intellectual relay by seven Puerto Rican authors for the nationalist newspaper *Claridad.* This was later collected as *El tramo ancla* (1988; The anchor lap).

In 1990 and 1991 Vega published two more collections of fiction: *Pasión de historia* (Passion of history), which addresses domestic violence by parodying detective fiction, and *Falsas crónicas del sur* (False southern chronicles), whose opening novella parodies the conventions of gothic fiction. She published the collection of essays and lectures *Esperando a Loló y otros delirios generacionales* (Waiting for Lolo and other generational deliriums) in 1993. An important essay of Vega's, dating to 1998, is "Carta abierta a Pandora" (Open Letter to Pandora), published in *El Nuevo Día* as a public response to a *New York*

Times piece in which writer Rosario Ferré openly endorses Puerto Rican statehood.

Bibliography

Henao, Eda B. *The Colonial Subject's Search for Nation, Culture, and Identity in the Works of Julia Alvarez, Rosario Ferré, and Ana Lydia Vega.* Lewiston, N.Y.: E. Mellen Press, 2003.

Vega, Ana Lydia. *Encancaranublado y otros cueos de naufragio.* Havana, Cuba: Casa de las Américas, 1982.

———. *Esperando a Loló y otros delirios generacionales.* San Juan: Editorial de la Universidad de Puerto Rico, 1994.

———. *Falsas crónicas del sur.* Río Piedras: Editorial de la Universidad de Puerto Rico, 1991.

———. *Pasión de historia y otras historias de pasión.* Buenos Aires, Argentina: Ediciones de la Flor, 1990.

———. *El tramo ancla: Ensayos puertorriqueños de hoy.* Río Piedras: Editorial de la Universidad de Puerto Rico, 1988.

———. *True and False Romances: Stories and a Novella.* New York: Serpent's Tail, 1994.

Vega, Ana Lydia, and Carmen Lugo Filippi. *Vírgenes y mártires.* Río Piedras, P.R.: Editorial Antillana, 1982.

Roberto Carlos Ortiz

Vega Yunqué, Edgardo (Ed Vega)
(1936–   ) *(novelist, short story writer)*

Edgardo Vega Yunqué is one of the most prolific Puerto Rican writers in the United States. He was born in Ponce, Puerto Rico, in 1936 and grew up in Cidra, a small northern town on the island. His family moved to New York in 1949, when his father became the Baptist minister of a Hispanic congregation in the South Bronx. After he graduated from high school Vega joined the U.S. Air Force in 1954. During this period Vega began reading the works of Ernest Hemingway, William Faulkner, John Steinbeck, and F. Scott Fitzgerald.

In 1977 Vega published his first short story, "Wild Horses." He has taught at Hostos University, Hunter College, and the State University of New York, Old Westbury. He has also worked in community projects such as Addiction Service Agency and Aspira. He was founder and president of the Clemente Soto Vélez Cultural and Educational Center in New York City.

His short story collections include *Mendoza's Dreams* (1987) and *Casualty Reports* (1991), but he is known mainly as a novelist. His novels include *The Comeback* (1985), *No Matter How Much You Promise to Cook or Pay the Rent You Blew It Cauze Bill Bailey Ain't Never Coming Home Again* (2003), *The Lamentable Journey of Omaha Bigelow into the Impenetrable Loisaida Jungle* (2004), and more recently *Blood Fugues* (2005).

Vega writes mainly in English, his language of education. Like many Latino writers, he has been influenced by Latin American authors such as Gabriel García Márquez and Jorge Luis Borges, especially in their use of MAGICAL REALISM. Vega portrays in his works the Puerto Rican experience of living on the mainland by using multiple voices and perspectives. He also explores racial relations with a critical perspective yet also with distinctly comic effects, as in his first novel, *The Comeback,* which is about a Gypsy–Eskimo–Puerto Rican hockey player who becomes a revolutionary. In *Mendoza's Dreams* Vega constructs different representations of barrio life and Puerto Rican versions of the success story. The main character, a barrio writer called Mendoza, writes about Puerto Rican dreams of overcoming the barrio's negative reality. In the story "Mercury Gómez," a small Puerto Rican black man who had always been "invisible" for white Americans and would never fit the image of the successful businessman, becomes powerful and rich by building an empire of media companies from a messenger service. He organizes a group of small black men who carry packages quickly, making the customer believe that only one black man makes the deliveries. Merc's success emerges from his own marginality; he subverts the system to benefit from his own social invisibility.

Vega's novels also present a biting vision on intercultural relations in the United States. In *No Matter How Much You Promise to Cook or Pay the Rent You Blew It Cauze Bill Bailey Ain't Never*

Coming Home Again, half Puerto Rican, half Irish Vidamía Farrel searches for a father she has never known. In a story featuring a full orchestra of characters, Vidamía discovers the roots of her ethnic identity. *The Lamentable Journey of Omaha Bigelow into the Impenetrable Loisaida Jungle* explores the complex issue of race through the use of a colorful characters and incredible situations. "Loisaida" is the Latino term used to refer to the Lower East Side of New York City. Vega humorously attacks xenophobia by making a political commentary on cultural stereotypes and combining unlikely ethnic personalities. Omaha Bigelow, a punk rocker, meets Maruquita Salsipuedes, a Nuyorican girl with magical powers who can help him solve his sexual problems. Their love affair is explored through passages of magical realism and political digression. Meanwhile, *Blood Fugues* is a tale of action and mystery that narrates how family ties and secrets come back to the present in the stories of two characters, Kenny Romero and Claudia, and their Puerto Rican and Irish families.

Bibliography

Binder, Wolfgang. "Interview: Ed Vega." In *American Contradictions: Interviews with Nine American Writers,* edited by Wolfgang Binder and Helmbrecht Breining, 125–142. Hanover and London: Wesleyan University Press, University Press of New England, 1995.

Hernández, Carmen Dolores. *Puerto Rican Voices in English: Interview with Writers.* Westport, Conn.: Praeger, 1997.

Pérez, Richard. "Literary Pre/occupations: An Interview with Puerto Rican Author Edgardo Vega Yunqué." *Centro Journal* 18, no. 1 (2006): 188–205.

Vega, Ed. *Casualty Report.* Houston, Tex.: Arte Público Press, 1991.

———. *The Comeback.* Houston, Tex.: Arte Público Press, 1985.

———. *Mendoza's Dreams.* Houston, Tex.: Arte Público Press, 1987.

Vega Yunqué, Edgardo. *Blood Fugues.* New York: Rayo, 2005.

———. *The Lamentable Journey of Omaha Bigelow into the Impenetrable Loisaida Jungle.* Woodstock, N.Y., and New York: Overlook Press, 2004.

———. *No Matter How Much You Promise to Cook or Pay the Rent You Blew It Cauze Bill Bailey Ain't Never Coming Home Again: A Symphonic Novel.* New York: Farrar, Straus & Giroux, 2003.

Antonia Domínguez Miguela

Vilar, Irene (1969–)

Irene Vilar was born in Arecibo, Puerto Rico, in 1969. She is the granddaughter of Lolita Lebrón, the famous Puerto Rican nationalist, who on March 1, 1954, walked into the U.S. House of Representatives with her comrades and opened fire and wounded five individuals. Lebrón spent the next 27 years of her life in a women's prison in West Virginia; her granddaughter, Vilar, spent the first few years of her life in Puerto Rico. Vilar graduated from Syracuse University in New York. In 1996 she published the memoir *A Message from God in the Atomic Age,* the title making reference to a letter her grandmother wrote. The work was republished the same year as *The Ladies' Gallery: A Memoir of Family Secrets* and was considered one of the best novels of the year by the *Detroit Free Press* and the *Philadelphia Inquirer.* Vilar has since been a visiting university lecturer, a magazine managing editor, and an acquisitions editor. For the University of Wisconsin Press she created the America series, which seeks to explore the varied perspectives of the Americas in relation to borders and historical perspectives.

Vilar's *The Ladies' Gallery* is the family history of farmers, landowners, priests, mothers, wives, gamblers, and a famous revolutionary who fought for her belief that Puerto Rico should be free of U.S. domination. The memoir becomes a search for Vilar's identity as she often questions and reflects upon who she is—"What was I" (44)—where and whom she is from, what homeland she belongs to, and her place in a world that defines her as the granddaughter of a great revolutionary, a suicidal mother, and a cheating father. As she struggles to find herself, Vilar introduces the reader to grandfathers, brothers, and the three women who define that family history. As she examines the legacy left to her by her grandmother and mother, she allows us a glimpse into her own tortured existence, from childhood traumas to her own attempted suicide that leads her into Hutchings Psychiatric Hospital. There Vilar gives us the most private of her thoughts, allowing us to look into the notes and stories from her time there as she comes to grasp her legacy and understand who she will one day become. This memoir is at the forefront of PUERTO RICAN LITERATURE, advancing a nationalist attitude and a reckoning with the island's commonwealth ties to the United States. The memoir allows us to think about the tumultuous history of Puerto Rico, from its foundation as a Spanish colony through its commonwealth status to its internal debate about becoming either a Caribbean nation or a U.S. state. Additionally, Vilar examines how tourism has affected the economy of Puerto Rico and those who work under its ruse.

Vilar begins her memoir with a prologue of her family history and then transitions into her time at the psychiatric hospital, asking herself monumental questions about why she is there and why she wants to die. The transition between those family struggles and her individual struggles "through a journey of madness" (19) defines the context of the memoir. How does the granddaughter of Lolita Lebrón, who became a hero of her nation and someone who had many followers, become a woman in her own right? How does she struggle with everyday sadness and her own attempts to take her life? As she tries to understand herself, Vilar travels back in time to the days when her grandfather was a distant stranger in her homeland and to family life on a sugar plantation. We follow her as she tries to accept her father's new wife, Blanquita, who burns her mother's possessions. She tells us of her time at the university and her struggle with bad grades, of her relationship with her boyfriend Ivan and his attitude toward her once he finds out about her family history.

Interwoven throughout her stories, are her tales of nightmares at the psychiatric hospital and her inability to explain to doctors, nurses, and other patients the reason why she is there. Vilar allows us to understand how her experience and the experiences of others in the hospital (an anorexic, agoraphobics, manic-depressives) are similar and haunting and how each is simply trying to survive their own familial legacies.

In the narration of the memoir Vilar incorporates Puerto Rican stories, and a parallel begins to form between the relationship between Vilar and her family and Puerto Rico's history with the United States. As such, Vilar is able to examine the struggle to achieve the American Dream as a Puerto Rican. She vividly recalls for the reader the moment her grandmother takes the fate of the island in her hands and her detail to what Lolita was thinking and feeling at that moment. She allows us to realize what the fight for freedom meant for Lolita and her nation. Midway through the story Vilar shares a poignant image of the funeral of her mother and how that image became a haunting reminder of her own effort to escape the Vilar legacy. Ultimately, this memoir is Vilar's endeavor to understand herself and find a place in her family, from Puerto Rican martyr to her mother's death. In the end Vilar does finally give us the possibility of healing in her relationship with her grandmother, who after 27 years of prison is released back to her island homeland. She is able to meet up with her in Puerto Rico, and the two women begin to heal together. Although there is no complete sense of resolution—Vilar, in fact, leaves us with the tale of her brother's death to drugs—Vilar and her grandmother's encounter gives us hope for a family's future. This future is bound up in questions of identity, nationhood, Americanization, and the roles of women on a journey of self-discovery.

Bibliography

Vilar, Irene. *The Ladies' Gallery: A Memoir of Family Secrets.* New York: Vintage Books, 1996.

Rosa Soto

Villagrá, Gaspar Pérez de (1555–1620)
(explorer, historian)

Born in 1555, Gaspar Pérez de Villagrá was a *criollo* (Creole) born in Puebla de los Ángeles in Mexico. Villagrá attended the University of Salamanca and joined the expedition of Juan de Oñate in 1596 following his return to Mexico from Spain. After three years of bureaucratic delays Villagrá and the other members of the Oñate expedition (soldiers, Franciscan friars, and contractually obliged settlers) departed for New Mexico on January 26, 1598. Villagrá's epic poem, *Historia de la Nueva México,* is a foundational narrative from the colonial era of exploration and settlement in New Mexico. Published in 1610, the account is a justification of the 1598 Oñate *entrada* (expeditionary colonization) in New Mexico, where Villagrá served as captain and legal officer. Written at a critical moment in Indo-Hispano relations in the Southwest, prefiguring the Pueblo Revolt of 1680, the *Historia* is the earliest published work concerning part of the territory that would later become the United States.

After crossing the perilous Jornada del Muerto in southern New Mexico, the party continued north and successfully established the first permanent Spanish settlement in the territory at San Juan de los Caballeros (north of present-day Española) in July 1598. Oñate later commissioned several expeditions to the surrounding areas, from the Arkansas River in the east, to the Colorado River in the west. The settlement expedition that Villagrá recounts involved significant and brutal encounters, among the Spanish themselves and between the Spanish and Indian tribes (the Acoma). In one such instance Villagrá and his fellow soldiers were sent to apprehend four deserters, two of whom were punished by beheading.

In what literary critic Luis Leal deems "the most memorable and most important passage in the *Historia*" (109), Villagrá narrates the terrible battle between Oñate's men and the tribal members from the mesa-top pueblo of Acoma. In December 1598 Oñate had sent his nephew, Juan de Saldívar, to demand that the Acoma yield to Spanish rule and adhere to the colonial *encomienda* (tributary labor) system. The pueblo leadership refused and, rising against Saldívar, killed him and his men.

To punish the pueblo for its insubordination and make an example of the Acoma, Oñate commanded his men to return to the pueblo, insist that the tribe surrender, and turn over the leaders of the rebellion. If the Acoma refused to capitulate, the Spanish soldiers, led by Saldívar's brother Vicente, were permitted to initiate a war without quarter on the community. The Acoma again refused to submit to Oñate's conditions, and on January 22, 1599, the Spanish laid siege to Acoma, capturing and killing tribal members and burning down the pueblo.

When his nephew returned to Santo Domingo pueblo with the captives, Oñate displayed no compassion for the Acoma. In addition to ordering most of the tribal members into servitude or exile, he decreed that all men over the age of 25 would have one foot cut off and be enslaved for a period of 20 years. The colonists protested this treatment, and some even helped imprisoned Acomas escape before their sentences could be carried out.

Oñate, Saldívar, and Villagrá returned to Spain after several years, and there they were charged for the atrocities committed in New Mexico. Following a trial that lasted from 1612 to 1614, the three men were sentenced: Oñate and Vicente de Saldívar were fined and banished from New Mexico forever, and Villagrá was banned from New Mexico for a period of six years. Although Villagrá's punishment was later mitigated by his appointment to the governorship of Zapotitlán, Guatemala, Miguel López suggests that perhaps the Cortes would have overlooked Oñate's offenses altogether if his expedition had found wealth in the New Mexico territory (44).

Given this historical context, Villagrá's *Historia* may be read as a poetic rendering of the events of the Oñate *entrada* and as an exoneration of its leaders. Often compared to other colonial-era Latin American chronicle poetry, such as Alonso de Ercilla's Chilean epic *La Araucana* (1569–89) and Antonio Saavedra de Guzmán's *El peregrino indiano* (1599), Villagrá's work has been mistakenly disregarded as a work of inferior literary value. More recently, however, its importance as a foundational text of New Mexican literature has been recognized.

Villagrá was educated in rhetoric and poetry during the Renaissance, a vibrant period of literary production that coincided with New World exploration. The theme of arms and letters arises explicitly in the *Historia* and is reflected in the poem's literary qualities. Villagrá wrote its 34 varied-length cantos in mostly hendecasyllabic blank verse (11 syllables per line), ending each canto with a rhyming couplet; the work occasionally falls into an irregular meter, though this is not that unusual in Renaissance works.

In discussing the subject matter of the poem both López and Phil Jaramillo divide the work into three segments: Cantos 1–9, Cantos 10–27, and Cantos 28–34. In the first segment Villagrá briefly chronicles the conquest of Mexico, establishes the legitimacy of the Oñate family in New Spain, recounts previous explorations of the New Mexico territory, and describes the delays the party experienced in securing permission to depart for New Mexico.

In the second section the *Historia* narrates the entourage's journey from the valley of San Bartolomé to the site of San Juan de los Caballeros. After many difficulties (lack of water, rough terrain) Oñate discovers the resources of the northern pueblos and the colonists establish their settlement. The third section of the *Historia* describes the battle between the Spanish and the Acoma at their pueblo. The tribe fights nobly, but the Spanish eventually force their surrender. In the *Historia*'s final canto, among the smoldering ruins of Acoma, the remaining tribal members are promised by the Spanish that they will keep their lives, as two of their leaders, Tempal and Cotumbo, hang themselves in the middle of the pueblo. As they do so, the Acoma men utter a curse at the Spanish, which closes the work:

> *Mas de vna cosa ciertos os hazemos,*
> *Que si bolver podemos a vengarnos*
> *Que no parieron madres Castellanas,*

> *Ni bárbaras tampoco, en todo el mundo*
> *Más desdichados hijos que a vosotros.*

> But yet of one thing we do assure you:
> That if we can return for our vengeance,
> Castilian mothers shall not bear,
> Barbarian either, throughout all the world,
> Sons more unfortunate than all of you (302).

Though fighting for the Spanish and supporting the conquest of New Mexico, Villagrá recognized the struggle of his Acoma enemies, their valor, and the import of the curse that closes this history of conquest. This curse resonates with the "last words" uttered in other Native American contests with white settlers. Villagrá's account provides a historical context for BORDER LITERATURE.

Bibliography

Jaramillo, Phil. "The Homeric Image in Gaspar de Villagra's *Historia de la Nueva México.*" *Bilingual Review/Revista Bilingüe* 23 (1998): 137–144.

Leal, Luis. "Poetic Discourse in Pérez de Villagrá's *Historia de la Nueva México.*" In *Reconstructing a Chicano/a Literary Heritage,* edited by María Herrera-Sobek, 95–117. Tucson: University of Arizona Press, 1993.

López, Miguel. "Disputed History and Poetry: Gaspar Pérez de Villagrá's *Historia de la Nueva México.*" *Bilingual Review/Revista Bilingüe* 26 (2002): 43–55.

Villagrá, Gaspar Pérez de. *Historia de la Nueva México: A Critical and Annotated Spanish/English Edition.* Translated and edited by Miguel Encinias, Alfred Rodríguez, and Joseph P. Sánchez. Albuquerque: University of New Mexico Press, 1992.

Anna Nogar

Villarreal, José Antonio (1924–)
(fiction writer)

Although José Antonio Villarreal has produced work in several other genres, his literary reputation rests largely on his novel POCHO (1959). Because *Pocho* was one of the first literary works by a Mexican American to receive widespread attention, Villarreal has been regarded as one of the founders of CHICANO LITERATURE.

Villarreal was born in Los Angeles to Mexican immigrants on July 30, 1924. His father had fought with Pancho Villa during the decade-long MEXICAN REVOLUTION (1910–20). Villarreal himself served from 1942 to 1945 in the U.S. Navy. After his discharge he enrolled at the University of California, Berkeley, completing a bachelor's degree in 1950. He was married in 1953 and supported his wife, Barbara, and their three children by working ordinary jobs. He took graduate courses in 1958. From 1960 to 1968 Villarreal was employed as a technical writer by Lockheed Aircraft in California. From 1968 to 1971 he worked at Ball Brothers Research Corporation in Boulder, Colorado. He has held visiting professorships as a writer-in-residence at almost a dozen universities in the United States and Mexico, first at the University of Colorado, Boulder, and subsequently at such institutions as the University of Texas, El Paso; the University of California, Santa Clara; the University of the Americas in Mexico City; and the University of Texas–Pan American. In between his academic appointments he has been employed as a magazine editor, journalist, and radio commentator. In 1973 Villarreal applied for and was granted Mexican citizenship.

Pocho is a coming-of-age story, focusing on the experiences of a Mexican-American teen named Richard Rubio. It describes his formative experiences while growing up in central California during the Great Depression. His adolescent experiences are in many ways typical of any American youth, but the central issue that Richard grapples with is how to be a typical American when his Mexican ancestry makes him automatically an "atypical" American. The title of the novel comes from a slang term for first-generation Mexican Americans who are caught between the two cultures. As Richard begins to gain a mature understanding of his family's past and of the difficulties that his parents have faced, both before and after their immigration to the United States, the tensions between his Mexican and his American identities are both clarified and deepened. Villarreal describes in flashback the

formative experiences of Richard's father, Juan; thus, the novel achieves the dimensions of a historical saga, and as he describes Richard's mother's gradual rebellion against his father's attempts to dominate her, the novel explores familial and cultural issues typically associated with works of social realism. The novel has sufficient range and impact that its deficiencies seem much outweighed by the scope of his achievement. Critics look at the accommodationist resolution of the narrative.

Given the stature of *Pocho*, it is surprising that Villarreal's second and third novels have occasioned so little comment. His later work has been published in a period in which American ethnic literatures, and Latino literature in particular, have been marketed extensively, have been reviewed widely, and have become the subjects of considerable formal study. Villarreal's second and third novels are of special interest because they provide a sort of prequel and sequel to *Pocho*. *The Fifth Horseman: A Novel of the Mexican Revolution* (1974) is Villarreal's longest novel and, in form and technique, a fairly conventional historical saga. The action is centered on the events of the early years of the Mexican Revolution, though the novel ranges from the oppression of the prerevolutionary period into the decades following the creation of modern Mexico. Thematically, the novel explores not only the conflicts that did much to define the Mexican national identity but also the issues that such a watershed event may leave unresolved. *The Fifth Horseman* can be read alongside the work of NELLI CAMPOBELLO and other writers who explore the effects of the revolution on Mexican life.

Villarreal's third novel, *Clemente Chacón* (1984), is a character study of a *pocho*. The protagonist starts out among the poorest of the poor in Mexico but then crosses the border into the United States to seek the American Dream. The protagonist's experiences represent the possibilities of material success for Mexican Americans and the cultural compromises that may be largely unavoidable costs of that success.

Along with his three novels Villarreal has authored a number of short stories published in literary journals and other periodicals but not yet collected in book form. Several of his stories have been chosen for inclusion in anthologies such as *Iguana Dreams* (1992). Meanwhile, his most notable nonfiction includes two articles he contributed to *Holiday* in 1965, "California: The Mexican Heritage" and "The Fires of Revolution," and two articles published in 1966 in *West Magazine*, "Mexican-Americans and the Leadership Crisis" and "Mexican Americans in Upheaval." Although not a prolific novelist, Villarreal's contributions to Chicano literature are significant.

Bibliography

Gingerich, Willard. "Aspects of Prose Style in Three Chicano Novels: *Pocho, Bless Me, Última,* and *The Road to Tamazunchale.*" In *Form and Function in Chicano English,* edited by Jacob Orstein-Galicia, 206–228. Rowley, Mass.: Newbury House, 1984.

Hernandez-G., Manuel de Jesús. "Villarreal's *Clemente Chacón* (1984): A Precursor's Accommodationist Dialogue." *Bilingual Review/Revista Bilingüe* 16, no. 1 (January–April 1991): 35–43.

Myers, Inma Minoves. "Language and Style in *Pocho.*" *Bilingual Review/Revista Bilingüe* 16, nos. 2–3 (May–December 1991): 180–187.

Parotti, Phillip. "Heroic Conventions in José Antonio Villarreal's *The Fifth Horseman.*" *Bilingual Review/ Revista Bilingüe* 17, no. 3 (September–December 1992): 237–241.

Sedore, Timothy S. "'Everything I Wrote Was Truth': An Interview with Jose Antonio Villarreal." *Northwest Review* 39, no. 1 (2001): 77–89.

———. "Solace in Solitude: An American Adamic Alienation and José Antonio Villarreal's *Pocho.*" *Literature* 11, no. 2 (August 2000): 239–259.

Villarreal, José Antonio. *Clemente Chacón.* Binghamton, N.Y.: Bilingual Review Press, 1984.

———. *The Fifth Horseman: A Novel of the Mexican Revolution.* New York: Doubleday, 1974.

———. *Pocho.* New York: Doubleday, 1959.

Martin Kich

Villaseñor, Victor Edmundo (1940–   )

The challenge in classifying the work of Victor Edmundo Villaseñor is due to the strong autobiographical nature of his fiction and the novelistic techniques that he has employed with great success in his nonfiction. Indeed, his nonfiction very much warrants classification as "creative nonfiction."

Born in Carlsbad, California, on May 11, 1940, Villaseñor grew up in a rural setting near Oceanside. Because his family spoke only Spanish at home, and because he suffered from undiagnosed dyslexia, he had great difficulty in school. He dropped out before completing the 11th grade. Afterward he made his way into Mexico, where he was exposed to Mexican history, customs, literature, and art; this gave him a satisfying sense of his heritage and of his own identity. When he returned to California he worked at ordinary jobs, including a stretch as a construction worker from 1965 to 1970. Although he attended classes at the University of San Diego and Santa Clara University, he did not complete the requirements for a degree. Inspired by James Joyce's *A Portrait of the Artist as a Young Man,* he did, however, apply himself strenuously to his own writing. He felt a great release in his self-expression and became determined to communicate this experience to readers, particularly readers of CHICANO LITERATURE. This perseverance is reflected in the statistics that he provides on his own Web site: Before he sold his first novel, he had written nine other novels and 65 short stories and had received 265 rejection slips for his efforts.

Published during the much-publicized effort to organize the migrant farm workers of California's Central Valley, *Macho!* (1973), Villaseñor's first novel, focuses on the experiences of Roberto García, an illegal immigrant from Mexico who finds work as a migrant farm laborer. Broad in its literary appeal, the novel sensitively explores Roberto García's culture shock at moving from a traditional Mexican village to the multiethnic and often socially volatile communities of California. Although García and his fellow farmworkers live in poverty in both Mexico and the United States, the notion of poverty is very different within the two cultural contexts. In the United States the distinctions between wealth and poverty, between the rich and the poor, are much more elastic than in Mexico. In the United States the poor are surrounded by material evidence of what escaping poverty means. There is always hope of such an escape, as well as a more acute bitterness each time such hope is disappointed. Roberto García's experiences in the United States most pointedly reflect his compounded exploitation as an unskilled laborer who is also an illegal immigrant. Interestingly, although these experiences lead him to return to Mexico, he does so with a more discriminating awareness of his native culture and an unwillingness to accept those aspects of village life that have become destructive.

Villaseñor's reputation rests on his trilogy of nonfiction books about his family's experiences as Mexican Americans: *Rain of Gold* (1991), *Wild Steps of Heaven* (1996), and *Thirteen Senses: A Memoir* (2001). When *Rain of Gold* was initially published, it received some extra attention because of reports that Villaseñor had withdrawn it from several publishers who had intended to sell it as a novel, whereas he wished it to be marketed as nonfiction; nonetheless, in a number of reviews *Rain of Gold* was treated as a novel. The book presents the stories of Juan Salvador and Lupe, the author's parents, who grew up in different parts of Mexico during the worst years of the MEXICAN REVOLUTION. Both families gradually make their way to California, where Juan Salvador and Lupe meet, fall in love, and start their own family. The narrative contains elements seemingly borrowed from MAGICAL REALISM—ordinary characters and everyday incidents invested with mysterious and supernatural possibilities. But, for all of its emphasis on the distinctive aspects of Mexican-American culture, *Rain of Gold* also fits within the broad tradition of the American frontier tale, mixing moments of casual brutality, uproarious comedy and unrestrained crudity, and unexpected pathos.

Wild Steps of Heaven (1996) acts a sort of prequel to *Rain of Gold*, tracing the families' roots in prerevolutionary Mexico. As the subtitle suggests, *Thirteen Senses: A Memoir* (2001) is more of a sequel to *Rain of Gold*, focusing primarily on Villaseñor's own experiences. *Walking Stars: Stories of Magic and Power* (1994) is a collection of short fiction in which Villaseñor attempts to reapproach his parents' formative experiences, detailed in *Rain of Gold*, from a less constrained, more imaginative perspective. Although all of these books have been written in much the same style as *Rain of Gold*, Villaseñor has become more aware of the appeal of his books among younger readers. As a result the narratives have become a little more accessible in form and considerably more straightforward in their themes. Villaseñor has collaborated on a number of children's books, including *Little Crow to the Rescue* (2005) and *Frog and His Friends Save Humanity* (2005). His most recent publication is *Crazy Loco Love: A Memoir* (2006).

Bibliography

Hubbard, Kim. "Rain Maker." *People* (September 28, 1992), 95–96.

Kelsey, Verlene. "Mining for a Usable Past: Acts of Recovery, Resistance, and Continuity in Victor Villaseñor's *Rain of Gold*." *Bilingual Review* 18 (January–April 1993): 79–86.

Miller, S. "Caught between Two Cultures." *Newsweek* (April 20, 1992), 78–79.

Villaseñor, Victor. *Crazy Loco Love: A Memoir*. New York: Rayo, 2006.

———. *Macho!* Houston, Tex.: Arte Público Press, 1996.

———. *Rain of Gold*. New York: Dell, 1992.

———. *Thirteen Senses: A Memoir*. New York: Rayo, 2001.

———. *Walking Stars: Stories of Magic and Power*. Houston, Tex.: Arte Público Press, 1994.

———. *Wild Steps of Heaven*. New York: Dell, 1996.

Martin Kich

Viramontes, Helena María (1954–)

Mexican-American writer Helena María Viramontes was born in East Los Angeles in 1954. Her father, Serafin Bermúdes Viramontes, worked in construction as a hod carrier and her mother, Mary Louise La Brada Viramontes, stretched the household budget to feed six daughters and three sons. Despite the family's limited means, Viramontes's mother generously opened the household doors to others who needed temporary refuge. Viramontes recalls the stories of people seated around her family's kitchen table, stories of struggle, heartbreak, and triumph. In what Viramontes describes as a "bookless home" that only contained the *Encyclopaedia Britannica* and the Bible, these late-night talk sessions were her earliest experiences with storytelling.

Viramontes graduated from James A. Garfield High School and attended Immaculate Heart College on scholarship. She received a B.A. in English literature in 1975 and an M.F.A. from the University of California, Irvine, in 1994. Viramontes won the 1977 and 1978 first prize for fiction from *Statement Magazine* and the 1979 first prize for fiction in University of California, Irvine's Chicano Literary Contest. Active in the Los Angeles greater community of writers, she has served as literary editor of the journal *XhismeArte* and as coordinator of the Los Angeles Latino/a Writers Association. In 1989 she was awarded a National Endowment for the Arts fellowship to attend a workshop directed by Nobel Prize–winning author Gabriel García Márquez, and by 1990 she had cofounded the nonprofit group Latino Writers and Filmmakers. In 1996 Viramontes was awarded the 16th annual John Dos Passos Prize for literature. Currently Viramontes is an associate professor at Cornell University.

Viramontes describes writing as a spiritual and political activity. She hopes to raise awareness about the experiences of people too often silenced in society—women, the politically dispossessed, and the economically disadvantaged. Her stories and novels focus on the everyday lives of people in order to expose racial, economic, and social disparities. Her stories and novels, often characterized by a sense of fragmentation, have been read through the lenses of feminism, ethnic studies, and reader response. The stories include references to Chicano folklore, thereby addressing deep-seated cultural beliefs, while simultaneously challenging them. In much of Viramontes's writing women become the individuals who negotiate the struggle for power in gender relations as well as the interplay between race and class. She is especially known for

her collection of short fiction *The Moths and Other Stories* (1985) and her novel UNDER THE FEET OF JESUS (1995).

Much of *The Moths and Other Stories* centers on individuals who are contending with economic constraints and social oppression. The stories explore the complexities of urban Latino life without providing answers to the characters' most difficult and compelling questions. The collection includes the much analyzed stories "The Cariboo Café" and "Neighbors." "The Cariboo Café" traces issues of displacement and misunderstanding between English- and Spanish-speaking cultures as it weaves together three different story lines: that of two Mexican-American children who become lost in East Los Angeles, a political refugee from El Salvador whose young son was murdered, and the proprietor of a hole-in-the-wall restaurant, the Cariboo Café. "Neighbors," meanwhile, focuses on the detriments of miscommunication within a community as an elderly woman calls the police when she finds the young men of her neighborhood too disorderly. Both stories foreground issues of community and the necessities and failures of intercultural relationships.

Under the Feet of Jesus follows the coming of age of a migrant farmworker, Estrella. Focusing on the day-to-day existence and the emotional and physical lives of the characters, Viramontes shows just how strong the spirit must be in the face of an overarching culture that often exists by consuming the fruits of migrant labor while undervaluing the experiences of the people who work in the fields. When a close friend falls ill, Estrella discovers that she herself must find the strength to bring him help. Gathering all of her understanding, experience, and love, Estrella finds a way to help her friend Alejo and also to pull her family closer together. Through Estrella's growing consciousness the home, family, and community begin growing, too, and are sustained by individual understanding for others. While the novel primarily follows the thoughts of Estrella, Viramontes also stylistically enhances the sense of community. The novel weaves together the perspectives of its different characters; no single perspective takes complete control of the narrative. Instead, like grape pickers working side by side in the rows of the field, the story moves fluidly among several characters who speak their own perspectives equally, one beside the other. For its characters and themes Viramontes's fiction can be read within the context of CHICANO LITERATURE.

Bibliography

Moore, Deborah Owen. "La Llorona Dines at the Cariboo Café: Structure and Legend in the Work of Helena María Viramontes." *Studies in Short Fiction* 35, no. 3 (1998): 277–286.

Rodríguez, Ana Patricia. "Refugees of the South: Central Americans in the U.S. Latino Imaginary." *American Literature.* 73, no. 2 (2001): 387–412.

Saldívar-Hull, Sonia. "Feminism on the Border: From Gender Politics to Geopolitics." In *Criticism in the Borderlands: Studies in Chicano Literature, Culture, and Ideology,* edited by Héctor Calderón and José David Saldívar, 203–220. Durham, N.C.: Duke University Press, 1991.

Shea, Anne. "'Don't Let Them Make You Feel You Did a Crime': Immigration Law, Labor Rights, and Farmworker Testimony." *MELUS* 28, no. 1 (2003): 123–144.

Viramontes, Helena María. *The Moths and Other Stories.* Houston, Tex.: Arte Público Press, 1985.

———. *Under the Feet of Jesus.* New York: Dutton, 1995.

Viramontes, Helena María, and María Herrera-Sobek, eds. *Chicana Creativity and Criticism.* Houston, Tex.: Arte Público Press, 1988.

———. *Chicana (W)rites on Word and Film.* Berkeley, Calif.: Third Woman Press, 1995.

Irena Praitis

Warrior for Gringostroika: Essays, Performance Texts, and Poetry
Guillermo Gómez-Peña (1993)

Performance artist GUILLERMO GÓMEZ-PEÑA published *Warrior for Gringostroika: Essays, Performance Texts, and Poetry* in 1993. The work covers his activities during the period 1979–93 and features a collection of Gómez-Peña's projects, including transcripts from his performance pieces, samples of his poetry, and several of his political essays. *Warrior for Gringostroika* draws predominantly from work Gómez-Peña produced after founding the Border Arts Workshop/Taller de Arte Fronterizo. A politically conscious ensemble, the Border Arts Workshop was inspired in part by the 1985 Mexico City earthquake and the desire to address separatism among Chicanos and Latinos in the art community. *Warrior for Gringostroika* documents the projects that the Border Arts Workshop produced and provides readers unfamiliar with Gómez-Peña's art insight into his political consciousness as a border artist.

Gringostroika chronicles Gómez-Peña's artistic projects after immigrating to the United States from Mexico City in 1978. To this end the author explores the ever-changing formation of Mexican-American identities in the *borderlands,* a term many Mexican Americans use to denote the geographical and cultural frontier that simultaneously separates and connects the United States and Mex-

ico. Gómez-Peña uses the term *Gringostroika* to describe the opening up of borders in North-South relations in the era of globalization. The author expresses the dynamic situation of the Mexican American on the cusp of the 21st century through his various performances and observations.

Gringostroika is broken down into several smaller sections, each representing the many different types of work Gómez-Peña engages in as a performance artist. He uses his body, language, and wit to express and challenge conventional notions of race, culture, and class. The first work, "A Binational Performance Pilgrimage" (1991), presents excerpts from his performance diaries and chronicles the two decades of projects, social movements, and cultural issues that shaped his generation of Chicano artists. The essay functions as an ideological map that reveals Gómez-Peña's expanding political consciousness. The first two sections look at his political essays and performance texts and close with a lengthy photo gallery of onsite performance installations. The final and longest section, entitled "Sin/Translation," features more than a decade's worth of Gómez-Peña's "poetical texts" written in Spanish, English, and SPANGLISH. This section serves as a useful index of the dynamic fusion of Mexican and white, English-speaking cultures. Among Gómez-Peña's other publications are *NEW WORLD BORDER: PROPHECIES, POEMS AND LOQUERAS FOR THE END OF THE CENTURY* (1996),

FRIENDLY CANNIBALS (1996), and DANGEROUS BORDER CROSSERS: THE ARTIST TALKS BACK (2000).

Bibliography

Gómez-Peña, Guillermo. *Warrior for Gringostroika: Essays, Performance Texts, and Poetry.* St. Paul, Minn.: Graywolf Press, 1993.

Lysa Rivera

We Fed Them Cactus Fabiola Cabeza de Baca (1954)

Fabiola Cabeza de Baca was born on May 16, 1894, near Las Vegas, New Mexico, and died in 1991. She received her B.A. from New Mexico Normal in 1921 and a B.S. degree in home economics from New Mexico State University in 1927. As an agent for the Agricultural Extension Service for more than 30 years, she assisted women with home management skills in rural New Mexican communities. She also supported Tarascan Indians with home maintenance as a representative of the United Nations in Mexico in the 1950s. Although Cabeza de Baca was an Americanization agent, who stressed mainstream U.S. standards, she also believed it was important to incorporate the values of the communities she worked with. Her concern with preserving native culture is reflected in several of her texts that affirm Mexican-American culture. These publications include "Los alimentos y su preparación" (1934; Food and its preparation), "New Mexican Diets" (1942), *Historic Cookery* (1942), *The Good Life* (1949), *We Fed Them Cactus* (1954), and several articles for the *Santa Fe Scene* and the *New Mexican*.

Cabeza de Baca, similar to other New Mexican women writers of this period, such as CLEOFAS MARTINEZ JARAMILLO and Nina Otero-Warren, preserved Hispanic culture by collecting stories, poems, and recipes. It is remarkable that Cabeza de Baca and these other Hispanic women wrote given the tremendous power of Anglo-American culture, language, and patriarchy (a system based on the governance of men) under which they lived. Since very few Hispanic women were writing and publishing during this time, Cabeza de Baca's con-

tributions to Hispanic and American literature are significant; she asserts the importance of Mexican-American cultural traditions, specifically those of women, to both Hispanic and American history.

Cabeza de Baca's most widely known text is *We Fed Them Cactus*. It records the lives of Hispanic pioneers who established ranches and communities on the Llano Estacado in the 1830s and their gradual loss of this land up through the 1940s due to the Treaty of GUADALUPE HIDALGO (1848). The cactus of the title refers to the drought of 1918 that led Hispanic farmers to feed cactus to their cattle for survival. The title also references how the people in Cabeza de Baca's community, similar to the cactus that preserves water and protects itself with thorns, were able to withstand both natural and social misfortunes.

Cabeza de Baca uses the collective voices of her community to narrate her text. She underscores how these stories are not simply her own but part of a complex history of New Mexicans. For instance, she incorporates the tales of the following storytellers, who each represent different aspects of the Hispanic pioneer experience. These storytellers include family members, such as her grandmother and her father, as well as local personalities such as El Cuate, her family's cook; Doña Jesusita García de Chávez and Lola Otero de García, both CURANDERAS (healers); the bandit Black Jack Ketchem; and Don Miguel Benavides and Señor Antonio Trujillo, both taken captive by Indians as children. By narrating her life with these distinct characters, Cabeza de Baca highlights both the importance of the oral tradition and how her personal story is a collective one.

A central theme of the text is the importance of land in the lives of the early Hispanic pioneers. Descriptions of landscape parallel the gradual loss of Hispanic land to Anglo settlers. In the beginning of the text the New Mexican landscape is described as rich, nourishing, and fruitful. By the end of the narrative it is depicted as a barren wasteland. Despite this loss, Cabeza de Baca points to the Spanish names that are still used to describe the area, thereby affirming the importance of Hispanic culture to the region. She observes: "The Hispano has almost vanished from the land and most of the chapels are nonexistent, but the names of the hills, rivers, arroyos, canyons and defunct plazas linger as monuments to a people who pioneered into the land of the buffalo and the Comanche" (66). Accordingly, Cabeza de Baca confounds the view that Hispanic culture is foreign or outside the nation, and in this way her narrative resists Anglo cultural domination.

The text also depicts the significant role of Hispanic women in the history and settlement of the land. Cabeza de Baca portrays the work women performed as *curanderas* or *médicas*. By writing down the oral traditions of the *curandera*, which she also details in *The Good Life* and *Historic Cookery*, Cabeza de Baca preserves traditional Hispanic healing practices carried on by women. The *curandera's* methods of healing are distinct from mainstream medical practices; thus, Cabeza de Baca represents Mexican-American women as figures of resistance to U.S. cultural domination. She also portrays the important role of the wives of the *patrones* (ranch owners) in the villages and ranches of the Llano. Although subservient to the patron who ruled the ranch, these women ruled the spiritual and physical life of his employees and their families. By detailing women's lives, Cabeza de Baca depicts a female perspective of Hispanic history and culture. By doing so, she places herself within the conventions of BORDER LITERATURE, as well as a feminist tradition of CHICANO LITERATURE.

Bibliography

Cabeza de Baca, Fabiola. *The Good Life: New Mexico Traditions and Food*. Santa Fe, N.Mex.: Museum of New Mexico Press, 2005.

———. *Historic Cookery*. Santa Fe, N.Mex.: Ancient City Press, 1997.

———. *We Fed Them Cactus*. Albuquerque: University of New Mexico Press, 1994.

Rebolledo, Tey Diana. "Tradition and Mythology: Signatures of Landscape in Chicana Literature." *The Desert Is No Lady: Southwestern Landscapes in Women's Writing and Art*, edited by Vera Norwood and Janice Monk, 96–124. New Haven, Conn.: Yale University Press, 1987.

———. *Women Singing in the Snow: A Cultural Analysis of Chicana Literature*. Tucson: University of Arizona Press, 1995.

Rebolledo, Tey Diana, and Eliana S. Rivero, eds. *Infinite Divisions: An Anthology of Chicana Literature*. Tucson: University of Arizona Press, 1993.

Marci R. McMahon

When I Was Puerto Rican Esmeralda Santiago (1993)

ESMERALDA SANTIAGO's first memoir, *When I Was Puerto Rican*, is an autobiographical novel concerned with themes of loss, alienation, and migration. Santiago's work can be read both alongside the coming-of-age narratives of JUDITH ORTIZ COFER as well as the gritty poetry of MIGUEL PIÑERO. Like other contributors to PUERTO RICAN LITERATURE, Santiago tackles the issue of hybridity (the cultural and geographic complexity of being Latina and, more specifically, Puerto Rican) and writes with an awareness of both island and mainland Puerto Rican communities. The overall effect of *When I Was Puerto Rican* is not integration; rather, her memoir delivers the sometimes unsettling bildungsroman (coming-of-age story) of Esmeralda Santiago. The question that the title poses—when was Santiago Puerto Rican?—is not answered by asserting Puerto Rican identity on the mainland (and specifically New York) but is instead the formulation of a personal and painful journey of growth and displacement.

The text, which begins when Santiago's childhood protagonist, Negi, is around four year old, chronicles Santiago's journey from rural Puerto Rico to the suburban slums of San Juan, to the urban jungle of Brooklyn and surprisingly ends in mid-story when Negi is 13. Though the text is sandwiched between a prologue and epilogue (which provide a glimpse into Santiago's adult life as a Harvard graduate living in New York City), the narrative strand of the abruptly concluded first memoir is not picked up until the second text, *ALMOST A WOMAN* (1998). The effect of the first text's abrupt conclusion is an impression that Santiago's life story is very akin to the classic

American "Ragged Dick" narrative, in this case the story of an extremely impoverished and disadvantaged Puerto Rican girl who comes to New York, works hard, and eventually achieves a great deal. The difference between Santiago's text and a more classical rags-to-riches narrative is the negotiation of ethnic identity that Santiago makes central to the text. Unlike other prominent Latina writers, Santiago's struggle does not end with an affirmation of hybrid identity; it is more appropriately a struggle with it.

Negi's struggle with hybridity drives the plot throughout the narrative—both on the island with its Americanization programs and in Brooklyn with its tough neighborhoods and immigrant communities. The family's moves to various locations on the island reveal their economic hardships as well as the tumultuous nature of the parents' relationship. Likewise, these moves bring to the reader's attention Negi's responsibilities as the eldest sibling and the dynamics of living in a commonwealth society—Puerto Rico is neither a nation nor a state. The move to Brooklyn acts as a devastating crack in Santiago's identity, the crack that leaves her a misplaced migrant. She learns to change her sense of self while learning a new set of urban rules and American expectations.

Once on the mainland Negi tries to understand a drastically different language, culture, and society. Her mishaps in Brooklyn, which make up only the last few chapters of the book, read much like other migrant narratives. Her family struggles with poverty, fear, urban alienation, alcoholism, sexual predators, violence, and death, all the while firmly believing that life will eventually become better in the United States. Amid all this Negi becomes the intermediary between U.S. society and her family as she is the first to learn English (a task that requires translating for her mother at the welfare office and at school), the first to attend school, and the first to become "incorporated" into Brooklyn culture. This incorporation, however, is not seamless, as Negi must also learn her place in the hierarchy of race, class, generation, and gender that dominates the urban environment. Not surprisingly, Negi determines that one day she will escape

from the violence, poverty, and alienation that characterize her life in Brooklyn and earns admission into Manhattan's prestigious Performing Arts High School.

Negi's achievements reflect the singularity of Santiago's text. *When I Was Puerto Rican* is the complicated story of a Puerto Rican teenager. This first memoir is a classic bildungsroman marked by the rugged individualism and hard work that defined U.S. national character a century earlier; at the same time readers cannot ignore the colonial history that gave rise to the narrative. For its themes and setting Santiago's work can be read within the context of Puerto Rican litèrautre.

Bibliography

González, Lisa Sánchez. *Boricua Literature: A Literary History of the Puerto Rican Diaspora.* New York: New York University Press, 2001.

Rivera, Carmen S. *Kissing the Mango Tree: Puerto Rican Women Rewriting American Literature.* Houston, Tex.: Arté Público Press, 2002.

Santiago, Esmeralda. *Almost a Woman.* New York: Vintage Books, 1998.

———. *When I Was Puerto Rican.* New York: Vintage–Random House, 1993.

Thomas, Piri. *Down These Mean Streets.* New York: Vintage, 1997.

Lorna Pérez

Where Horizons Go Rhina Espaillat (1998)

Dominican-American writer RHINA ESPAILLAT was awarded the T. S. Eliot Prize for Poetry for her 1998 collection, *Where Horizons Go.* In this collection, which follows her first book, LAPSING TO GRACE (1992), Espaillat addresses such subjects as love, loss, family, discovery, memory, and living in a bilingual culture. She continues a thematic thread begun in her first collection as a number of the poems included in *Where Horizons Go* illustrate many of the realities of exile and migration, revealing the liminal quality of this poet who stands on the threshold of two places, two temporal spaces, and two languages. Throughout her verses Espaillat articulates the negotiation of a hyphenated ethnic identity while affirming cultural hybridity as a natural and enriching human process.

Espaillat's work reinforces a multicultural view of the world, and her poetic vision is one of inclusion rather than exclusion, of unity rather than division. Poems such as "Para mi tataranieto el astropionero," for which she provides her own translation—"For My Great-Great-Grandson the Space Pioneer"—remind her descendant (and other immigrants) to preserve the link with ancestral roots while living in a new land. Its concluding lines, "in this little case of bones / I've left you the perfume of the seas" (11–12), suggest the smells and sounds of the Caribbean Sea—integral parts of the poet and her memories. The poem's speaker treasures the sights, the scents, and the rhythms of the island and values the connection with the ancestral landscape and all that it represents. Espaillat understands that the act of recollection is a part of forming a self-identity. Our memories make us who we are, reminding us of our history and heritage. The poem "Rainy Sunday" uses memory to transport the audience and speaker to the past and, in the process, to ask for acceptance of the present. In this poem the speaker is transported to when she "was a child caught in the long ago / And pinioned to the wake of alien stars" (11–12). Through her memories—imbedded with images, sounds, smells, and sensations—she feels that "the dead were with [her]" (13) and in this way maintains a tangible bond with her ethnic core. However, the speaker also points out that she cannot stay exclusively in the past because she hears "the present sing its song" (15). Since Espaillat inhabits two cultures, she explores bicultural memories, the past and the present, fusing them to shape the whole.

This effort of fusing past and present, the traditions of two different cultures, causes many immigrants to experience ambivalence concerning their simultaneous commitment to the United States and their island homeland. The poem "Bra" explores the dual allegiances experienced by many U.S. Latinos, who feel torn between their loyalty for their respective country of origin (and/or for Latin America as whole) and their pledge to U.S.

society, since they live, love, and work in this land. They may demonstrate overt social and political loyalties to the United States, yet part of them remains keenly aware of the cultural, racial, and linguistic ties that bind them to the Latino world. "Bra" proposes that one culture cannot be chosen over the other, as bicultural individuals inhabit two worlds simultaneously:

> If only the heart could be worn like the
> breast, divided,
> nosing in two directions for news of the
> wide world,
> sniffing here and there for justice, for mercy.
> How burdened every choice is with politics,
> guilt,
> expensive with duty, heavy as breasts in
> need of
> this perfect fit whose label says Honduras
> (13–18).

Here Espaillat reveals her awareness of globalization—the manufacturing of lingerie in Latin American countries such as Honduras—while contemplating the tension on a more intimate level between unity and division in the human spirit.

Another poem that expresses Espaillat's sense of dual cultural allegiances is titled "Bilingual/ Bilingüe." It is written in English and Spanish, using a linguistic device called CODE SWITCHING. The poet shifts back and forth between languages to re-create the experience of bilingualism and, by extension, biculturalism. This poem illustrates the differing individual approaches to acculturation, emphasizing generational distinctions. In an essay of the same title, "Bilingual/Bilingüe," published as the afterword of *Where Horizons Go*, Espaillat expands on reasons for these generational differences. She explains, the Espaillat family went into political exile, and her father "lived in the hope of return," believing that the "new home, the new speech, were temporary" (67). In the first lines of the poem the speaker states her father's theory on bilingualism: "My father liked them separate, one there / one here (allá y aquí)" (1–2). He believed that "if it could be said at all, it could be said best in the language of those authors whose words were the core of his education" (67), as elaborated in her afterword. The father's attitude about language echoes research stating, "while there exists a number of markers of identity, such as social group, geography, cultural traditions, and race, for many Dominicans, language is the most significant criterion of self-identification" (Toribio 1,135).

The poem "Bilingual/Bilingüe" suggests that the father needed a separation between English and Spanish out of the fear that dual linguistic and cultural allegiances force her to choose English and, by implication, U.S. culture over her original Spanish language and Dominican cultural identity. Like many Latino authors, Espaillat reflects on her father's desire to maintain a Spanish-speaking identity. Linguists report that Dominicans "remain fiercely loyal to their native dialect, which serves as an immutable marker of Dominican identity" (Toribio 1,135). The speaker's father does not want English to define his daughter's identity, both culturally and linguistically. It is aptly ironic that the father considers English and U.S. customs the "alien part," yet, legally, he and his family were designated as "alien" political exiles by the U.S. government, and by most in the mainstream society.

For the father, his Spanish "name" represents more than a given name at birth or the surname of his father; it is the collection of customs, beliefs, and memories that make him who he is—both his personal and ethnic identities—and which he wants his own offspring to retain and pass on to future generations. The father experiences a sense of betrayal, exemplified by his daughter's process of learning another language and acculturating to a new set of cultural norms. In an effort to hold onto his own cultural identity the father commands: "English outside this door, Spanish inside" (7). This paternally imposed linguistic split causes the poem's speaker to experience discomfort and perhaps guilt of adapting to a new land and language. These conflicting emotions are illustrated by the poignant question: "But who can / divide the world, the word (mundo y palabra) from / any child?" (8–10).

Espaillat recollects the difficulties of this time with a father who demanded the exclusive use of Spanish in the home: "His insistence on pure Spanish made it difficult, sometimes impossible, to bring home and share the jokes of friends, puns, pop lyrics, and other staples of seven-year-old conversation. Table talk sometimes ended with tears or sullen silence" (67). For Espaillat's treatment of issues of language and identity, this poem and others by her are characteristic of DOMINICAN-AMERICAN LITERATURE.

Ultimately, and regardless of the frictions at home, the poem declares the speaker's resolve to learn English: a determination to acculturate. Yet, this crossing of boundaries does not come without emotional and psychological penalties, which Espaillat mentions in her epilogue:

> *Memory, folklore, and food all become part of the receding landscape that language sets out to preserve. Guilt, too, adds to the mix, the suspicion that to love the second language too much is to betray those ancestors who spoke the first and could not communicate with us in the vocabulary of our education, our new thoughts . . . a sense of grievance and loss may spur hostility toward the new language and those who speak it, as if the common speech of the perceived majority could weld together a disparate population into a huge, monolithic, and threatening Other. That Other is then assigned traits and habits that preclude sympathy and mold "Us" into a unity whose cohesiveness gives comfort (68).*

This alienation does not however have to be the final reality for the bilingual-bicultural individual. The poem's speaker makes a stand against the monolingual (and implied unicultural) paternal dictums. She decides to embrace two languages and two cultures and finds that "still the heart was one" (14). Here is the poet's central belief concerning the human capacity to exhibit multiple linguistic abilities, and the potential of maintaining multiple cultural allegiances, and still remain a whole, unified individual with broader perspectives and understandings of the human condition.

Although Espaillat addresses some of the difficulties encountered by many U.S. immigrants in acculturation, her work emphasizes the need to avoid both personal and collective perceptions that may lead toward belief systems that exclude others based on their ethnicity, race, country of origin, and/or language. She concentrates on group similarities rather than the differences, advocating a worldview of cultural inclusion, and warns against the tendency toward ethnocentrism. After all, during different times and places throughout history people from diverse backgrounds have experienced analogous processes of migration, cultural adaptation, and internal and/or external alienation from their host societies. Espaillat's poems advocate an appreciation of both the ethnic resemblances, as well as the distinctions, because the conscious incorporation of diverse cultural characteristics is ultimately beneficial to the individual and to society as a whole.

Bibliography

Espaillat, Rhina P. *Where Horizons Go.* Kirksville, Mo.: New Odyssey Press, 1998.

Toribio, Almeida Jacqueline. "Language Variation and the Linguistic Enactment of Identity among Dominicans." *Linguistics* 38, no. 5 (2000): 1,133–1,159.

Alba Cruz-Hacker

Whispering to Fool the Wind: Poems
Alberto Alvaro Ríos (1982)

Whispering to Fool the Wind: Poems, by Mexican-American writer ALBERTO ALVARO RÍOS, won the 1982 Walt Whitman Award. As with Ríos's collection *The SMALLEST MUSCLE IN THE HUMAN BODY* (2002), *Whispering to Fool the Wind* draws on the conventions of MAGICAL REALISM to contribute to the canon of BORDER LITERATURE. In these poems Ríos, who was born and raised in Nogales, Arizona, delves into the emotions, geography, and psychology of the border region.

In this, his first, book of poetry Ríos introduces many of the themes that he will continue to explore in subsequent volumes. The collection offers a sharp insight into the complexities and possibilities of language. Exploring personalities, terrain, and emotions, the book offers a distinct impression of life in a border town. Informed by multiple cultures, languages, and places, the poems blur the distinctions between reality and dreams and between imagination and materiality. Family, and the joys and strains associated with it, also feature prominently in this collection.

In the widely anthologized sestina "Nani," a child speaker expresses the wonders of his grandmother's kitchen. While the grandmother and the child are separated by language, as the grandmother speaks the "now-foreign words" the child "used to speak" (17), they are closely connected by the ties of family and by the food that the grandmother serves. The child sees himself and his family in the wrinkles on his grandmother's skin and sees her love for him in the food she serves. By the end of the poem language becomes secondary as the child declares, "Even before I speak, she serves" (39). Their language differences threaten to divide them, but their family ties and love keep them closely connected.

In another widely anthologized poem, "Madre Sofía," Ríos explores the many ways that "wisdom" manifests in the world. The speaker recalls a visit to a fortune-teller because his mother "couldn't / wait the second ten years to know" (1–2). Again, in the context of the poem, language becomes a secondary mode of communication. As the speaker asserts, "She did not speak, and as a child / I could only answer, so that together / we were silent" (18–20). Rather than communicating directly, the speaker relies on his sensory observations, and the poem ends with Madre Sofía's declaration of the speaker's fortune: "The future will make you tall" (62). The wisdom of Madre Sofía, a wisdom of magic and dream, exemplifies the reality presented in the book.

The poems express compassionately the stories of those who are misshapen and outcast, such as "The Man Who Became Old." This man "grew a new tooth" (1) every year and became too wolflike for his friends, who turned away from him and forgot him. The amazing resilience and active creativity of the world emerges in poems such as "At Kino Viejo, Mexico," where "the potatoes of the corner store sing" (1). The boundaries between reality and dream blur in poems such as "The Man Who Has Waited, Not Out of Patience," where "The eagles came / from out of the night / pulling me from my room / with their beaks" (1–4). Again and again we see the people of a town who give it its character such as "Palomino" with his "thousand filthy hats" (7) and Graciela, from the poem "True Story of the Pins," who is a seamstress and "has pins it is rumored / even in hard times" (9–10). Death, too, inhabits these poems. In "Mi Abuelo" a dead grandfather speaks to his grandson from "out of the ground" (16) about the hills as *"slowest waves"* (34), and in the poem "Some Years" the speaker asserts, "Some years, people just die / and everybody says isn't it strange" (1–2). Moving through the wonder of childhood, the awkwardness of adolescence, and the grief and somberness of old age, these poems span the lifetimes lived by the people who dwell in and make up the border that serves as home for them.

Bibliography

Ríos, Alberto. *Five Indiscretions.* New York: Sheep Meadow Press, 1985.

———. *The Lime Orchard Woman.* New York: Sheep Meadow Press, 1988.

———. *The Smallest Muscle in the Human Body.* Port Townsend, Wash.: Copper Canyon Press, 2002.

———. *Teodoro Luna's Two Kisses.* New York: W. W. Norton, 1990.

———. *Whispering to Fool the Wind.* New York: Sheep Meadow Press, 1982.

Thielen, Greg. "The Language of Listening." *University Planet* 1, no. 6 (1993): 19.

Wild, Peter. *Alberto Ríos.* Boise, Idaho: Boise State University Press, 1998.

Wooten, Leslie. "At the Kitchen Table: A Conversation with Alberto Ríos." *Bloomsbury Review* 23, no. 4 (2003): 5.

Irene Praitis

With His Pistol in His Hand: A Border Ballad and Its Hero Américo Paredes (1958)

With His Pistol in His Hand: A Border Ballad and Its Hero is based on AMÉRICO PAREDES's dissertation in cultural anthropology. Paredes was one of the first Mexican Americans to receive a Ph.D. from the University of Texas. *With His Pistol in His Hand* established Paredes's reputation as one of the founders of CHICANO LITERATURE. This study of a popular folk song of the south Texan border region, "El corrido de Gregorio Cortez," has been acknowledged as one of the most influential contributions to the emergence of Mexican-American studies and is a foundational text in BORDER LITERATURE. Published in 1958, prior to the beginning of the Chicano movement, *With His Pistol in His Hand* takes up many of the topics that the following generation of Chicano writers would deal with in fiction, drama, and poetry.

"The Ballad of Gregorio Cortez" was popular in southern Texas and northern Mexico in the first part of the 20th century. It was sung in Spanish in the local communities, accompanied on guitar. The ballad's history represents, within a broader context, songs and poems of the borderlands and especially the Rio Grande valley. The ballad refers to and grew out of an incident of the year 1901. In search of a horse thief Sheriff Morris and two deputies came to the small farm that Cortez had rented in Karnes County, Texas. As the sheriff did not speak any Spanish, one of his deputies translated Cortez's and his brother's words; however, the deputy's Spanish was deficient. As he did not know the Spanish word for "mare," a misunderstanding ended in the lawmen shooting at Cortez. Cortez shot the sheriff in self-defense.

Knowing that he could not expect a just trial, Cortez fled. A few hundred men, including sheriffs and Texas Rangers, chased Cortez through the border region. Believing that Cortez was the head of a gang, more and more men joined in the chase. Local and national newspapers and magazines covered the event, which was perceived as a conflict between European Americans and Mexican

Americans. Cortez was not captured until he was betrayed by a Mexican American. The chase lasted for 10 days, during which Cortez walked more than 100 miles and rode more than 400 miles on horses. During his flight Cortez was repeatedly assisted by the local Mexican-American population. The original *corrido* was composed by folk poets soon after Cortez's capture on June 22, 1901. The legend of the chase and his capture spread rapidly in Texas and northern Mexico, and Cortez became a Mexican-American folk hero.

With His Pistol in His Hand consists of two parts. The first part, entitled "Gregorio Cortez, the Legend and the Life," provides a historical background for the analysis of different versions of the ballad that we find in the second part, entitled "*El corrido de Gregorio Cortez,* a Ballad of Border Conflict." In the first part Paredes also reads different legends of the life of Gregorio Cortez in the context of the history of southern Texas. Paredes examined court records, conducted interviews with Cortez's relatives, and carried out historical research for his in-depth study. He used this material to write a biography of the hero of the ballad and to write a book about the culture of the Rio Grande valley.

Although Paredes traces the *corrido* back to Spanish poetry of the colonial period, he emphasizes that the specific "border *corrido*" is a product of the conflicts between Anglo-American and Mexican-American populations in Texas after the U.S.-Mexican War (1846–48). Paredes argues that the ballads, as oral literature, were a way of forming a collective identity and of criticizing the social conditions in the border region. The lyrics of the ballads, argues Paredes, almost always repeat the same pattern: A Mexican-American hero fights representatives of Anglo-American social and cultural dominance, as, for example, the Texas Rangers. The Mexican American is framed as the heroic figure that has to surrender to the cowardly white authorities only because they are more numerous. His analysis of "The Ballad of Gregorio Cortez" makes Paredes read the entire tradition of the border *corrido* as a form of ethnic empowerment. They provided, argues Paredes, a

subtle symbolic expression of resistance against racism, exclusion, and discrimination in a time when anti-Mexican sentiments and segregation were still powerful in Texas. However, Paredes makes strong that beginning in the late 1930s, with the commercial exploitation of the *corridos* in Mexican mass media, particularly the radio, the ballads lost their traditional function of social criticism (149).

With this study of the border *corrido* Paredes provided the first study of the Mexican-American oral traditions from an ethnic perspective. His analysis of ethnic conflict has strongly influenced other writers such as TOMÁS RIVERA. Rivera explains that *With His Pistol in His Hand,* "fascinated me because, one, it proved it was possible for a Chicano to publish; two, it was about a Chicano, Gregorio Cortez, *y sus azañas* [sic; and his deeds]. . . . That book indicated to me that it was possible to talk about a Chicano as a complete figure. . . . More importantly, *With His Pistol in His Hand* indicated to me a whole imaginative possibility for us to explore" (Bruce-Novoa 150).

Bibliography

Bruce-Novoa, Juan. *Chicano Authors: Inquiry by Interview.* Austin: University of Texas Press, 1980.

Limón, José E. *Dancing with the Devil: Society and Cultural Poetics in Mexican-American South Texas.* Madison: University of Wisconsin Press, 1994.

———. *Mexican Ballads, Chicano Poems: History and Influence in Mexican-American Social Poetry.* Berkeley: University of California Press, 1992.

Paredes, Américo. *Between Two Worlds.* Houston, Tex.: Arte Público Press, 1991.

———. *With His Pistol in His Hand: A Border Ballad and Its Hero.* Austin: University of Texas Press, 1958.

Markus Heide

Woman Hollering Creek and Other Stories
Sandra Cisneros (1991)

Woman Hollering Creek and Other Stories (1991) is a collection of 22 stories by SANDRA CISNEROS, an internationally acclaimed writer. Set in San Antonio, Texas, this collection combines stories of painful love, anguished hope, and the strength of Mexican-American girls and women. By CODE SWITCHING between Spanish and English, Cisneros allows us to get to know female characters living in the urban borderlands. This volume features raped and battered Mexican-American women who reflect, to some extent, the casualties of a patriarchal judicial system. Ultimately, though, Cisneros's characters are able to see the reality of their situation and eventually become empowered through their painful experiences.

Woman Hollering Creek and Other Stories is divided into three sections that explore childhood, adolescence, and adulthood of Mexican-American life. The first section has seven stories narrated by the voices of preadolescent girls. The first story, "My Lucy Friend Who Smells Like Corn," creates a sisterhood of little girls as a replacement for absent parents: a father who is never home and a mother who is always tired. The story "Eleven" is primarily concerned with self-discovery. Featuring the 11-year-old protagonist, Rachel. On her birthday, she cries like a little girl would but prevails in her disappointment to discover a complex sense of self "like an onion or like the rings inside a tree trunk or like my little wooden dolls that fit inside the other" (6). In "Salvador Late or Early" we meet a child devoid of childhood as the result of an absent father and a busy mother. Meanwhile, in the stories "Mexican Movies," "Barbie-Q," "Mericans," and "Tepeya" Cisneros exposes the cultural artifice that perpetuates racial and gender stereotypes. ""Mexican Movies," for example, suggests that popular Mexican romance films draw a curtain of false happiness over a harsh reality in the relations between men and women. In many ways this first section of *Woman Hollering Creek* coincides with Cisneros's critically acclaimed book, *The HOUSE ON MANGO STREET* (1984). The stories in *Women Hollering Creek* reveal the collision of childhood innocence with a sometimes predatory adult world.

The second section contains only two stories, both of which are portrayed through the perspective of vulnerable teenage girls. In "One Holy Night" the teenage Ixchel is seduced, impregnated, and abandoned by her vagrant lover, Boy Baby. After Ixchel's deflowering we learn of other teenage girls who are taken in by the possibility of mothering a descendant of Mayan kings. The story takes a sinister twist when the reader discovers that, over the course of seven years, Boy Baby has killed 11 girls. Cisneros shows that society fails to protect these girls who, like Ixchel, become "a part of history" as they follow the unfortunate path of their adolescent counterparts, mothers, and grandmothers (30). In "My Tocaya" we encounter more violence; in this story Cisneros focuses on a female body left in a drainage ditch. This is, unfortunately, a common image in newspapers published along the border. The corpse is identified as the narrator's runaway friend, Patricia, until she rises "from the dead three days later" (40). In this section Cisneros juxtaposes the body of the Mexican-American runaway with the anonymity of female bodies left to rot along the border. But the idea that Patricia rises again perhaps offers a sense of hope; at the least this plot turn reveals Cisneros's use of MAGICAL REALISM, where the supernatural world and the material world overlap with each other.

The last section consists of 13 stories that deal with mature women. While the central theme of the previous section is female victimization, this section considers female resistance to traditional gender roles and male violence. The title story of the collection, "Woman Hollering Creek," which is a literal translation of Arroyo La Gritona, features the newlywed Cleófilas, the strong and helpful Felice, and the widowed Dolores. The young Cleófilas is a modern version of La LLORONA, the Weeping Woman of Aztec folklore. By crossing borders to live with her abusive husband, Juan Pedrito, Cleófilas is trapped between a real-life soap opera, which terrifies her, and a romantic *telenovela* soap opera, which idealizes feminine suffering. Cleófilas eventually escapes the oppressive house with Felice's help, an optimistic transformation from a stereotypical female victim, the beaten wife, to a woman of survival and strong mother. In the end, unlike La Llorona, who loses her children, Cleófilas keeps her children, laughing "a long ribbon of laughter like water" (56).

One of Cisneros's powerful female characters is Clemencia, the female sexual conqueror in "Never Marry a Mexican." Clemencia defines her living as simply, "a form of prostitution" (71). Unlike Cleófilas, who believes in romantic marriage, Clemencia is realistically aware that she is too romantic to marry. Having sexual relationships with her lover and his son, Clemencia seems to resist a culturally defined gender role. At the same time, however, she is trapped within feelings of guilt and isolation because she acts in favor of masculinity.

In this collection Cisneros also offers fascinating portraits of Tristán, a transvestite dancer, in "Remember the Alamo"; Inés, a witch woman, in "Eyes of Zapata"; and Lupe, a talented artist, in "*Bien* Pretty." Cisneros finishes her poetic stories by encouraging the wounded women to do something about their broken or limited lives "with no thought of the future or past. Today. Hurray. Hurray!" (165). On the whole, and without idealizing her heroines, Cisneros offers a compelling portrait of women who live in the dynamic space between Mexico and the United States. As a poet and short story writer she has made a critical contribution to CHICANO LITERATURE.

Bibliography

Cisneros, Sandra. *Woman Hollering Creek and Other Stories*. New York: Random, 1991.

Mullen, Harryette. "'A Silence Between Us Like a Language': The Untranslatability of Experience in Sandra Cisneros's *Woman Hollering Creek*." *MELUS* 21 (1996): 3–20.

Thomson, Jeff. "What Is Called Heaven: Identity in Sandra Cisnero's *Woman Hollering Creek*." *Studies in Short Fiction* 31 (1994): 415–424.

Heejung Cha

Year of Our Revolution, The Judith Ortiz Cofer (1998)

Like her earlier collection *The LATIN DELI* (1993), JUDITH ORTIZ COFER's *The Year of Our Revolution* is a compilation of poems and narratives. *The Year of Our Revolution* is a book that defies easy categorization, just as its speakers and characters resist stereotyping. In it the author has artfully arranged seven poems and nine stories, some of which had already been published. The mixing of genres captures the lives of Puerto Rican immigrants in the United States. One of the book's young protagonists, an aspiring poet, seems to speak for Cofer's vision of form and content when she observes, "My own pupa-stage poems were seeking out the concrete image that would years later give shape, form and meaning to my fragmented world" (83). With the phrase, "a fragmented world," Cofer brings to life the struggle between generations of children, parents, and grandparents as well as the changes that come about from migration, resistance to custom, and adaptation to a new land and language. *The Year of Our Revolution* depicts a younger generation of Puerto Ricans for whom all these inherited familiarities of life, including the use of Spanish, are dissolving and being replaced by a new set of exciting sensations. One teenage narrator, Elenita, describes the phenomenon and its causes this way:

I could never ask any of my friends over to our apartment. They would have suffered culture shock. So I divided myself into two people—actually three. . . . It was not always easy to shuffle out of my visionary self and into the binding coat of propriety the Puerto Rican girl was supposed to wear (44).

While Elenita's confession indicates domestic tensions, it also introduces, with "the binding coat of propriety," the parental weapon of choice against fragmentation: restraint. The imagery of being bound and restricted appears prominently too in the poem "They Say," an account of the speaker's difficult birth, though, as the reader quickly notices, the delivery is unremarkable. The complication arises after the speaker "slips" into the attending hands and is attended by prayers, hinting at the restraints of a home-grown Catholicism that begins at birth.

The book's final selections, two lyric poems, turn with a degree of resolution to the battle between generations and the burdens of memory. We can read "So Much for Mañana" as an intergenerational exchange of letters in which the matriarchal figure "Mamacita" has returned to Puerto Rico. Her daughter, however, has no sure intention of returning to her island homeland: "I write back: 'Someday I will go back / to your Island and get fat, / but not now, Mama, maybe mañana.'" The "your Island" indicates who comfortably possesses the island homeland and who has made another land her home.

The last lyric, "El Olvido," declares at its beginning that "It is a dangerous thing / to forget the climate of / your birthplace" (97). Readers will find in this piece a catalog of cultural artifacts and perspectives, including the voices of dead relatives, traditional clothes, and plaster saints. Ultimately then, while "So Much for Mañana" teases the reader to reconcile the demands of tradition and assimilation, as between mother and daughter, this last poem presents the perils of isolation in an adopted homeland. In such a "forgetting place," the danger is both forgetting and being forgotten, and the reversion to prayer and the mother tongue at the poem's end marks the anxious glance of the migrant.

Overall *The Year of Our Revolution,* with its explicit plural pronoun, unveils the consequence inherent in migration from the island to the mainland. One generation's desire for a better life inevitably exposes the next generation to the likely death of Puerto Rican customs, the formality of the Spanish language (with its *tú* and *usted*), and the familiarity with life in the Tropics. Thus, Cofer points out how in migration and adaptation we find the end of the very idea of what *home* means. For her characters and themes in this work and elsewhere Cofer's work can be read within the context of PUERTO RICAN LITERATURE.

Bibliography
Acosta-Belén, Edna. "A *MELUS* Interview: Judith Ortiz Cofer." *MELUS* 18, no. 3 (1993): 83–97.

Cofer, Judith Ortiz. *Reaching for the Mainland and Selected New Poems.* Phoenix, Ariz.: Bilingual Press, 1995.

———. *Woman in Front of the Sun: On Becoming a Writer.* Athens: University of Georgia Press, 2000.

———. *The Year of Our Revolution.* Houston, Tex.: Arte Público Press, 1998.

McConnell, Thomas. "Assimilation and Fragmentation in Judith Ortiz Cofer's *Latin Deli* and *Year of Our Revolution.*" *Atenea* 23, nos. 1–2 (2002): 57–63.

Thomas McConnell

. . . Y no se lo tragó la tierra
See *THIS MIGRANT EARTH.*

¡Yo! Julia Alvarez (1996)

JULIA ALVAREZ is a Dominican-American writer who was born in New York but raised in the Dominican Republic until the age of 10. Both *¡Yo!* and its prequel, *HOW THE GARCÍA GIRLS LOST THEIR ACCENTS* (1991) are fictional autobiographies that draw on the author's own experiences of translocation. In *¡Yo!* Alvarez depicts the lives of the García sisters and their adjustment to life in New York. The protagonist, Yolanda (Yo) García, moves to Queens at 10 years of age after the family flees the Dominican Republic under Rafael Trujillo's violent regime (1930–61). Yo's displacement and immersion in a new language lead to a sense of dislocation that lands her in psychotherapy. Though she is only a little girl when Trujillo is in power, she is haunted by life under his regime; as an adult, she has problems with sexuality and intimacy and with her own role as a childless writer in a patriarchal Catholic culture. She feels compelled to return to her island homeland in order to face the past; but when she returns to visit her aunts and cousins, it becomes clear to the reader that she is neither wholly Dominican nor American. Whereas *How the García Girls Lost Their Accents* leaves us with Yolanda's decision to move back to the island, *¡Yo!* suggests that the attempt to go back "home" has failed, and in this regard Alvarez highlights the difficulty of determining where home is.

Alvarez's mode of representation embodies a migrant aesthetic insofar as it challenges the opposition between the modern and the traditional, the country of destination and the country of origin. Yolanda's relation to both the Dominican Republic (her "homeland") and the host country (the States) is characterized by ambivalence. She belongs neither here nor there. She is perceived as "Americanized" by her island relatives and as "a Latin lady" by her American boyfriend. Despite her repeated efforts at belonging she never manages to feel rooted in any culture. She is alienated from the island she left behind as evidenced by her vain attempts at retracing her lost roots. And although she now lives in the States, the legacy of her island's culture prevents her from ever quite feeling at home away from the Dominican Republic.

Throughout the narrative the concept of home is rendered as a space that is dynamic and vital; that is, through Yolanda's move from the Dominican Republic to New York and from New York to regions all over the United States, Alvarez reconceptualizes the conventional notion of "home" as a stable and secure place. Instead, home is a site of constant renegotiation of the migrant's identity. In this context the act of returning to the Caribbean reveals a time and place in Yo's life that cannot be reclaimed but can only be envisioned through memory. At the same time the United States fails to function as a new "home" because of the cultural baggage Yo brings with her. Thus, the idea of "home" as belonging and community is exposed as a myth. If the Dominican Republic continues to be referred to as "home" in the novel, it is only with the understanding that the reader's conventional idea of home needs to be revised to emphasize ambivalence.

Significantly, the novel also thwarts any attempt to read Yo's arrival in the States as a narrative of progress from oppression to freedom. Such reading is often enhanced by our knowledge of the sexual oppressiveness and the volatile political situation that migrants often leave behind in their home country. In *¡Yo!* the temptation to associate the Caribbean with repressive sexual mores and the United States with liberation is checked through the ways in which the various sections comment on one another once they are considered in juxtaposition. In part 1 a Dominican peasant woman who is accustomed to following patriarchal authority justifies her daughter's victimization. This scenario corresponds with a Vermont landlady's resignation to domestic violence in part 2. Conversely, the liberated sexual behavior of U.S. women is exposed as a fear of intimacy, merely another form of enslavement rather than as a genuine sign of freedom. Similarly, Yolanda's interventions as a feminist crusader in lower-class Dominican women's lives ultimately reveal her blindness to the gender dynamics that underlie her own identity crisis rather than her insight about their situations.

In *¡Yo!* we are far from the model of identity offered by autobiographical novels in which the protagonist's sense of self takes center stage. The title *¡Yo!* refers to both the name of the central character and the pronoun "I" in Spanish, but we learn about Yo mostly through other perspectives, a remarkable decision on the author's part because the novel is centered around the protagonist's struggle to "find her voice." Our only access to Yo's voice is in fact through the narratives of relatives, friends, servants, and even enemies (for example, her stalker) who relate their conflicting impressions and give us insight into her character, either directly focalized through their individual consciousness or indirectly through the third-person narration of the implied author. In circling a central character we never hear from directly the novel offers a portrait of the self as constructed within a countless number of interlocking identities. It challenges the possibility of any totalizing picture, as the self is situated in relation to the viewpoints and memories of others. Identity is thus reconfigured as a collective process that occurs through others rather than in opposition to them. For its themes and characters Alvarez's novel can be read within the context of DOMINICAN-AMERICAN LITERATURE.

Bibliography

Alvarez, Julia. *How the García Girls Lost Their Accents.* Chapel Hill, N.C.: Algonquin Books, 1991.

———. *¡Yo!* Chapel Hill, N.C.: Algonquin Books, 1996.

Henao, Eda B. *The Colonial Subject's Search for Nation, Culture, and Identity in the Works of Julia Alvarez, Rosario Ferré, and Ana Lydia Vega.* Lewiston, N.Y.: E. Mellen Press, 2003.

Johnson, Kelli Lyon. *Julia Alvarez: Writing a New Place on the Map.* Albuquerque: University of New Mexico Press, 2005.

Carine Mardorossian

Yo Soy Joaquín

See *I Am Joaquín*.

Yo-Yo Boing Giannina Braschi (1998)

In her novel *Yo-Yo Boing* Giannina Braschi (1953–) combines passages that are written in both Spanish and English. This use of CODE SWITCHING reveals the duality and contradiction of Puerto Rican identity, seen through a somewhat cynical lens. Optimistic and self-assuring, duality and pluralism reveal an intensity of thought and soul. Paradoxical coexistence between two apparently dissimilar elements is in evidence from the beginning of the novel. The protagonist is first introduced in the bathroom performing her toilet. By bringing the lens/text close to this performatory act, the author attempts to disclose what is hidden behind appearances, to bring out all the most essential and animalistic nature in all human beings. The paradoxical situation of the act of primping, which consists of exposing the ugly in order to attain the beautiful, is also evidenced in this moment where every trivial act is meaningful, where the simple fact of putting on some makeup becomes a sign of the artificial, the social representation of our selves.

The novel starts and finishes in a beautiful and rich Spanish prose that results in meticulous metaphorical work, but the central part is written in both English and Spanish combined in every kind of arrangement imaginable. Call it code switching or SPANGLISH, it is a reflection of the easy flowing language that Latinos speak in New York. This blend of English and Spanish is a current phenomenon evidenced by the increasing number of Latino authors that practice code switching in the States. The novelty is that these writers usually publish in small publishing houses due to the limited number of readers their use of a double language implies. In the case of *Yo-Yo Boing!* the nomination for the Pulitzer Prize entailed an unprecedented diffusion for a work of these characteristics. And yet, the author is convinced that her bicephalous language does not limit her audience but rather expands it.

Braschi draws the attention of the reader toward a complex and intercultural society where essentialist mythologies of origin are dissolved. This work becomes thus an example of the fusion of aesthetics inherited not only from Federico García Lorca, Pablo Neruda, and Jorge Luis Borges but also from James Joyce, Gertrude Stein, Luce Irigaray, and Hélène Cixous. In *Yo-Yo Boing!* the image of the yo-yo becomes a metaphor of the author's inner division resulting from moving between two languages. The title operates dynamically as a word play on the toy and also as the representation of the inherent duality of being a Latino in New York, moving between one language and another, one tradition and another, and belonging to both at the same time.

Hybridity in *Yo-Yo Boing!* is paradoxically a differential trait in a society that seeks to celebrate difference but that privileges sameness, hence the critique of multiculturalism that appears in the novel. The central part of the novel, "Blow-up," is a continuous exhibition of the dramatic possibilities and limits of a dialogue. Some critics have read it as a text about love in modern times. If the body was the protagonist of the first part of the novel, now the protagonist is the spoken word: the word in action, the word being performed. From food to movies, from academia to sex, everything that may be of current interest is discussed in this anti–comedy of manners.

In the last part of this nonconventional novel, "Black out," the language is Spanish again. If the beginning focused on the body and the central part on the social, this final part foregrounds what we could call the spiritual or the soul. The protagonist analyzes her feelings, her anguishes, exercising a total self-examination. Aware of her inner dissociation, Braschi tries to come to terms with her body and her spirit in an attempt to reconcile the two. Rejecting her physical limitations, she wants to go beyond her human being to attain a state of purity that is impossible in a material world. She also wants to overcome the limitations of language, writing the text in a quasi-continuous sentence, where the punctuation signs are not obstacles anymore: They do not establish relationships but have almost disappeared to let the author be alone with her thoughts.

The novel ends at the Statue of Liberty, with a dialogue between Zaratustra (Zoroaster), Hamlet, and Braschi. It is a dialogue between the past and the present, between philosophy, literature, and reality. Hamlet and Zaratustra have their own dead bodies to bury. Braschi is there to bury the 20th century. She believes that it is necessary to bury the past in order to be ready for the future. *Yo-Yo Boing!* marks Braschi's contribution to postmodern PUERTO RICAN LITERATURE.

Bibliography

Braschi, Giannina. *Yo-Yo Boing!* Pittsburg, Pa.: Latin American Literary Review Press, 1998.

Stavans, Ilan. *Spanglish, the Making of a New Language.* New York: Rayo, 2003.

Cristina Garrigós

Zamora, Bernice (1938–) (poet)

Bernice Zamora was born on January 20, 1938, in Aguilar, a small town in south central Colorado. For six generations her Mexican ancestors made their living as farmers and coal miners in Colorado. Zamora spent most of her formative years in Denver and Pueblo, and her schooling took place in parochial schools. She worked as a bank teller during the day and studied at night at Southern Colorado State University, where she received a B.A. in French and English in 1969 and an M.A. in English in 1972. Zamora completed her Ph.D. in English and American literatures at Stanford University, where she worked with Chicano writer Arturo Islas and wrote one of the first dissertations on Chicano poetry. From 1990 to 1996 Zamora was a professor of English at Santa Clara University. She currently lives in Colorado and teaches at Southern Colorado University.

Zamora is considered a pioneer in Chicano literature. In 1976 Zamora copublished *Restless Serpents* with Chicano artist José Antonio Burciaga. Her highly crafted poetry and her feminist themes gained the respect of Juan Bruce-Novoa and Marta Sánchez, who proclaimed her one of the most talented voices in Chicano poetry. In 1994 Zamora republished her poems from her first collection along with newer poems in a book entitled *Releasing Serpents*.

The main theme in Zamora's poetry is oppression, whether economic, sexual, or political. For instance, in "Gata Poem," one of her most anthologized poems, she destroys the myth of the Mexican-American male as a virile bronze god. The poem opens with the god calling the *gata* (female cat) from the summit. The summit symbolizes the high position and power that the Chicano exerts over his community and this woman. The *gata* falls under his spell and follows him. They make love, but he is unable to perform sexually. Once again the Chicano begs her to go with him, promising her a shining sun and trips around the seven worlds. The *gata* is not enticed by his offers. Once the prowess of the Chicano was brought into question, the *gata* is disillusioned and opts to walk away from him.

While Zamora writes about the liberation of women, she also speaks about the struggle for the equal rights of Mexican Americans in general. In "The Sovereign" she celebrates the commitment of Mexican-American labor rights leader Cesar Chavez. The poet compares Chavez to Atlas, the Greek god who carries the world on his shoulder. Unlike Atlas, Chavez's strength is not physical, but rather moral and spiritual. She portrays as a true steadfast hero.

Another important theme developed in Zamora's poetry is the act of writing as a female activity, evidenced in her title poem, "Restless Serpents." Here the poet represents cobras that have pricked their master's veins to gain his attention since he has neglected them. It is only when the master begins to play music for them that they are at rest. Toward the end of the poem the serpents have shed their skins and are resurrected. Subsequently they strike again their master, this time ending his life. The serpents symbolize life, death, rebirth, and creativity. Lyrics, in turn, are equated with poems. The noun "strokes" renders two appropriate readings: pen strokes (the act of writing) and physical strokes (the act of striking with a weapon).

Zamora offers her readers political themes and complex poetry. Influenced by the Beat poets of the 1960s and 1970s, who promoted a spiritual, civic, and sexual revolution, Zamora's work has received wide attention for its rich imagery and metaphors.

Bibliography

Bruce-Novoa, Juan. *Chicano Authors: Inquiry by Interview.* Austin: University of Texas Press, 1990.

Calendaria, Cordelia. *Chicano Poetry: A Response to Chaos.* Westport, Conn.: Greenwood, 1986.

Madsen, Deborah L. *Understanding Contemporary Chicana Literature.* Columbia: University of South Carolina Press, 2000.

Sánchez, Marta E. *Contemporary Chicana Poetry: A Critical Approach to an Emerging Literature.* Berkeley: University of California Press, 1985.

Zamora, Bernice. *Releasing Serpents.* Tempe, Ariz.: Bilingual Review Press, 1994.

Sonia Gonzalez

Zeno Gandía, Manuel (1855–1930) *(poet, novelist, doctor, political leader)*

Manuel Zeno Gandía helped to record the changes that Puerto Rico underwent as it transitioned from being a colony of Spain to a commonwealth of the United States. The island, which had been held by Spain for more than 400 years, became an American possession as a condition of the Treaty of Paris of 1898, ending the Spanish-American War. A well-respected doctor who proposed the establishment of an island-wide department of health, Zeno Gandía dedicated his life to protecting the island's political, literary, and cultural welfare, as well. He is a major figure in PUERTO RICAN LITEARATURE and SPANISH-AMERICAN CARIBBEAN LITERATURE.

Although he first became known as a poet, Zeno Gandía is best known now for Crónicas de un mundo enfermo (Chronicles of a sick world), a collection of four novels—*La Charca* (1894; *The Pond*), *La Garduña* (1896; The pickpocket), *El Negocio* (1916; The business), and *Redentores* (1925; Redeemers)—in which he details the island's economic and social struggles in the late 19th and early 20th centuries. A prolific writer in several genres, Zeno Gandía also wrote a book on the island's literary tradition, and in 1888, he published a history of famous Puerto Ricans and their significance in *Pero si no tenemos historia* (But if we don't have a history). Zeno Gandía also authored several Spanish-language grammar books and at the time of his death in 1930 was preparing a book on the language of the Tainos, the native peoples who inhabited the island at the time of Christopher Columbus's arrival.

The eldest son of a high-ranking military officer, the author was born into two of the island's prominent families, the Zenos and the Gandías. Zeno Gandía spent his adolescence in Spain, leaving with his family in 1866 at the age of 11 when his father received a commission. Like most of the sons from the island's well-connected class, Zeno Gandía was educated in Spain and France. During the final year of his medical studies he published a medical book entitled *Influencia del clima en las enfermedades del hombre* (The influence of climate on illness).

Some of Zeno Gandía's earliest works, those published while he was still living in Spain, include a comedic play entitled *Un matrimonio a oscuras o el Demonio son los celos* (1873; A marriage in the dark, or jealousy is the devil) and several poems. In 1874, shortly before his return to the island, two of Zeno Gandía's poems appeared in print in Puerto Rico, "El recuerdo de un ángel" (The memory of an angel) and "Comparaciones" (Comparisons). Once back on the island he established his medical practice, working to stem smallpox and yellow fever epidemics and continued writing poetry, receiving in 1880 an invitation to read at the Teatro La Perla, a renowned cultural center in Ponce. By the late 1880s Zeno Gandía was widely known for two poems, "Abismos" (Abysses) and "La señora duquesa" (The lady duchess), and two short novels, *Rosa de mármol* (Marble rose) and *Píccola.* Several literary critics have noted the influence of Zola and naturalism already evident in Zeno Gandía's early works.

The study of the "human beast," as Abril called it, becomes the focus of an ambitious collection of novels planned by Zeno Gandía at the same time he was publishing his poetry. The collection was to consist of 11 volumes, which together would be referred to as *Crónicas de un mundo enfermo.* Each novel in the proposed collection would be a record of a specific aspect of life in 19th-century Puerto Rico, a practice and philosophy of writing Zeno Gandía promoted all this life. In the end only four novels would come to make up this project: *La Charca* (1894); *Garduña* (1896); *El Negocio* (1922), and lastly, *Redentores,* serialized in the San Juan newspaper *El Imparcial* from February to October 1925. At the time of his death in 1930 Zeno Gandía was at work on another novel with the working title *Hubo un escándalo in Nueva York* (There was a scandal in New York).

In light of Zeno Gandía's position in Puerto Rican society and politics it is not surprising that issues of class, colonialism, and gender are themes that run through these novels. The first of the Crónicas published, *La charca,* got its title, explains the novel's English translator Kal Wagenheim, from "the colloquial Spanish of Puerto Rico's hill country . . . [*una charca* is] a stagnant pond, a small body of brackish water that emits a miasmic stench" (Auffant Vázquez 22). For Zeno Gandía, argues Wagenheim in the preface to his translation of *The Pond, la charca* was the perfect metaphor for the island: "Puerto Rico's Spanish colonial society . . . was an immense *charca* of human beings, oppressed by poverty, ignorance and disease" (7).

Themes and images that will be repeated in the other Crónicas are included in *La charca*: pious virgins who must face the traumas of poverty and sexual violence; an unscrupulous middle class that commits much of the violence and deception; well-intentioned but enfeebled individuals who, despite the resources and awareness to initiate a change in the lives of other Puerto Ricans, are too overwhelmed to follow up with that change; and political activists who struggle against the stagnation of life on the island.

Although no exact years are offered as settings for the novels, literary critic Vivian Auffant Vázquez proposes some possibilities (39). Set around 1868—the year of Spain's September Revolution and Puerto Rico's El Grito de Lares—*La charca* is regarded as a classic in Puerto Rican literature and the strongest of Zeno Gandía's tetralogy. Centering on the coffee ranches of the island, the novel opens with the young and beautiful Silvina shouting for her mother, Leonarda, and closes with Leonarda weeping over her daughter's body. In *La Garduña*, Zeno Gandía focuses on the dealings of the island's ruthless sugar industry during the mid-19th century. In *El negocio* he moves his characters (some from *La charca*) into an urban setting, the southern city of Ponce, and offers a criticism of business and commerce during the years preceding and succeeding 1868. Set in San Juan, *Redentores* focuses on conflicts that the island faced in the early years of the American presence. In *Redentores* some characters are frustrated by the United States's treatment of the island and commit themselves to fight for autonomy, while others try to exploit the situation for personal gains. Still other characters, such as Áureo del Sol, are torn between representing the island's best interests and prospering personally under the new insular government.

By calling his novels Crónicas, Zeno Gandía recalls, with a simple wordplay, his own vocation and training as a scholar and healer of chronic conditions but also his desire to document the events in Puerto Rican life at a time of colonial transition.

By 1902 Zeno Gandía had committed himself to a life in politics and government, having essentially ended his private medical practice. This shift is due in large part to his increasing frustration with

American inaction at the dire economic conditions on the island. By 1904 Zeno Gandía had formed the Partido Unión (Union Party) with Luis Muñoz Rivera and José de Diego. The main goal of the party was to promote autonomy, or self-government, whether within the United States or separated from it. Within 10 years, however, Zeno Gandía and de Diego broke publicly with Muñoz Rivera and de Diego formed the Partido Independista (Independence Party).

In 1902 Zeno Gandía purchased the San Juan newspaper *La Correspondencia,* moving him permanently into the role of chronicler of the island's state of affairs. As editor, Zeno Gandía became the plaintiff of a libel case that reached the U.S. Supreme Court. In a series of editorials Zeno Gandía criticized N. B. K. Pettingill for serving as a U.S. attorney for the island, representing the island in several cases, while also maintaining a private practice in which he represented clients bringing suits against the island. The Supreme Court ruled in favor of the lower court's ruling, which had declared that the articles were not libelous and that Pettingill's behavior was inappropriate. At his death in 1930 Zeno Gandía was hailed as one of the island's premier writers, statesmen, and citizens.

Bibliography

Alvarez, Ernesto. *Manuel Zeno Gandía: Estética y sociedad.* Río Piedras: Universidad de Puerto Rico, 1987.

Auffant Vázquez, Vivian. *El concepto de crónicas en Crónicas de un mundo enfermo de Manuel Zeno Gandía.* San Juan: Publicaciones Puertorriqueñas Editores, 1998.

Gandía v. Pettingill, No. 97. Supreme Court of the United States. January 9, 1912.

Gardón Franceschi, Margarita. *Manuel Zeno Gandía, vida y poesía.* San Juan: Ediciones Borinquen/Editorial Coqui, 1969.

Garrastegui, Anagilda. *Redentores, "un roman à clef."* San Juan: Instituto de Cultura Puertorriqueño, 1998.

Janer, Zilkia. "Impossible Romance: Nation and Gender in Puerto Rican Literature." Latin American Studies Association Meeting, April 17, 1997, Continental Plaza Hotel, Guadalajara, Mexico.

Palmer de Dueño, Rosa. *Sentido, forma, y estilo de Redentores de Manuel Zeno Gandía.* Río Piedras, P.R.: Colección UPREX, 1974.

Zeno Gandía, Manuel. *Cuentos.* New York: Las Américas Press, 1958.

———. *The Pond.* Translated by Kal Wagenheim. Maplewood, N.J.: Waterfront Press, 1982.

Zeno Matos, Elena. *Manuel Zeno Gandía: Documentos biográficos y críticos.* San Juan, P.R.: Gráficas Yagües, 1955.

Arlene Rodríguez

Zia Summer Rudolfo Anaya (1995)

In *Zia Summer* RUDOLFO ANAYA turns to conventions of the detective fiction in his characterization of Sonny Baca. Readers of *ALBURQUERQUE* (1992) will recognize the character of Sonny Baca; we know that he is the great-grandson of a real person from the history of the Southwest: Elfego Baca, a charismatic lawman. In *Zia Summer* we learn more about Sonny as a college-educated Mexican American who has moved from teaching into the private detective business. He straddles the divide between the younger generation of Chicanos who often lose faith in Mexican-American traditions and instead assimilate into white, English-speaking society and the older generation with their wisdom and spiritual insights. Don Elisio, Sonny's aged neighbor, exemplifies the old ways and warns Sonny about the struggle between good and evil in this narrative that concerns Gloria's death and her spirit. This struggle takes the form of a confrontation between Sonny and *brujos* (witches). Don Elisio and his two elderly friends, Doña Concha and Don Toto, lead Sonny to key evidence in Gloria's case, even as they serve as comic relief.

In *Zia Summer,* as in all of his work, Anaya is concerned with Mexican mythology, which combines Aztec folklore with elements of Catholicism; likewise, Anaya explores in his writing the dynamic and forceful relationship between humans and nature. This infuses the conventional detective novel action with prophetic dreams and shamanic magic. In *Zia Summer* Sonny searches for the murderer of his cousin and first love. The wife of a wealthy Anglo developer and mayoral candidate, Frank Dominic, Gloria was drained of blood and marked with the *Zia* (Pueblo Indian sun god) sign in what seems to be a cult murder. Sonny feels her spirit has invaded his soul to urge him to avenge her. His aunt pays him 20 hard-earned dollars to find out who killed her daughter. So, his quest to find the killer becomes threefold: to satisfy family feelings, to resolve his own need for justice, and to exorcise Gloria's ghost.

In his characteristic treatment of the spirit world and concern with the sacredness of nature the environment becomes a subplot to the murder of Gloria: The government has forced the city of Albuquerque to store the nation's worst nuclear wastes. We also meet Raven, the novel's villain and Sonny's nemesis, who has four cult wives at a bizarre compound in the foothills above Albuquerque, is also a shaman and *brujo* who uses evil magic to fulfill his plans and lead Sonny astray.

Even more than in Anaya's earlier novels the female CURANDERA (healer) figure is central to the plot. Sonny's lover, Rita López, grows herbs and uses traditional remedies, though she does not actively practice as a *curandera*. Her friend, Lorenza Villa, is not only a *curandera* but also a shaman, who has a spiritual connection with the *nagual* (animal spirits). Both women use their *curandera* skills to aid Sonny in his quest. In the course of the book Sonny learns from Lorenza that he also has shamanic potential within him, the coyote being his *nagual*.

In an evil reverse of the *curanderas,* as Raven is a reverse of Sonny's powers for good, Tamara Dubronsky, Raven's lover, also seeks Sonny's love and uses her sex appeal and psychic gifts to try to corrupt him. She believes she is the reincarnation of high priestesses and that Sonny, her lover in another life, is destined to repeat the role. In the end, after foiling Raven's plans for a nuclear incident, Sonny learns that Tamara is responsible, with Raven, for directing the cult wives in the murder of Gloria. He recovers Gloria's blood mixed with earth to bury with her ashes.

Anaya's move to the mystery novel as a way of broadening the audience for his spiritual and cultural message is explored by Ann Catherine Geuder, and Carmen Flys Junquera looks at his detective novels in the context of other ethnic mysteries, as well as exploring the ecological concerns he raises in these works. Anaya's novel—and others in the Alburquerque series—can be read within the context of CHICANO LITERATURE.

Bibliography

Anaya, Rudolfo. *Zia Summer.* New York: Warner Books, 1995.

Dick, Bruce, and Silvia Sirias, eds. *Conversations with Rudolfo Anaya.* Jackson: University of Mississippi Press, 1998.

Fernandez Olmos, Margarite. *Rudolfo A. Anaya: A Critical Companion.* Westport, Conn.: Greenwood, 1999.

Flys Junquera, Carmen. "Detectives, Hoodoo, and *Brujeria*: Subverting the Dominant U.S. Cultural Ethos." In *Sleuthing Ethnicity: The Detective in Multiethnic Crime Fiction,* edited by Dorothy Fischer-Hornung and Monika Mueller, 97–113. Madison, N.J.: Fairleigh Dickinson University Press, 2003.

———. "Nature's Voice: Ecological Consciousness in Rudolfo Anaya's Albuquerque Quartet." *Aztlán* 27, no. 2 (2002): 119–138.

Geuder, Ann Catherine. "Marketing Mystical Mysteries." In *Sleuthing Ethnicity: The Detective in Multiethnic Crime Fiction,* edited by Dorothy Fischer-Hornung and Monika Mueller, 81–94. Madison, N.J.: Fairleigh Dickinson University Press, 2003.

Vasallo, Paul, ed. *The Magic of Words: Rudolfo A. Anaya and His Writings.* Albuquerque: University of New Mexico, 1982.

Linda Rodriguez

Zoot Suit Luis Valdez (1978)

The 1978 opening of LUIS VALDEZ's *Zoot Suit* reflects a turn in the development of El TEATRO CAMPESINO because of Valdez's mainstreaming of Chicano theater. Coproduced with the Center Theater Group of Los Angeles, the play explores two of the most important events of Chicano history: the Sleepy Lagoon murder of 1942, a case involving 17 Chicano youths who were indicted in the largest conspiracy trial in California history, and the week-long Zoot Suit Riots of 1943, in which thousands of Mexican Americans were stripped and beaten by U.S. sailors, soldiers, and marines.

Valdez presents the play within a mythic and historical setting. On August 2, 1942, José Díaz (renamed José Williams in the play) was found dead on a dirt road near Los Angeles's "Sleepy Lagoon" reservoir. In January 1943, after a sensationalized trial that was characterized by judicial irregularities and a hostile press, 12 defendants were found guilty of murder and sentenced to San Quentin. In August 1944 the district court of appeals unanimously reversed the convictions because of lack of evidence. During the two years between the killing and the acquittal the negative press coverage of the trial both fueled and was fueled by a growing anti-Mexican-American sentiment. Racial tensions came to a head in June 1943, when, over the course of a week, soldiers and sailors from as far away as San Diego entered East Los Angeles and systematically began beating anyone wearing a zoot suit.

Valdez evokes the period through elaborate costumes, giant facsimiles of newspaper headlines, and musical collages of popular songs. He supplements these historical markers with the *acto* (the short political sketch), *mito* (the mythical examination of pre-Columbian culture), and *corrido* (folk songs celebrating the border hero). He merges the alienation effects of Bertolt Brecht with Aztec symbolism (such as dressing El Pachuco in the colors of the Aztec deity Quetzalcóatl) in order to add depth and complexity to the drama and to appeal to both mainstream and Latino audiences.

In his earlier work with El Teatro Campesino Valdez had used the pachuco (the zoot suiter) as a figure of defiance against a confluence of governmental, judicial, and media forces. By using the figure in this way, he argued against earlier writers, such as the Mexican poet OCTAVIO PAZ, who had criticized these young men for dressing in

burlesque variants of the bourgeois business suit and for speaking their own slang. As Guillermo Hernández explains, the figure of the pachuco, like the figure of the assimilated *pocho,* had become an object of satire for failing to maintain a healthy respect for the Mexican-American community.

In *Zoot Suit* Valdez presents El Pachuco as the *nagual* (the other self) for the leader of the 38th Street Gang, Henry Reyna (renamed from the historical Henry Leyvas). By telling the story through Henry's perspective, Valdez creates a theater of the mind in which the plot develops either through Henry's memories of killing or through fantastic representations of events outside Henry's direct experience. As Mark Pizzato argues, Valdez uses the ritual quality of Chicano theater to ensure that his audience can participate in the re-creation of these historical events. Act 1 presents the confusing chronology of the night before the killing—Henry, on the eve of his induction into the U.S. Navy, decides to don his *tachuche* (zoot suit) for a final evening with his girl, Della Barrios, and his gang—and highlights the irregularities of the trial in which the Press plays the prosecutor. Act 2 presents the successful activism of the Sleepy Lagoon Defense Fund and depicts how the 38th Street neighborhood has changed in the wake of the riots. While the historical markers connect with the *acto* and the musical numbers connect with the *corrido,* it is in the depiction of the actual riots that Valdez directly connects the figure of El Pachuco with the *mito.* After being beaten and stripped by soldiers and sailors El Pachuco rises and—naked except for a loin cloth—presents himself as an Aztec underneath the outrageous pachuco costume.

Rather than end with the acquittal of the 38th Street Gang—a scene that would have provided a happy ending—Valdez avoids any easy conclusion to the past injustices presented in the play. In the final scene, "Return to the Barrio," Henry is confronted with a choice between marrying Della and exploring a romantic relationship with the white activist who has led his defense, Alice Bloomfield (renamed from the historical Alice

McGrath). After Henry reasserts his commitment to the Chicano community by choosing Della, Valdez grants the character three alternate futures: the recalcitrant drug addict who dies traumatically in the 1970s, the Korean War hero who is posthumously awarded the Medal of Honor, and the father of college-educated children who are capable of speaking both academic English and pachuco slang.

Zoot Suit began as a production of the Mark Taper Forum's New Theatre for Now series in April 1978 and moved into the theater's main space in July. In October the play moved to the 1,200-seat Aquarius Theatre in downtown Los Angeles, where it remained until the summer of 1980. Due to the play's success in Los Angeles, Valdez modified the plot in order to perform in New York's Winter Garden Theatre, making Valdez the first Chicano playwright to open on Broadway. The play opened on March 25, 1979, but due to poor reviews closed after only 17 performances. *Zoot Suit* eventually won the Los Angeles Critics Circle Award for Distinguished Production and eight Drama-Logue Awards for Outstanding Achievement in Theater. Because Valdez is selective to whom he grants production rights, the play was not often performed after the 1980s, although El Teatro Campesino held a 25th-anniversary national tour in 2004. The success of *Zoot Suit* began a new phase in Valdez's career. Despite the poor reviews for the New York production Valdez successfully wrote a screenplay for a film adaptation, *Zoot Suit* (1981), which featured Edward James Olmos as El Pachuco and Daniel Valdez as Henry. Filmed in the Aquarius Theatre in Hollywood, the film attempts to capture some of the original theatergoing experience.

Bibliography

Escobar, Edward J. *Race, Police, and the Making of a Political Identity: Mexican Americans and the Los Angeles Police Department, 1900–1945.* Berkeley: University of California Press, 1999.

Hernández, Guillermo. *Chicano Satire: A Study in Literary Culture.* Austin: University of Texas Press, 1991.

Huerta, Jorge A. *Chicano Drama: Performance, Society, and Myth.* Cambridge: Cambridge University Press, 2000.

Noriega, Chon A. "Fashion Crimes." *Aztlán* 26, no. 1 (Spring 2001): 1–13.

Paz, Octavio. *El Laberinto de la Soledad.* Mexico City: Fondo de Cultura Económica, 1993.

Valdez, Luis. *Zoot Suit and Other Plays.* Houston, Tex.: Arte Público Press, 1992.

Jeffrey Charis-Carlson

BIBLIOGRAPHY OF SECONDARY SOURCES

Adorno, Rolena
The Polemics of Possession in Spanish American Narrative. New Haven, Conn.: Yale University Press, 2007.

Allaton, Paul
Key Terms in Latino/a Cultural and Literary Studies. Malden, Mass: Blackwell, 2007.

Alvarez, Alma Rosa
Liberation Theology in Chicana/o Literature: Manifestations of Feminist and Gay Identities. New York: Routledge, 2007.

Alvarez-Borland, Isabel
Cuban-American Literature of Exile: From Person to Persona. Charlottesville: University Press of Virginia, 1998.

**Aparicio, Frances R.,
and Susana Chávez-Silverman, eds.**
Tropicalizations: Transcultural Representations of Latinidad. Reencounters with Colonialism: New Perspectives on the Americas. Hanover, N.H.: Dartmouth College Press, 1997.

Bender, Steven
Greasers and Gringos: Latinos, Law, and the American Imagination. New York: New York University Press, 2005.

Benson, Sonia, and Nicolás Kanellos, eds.
The Hispanic American Almanac: A Reference Work on Hispanics in the United States. 3rd ed. Farmington Hills, Mich.: Gale Cengage, 2002.

Caminero-Santangelo, Marta
Latinidad: U.S. Latino Literature and the Construction of Ethnicity. Gainesville: University Press of Florida, 2007.
"Contesting the Boundaries of Exile Latino/a Literature." *World Literature Today* 74, no. 3 (June 22, 2000): 507.

Chávez-Silverman, Susana
Killer Crónicas: Bilingual Memories/Writing in Latinidad. Madison: University of Wisconsin Press, 2004.

Christie, John S.
Latino Fiction and the Modernist Imagination: Literature of the Borderlands. New York: Routledge, 1998.

**Conner, Randy P.,
with David Hatfield Sparks**
Queering Creole Spiritual Traditions: Lesbian, Gay, Bisexual, and Transgender Participation in African-Inspired Traditions in the Americas. New York: Harrington Park Press, 2004.

Dalleo, Raphael, and Elena Machado Sáez
The Latino/a Canon and the Emergence of Post-Sixties Literature. Westport, Conn.: Greenwood Press, 2003.

Fahey, Felicia Lynne
The Will to Heal: Psychological Recovery in the Novels of Latina Writers. Albuquerque: University of New Mexico Press, 2007

Gutiérrez y Muhs, Gabriella
Communal Feminisms: Chicanas, Chilenas, and Cultural Exile: Theorizing the Space of Exile, Class, and Identity. Lanham, Md.: Lexington Books, 2007.

Hutchinson, Earl Ofari
The Latino Challenge to Black America: Towards a Conversation Between African Americans and Hispanics. Los Angeles: Middle Passage Press, 2007.

Jacobs, Elizabeth
Mexican American Literature: The Politics of Identity. New York: Routledge, 2006.

Janer, Zilkia
Puerto Rican Nation-Building Literature: Impossible Romance. Gainesville: University Press of Florida, 2005.

Johannessen, Lene
Threshold Time: Passage of Crisis in Chicano Literature. New York: Rodopi, 2008.

Kevane, Bridget
Latino Literature in America. Westport, Conn.: Greenwood Press, 2003.
Profane & Sacred: Latino/a American Writers Reveal the Interplay of the Secular and the Religious. Lanham, Md.: Rowman & Littlefield Publishers, 2008.

Laezman, Rick
100 Hispanic-Americans Who Shaped American History. San Mateo, Calif.: Bluewood Books, 2001.

Lima, Lázaro
The Latino Body: Crisis Identities in American Literary and Cultural Memory. New York: New York University Press, 2007.

López-Calvo, Igacio
God and Trujillo: Literacy and Cultural Representations of the Dominican Dictator. Gainesville: University Press of Florida, 2005.

López-Lozano, Miguel
Utopian Dreams, Apocalyptic Nightmares: Globalization in Recent Mexican and Chicano Narrative. West Lafayette, Ind.: Purdue University Press, 2008.

Luís, William
Dance between Two Cultures: Latino Caribbean Literature Written in the United States. Nashville, Tenn.: Vanderbilt University Press, 1997.

Martinez Wood, Jamie
Latino Writers and Journalists. New York: Facts On File, 2007.

Mirabal, Nancy Raquel, and Agustin Laó-Montes, eds.
Technofuturos: Critical Interventions in Latina/o studies. Lanham, Md.: Lexington Books, 2007.

Montero-Sieburth, Martha, and Edwin Melendez, eds.
Latinos in a Changing Society. Westport, Conn.: Praeger Publishers, 2007.

Montes, Rafael Miguel
Generational Traumas in Contemporary Cuban-American Literature: Making Places/Haciendo Lugares. Lewiston, Me.: Edwin Mellen Press, 2006.

Ortiz, Ricardo L.
Cultural Erotics in Cuban America. Minneapolis: University of Minnesota Press, 2007.

Quintana, Alvina E.
Reading U.S. Latina Writers: Remapping American Literature. New York: Palgrave Macmillan, 2003.

Reyes, Israel
Humor and the Eccentric Text in Puerto Rican Literature. Gainesville: University Press of Florida, 2005.

Rivera, Carmen S.
Kissing the Mango Tree: Puerto Rican Women Rewriting American Literature. Houston: Arte Público Press, 2002.

Roy-Féquière, Magali
Women, Creole Identity, and Intellectual Life in Early Twentieth-Century Puerto Rico. Philadelphia: Temple University Press, 2004.

Sadowski-Smith, Claudia
Border Fictions: Globalization, Empire, and Writing at the Boundaries of the United States. Charlottesville: University Press of Virginia, 2008.

Sagás, Ernesto, and Sintia E. Molina
Dominican Migration: Transnational Perspectives. Gainesville: University Press of Florida, 2004.

Sanchez, Marta Ester
"Shakin' Up" Race and Gender: Intercultural Connections in Puerto Rican, African American, and Chicano Narratives and Culture (1965–1995). Austin: University of Texas Press, 2005.

Sánchez-González, Lisa
Boricua Literature: A Literary History of the Puerto Rican Diaspora. New York: New York University Press, 2001.

Silva Gruesz, Kirsten
Ambassadors of Culture: The Transamerican Origins of Latino Writing. Princeton, N.J.: Princeton University Press, 2001.

Smorkaloff, Pamela Maria
Cuban Writers on and off the Island: Contemporary Narrative Fiction. New York: Twayne Publishers, 1999.

Sommer, Doris, ed.
Bilingual Games: Some Literary Investigations. New York: Palgrave Macmillan, 2003.

Stavans, Ilan, ed.
Wáchale!: Poetry and Prose about Growing Up Latino in America. Chicago: Cricket Books, 2001.

Stevens, Camilla
Family and Identity in Contemporary Cuban and Puerto Rican Drama. Gainesville: University Press of Florida, 2004.

Tatum, Chuck
Mexican American Literature. New York: Harcourt. 1990.

**Tatum, Chuck, and
Erlinda Gonzales-Berry, eds.**
Recovering the U.S. Hispanic Literary Heritage. Vol. 2. Houston: Arte Público, 1996.

Torres, Hector A.
Conversations with Contemporary Chicana and Chicano Writers. Albuquerque: University of New Mexico Press, 2007.

West, John
Mexican American Folklore. Atlanta, Ga.: August House, 2007.

BIBLIOGRAPHY OF MAJOR WORKS BY HISPANIC-AMERICAN WRITERS

৯৯৯৯

Entries appear for all authors whose work is analyzed in this volume; the originals were published in English or have been translated into English. The works selected tend to be major texts or works that have gained critical attention. With few exceptions the items listed in the bibliography are written solely by the author rather than the product of collaboration or editing. Items also tend to be recent editions rather than out-of-print or obscure editions. Finally, the focus is on literature for adult audiences rather than on children's literature.

Acosta, Oscar Zeta

The Autobiography of a Brown Buffalo. San Francisco: Straight Arrow Books, 1972.

The Revolt of the Cockroach People. New York: Vintage Books, 1989.

Acuña, Rodolfo

Anything but Mexican: Chicanos in Contemporary Los Angeles. New York: Verso, 1996.

Corridors of Migration: The Odyssey of Mexican Laborers, 1600–1933. Tucson: University of Arizona Press, 2007.

Occupied America: A History of Chicanos. 5th ed. New York: Pearson Longman, 2004.

Sometimes There Is No Other Side: Chicanos and the Myth of Equality. Notre Dame, Ind.: University of Notre Dame Press, 1998.

U.S. Latino Issues. Westport, Conn.: Greenwood Press, 2003.

Agosín, Marjorie

The Alphabet in My Hands: A Writing Life. Translated by Nancy Abraham Hall. New Brunswick, N.J.: Rutgers University Press, 2000.

Always from Somewhere Else: A Memoir of My Chilean Jewish Father. New York: Feminist Press at the City University of New York, 1998.

A Cross and a Star: Memoirs of a Jewish Girl in Chile. Translated by Celeste Kostopulos-Cooperman. Albuquerque: University of New Mexico Press, 1995.

Invisible Dreamer: Memory, Judaism, and Human Rights. Santa Fe, N.Mex.: Sherman Asher Publishing, 2001.

Secrets in the Sand: The Young Women of Ciudad Juárez. Translated by Celeste Kostopulos-Cooperman. Buffalo, N.Y.: White Pine Press, 2006.

Alcalá, Kathleen

The Desert Remembers My Name: On Family and Writing. Tucson: University of Arizona Press, 2007.

The Flower in the Skull. San Francisco, Calif.: Chronicle Books, 1998.

Mrs. Vargas and the Dead Naturalist. Corvallis, Oreg.: Calyx Books, 1992.

Spirits of the Ordinary: A Tale of Casas Grandes. San Francisco, Calif.: Chronicle Books, 1997.

Treasures in Heaven. San Francisco, Calif.: Chronicle Books, 2000.

Algarín, Miguel

Body Bee Calling from the 21st Century. Houston, Tex.: Arte Público Press, 1982.

Love Is Hard Work: Memorias de Loisaida. New York: Scribner, 1997.

On Call. Houston, Tex.: Arte Público Press, 1980.

Time's Now/Ya es tiempo. Houston, Tex.: Arte Público Press, 1985.

Allende, Isabel

Daughter of Fortune. Translated by Margaret Sayers Peden. New York: HarperCollins, 1999.

Eva Luna. Translated by Margaret Sayers Peden. Franklin Center, Pa.: Franklin Library, 1988.

Forest of the Pygmies. Translated by Margaret Sayers Peden. New York: HarperCollins, 2005.

The House of the Spirits. Translated by Magda Bogin. New York: Knopf, 1985.

Inés of My Soul. Translated by Margaret Sayers Peden. New York: HarperCollins, 2006.

The Infinite Plan. Translated by Margaret Sayers Peden. Franklin Center, Pa.: Franklin Library, 1993.

My Invented Country: A Nostalgic Journey Through Chile. Translated by Margaret Sayers Peden. New York: HarperCollins, 2003.

Paula. Translated by Margaret Sayers Peden. New York: HarperCollins, 1995.

Portrait in Sepia. Translated by Margaret Sayers Peden. New York: HarperCollins, 2001.

Alurista

Floricanto en Aztlán: Poetry. Los Angeles: Chicano Studies Center, University of California, 1976.

Return: Poems Collected and New. Tempe, Ariz.: Bilingual Review Press, 1982.

Spik in Glyph. Houston, Tex.: Arte Público Press, 1981.

Timespace Huracán: Poems, 1972–1975. Albuquerque, N.Mex.: Pajarito Publications, 1976.

Z Eros. Tempe, Ariz.: Bilingual Press/Editorial Bilingüe, 1995.

Alvarez, Aldo

Interesting Monsters. St. Paul, Minn.: Graywolf Press, 2001.

Alvarez, Julia

Before We Were Free. New York: A. Knopf, 2002.

How the García Girls Lost Their Accents. Chapel Hill, N.C.: Algonquin Books, 1991.

In the Name of Salomé. Chapel Hill, N.C.: Algonquin Books, 2000.

In the Time of the Butterflies. Chapel Hill, N.C.: Algonquin Books, 1994.

Once Upon a Quinceañera. New York: Viking, 2007.

Saving the World. Chapel Hill, N.C.: Algonquin Books, 2006.

¡Yo! Chapel Hill, N.C.: Algonquin Books, 1997.

Anaya, Rudolfo Alfonso

The Adventures of Juan Chicaspatas. Houston, Tex.: Arte Público Press, 1985.

Alburquerque. Albuquerque: University of New Mexico Press, 1992.

The Anaya Reader. New York: Warner Books, 1995.

Bless Me, Última. New York: Warner Books, 1994.

Heart of Aztlán. Albuquerque: University of New Mexico Press, 1988.

Jalamanta: A Message from the Desert. New York: Warner Books, 1996.

Jemez Spring. Albuquerque: University of New Mexico Press, 2005.

The Legend of La Llorona: A Short Novel. Berkeley, Calif.: Tonatiuh–Quinto Sol International, 1984.

Rio Grande Fall. New York: Warner Books, 1996.

Shaman Winter. New York: Warner Books, 1999.

Tortuga. Albuquerque: University of New Mexico Press, 2004.

Zia Summer. New York: Warner Books, 1995.

Anzaldúa, Gloria

Borderlands/La frontera: The New Mestiza. San Francisco, Calif.: Aunt Lute Books, 2007.

Interviews/Entrevistas. New York: Routledge, 2000.

This Bridge Called My Back: Writings by Radical Women of Color. Edited by Gloria Anzaldúa and Cherríe Moraga. Berkeley, Calif.: Third Woman Press, 2001.

Arenas, Reinaldo
Before Night Falls. Translated by Dolores M. Koch. New York: Viking, 1993.
The Color of Summer, or The New Garden of Earthly Delights. Translated by Andrew Hurley. New York: Viking, 2000.
The Doorman. Translated by Dolores M. Koch. New York: Grove Weidenfeld, 1991.
El Central: A Cuban Sugar Mill. Translated by Anthony Kerrigan. New York: Avon Books, 1984.
Farewell to the Sea: A Novel of Cuba. Translated by Andrew Hurley. New York: Viking, 1986.

Arias, Ron
Five Against the Sea: A True Story of Courage and Survival. New York: New American Library, 1989.
Moving Target: A Memoir of Pursuit. Tempe, Ariz.: Bilingual Press/Editorial Bilingüe, 2003.
The Road to Tamazunchale. Albuquerque, N.Mex.: Pajarito Publications, 1978.

Baca, Jimmy Santiago
Black Mesa Poems. New York: New Directions Publishing, 1989.
C-train (Dream Boy's Story); and, Thirteen Mexicans: Poems. New York: Grove Press, 2002.
Healing Earthquakes: A Love Story in Poems. New York: Grove Press, 2001.
The Importance of a Piece of Paper. New York: Grove Press, 2004.
Martín and Meditations on the South Valley. New York: New Directions, 1987.
A Place to Stand: The Making of a Poet. New York: Grove Press, 2001.
Spring Poems Along the Rio Grande. New York: New Directions Publishing, 2007.
Winter Poems Along the Rio Grande. New York: New Directions Publishing, 2004.

Belli, Gioconda
The Country Under My Skin: A Memoir of Love and War. New York: Alfred A. Knopf, 2002.
From Eve's Rib. Translated by Steven F. White. Willimantic, Conn.: Curbstone Press, 1989.
The Inhabited Woman: A Novel. Translated by Kathleen March. Madison: University of Wisconsin Press, 2004.

The Scroll of Seduction: A Novel. Translated by Lisa Dillman. New York: HarperCollins, 2006.

Benítez, Sandra
Bag Lady: A Memoir. Edina, Minn.: Benítez Books, 2005.
Bitter Grounds. New York: Hyperion, 1997.
Night of the Radishes. New York: Theia, 2003.
A Place Where the Sea Remembers. Minneapolis: Coffee House Press, 1993.
Weight of All Things. New York: Hyperion, 2000.

Braschi, Giannina
Empire of Dreams. Translated by Tess O'Dwyer. New Haven: Yale University Press, 1994.
Yo-Yo Boing! Pittsburgh: Latin American Literary Review Press, 1998.

Burgos, Julia de
Roses in the Mirror. Edited and translated by Carmen D. Lucca. San Juan, P.R.: Ediciones Mairena, 1992.
Song of the Simple Truth: The Complete Poems. Translated by Jack Agüeros. Willimantic, Conn.: Curbstone Press, 1997.

Cabeza de Baca, Fabiola
The Good Life, New Mexico Traditions and Food. Santa Fe: Museum of New Mexico Press, 1982.
We Fed Them Cactus. Albuquerque: University of New Mexico Press, 1994.

Cabeza de Vaca, Álvar Núñez
The Account: Alvar Núñez Cabeza de Vaca's Relación. Translated by Martin A. Favata and José B. Fernández. Houston, Tex.: Arte Público Press, 1993.
Alvar Núñez Cabeza de Vaca: His Account, His Life, and the Expedition of Pánfilo de Narváez. Edited by Rolena Adorno and Patrick Charles Pautz. Lincoln: University of Nebraska Press, 1999.

Cambeira, Alan
Azúcar's Sweet Hope: Her Story Continues. Frederick, Md.: PublishAmerica, 2004.
Azúcar! The Story of Sugar. Belecam and Associates, 2001.

Quisqueya la bella: The Dominican Republic in Historical and Cultural Perspective. Armonk, N.Y., and London: M. E. Sharpe, 1997.

Tattered Paradise: Azúcar's Trilogy Ends! Frederick, Md.: PublishAmerica, 2007.

Campobello, Nellie

Cartucho; and My Mother's Hands. Translated by Doris Meyer and Irene Matthews. Austin: University of Texas Press, 1988.

Cantú, Norma Elia

Canícula: Snapshots of a Girlhood en la frontera. Albuquerque: University of New Mexico Press, 1995.

Castañeda, Omar S.

Among the Volcanoes. New York: Lodestar Books, 1991.

Cunuman. Sarasota, Fla.: Pineapple Press, 1987.

Imagining Isabel. New York: Lodestar Books, 1994.

Naranjo the Muse: A Collection of Stories. Houston, Tex.: Arte Público Press, 1997.

Remembering to Say "Mouth" or "Face." Boulder, Colo.: Fiction Collective Two, 1993.

Castillo, Ana

Goddess of the Americas: Writings on the Virgin of Guadalupe. Edited by Ana Castillo. New York: Riverhead Books, 1996.

Guardians: A Novel. New York: Random House, 2007.

Loverboys: Stories. New York: Plume, 1997.

Massacre of the Dreamers. Albuquerque: University of New Mexico Press, 1994.

The Mixquiahuala Letters. Binghamton, N.Y.: Bilingual Press/Editorial Bilingüe, 1986.

Peel My Love Like An Onion. New York: Doubleday, 1999.

Sapogonia: An Anti-romance in 3/8 Meter. Tempe, Ariz.: Bilingual Press/Editorial Bilingüe, 1990.

So Far from God. New York: W. W. Norton, 1993.

Watercolor Women, Opaque Men: A Novel in Verse. Willimantic, Conn.: Curbstone Press, 2005.

Castro, Fidel

Che, a Memoir. New York: Ocean Press, 2006.

The Fidel Castro Reader. Edited by Deborah Shnookal and David Deutschmann. New York: Ocean Press, 2007.

History Will Absolve Me. Havana: Guairas, 1967.

The Second Declaration of Havana, with the First Declaration of Havana: Cuba's 1962 Manifesto of Revolutionary Struggle in the Americas. New York: Pathfinder, 1994.

Cervantes, Lorna Dee

Drive: The First Quartet. San Antonio, Tex.: Wings Press, 2006.

Emplumada. Pittsburgh, Pa.: University of Pittsburgh Press, 1981.

From the Cables of Genocide. Houston, Tex.: Arte Público Press, 1991.

Chacón, Daniel

And the Shadows Took Him. New York: Atria Books, 2004.

Chicano Chicanery: Short Stories. Houston, Tex.: Arte Público Press, 2000.

Chavez, Cesar

The Words of Cesar Chavez. Edited by Richard J. Jensen and John C. Hammerback. College Station: Texas A&M University Press, 2002.

Chávez, Denise

Face of an Angel. New York: Farrar, Straus, & Giroux, 1994.

Last of the Menu Girls. New York: Vintage Contemporaries, 2004.

Loving Pedro Infante. New York: Farrar, Straus, & Giroux, 2001.

A Taco Testimony: Meditations on Family, Food and Culture. Tucson, Ariz.: Rio Nuevo Publishers, 2006.

Cisneros, Sandra

Caramelo, or Puro cuento. New York: Knopf, 2002.

The House on Mango Street. Houston, Tex.: Arte Público Press, 1984.

My Wicked, Wicked Ways. New York: Turtle Bay Books, 1992.

Woman Hollering Creek, and Other Stories. New York: Random House, 1991.

Cofer, Judith Ortiz

Call Me Maria: A Novel. New York: Orchard Books, 2004.

An Island Like You: Stories of the Barrio. New York: Puffin Books, 1996.

The Latin Deli: Poetry and Prose. Athens: University of Georgia Press, 1993.

The Line of the Sun. Athens: University of Georgia Press, 1989.

The Meaning of Consuelo. New York: Farrar, Straus, & Giroux, 2003.

Silent Dancing: A Partial Remembrance of a Puerto Rican Childhood. Houston, Tex.: Arte Público Press, 1990.

Year of Our Revolution: New and Selected Stories and Poems. Houston, Tex.: Piñata Books, 1998.

Corpi, Lucha

Black Widow's Wardrobe. Houston, Tex.: Arte Público Press, 1999.

Cactus Blood: A Mystery Novel. Houston, Tex.: Arte Público Press, 1995.

Crimson Moon: A Brown Angel Mystery. Houston, Tex.: Arte Público Press, 2004.

Delia's Song. Houston, Tex.: Arte Público Press, 1989.

Eulogy for a Brown Angel: A Mystery Novel. Houston, Tex.: Arte Público Press, 1992.

Cruz, Victor Hernández

By Lingual Wholes. San Francisco, Calif.: Momo's Press, 1982.

Maraca: New and Selected Poems, 1966–2000. Minneapolis, Minn.: Coffee House Press, 2001.

The Mountain in the Sea: Poems. Minneapolis, Minn.: Coffee House Press, 2006.

Panoramas. Minneapolis, Minn.: Coffee House Press, 1997.

Rhythm, Content, and Flavor. Houston, Tex.: Arte Público Press, 1988.

Díaz, Junot

Drown. New York: Riverhead Books, 1996.

The Brief Wondrous Life of Oscar Wao. New York: Riverhead Books, 2007.

Dorfman, Ariel

Blake's Therapy: A Novel. New York: Seven Stories Press, 2001.

Death and the Maiden. New York: Penguin Books, 1992.

Heading South, Looking North: A Bilingual Journey. New York: Farrar, Straus, & Giroux, 1998.

In Case of Fire in a Foreign Land: New and Collected Poems from Two Languages. Translated by Edith Grossman and Ariel Dorfman. Durham, N.C.: Duke University Press, 2002.

The Last Song of Manuel Sendero. Translated by George R. Shivers and Ariel Dorfman. New York: Penguin Books, 1988.

Last Waltz in Santiago and Other Poems of Exile and Disappearance. Translated by Edith Grossman and Ariel Dorfman. New York: Penguin Books, 1988.

Mascara: A Novel. New York: Seven Stories Press, 2004.

Other Septembers, Many Americas: Selected Provocations, 1980–2004. New York: Seven Stories Press, 2004.

The Other Side. New York: Samuel French, 2006.

Widows: A Novel. Translated by Stephen Kessler. New York: Seven Stories Press, 2002.

Engle, Margarita

The Poet Slave of Cuba: A Biography of Juan Francisco Manzano. New York: Henry Holt, 2006.

Singing to Cuba. Houston, Tex.: Arte Público Press, 1993.

Skywriting: A Novel of Cuba. New York: Bantam Books, 1995.

Escandón, María Amparo

Esperanza's Box of Saints. New York: Scribner Paperback Fiction, 1999.

González and Daughter Trucking Co.: A Road Novel with Literary License. New York: Three Rivers Press, 2005.

Espada, Martín

Alabanza: New and Selected Poems, 1982–2002. New York: W. W. Norton, 2003.

City of Coughing and Dead Radiators: Poems. New York: W. W. Norton, 1993.

Imagine the Angels of Bread. New York: W. W. Norton, 1996.

A Mayan Astronomer in Hell's Kitchen: Poems. New York: W. W. Norton, 2000.

The Republic of Poetry. New York: W. W. Norton, 2006.

Trumpets from the Islands of Their Eviction. Tempe, Ariz.: Bilingual Press/Editorial Bilingüe, 1994.

Zapata's Disciple: Essays. Cambridge, Mass.: South End Press, 1998.

Espaillat, Rhina

Lapsing to Grace. East Lansing, Mich.: Bennett and Kitchel, 1992.

Playing at Stillness. Kirksville, Mo.: Truman State University Press, 2005.

Rehearsing Absence: Poems. Evansville: University of Indiana Press, 2001.

The Shadow I Dress In: Poems. Cincinnati, Ohio: David Robert Books, 2004.

Where Horizons Go. Kirksville, Mo.: New Odyssey Press, 1998.

Esteves, Sandra María

Bluestown Mockingbird Mambo. Houston, Tex.: Arte Público Press, 1990.

Esteves, Sandra Maria. *Yerba buena: dibujos y poemas.* Greenfield Center, N.Y.: Greenfield Review Press, 1980.

Fernández, Roberta

Intaglio: A Novel in Six Stories Houston, Tex.: Arte Público Press, 1990.

Fontes, Montserrat

Dreams of the Centaur: A Novel. New York: W. W. Norton, 1996.

First Confession. New York: W. W. Norton, 1991.

Fornes, Maria Irene

Fefu and Her Friends. New York: PAJ Publications, 1990.

Plays. New York: PAJ Publications, 1986.

García, Cristina

The Agüero Sisters. New York: One World, 1998.

Dreaming in Cuban. New York: Knopf, 1992.

A Handbook to Luck. New York: Alfred A. Knopf, 2007.

Monkey Hunting. New York: Ballantine Books, 2004.

García Ramis, Magali

Happy Days, Uncle Sergio. Translated by Carmen C. Esteves. Fredonia, N.Y.: White Pine Press, 1995.

Gaspar de Alba, Alicia

Calligraphy of the Witch. New York: St. Martin's Press, 2007.

Desert Blood: The Júarez Murders. Houston, Tex.: Arte Público Press, 2005.

La Llorona on the Longfellow Bridge: Poetry y otras movidas, 1985–2001. Houston, Tex.: Arte Público Press, 2003.

The Mystery of Survival and Other Stories. Tempe, Ariz.: Bilingual Press/Editorial Bilingüe, 1993.

Sor Juana's Second Dream: A Novel. Albuquerque: University of New Mexico Press, 1999.

Goldman, Francisco

The Divine Husband. New York: Atlantic Monthly Press, 2004.

Long Night of White Chickens. New York: Atlantic Monthly Press, 1992.

The Ordinary Seaman. New York: Atlantic Monthly Press, 1997.

Gómez-Peña, Guillermo

Dangerous Border Crossers: The Artist Talks Back. New York: Routledge, 2000.

Ethno-Techno: Writings on Performance, Activism, and Pedagogy. Edited by Elaine Peña. New York: Routledge, 2005.

Friendly Cannibals. San Francisco, Calif.: Artspace Books, 1996.

New World Border: Prophecies, Poems and Loqueras for the End of the Century. San Francisco, Calif.: City Lights, 1996.

Warrior for Gringostroika: Essays, Performance Texts, and Poetry. St. Paul, Minn.: Graywolf Press, 1993.

Gonzales, Rodolfo "Corky"

I Am Joaquín/ Yo soy Joaquín: With a Chronology of People and Events in Mexican and Mexican American History. New York: Bantam Books, 1972.

Message to Aztlán: Selected Writings of Rodolfo "Corky" Gonzales. Edited by Henry A. J. Ramos. Introduction by Antonio Esquibel. Houston, Tex.: Arte Público Press, 2001.

González, José Luis

Ballad of Another Time. Translated by Asa Zatz. Madison: University of Wisconsin Press/Terrace Books, 2004.

Puerto Rico: The Four-Storeyed Country and Other Essays. Translated by Gerald Guinness. Princeton, N.J.: M. Wiener Publishing, 1993.

Grillo, Evelio

Black Cuban, Black American, a Memoir. Houston, Tex.: Arte Público Press, 2000.

Herrera, Andrea O'Reilly

The Pearl of the Antilles. Tempe, Ariz.: Bilingual Press/Editorial Bilingüe, 2001.

Herrera, Juan Felipe

Border-Crosser with a Lamborghini Dream: Poems. Tucson: University of Arizona Press, 1999.

Cinnamon Girl: Letters Found Inside a Cereal Box. New York: Joanna Cotler Books, 2005.

CrashBoomLove: A Novel in Verse. Albuquerque: University of New Mexico Press, 1999.

Downtown Boy. New York: Scholastic Press, 2005.

Exiles of Desire. Houston, Tex.: Arte Público Press, 1985.

Mayan Drifter: Chicano Poet in the Lowlands of America. Philadelphia: Temple University Press, 1997.

Night Train to Tuxtla. Tucson: University of Arizona Press, 2004.

Notebooks of a Chile Verde Smuggler. Tucson: University of Arizona Press, 2002.

187 Reasons Mexicanos Can't Cross the Border: Undocuments, 1971–2007. San Francisco, Calif.: City Lights Books, 2007.

Hijuelos, Oscar

Empress of the Splendid Season. New York: HarperFlamingo, 1999.

The Fourteen Sisters of Emilio Montez O'Brien: A Novel. New York: Farrar, Straus & Giroux, 1993.

The Mambo Kings Play Songs of Love. New York: Perennial Classics, 2000.

Mr. Ives' Christmas. New York: HarperCollins, 1995.

Our House in the Last World: A Novel. New York: Persea Books, 1983.

Simple Habana Melody: From When the World Was Good. New York: HarperCollins, 2002.

Hinojosa Smith, Rolando

Ask a Policeman. Houston, Tex.: Arte Público Press, 1998.

Becky and Her Friends. Houston, Tex.: Arte Público Press, 1990.

Dear Rafe. Houston, Tex.: Arte Público Press, 1985.

Klail City: A Novel. Houston, Tex.: Arte Público Press, 1987.

The Useless Servants. Houston, Tex.: Arte Público Press, 1993.

We Happy Few. Houston, Tex.: Arte Público Press, 2006.

Hoyos, Angela de

Arise, Chicano! and Other Poems. San Antonio, Tex.: M&A Editions, 1980.

Selected Poems. San Antonio, Tex.: Dezkalzo Press, 1979.

Woman, Woman. Houston, Tex.: Arte Público Press, 1985.

Islas, Arturo

Arturo Islas: The Uncollected Works. Edited by Frederick Luis Aldama. Houston, Tex.: Arte Público Press, 2003.

La Mollie and the King of Tears. Edited by Paul Skenazy. Albuquerque: University of New Mexico Press, 1996.

Migrant Souls. New York: Morrow, 1990.

The Rain God. Palo Alto, Calif.: Alexandrian Press, 1984.

Jaramillo, Cleofas Martinez

Romance of a Little Village Girl. Albuquerque: University of New Mexico Press, 2000.

Shadows of the Past. Santa Fe, N.Mex.: Seton Village Press, 1941.

Lamazares, Ivonne
The Sugar Island. Boston: Houghton Mifflin, 2000.

Las Casas, Bartolomé de
An Account, Much Abbreviated, of the Destruction of the Indies, with Related Texts. Edited by Franklin W. Knight. Translated by Andrew Hurley. Indianapolis, Ind.: Hackett Publishing, 2003.

In Defense of the Indians: The Defense of the Most Reverend Lord, Don Fray Bartolomé de las Casas, of the Order of Preachers, Late Bishop of Chiapa, against the Persecutors and Slanderers of the Peoples of the New World Discovered Across the Seas. Edited and translated by Stafford Poole. DeKalb: Northern Illinois University Press, 1992.

Laviera, Tato
AmeRícan. Houston, Tex.: Arte Público Press, 2003.
Enclave. Houston, Tex.: Arte Público Press, 1985.
La Carreta Made a U-turn. Houston, Tex.: Arte Público Press, 1992.
Mainstream Ethics/Etica corriente. Houston, Tex.: Arte Público Press, 1988.

Leguizamo, John
Freak: A Semi-Demi-Quasi-Pseudo Autobiography. New York: Riverhead Books, 1997.
Pimps, Hos, Playa Hatas, and All the Rest of My Hollywood Friends: My Life. New York: Ecco, 2006.
The Works of John Leguizamo. New York: Harper, 2006.

Levins Morales, Aurora
Medicine Stories: History, Culture, and the Politics of Integrity. Cambridge, Mass.: South End Press, 1998.
Remedios: Stories of Earth and Iron from the History of Puertorriqueñas. Boston: Beacon Press, 1998.

Limón, Graciela
The Day of the Moon. Houston, Tex.: Arte Público Press, 1999.
Erased Faces. Houston, Tex.: Arte Público Press, 2001.
In Search of Bernabé. Houston, Tex.: Arte Público Press, 1993.

Left Alive. Houston, Tex.: Arte Público Press, 2005.
The Memories of Ana Calderón: A Novel. Houston, Tex.: Arte Público Press, 1994.
Song of the Hummingbird. Houston, Tex.: Arte Público Press, 1996.

Lopez, Erika
Flaming Iguanas: An Illustrated All-Girl Road Novel Thing. New York: Simon & Schuster, 1997.
Hoochie Mama: La otra carne blanca. New York: Simon & Schuster, 2001.
Lap Dancing for Mommy: Tender Stories of Disgust, Blame, and Inspiration. Seattle, Wash.: Seal Press, 1997.
They Call Me Mad Dog! A Story for Bitter, Lonely People. New York: Simon & Schuster, 1998.

López, Lorraine
Call Me Henri. Willimantic, Conn.: Curbstone Press, 2006.
Soy la Avon Lady and Other Stories. Willimantic, Conn.: Curbstone Press, 2002.

Marqués, René
The Docile Puerto Rican: Essays. Translated by Barbara Bockus Aponte. Philadelphia: Temple University Press, 1976.
The Look/La mirada. Translated by Charles Pilditch. New York: Senda Nueva de Ediciones, 1983.
The Oxcart/La carreta. Translated by Charles Pilditch. New York: Scribner, 1969.

Martí, José
Ismaelillo. Translated by Tyler Fisher. San Antonio, Tex.: Wings Press, 2007.
José Martí: Doctrines, Maxims, and Aphorisms, a Bilingual Anthology, with a Concordance. Translated by Carlos Ripol. Miami: Moderna Poesía, 2000.
José Martí Reader: Writings on the Americas. Edited by Deborah Shnookal and Mirta Muñiz. New York: Ocean Press, 1999.

Martínez, Demetria
Breathing Between the Lines: Poems. Tucson: University of Arizona Press, 1997.

Confessions of a Berlitz-Tape Chicana. Norman: University of Oklahoma Press, 2005.

Devil's Workshop. Tucson: University of Arizona Press, 2002.

Mother Tongue. New York: One World, 1996.

Medina, Rubén

Amor de lejos/Fools' Love. Translated by Jennifer Sternbach and Robert Jones. Houston, Tex.: Arte Público Press, 1986.

Menéndez, Ana

In Cuba I Was a German Shepherd. New York: Grove Press, 2001.

Loving Che. New York: Atlantic Monthly Press, 2003.

Mercado, Nancy

It Concerns the Madness. Hoboken, N.J.: Long Shot, 2000.

Mohr, Nicholasa

El Bronx Remembered: A Novella and Other Stories. New York: Harper & Row, 1975.

Growing Up Inside the Sanctuary of My Imagination. New York: J. Messner, 1994.

In Nueva York. Houston, Tex.: Arte Público Press, 1988.

Matter of Pride and Other Stories. Houston, Tex.: Arte Público Press, 1997.

Nilda. Houston, Tex.: Arte Público Press, 1985.

Rituals of Survival: A Woman's Portfolio. Houston, Tex.: Arte Público Press, 1985.

Mora, Pat

Agua santa/Holy Water. Tucson: University of Arizona Press, 2007.

Chants. Houston, Tex.: Arte Público Press, 1984.

Communion. Houston, Tex.: Arte Público Press, 1991.

The Desert Is My Mother/El desierto es mi madre. Houston, Tex.: Piñata Books, 1994.

House of Houses. Boston: Beacon Press, 1997.

A Library for Juana: The World of Sor Juana Inés. Translated by Alan S. Trueblood. New York: Alfred A. Knopf, 2002.

Nepantla: Essays from the Land in the Middle. Albuquerque: University of New Mexico Press, 1993.

Moraga, Cherríe

Giving Up the Ghost: Teatro in Two Acts. Los Angeles: West End Press, 1986.

The Last Generation. Boston: South End Press, 1993.

Loving in the War Years: Lo que nunca pasó por sus labios. Cambridge, Mass.: South End Press, 2000.

This Bridge Called My Back: Writings by Radical Women of Color. Edited by Cherríe Moraga and Gloria Anzaldúa. Berkeley, Calif.: Third Woman Press, 2001.

Waiting in the Wings: Portrait of a Queer Motherhood. Ithaca, N.Y.: Firebrand Books, 1997.

Morales, Alejandro

The Brick People. Houston, Tex.: Arte Público Press, 1988.

The Captain of All These Men of Death. Tempe, Ariz.: Bilingual Press/Editorial Bilingüe, 2006.

Death of an Anglo. Translated by Judith Ginsberg. Tempe, Ariz.: Bilingual Press, 1988.

Old Faces and New Wine. Translated by Max Martinez. San Diego, Calif.: Maize Press, 1981.

The Rag Doll Plagues. Houston, Tex.: Arte Público Press, 1992.

Muñoz, Elías Miguel

Brand New Memory. Houston, Tex.: Arte Público Press, 1998.

Crazy Love. Houston, Tex.: Arte Público Press, 1989.

The Greatest Performance. Houston, Tex.: Arte Público Press, 1991.

Niggli, Josephina

Mexican Folk Plays. New York: Arno Press, 1976.

Mexican Village. Albuquerque: University of New Mexico Press, 1994.

Step Down, Elder Brother: A Novel. New York: Rinehart, 1947.

Obejas, Achy

Days of Awe. New York: Ballantine Books, 2001.

Memory Mambo: A Novel. Pittsburgh, Pa.: Cleis Press, 1996.

We Came All the Way from Cuba So You Could Dress Like This? Stories. Pittsburgh, Pa.: Cleis Press, 1994.

Paredes, Américo

Between Two Worlds. Houston, Tex.: Arte Público Press, 1991.

George Washington Gómez: A Mexicotexan Novel. Houston, Tex.: Arte Público Press, 1990.

The Shadow. Houston, Tex.: Arte Público Press, 1998.

With His Pistol in His Hand: A Border Ballad and Its Hero. Austin: University of Texas Press, 1958.

Paz, Octavio

¿Aguila o sol?/Eagle or Sun? Translated by Eliot Weinberger. London: P. Owen, 1990.

Alternating Current. Translated by Helen R. Lane. New York: Viking Press, 1973.

The Bow and the Lyre (El arco y la lira): The Poem, the Poetic Revelation, Poetry and History. Translated by Ruth L. C. Simms. Austin: University of Texas Press, 1973.

Conjunctions and Disjunctions. Translated by Helen Lane. New York: Arcade Publishing, 1990.

In Search of the Present: Nobel Lecture, 1990. Translated by Anthony Stanton. San Diego, Calif.: Harcourt Brace Jovanovich, 1990.

The Labyrinth of Solitude: Life and Thought in Mexico. Translated by Lysander Kemp. New York: Viking Penguin, 1985.

One Earth, Four or Five Worlds: Reflections on Contemporary History. Translated by Helen Lane. San Diego, Calif.: Harcourt Brace Jovanovich, 1985.

Sor Juana, or The Traps of Faith. Translated by Margaret Sayers Peden. Cambridge, Mass.: Belknap Press, 1988.

Perdomo, Willie

Postcards of El Barrio. San Juan, P.R.: Isla Negra Editores, 2002.

Where a Nickel Costs a Dime. New York: W. W. Norton, 1996.

Perez, Loida Maritza

Geographies of Home. New York: Viking, 1999.

Pérez, Ramón "Tianguis"

Diary of a Guerrilla. Translated by Dick J. Reavis. Houston, Tex.: Arte Público Press, 1999.

Diary of an Undocumented Immigrant. Translated by Dick J. Reavis. Houston, Tex.: Arte Público Press, 1991.

Pérez Firmat, Gustavo

Anything but Love. Houston, Tex.: Arte Público Press, 2000.

Bilingual Blues. Tempe, Ariz.: Bilingual Press/Editorial Bilingüe, 1995.

The Cuban Condition: Translation and Identity in Modern Cuban Literature. New York: Cambridge University Press, 1989.

Life on the Hyphen: The Cuban-American Way. Austin: University of Texas Press, 1994.

Literature and Liminality: Festive Readings in the Hispanic Tradition. Durham, N.C.: Duke University Press, 1986.

Next Year in Cuba: A Cubano's Coming-of-Age in America. Houston, Tex.: Arte Público Press, 2005.

Scar Tissue. Tempe, Ariz.: Bilingual Press/Editorial Bilingüe, 2005.

Tongue Ties: Logo-Eroticism in Anglo-Hispanic Literature. New York: Palgrave Macmillan, 2003.

Pietri, Pedro

Illusions of a Revolving Door: Plays, Teatro. Río Piedras: Editorial de la Universidad de Puerto Rico, 1992.

Puerto Rican Obituary. New York: Monthly Review Press, 1974.

Piñero, Miguel

La Bodega Sold Dreams. Houston, Tex.: Arte Público Press, 1980.

Outrageous: One Act Plays. Houston, Tex.: Arte Público Press, 1986.

Short Eyes. New York: Hill & Wang, 1975.

Quinn, Anthony

One Man Tango. Anthony Quinn, with Daniel Paisner. New York: HarperCollins, 1995.

The Original Sin: A Self-Portrait. Boston: Little, Brown, 1972.

Quiñonez, Ernesto

Bodega Dreams. New York: Vintage Contemporaries, 2000.

Chango's Fire. New York: Rayo, 2004.

Rechy, John

Bodies and Souls: A Novel. New York: Carroll & Graf, 1983.

City of Night. New York: Grove Press, 1984.

Coming of the Night. New York: Grove Press, 1999.

Fourth Night. New York: W. H. Allen, 1972.

The Life and Adventures of Lyle Clemens: A Novel. New York: Grove Press, 2003.

Marylin's Daughter. New York: Carroll & Graf, 1988.

The Miraculous Day of Amalia Gómez. New York: Grove Press, 2001.

Numbers. New York: Grove Press, 1984.

Our Lady of Babylon: A Novel. New York: Arcade Publishing, 1996.

Rushes. New York: Grove Press, 1979.

The Sexual Outlaw: A Documentary. New York: Grove Press, 1985.

Retamar, Roberto Fernández

Caliban and Other Essays. Translated by Edward Baker. Minneapolis: University of Minnesota Press, 1989.

Ríos, Alberto Alvaro

Capirotada: A Nogales Memoir. Albuquerque: University of New Mexico Press, 1999.

The Curtain of Trees: Stories. Albuquerque: University of New Mexico Press, 1999.

The Iguana Killer: Twelve Stories of the Heart. Albuquerque: University of New Mexico Press, 1999.

The Smallest Muscle in the Human Body. Port Townsend, Wash.: Copper Canyon Press, 2002.

Whispering to Fool the Wind. New York: Sheep Meadow Press, 1982.

Rivera, Tomás

Tomas Rivera: The Complete Works. Edited by Julián Olivares. Houston, Tex.: Arte Público Press, 1991.

This Migrant Earth. Translated by Rolando Hinojosa. Houston, Tex.: Arte Público Press, 1987.

. . . Y no se lo tragó la tierra/. . . And the Earth Did Not Devour Him. Translated by Evangelina Vigil-Piñon. Houston, Tex.: Arte Público Press, 1990.

Rodríguez, Luis J.

Always Running: La vida loca, Gang Days in L.A. Willimantic, Conn.: Curbstone Press, 1993.

Rodriguez, Richard

Brown: The Last Discovery of America. New York: Viking, 2002.

Days of Obligation: An Argument with My Mexican Father New York: Viking, 2002.

Hunger of Memory: The Education of Richard Rodriguez, an Autobiography. Boston: D. R. Godine, 1982.

Roqué, Ana

Luz y sombra: Estudio crítico, notas y esquema biográfico. Río Piedras: Editorial de la Universidad de Puerto Rico, 1991.

Ruiz de Burton, María Amparo

Conflicts of Interest: The Letters of María Amparo Ruiz de Burton. Edited by Rosaura Sánchez and Beatrice Pita. Houston, Tex.: Arte Público Press, 2001.

The Squatter and the Don: A Novel Descriptive of Contemporary Occurrences in California. Edited by Rosaura Sánchez and Beatrice Pita. Houston, Tex.: Arte Público Press, 1992.

Who World Have Thought It? Edited by Rosaura Sánchez and Beatrice Pita. Houston, Tex.: Arte Público Press, 1995.

Ryan, Pam Muñoz

Becoming Naomi. New York: Scholastic Press, 2004.

Esperanza Rising. New York: Scholastic Press, 2000.

Sáenz, Benjamín Alire

Calendar of Dust. Seattle, Wash.: Broken Moon Press, 1991.

Carry Me Like Water. New York: Hyperion, 1995.

Dark and Perfect Angels. El Paso, Tex.: Cinco Puntos Press, 1995.

Dreaming the End of War. Port Townsend, Wash.: Copper Canyon Press, 2006.

Elegies in Blue: Poems. El Paso, Tex.: Cinco Puntos Press, 2002.

Flowers for the Broken: Stories. Seattle, Wash.: Broken Moon Press, 1992.

House of Forgetting. New York: HarperCollins, 1997.

In Perfect Light: A Novel. New York: Rayo, 2005.

Sahagún, Bernardino de

Bernardino de Sahagún's Psmalmodia Christiana. Translated by Arthur J. O. Anderson. Salt Lake City: University of Utah Press, 1993.

Conquest of New Spain: 1585 Revision by Bernardino de Sahagún. Translated by Howard F. Cline. Edited by S. L. Cline. Salt Lake City: University of Utah Press, 1989.

Florentine Codex: General History of the Things of New Spain. Translated by Arthur J. O. Anderson and Charles E. Dibble. Santa Fe, N.Mex., and Salt Lake City, Utah: School of American Research and University of Utah Press, 1975.

War of Conquest: How It Was Waged Here in Mexico. The Aztecs' Own Story as Given to Bernardino de Sahagún. Rendered by Arthur J. O. Anderson and Charles E. Dibble. Santa Fe, N.Mex., and Salt Lake City, Utah: School of American Research and University of Utah Press, 1978.

Salinas, Raúl

East of the Freeway: Reflections de mi pueblo, Poems. Austin, Tex.: Red Salmon Press, 1995.

Indio Trails: A Xicano Odyssey Through Indian Country. San Antonio, Tex.: Wings Press, 2006.

raúlrsalinas and the Jail Machine: My Weapon Is My Pen, Selected Writings. Austin: University of Texas Press, 2006.

Un Trip Through the Mind y otras Excursions: Poems. Houston, Tex.: Arte Público Press, 1999.

Sánchez, Ricardo

Eagle-Visioned/Feathered Adobes: Manito Sojourns and Pachuco Ramblings October 4th to 24th, 1981. El Paso, Tex.: Cinco Puntos Press, 1990.

The Loves of Ricardo. Chicago: Tia Chucha Press, 1997.

Selected Poems. Houston, Tex.: Arte Público Press, 1985.

Santiago, Esmeralda

Almost a Woman. New York: Vintage Books, 1999.

América's Dream. New York: HarperCollins, 1996.

Turkish Lover. Cambridge, Mass.: Da Capo Press, 2004.

When I Was Puerto Rican. New York: Vintage Books, 1994.

Seguín, Juan Nepomuceno

Revolution Remembered: The Memoirs and Selected Correspondence of Juan N. Seguín. Edited by Jesús F. de la Teja. Austin: Texas State Historical Association, 2002.

Sommer, Doris

Bilingual Aesthetics: A New Sentimental Education. Durham, N.C.: Duke University Press, 2004.

Bilingual Games: Some Literary Investigations. New York: Palgrave Macmillan, 2003.

Foundational Fictions: The National Romances of Latin America. Berkeley: University Press of California, 1991.

One Master for Another: Populism as Patriarchal Rhetoric in Dominican Novels. Lanham, Md.: University Press of America, 1983.

Proceed with Caution, When Engaged by Minority Writing in the Americas. Cambridge, Mass.: Harvard University Press, 1999.

Soto, Gary

Accidental Love. Orlando, Fla.: Harcourt, 2006.

The Afterlife. Orlando, Fla.: Harcourt, 2003.

Amnesia in a Republican County. Albuquerque: University of New Mexico Press, 2003.

Black Hair. Pittsburgh, Pa.: University of Pittsburgh Press, 1985.

Buried Onions. New York: HarperCollins, 1999.

Canto Familiar. San Diego, Calif.: Harcourt Brace, 1995.

Cesar Chavez: A Hero for Everyone. New York: Aladdin, 2003.

Crazy Weekend. New York: Scholastic, 1994.

The Effects of Knut Hamsun on a Fresno Boy. New York: Persea Books, 2000.

Elements of San Joaquin. Pittsburgh, Pa.: University of Pittsburgh Press, 1977.

A Fire in My Hands. Orlando, Fla.: Harcourt, 2006.

Home Course in Religion: New Poems. San Francisco, Calif.: Chronicle Books, 1991.

Jesse. Orlando, Fla.: Harcourt, 2006.

Junior College. San Francisco, Calif.: Chronicle Books, 1997.

Living up the Street. New York: Bantam, 1985.

Natural Man. San Francisco, Calif.: Chronicle Books, 1999.

Nerlandia: A Play. New York: Penguin, 1999.

New and Selected Poems. San Francisco, Calif.: Chronicle Books, 1995.

Nickel and Dime. Albuquerque: University of New Mexico Press, 2000.

Novio Boy, a Play. Orlando, Fla.: Harcourt, 2006.

One Kind of Faith. San Francisco, Calif.: Chronicle Books, 2003.

Poetry Lover. Albuquerque: University of New Mexico Press, 2001.

A Simple Plan. San Francisco, Calif.: Chronicle Books, 2007.

A Summer Life. Hanover, N.H.: University Press of New England, 1990.

Tale of Sunlight. Pittsburgh, Pa.: University of Pittsburgh Press, 1978.

Where Sparrows Work Hard. Pittsburgh, Pa.: University of Pittsburgh Press, 1981.

Who Will Know Us? San Francisco, Calif.: Chronicle Books, 1990.

Soto, Pedro Juan

Spiks, Stories. Translated by Victoria Ortiz. New York: Monthly Review Press, 1973.

Usmaíl. Translated by Myrna Pagán and Charlie Connelly. St. John, Virgin Islands: Sombero Publishing, 2007.

Stavans, Ilan

Bandido: The Death and Resurrection of Oscar "Zeta" Acosta. Evanston, Ill.: Vidas/Northwestern University Press, 2003.

Bandido: Oscar "Zeta" Acosta and the Chicano Experience. New York: IconEditions, 1995.

Conversations with Ilan Stavans. Tucson: University of Arizona Press, 2005.

The Disappearance: A Novella and Stories. Evanston, Ill.: TriQuarterly Books/Northwestern University Press, 2006.

The Hispanic Condition: Reflections on Culture and Identity in America. New York: HarperCollins, 1995.

Imagining Columbus: The Literary Voyage. New York: Palgrave, 2001.

Latino History and Culture. New York: Collins, 2007.

Octavio Paz: A Meditation. Tucson: University of Arizona Press, 2001.

On Borrowed Words: A Memoir of Language. New York: Viking, 2001.

The One-Handed Pianist and Other Stories. Albuquerque: University of New Mexico Press, 1996.

Spanglish: The Making of a New American Language. New York: Rayo, 2003.

Suárez, Virgil

Banyan: Poems. Baton Rouge: Louisiana State University, 2001.

The Cutter: A Novel. Houston, Tex.: Arte Público Press, 1999.

Going Under. Houston, Tex.: Arte Público Press, 1996.

Guide to the Blue Tongue. Urbana: University of Illinois Press, 2002.

Havana Thursdays: A Novel. Houston, Tex.: Arte Público Press, 1995.

Infinite Refuge. Houston, Tex.: Arte Público Press, 2002.

In the Republic of Longing: Poems. Tempe, Ariz.: Bilingual Press, 1999.

Latin Jazz. Baton Rouge: Louisiana State University, 2002.

90 Miles: Selected and New Poems. Pittsburgh, Pa.: University of Pittsburgh Press, 2005.

Palm Crows. Tucson: University of Arizona Press, 2001.

Spared Angola: Memories from a Cuban-American Childhood. Houston, Tex.: Arte Público Press, 1997.

Welcome to the Oasis and Other Stories. Houston, Tex.: Arte Público Press, 1992.

Thomas, Piri

Down These Mean Streets. New York: Vistage Books, 1997.

Saviour, Saviour, Hold My Hand. Garden City, N.Y.: Doubleday, 1972.

Seven Long Times. Houston, Tex.: Arte Público Press, 1994.

Stories from El Barrio. New York: Knopf, 1978.

Trevino, Jesús Salvador

Eyewitness: A Filmmaker's Memoir of the Chicano Movement. Houston, Tex.: Arte Público Press, 2001.

The Fabulous Sinkhole and Other Stories. Houston, Tex.: Arte Público Press, 1995.

The Skyscraper That Flew and Other Stories. Houston, Tex.: Arte Público Press, 2005.

Ulibarrí, Sabine

The Best of Sabine R. Ulibarrí: Selected Stories. Edited by Dick Gerdes. Albuquerque: University of New Mexico Press, 1993.

El Cóndor and Other Stories. Houston, Tex.: Arte Público Press, 1989.

Governor Glu-Glu and Other Stories. Tempe, Ariz.: Bilingual Press, 1988.

Mayhem Was Our Business/Memorias de un veterano. Tempe, Ariz.: Bilingual Press, 1997.

Tierra Amarilla: Stories of New Mexico/Cuentos de Nuevo México. Translated by Thelma Campbell. Albuquerque: University of New Mexico Press, 1993.

Urrea, Luis Alberto

Across the Wire: Life and Hard Times on the Mexican Border. New York: Anchor Books, 1993.

By the Lake of the Sleeping Children: The Secret Life of the Mexican Border. New York, 1996.

The Devil's Highway: A True Story. New York: Little Brown, 2004.

Ghost Sickness. El Paso, Tex.: Cinco Puntos Press, 1997.

Hummingbird's Daughter: A Novel. New York: Little Brown, 2005.

In Search of Snow: A Novel. Tucson: University of Arizona Press, 1999.

Nobody's Son: Notes from an American Life. Tucson: University of Arizona Press, 1998.

Six Kinds of Sky: A Collection of Short Fiction. El Paso: Cinco Puntos Press, 2002.

Valdez, Luis

Luis Valdez—Early Works: Actos, Bernabé, and Pensamiento serpentino. Houston, Tex.: Arte Público Press, 1990.

Mummified Deer and Other Plays. Houston, Tex.: Arte Público Press, 2005.

Zoot Suit and Other Plays. Houston, Tex.: Arte Público Press, 1992.

Vega, Ana Lydia

True and False Romances: Stories and a Novella. Translated by Andrew Hurley. New York: Serpent's Tail, 1994.

Vega Yunqué, Edgardo

Blood Figures. New York: Rayo, 2005.

Casualty Report. Houston, Tex.: Arte Público Press, 1991.

Comeback. Houston, Tex.: Arte Público Press, 1985.

Coming Home Again. New York: Farrar, Straus, & Giroux, 2003.

The Lamentable Journey of Omaha Bigelow into the Impenetrable Jungle. Woodstock, N.Y.: Overlook Press, 2004.

Mendoza's Dreams. Houston, Tex.: Arte Público Press, 1987.

No Matter How Much You Promise to Cook or Pay the Rent You Blew it Cauze Bill Bailey Ain't Never Coming Home Again: A Symphonic Novel. New York: Farrar, Straus & Giroux, 2003.

Vilar, Irene

A Message from God in the Atomic Age. Translated by Gregory Rabassa. New York: Pantheon Books, 1996.

Villagrá, Gaspar Pérez de

History of New Mexico, Alcalá, 1610. Translated by Gilberto Espinosa. Los Angeles: Quivira Society, 1933.

Zaldívar and the Cattle of Cíbola: Vicente de Zaldívar's Report of His Expedition to the Buffalo Plains in 1598. Translated by John H. R. Polt. Dallas, Tex.: William P. Clements Center for Southwest Studies, Southern Methodist University, 1999.

Villarreal, José Antonio

Clemente Chacón: A Novel. Binghamton, N.Y.: Bilingual Press, 1984.

The Fifth Horseman. Garden City, N.Y.: Doubleday, 1974.

Pocho. New York: Anchor Books, 1989.

Villaseñor, Victor Edmundo

Burro Genius: A Memoir. New York: Rayo, 2004.

Macho! Houston, Tex.: Arte Público Press, 1991.

Rain of Gold. Houston, Tex.: Arte Público Press, 1991.

Thirteen Senses: A Memoir. New York: Rayo, 2001.

Walking Stars: Stories of Magic and Power. Houston, Tex.: Piñata Books, 1994.

Wild Steps of Heaven. New York: Delacorte Press, 1996.

Viramontes, Helena María

Moths and Other Stories. Houston, Tex.: Arte Público Press, 1995.

Their Dogs Came with Them: A Novel. New York: Dutton, 2000.

Under the Feet of Jesus. New York: Dutton, 1995.

Zamora, Bernice

Releasing Serpents. Tempe, Ariz.: Bilingual Press, 1994.

Restless Serpents. Menlo Park, Calif.: Diseños Literarios, 1976.

Zeno Gandía, Manuel

The Pond: Puerto Rico's 19th-Century Masterpiece. Translated by Kal Wagenhem. Markus Wiener Publishing, 1999.

LIST OF CONTRIBUTORS

Grisel Y. Acosta, University of Texas at San Antonio

Donna Bickford, The University of North Carolina, Chapel Hill

Sarah Boslaugh, Washington University in Saint Louis

Patricia Bostian, Central Piedmont Community College

Ethriam Brammer, Wayne State University

Diane Todd Bucci, Robert Morris University

John P. Buentello, University of Texas at San Antonio

Ritch Calvin, State University of New York, Stony Brook

Alan Cambeira, The Citadel

Heejung Cha, Indiana University of Pennsylvania

Jeffrey Charis-Carlson, University of Iowa

Selfa Chew, University of Texas at El Paso

Kevin L. Cole, University of Sioux Falls

Dustin Crawford, Utah State University

Alba Cruz-Hacker, University of California, Riverside

Catherine Cucinella, California State University, San Marcos

Isabel M. Andrés Cuevas, Universidad de Granada

Deb Cunningham, Texas A&M University

Sandra L. Dahlberg, University of Houston, Downtown

Analisa DeGrave, University of Wisconsin, Eau Claire

Kevin De Ornellas, University of Ulster

Khamla Dhouti, California State University, San Bernardino

Brian Doherty, University of Texas at Austin

Antonia Domínguez Miguela, University of Huelva

Alex Feerst, Macalester College

Anne Marie Fowler, Keiser University

Cristina Garrigos, Universidad de León

Alexandra Ganser, University of Vienna/University of Erlangen-Nuremberg

Patricia González, Texas A&M International University

Sonia V. González, Purdue University

Hedwig Gorski, University of Louisiana at Lafayette

Luis Duno Gottberg, Florida Atlantic University

Paul Guajardo, University of Houston

Nicole Guidotti-Hernández, University of Arizona, Tucson

Gabrielle Halko, West Chester University

Rebekah Hamilton, University of Texas–Pan American

Jean Hamm, East Tennessee State University

Markus Heide, Humboldt University, Berlin

Karen Holleran, Kaplan University

Amanda Holmes, McGill University

Martin Kich, Wright State University, Lake Campus

Shimberlee King, Stanford University

Marilyn Kiss, Wagner College

Lawrence La Fountain-Stokes, University of Michigan, Ann Arbor

Michelle Lin, North Carolina State University

Bernhard Malkmus, Ohio State University, Columbus

Carine Mardorossian, University at Buffalo

Imelda Martín-Junquera, Universidad de León

Yolanda P. Martínez, University of Birmingham (U.K.)

Thomas McConnell, University of South Carolina Upstate

Marci R. McMahon, University of Southern California

Amparo McWatt, University of West Indies, Barbados

Nancy Mercado, Boricua College

G. Douglas Meyers, University of Texas at El Paso

Seth Michelson, University of Southern California

John Charles Miller, Professor Emeritus, University of Colorado, Colorado Springs

Dylan A. T. Miner, Michigan State University

Jeanetta Calhoun Mish, University of Oklahoma

Marian Pozo-Montaño, University of North Carolina, Chapel Hill

Rafael Miguel Montes, St. Thomas University

Enrique Morales-Díaz, Hartwick College

Timothy K. Nixon, Shepherd University

Cindy Noble Marsh, California State University, San Bernardino

Anna M. Nogar, University of Texas at Austin

Megan Obourn, State University of New York, College at Brockport

Roberto Carlos Ortiz, Tulane University

Lorna Pérez, University at Buffalo

Rolando Pérez, Hunter College

Tony Perrello, California State University, Stanislaus

Bryan Peters, Miami University

Kati Pletsch de García, Texas A&M International University

Irena Praitis, California State University, Fullerton

María de la Cinta Ramblado-Minero, University of Limerick (Ireland)

Luz Elena Ramirez, California State University, San Bernardino

Lysa Rivera, Western Washington University

Carolyn Roark, Baylor University

Andrés Rodríguez, Kansas City, Missouri.

Arlene Rodríguez, Springfield Technical Community College

Linda Rodriguez

Jaime Rodríguez-Matos, University of Michigan, Ann Arbor

Jon D. Rossini, University of California, Davis

Raúl Rubio, Wellesley College

Betsy Sandlin, University of the South

Nhora Lucia Serrano, California State University, Long Beach

Dorsía Smith Silva, University of Puerto Rico, Río Piedras

Rosa E. Soto, William Paterson University

Paula Straile-Costa, Ramapo University of New Jersey

Jo-Anne Suriel, New York University

tatiana de la tierra, University at Buffalo

Yeliz Biber Tilbe, University of Leeds

Luz Consuelo Triana-Echeverría, St. Cloud State University

Gustavo Adolfo Guerra Vásquez, University of California, Berkeley

Gabriela Baeza Ventura, University of Houston

Marta Vizcaya Echano, University of Northampton (U.K.)

Zach Weir, Miami University

Tamar Diana Wilson, University of Missouri, St. Louis

Kristina Wright, Tufts University

Alberto Zambrana, University of North Carolina

INDEX

N